WESTMINSTER COMMENTARIES
EDITED BY WALTER LOCK D.D.
IRELAND PROFESSOR OF THE EXEGESIS
OF HOLY SCRIPTURE

THE BOOK OF THE PROPHET
JEREMIAH

THE BOOK OF THE PROPHET
JEREMIAH

WITH INTRODUCTION AND NOTES

BY

L. ELLIOTT BINNS, M.A.

LATE SCHOLAR OF EMMANUEL COLLEGE;
AND SOMETIME CHAPLAIN AND LECTURER IN OLD TESTAMENT HISTORY,
RIDLEY HALL, CAMBRIDGE

METHUEN & CO. LTD.
36 ESSEX STREET W.C.
LONDON

First Published in 1919

PREFATORY NOTE BY THE GENERAL EDITOR

THE primary object of these Commentaries is to be exe-
getical, to interpret the meaning of each book of the
Bible in the light of modern knowledge to English readers.
The Editors will not deal, except subordinately, with questions
of textual criticism or philology ; but taking the English text
in the Revised Version as their basis, they will aim at combining a hearty acceptance of critical principles with loyalty to
the Catholic Faith.

The series will be less elementary than the Cambridge Bible
for Schools, less critical than the International Critical Commentary, less didactic than the Expositor's Bible ; and it is
hoped that it may be of use both to theological students and to
the clergy, as well as to the growing number of educated laymen
and laywomen who wish to read the Bible intelligently and
reverently.

Each commentary will therefore have

(i) An Introduction stating the bearing of modern criticism
and research upon the historical character of the book, and
drawing out the contribution which the book, as a whole, makes
to the body of religious truth.

(ii) A careful paraphrase of the text with notes on the
more difficult passages and, if need be, excursuses on any points
of special importance either for doctrine, or ecclesiastical or-
ganization, or spiritual life.

But the books of the Bible are so varied in character that

considerable latitude is needed, as to the proportion which the various parts should hold to each other. The General Editor will therefore only endeavour to secure a general uniformity in scope and character : but the exact method adopted in each case and the final responsibility for the statements made will rest with the individual contributors.

By permission of the Delegates of the Oxford University Press and of the Syndics of the Cambridge University Press the Text used in this Series of Commentaries is the Revised Version of the Holy Scriptures.

WALTER LOCK

PREFACE

D URING the past few years the importance of Jeremiah amongst the prophets of the Old Testament has been increasingly recognised; no longer is he overshadowed by the massive figure of Isaiah, but rather have the two prophets come to be regarded as twin peaks standing side by side and pointing the soul to the things of God. If, however, the number of books written upon the earlier prophet be compared with those written upon the later, it will be found that there is a very great disproportion between them. It would seem therefore that room is left for another Commentary on the Book of the prophet Jeremiah.

Much that is valuable has been written on the book, but not much that is recent, at any rate in Great Britain. Exceptions to the last statement are to be found in Dr Peake's two volumes in the *Century Bible* (1910 and 1911), and in the last edition of Dr Streane's volume in the *Cambridge Bible* (1913), the revision of which he completed only a short time before his lamented death. In writing my own Commentary, however, I have not made any very great use of these two works, valuable though they be, having preferred to go behind them to the great work of Cornill (*Das Buch Jeremia*, 1905), a work which must form the basis of every modern Commentary on the prophet.

In his translation and arrangement of Jeremiah (1906) the late Dr Driver, writing of the Commentaries of Keil (1872) and Duhm (1901), said that 'the principal task of the future Commentator on Jeremiah will be to discover the right mean between them.' In a humble way I have tried to follow out his advice. Other Commentators whom I have found useful are Graf (1862) and Giesebrecht (1894 and 1907). To Cheyne's *Jeremiah: His Life and Times* in the 'Men of the Bible' series I owe many fruitful ideas, as I do also to Dr Moses Buttenwieser's *Prophets of Israel* (Part I, 1914). My debt to the writers named above is very large as will be seen by the constant references to them contained in the following Commentary, references which by no means disclose the fulness of my obligation to them.

The scope of the series in which this Commentary appears does not permit of any large dealing with the Hebrew text of Jeremiah; hence many points of interest to Hebrew scholars have had to be passed by almost unnoticed. For a similar reason the question of Jeremiah's use of metre, a highly controversial and technical subject, has received but slight treatment. In the present volume no general review of the origin and development of Hebrew prophecy has been attempted, the subject having already received admirable treatment in the series, and the reader who desires more detailed information on the subject cannot do better than consult Dr Wade's note *Hebrew Prophecy and its Credentials* in his Commentary on Isaiah, pp. viii—xvii.

In conclusion I wish to express my deep gratitude to the General Editor, Dr Lock. Dr Lock has been most patient and kind in reading through both the MS and proofs of the Commentary, and to his wise advice and varied learning I have frequently been indebted. Canon R. H. Kennett, the Regius Professor of Hebrew in Cambridge University, very kindly read through the MS of the Introduction and made valuable suggestions in regard to it for which I am very grateful, as I am for the care and affection which he lavished upon me—as upon his other pupils—during the years that I studied under his guidance.

L. E. B.

PLYMOUTH,
Lent, 1919.

CONTENTS

LIST OF PRINCIPAL ABBREVIATIONS

AJTh.   *American Journal of Theology.*

Aq.   The Version of Aquila.

AV.   The Authorised Version.

BDB.   *A Hebrew and English Lexicon of the Old Testament* &c.   By Francis Brown, D.D., S. R. Driver, D.D., and C. A. Briggs, D.D.

Buhl *Pal.*   F. Buhl, *Geographie des alten Palästina.*

CB.   *Cambridge Bible.*

cf.   Compare.

CIS.   *Corpus Inscriptionum Semiticarum* (Paris).

COT.   Eb. Schrader, *The Cuneiform Inscriptions and the O.T.*   (English Translation.)   See also *KAT.*

D.   The Deuteronomic Document of the Pentateuch.

DB.   W. Smith, *A Dictionary of the Bible.*

E.   The Elohistic Document of the Pentateuch.

Enc. Bib.   *Encyclopaedia Biblica,* edited by the Rev. T. K. Cheyne, D.D., and J. Sutherland Black, LL.D.

Enc. Brit.   *Encyclopaedia Britannica.*

ET.   English Translation.

EVV.   English Versions of the Bible.

fr.   Fragment.

Ges.-K.   *Gesenius' Hebrew Grammar, as edited and enlarged by E. Kautzsch.*   Translated from the 28th German edition by A. E. Cowley, D.D.

H.   The Holiness Document of the Pentateuch.

HDB.   *A Dictionary of the Bible,* edited by J. Hastings, D.D.

HDRE or *HD Rel. & E.*   *A Dictionary of Religion and Ethics,* edited by J. Hastings, D.D.

ICC.   *The International Critical Commentary,* edited by S. R. Driver, D.D., A. Plummer, D.D., and C. A. Briggs, D.D.

J.   The Jehovistic Document of the Pentateuch.

JBL.   *The Journal of Biblical Literature.*

Jew. Enc.   *The Jewish Encyclopaedia.*

JQR.   *Jewish Quarterly Review,* edited by I. Abrahams, M.A., and C. G. Montefiore, M.A.

J. Th. S.   *Journal of Theological Studies,* edited by J. F. Bethune-Baker, D.D., and F. E. Brightman, M.A.

KAT.   Eb. Schrader, *Die Keilinschriften und das Alte Testament.*

KB.   *Keilinschriftliche Bibliothek* (Berlin).

B.   *b*

LOT.   S. R. Driver, D.D., *Introduction to the Literature of O.T.*

LXX.   The Septuagint Version.

mg. or marg.   Margin.

MT.   The Massoretic Text of the Hebrew O.T.

N.S.   New Series.

NSI.   G. A. Cooke, D.D., *North Semitic Inscriptions.*

NT.   The New Testament.

OT.   The Old Testament.

OTJC.   The O.T. in the Jewish Church.

P.   The Priestly Document of the Pentateuch.

Parad.   Friedrich Delitzsch, *Wo lag das Paradies?*

PEFQS.   The Palestine Exploration Fund Quarterly Statement.

Rel. Sem.   W. Robertson Smith, *The Religion of the Semites.*

Rev. Bib.   Revue Biblique.

Rev. Et. Juives.   Revue des Études Juives.

R.V.   The Revised Version.

SBOT.   The Sacred Books of the O.T. edited by Paul Haupt.   The vol. on Jeremiah is by C. H. Cornill.

S. & P. or *Sin. & Pal.*   A. P. Stanley, D.D., *Sinai and Palestine in connexion with their history.*

Symm.   The Version of Symmachus.

Syr.   The Syriac Version.

Targ.   The Targum.

Theod.   The Version of Theodotion.

Vg. or Vulg.   The Vulgate Version.

ZATW.   Zeitschrift für die alttestamentliche Wissenschaft, edited by B. Stade.

INTRODUCTION

§ 1. THE IMPORTANCE OF JEREMIAH

The book of the prophet Jeremiah is the longest in the Bible[1], and though the mere volume of matter contained in even an inspired writing is no sure or final test of its importance—such a test, for example, would make Ecclesiastes of higher value than the Epistles of St John—yet in view of the disappearance of many of the prophetic utterances, it is evidence of the regard in which Jeremiah was held by the men of the Jewish Church, that they were at pains to collect and preserve so many narratives concerning his life, as well as writings attributed to him. The importance of the book, however, does not depend on its bulk, and had there come down to us only such fragments as chh. ix., xv. 15 ff., xvii. 12 ff., and xx. 7 ff. it would hardly be an exaggeration to say that Jeremiah was still the most valuable book in OT.

But wherein lies the value of the OT. writings, and what inherent and quickening quality has enabled them to survive the lapse of time and the dangers which arise alike from persecution and from indifference? Is it that they throw an unique light on the primitive customs and folklore of the Semitic race? Surely not; for, though the subject aroused the occasional curiosity of the ancients, a deep and sustained interest in the *origines* of nations is of modern growth and in itself would hardly have been sufficiently strong to protect and preserve so much of the literature of a comparatively obscure and despised people[2]. Nor is it that the writers of OT., taken as a whole, were gifted above other men with either critical or literary ability. The literature itself *qua* literature is of very uneven quality and in many places the text is

---

[1] That is if 1 and 2 Samuel, Kings, and Chronicles, respectively, be counted as separate books.

[2] To the Jews themselves, who first collected the writings, as to the Christians, they were not an obscure people; but their importance was religious not political.

so corrupt that no certain clue can be found to its meaning[1]. Even in some of the finest passages the heavy hand of a later editor has often all but succeeded in destroying the noble workmanship of the true and skilful artist. It seems impossible to imagine, however, that the whole of the poetry of the Psalmists and the noble prose of the prophets could ever have been permanently lost. Again, though OT., or much of it, does come within Gibbon's definition of history as being 'little more than a register of the crimes, follies and misfortunes of mankind[2],' yet the Jewish writers were notoriously lacking in many of the gifts which are necessary for the student of history; even in the books popularly called 'historical,' that sense of proportion, that freedom from prejudice, which are so requisite in the true historian, are conspicuously absent[3]. No, the value of OT. lies elsewhere than in the chronicling of the pomp of kings and the petty majesty of war; it lies rather in its being a record of the gradual revelation of what was to the Jews—or at any rate to the higher minds amongst them—the supreme good in life, the knowledge of the living God.

The peculiar value of OT., nay of the whole Bible, is not therefore historical but spiritual or, one might almost say, psychological. Its value is psychological because it is through the mind of man quickened by the Holy Spirit that God has given the most intimate revelation of Himself. Much can be learned of God by studying His handiwork in Nature, that open book in which he 'who runs may read'; much can be learned from His guiding of the events of history, especially in the work of preparation for the Incarnation[4]: but it is from His dealings with the souls of men—both collectively and as individuals—that God is to be known most certainly. The unique position which the Bible occupies, even amongst religious literature, lies in the fact that it contains a number of records of such dealings[5], and moreover records

---

[1] Cf. Driver, *Schweich Lectures*, p. 11 note. 'Hebrew texts, from the character of the script, are...more liable to corruption than Greek texts, and the Ancient Versions afford convincing evidence that the Old Testament has in very many places been corrupted seriously.'

[2] *Decline and Fall*, &c. I. p. 77 (Methuen's Standard Library Edition).

[3] The Jewish writers did not claim to write 'history'; even books like Joshua, Judges, Samuel and Kings were included amongst the prophets (see p. lxxiii). The omission of the writer of 1 K. xvi. to give to the reign of Omri more than a few verses shews his non-historical point of view, for according to the evidence of the inscriptions the reign of Omri was perhaps the most important in the Northern Kingdom. The only writer in the whole Bible with anything like an adequate power of writing history in the modern sense was St Luke, and he was a Gentile; see Ramsay, *St Paul the Traveller*, &c. pp. 4 f.

[4] Cf. the Essay by the present Bishop of Winchester in *Lux Mundi*.

[5] Cf. W. Temple, *The Faith and Modern Thought*, p. 39: 'we should go back

that are inspired by that Word of God upon whose sojourn on earth all the scattered rays of revelation are centred and in the power of whose ascended life alone they are to be interpreted. It is because Jeremiah amongst the prophets has left the most intimate and impressive accounts of what God meant to his soul, of the variety and richness of his religious experience, that the book which bears his name—and which most assuredly contains much that comes directly from him—has such surpassing importance. The value of Jeremiah, estimated by this standard, is coming more and more to be realised, and the writer of a recent book on the prophets, referring to Jer. xx. 7—9, goes so far as to say that 'Any discussion of the faith of the prophets must centre finally in this fervid record of Jeremiah's[1].'

In the present day there is a tendency amongst the majority of people, including the professedly religious, to neglect and in many cases altogether to ignore the reading and study of the Bible. Even amongst Bible students themselves two equally dangerous attitudes of mind are not uncommon, attitudes of mind which regard the OT. on the one hand as a collection of obsolete documents, on the other as an armoury of proof texts[2]. The effect in each case is the same, the OT. falls into the background and its influence tends to become more and more like 'a lingering star with lessening ray.' This modern tendency to neglect OT. is fraught with much danger, because the two parts of Holy Scripture are so closely linked together that a study and appreciation of OT. is essential to a due and proper understanding of the New. It is not merely that the writers of NT. find in OT. a storehouse

---

to the inspired men of the past, not to find a short cut to truth (there is none), but to find out how to find truth. These men were in contact with the Divine. We can learn something of how their conception of the Divine grew in their own minds, and we can learn by what steps they established their communion with the Divine, so that following their example we may establish our own.'

[1] Buttenwieser, *The Prophets of Israel*, p. 10. Apart from his self-revelation Jeremiah has a place of tremendous importance in the history of religion from the fact that his conception of the relation of God and man was so highly spiritual: see further under *Teaching* and *Influence*.

[2] This latter weakness marked the learning of the period before the Reformation. 'The scholastic divines, holding to a traditional belief in the *plenary* and *verbal* inspiration of the whole Bible, and remorselessly pursuing this belief to its logical results, had fallen into a method of exposition almost exclusively *textarian*. The Bible, both in theory and in practice, had almost ceased to be a record of real events, and the lives and teaching of living men. It had become an arsenal of texts; and these texts were regarded as detached invincible weapons to be legitimately seized and wielded in theological warfare, for any purpose to which their words might be made to apply, without reference to their original meaning or context....Thus had the scholastic belief in the verbal inspiration of the sacred text led men blindly into a condition of mind in which they practically ignored the scriptures altogether.' Seebohm, *The Oxford Reformers*, ch. II. § 1.

of illustrations and a model of teaching, but, if the meaning of the Incarnation is to be apprehended in all its fulness, the preparatory work carried on in and through the people of Israel must be clearly understood.

But the teaching of OT. has a value its own, and in particular the teaching of those great forerunners of the Messiah, the prophets. Amongst the prophetical books there is none which has a more striking message for modern times than the book of Jeremiah. Even in the days before the great European War the value of a study of this book was recognised by so clear-sighted a judge as Bishop Westcott, who in the notice to the second edition of his commentary on the Epistle to the Hebrews (Sept. 1892) wrote as follows: 'The more I study the tendencies of the time in some of the busiest centres of English life, the more deeply I feel that the Spirit of GOD warns us of our most urgent civil and spiritual dangers through the prophecies of Jeremiah and the Epistle to the Hebrews.' But it is since the outbreak of the war and amidst all the shocks which the traditional faith has had to undergo, that the supreme importance of Jeremiah's teaching has come most clearly to be recognised ; and it has come to be recognised because the situation in which the prophet found himself has so much in common with that of the present day. His message was delivered during an age of transition, and delivered moreover to a people whose beliefs, founded on material conceptions of God, had been shattered by the course of events, by the harsh tragedies of actual life[1].

Jeremiah, like every true prophet, was the product of his age (cf. pp. xxxvi ff.), he had an actual living message for his contemporaries; but at the same time he was able to rise above his environment and to proclaim universal principles such as are valid for all time, and not least so for the time in which we are ourselves living. It is not within the scope of this commentary to work out detailed applications of the teaching of Jeremiah to the problems of the present day, but perhaps I may be allowed to point out that two of his great doctrines, one in the religious, the other in the social sphere, are still unrealised in our actual life as a Church and as a nation. In spite of the teaching of Jeremiah, and of our Lord Himself, religion still tends to substitute worship and ritual for obedience to God's commands and for efforts to make His will done ' on earth as it is in heaven'; how much of popular

---

[1] For a fuller treatment of this subject see Mr Oliver C. Quick's *Essays in Orthodoxy*, pp. xv ff.

religion, for example, exhausts itself in churchgoing[1]? Again in the matter of justice to the poor and needy, have we not much still to do before our methods of procedure would be approved by Jeremiah? People of the more comfortable classes hardly realise how heavily our legal system tells against the less influential classes and how the widow and the stranger are still the subjects of oppression for the benefit of the wealthy. This is seen in our system of punishing offences by fines, of inflicting a penalty which to one man may be a month's wages and to the other hardly the price of a single meal: and again, the expense of legal procedure, especially when appeals are taken from one court to the next, often makes it just as impossible for the poor man to get justice done for him in our own day as it was under a corrupt tyrant like Jehoiakim[2].

§ 2. THE TIMES OF JEREMIAH

In studying any part of the Bible which claims to be considered as history we are bound to take into account, much more fully than does OT., the records of contemporary nations. The old-fashioned view which would treat the history of the chosen people as though they were entirely separated from their neighbours is quite inadequate. God did indeed stand in a peculiar relationship to Israel, but that was because Israel had a peculiar ability for receiving God's revelation. Those who still cling to the old view tend to place all other nations outside God's providential dealings. The only worthy and Christian view of history is that it is all controlled by God, but that nations like individuals may resist the will of their creator. This statement applies equally to what we call secular matters and religious matters.

After the fall of Samaria in 722 B.C. and the consequent collapse of the Northern Kingdom, Judah alone remained as the representative of the house of Israel[3]. HEZEKIAH was then reigning in Jerusalem and

---

[1] Dr Rauschenbusch has made this point very clearly, though not without exaggeration, in *Christianity and the Social Crisis*, p. 7, where he says: 'This Christian ceremonial system does not differ essentially from that against which the prophets protested....But the point that here concerns us is that a very large part of the fervour of willing devotion which religion always generates in human hearts has spent itself on these religious acts. The force that would have been competent " to seek justice and relieve the oppressed " has been consumed in weaving the tinsel fringe for the garment of religion.'

[2] Cf. Dr Rauschenbusch, *Christianizing the Social Order*, pp. 332 ff. He is dealing primarily with America but his statements apply to Great Britain to an almost equal degree.

[3] By this statement I do not intend to deny that the province of Samaria exercised an important influence on Jewish thought after 722 B.C.

under the guidance of Isaiah he succeeded in preserving the independence of his kingdom, though at times it seemed as if the 'overflowing scourge' would engulf Judah as it had already engulfed Samaria. In addition to preserving the political existence of the nation from the threatening advance of Assyria, Hezekiah carried through a comprehensive reformation of religion; and during his reign, in spite of occasional relapses, such as the reception of the embassy from Merodach-baladan (Is. xxxix. 1 ff.), he seems to have followed the guidance of what may be called the prophetic party. Hezekiah was succeeded by his son MANASSEH, a boy of twelve years of age. The new king was evidently the instrument of that party in the state whose policy in both religious and secular affairs—the distinction was hardly noticeable in Israel— was exactly opposed to that of the late government. Manasseh occupied the throne for 55 years and his long reign served to undo all that had been accomplished during his father's lifetime; religion fell back once more into the old ruts from which it had been raised, and not only so, but fresh forms of heathenism and superstition were introduced by the royal power, and eagerly adopted by the people (2 K. xxi. 2 ff. &c.). This period is amongst the darkest of Hebrew history, though outwardly there was peace for the greatest part of the reign, and the true worshippers of Jehovah had to remain in hiding, hoping and praying for the coming of a new monarch and the reaction which would almost inevitably accompany his accession. Later ages looked back on the reign of Manasseh as finally sealing the doom of Judah and rendering unavoidable the captivity of the nation[1]. Manasseh was followed by AMON, but the son walked in all the ways of his father and his government brought no relief to the devout. Their time of waiting was however nearing an end; the reign of Amon was suddenly cut short by a palace intrigue, and the king was murdered. The conspirators do not seem to have had influential support and the movement apparently collapsed; at any rate the dynasty was preserved, Josiah the youthful son of Amon being placed on the vacant throne and his father's murderers being put to death.

JOSIAH was only eight years old when he came to the throne, and during the early part of his reign the government was evidently carried on by the princes of the royal house. Their policy followed the same lines as that of the two previous reigns, and one who looked upon their

---

[1] 2 K. xxiv. 3 f. and Jer. xv. 4. This latter *v.* is almost certainly not by the prophet himself as it is not in agreement with his constant teaching (see note *ad loc.*) but it represents the judgement of a later age.

administration with no kindly eye has described them as 'filling their master's house with violence[1].' For this cause therefore the first years of a reign which was destined to leave a permanent mark on the religious history of Israel were distinguished by no change of religious policy. Under the surface, however, there was growing up a strong movement towards a more spiritual religion; men were disgusted and wearied by the long barren years since the time of Hezekiah; everything was ready for a puritan reaction and the return to power of the prophetic party. But the return to power of the prophetic party was not likely to take place of itself; what was needed was some striking event to rouse men's minds and to stir the country to its very depths. Such an event was not long delayed. Josiah had hardly reached the thirteenth year of his reign when the dark and mysterious barriers of the North were uplifted, as they had been many times before, and the Scythian hordes came rushing forth to invade Palestine[2]. Not very much is known of the history of this people[3], who issued from their homes North of the Black Sea and spread terror and devastation wherever they went. The flood of invasion swept over Palestine as far as Egypt where the bribes of the reigning Pharaoh, supported by the strongly garrisoned frontier, succeeded in checking it. The Scythians retraced their steps through Palestine and turned aside into Mesopotamia which thus had one more element of disruption added to it for the next twenty years. Judah seems to have been left untouched by the invader, thanks no doubt to the natural inaccessibility of its situation and to the absence of attractive plunder, but the danger was sufficiently threatening to call forth the voice of prophecy, so long silent in the land, and it is to this period in all probability that the book of Zephaniah belongs, and even more important, the first utterances of Jeremiah. The advent of a prophet and the presence amongst them of messengers whose words stamped them as truly accredited of God roused the king and the people, and in the eighteenth year of his reign Josiah put himself at the head of the reforming party and began to repair the temple[4]. During the repairs

---

[1] Zeph. i. 9.

[2] Cf. i. 15 : 'out of the North shall evil break forth upon all the inhabitants of the land.'

[3] See Herod. I. 103 ff., IV. 64. The Scythians were looked upon by the Greeks as typical of all that was worst amongst the barbarians and their savagery was proverbial. However in the Kingdom of Jesus Christ there is hope even for the barbarous Scythian (cf. Col. iii. 11 ; Justin, *Dial.* § 28). For fuller details of the history of this people see Rawlinson, *Anct. Monarchies*[4], II. 225 f. ; Driver, *LOT.*[8] pp. 252 f.

[4] So 2 K. xxii. 3 : according to 2 Ch. xxxiv. 3, in the *twelfth* year. It may be noted in passing that the account in Kings makes the reform depend on the

'a book of Torah[1]' was discovered by Hilkiah the priest and handed on to Shaphan the scribe, who read it and, recognising its importance, immediately carried it to the king. The contents of the book filled Josiah with alarm, and rending his clothes he sent to make enquiries of a certain prophetess named Huldah who was the wife of one of his officers[2]. Huldah returned the answer that judgement must indeed fall upon the guilty nation but that it would not be in the lifetime of the king himself. In spite of this reply[3], which was calculated to check all attempts at reform, Josiah determined to make a vigorous effort to cleanse the religion of his country and to bring it nearer to the ideal which was presented in the newly discovered book. As a first step towards reform a popular assembly was convened in the temple area and the book was read to the people. At the close of the reading, which evidently moved all present to a sense of their peril, the king and people entered into a solemn covenant before God to adopt the commands of the book as the national law.

According to the somewhat idealised account in 2 K. xxiii. the reformation was effected in five main directions, though in all probability many of the abuses there stated to have been remedied succeeded in escaping, at any rate in part, the attentions of the reformers. (*a*) The temple was purified from all traces of Baal worship; and even the sacred objects, including the Asherim (see note on xvii. 2) and the pillars (see note on xxvii. 19), were destroyed. These had originally been taken over from the Canaanites, but by this time must have been considered a part of the national cultus (see *vv.* 4, 6, 11; cf. Dt. xii. 3, xvi. 22 and contrast Ex. xxiv. 4). (*b*) The 'idolatrous priests' were put down together with their altars and images (*v.* 5). The

---

finding of the book; whilst in 2 Ch. xxxiv.—xxxv. the reformation is carried out first and the book is discovered as a direct result of the reforms. Probably the later writer could not understand the king's action in continuing a reform when the prophetess had said that it would be of no avail in saving the nation. (Cf. especially 2 Ch. xxxiv. 8 with 2 K. xxiii. 2 ff.)

[1] See note on ii. 8 for the meaning of Torah. There has been much disagreement among critics as to what is here referred to, it can hardly be the whole Pentateuch as the document was read through in one sitting. Most scholars think that what Hilkiah discovered was Dt., or at any rate the kernel of it (see Driver, *Deut.* p. xlv). At the same time it ought perhaps to be pointed out that the account of the discovery in 2 K. xxii.—xxiii. shews marks of a Deuteronomic compiler and that many of the coincidences both of language and of matter may be due to his influence.

[2] It is strange that there is no mention of either Jeremiah or Zephaniah in connexion with the king's enquiry.

[3] The form of Huldah's reply, however, is probably due to the later Deuteronomic historian; cf. 1 K. xxi. 28 f.

'chariots and horses of the sun' (*v.* 11) were doubtless borrowed from Babylon where the sun-god was represented as riding in such a chariot (cf. Dt. xvii. 3)[1]. (*c*) Those who engaged in immoral rites in connexion with religion were destroyed, as well as all wizards and magicians (*vv.* 7, 24; cf. Dt. xxiii. 17 f., xviii. 10 *b*—14). (*d*) The offering of children to Molech was forbidden (*v.* 10; cf. Dt. xviii. 10 *a*). (*e*) The high places and local sanctuaries were destroyed (*vv.* 8 f.; cf. Dt. xii. 13 f.). This last reform was in effect the disestablishment of every sanctuary outside Jerusalem, together with its priests. There can be no doubt that in many of the local shrines the worship offered to Jehovah had become very corrupt; it must be remembered that there was much rivalry between the various sanctuaries (cf. Am. v. 5, viii. 14) and that their guardians in the endeavour to attract worshippers would be tempted to countenance every kind of vicious practice. Wellhausen compares the advice of Luther to the princes of Germany that the field chapels and churches should be destroyed, on the ground that they were 'devices of the devil used by him to strengthen covetousness, to set up a false and spurious faith, to weaken parish churches, to increase taverns and fornication, to squander money and labour to no purpose, and merely to lead the poor people about by the nose[2].' In as far as it did away with such abuses the policy of centralisation was a step in the right direction.

The actual carrying out of the reform must have been made much easier by the destruction of forty-six of the fenced cities of Judah at the time of Sennacherib's invasion (2 K. xviii. 13), a disaster from which they could hardly have recovered, but which had left Jerusalem untouched and consequently supreme in material power, and, what was even more important, with the reputation of being an inviolable sanctuary. At the same time the destruction of the local shrines meant that the priests whose livelihood was gained by attending them were thrown out of employment, and that ill-feeling was aroused against the 'Jerusalem monopoly.' The effect upon the common people could hardly fail to be to remove God out of their everyday life and to make the outward part of their religion mainly a matter of pilgrimages and visits to the distant capital[3]. It must, however, be remembered that Jerusalem

---

[1] The ancient Greeks dedicated chariots and horses to the sun who needed them, so they believed, for his journey across the sky: cf. J. G. Frazer, *Magic Art*, i. p. 315; H. Zimmern in *KAT*.[3] pp. 369 ff.

[2] *Prolegomena*, p. 27.

[3] Cf. Driver, *Deut.* p. xxix: 'The limitation of the public worship of Jehovah to Jerusalem...may seem indeed to *us* to be a retrograde step and inconsistent with

was not at a very great distance from any part of a kingdom whose total
area was not much more than that of an English county. According to
2 K. xxiii. 15 ff. the reform penetrated to Bethel which was outside
the nominal territory of Josiah. There is nothing improbable in this
extension, and other evidence exists of a close connexion in matters of
religion between Jerusalem and the inhabitants of what had been the
Northern Kingdom (Jer. xli. 5 ff.); and Josiah did not scruple to traverse
the territories of Assyria if he found it necessary (2 K. xxiii. 29)[1].
The weakness of the reformation seems to have been that it quite
evidently set a standard of religious life for which the nation as a whole
was not yet ready; the truth of this criticism is clearly demonstrated
by the violent reaction which followed the death of Josiah. The king
was apparently of an enthusiastic and even fanatical disposition[2] and
no doubt he carried with him in the movement many who had no real
desire for reform. It is almost certain that in this, as in all similar
enterprises, amongst the ranks of the reformers were men who were
moved by very mixed motives, who in the desire to obtain the favour
of those in power pretended to share in their lofty aims, members of

'That ungracious crew which feigns demurest grace.'

It is a strange and at the same time a notable fact that Jeremiah seems
to have taken no part in the revival—possibly there is a reference to
his having done so in xi. 1 ff. (see notes *ad loc.*)—and in his references
to Josiah's memory he praises him not for his efforts in purifying religion,
but for his just and upright rule (xxii. 15). Perhaps the prophet felt
that the reforms did not go far enough, especially in the matter of
sacrifice (cf. vii. 21 ff.); or he may have suspected the motives of the
reformers, or have felt that the king was being used as a tool by the

---

the author's (of Dt.) lofty conception of the Divine nature (x. 14): but partly it
was a result of the national feeling of Israel, to which the prophets, even in their
most exalted moments, were hardly ever wholly superior, and which looked up to
the national Temple on Zion as specially honoured by Jehovah's presence ; partly
it arose out of the circumstances of the age, which made the local sanctuaries
centres of impure or unspiritual rites.'

[1] Canon Kennett rejects the historicity of 2 K. xxiii. 15 ff., probably correctly,
see 'The Origin of the Aaronite Priesthood' in *J. Th. S.* for Jan. 1905.

[2] Commenting on Josiah's violence against those whose ways he condemned,
Dean Stanley remarks: 'It was the first direct persecution that the kingdom of
Judah had witnessed on behalf of the True Religion. Down to this time the
mournful distinction had been reserved for the half-pagan King Manasseh. But
the cruelty had here, as in all like cases, provoked a corresponding cruelty ; and
the reformation of Josiah, if from his youth and his zeal it has suggested his
likeness to our Edward VI, by its harsher features encouraged the rough acts
which disfigured so many of the best efforts of that and other like movements of
the Christian Church.' *Jewish Church*, II. p. 425.

Jerusalem Priesthood. The expedition against Pharaoh Necho in which Josiah met his death is probably another exhibition of the same enthusiastic and visionary spirit as inspired the reformation; whether this is so or not and whatever the motives or hopes which may have prompted it, the expedition to Megiddo was a disastrous failure, and as Dr Pusey has well said 'in Josiah's death the last gleam of the sunset of Judah faded into night[1].' After the battle of Megiddo Necho evidently continued his advance, leaving Jerusalem for the time in peace. The opportunity was thereupon seized by the people of the land to choose their own king and to place on the throne Josiah's younger son JEHOAHAZ. The new king almost certainly intended to continue his father's anti-Egyptian policy and his election was no doubt inspired by the prophetic party. It is to be noticed that in Jeremiah's lament over Jehoahaz under the name of Shallum (xxii. 10—12) there is no trace of any disapproval or criticism (contrast the conventional and late comment of 2 K. xxiii. 32); and according to Ezekiel the king was already famous as a warrior (xix. 3 f.). If the prophetic party entertained any hopes from the prowess of Jehoahaz and the similarity of his policy to that of Josiah, their hopes were speedily disappointed, for his brief reign of three months was ended by a summons to appear before Necho at Riblah. No record remains of what took place at the interview but the Judean king was deposed and carried in chains to Egypt.

Having disposed of Jehoahaz in this summary manner, Necho proceeded to place on the throne his elder brother Eliakim and changed his name to JEHOIAKIM. He also imposed a tribute upon the land of 100 talents of silver and one of gold (2 K. xxiii. 33). In view of the long period of peace during the reign of Josiah and the opportunities which it must have given for increasing the prosperity of the kingdom, this tribute was not an excessive amount; Jehoiakim, at any rate, does not seem to have looked upon it as exhausting the wealth of his people and he raised heavy taxes from them for his own private building schemes[2]. These operations were evidently conducted on a large and generous scale and the chief ambition of the king appears to have been to rival the courts of neighbouring powers. In the historical books this extra taxation is barely mentioned (2 K. xxiii. 35); Jeremiah, however,

---

[1] The motives which underlay Josiah's action are very obscure owing to our lack of information and I have discussed them elsewhere (see *J. Th. S.* xviii. pp. 40 f.); possibly he felt it was his duty as the vassal of Assyria to endeavour to stop the Egyptians; or it may well have been that he hoped to restore the boundaries of the ancient Jewish monarchy.

[2] Hitzig compares Sallust, *Bell. Jug.* 31; Tacitus, *Hist.* iv. 2.

gives a much more detailed account, also stating that the new king was extravagant and unjust in the use which he made of forced labour (xxii. 13—17). It has been suggested that Jehoiakim's efforts were intended to strengthen the kingdom against its foes (cf. xxii. 23), but it is hardly likely that Necho would allow a vassal to add to the fortifications in his territory. The king seems to have been a bitter opponent of the prophetic party and had at least one prophet put to death (xxvi. 20—23); his efforts against Jeremiah and Baruch were less successful owing to the protection which was afforded them by some of the princes (xxxvi. 26; cf. v. 25 and xxvi. 24). Jehoiakim may have been, as Josephus says, 'unjust and malignant; neither holy towards God, nor forbearing towards man[1],' but as he appears in Jer. he is a real man, one who is able to make up his mind and to carry out his plans. The kings of Judah are for the most part mere names and though Zedekiah is described with some detail, yet he is so feeble and characterless that he seems to glide across the prophet's life like a featureless ghost. Jehoiakim by the single incident narrated in xxxvi. 20 ff. is revealed as a person of strong and determined character. It is only necessary to study the action of the nobles in his reign, when even the strongest sympathisers with the prophets had to work in secret and in fear (xxxvi. 19), with the insolent and overbearing conduct of their inferior successors in the reign of Zedekiah (xxxviii. 24 ff. &c.), to realise the difference between the two men.

The Egyptian supremacy in Asia which had been the cause of Jehoiakim's elevation to the throne did not last very long; in 607 or 606 B.C. Nineveh fell before the Medes and Babylonians, and in 605 Necho himself was completely crushed at Carchemish by Nebuchadrezzar, the son and general of Nabopolassar the new Babylonian monarch. A description of the battle, one of the most important in the world's history, has been preserved in Jer. xlvi. 1—12, which tells how Egypt's 'mighty ones were beaten down, they fled away and looked not back; their swift and mighty men stumbled and fled.' Nebuchadrezzar was not able to take immediate advantage of his victory, as the death of his father and the consequent unsettlement demanded the presence in Babylon of the new monarch. The Chaldeans, however, eventually returned and Jehoiakim had perforce to submit. As the nominee of Egypt Jehoiakim may be presumed to have been pro-Egyptian in his sympathies, and he seems to have found the yoke of Babylon very

---

[1] *Ant.* x. v. 2.

heavy; accordingly after three years he refused tribute and entered into open rebellion (2 K. xxiv. 1). Josephus tells us that it was in reliance upon the assistance of Egypt that he took this step[1]. If the people of Judah expected to receive help from their neighbours such expectations were soon proved to be vain; on the contrary the nations round about looked upon Judah as a lawful prey, and bands of Chaldeans, Syrians (? Edomites), Moabites and Ammonites speedily invaded the doomed country intent on plunder (2 K. xxiv. 2). Jehoiakim died before the extent of his folly became visible and his son Coniah was left to face the fury of the Babylonian advance[2].

The new king adopted the name of JEHOIACHIN (he is called Coniah in xxii. 24, and Jeconiah in xxiv. 1 and in 1 Ch. iii. 16). His reign like that of Jehoahaz lasted only three months and he seems to have been very much under the influence of the queen-mother Nehushta (see note on xiii. 18). The men of Jerusalem were wise enough to submit after a very short siege and so the city was spared, for the time, the horrors which afterwards came upon it; the king however and his principal nobles, together with the craftsmen and warriors, were carried away to Babylon[3]. Jehoiachin was perhaps the most fortunate of the later kings of Judah as he was apparently well treated by his captors, and Evil-merodach, the successor of Nebuchadrezzar, released him from confinement and 'spake kindly to him, and set his throne above the thrones of the kings that were with him in Babylon' (Jer. lii. 32). Nebuchadrezzar placed on the throne of the enfeebled kingdom the youngest of Josiah's sons and therefore the uncle of the last king. He exercised what seems to have been the suzerain's right by changing the king's name from Mattaniah to ZEDEKIAH. Zedekiah seems to have been chosen for his weakness of character, and all through his unhappy reign he appears to have been at the mercy of the man or the party which was nearest to him for the time being. In considering the people

---

[1] *Ant.* x. vi. 2.

[2] I follow the account contained in 2 K. xxiv., which says that Jehoiakim was buried in peace (*v.* 6), and that Jerusalem did not fall until the next reign (*v.* 12). The chronicler makes Nebuchadrezzar carry Jehoiakim in chains to Babylon (2 Ch. xxxvi. 6) but his account evidently confuses Jehoiakim and Jehoiachin; Josephus (*Ant.* x. vi. 3) states that Jerusalem was entered by the Chaldeans on friendly terms and that the king was treacherously murdered by them.

[3] It should be noticed that among the captives taken to Babylon in the first deportation was the prophet Ezekiel, and that he dates the beginning of the Captivity from the first fall of Jerusalem. There is some difficulty in arriving at the actual date of the city's fall; in 2 K. xxiv. 12 it is said to have been in the *eighth* year of Nebuchadrezzar (i.e. 597 B.C.) but in Jer. lii. 28 the *seventh* year is given as the date of the beginning of the Captivity; this latter date agrees with the statement in 2 K. xxv. 27, where see Skinner's note.

who controlled him it must be remembered that all the best and most experienced of the nation had been carried away to Babylon.

Jeremiah spent all his energies in trying to keep the king faithful to the oath of allegiance which he had sworn to Nebuchadrezzar (Ez. xvii. 13 ff.) and for a time he was successful, though in the fourth year of his reign (594—593 B.C.) the king entered into certain negotiations with Moab, Ammon and Tyre (xxvii. 1 ff.). Necho had died in 594 and it is possible that the plotting against Babylon which broke out about this time in Palestine was inspired by his successor Psamme-tichus II. Cornill thinks that the conspiracy failed to come to a head because war broke out suddenly between Egypt and Ethiopia and so deprived the smaller states of that support without which any attempt to throw off the yoke of Babylon would have been mere foolishness[1]. According to Jer. li. 59, Zedekiah made a journey to Babylon about this time probably to explain his conduct to his overlord and to give pledges of his loyalty. The inevitable end, however, could not be long delayed; the weak king surrounded by ambitious courtiers and tempted by the promises of the neighbouring peoples made common cause with Moab and Ammon and appealed to Egypt for protection. Jerusalem was immediately invested; it held out stubbornly for a year and a half but at length a breach was made in the North side (2 K. xxv. 2—3) and the king and his army fled out by the opposite gate. The fugitives were captured near Jericho and taken to Nebuchadrezzar at Riblah. The long and troublesome resistance of Jerusalem made any plea for mercy vain; the king's sons were slain in their father's sight; his own eyes were put out, and he was taken to Babylon in chains, there to remain until his death. The temple and palaces of Jerusalem were razed to the ground together with the walls, and the bulk of the population was taken captive to Babylon, seventy of the principal men being exe-cuted (2 K. xxv. 4—10). This final and overwhelming disaster was undoubtedly due to the feeble and vacillating character of the king, who in words which Bishop Stubbs applied to John of England had 'neither grace nor splendour, strength nor patriotism.' Zedekiah is indeed a pitiable example of a man occupying a position of responsi-bility for which he was not fitted and for which he probably had no desire. The gifts of kindly feeling and the desire to do what was right which he possessed would have been estimable virtues in private life, but, unsupported as they were by strength of character or the power of taking any decisive step, they brought about the ruin of his country.

---

[1] *Das Buch Jeremia*, pp. 305 f.

Zedekiah had just enough power to retain his throne, yet not enough
to be the real ruler of the nation; he had just enough fear of God to
prevent his doing anything violently wrong, but not enough to make
him active in God's service. He is a typical example of lukewarmness,
one who was neither hot nor cold and whose final doom was worse than
that of a thoroughgoing and determined despot like Jehoiakim.

GEDALIAH, the son of Ahikam Jeremiah's protector, was put in charge
of the ruined province. Jeremiah himself went at first with the other
captives as far as Ramah, but on permission being given to him he
returned and threw in his lot with those who remained in the land.
Jerusalem having been destroyed, the headquarters of the new community were fixed at Mizpah, and to this centre there gradually collected the roving bands which had escaped from the Babylonians. For
two months all went well and the beginnings of what must have seemed
to the prophet a new social order were successfully made, when an
unexpected disaster overtook the community[1]. The governor was slain
by Ishmael, son of Nethaniah, acting for the king of Ammon; whereupon the remnant of the people fled to Egypt, taking the reluctant
prophet with them.

The experiment which Nebuchadrezzar made in appointing a Jew
as governor of the conquered province exhibits the Babylonians in a
very favourable light. It was a policy attended with grave risks in
view of the continued rebellions of the people of Judah in the past, and
though the experiment failed it was through no fault on the part of the
new governor, unless indeed excessive trust in the good faith of others
can be termed a fault. Gedaliah had evidently been chosen with great
care, and he seems to have gained the trust of the Jews as well as of
the Babylonians, as is shewn by the crowds of fugitives who returned
to take refuge under his protection. His murder was most probably
the act of one who was utterly opposed to any submission to Babylon
and to any recognition of its right to appoint a governor. Ishmael

---

[1] Canon Kennett thinks that the governorship of Gedaliah may have lasted for
a much longer time than is usually supposed. He writes to me as follows: ' The
date of the murder of Gedaliah is very doubtful. Jerusalem did not fall till the
7th day of the 6th month of the 11th year of Zedekiah. After that the incidents
related in Jer. xxix. 4 ff. must have taken some time, and also the return of the
fugitives related in xl. 11, 12. If Gedaliah was murdered in the 7th month there
scarcely seems time for all this to happen. Jer. lii. 30 mentions a third deportation
not recorded in Kings, and this third deportation must have been in consequence
of some insurrection. It seems to me probable that it was in consequence of the
murder of Gedaliah, and I should therefore regard his governorship as lasting
seven years.'

may also have been disgusted that a member of the royal house should accept such a degrading position and act in a subordinate post under a conqueror.

§ 3. The Life of Jeremiah

There are men to whom God's voice comes as they wander in some lonely garden at the cool of the day; there are others who hear it amidst the blaze of a midday sun upon the open highway; but, whenever the hour and wherever the place, the true servant of God is always ready to welcome the Divine message, to receive which his mind and conscience have long been preparing him. But though this preparation may have been long, going behind even the birth of the person concerned[1], yet it does not follow that he himself has been conscious of the process. Such seems to have been the case with Jeremiah, who evidently first realised his vocation at the time when he was called to fulfil it, and who had remained ignorant of the Divine care which had watched over him from his very birth.

The name of the prophet's father according to the heading of the book (i. 1) was Hilkiah, but nothing is known of his history or character (there is no reason for identifying him with the high priest of the same name mentioned in 2 K. xxii.). His home was at Anathoth, a small village lying amongst the heights of Benjamin, 'just out of sight of Jerusalem[2],' but on the great highway from it to the North. The outlook from Anathoth towards the wilderness was stern and desolate and doubtless influenced the mind of Jeremiah, as is shewn by the images which he used (cf. ii. 31, iv. 11, &c.); 'from its site the land falls away in broken barren hills to the North end of the Dead Sea. The vision of that desert maze was burnt into the prophet's mind, and he contrasted it with the clear ordered word of God[3].' Anathoth is included in the list of priestly cities in Josh. xxi. 18 and is associated with the priestly family of Abiathar (1 K. ii. 26), but it is quite uncertain whether Jeremiah or even his father were members of the priestly guild (see on i. 1)[4].

---

[1] Cf. H. P. Liddon, 'When God forms a human life to do some appointed task, His preparatory action may be traced in the circumstances of hereditary descent not less than in other provisions whether of Nature or of Grace.'

[2] Dean Stanley, *Sin. and Pal.* p. 166.

[3] G. A. Smith, *Hist. Geog.* p. 315.

[4] If Jeremiah was a priest when the call came to him he must be reckoned as the first of the canonical prophets who had such an origin.

It is greatly to be regretted that no descriptions of the appearance of Jeremiah have come down to us; what would we not give to have some slight sketch, it may be, of the young prophet as he was when first God's voice came to him, sketches such as St Thomas of Celano has preserved of St Francis in his early days when he was pondering over the claims of the Divine will upon his life and allegiance? And even if such a detailed picture be denied to us, some single illuminating touch—as when it is said of David that 'he was ruddy, and withal of a beautiful countenance, and goodly to look upon[1]'; or of Saul that 'he was higher than any of the people from his shoulders and upwards[2]'—would be of untold value in helping us to realise that Jeremiah was an actual living and suffering man such as we ourselves are. We tend so constantly to look upon the prophets as 'personified qualities in an allegory' and quite fail to invest them 'with the reality of human flesh and blood.' The Hebrews as a whole seem to have had but little interest in the physical appearance of their great men, nor do they seem to have regarded that other aspect of their physical being, bodily health. Jeremiah can talk of the state as being sick unto death, and can liken the false prophets to unskilled physicians, but he does not seem to have realised that his own constant change of mood, now unduly depressed, now too highly exalted, may have been, in part at any rate, the result of the humours of the body.

Jeremiah reveals nothing of his inner life before God's call came to him, though from his general attitude it seems certain that his longings and desires were of a religious nature. He had probably studied the works of the earlier prophets, his predecessors, with a loving diligence[3], and was no doubt familiar with their histories as handed down to his own times, and this knowledge may have had much to do with his hesitation and shrinking back when he was called to the same office. Who was he that he should dare to take his place beside the prophets of old, beside Amos and Hosea, Isaiah and Micah?

The call evidently came to him when he was still quite young (though 'child' in i. 6 is not to be taken literally, see note *ad loc.*). It came to him first in the thirteenth year of Josiah (626 B.C.), which was also the year in which Esarhaddon's long reign of forty-two years

---

[1] 1 S. xvi. 12.
[2] 1 S. x. 23.
[3] His writings bear marks of the influence of Hosea especially (see p. lxix); it must not, however, be taken for granted that Jeremiah's study of these writings antedated his call, though from the nature of the case it is exceedingly likely.

came to an end : possibly some disturbance in connexion with the succession unknown to us may have quickened Jeremiah's prophetic instincts, but it is much more likely that he first realised the state of his nation and the imminence of judgement by the near approach of the Scythians which took place about this time (see p. xix.). Jerusalem itself escaped the danger, and Jeremiah's credit as a prophet must have been severely shaken; he knew however that he was not mistaken as to the final fate of the nation if repentance were delayed, and during the remaining eighteen years of the reign of Josiah he continued to attack abuses and corruptions both in the moral and in the ecclesiastical life around him. It was stated above that Jeremiah took no active or at least no prominent part in the reformation of Josiah, but even so his teaching must have prepared for it and reinforced its lessons. At the same time he warns the people that mere ceremonial is useless, even though it be performed at a purified sanctuary. Such opposition as Jeremiah encountered during the reign of Josiah, and apparently he exercised his ministry continually (xxv. 3), must have been of a private and spiteful character as he was probably countenanced by the king. With the accession of Jehoiakim, however, all was changed, the prophet's life became a burden to him and constant persecution was his lot for the remainder of his life.

Such a series of experiences was involved in his acceptance of God's call to him, as he doubtless realised at the time, for though the philosopher may, as Plato says, 'stand out of the way under a wall until the driving storm of sleet and rain be overpast,' the prophet of God can never think of himself or the dangers of his mission and the hardships which it will involve; if he does so, he will assuredly unfit himself for his vocation and be put to shame in the presence of those who oppose him (i. 17). Until his message is delivered the prophet should know that nothing that he fears can overwhelm him, and so he must go about amongst his people with perfect confidence, sharing if need be in the dangers and discomforts of their situation, making them aware of the source from which these have come and of the sin which is their ultimate cause. But at the same time it is no necessary part of the work of the prophet to find solutions for all the problems of the times in which he lives. His duty is rather to point them out, to discover their significance, and to define the limits within which they are really vital; and if in addition he points men's minds to the ever-present reality of a living God in whom all problems find their solution, then may he entrust to others the working out of the details

of his teaching. In other words, the function of the prophet is to deal
with principles, and to leave to the priest and the ruler their application
to everyday life.

Such a course of action is always bound to result in suffering and
persecution, and the prophet often finds himself standing alone as the
witness of righteousness. Loyalty to his mission and to the convictions which inspire and sustain him compels him to attack customs
and beliefs which are the cherished possessions of those in power, the
sacred deposit which must be defended by every means against the
desecration of the profane. In a state like Judah where religion and
politics were hardly to be distinguished, and where, in the words of a
recent writer, 'religious conceptions' were 'mixed up with angry
political passions and carnal dreams[1],' any attack on the one could not
be carried out without a collision with the other. The prince and the
ecclesiastic were the joint guardians of the established order. If
Jeremiah had restricted his teaching to the promulgation of the mystic
truth that God is a spirit and that therefore He demands spiritual
worship (without definitely stating that sacrifices and offerings were
not spiritual), very possibly he would have been allowed to go on
his way as a harmless enthusiast; but when he attacked the temple
worship and the maladministration of the authorities he became
dangerous, the threat to vested interests was too obvious and pressing
to be ignored; all parties combined to crush him. Once the true
inwardness of his teaching and all that it involved were discovered,
his life became a burden to him, and his sensitive soul was wrung by
the hatred of those around him (xv. 10, 17 f.). He was openly contradicted (xxiii. 17, xxvii. 9 ff., xxviii., xxix.) and mocked (xvii. 15,
xx. 7 f., xxiii. 33); false accusations were brought against him (xx. 10,
xxxvii. 13, xxxviii. 4); he was repeatedly imprisoned (xx. 2, xxxii. 3,
xxxiii. 1, xxxvii. 13—21, xxxviii. 6—13); twice he was beaten (xx.
1—3, xxxvii. 11—16); and on at least four occasions his life was
threatened, sometimes by treacherous attacks (xi. 18—21, xviii. 18—
23), once by the royal command (xxxvi. 26), and once by the more
subtle methods of legal procedure (xxvi. 8 f.).

Of the prophet's life during the later years of Jehoiakim the book
gives us little information. After his attack on the temple and the

---

[1] The author of *Pro Christo et Ecclesia* in the volume entitled *Concerning
Prayer*, p. 148. In their original context the words are applied to a later period of
Jewish history, but they are equally true of the times of Jeremiah.

whole sacrificial system[1], an attack which nearly cost him his life, Jeremiah seems to have gone into retirement[2]. But such a with-drawal from actual preaching did not mean that the prophet was inactive; on the contrary, he seized the opportunity to dictate, in response to the Divine command, a summary of his discourses, which he thereupon had presented to the king by the hand of his scribe Baruch, son of Neriah. The indignant and blasphemous conduct of the king has already been referred to, he burnt the roll and tried to apprehend its author, but without success, Jeremiah was 'hidden by the Lord[3].'

We are told nothing of the prophet's fortunes during the first siege of Jerusalem, but on the accession of Zedekiah he once more appears upon the scene. During this, the last reign of Jewish history, Jeremiah had to meet with much opposition from prophets whose claim to be representatives of Jehovah was exactly the same as his own[4]. The message of these prophets was, however, unlike his, one of hope, the exiles were to return from Babylon and to bring with them the vessels of the temple which had been conveyed thither after the fall of the city. The encounter between Jeremiah and one of these prophets, Hananiah by name, is described in detail, together with the subsequent fate of the latter, and there can be but little doubt that this incident is only one instance of what was continually occurring[5]. In spite of his gloomy views of their future and his denial of the possibility of any speedy return, Jeremiah had a very high regard for the members of the first deportation, that is in comparison with those who remained behind, the difference between them was similar to that between good figs and bad[6]. He further shewed his interest in them by sending to Babylon a letter of warning and advice, a letter which aroused some amount of indignation both in Babylon and in Judah itself[7]. When Zedekiah finally threw in his lot with the Anti-Babylonian party and revolted, Jeremiah's position became one of great difficulty, and he suffered at this time many of the indignities to which reference was made above, on one occasion his life was only preserved by the courage and humanity of an Ethiopian eunuch[8]. During the course of the siege the prophet was frequently consulted by the king, and

[1] See vii. 1 ff. and xxvi. 1 ff. with notes.
[2] Whether this retirement was compulsory or voluntary it is impossible to say ; see on xxxvi. 5.
[3] xxxvi. 26. [4] See Additional Note, pp. 182 ff.
[5] xxviii. 1 ff., cf. also xxiii. 9 ff.
[6] xxiv. [7] xxix. [8] xxxviii. 1 ff.

appeals were made to him for some promise of consolation and hope[1], but he remained steadfast to his message that in surrender alone lay the hope of safety. Teaching such as this was bound to be resented by those responsible for the defence of the city, and when, in an interval of the siege caused by the advance of an army of relief from Egypt, Jeremiah essayed to go down to his native village, they seized the opportunity of arresting him as a deserter[2]. This attempt of the Egyptians to relieve Jerusalem, which in the end proved abortive, was a cause of the prophet's gaining further disfavour with his fellow-countrymen. Inspired by fear of punishment and perhaps hoping for Jehovah's favour, the men of Jerusalem had released their slaves in accordance with the requirements of the law ; but when the Babylonians withdrew they once more enforced their claims for service. Such contempt for the rights of God and man could not be allowed to pass uncondemned by the representative of Jehovah, and the prophet was unmeasured in his denunciations[3]. When the Chaldeans finally entered the city Jeremiah received special care at their hands, though the exact sequence of events is hard to follow[4], and in spite of the opportunity of going to Babylon he chose to remain with the scanty remnant of the nation gathering round Gedaliah at Mizpah. For a short time a new hope seemed to dawn and then darkness once more descended for ever, Gedaliah was slain and the prophet taken down to Egypt, where, so tradition says, he met his death at the hands of his fellow-exiles. If this tradition is true, as it well may be in spite of its late date, his death was a fitting climax to a life spent in the devoted service of an ungrateful nation[5].

If the life of Jeremiah be judged according to the standards of worldly success and failure, that is by reference to the ends which he set before himself, or even by comparison with the achievements of other prophets and reformers, it must be reckoned a failure. A study of his utterances shews that the prophet's ministry had two main objectives ; first, to arouse the people to a more worthy conception of the character of God, and of the worship due to Him ; and then by means of

---

[1] xxi., xxxvii. 1 ff., xxxviii. 14 ff.
[2] xxxviii. 11 ff.
[3] xxxiv. 8 ff.   [4] See notes on xl. 1—6.
[5] For a collection of traditions regarding Jeremiah's sojourn in Egypt and his subsequent fate see *Enc. Bib.* 2368. The tradition that the prophet was stoned comes from Christian sources (Tert. *Scorpiace* 8 ; Jerome, *adv. Jov.* II. 37). According to the Jews he escaped from Egypt and went with Baruch to Babylon where he died.

a newly-awakened national conscience to influence the rulers in such a way as to banish injustice and oppression at home, and to bring to an end the system of petty intrigues and alliances which had become traditional in the foreign politics of the nation.

A comparison between the two somewhat similar ministries of Isaiah and Jeremiah—similar that is in aim rather than in performance, though both prophets were witnesses of reforms in religion and both went through the experience of a foreign invasion—suggests that the reasons for the success of the one and the failure of the other lay in the difference between (a) their outward circumstances ; and (b) their inward character.

(a) Jeremiah had an infinitely harder task to perform than had Isaiah, for the period which elapsed between them had been one of decline in nearly every department of the national life[1]. Though the ministry of Isaiah had been a success and the policy suggested by him had been adopted by the leaders of the people[2], yet his warnings and the more spiritual parts of his teaching had been ignored. In fact the very success of his policy had tended to confirm the men of Judah in their conviction that Jehovah would never desert Jerusalem and that it was therefore inviolable. Furthermore, Isaiah was able to command the support of an influential party and of the king himself during the greater part of his ministry ; Jeremiah, on the other hand, always gives the impression of one who stands alone[3], and though he probably had the support of Josiah, yet after the decease of that monarch he had to undergo the opposition of the successive rulers of the nation or at best their languid patronage. The death of Josiah and the failure of the reformation which he had attempted made the work of the prophet exceedingly hard, as these events seemed to be a Divine judgement upon all attempts at purifying the worship of the nation and raising its standard of life ; moreover, the tradition that Jerusalem was God's holy seat and that He would protect it, which had been so strikingly upheld in Isaiah's day, had hardened into a superstition, and one which had become quite divorced from the moral and religious context which it occupied in the teaching of that prophet himself[4].

---

[1] Cf. pp. xlix ff.

[2] There was a reaction, however, against the teaching of Isaiah, in the reign of Manasseh, under whom the prophet, according to a late tradition, was sawn asunder.

[3] It must be admitted that Jeremiah was apt to be pessimistic and like Elijah to overlook the seven thousand who had not bowed the knee to Baal.

[4] The comparison between the prophetic careers of Isaiah and Jeremiah reveals

'There are times,' as Dean Stanley said, 'when ancient truths become modern falsehoods[1].'

(b) Jeremiah's failure, however, was largely due to his own personal limitations. In the first place, he seems to have been unable sufficiently to sympathise with those to whom he was sent, or perhaps it would be more accurate to say that he was unable to shew his sympathy; his attitude was too uncompromising, and his preaching often gives the impression of one who desired to put things as bluntly as possible, and even to shock people. Doubtless such a course was necessary with the self-satisfied audiences whom he addressed, but he seems at times to be needlessly harsh. Very possibly this seeming harshness arose from his love for those whom he was compelled to condemn, for paradoxical as it may sound, a teacher is often most fierce, when he has to criticise those whom he most loves. Jeremiah's love for his country was also a handicap to his preaching in another way, in that it tended to make him seemingly inconsistent, and therefore hard to understand. There were ever two impulses stirring within him, which issued sometimes in stern denunciations, sometimes in tender appeals. After all it must be remembered that the prophet is not the inventor of a perfect system by means of which every little detail of life can be fitted into its appropriate place, and play its part in contributing to a logical and balanced whole[2]. He is not one who depends largely on the promptings of his intellect at all; but he is above all one who follows the guidance of the voice within and who feels deeply the truths for which he has made his stand[3]. It therefore happened that Jeremiah, like the other prophets, had a strong and almost fanatical grasp of a few great principles which he did not hesitate to apply to every object of thought or discussion, and in so doing he was quite regardless of the effect upon other men's minds. He was essentially deductive in his methods and not concerned with the actual facts of the matter in hand, the principle was to be followed at all costs, the facts must find their own place. In other words, he was according to present-day judgements unpractical, a dreamer, and a visionary. He

---

an apparent paradox: Isaiah was a success as far as men could judge, Jeremiah a failure; yet the teaching of the former was perverted and became a stumbling-block, the teaching of the latter became the basis of all future progress in Hebrew religion and culminated in Christianity itself.

[1] *Jewish Church*, II. 441.

[2] Cf. pp. xxx f.

[3] 'The modern reformer may study tactics and opportunities, but the great prophets of old on great occasions follow without questioning the admonition of an inner voice.' Canon Streeter, *Foundations*, p. 123.

was lacking in that sense of statesmanship which enabled Isaiah to seize and use his opportunities, and he does not seem to have had the same sure touch in dealing with practical problems. In this respect there are many parallels to be drawn between him and the gentle saint of Assisi, for St Francis too was quite unable to cope with problems of government and practical politics[1].

Jeremiah, in spite of the fact that many of his proposed reforms must have seemed utterly radical to his fellow-countrymen, was in reality a conservative; his great object was to bring back the purer conditions of that past upon which his heart so frequently meditated[2]. But he was not able to sway men's minds and to make them sharers in the same vision; his influence, however, survived his lifetime, and the ideals which then seemed impossible have not in later times been without their measure of realisation; and, moreover, it is in them that the hope of the future lies[3]. Jeremiah failed, not because like the Stoic, he 'revealed a disease and palsy of human nature which he could not cure[4],' but because he was unable to make the patient realise the seriousness of his state, or to get him to adopt the only possible way of health and safety. But it must not be forgotten that the prophet was chosen by God for his task, and, as will be seen later, his apparent failure brought about the teaching of the New Covenant. The Almighty, if He had so wished, could have forged an instrument which would have saved Judah as a nation, He chose one rather which made possible Judah as a church.

§ 4. The Character of Jeremiah

God's revelation through a prophet has always to be mediated by means of the prophet's personality[5]. If God makes use of a messenger, that messenger is bound to influence the form in which the message is delivered. The message which was entrusted to the various prophets came to them in various ways but almost always by means of the incidents of their ordinary occupations or by the events of contem-

---

[1] Cf. Father Cuthbert, *Life of St Francis of Assisi*, pp. 270 f.
[2] Cf. ii. 1, vi. 16 ff., xxxv. 1 ff. with notes.
[3] For the influence of Jeremiah's teaching see pp. lxxxiii ff.
[4] The Bishop of Winchester in *Lux Mundi*[15], p. 106.
[5] Cf. Dean Stanley, *The Jewish Church*, I. p. 94, 'In grace, as in nature, God, if we may use the well-known expression, *abhorret saltum*, abhors a sudden unprepared transition. "The child is father of the man": the man is father of the prophet.'

porary history. They realised God's voice speaking to them through
their surroundings; then they declared His will to the people amongst
whom they dwelt. In the case of Jeremiah, as of Hosea with whom he
has remarkable similarities of teaching, the experience of his own life
led the prophet to a conception of God such as had been reached
by none before him. This being so, a short sketch of the prophet's
character and its development is a necessary preliminary to the study
of his teaching, as well as being a fitting sequel to the narrative of his
life.

The character of a living person can be estimated and described
after some acquaintance with him and after some enquiry amongst his
familiars; but even here a certain amount of difficulty arises because
every man, even the most simple, leads to some extent a dual existence;
there is the outward life known to his acquaintances, and the inward
life known only to himself. In estimating the character of Jeremiah
both classes of evidence are fortunately available; as was seen above
(pp. xiv f.) the book which bears his name, though much of it is the
record of others, contains passages of priceless value as being sincere
and unreserved revelations of the prophet's secret soul in its highest
relations[1]. This help to the understanding of Jeremiah's character is
all the more valuable as that character is one of much complexity and
its outward seeming must often have deceived his contemporaries; few,
if any, imagined that beneath 'the pillar of iron and brass' there beat
the nervous and hesitating heart of one who confessed that he was but
'a child.' The prophet's inner life might be pictured as some lonely
mountain tarn, sometimes visited by fierce winds, sometimes smiled
upon by the sun and the tender myriads of the stars, but always upborne
by the might of the everlasting hills. Jeremiah, like every other true
prophet, was the human agent of a Divine master, and the weakness of
the agent was ever shrinking back from the compelling power of the
Master[2]. Deeply sensitive and tender hearted, he was at the same time
intrepidly brave; liable to fits of deep emotion, he had a piercing judgement and was also capable of great endurance. His judgement and
knowledge had not been formed like those of Elijah or Amos in the

---

[1] Fortunately there is little question of the genuineness of all the most important autobiographical passages which throw so much light on the prophet's
character and teaching. There is one exception to this—and it is a great exception
—that is the question of the New Covenant (see Additional Note, pp. 241 ff.).

[2] Bishop Gore contrasts 'the life of divinely given authority in insight and
foresight, based upon the divine word communicated and the vision of God vouchsafed: and side by side with it, the life of intense personal trial and dismay.'
Bampton Lectures[2], p. 155.

loneliness of the desert, but he was a townsman and familiar from childhood with the scene of his future ministry[1]. At the same time his affectionate and sympathetic nature enabled him to enter into the feelings even of those whom he condemned, little though they might realise it, and so he never really seems to be detached from them as was Amos or Ezekiel; on the contrary he uttered his condemnations with an aching and broken heart.

Such was the character of Jeremiah in general terms, but a more detailed treatment is necessary in regard to certain outstanding traits.

(*a*) *His timidity*. As was seen above the book of Jeremiah contains a number of self-revelations by the prophet which shew that the outward sternness of his life only concealed an inward conflict. These records of his physical cowardice and shrinking make Jeremiah a figure much more human and like unto the ordinary Christian of to-day; and those who share in his weakness have the consolation of knowing that they can also learn the secret of his strength. There are not many men who are heroes by nature, but there are fewer still who may not become heroes by grace[2]. The call of Jeremiah is the first event narrated in the book which bears his name and it is a record of the spirit in which the prophet carried out his whole life-work. Great self-distrust and inward fear overcome by the power of God are the marks of Jeremiah's ministry. He did not like Isaiah[3] volunteer to go on God's errand, but like Moses[4] he shrank back from it. God gave him power by touching his lips, and then commanded him to speak out all the words which had been given him, otherwise his cowardice would be openly shewn in the sight of his enemies[5]. There can have been few men in the history of the world who have undertaken tasks less congenial to them than did Jeremiah when he became the prophet of Jehovah; the weakness of his nature made his life one long perpetual struggle, he cursed the day on which he was born and even rose to the height of blaming God Himself. His timid spirit and the extremity of suffering which he had to undergo drove him almost to madness; hence his strange boldness towards God. He felt that it was for His sake that he had borne reproach, and that God, as it were, had forced him against his own will to undertake the life of pain which oppressed him and at times threatened to overwhelm him[6]. These strange outbursts are the strongest possible evidence of

---

[1] Duhm's theory that Jeremiah had not visited Jerusalem before the incidents described in v. 1 ff. can hardly be correct, see the introd. to that chapter.

[2] Cf. Cheyne, *Life and Times*, p. 36.

[3] Is. vi. 8.   [4] Ex. iv. 1 ff.   [5] i. 6 ff., 17.

[6] xv. 15—18, xx. 7—12.

the desperate state to which the prophet had been reduced, a state of despair such as comes to 'many a lofty soul which feels itself misunderstood by men, which can hardly believe that it is not deserted by God[1].'

(b) *His power of endurance.* Jeremiah then was timid and aware of the horrors and difficulties of his heavy task; and the more one studies his life, the greater becomes one's wonder that he was able to endure at all. For the most considerable part of his ministry he had to stand practically alone; he had no enthusiastic body of followers who might on the one hand have supported him in his policy and urged him on to fresh efforts, and at the same time concealed from him the strength and ruthlessness of those by whom he was opposed. But as Dr Payne Smith has said: 'Naturally despondent and self-distrustful, there was no feebleness in his character; and he possessed a far higher quality than physical courage in his power of patient endurance[2].' All Jeremiah's powers of patient endurance were needed as his ministry proceeded and as he became more and more convinced that Judah would not give heed to his message. The secret of his courage and endurance was to be found in the God who had called him to His service and whose promise of continual help never failed him. At the same time the Divine power acted as a compelling as well as a helping force. The prophet was decidedly not one of those who from the desire for publicity or fame preach startling sermons, and his shrinking and retiring nature needed the stimulus of God's awful compulsion before the proclamation of his message was possible. Newman's description of the steadfastness of the Christian might well be applied to Jeremiah. 'The foundations of the ocean' he says, 'the vast realms of water which girdle the earth, are as tranquil and as silent in the storm as in the calm. So it is with the souls of holy men. They have a well of peace springing up within them unfathomable; and though the accidents of the hour may make them seem agitated, yet in their hearts they are not so[3].'

(c) *His sensitiveness.* Jeremiah has come down to later ages as the 'weeping prophet,' mainly it may be supposed because the book of Lamentations was traditionally attributed to him, and his name has

---

[1] Stanley, *The Jewish Church*, II. 454.
[2] In the *Speaker's Commentary* on i. 17.
[3] *Parochial and Plain Sermons*, v. p. 69; cf. also John Keble's lines in his poem for the Twenty-third Sunday after Trinity in *The Christian Year*:

'Watching in trance nor dark nor clear,
Th'appalling Future as it nearer draws:
His spirit calmed the storm to meet,
Feeling the rock beneath his feet
And tracing through the cloud the eternal Cause.'

been turned into a byword for pessimistic denunciations. But Jeremiah's denunciations were no more severe than those of the other prophets, his outlook on the future no darker. Why then was it that he above all other prophets should be chosen out to bear the term of reproach? It is almost undoubtedly for two reasons amongst others. (i) The soul of Jeremiah, with the possible exception of Hosea, was more sensitive than that of the others. He was not one who heard the deep sighing of the poor and left it unheeded, rather was he one of that noble but suffering band

> 'to whom the miseries of the world
> Are misery, and will not let them rest.'

It is true that to him as to them all there came times when (to continue the quotation) he did desire to 'find a haven,' not indeed 'in the world' but rather from it. This longing, due to natural reaction in one of a highly strung and sensitive nature, is evidence of the extremity of his suffering rather than of his desire to avoid responsibility, and was soon put aside and no doubt repented of with tears. (ii) Just as Jeremiah felt the miseries of the individual Israelites so he felt the horrors of the fate which was coming upon the nation at large. His naturally affectionate disposition, cut off from the love of wife or child, poured itself out in overflowing measure upon his country. Isaiah or Ezekiel could utter the most scathing condemnations of Israel or Judah, could forecast for them the most desperate fortunes and apparently remain unaffected themselves; but such was not the case with Jeremiah, he was no mere 'looker on of this world's stage' and the sorrows of the nation were as his own, its hopeless and pitiable fate moved him till as he himself said his eyes became 'fountains of water.' The horrors which were coming seemed to fascinate him, he could not take his mind from them, and so it is that he seems almost to delight in dwelling on scenes of destruction and in picturing God's thirst for vengeance slaking itself in the most awful carnage[1]. Jeremiah's life as a prophet was constantly darkened by the character of the message which he had to deliver; and like a judge compelled to sentence his only child, his soul shrank in dread from the words of condemnation which his lips were bidden to utter. What made the position harder for the prophet was the knowledge that by warning the people of the coming of judgement he was making more certain their ultimate punishment, for it has been proved time and again that 'the judgements of God, public or personal, though

---

[1] Cf. xii. 12, xxv. 30—33, xlvi. 10, l. 25—29.

they ought' as Coleridge says 'to drive us to God, yet the heart, unchanged, runs the further from God[1].' Again and again he even ventures to expostulate with God Himself on behalf of the people, sometimes with a boldness which is surprising, verging as it does on irreverence. This attitude of mind is brought out more clearly still by a comparison with Jeremiah's younger contemporary Ezekiel, whose message had so many points in common with his own. Ezekiel had no mental conflict, all was clear to him, nay he ever delighted to carry the Divine message even if it involved the destruction of his native land. Ezekiel is always on the Lord's side, and sees nothing but the sin and wickedness which have called forth the Divine anger; there is indeed something grim and stern about his attitude which is in strong contrast to the tender yearning of the earlier prophet, who often dares to take the part of his people even against their rightful Lord and to defend and excuse them (cf. xiv. 13, &c.).

Jeremiah loved Jerusalem and all that it stood for 'as an Athenian loved the city of the violet crown, as a Roman loved the city of the seven hills,' and it was this wonderful love that enabled him to pierce below the surface of the national life and to discern the evil which was slowly sapping its strength. He alone of all those who took in hand the cure of the unhappy country could heal its malady because he alone had sufficient insight to diagnose the disease from which it suffered. The politician and the religionist cried 'Peace, peace' when there was no peace, trying to soothe with soft words the patient whose ills they had never investigated; but Jeremiah's purpose went far deeper, he was determined, in Bacon's words, 'to search the wounds of the country, not to skim them over'; and whilst they poured in the oil of the physician, he constantly declared that the only hope of salvation lay in the surgeon's knife. But in all truth he had a hopeless and distressing task and his experience might well be described in words which were written of another. 'It is difficult to conceive any situation more painful than that of a great man, condemned to watch the lingering agony of an exhausted country, to tend it during the alternate fits of stupefaction and raving which precede its dissolution, and to see the symptoms of vitality disappear one by one, till nothing is left but coldness, darkness and corruption[2].' Jeremiah remained constant in his love in spite of the apostasy of the nation, in spite of the sufferings

---

[1] *Aids to Reflection*, xcvii.
[2] Macaulay, *Essay on Machiavelli*. This same quotation has been applied to Jeremiah quite independently by Dr Streane.

which he endured at the hands of its rulers. He knew that the political future was dark and so he counselled submission and thus brought upon himself the hatred of his fellow-countrymen, and at the end when the rulers and the nobles had gone into exile he still clung to the broken remnant left in the land.

(*d*) *His desire for sympathy.* One point which must strike every student of the life and writings of the prophet is his great loneliness. It is as though throughout his whole life he was lavishing his affection upon objects from which he vainly expected some return. Cut off from his countrymen as Jeremiah was by the message of condemnation which he had to deliver, and hated by his brethren, one might have thought that he would have been allowed to find a natural solace in the love of a wife and children. The whole nature of the prophet seemed to demand such a consolation, for Jeremiah was no ascetic and hater of pleasure, and he took a gladsome delight in the young life growing up around him; the first picture which comes to his mind when he tries to imagine the approaching ruin is of the fate of the innocent children playing in the streets[1]. But these natural instincts and desires were not to be fulfilled, marriage was denied to him[2], and the prophet knew in his heart that his life must be dedicated to the delivery of his message. Jeremiah was unique amongst the prophets in this respect, so far as we know, though Hosea was unfortunate in his married life[3], and Ezekiel was forbidden to mourn for the loss of a dearly loved wife, 'the desire of his eyes' as he called her, who was suddenly snatched from him[4]. As was seen above, the affection which Jeremiah poured out upon his nation was turned back into his own bosom and his efforts on its behalf entirely misunderstood; some few indeed of his countrymen seem to have given him a tardy sympathy and an effective protection, and one at least was not afraid to stand by his side and even to represent him at the peril of his life; but on the whole Jeremiah received more favour and consideration from the enemies of his people than from the people themselves. Yet the prophet longed for the love of his fellows, and the fact that they misinterpreted his motives and suspected his teaching was a great grief to him. It was probably in order to gain the ear of the nation and to make an *apologia pro vita sua* that Jeremiah made public those intimate experiences between his soul and God which are of such inestimable value to later generations. The prophet was

---

[1] vi. 11 and ix. 20 (see Cornill's note on the former passage).
[2] xvi. 1 f. where see notes.
[3] Hos. i.—iii.   [4] Ez. xxiv. 15—24.

reticent by nature, such at least is the conclusion suggested by the account of his call, where no attempt is made to describe the appearance of the Almighty, or the phenomena which accompanied and heralded His approach, though at the same time the prophet does not hesitate to claim that it was no seraph who touched his lips but Jehovah Himself[1]. It seems therefore that these passages, unique as they are in prophetic literature, are the outstretchings of a deeply wronged and suffering man towards those who have done him hurt, but whom he still loves and longs to save. In their eyes he had shewn himself to be harsh, unfeeling, and one whose denunciations of his country reached the point of barely concealed treachery. By his self-revelation the prophet wished to let the people see the other side of the picture, he wished them to know of all his vain longings and pleadings on their behalf and to realise something of the sufferings which were inflicted upon him by the fate of his beloved land. This motive seems alone sufficient to account for the laying bare of Jeremiah's soul.

Jeremiah has been likened to many personages in history, generally in regard to the bitter experience of his life. He has been likened 'to Cassandra, the Trojan prophetess, whose fate it was never to be believed, though prophesying nothing but the truth; to Phocion, the rival of Demosthenes in the last generation of Athenian greatness[2], who maintained the unpopular but sound doctrine that, if Athens were to escape worse evils, she must submit peaceably to the growing power of Macedon; to Dante, whose native state, Florence, was in relation to France and the Empire as Palestine was to Egypt and Babylon, while the poet like the prophet could only protest without effect against the ever-growing dangers[3].' All these comparisons, as was said above, deal with the fate of the prophet rather than with his character. It may perhaps be allowable to introduce another comparison regarding the latter aspect. Readers of Miss Evelyn Underhill's *Mysticism* will hardly fail to recognise the justice of likening Jeremiah to Suso, the German mystic of the fourteenth century. Suso was indeed the Jeremiah amongst contemplatives, both for his sensitiveness to the hardships of his lot and for the habit of self-analysis and self-revelation which made him record them[4]. He had at the same time much of the prophet's boldness

---

[1] i. 9 ; cf. Is. vi. 1—7 ; and Ez. i.—iii.

[2] This comparison was first made, I believe, by Bunsen, *Gott in der Geschichte*, p. 144.

[3] Dr Streane in *Camb. Bible*, p. xxxii.

[4] Cf. p. 488, 'There is no grim endurance about Suso : he feels every hard knock, and all the instincts of his nature are in favour of telling his griefs.'

B.   *d*

and endurance in facing the difficulties of his position and the enmity of his friends. Nor was he lacking in the insight which made him see in the casual incidents of everyday life symbols of his own life in relation to God[1].

§ 5. The Teaching of Jeremiah

i. *His conception of God*

The teaching of Jeremiah, as of the other prophets, was based ultimately on his conception of Jehovah. The religious teachers of Israel as was said above were deductive in their methods, in other words they began by accepting the truth of certain great principles regarding the Divine Nature and deduced from them their duty towards both God and man. The deductive methods of the prophets, however, did not apparently lessen their wonderful powers of observation and of reflection, though inevitably they tended to make the facts of life and thought which they discovered conform to their preconceived ideas. Jeremiah, like his forerunners, assumed the existence of the God whom he worshipped and whose will he declared. To a Semite the atheism which follows on reflection was unknown, every Semite believed in God and paid Him the dues of worship and sacrifice, though this belief in God might be accompanied by that more terrible form of atheism, which leaves God out of all account in the practical life of the individual and nation alike. Such a conception of God as this was naturally based on a much narrower review of the facts of life than the similar conceptions of modern teachers. It was a conception of God which was fundamentally and entirely religious, and one which owed nothing either to natural science on the one side or to philosophy on the other.

(*a*) *Jehovah is a living God.* The book of Jeremiah then contains no apologetic, no 'proofs' of the existence of God; He is there, as real to the prophet as the nation itself, as real as his own soul. This absence of apologetic, which seems so remarkable to a western mind, is accompanied by the omission of any systematic statements regarding the Divine Nature. For whilst it may be confidently asserted that the conception of the character of Jehovah which each prophet held was the basis of his teaching, yet, paradoxical as it may sound, what that conception was in each case can only be gathered from incidental allusions. The mark of the pre-exilic Hebrew writings was *life* rather

---

[1] Cf. his conversation with the knight, *op. cit.* pp. 488 f.

than *thought*; the writers had known Jehovah and felt His influence in their souls; they had not yet been able to find for such knowledge a systematic and ordered expression, nay they had hardly felt the need for it. Life comes before thought in the spiritual, as in the natural world, and experience must ever be the forerunner of reflection; as Aubrey Moore has well put it, 'Religion in its earliest stages is instinctive not reasoned[1].' Jeremiah's own conception of God was derived from the teaching of the older prophets, as that teaching was current in Judah, and as it was interpreted by his own intense spiritual experiences, experiences which whilst they interpreted the older ideas at the same time modified them.

The predominant mark of the prophetic conception of God was as we have seen its unswerving grasp of His reality, that belief in a living God which must be the basis of any true religion. The period during which Jeremiah was called upon to exercise his ministry was one which demanded reality in religion as in everything else, for he lived in a time of crisis. There is a sense in which it is true to say that every moment marks a crisis, inasmuch as every moment is the meeting place of the whole of the past and the departing point of all the future, it is the daughter of the ages, and the mother of the years that are yet to be. But in Jeremiah's days the sense of crisis, of a time of testing, was something more insistent than this; hence the demand for reality.

(*b*) *Jehovah is the only God.* It is not quite clear whether Jeremiah looked upon Jehovah as the sole God of the universe, the majority of his contemporaries certainly did not, but he was at any rate a practical monotheist, and in his eyes the gods of the heathen when compared with Jehovah were but nothingness (iv. 1, vii. 30) and vanity (xiv. 22, xvi. 19 ff., xviii. 15)[2], the work of men's hands (ii. 27 f., xvi. 19 ff.), and as such entirely subordinate to the God of Israel (ii. 11; cf. Dt. iv. 19 f.). Jeremiah's monotheism is further shewn by his unquestioning belief that it was not Israel alone which was under the

---

[1] *Lux Mundi*[15], p. 48; cf. the quotation from Newman in the same essay, p. 64: 'As the intellect is cultivated and expanded, it cannot refrain from the attempt to analyse the vision which influences the heart, and the object in which it centres; nor does it stop till it has, in some sort, succeeded in expressing in words, what has all along been a principle both of the affections and of practical obedience.' *Arians*, ch. II. § 1. See also W. Temple, *The Faith and Modern Thought*, pp. 43 f.: 'it is possible that the man who has the most vital communion with God will be least able to make a scientific theory of that experience. I suppose that Shakespeare knew very much less about the method on which he constructed his plays than either Coleridge or Professor Bradley.'

[2] This view may be compared with the idea current in early Christian literature that they were demons.

control of Jehovah, but that His rule extended over other nations as well (xviii. 7 ff., xxvii. 7, xxviii. 14). The prophet though he recognised Jehovah's power over the heathen, still felt that there was a relationship of an especial character between Him and Judah. This can clearly be gathered from the titles by which God is addressed, titles such as 'the Hope of Israel' (xiv. 8, xvii. 13), 'the Saviour thereof' (xiv. 8), He who is in the midst of His people (xiv. 9), as well as by the more usual title 'Jehovah, the God of Israel.'

(c) *The attributes of God.* It will be convenient to arrange these under two heads, those which may be called the physical and those which may be called the moral attributes of God.

(a) *The physical attributes.* In the prophet's eyes Jehovah is the creator of the universe (xxvii. 5, xxxi. 37), highly exalted (xvii. 12), and omnipotent (xviii. 6, xxxii. 26 f.). It is He also who sustains the world, ruling it by His ordinances (xxxi. 35), and keeping the various parts of the natural creation in due subordination to the whole, and even though

'The ambitious ocean swell and rage and foam
To be exalted with the threatening clouds'

it cannot overpass its lawful bounds (v. 22). God who restrains the sea, also controls the waters above the firmament and at His will can bring rain upon the earth (v. 24), thus meeting what was one of the great tests of Divine power in the ancient world (xiv. 22). Although Jeremiah makes use of anthropomorphic expressions, he is very careful, as are most of the prophets, to avoid the use of those cruder forms of expression such as are found in the Pentateuch, expressions by which Jehovah is represented as delighting in the smell of sacrifices (Gen. viii. 21; cf. Ps. li. 16); and as needing to descend to earth in order to become acquainted with the doings of men (Gen. xi. 5). Jehovah, to Jeremiah, is one who knows all the thoughts of men and is the searcher out of the reins and the heart (xvii. 10, xx. 12, xxiii. 24). It is true that in one passage weariness is ascribed to the Deity (xv. 6), but the use is obviously metaphorical. The prophetic conception of the physical attributes of God was not without its weakness, in that it laid undue stress on His transcendence and power. As the present Dean of St Paul's has well said, 'There is not necessarily anything divine about omnipotence[1].' Even in Jeremiah's doctrine of the New Covenant God is still transcend-

---

[1] *Contentio Veritatis*, p. 100; the passage continues, ' It is conceivable that the universe might have been ruled by an omnipotent devil; in which case men would have been found to defy him, and to go to his hell coerced, but unsubdued.'

ent, He is outside and above mankind, and it is the covenant which is
to be written in their hearts, not God who is to make them His abode
(cf. the teaching of NT.: Eph. iii. 17, &c.). The stress on the transcendence of God which was so strongly marked in Hebrew religion
was not, however, without its good side, for it taught men to reverence
God, and as a result 'their religion, alone among the primitive religions
of the world, remained free from degrading myths and untainted by
any association with sensuality[1].'

(β) *The moral attributes.* Any conception of God which lays too
much stress on the physical attributes of the Deity tends either to
over-emphasise His power and transcendence, as did the Hebrew;
or going to the other extreme, to bring Him down to the level of
His worshippers, whom He then exceeds only by the greater licence
of His passions, and the more abundant means which He possesses
of gratifying them. Such was the conception of the Divine Nature
held by the popular religion of the Greeks, hence its utter failure
to secure the allegiance of the better minds amongst them and its
eventual displacement by various systems of philosophy; systems
which, during the period of highest development, more and more
tended to ignore metaphysics altogether and to find all their interest
in the sphere of ethics. Amongst the Hebrews, however, religion
and morality were ever closely allied, and in the prophets this alliance
becomes almost a unity, religion is morality, at any rate as regards
the duty of man to man; 'He hath shewed thee, O man, what is
good; and what doth the Lord require of thee, but to do justly, and
to love mercy, and to walk humbly with thy God[2]?' Jehovah was
Himself a righteous God and above all things He required in those
who worshipped Him the same love of justice and righteous dealing
(ix. 24). The righteousness of God was also shewn by His sternness
towards sin and those who persisted in it, against such the Divine
wrath went forth like the sudden blast of a trumpet (xxiii. 19 ff.),
and even the natural world (iv. 26) and the very beasts of the field
were shaken by it (vii. 20). There is something almost unloving
about Jeremiah's conception of God, something which suggests only
the twilight of revelation, and which has hardly approached the truer
conception of God as the loving Father who sent His Son to die for

---

[1] Inge, *op. cit.* p. 66. The last part of this statement is true only of the highest
type of Hebrew religion, the prophets were constantly denouncing the immoral
practices associated with the popular worship (see pp. xlix f. below).
[2] Mic. vi. 8.

the world Even in his own relations with the Almighty, Jeremiah often seems to regard Him as a stern taskmaster (xx. 7 ff. &c.). There is, however, another aspect of his teaching, and he holds out to those who are penitent and desirous of returning from their sinful ways the loving-kindness and mercy of the Lord (iii. 12, ix. 24, xxxi. 20). At the same time one cannot help feeling that the repeated acts of apostasy of which many individual Hebrews were guilty at this time came not only from the doubt of Jehovah's power (xliv. 18; Ez. viii. 12), but also from unwillingness to comply with the conditions necessary for worshipping Him. The teaching of the prophets made men begin to realise that Jehovah could only be approached by those who had 'clean hands and a pure heart'; but other deities, so the people thought, might possess equal power and be less particular as to the morals of those who came to them as suppliants. Such action on the part of the people is no condemnation of the prophetic teaching for the stress which it laid on morality, but morality in itself is not attractive, and the phrases so often on the lips of Jeremiah 'to provoke Jehovah to anger' (vii. 19), 'the wrath of Jehovah' (xviii. 20, &c.), may have made his countrymen afraid of their God. The idea of God's wrath, though a very necessary complement to the idea of His love, is liable to misinterpretation and when emphasised in the present day often originates in our own blinded and wrathful hearts[2]. The Lady Julian of Norwich, speaking of a vision of God which came to her, says, 'I saw no wrath but on man's part; and that forgiveth He in us. For wrath is nought else but a frowardness and contrariness to peace and love; and either it cometh of failing of might, or of failing of wisdom, or of failing of goodness, which failing is not in God but on our part[3].'

(*d*) *Summary.* Such was the conception of God which formed the basis of Jeremiah's teaching: Jehovah was high and lifted up, the creator and sustainer of the universe, yet not ignoring His people, and above everything else He was a just and holy being demanding justice and holiness in those who professed to serve Him. This conception Jeremiah owed in its main outlines to the teaching of the older prophets. There are, however, certain points in the rest of Jeremiah's teaching which are in an especial manner his own, and which form his

---

[1] It is not intended to suggest that Jeremiah's conception of God was harsher than that of the other OT. prophets.

[2] It should be remembered that to the Hebrews every disaster was directly due to the Divine action; cf. pp. 10 ff.

[3] Quoted by Inge, *Studies in the English Mystics*, p. 67.

contribution to the ever-growing revelation of God. These points must be dealt with at much greater length. Before going on to deal with them, however, and indeed as an introduction to them it will perhaps be not unprofitable briefly to summarise the condition of popular religion during the period covered by the prophet's ministry.

ii. *The religious condition of the Nation*

By the time of Jeremiah the pure worship of Jehovah, which the Israelites had brought from the desert (ii. 2 f. &c.), had ceased to exist amongst the nation at large, although it was still preserved amongst communities like the Rechabites[1]. When the primitive Israelites invaded Palestine, and began to settle down in the land, they were compelled to exchange the simple life of the nomad for the more complicated existence of the agriculturist, and no doubt they had to depend for their knowledge of the new arts upon their conquered neighbours, the Canaanites. With the arts of agriculture, and as a most important part of them, would go the cult of the local Baal, the patron from immemorial antiquity of each several tract of land. The new conditions of life required new habits of worship[2]. As a result many degrading customs and many horrible superstitions were incorporated into the religion of Jehovah; for it must not be forgotten that ancient religions, at any rate in their popular forms, were essentially eclectic, and that the common people in worshipping the Baalim were conscious of no disloyalty to the God of Israel (ii. 23, ix. 14, xi. 13, xix. 5). This habit of mind is invariably the mark of periods of transition from one religion to another, and such periods are often indefinitely prolonged. Christianity itself has borrowed largely from outside sources in developing its forms of worship and even its doctrinal statements. In this connexion the account of the Goths preserved in Gregory of Tours, *Hist. Franc.* v. 44 is not without interest: 'We do not reckon it a crime to worship this or that; for we say in our common speech, it is no harm

---

[1] See xxxv. 1 ff. with notes.

[2] Cf. A. C. Turner in *Concerning Prayer*, p. 376. 'Jehovah was a great God of War, and had driven the gods of Canaan before him; but, once in, it was not so certain that he could ensure the kindly fruits of the earth in due season. Agriculture was not in his line. Would it not be as well to make doubly sure by setting up a high place to the local Baal who had tended the ground from all time?' In a similar way when the Aryan peoples invaded India they borrowed many superstitions and beliefs from the aborigines, and these found expression both in their religious life and also in their literature. See Poussin, *The Way of Nirvāna*, pp. 16 ff.

if a man passing between heathen altars and a church of God makes his reverence in both directions[1].'

The worship of the Canaanite Baalim and of Jehovah under conceptions which were practically identical, as well as of the female counterparts of the Baalim, the goddesses of fecundity, was accompanied by a variety of sexual crimes which the better feeling of a later age has striven to conceal, but which must have accounted in no small measure for the unswerving opposition of the prophets and of the higher minds of the community to the manner in which the local sanctuaries were conducted, and which in the end led to their suppression (see pp. xxi f.). Traces of these practices can be found in the statements in 1 K. xiv. 24; 2 K. xxiii. 7; and in the law in Dt. xxiii. 17 f.[2] When Jeremiah spoke of Judah as 'playing the harlot' and as 'committing adultery' his words had a literal as well as a metaphorical truth behind them. In addition to these abuses which were of long standing, other more recent superstitions had been introduced by Manasseh. These superstitions owed their introduction to the much closer contact between Judah and the great nations of the East which was then beginning. In addition to the condemnation of the worship of the Baalim (vii. 9, ix. 14, &c.; Zeph. i. 4), of stocks and stones (ii. 27, xxv. 6), and of other gods (i. 16, iii. 9, &c.), condemnations such as had been frequent in the earlier prophets, there are to be found in Jeremiah and his contemporaries notices of the adoration of the heavenly bodies (v. 18, viii. 2, xix. 13; Zeph. i. 5), especially of the Queen of Heaven (xliv. 15 ff.), of devotions to Tammuz (Ez. viii. 14) and other nameless superstitions (Ez. viii. 10 ff.), as well as of the spread of the custom of infant sacrifice (vii. 31, xix. 5) and of 'making children pass through the fire to Molech' (xxxii. 35; Ez. xvi. 21, xx. 26, 31; cf. also Zeph. i. 5). In all these habits and customs of worship, habits and customs which made the prophet refer to his contemporaries as 'the generation of God's wrath' (vii. 29), the people were encouraged by the example of those who were their rulers in both the religious and the political sphere (xxiii. 2, 15 f.). Under circumstances such as these the backsliding of the people was continuous (viii. 4), and even the striking and tragic fate of the Northern Kingdom had failed utterly to be a warning to them (iii. 6 ff.); on the contrary, so blinded were the men of Judah to their

---

[1] Quoted by Gore, *Bampton Lectures*[2], p. 92.
[2] The word which is translated *sodomite* in EVV. is literally 'sacred person,' that is to say one consecrated to the service of the deity; see Driver's note on Dt. xxiii. 17; Frazer, *Adonis*, &c. I. 17, 57 ff.

true condition, that the fact that they had escaped when Samaria was overthrown was to them a pledge and token of the favour with which Jehovah regarded them[1].

iii.   *The New Covenant*

Early in his ministry 'in the days of Josiah' (iii. 6), Jeremiah looked forward to a time when Israel would have shepherds after Jehovah's own heart who would give the people knowledge of their God. This conception of religion as communion with Him 'in knowledge of whom standeth our eternal life' became deeper and ever deeper in the prophet's mind during the course of his life, in spite of the bitter experience in which every fresh insight into the state of the nation involved him. That religion as he understood it was ever to become the possession of the nation as a whole seemed to him something impossible; those who were accustomed to do evil could no more do good than the Ethiopian could change his skin, the leopard his spots (xiii. 23). God had indeed revealed Himself to the fathers of the race, and at Sinai had entered into a covenant with them, but how were they to keep their side of the covenant? How could man know and do the will of God? The prophet had to go through that agony of perplexity and despair which has been the lot of so many and which has been described for all time by St Paul in Rom. vii. 15 ff. At last he saw the solution, not as the apostle saw it, or as we may see it with a full experience of the power of the risen and ascended Christ, but as something 'dimly and faintly hidden and afar.' Man can only keep God's law by its being written in his under-

---

[1] Some scholars have seen in Israel's readiness to submit to foreign influence both in the way of thought and of institutions a mark of the vitality of the nation and one of the causes of its true greatness. Professor W. R. Harper, for example, says 'A striking characteristic of Israel, in comparison with its sister nations, was a readiness to receive, from the outside, contributions in the form of new institutions and new thought. Much of this was bad and in time was lost; but much of it, being good, was retained. The gradual accumulation and assimilation of this outside material, under the guidance of an all-wise Providence, ultimately lifted Israel to a position of influence in world-history.' *Amos and Hosea* (*ICC.*), p. xxxi note. Whilst one rejoices to recognise with Newman that 'He who had taken the seed of Jacob for His elect people had not therefore cast the rest of mankind out of His sight' and that 'The Greek poets and sages were in a certain sense prophets,' and whilst one hesitates to criticise so high an authority as Dr Harper, yet this and similar statements seem to the present writer to contain a two-fold exaggeration, in that they exaggerate on the one hand the extent of the outside influences which entered into the life of Israel—especially in comparison with other nations—and on the other they attribute to such influences greater benefits than were actually obtained from them. The influences above all others which made Israel great were its own native influences.

standing and by his having such a knowledge of the Divine as will keep him in constant communion with his heavenly Father.

But it was not the consideration of the nation's failure to keep the covenant of Sinai that alone led Jeremiah to his discovery; the circumstances of his own life had already forced him to realise the necessity for communion between God and man. To the early Semites men were part of a nation and as such had a relation to the God of the tribe or race; any other ground of acceptance had hardly been thought of. The prophets of Israel, almost from the first, realised the limitations of this theory of man's relation to God, but it required the lapse of many generations before the clear doctrine of the possibility of communion between each individual soul and God was plainly taught by Jeremiah and Ezekiel. The idea was not, however, entirely new for, as Jowett pointed out, in the answer to Elijah 'yet have I seven thousand who have not bowed the knee to Baal,' there is an indication of a 'change in God's mode of dealing with His people...the whole people were not regarded as one; there were a few who still preserved amidst the general corruption, the worship of the true God[1].' These scattered hints and vague anticipations of the doctrine of God's dealings with individuals first found open and clear expression in the teaching of Jeremiah. The experiences of the prophet's life were such as to drive him back, as it were, on God at every point—the deep affectionateness of his nature which seemed for ever doomed to be thwarted in its efforts to find any human outlet; the isolation in which his mission involved him; the weakness and infirmity of his 'flesh' which needed constant renewals of the Divine refreshment; the harsh treatment at the hands of the beloved nation, the only earthly object his affections ever really found upon which to lavish themselves; all these experiences tended to force the prophet back upon God Himself, recognised as to be known and loved as a person, and as the only satisfying object of the prophet's love. In view of his own knowledge Jeremiah was enabled to grasp the fact that all men needed a God and that all might know Him; hence the doctrine of the New Covenant and his realisation of the true nature of religion, or rather of its necessary basis, the personal knowledge of God by the individual. The failure of Josiah's reformation shewed him unmistakably that something more than a mere external law was needed to make men obey God, and in this as in his teaching on circumcision, he anticipated St Paul. If Josiah's efforts with all the influences behind

---

[1] *The Epistles of St Paul*, II. 148 f.

them came to nothing, was another likely to succeed where he had
failed ? Jeremiah, then, despaired of the religion of his country as he
found it; the Old Covenant must, he was convinced, give place to a
New, and a different and purer conception of religion be substituted
for the easygoing, popular worship of the temple. But though Jeremiah
in his teaching looked forward to a time when the Old Covenant would
have been superseded by the New (xxxi. 31 ff.), yet he did not deny
the Divine origin of the former, and indeed he complains that men do
not keep it (viii. 8, ix. 13, xi. 9—17). The Old Covenant had been
made with the nation as a whole, his higher conception of religion
demanded that the new spiritual relation between God and man should
be inaugurated by a personal covenant; 'this is the covenant that I
will make with the house of Israel after those days, saith the Lord;
I will put my law in their inward parts, and in their heart will I write
it; and I will be their God, and they shall be my people: and they
shall teach no more every man his brother, saying, Know the Lord; for
they shall all know me, from the least of them unto the greatest[1].' These
few verses form the crown of Jeremiah's teaching, and indeed of the
whole of the OT. and that not so much because of what they meant to
those who first received them, as because they are a summing up of all
the aspirations of the whole human race, aspirations which are in many
cases dumb and inarticulate, for the personal knowledge of a personal
God. The notable thing about the passage is the fact that there is in
it, not the promise of a new law—such a promise would have been no
novelty—but that men are to receive power to keep the provisions of
the law inasmuch as it will be written in their hearts. It is the glorious
claim of the gospel that in Jesus Christ this promise is fulfilled. 'I
thank God through Jesus Christ...For the law of the Spirit of life in
Christ Jesus hath made me free from the law of sin and death[2].'

The doctrine of the New Covenant as set forth by Jeremiah had but
little influence on his successors, and post-exilic Judaism developed
on lines which were so different as almost to be opposed to such a
spiritual conception of religion. That this should have been so is not
so surprising as it seems at the first glance. Jeremiah was much in
advance of his times and the nation was not ripe for such teaching,

---

[1] xxxi. 33 f. In actual fact each male Israelite was brought into covenant
relation with Jehovah in the rite of circumcision (Gen. xvii. 11), but Jeremiah's
conception was something much more spiritual.
[2] Rom. vii. 25 a, viii. 2 : cf. Bishop Westcott on Heb. viii. 8, 'under this covenant (i.e. the New Covenant) grace not law is the foundation of fellowship. God
comes to man as giving and not as requiring.'

men preferred less exalted ideas of the meaning of religion and found in the due performance of the ritual and ceremonial requirements of the law a sufficient tax on their piety. In the present day the same difficulty has to be faced, there is the same task of persuading men of the wonderful privileges to which they have a right, and of applying to the individual the powers which have been so lavishly poured out upon the Church—the great problem is still that of awakening individual Christians to the realisation of their privileges as members of the body of Christ and living temples of the Holy Ghost.

Jeremiah, then, looked upon the Old Covenant of legal requirements as ready to pass away, but, like St Paul, he would hardly have allowed men to be free from restrictions entirely; he who had the law written on his heart would obey it more readily than he who had to consult some external ordinance to discover what it was. Life according to rule has its place under the new dispensation as well as under the old; and no merely emotional religion, however highly it may exalt the feelings of him who experiences it, can be a complete substitute for a religion which lays stress on the due performance of ethical commands. It is indeed true that the Christian is a new creature, but discipline is necessary none the less, so long as undue value is not attached to the 'rule of life' and so long as the source of strength is recognised to be in God (cf. Phil. ii. 12 f.). 'There is no more certain fact,' to quote Dean Church, 'in the range of human experience than that with strong and earnest religious feeling there may be a feeble and imperfect hold on the moral law, often a very loose sense of justice, truth and purity.... The kindling and absorbing earnestness which has given itself with ardour to some high religious object is not safe, wants its only solid and trustworthy foundation, unless it has full in view, unforgotten and deeply reverenced, the great fixed law of moral right ruling with no reserves over the inner and unseen life[1].'

iv. *The punishment of the innocent*

One provision of the law as laid down by his predecessors Jeremiah, in view of his new conception of the relation of God and man, felt bound to oppose. There existed in ancient times a widely held view that the sins of a parent might be punished in the persons of his descendants, such, for example, was the teaching of the Code of Hammurabi[2], and of

---

[1] *The Discipline of the Christian Character*, p. 41.
[2] See S. A. Cook, *The Laws of Moses*, &c. p. 261.

many passages of OT. (e.g. Ex. xx. 5; Josh. vii. 24 f.; 1 S. xxii. 16 f.; 2 S. xxi. 1—9). Nor was this idea confined to the Semitic branch of the human family, similar pronouncements are found amongst the Greeks. Solon, for example, expressly declares that 'if the guilty escape, and the doom ordained by Heaven fall not upon themselves, it will surely fall hereafter; the innocent will suffer for the guilty, their children perhaps or later generations[1].' In a somewhat higher strain, and looking at the matter not from the point of view of a legislator but of the innocent sufferers, Theognis prays 'when children of an unjust father follow after justice in thought and act...let them not pay for the transgressions of their sires[2].' The belief no doubt originally arose partly because of the widespread idea that the real unit was not the individual but the tribe, and especially the family; partly as an explanation of the suffering of the apparently innocent (cf. Jn. ix. 1 ff.). There is a sense in which the old idea is valid as the study of natural science has shewn; children do suffer for the sins of their parents; but the explanation is different. In OT. times there was no conception of the Laws of Nature (cf. pp. xlviii. 10 ff.), or of any intermediary forces—God Himself was the direct agent in every transaction. Therefore any evil came from Him and was regarded as the expression of His anger against the guilty offender. More enlightened ages have recognised a distinction between the *consequences* of sins and their punishment, and to regard the former as judgements introduces a limitation and depicts God as a harsh despot[3]. Jeremiah taught, as did Ezekiel after him, that men must suffer for their own sins and in his teaching, let it not be forgotten, Hebrew religion arrived at a point which was not reached by Greek philosophy until some two centuries later in the time of Plato[4].

v. *The value of ritual*

Believing as Jeremiah did, that religion was a relation of a spiritual character between God and the individual, he found himself opposed

---

[1] xii. 17 ff. Cf. J. Adam, *Religious Teachers of Greece*, pp. 86 f., to whom I am indebted for this and the following quotations.

[2] 737 ff. Cf. Ez. xviii. 21 f.; the similarity, however, is only verbal as the prophet is dealing with the case of an unrighteous man who himself turns from the evil of his ways.

[3] Cf. S. Schechter, *Studies in Judaism*, p. 265, 'There is no possibility of overcoming the moral objection against punishment of people for sins which they have not committed.'

[4] xxxi. 29 f.; Ez. xviii.; cf. Dt. xxiv. 16; Wisd. iii. 16; and for a discussion of the treatment of the whole question in Apocryphal Literature see Wicks, *The Doctrine of God in Jew. Apoc. Lit.* pp. 257 ff.

to the popular ideas in another respect, namely in regard to the value of ritual. Jeremiah was a typical 'prophet' in his outlook, and the priestly and institutional elements of religion were for him of comparatively little importance,—an attitude of mind which was strongly in contrast with that of Ezekiel (see pp. lxxxiv f.), and he even goes so far as to deny the divine origin of the temple sacrificial system[1]. The truth of the matter was that Jeremiah, like the English Puritans, had within him 'the consciousness of a spiritual life which no outward ordinances could adequately express[2].' The position of ritual in religion and the outward expression of the spiritual life will always remain a problem to worshipping man, some form of ritual expression seems necessary, as the banner of the Salvationist and the handshake of the Quaker plainly shew. Ritual becomes dangerous when its observance is made a substitute for righteousness, or when it is used for the setting forth of what are looked upon as false doctrines.

In primitive communities where religion has scarcely struggled above the level of magic the due and proper performance of the correct ritual acts is of the utmost importance, more important by far than the observance of any merely ethical precepts; such was the conception prevailing amongst the Greeks in Homeric times[3]. 'The Magical Fallacy is far older than Christianity, almost as old as the mind of man. Everywhere in primitive religion we come upon the belief that supernatural powers can be forced into the service of man by a knowledge and use of the right form of words, or of the right ceremonial. The god is bound to grant the desires of the worshipper who knows the secret. Not faith but exact ritual can move mountains;

"Carmina vel caelo possunt deducere lunam[4]."

Hence followed the necessity of concealing the right method of approaching the gods, lest it should be copied and used against its proper owner or neutralised by still more potent charms[5].'

The estimation of the value of ritual in the worship of God held by Jeremiah's contemporaries was evidently very similar to that described above, and it seems to have been widespread amongst them, receiving naturally enough the ready and anxious support of the priests. Jere-

---

[1] See Additional Note on vii. 22 ff.
[2] Cf. T. H. Green, *Works*, iii. p. 125.
[3] See *Odys.* xix. 365 f.; *Iliad* ix. 535 ff., 499 ff.
[4] Virgil, *Eclogue* viii. 69.
[5] J. H. F. Peile, *The Reproach of the Gospel*, p. 69.

miah condemned, as did Plato in later times and beneath other skies, such a degraded idea of the worship demanded by Almighty God[1].

vi. *The religious duties of man*

Man's religious nature has two channels through which it may seek an outlet, and these two channels represent or correspond to his two-fold relationship with the things outside himself; his relation to God on the one hand, and his relation to his fellow-men on the other. What then was Jeremiah's teaching on these two points?

(*a*) *Duty towards God.* Jeremiah recognises that men are free to worship and obey Jehovah or they are free to ignore Him; the choice is a voluntary one (ii. 19); but to know God is man's greatest glory, greater by far than the possession of power or wealth (ix. 23 f.). The doctrine of the New Covenant with its high ideal came to Jeremiah's contemporaries as something which was quite beyond their comprehension or power to realise; and indeed this doctrine never really had much influence in Judaism before the coming of our Lord; but since His day the communion of the soul with its Maker has been the foundation of all religion and a modern writer can even go so far as to say that 'religion...assumes a moral relationship, the relationship of personal beings as existing between man and the Object of his worship[2].' Further, man owes to God the duty of worship (ii. 5 ff.), and this worship was mainly that of the sacrificial system which Jeremiah elsewhere condemned on account of its being offered from hypocritical, or at best, ignorant hearts (vii. 10, 21 ff.). When Jeremiah questioned the antiquity of the whole method of worshipping Jehovah he was not necessarily wishing that the system should be abolished, nor did he think, as has been suggested, that the outward ordinances were merely a concession to the weakness of the Jews, and instituted to prevent the introduction of unlawful images such as the golden calf[3]. As Bishop Paget pointed out, the sacrifices of the Old Covenant were a training and preparation for the sacraments of the New and a recognition of the fact that the body has its part to play in the true worship of God[4].

Jeremiah objected to the sacrificial system because it was made a substitute for justice and true holiness; God demanded from man not

---

[1] vii. 5, see notes; and cf. iii. 16, v. 30, vii. 1—28; and for Plato's opinion see *Euth.* 14 E.
[2] Aubrey Moore, *Lux Mundi*[15], p. 47.
[3] Cf. St Jerome on vii. 21.
[4] Essay on ' Sacraments ' in *Lux Mundi*[15], pp. 302 f.

only worship, but also obedience (iii. 25, v. 19, vii. 23, xii. 4, 7, &c.), and if God's kindness in providing the bountiful gifts of the earth was not sufficient to make men obey Him appeal must be made to their sense of fear (v. 22; cf. *v.* 24). Though God through His own appointed messengers might endeavour to raise man's awe by confronting him with the wonders of nature, yet the main function of these phenomena was to persuade him that God was the only sufficient object of his trust (xvii. 5 ff.). The prophet himself, by the purchase of the field at Anathoth (xxxii.), shewed his own perfect confidence in God's power, and indeed he had seen too much of man's weakness to place any confidence in princes. He had seen no doubt Josiah, with his magnificent army, marching out of Jerusalem in all the glow of trust in Jehovah of Hosts and in the confidence of being His chosen instrument; and then there had come back to the terrified city the tidings of Megiddo. He had seen men trembling before Jehoiakim, and then he had doubtless seen the corpse of the king dragged away to a disgraceful and unhallowed burial. The tragic death of Josiah and the dishonours done to the dead body of Jehoiakim had taught him the same lesson as was burnt in upon the mind of the Norman chronicler Orderic by the events following the death of William the Conqueror. 'O magnificence of the world, how worthless thou art, and how vain and frail: like the rain bubbles of the shower, swollen one moment, burst into nothing the next. Here was a most mighty lord, whom more than a hundred thousand warriors just now eagerly served, and before whom many nations feared and trembled; and now by his own servants, in a house not his own, he lies foully stripped, and from the first to the third hour of morning is left deserted on the bare floor[1].'

(*b*) *Duty to man.* Jeremiah's contemporaries failed to realise, as their fathers had done before them, that God cared more for justice between a man and his fellow than He did for incense and sacrifices[2]; and as a result the social conditions of Judah had become by the time of the prophet distressing in the extreme. It was not that there was any widespread ignorance of the rights of those who were oppressed and defrauded, excuses on this ground could not have been upheld in

---

[1] Quoted by Dean Church, *St Anselm*, pp. 184 ff.

[2] The same statements would be true of the religion of the present day to a very large extent. By our habit of spiritualising so much of the teaching of the Old Testament we have been led to ignore or at any rate to obscure the main emphasis of the prophetic message. That emphasis is on what are called the social virtues and especially upon that cardinal virtue of all community life—justice between man and man.

face of the clear teaching of the prophets. It is quite true that in the early stages of the life of any community there are sometimes, owing to the fewness and elementary nature of the accepted conventions, uncertainties as to moral laws; but such was not the case in Judah at the beginning of the sixth century B.C., and herein lay the hopelessness of the situation; the chaos and confusion which reigned were not the birth-pangs of a new order, rather were they the forerunners and heralds of the 'dread disorder of decay.'

Jeremiah began his ministry about a hundred years after that of Isaiah and during the century which had elapsed the social condition of the people had not tended to improve; the abuses which had called forth the vehement denunciations of Isaiah had found no remedy, on the contrary they had increased their hold on the community. By the time of Jeremiah, indeed, the small peasant farmers, the great bulwark of the state in peace as in war, had largely been crushed out of existence by the exactions and greed of the larger proprietors, and in their place had risen up a host of slaves and serfs who had no interest in improving the land they were compelled to cultivate or in defending a system which was the mainstay of their oppressors. The economical and political stability of the community was thus being sacrificed to the ambition of a few individuals. The ancient simplicity of life, which had always marked the Judean peasantry and even the nobles, had almost entirely vanished before the influence of Assyrian customs; and society, as it became ever more complicated, became ever more corrupt. The breezy life of the Judean uplands had given place to the artificial atmosphere of an Oriental court; the eunuch had become more important than the shepherd; among the upper classes luxury had been substituted for manliness, and in the lower freedom had become pauperism.

Such was the state of the people when Jeremiah began his ministry, and as that ministry proceeded many causes combined to undermine the remnants of the moral stability of the nation. The death of Josiah apparently entirely discredited the reformation which he had inaugurated[1], and everything in the political world grew more and more perplexing and confused. At such a time the upholding of the moral laws, laws which depend for their force almost entirely upon a fixed public opinion, is notoriously difficult[2]. The internal conflict in the

---

[1] The law of the single sanctuary is an exception to this statement.
[2] Cf. Creighton, *Wolsey*, p. 4.

B.   *e*

state between the prophetic party and its opponents, as well as the rivalry which no doubt existed between the great landowners, must have had a disintegrating effect in the moral as in the material sphere[1]. A catalogue of the sins and abuses denounced by Jeremiah would cover practically all the last six commandments; and such a catalogue would have been but a record of the outward manifestation of a state of society in which all mutual trust and confidence had been destroyed, where brother plotted against brother, and friend against friend (ix. 5 ff.). Violence and oppression were the lot of the poor and the hireling (vi. 6, xxi. 12, xxii. 13, 17) and even the right of bare justice was denied to those whose weakness prevented them from enforcing their lawful claims (v. 28, xxii. 3, xxxiv. 8 ff.). But deeds of wickedness were by no means confined to the wealthy or the great, rich and poor alike sinned each according to his opportunity, all were adulterers and fornicators (v. 7 f., ix. 2, xxiii. 10), covetous (vi. 13), murders were very frequent (xxii. 3, 17), and usury so common as to supply a figure which would be known to all (xv. 10). With this weight of sin there went an entire failure to recognise its heinousness, a failure which shewed itself in a moral levity of outward conduct corresponding to the state of deadness of conscience within (xv. 17, xvi. 9).

The poor and the oppressed evidently looked to God Himself for direct help, and social reform in the sense in which it is understood to-day was unknown, except so far as the words of the prophets touched the hearts of those in power. But in truth the state of affairs was beyond the healing ability of mortal physicians, in God was the only help of the poor and He would relieve them in His own way and time. Such an attitude of mind is far removed from modern conceptions of how best to deal with the problems raised by social inequalities, but it recognises a truth which can be neglected only to our hurt and peril. The student of sociology has gone to the opposite extreme and tends to leave God entirely out of account. The race has attained to such a measure of perfection by its own efforts that there is a strong temptation for it to rely on the continuance of those efforts alone for its ultimate salvation. This salvation, so it would seem, is to be achieved by means of either improved education, or by a more perfect organisation of industrial life, or by some other form of legal enactment. Civilised man so constantly depends upon his reasoning powers that he is in danger of losing his instincts, and amongst them that instinctive

---

[1] Cf. J. R. Lowell, *The English Poets*, p. 34, 'A conflict of opposing ambitions wears out the moral no less than the material forces of a people.'

regard for the God who alone can guide him to the light and the truth. Jeremiah, however, had been taught by the bitterness of his own disappointments to distrust the arm of flesh and his one remedy for the evils of his day was repentance and a fresh turning to God.

The most pressing problems with which the prophet was confronted were international, and therefore he did not spend so much of his energy as did Micah, for example, in denouncing social abuses. None the less it was no mere coincidence that led men to see in him another Micah (xxvi. 18), for he was possessed by the same burning indignation against the oppressors of the poor and needy, by the same outward fearlessness in denouncing wrongs of every kind, and by the same carelessness as to his own fate, which had upheld the earlier prophet. In his teaching Jeremiah never attempted to change the economic system upon which the life of the nation was organised, his endeavour was to transform the relations of man with man, to make his people realise their mutual dependence and their duty one to another. When the prophets represented Israel under the figure of the vine, or they spoke of 'the virgin daughter of my people,' they were attempting to express an idea which corresponded with what we should now call the 'organic and social life' of the nation. To them the nation was a kind of 'gigantic personality' and the sins they were concerned especially to denounce were those which tended to destroy the body politic. Hence Jeremiah is always calling upon men to do judgement (xxi. 2, xxii. 3), which he even goes so far as to equate with that great end of man's life—to know God (xxii. 16).

vii. *The Future*

To the popular mind a prophet is one who foresees the future, and foretells things yet to be; and this conception of the prophetic office has been enshrined and perpetuated in everyday language by the meaning attached to the word itself, even when used with no religious connotation—a prophet is one who foretells. The Hebrew prophets, however, as God's representatives were not mainly concerned with the future (cf. pp. xvi, xxx f.); their first concern was with the things of the present; and their task, to deal with the needs of the day, to find solutions for the difficulties and perplexities of their contemporaries. But such difficulties and perplexities had their beginnings in the past, for history does not consist of a mere vague succession of isolated events and disconnected incidents; rather is it the working out of a divinely controlled plan in which the past and the present are linked with one another, and with the future, by the closest possible connexion of cause and effect. Hence the servant of the Most High, although his primary concern is with the happenings of the present, must inevitably look beyond them to the unknown years that are coming.

The desire to penetrate into the future, and to build upon its level and unspoiled plains a noble edifice—an edifice often enough fashioned from the ruins of the past and consecrated by the pains and hopes of the present—is not peculiar to the canonical prophets, or even to the Hebrew nation. At all times and amongst every race teachers have arisen who have discerned, beyond the mists of the present, visions of a better state of things: and almost invariably the motive which has stimulated the imagination of the seer has been despair of society as he found it in his own day. Take some of the best known of such idealists—Plato, St Augustine, Dante, Sir Thomas More,—they, quite as much as the writers of the innumerable works which belong to what is technically known as Apocalyptic literature, wrote under the pressure of a strong sense of failure and from a deficiency of hope in their own age and environment. The *Republic* was contemporary with the decay of Greek power and Greek ideals; the *De Civitate Dei* was put forth to describe a new and more abiding polity arising from the ruins of the Roman Empire; the *De Monarchia* was a vision of that self-same Empire—which Dante held, it must be remembered, to have Divine sanction—healing the miseries of the world around; and doing so by absorbing into itself the warring fragments of divided rule; in order that, as he so pathetically put it, 'in the little plot of earth belonging to mortal man life may pass in freedom and peace'; and finally, the *Utopia* was produced by one who lived in the period of exhaustion which followed the Wars of the Roses and amidst the ever increasing corruptions of an unreformed church[1]. The present age no less than its predecessors, has also had its prophets; men who, from amidst the perplexities of modern social and international conditions, raised their eyes above, and endeavoured to describe the visions, which came to them in their turn, of newer and better Utopias.

So it was with Jeremiah. His own sufferings and disappointments were perhaps greater than were those of any other Hebrew prophet; it was his appointed lot to live at a time when

'days decrease
And autumn grows autumn in everything.'

---

[1] See Jowett, *Republic*, iii. pp. ccxviii—xxviii for a fuller working out of these and other instances.

Jeremiah did indeed live in a season of decay, and it was his lot to see the nation gradually slipping from one folly to another. As a result, pessimism in regard to the nation's immediate future took a deeper tone in his prophecies than in those of any other canonical writer. It is no paradox, however, that from this prophet of gloom and disaster came the brightest and most glowing pictures of the ultimate future.

Jeremiah's vision of the future, however, was no vague and fantastic dream dealing with abstract and indefinite objects, and tricked out with all the finery of the later apocalypse; it was a practical scheme intended for actual human beings living in the very land that he himself trod, and moreover a scheme which it would be possible to make a reality if once the conditions became favourable. The future as conceived by him concerned itself with men and the problems which they have to face, whether they beset them as individuals or as organised into communities, and the most convenient method of treating his teaching regarding the future is to divide it up under these heads. But since the hope for the individual was dealt with in connexion with the doctrine of the New Covenant, the communal or national aspect of the question alone remains to be considered here.

To the Israelite mankind was divided into two unequal parts; the nation *par excellence*, the chosen people, and the rest of the world, those, that is to say, who were outside the covenant, and who are referred to as the nations, or the heathen, or the Gentiles[1]. In Jeremiah's day no one had yet risen above this distinction, not even the prophet himself, though the underlying principle of the New Covenant, if pressed to its logical conclusion, would destroy any real distinction, and was indeed a forecast of that time when there should be neither Jew nor Gentile, bond nor free. It will therefore be convenient to divide the prophet's teaching concerning the future of the race into two parts, as it affected (*a*) the people of Israel; and (*b*) the nations.

(*a*) *The people of Israel*. The New Covenant which was the basis of the future hope was to be made between Jehovah and the House of Israel[2] (xxxi. 31 ff.); but with them as individuals, with all an individual's privileges and responsibilities. It is to be noted that the phrase 'house of Israel' may include the men of the Northern Kingdom

---

[1] This variety of names is mainly due to the translators of EVV. One of two Hebrew words גּוֹים and עַמִּים is generally used. The latter word in the singular is usually reserved for Israel.

[2] 'The house of Judah' which occurs in MT. is probably an insertion (see notes *ad loc.*).

in this context, or it may refer to Judah only, as being the sole surviving heir to the promise left to Jacob (see p. xvii). In the early days of his ministry Jeremiah had hoped for a speedy return of the scattered exiles of Ephraim (iii. 11 f.); and even in the later period, during the reign of Zedekiah, he foretold that 'Judah shall be saved, and Israel shall dwell safely[1],' though in this last quotation it is not certain from the parallelism whether the content of the two words 'Judah' and 'Israel' is the same or not. The prophet's hopes for the Northern Kingdom were fruitless, for not only did they not return at his invitation, but on the contrary the rest of the nation quickly sank to equality in misfortune; Judah followed Samaria into exile, as, in spite of the prophet's warnings, she had followed her into sin (iii. 6 ff.). But the exile of Judah had been foreseen by Jeremiah, who recognised that the deeps of national sin could only be cleansed by some such period of testing and purification. The nation as a whole would never return, so the prophet taught, but only a remnant selected by a process of fierce and bitter trial. The doctrine of the Remnant at first used as a threat of almost complete national destruction (cf. Is. iv. 2, x. 22), was now used as a message of hope and of spiritual regeneration. Jeremiah had indeed high and ardent hopes for the generation that would return from Babylon, and his own contemporaries were warned that the people must not be suffered to diminish in number even though they were to dwell in a strange land for some seventy years (xxix. 6, 10). When the release from captivity did eventually take place it was to be, so he promised, of such a nature that the redemption from Egypt and the wonders of the Exodus would speedily be forgotten (xxiii. 7 f.).

In trying to understand any prophetic vision of an apocalyptic nature great difficulty is always experienced, and such difficulty is almost unavoidable, in separating the various layers, if one may use that term of a vision, of the future which is coming. A well-known illustration is the account recorded in Matt. xxiv. of our Lord's forecasts of approaching destructions. As the sayings are there preserved it is almost impossible to say how much of them refers to the immediate future—the Fall of Jerusalem—and how much refers to that which is remote—the last judgement. So it is with Jeremiah's forecasts, some quite clearly refer to the time of the return at the end of the seventy years, while some seem to have in view a much later period. In this last connexion it should be pointed out that a large portion of the

---

[1] xxiii. 6. For the date of the passage see notes thereon.

eschatological matter included in the prophecies is almost certainly
editorial and late. This much, at any rate, is certain, Jeremiah anticipated a speedy return to Palestine for the nation when once the power
of Babylon was broken, and he shewed his confidence in its future by
buying up the field of Anathoth (xxxii. 1—15). It thus came to pass
that just as the field of Machpelah with its lonely grave was the pledge
to the Israelites throughout the wanderings of the Exodus of the future
possession of the promised land, so was the memory of this simple act
of faith to be a sacred pledge throughout the long years of exile in
Babylon that Judah should once more become their own. By a simple
act of purchase, an everyday transaction, both patriarch and prophet
sought to arouse in their countrymen a sense of national vocation and
a trust in the Divine protection. The later Apocalyptical writers as a
rule despaired of any regeneration of this earth, and even St John looked
for a New Jerusalem to descend from heaven; though at the same time
it should be noticed that it was Jerusalem, and no strange city, which
was thus to realise his longings, in fact one might almost read into the
seer's mind a definite hope of a regenerate city. In writing of the future
as he saw it, Jeremiah had no doubts as to the possibility and the hope
of its being realised here on earth, and in the holy city itself, which was
to be re-built together with the temple (xxx. 18). One great difference
there was to be, however, the ark was no more to be an object of veneration[1]. Furthermore the new community, which was to inherit these
good things to come, was no longer to be at the mercy of unjust and
grasping rulers, the 'shepherds' who sought their own gain and not the
good of the sheep; but it was to have a body of righteous judges (xxiii.
4), culminating in a king of the house of David, a king whose very
name would declare his character, 'The Lord our righteousness' (xxiii.
5 ff., xxx. 9). It is quite in keeping with what we know of Jeremiah
that his soul should soar above the evil rulers of his own day and
should discern in the dim future the promise of the ideal king. The
times cried out for a just ruler, and as the spokesman of the oppressed
and despised classes, the prophet could well have anticipated Dante's
protest:

> 'A king we need whose eyes at least shall see
> That city's towers where dwells true righteousness[2].'

---

[1] iii. 16 f.; these *vv.* come from the early period of the prophet's ministry, but
there is no reason for thinking that his opinion was modified later, rather the
contrary as the utterance has been preserved.

[2] *Purg.* xvi. 95 f.

It should be noticed that Jeremiah has no new type of ruler to suggest, but that his ideas naturally express themselves through the medium of that kind of government to which he has been accustomed, for the pre-exilic prophets instinctively pictured 'their Utopia, their ideal state as an ideal monarchy; for patriarchal monarchy was the only form of state they knew[1].' In xxx. 21 it is declared that the 'ruler' is to 'approach' God, that is to say he is to be a priest as well as a prince; such ideas belong rather to the exilic school of Ezekiel and to still later times, and there are many reasons for regarding the passage as late (see notes *ad loc.*). At the same time Jeremiah's conception of the future is distinctly spiritual and in strong contrast to some of the material anticipations of later writers, and of some even who lived in Christian times[2]. It is quite true to say that if 'Jeremiah's picture of the Messianic king and his kingdom is less magnificent than Isaiah's, the true glory of that rule comes into fuller prominence in proportion as the outward splendour falls away; and we make a long step forward towards the idea of that spiritual kingdom which was to be the true fulfilment of the hopes of Israel[3].'

(*b*) *The Nations.* Jeremiah was called to be a prophet of the nations (i. 5), and such an office had a two-fold scope or reference; on the one hand to the *political*, and on the other to the *religious*, future of those with whom his message was concerned. As was said above the most pressing problems of Jeremiah's times in the sphere of politics were international. Judah, deserting the policy of Isaiah and led on by the wild ambition of her kings, had plunged once more into the vast whirl-pool of contemporary politics, and her counsels were swayed by the rival claims of Egypt and of Babylon. Jeremiah himself was pronouncedly in favour of a pro-Babylonian policy, and indeed saw in the Chaldeans an instrument specially raised up by Jehovah for bringing vengeance upon the world. So convinced was the prophet of the lawful and ultimate triumph of Nebuchadrezzar that resistance, even on behalf of the beloved city itself, was useless and wrong (xxvii. 8, xxxviii. 2 f.)[4]. Jerusalem

---

[1] Canon Streeter, *Foundations*, p. 87.

[2] The strange beliefs held by Papias and other early Christians are well known, and even one who prided himself upon his discernment so much as Eusebius could see in the decorations put up by the Emperor Constantine a fulfilment of the Golden Future of the Prophets, if not the coming of the New Jerusalem itself (*Vit. Const.* ii. 33). It is perhaps necessary to look upon this as one of the not uncommon cases of the insight of the historian being forgotten in the zeal of the panegyrist.

[3] A. F. Kirkpatrick, *The Doctrine of the Prophets*[3], p. 323.

[4] In a similar manner Luther in his earlier years regarded the Turks as an instrument raised up by God for the punishment of Christendom, and therefore not

was bound to fall because of the sins of her children. This teaching was a strange reversal of the confident pledges of Isaiah that Zion was inviolable, and to the men of the siege seemed little less than blasphemy against God and treachery to the state (xxxviii. 4). But the forecasts of Jeremiah were fulfilled and the holy city burnt by the alien conquerors, and in the providence of God the very forecasts which had seemed to be blasphemy were used for the purifying and sustaining of the worship offered to Himself[1]. Punishment did indeed begin at Jerusalem, but God who rules all the nations of the world and not merely His own people did not allow it to end there (xxv. 29); He had a controversy with all the nations and Babylon was His weapon against them (xxv. 15 ff.). Even Babylon itself was not to escape unpunished, but the Divine vengeance was at length to seek it out also (xxv. 12). In some passages of OT. itself the final doom of the nations is regarded as certain[2], and in the later non-canonical writers still further emphasis is laid on their coming extermination[3]. In Jeremiah the nearest approach to this attitude of mind is found in x. 25 where Jehovah is implored 'to pour out His fury' upon the heathen for they have devoured Jacob. In the list of prophecies at the end of the book the treatment which is to be awarded to the various nations differs considerably, and some are promised a time of revived prosperity, e.g. Egypt (xlvi. 26), Ammon (xlix. 6), Elam (xlix. 29)[4]. In one passage at least a striking feature is introduced, and that is, that the survival of the nations will depend on their attitude towards Jehovah; 'if they will diligently learn the ways of my people, to swear by my name...then shall they be built up in the midst of my people. But if they will not hear, then will I pluck up that nation, plucking up and destroying it[5].' The double scope of the prophet's office towards the nations is thus coordinated, and their political and religious future closely connected. On the other hand the means by which the nations were to be attracted towards Jehovah was the desire to share in the blessings which would be poured upon the penitent nation when Judah had once more turned to Him (iv. 1 f.;

---

to be resisted. The siege of Vienna and the nearer approach of the Ottomans however quickly changed his attitude.

[1] Cf. pp. lxxxiii f.

[2] E.g. Is. xxiv., xxxiv.; Mic. iv. 11; Zeph. ii., iii. 8—10; Zech. i. 19 ff., xii. 3 f., xiv. 1—4; Hag. ii. 21 f.

[3] Cf. Eth. En. xci. 9; 4 Esdr. xiii. 37 f., 49; Ps. Sol. xvii. 25, 27; Apoc. Bar. xxxix. 7—10.

[4] The promise to Moab (xlviii. 47) is of doubtful authenticity, being absent from LXX.

[5] xii. 14 ff.

cf. Driver on Gen. xii. 3)[1]. At the same time Jeremiah recognised that between the soul of every man and his Maker there is a natural affinity; and the doctrine of the New Covenant, by its recognition of the principle that a man's relation to God is his by virtue of his humanity, and not by reason of his being a member of any particular race, paved the way for the inclusion of all nations within the Church of God. Moreover it should be noticed that it is because of his own personal faith in Jehovah that the prophet can look forward to the time when the Gentiles shall turn to Him in worship; 'O Lord, my strength, and my strong hold, and my refuge in the day of affliction, unto thee shall the nations come from the ends of the earth, and shall say, Our fathers have inherited nought but lies, *even* vanity and things wherein there is no profit[2].'

viii. *Jeremiah's Debt to the Past*

Whatever view may be held of inspiration, and of the manner in which the revelation entrusted to each individual prophet came to him, it is impossible to regard these individual prophets as being each independent of his fellows, without ancestor or descendant in the spiritual world. On the contrary the religious leaders of Israel, though they may not refer to one another by name, undoubtedly belong to a single stream of revelation, 'a school of the knowledge of God for all the world' as St Athanasius so happily named them[3]. And it is natural that they should be thus connected, for however original a teacher may seem to be and in whatever sphere he moves, be it religious, or social, or literary, unless he have his roots deep in the past he cannot be really great. It is not seldom indeed that the most significant contribution to the race made by such an one is to be found in his bringing once more to the light some truth or ideal which had been allowed to fade from the knowledge of his contemporaries. It is not in religion alone that revivals take place; nor is a renaissance peculiar to culture. The prophets have every right to be numbered amongst those who

> 'share the poet's privilege,
> Bring forth new good, new beauty from the old.'

For, as Lowell has put it, 'A great man without a past, if he be not an impossibility, will certainly have no future....The only privilege of

---

[1] The same idea that the salvation of the Gentiles is in some way dependent upon Israel runs through 2 Is. and is common in the later literature; cf. Tob. xiv. 6 ff.; Test. xii. Patr. *Jud.* xxiv. 6, *Lev.* ii. 11, xiv. 4; Ps. Sol. xvii. 3 f.

[2] xvi. 19; cf. Is. xlv. 14 ff.; Zech. ii. 11.

[3] *De Inc.* xii. 5.

the original man is, that like other sovereign princes, he has the right
to call in the current coin and re-issue it stamped with his own image[1].'

Jeremiah was no exception to this universal rule, his debt to the
past cannot be overlooked, and though his contribution to that river
of truth which 'receives tributaries from every side' may seem dis-
tinctive and original, yet it would never have been made but for the
life-giving power of that river itself, and of some even of its smallest
and least known tributaries. The outside influences which moulded
the youth of Jeremiah are in their entirety known only to the God who
chose him to be His instrument: the pious home; the godly parents;
the older friends who shaped the religious consciousness of the growing
boy; all these we can never know; nor can we rule out the possible
influence of prophetic writers of whose very existence we are ignorant.
Jeremiah's mind had an instinctive reverence for the past, a clear and
loving recognition of the value of tradition, of those old paths from
which men's feet stray so readily; and if one may judge from his own
statements, the supreme task laid upon him was to restore to Israel the
pure religion of the wilderness period and to purge it from novel and
alien abuses which had been allowed to enter it.

Amongst canonical prophets he owed most to *Hosea*. Not only was
he indebted to him for many of his ideas, but he has even preserved
and re-expressed the very images in which the earlier prophet had
clothed them. It is not merely that the circumstances of the two prophets were very similar, Hosea being the herald of the Fall of Samaria,
as Jeremiah was of that of Judah, but the resemblance is so close
that there must have been definite borrowing on the part of the later
prophet[2]. It is to Hosea that Jeremiah owes the conception of Jehovah
as the loving husband of the nation, as well as the idea of God as
Father; it is through his influence that the service of other gods is
described as adultery and fornication; and doubtless it was from the
same source that Jeremiah got his figure of the wilderness period as
the espousal time[3]. From the prophet *Micah*, in addition to the quotation of Mic. iii. 12 in xxvi. 18, Jeremiah seems to have derived some

---

[1] *Lectures on the English Poets*, p. 270.

[2] Cf. Harper, *Amos and Hosea*, in *ICC*. p. cxli.

[3] Parallels between the two prophets have been worked out in some detail by
various scholars, e.g. Kirkpatrick in his *Doctrine of the Prophets*[3], p. 117. The
following list is by no means exhaustive: Jer. ii. 2 ff. and Hos. i.—iii., vi. 4,
xiii. 5; ii. 8 and iv. 4 ff., v. 1, vi. 9; ii. 18 and vii. 11; ii. 31 ff. and i. 2, ii. 2 ff.;
iii. 22 and xiv. 1, 4; iv. 3 and x. 12; v. 30 and vi. 10; vii. 9 and iv. 2; vii. 22 f.
and vi. 6; ix. 12 and xiv. 9; xiv. 10 and viii. 13, ix. 9; xviii. 13 and vi. 10; xxiii.
14 and vi. 10; xxx. 9 and iii. 5; xxx. 22 and ii. 23.

of his teaching, for the utterances of the two prophets have much in common[1]. It may well be, however, that this similarity, which seldom extends to actual wording, was due more to similarity of situation than to direct borrowing; as was pointed out above the fact that Jeremiah was recognised as a second Micah is evidence of some resemblance in character and teaching. The parallels between *Amos* and the book of Jeremiah are fairly numerous, though it is not certain that they originated with the prophet himself, being found as they are for the greater part in the section on the nations. Dr Harper sees distinct traces of Amos' influence and quotes several instances of it, the most striking being that in these two prophetic books only is there use made of the phrases 'virgin of Israel' and 'days are coming[2].' Jeremiah does not seem to have owed much to the teaching of his greatest predecessor *Isaiah*, at any rate as far as it is contained in OT.; and though there are resemblances between his prophecies and those of his contemporary *Zephaniah* they would appear to arise more from the similarity of environment than from any mutual influence. With *Nahum* and *Habakkuk*, who were also his contemporaries in all probability, Jeremiah's writings shew little kinship and the difference in point of view is so striking as to preclude the possibility of influence[3].

ix. *The Methods of Jeremiah's Teaching*

Those who have had a message for their fellows in every age and in every land have endeavoured to deliver it by means of the spoken word, and in cases where civilisation has advanced sufficiently, by means of writing also. It is not probable that by Jeremiah's time much use was made of writing—though we are told that he sent a letter to those who had been taken to Babylon after the first capture of Jerusalem (xxix.), and that he had records of his prophecies written down (xxxvi. 2). But to us his message comes entirely through the medium of a book, and the consideration of this method of arousing his contemporaries will be found in the section dealing with its composition (pp. lxxii ff.).

Jeremiah, like the other OT. prophets, did not limit his methods of

---

[1] Cf. Jer. xii. 16 and Mic. iv. 1 f.; xvi. 19 and iv. 1 f.; xxiii. 9 ff. and ii. 11, iii. 11; xxx. 9 and iv. 7, v. 2; xxxi.—xxxiii. and ii. 13.

[2] *Amos and Hosea*, p. cxxxvi. Cf. Jer. xlvii. 2, xlviii. 1, xlix. 1, 7, 28, 34 and Am. i. 3, 6 &c.; xlviii. 25, 44 &c., and i. 5, 8 &c.; xvii. 27 and ii. 5; xxi. 10 and ix. 4; xxv. 30 and i. 2; xlix. 13, 20 ff. and i. 12; xlviii. 7, xlix. 3 and i. 15. See also the list in the volume on *Amos* in the present series of Commentaries, p. xxiv.

[3] Cf. Davidson, *Nahum*, &c. in *Camb. Bible*, p. 63.

teaching merely to the spoken and the written word. He was quite aware that truth is most easily perceived and most firmly grasped when seen in action, and he endeavoured constantly so to exhibit it[1]. The prophet also made a varied but wise use of symbols, knowing that, next to exhibiting it in action, the most effective way of declaring and enforcing truth is, as it were, to embody it in a symbol[2]. As John Bunyan said, when defending himself for the use of so much allegory in *Pilgrim's Progress*:

> 'The prophets used much by metaphors
> To set forth truth.'

Closely akin to these symbolical actions was the use which Jeremiah made of visions, and indeed it is sometimes hard to say whether the prophet is describing an actual event or something which was performed merely in a vision[3]. In the case of the two baskets of figs (xxiv. 1 ff.) the vision may have been purely subjective, 'an inward event' as Keil calls it, 'a seeing with the eyes of the spirit, not of the body.' There seems to be one instance at least of a symbolical act which was performed in vision only, the giving of the cup of the fury of the Lord to the various nations (xxv.), an account which it is impossible to take literally. But the significance and importance of the visions cannot be exhausted by regarding them merely as a means of teaching, they were undoubtedly a channel of instruction and consolation to the soul of the prophet himself. There have always been those who claimed that knowledge was vouchsafed to them by the supranormal method of the vision, and such experiences are really beyond and outside the scope of criticism, except as regards their contents, for as Miss Evelyn Underhill has said, 'it is really as impossible for those who have never experienced a voice or a vision to discuss it with intelligence, as it is for stay-at-homes to discuss the passions of the battlefield on the materials supplied by war correspondents[4].' These visions and voices are beyond the scope of criticism, but it is perhaps necessary to point out that they are not for this reason to be taken as infallible guides to truth and knowledge; else would mankind have accepted some strange and contradictory teaching. It is further to be noticed that the greatest

---

[1] Cf. for example his purchase of the field at Anathoth (xxxii.).

[2] Instances of Jeremiah's use of symbolical actions are to be found in xix. (the broken vessel), xxviii. 10 (the wearing of the yoke), in xliii. 8 ff. (the hiding of stones in the brickwork of Pharaoh's palace).

[3] xliii. 8 ff. is really an instance of such a difficulty; see notes *ad loc.*

[4] *Mysticism*, p. 334.

mystics have always been careful not to attach too much importance to supposed revelations which came to them from these sources[1]. The visions which Jeremiah claimed to have seen were so natural and so reasonable that few would be inclined to condemn them as extravagances; they came to him so much in the course of his ordinary life and indeed seem to have been suggested by the common sights of such a life that to throw doubt upon them is hypercriticism. When the prophet saw the almond tree, for example, as when he saw the basket of figs, his mind was deeply occupied with his mission and the state of those to whom he was sent; the sudden realisation of the presence and significance of the objects before him must have come to him with all the force of signs from heaven, as indeed they were[2].

§ 6. THE BOOK OF JEREMIAH

i. *Its Composition*

In times past the various books which are attributed to the great prophets were looked upon as being their actual productions, written and composed by those whose names they bear. But this theory of the origin of the prophetic writings will hardly stand the test of a strict enquiry. The prophets, before Jeremiah at any rate, were probably not literary men in the sense that they left writings behind them; their utterances were delivered to a definite audience, at a particular time, and though some of them have survived in a written form, it is almost certain that the prophets had no deliberate intention when they uttered their message that such should be the case. The pre-exilic prophets were preachers and speakers, not authors and writers[3], and therefore did not make any complete written record of their sermons. The truth of this theory is proved for all practical purposes by Jeremiah's omission to write out his prophecies until he received a Divine command to do so some twenty-three years after many of them had been delivered[4].

---

[1] Underhill, *op. cit.* pp. 321, 325, &c.

[2] Cf. the story of Robert Bruce and the spider.

[3] They would probably have agreed with Plato's opinion that though ' the writing of books may be useful as an innocent pastime, or to preserve the records of oral discussion against the forgetfulness of age, or by way of guidance to those who may afterwards pursue the same track...literature is a much less efficient means of education than the spoken word.' (*Phaedrus*, 275 D—277 A, as summarised by J. Adam, in *The Religious Teachers of Greece*, p. 399.)

[4] The Lady Julian of Norwich, a famous English mystic, did not write down her visions until the end of a period of fifteen years. See Inge, *English Mystics*, pp. 38 ff.

Collections of such discourses would naturally arise from the desire of
the disciples of the prophets to preserve the teaching of their master,
and the fact that much of the prophetic teaching was given in a poetic
form would make it easier to remember. The earliest direct reference
to this method is in Is. viii. 16 'Bind thou up the testimony, seal
the law among my disciples,' the meaning of which is that since Israel
will not receive the message it must be treasured up by Isaiah's disciples until a more favourable time[1]. Similarly in the passage in
Jer. xxxvi. (referred to above) the prophet is deliberately told to write
down his prophecies in order to bring them back to the minds of the
people. At first the various utterances of the prophets would be
handed down and preserved by different groups or schools, with all care
and faithfulness indeed, but not without those small alterations and
additions which are inseparable from an oral tradition. In course of
time efforts would be made to systematise such fragments, and to
arrange them into something like a logical sequence; editorial matter
would also be provided to fill up gaps, and to give further information
about the prophet who gave the title to each particular book. The
result of this process is perhaps best seen in the book of Samuel. But
it would be a mistake to limit it to the books of the four Former
Prophets only, that is to say to Joshua, Judges, Samuel, Kings; the
books of the Latter Prophets doubtless owe as much to the work of
editors. A somewhat similar series of events accounts for the form of
the first three gospels as they have come down to us, as well as for
the collection of the Koran[2].

The preservation of the records must, in the first place, have been
due to those who were in some real sense the disciples of the prophet,
or at least to those who were in sympathy with his aims. The bulk
of the people would be not at all anxious that such records of sin,
of folly, and of failure should be handed down to later generations;
though a certain amount of superstition, and even of godly fear, might
prevent their going to the lengths of Jehoiakim and his courtiers
(xxxvi. 23 f.). Still, as Pascal has pointed out[3], it is an amazing thing

---

[1] Cf. Ewald, *Proph.* I. 48. 'Nothing is more instructive than what Isaiah tells
us in his own case. When his contemporaries refused to comprehend and believe
great truths which he had preached repeatedly, then especially the prophetic spirit
which had led him to speak summoned him also to write, that by this means he
might work for his own time, and lay down in an everlasting memorial for the ages
what he felt to be as true as his own life (viii. 1, 16; xxx. 8).'

[2] Cf. D. B. Macdonald, *Aspects of Islam*, pp. 77, 82; Leblois, *Le Koran et la
Bible Heb.*, pp. 37 ff.

[3] *Pensées*, II. vii. 2.

that such literature has been preserved at all, and especially by the descendants of the very men to condemn whom it was originally written. Much indeed of the prophetic preaching has undoubtedly perished; and that not because it was less truly inspired by God than that which has been preserved, but simply because it had not the same relation to the needs of later generations of the house of Israel; hence it was allowed to fall gradually into disuse, until finally it disappeared altogether. God may inspire a prophet or a messenger to meet a particular emergency or to perform a particular task, which once completed even the record of it perishes. In this way, it would seem, the disappearance of much of the prophetic preaching may be accounted for; it was truly inspired, and a message from God, but it was at the same time too incidental, too much involved in the circumstances of the age for men to treasure it up and for their posterity to preserve it. But with the writings of Jeremiah it was not so, and one cannot help thinking that as he dictated his roll to Baruch, the prophet, knowing that his book would be used by God to reprove the profanity of the king and 'the madness of the people,' knew also that it was 'something so written to after-times as they should not willingly let it die.'

Though there can be hardly a doubt that the book of Jeremiah, as it has come down to us, contains much that comes straight from the prophet's lips, yet as a whole it is not much more his work than the book of Samuel is the work of the prophet whose name it bears (cf. p. lxxiii). The lack of order and arrangement shews that the book is not the work of one man but rather a collection; and whilst some of the passages are written in the first person, many of them are in the third. It does not necessarily follow that all the latter passages are not the work of Jeremiah, yet on the other hand they make no claim on the face of them to come from him, and apart from later tradition would hardly have been held so to do. The narrative in xxxvi. tells us that the sermons delivered during the earlier part of his ministry were recorded in a roll for King Jehoiakim, and it is natural to suppose that the contents of this roll are included, not necessarily in their original order, in the canonical book. It is impossible to say whether the roll consisted merely of sermons and orations, and whether the framework as it has come down to later ages was entirely supplied by another. Probably it was so supplied, and the prophet's faithful scribe, Baruch the son of Neriah, is generally held to have been its author. At any rate it is the opinion of nearly all critics that the book as it stands owes much to the pen of Baruch. It is exceedingly likely that Baruch carried with him into Egypt the second roll (see xxxvi. 28) or some similar record of his master's teaching, and added to it from time to time, possibly with the knowledge, and even at the instigation of the prophet, reminiscences of his ministry[1]. Some of the accounts of events in which Baruch is said to have taken part shew signs of being the work of one who was an actual witness of and actor in the scenes which he describes (cf. xxxvi. 15 'Sit down now'). Jeremiah must have been a figure of great interest and some mystery to the exiles in Egypt, and doubtless many traditions arose around his name; and since this interest would not be limited to Egypt, the same process was probably in operation amongst the Jews in Babylon. After the exile these various traditions would be collected, and to them might be added other floating prophecies, the process continuing for many generations until the book was finally declared to be canonical and no further additions to it were allowed to be made. Some critics have endeavoured to split up the book into its component parts and to indicate the authors by letters in the margin, but though such a proceeding is possible in dealing with the Pentateuch, and indeed essential to a correct understanding of the various strata of the Mosaic law, it is too much a matter of conjecture in the prophetic books to be reliable. Those who are interested in such analyses will find Dr Peake's two volumes in the *Century Bible* exceedingly well done[2].

ii.   *Its Contents*

The contents of the book are hard to analyse and indeed bewildering in their present form which seems to follow no consistent scheme of arrangement; and this bewilderment is increased by the absence of any attempt to take advantage of the chronological notes, which in the later chapters, at all events, are sufficiently numerous. As Canon Nairne has said, 'The book of Jeremiah is not easily analysed. Attempts have been made to classify its contents. One attempt by the Jewish Synagogue provides the book as we know it in our English Bible. Probably the most helpful way of looking at the book is to think of it as a collection of manuscripts, stored in some corner of a library, not yet fully catalogued, but providing material of different kinds for the

---

[1] It is perhaps not necessary to point out that Baruch was no mere letter-writer of the bazaar, but a man of independent character and power, and one who was not altogether free from personal ambition (xlv. 5). In Jeremiah's old age he seems to have exercised a considerable influence over the prophet (xliii. 3; but see notes *ad loc.*).

[2] For later Jewish traditions regarding the prophet see pp. lxxxvi f.

illustration of a period of history. The period includes political and religious events of great significance, and people and scenes pass so quickly before our eyes that it is only natural we should find it difficult to put the papers in order.' Perhaps the best attempt to re-arrange the contents of Jeremiah is that of Cornill in *SBOT.*, yet even it can hardly be called final or really satisfactory. His arrangement is as follows:

(*a*) Discourses from the first twenty-three years of the prophet's ministry (i.e. up to the date of the compilation of the roll, 604 B.C.), i. 2, 4—19, ii. 1—13, 18—37, iii. 1—5, 19—25, iv. 3—9, 11—31, v. 1—19, 23—31, vi. 1—30, iii. 6—16, xi., xii. 1—3, 5 f., xviii., vii., viii., ix. 1—21, x. 17—24, xxv. 1—3, 7, 11, 13 *a*, 15—29, xlvi. 1—12, xlvii., xlviii. 1—21 *a*, 25, 28, 35—44, xlix. 1—33.

(*b*) Discourses from the later years of Jehoiakim, xiv., xv. 1—10, 15—21, xvi. 1—13, 16 ff., 21, xvii. 1—4, 14—18, xii. 7—17, xxxv. 1—14, 17 ff.

(*c*) Discourses from the reign of Jehoiachin, xiii.

(*d*) Discourses from the reign of Zedekiah, xxiv., xxix. 1, 3—15, 21—22 *a*, 31 *b*—32, xlix. 34—39, xxii., xxiii. 1—6, 9—18, 21—40, xxi. 1—10, 13 f., xx. 14—18, 7—12, xxxii. 1 *a*, 2 *a*, 6—15, 24—44, xxxiii. 1, 4—13, xxiii. 7 f. (= xvi. 14 f.).

(*e*) Discourses from the period after the fall of Jerusalem, xxx. 1—9, 13—21, xxxi. 1, 2—9, 15—34, 38 ff., xlvi. 13—26.

(*f*) Passages for which no satisfactory context can be found, ii. 14—17, ix. 22—25, xii. 4, xvi. 19 f., xvii. 5, 11—13.

(*g*) Biographical passages composed after the death of Jeremiah, xix., xx. 1—6, xxvi. 1—19, 24, 20—23, xxxvi., xlv., xxviii. 1 *a*, xxvii. 1 *b*, 6, 8—22, xxviii. 1 *b*—17, li. 59, 60 *a*, 61, 63, 64, xxxiv. 1—7, xxxvii. 5, 3, 6—10, xxxiv. 8—22, xxxvii. 4, 11—21, xxxviii. 1—28 *a*, xxxix. 15—18, xxxviii. 28 *b*, xxxix. 3, 14, xl. 6—16, xli., xlii., xliii., xliv. 1—28.

(*h*) Further biographical passages from a different author than the writer of those specified in (*g*), x. 1—4, 9, 5—8, 10, 12—16, xvii. 19—27, xxxix. 1, 2, 4—12, xl. 1—5, l., li., lii.

The remaining passages which it is needless to specify, consisting as they do in most cases of a few verses only, or even of parts of a verse, Cornill rejects as later glosses and interpolations.

Taking the book as it stands in EVV. the following is perhaps the best manner of dividing it up.

Part I. *Prophecies mainly included in the Roll*

(*a*) The prophet's call, i.
(*b*) The first collection of prophecies, ii.—vi.
(*c*) Prophecies at the temple gate, vii.—x.
(*d*) Prophecies on various occasions, xi.—xii.
(*e*) Warnings and Lamentations, xiii.
(*f*) Disaster and Despair, xiv.—xvii. 18.
(*g*) Concerning the Sabbath, xvii. 19—27.
(*h*) Lessons from the potter's art, xviii.—xx.

Part II. *Prophecies mainly from the siege and after*

(*a*) Judgements on Leaders and People, xxi.—xxiv.
(*b*) The cup of God's fury, xxv.
(*c*) The temple sermon and its sequel, xxvi.
(*d*) The false prophets and their teaching, xxvii.—xxix.
(*e*) The glories of the future, xxx.—xxxiii.
(*f*) Jeremiah's life during the siege, xxxiv.—xxxix.
(*g*) Jeremiah's life after the fall of Jerusalem, xl.—xlv.

Part III. *Prophecies on the Nations*

(*a*) Concerning the nations, xlvi.—li.
(*b*) Historical appendix, lii.

iii. *Its Text*

In the book of Jeremiah, as in several of the other books of OT.[1], there are found considerable divergences between the received Hebrew text and the LXX. version. In the present book these divergences are not merely matters of the omission of a few words here and there, or of errors due to mistranslation, and so forth, they even extend to the displacement of one whole section—and that an important one—of the book (see introduction to chh. xlvi.—li.). It has been suggested that the text implied by LXX. represents a later recension of the works of Jeremiah compiled by the prophet himself during his sojourn in Egypt and preserved by his fellow-exiles and their descendants[2]. There is, however, not much likelihood of this theory proving a correct one,

---

[1] E.g. Proverbs, Job, Esther, Daniel, &c.
[2] Cf. Blass's theory that the Western text of the writings of St Luke represents a different edition written by the evangelist himself.

f 2

though it contains this much of truth that it recognises that the differences between MT. and LXX. are so serious that they can only be accounted for by the supposition that the Greek translators had before them another text. To offer any really satisfactory explanation of the existence of such a double text is difficult, and in view of our ignorance of the history of the composition and transmission of the book as a whole, practically impossible[1].

§ 7. The Style of Jeremiah[2]

Though the God who inspired the prophets and teachers of old was one and the same, and though the revelation which came to them originated with that Father of Lights who is the source of every perfect boon, yet the style in which the message was ultimately expressed differed according to the differing personalities of each of the several messengers. It was given to these men to see visions of God and in the hidden recesses of the soul to hear the utterance of the Divine voice; but to tell out what they had seen and experienced was a hard, nay an impossible, task. Like St Paul they were lifted to the third heaven and were shewn unspeakable things, things which they might not utter, not because of any express prohibition laid upon them, but simply because they were unable to do so; to feel and to know is one thing, it is something diverse to find expression for that which has been felt and known. Language even when reinforced by passion and quickened by inspiration is but a poor means of conveying spiritual truths, for such truths are 'utterly beyond the powers of human understanding and therefore without equivalent in human speech[3].' The prophet then is always to

---

[1] For fuller details of this question see Dr Streane, *The Double Text of Jeremiah*, and Workman, *The Text of Jeremiah*—the latter with some amount of caution. Mr H. St John Thackeray has recently advanced the theory that LXX. of Jeremiah is the work of three translators, the first of whom did chh. i.—xxviii. (LXX.) and who shews close affinities with the translator of part of Ez. and the Minor Prophets; the second, who did chh. xxix.—li. (LXX.), resembles the style of the first part of Baruch; the third hand is responsible for ch. lii. only. See *J. Th. S.* IV. 245 ff. and *Gram. of OT. in Greek*, pp. 11 f.

[2] The question of the vocabulary of the prophet and his use of certain favourite phrases is not discussed here but the reader may be referred to the list in Driver, *LOT.*[8] pp. 275 ff.

[3] Evelyn Underhill, *Mysticism*, p. 500: cf. also the similar testimony of John Ruskin: 'For what revelations have been made to humanity inspired or caught up to heaven...have been either by unspeakable words, or else by their very nature incommunicable, except in types and shadows...for, of things different from the visible, words appropriated to the visible can convey no image.' *Modern Painters*, Bk. II. ch. xv. § 1.

be regarded as one who is trying to express, through a pathetically in-adequate medium, an inward and valuable experience.

The book of Jeremiah as it is contained in the Canonical Scriptures comes mainly, at any rate as regards the narratives, from the pen of Baruch[1], and in considering the style of Jeremiah it will be necessary to treat these sections as only of secondary value. The first mark of the prophet's style, and one indeed which is typical of nearly all Hebrew literature, is its *reality*. The Hebrew prophets wrote as they spoke, and indeed, as was said above, it is doubtful whether they had any conception of the value of the written word, except as a record of that which had already been spoken; hence the impression of sincerity and naturalness which their works never fail to leave behind. In the case of Jeremiah's prophecies, the reader cannot but feel that they are the utterances of one who had a message to deliver and who was more concerned with what he said than how he said it; the form is only incidental, the contents all supreme. This characteristic is seen in a striking way in the use which Jeremiah made of metaphors and figures; he never allows himself to be turned aside by them, or to forget that they are but means to an end; the human and didactic interest is pre-dominant, and the purely artistic always subordinate; allegory is never introduced for its own sake, but only to elucidate, as far as may be, the thoughts of the prophet, and to impress them upon the minds of his hearers.

Arising from the reality of the prophet's style is its *simplicity and vividness*. The language as a whole is terse and compact and goes directly to the point without pausing, with all that vigour and energy which we should expect to find in the writings of a man of Jeremiah's character. To give one example of his powers of description is sufficient, though many others could be found, and this passage is unequalled in the whole of prophetic literature for vividness of effect produced by quite simple methods:

> I beheld the earth, and, lo, it was waste and void;
> And the heavens, and they had no light.
> I beheld the mountains, and, lo, they trembled,
> And all the hills moved to and fro.
> I beheld, and, lo, there was no man,
> And all the birds of the heavens were fled.
> I beheld, and, lo, the fruitful field was a wilderness,
> And all the cities thereof were broken down
>   At the presence of the LORD
>   *And* before his fierce anger[2].

---

[1] See pp. lxxiv f. above. [2] iv. 23 ff.

In this and other passages of denunciation and woe the very simplicity of the utterance is often more dreadful and awe-inspiring than would be a series of vague and tedious lamentations such as those of him whom Gibbon has somewhat arbitrarily called 'the British Jeremiah[1].'

But it is not only in his language that Jeremiah exhibits the simplicity and directness of his style, it comes out also in his use of imagery and symbolical figures. As was pointed out above the prophet's use of allegory is generally judicious and restrained; one need only compare the parable of the two baskets of figs (ch. xxiv.) with, say, the elaborate allegory of the cave in Book VII. of *The Republic* to realise the simplicity of Jeremiah's mind.

In some passages which are generally admitted to come from the prophet himself there is an appearance of discursiveness and unnecessary repetition, but in nearly every case this will be found to be due to later editors who have either joined together several similar though disconnected fragments, or else have tried to drive home the moral of the prophet's teaching by interpolating into it their own prosaic paraphrases. So far the two marks of the prophet's style to which attention has been drawn have been those characteristics of all true Hebrew literature, reality and simplicity; the next feature to be considered is that of *passion*. Jeremiah's style is eminently embrued with passion and in some of his writings, especially those which describe his own spiritual experiences, his emotion raises him to a height of lyric grandeur which is seldom equalled even amongst the Hebrew poets themselves. His passion, indeed, is often so great that he comes near to breaking that canon which Lessing laid down for the art of sculpture—not only does he writhe, he almost screams.

Cursed be the day wherein I was born:
Let not the day wherein my mother bare me be blessed.
Cursed be the man who brought tidings to my father,
Saying, A man child is born unto thee;
Making him very glad.
And let that man be as the cities
Which the LORD overthrew and repented not:
And let him hear a cry in the morning
And shouting at noontide;
Because he slew me not from the womb;
And so my mother should have been my grave[2].

---

[1] Gildas. See *The Decline and Fall, &c.* (Methuen's Standard Library Edition), IV. p. 152 n. The directness of the prophet's style is also seen in his fondness for short, abrupt questions: e.g. ii. 14, viii. 19, xiv. 19, xviii. 14, 20, xxii. 28, xxx. 6, &c.
[2] xx. 14 ff.

In these and other passages the emotions pent up in the prophet's breast were so strong that, once an outlet was found for their expression, they were almost certain to overflow the bounds of literary convention; such a glowing stream, tested and purified in the Divine furnace, could not be contained in the mould of any merely human art. It is to this excess of passion, no doubt, that we often attribute the not infrequent changes of person, for example, which occur even in the same passage; changes which have led prosaic critics to imagine that either an alteration of speaker has taken place, or else that they have discovered another instance of composite documents. But examples of such 'passionate changes,' as Leigh Hunt once called them, are not far to seek even amongst our own poets, it is sufficient to quote the instance which called forth the above description:

> 'my noble lord,
> How does he find in cruel heart to hate
> Her, that him loved, and ever most adored
> As the god of my life? Why hath he me abhorred[1]?'

But however much Jeremiah may be led away by the force of his emotions, sometimes almost to the verge of loss of dignity, he never loses his impressiveness. This is so partly on account of the natural impressiveness of his subject matter, dealing as it does with things sacred, and partly because he speaks always from the depths of a troubled and struggling human heart.

Another quality of Jeremiah's style which must not be overlooked is its *picturesqueness*. This quality is shewn mainly in the use of vivid and striking images. For his choice of imagery Jeremiah usually draws upon a mind which has long observed the ways of nature, and which is filled with beautiful and glowing pictures, each in its turn capable of suggesting to the prophet 'the spiritual presences of absent things.' Jeremiah's love of nature was something exceptional amongst the Hebrew prophets, and one need only compare his simple and obvious illustrations derived therefrom with the involved and complicated visions of Ezekiel, for example, to see how greatly it stimulated his descriptive powers[2]. Jeremiah's imagery, to put the matter in a word, was the result of observation not of imagination, and his figures were the fruit not of art but of nature. Hence his writings hardly ever fail to be picturesque.

Finally the prophet's style, where it is truly his own, is *poetic*. By this is not meant that it conforms invariably to any definite rules of

---

[1] Spenser, *Faery Queen*, I. iii. 7 ff.

[2] For Jeremiah's love of Nature see the Additional Note pp. 10 ff., and for his use of symbolism cf. pp. lxx f.

metre, except in the case of those passages which are deliberately so written, but that even in the prose passages of Jeremiah there may always be detected, to use the phrase of Sir Philip Sidney, the movement of 'poetical sinews.' In his avowedly poetic passages Jeremiah rises to heights of lyric power which can hardly be equalled in the whole range of literature, for, as Mr Watts-Dunton has said, the greatest lyric poetry is found amongst the Hebrews only. It is with them alone that the combination of 'unconscious power' with 'unconscious grace' is found in its highest perfection, because it is with them alone that there is the intense yearning 'always to look straight into the face of God and live[1].'

A considerable part of the prophetic discourses included in the book of Jeremiah are written in a metrical form, and especially in that particular measure called the Qinah: Duhm even goes so far as to question the genuineness of any passage which is not written in this measure, or does not bear marks of having been originally so written. The whole question of Hebrew verse is very obscure, and experts are not even agreed as to what constituted the unit of measurement. It may suffice to say that many of the proposed attempts at re-arrangement, though often extremely ingenious, cannot, in view of our ignorance of the rules governing Hebrew prosody, be looked upon as more than provisional. Certainly the requirements of any particular system of versification are not by themselves a sufficient test of the genuineness of a particular passage; metrical considerations, however, may often have their share in deciding questions of criticism. The general principle that interpolations, possibly in many cases of a very early date, have been made into not a few passages, must be admitted; serious difficulties arise when attempts are made to apply it[2].

An interesting suggestion has been made as regards the peculiar rhythmic prose in which some of the prophetic writings appear. It is suggested that they owe this character to a species of self-hypnotism

---

[1] See article 'Poetry' in *Enc. Brit.*[9], xix. p. 257. 'The Great Lyric must be religious—it must, it would seem, be an outpouring of the soul, not towards man but towards God, like that of the God-intoxicated prophets and psalmists of Scripture. Even the lyric fire of Pindar owes much to the fact that he had a child-like belief in the myths to which so many of his contemporaries had begun to give a languid assent. But there is nothing in Pindar, or indeed elsewhere in Greek poetry, like the rapturous song, combining unconscious power with unconscious grace, which we have called the Great Lyric. It might perhaps be said indeed that the Great Lyric is purely Hebrew.'

[2] Those who are interested in the subject and desire further information should consult E. G. King, *Early Heb. Poetry*, and for a more advanced treatment G. B. Gray, *The Forms of Heb. Poetry*, and the books there referred to.

similar to that found in those who produce what is known as automatic writing. It is true that there are but few instances in OT. of the prophets speaking in trance, but there is no reason to suppose that the experiences of Balaam (Num. xxiv. 4) and of Elisha (2 K. iii. 15), which seem to require some kind of trance condition, were entirely without parallel. Miss Evelyn Underhill's remarks on the style of writing found in the works of some of the mystics are interesting in this connexion: 'The peculiar rhythmic language of genuine mystic dialogue' she says 'is an indication of its automatic character. Expression once it is divorced from the critical action of the surface intelligence always tends to assume a dithyrambic form. Measure and colour, exaltation of language, here take a more important place than the analytic intellect will generally permit[1].'

§ 8. THE INFLUENCE OF JEREMIAH

Viewed from the limited standpoint of his own day the life of Jeremiah, like the lives of so many of the world's greatest benefactors, was a failure[2]. But a careful examination of the history of the Jewish people, and indeed of the history of religion in the world at large, shews how the influence of the prophet did not cease with his death, but survived to become a factor of tremendous importance in deciding the spiritual destinies of the race.

It would also be true to say that, even before Jeremiah's death, the effect of his teaching was manifestly to be seen in operation; there can be but little doubt that but for the teaching of Jeremiah, the Fall of Jerusalem and the deportation of the men of Judah would, humanly speaking, have been as fatal to the survival of the religion of Jehovah amongst the Jews, as the Fall of Samaria had been to its survival amongst their kinsmen of the Northern Kingdom. When other Semitic nations fell their gods fell with them, and it was no idle boast that prompted Rabshakeh's question, 'Where are the gods of Hamath, and of Arpad[3]?' But Judah was overcome and still Jehovah had His faithful worshippers. 'The preservation of pure religion after the downfall of the nation depended,' says Dr Skinner[4], 'on the fact that the event had been clearly foretold. Two religions and two conceptions of God were then struggling for the mastery in Israel. (1) The religion of the prophets who set the moral holiness of Jehovah above every

---

[1] *Mysticism*, p. 333.   [2] See above pp. xxxiii ff.
[3] 2 K. xviii. 34.   [4] Ezekiel in the *Expositor's Bible*, p. 51.

other consideration and affirmed that His righteousness must be vindicated even at the cost of His people's destruction. (2) The popular religion which clung to the belief that Jehovah could not for any reason abandon His people without ceasing to be God....The destruction of Jerusalem cleared the issues. It was then seen that the prophets afforded the only possible explanation of the course of events.' In this way Jeremiah's teaching had a real, if only partly conscious, influence on the people at large even during his lifetime.

What was Jeremiah's influence upon his fellow-prophets? What special effect had he, above all, upon his younger contemporary Ezekiel? It is one of the most remarkable things in OT. that with a single exception[1], no prophet is mentioned by any of his fellows, though the influence of the teaching of one prophet upon another can be clearly traced. Jeremiah and Ezekiel, whilst often referring to the false prophets by whom they were opposed, never mention one another either by way of approval or otherwise, and, indeed, one might almost go so far as to say, seem to have been ignorant of each other's existence[2]. In spite of Ezekiel's failure to refer to Jeremiah there is so much in common between the teaching of the two prophets both in form and substance that some dependence of the one on the other seems almost certain. As Ezekiel did not receive his call till the older prophet had been proclaiming God's message for more than thirty years, any debt must be on his side. There is indeed hardly any part of Ezekiel's writings, except of course the final section which deals with the restored Temple, which does not shew some evidence of the teaching of Jeremiah. A comparison of the following passages will make this clear: Jer. ii. 7, Ez. xx. 27 ff.; iii. 11, xvi. 51; iv. 5—9, vii. 14, 27; v. 3, iii. 9; v. 20 ff., xii. 2; vi. 14, xxxviii. 15; vi. 17, iii. 17; vi. 22, xiii. 10; xi. 3—8, xx.; xiv. 13 ff., xiii.; xv. 16, ii. 8—iii. 3; xvi. 3—9, xxiv. 16—23; xxiii. 1—4, xxxiv.; xxiv. 7, xxxvi. 26; xxx. 9, xxxvii. 24; xxxi. 27, xxxvi. 9—11; xxxi. 29 f., xviii.; xlvi., xxix.—xxxi.

In spite, however, of the close relation of their teaching on so many points, Jeremiah and Ezekiel differ considerably in their point of view. If one may be allowed to apply present-day party names to the prophets of the old dispensation, Jeremiah is a Protestant, Ezekiel

---

[1] The exception is the mention of the prophet Micah in Jer. xxvi. 18. Even here the words are spoken not by Jeremiah himself but by the elders of the land.

[2] Cf. Ez. xxii. 30 which implies that there was no true prophet amongst the people in Palestine.

a Catholic. Jeremiah lays stress on personal religion, the intercourse of the soul with its Divine Lord, he seems to demand that the revelation once given should be continually repeated to him, he will receive nothing on authority. Ezekiel, on the other hand, accepts the Divine message, and at once attempts to carry it out, not in any emotional way, but with the strong disciplined spirit which characterised him. God had spoken, man knew what was right and therefore he must do it. Unlike his contemporary, Ezekiel did not require the stimulus of repeated emotional experiences. The two prophets, like the two parties in the Church, represent different dispositions[1]. The chief difference in actual teaching between them is in the matter of ritual. Jeremiah apparently condemned ritual as not being part of the original religion of Jehovah, and as having become, through the superstitions which had gathered round it, a substitute for justice and goodness[2]. Ezekiel, on the other hand, seemed to regard pure worship as being necessary to fellowship with God, and he looked upon the ritual as enshrining the truths of the religion of which it formed a part. The new spirit and the new covenant which is to be made with the House of Israel is to be preserved in the ceremonies of an institutional Church. Jeremiah was the first to lay stress on the personal relation of the individual with his God; Ezekiel supplemented this with his conception of the Church, which is to take the place formerly assigned to the nation in the scheme of the Divine economy.

Upon the later prophets Jeremiah does not seem to have exercised any great influence—though the figure of the Branch for the Messiah in Zech. iii. 8, vi. 12 is probably taken from the use in Jer. xxiii. 5— with the notable exception of the Second Isaiah. The coining of the phrase Servant of the LORD may be due to Jeremiah as its first use seems to have been in Jer. xxx. 10, and furthermore the portrait of the Servant contained in the later part of Isaiah owes many of its

---

[1] Bishop Creighton has well summed up the difference between the two types in one of his early letters. 'Some persons,' he says, 'seize hold of the love of God and exalt this to a spasmodic passion, having impressionable natures capable of momentary intensity, not of the continuous strain required for a moral life : such natures tend to monasticism, to religiosity, to formalism, or other things according to their surroundings. Others taking the love of God for their standard, translate their main principles into a number of practical axioms, and refer their separate acts to these axioms as rules: their danger is to forget their main principle, or rather put it in the background, and so gradually tend to lower the strictness of the rules by submitting them too much to the considerations of expediency which necessarily follow upon practice.' *Life and Letters*, I. pp. 94 f.

[2] vii. 22 f. with Additional Note.

traits to the character and history of Jeremiah, such at least is the opinion of many able critics[1].

Of the literature contained in the third division of the Hebrew Canon the book of Job has affinities with Jeremiah[2], and likewise the book of Psalms of which no less than nine have been attributed to the authorship of the prophet, viz.: xxii., xxxi., xxxv., xxxviii., xl., lv., lxix., lxxi., lxxxviii., and many others shew marked traces of the influence of his language and ideas[3].

Concerning the connexion of Jeremiah with one book of OT. nothing has as yet been said. As is well known the majority of critics consider that Deuteronomy, or at any rate its main kernel, is older than Jeremiah —that in fact it was the book found by Hilkiah in the Temple. According to this view any indebtedness between the two books—and such indebtedness must be acknowledged to be large both in teaching and style—must be due to borrowing by the prophetic writer. During the past few years, however, the opinion has been growing that Deuteronomy is of later date than had been generally supposed. This opinion has found its clearest expression in the writings of Canon Kennett, who, approaching the subject from the point of view of the time required for the composition of the separate documents of the Pentateuch and for their amalgamation, would place the date of Deuteronomy during the exile[4]. The subject is full of difficulties owing to our lack of knowledge, and to the student of Jeremiah the theory that the law-book was produced under the influence of the prophet's teaching rather than that the book produced the prophet has singular attractions[5]. On these and other grounds, the arguments for which are too technical and too lengthy to be produced here, the present writer after working on the subject for some years feels bound to express his substantial agreement with the position taken up by Canon Kennett, to whose writings he would refer those who are interested in the suggestion.

Interest in Jeremiah seems steadily to have increased during the period which elapsed between the exile and the coming of our Lord, and

---

[1] See Skinner in *Camb. Bible*, pp. 103, 111; G. A. Smith in the *Expositor's Bible*, pp. 275, 358 ff. Dr Mitchell sees traces of the influence of Jeremiah on the *style* of Haggai and Zechariah; see his commentary on these books in *ICC.* p. 101.

[2] See Davidson in *Camb. Bible*, pp. lxv f.

[3] In *Camb. Bible*, p. xxxvi.

[4] See his article 'The Date of Deuteronomy' in *J.Th.S.* vii. pp. 481 ff. and the article 'Israel' in Hastings' *Dict. Rel. and Ethics*.

[5] Cf. Dr Peake, *Jeremiah*, I. p. 60, 'this is a tempting suggestion to one who would gladly claim an even fuller originality for Jeremiah.' Dr Peake, however, is not convinced of the truth of Canon Kennett's theory.

this interest may be seen in the large number of legends which clustered around his name. An examination of some of these legends, however, tends to shew that his reputation rested on his supposed authorship of the book of Lamentations rather than on his prophetic writings[1]. Some indeed of the traditions connected with his name would appear to have arisen in quarters where there was very little real appreciation of his religious teaching, if not actual ignorance: e.g. the legend that Jeremiah carried away the tabernacle, the ark, and the altar of incense from the Temple and hid them on Mount Sinai[2]. It was Jeremiah rather than any other of the prophets who came to be regarded in much the same way as men in later ages regarded the Patron Saint of the nation, as in the famous vision of Judas Maccabaeus before his victorious encounter with Nicanor[3]. The same passage shews Jeremiah in another similar aspect as engaged in constant intercession for the people and the Holy City. Coming down to still later times it is curious to notice the great reverence with which the prophet was regarded by Philo[4].

By the time of our Blessed Lord's earthly ministry Jeremiah had seemingly been exalted to a supreme place amongst the written prophets (cf. Matt. xvi. 14). This exaltation may have been due to the fact that according to certain reckonings the book of Jeremiah occurs first in the Canon of the prophets[5]. In another passage (Matt. xxvii. 9) a quotation from Zech. xi. 13 is attributed to Jeremiah possibly for the same reason, i.e. Jeremiah's name was held to cover any extract from the prophets. At the same time it should be remembered that the last six chapters of Zech. are held by the majority of critics to have no connexion with the first eight, or with the prophet whose name they now bear. It is not without interest to recall the fact that the earliest recorded attempt to divide up the book was made as long ago as 1632, and then in order to avoid impugning the accuracy of the Gospel ascription of the passage[6]. But evidence of the high regard in which Jeremiah was held in NT. times is not limited merely to casual references to him

---

[1] This statement refers mainly to the popular conception of Jeremiah as 'the weeping prophet.' Cf. also the legend in the Talmud, which may be early, that to dream of Jeremiah was a sign of coming misfortune (*Berakhoth* 57 b).

[2] 2 Macc. ii. 1—8 ; contrast Jer. iii. 16.

[3] 2 Macc. xv. 13 ff.

[4] *De Cher.* § 14.

[5] Cf. J. Lightfoot on Matt. xxvii. 9.

[6] The attempt was made by Joseph Mede of Cambridge who tried to shew that the later part of Zech. was written by Jeremiah. See G. A. Smith, *The Twelve Prophets*, ii. 450.

by name. His influence is to be discovered in much of our Lord's own teaching, and in the hour before His passion it was to Jeremiah's doctrine of the New Covenant that the Master went back most naturally as a forecast of His own sacrificial work. So too in the Apostolic Age, 'it is,' as Dean Stanley says, 'to Jeremiah, even more than to Isaiah, that the writers...look back when they wish to describe the Dispensation of the Spirit.' (Cf. Heb. viii. 8 ff., x. 16 f.)[1]

Perhaps, however, the influence of Jeremiah had the most important results for the development of religion in the effect which both his life and his teaching had upon St Paul. This influence cannot be proved by any direct evidence; but to a close student of the Old Testament scriptures, such as Saul of Tarsus undoubtedly was, the teaching of Jeremiah upon the spiritual nature of religion could not have been passed by unnoticed. Whether St Paul was conscious of what he owed to Jeremiah or not the debt was none the less incurred, and one has only to compare passages such as Jer. iv. 4, ix. 25 f. with Gal. v., &c. to see the close connexion between the thoughts of the writers, a connexion which could hardly have been accidental. There was much also in the lives of the two men which was similar. Both were conscious that God had chosen them for His service even from their very birth (Jer. i. 5; Gal. i. 15); both had a mission to those who were not of their own race, and indeed the terms 'prophet of the nations' and 'apostle of the Gentiles' are practically synonymous; both had a passionate love for their country (Jer. iv. 19, ix. 1; Rom. ix.—xi.); and both suffered constant persecution from those whom they loved. It has been suggested by the present Bishop of Ely that St Paul regarded himself as a second Jeremiah, or at least that he recognised the likeness between his own experiences and those of the OT. prophet[2]. It would seem therefore that there is justification for assuming that Jeremiah was one of the great moulding influences upon St Paul.

The passages in NT. which shew the influence of Jeremiah are very numerous; the following list is taken from the appendix to Westcott and Hort's Greek Testament: Matt. ii. 18, Jer. xxxi. 15; vii. 22, xxvii. 15 and xiv. 14; xi. 29, vi. 16 (Heb.); xxi. 13, vii. 11; xxiii. 38, xxii. 5 and xii. 7. Mk. viii. 18, v. 21; xi. 17, vii. 11. Lk. xiii. 35, xxii. 5 and xii. 7; xix. 46, vii. 11. Acts vii. 42, vii. 18 (LXX.) and xix. 13; vii. 51, ix. 26 and vi. 10; xv. 16, xii. 15; xviii. 9 f., i. 8; xxvi.

---

[1] *The Jewish Church*, II. 446.
[2] F. H. Chase, *Credibility of the Acts*, p. 71. I am indebted to Dr Lock for this reference.

17, i. 7 f. Rom. ix. 21, xviii. 6; ix. 22, l. 7. 1 Cor. i. 31, ix. 24.
2 Cor. vi. 17, li. 45 (Heb.); x. 17, ix. 24. 1 Thes. ii. 4, xi. 20; iv. 5,
x. 25. 2 Thes. i. 8, x. 25. Heb. viii. 8—13, xxxi. 31—34; x. 16 f.,
xxxi. 33 f. Jas. v. 5, xii. 3; v. 7, v. 24. 1 Pet. i. 17, iii. 19. Apoc.
ii. 23, xvii. 10; vi. 15, iv. 29; vii. 17, ii. 13 and xxxi. 16; viii. 8, li.
25; x. 11, i. 10 and xxv. 30; xi. 5, v. 14; xiii. 10, xv. 2; xiv. 8, li.
7 f.; xv. 3, x. 10 (Heb.); xv. 4, x. 7 (Heb.); xvi. 1, x. 25; xvi. 12,
l. 38; xvii. 1 f., li. 13; xvii. 4, li. 7; xvii. 15, li. 13; xviii. 2, ix. 11;
xviii. 3, li. 7 and xxv. 16 f.; xviii. 4 f., li. 6, 9, 45; xviii. 6, l. 29; xviii.
8, l. 34; xviii. 21, li. 63 f.; xviii. 22 f., xxv. 10 (Heb.); xviii. 24, li.
49; xx. 9, xi. 15 and xii. 7; xx. 12 f., xvii. 10; xxi. 4, xxxi. 16; xxii.
12, xvii. 10.

In the Book of Common Prayer Jeremiah is read—with certain
omissions—as the first Lesson at Matins and Evensong from August 9th
to 26th, and the following portions from it are used as Proper Lessons:
chh. v. at Matins and xxii. or xxxv. at Evensong on Trin. XVII.;
ch. xxxvi. at Matins on Trin. XVIII.; xxxvi. 1—18 at Matins on
Innocents' Day; i. 1—11 at Evensong on the Feast of the Conversion
of St Paul; xxvi. 8—16 at Evensong on St James' Day; iii. 12—19 at
Evensong on SS. Simon and Jude's Day. In addition to these passages
read in the Lessons, xxiii. 5 ff. is the Special Portion read as the Epistle
on Trin. XXV.; x. 24 (= Ps. vi. 1) is among the Sentences at the opening of Matins and Evensong; and xvii. 5 is the basis of one of the
'curses' in the Commination Service.

Chronological Table

The notices of time in OT. if they stood by themselves would be of
little value owing firstly to the difficulty of relating them to outside
events, and secondly to the fondness of the Hebrews for the use of round
numbers and approximate calculations. Fortunately the Assyrians
had an elaborate and most accurate system of chronology with which
OT. history can easily be related. Like the Greeks they designated
each year by the name of a certain officer and lists of these officers
have survived, often in duplicate, and their substantial accuracy has
been proved by comparing the dates which they record for certain
eclipses and other astronomical phenomena with the dates required by
modern astronomers. Wherever, then, Jewish and Assyrian history
touch we have means of discovering fixed dates from which the others
can be calculated.

B.C.

c. 722. The Fall of Samaria.

c. 697. MANASSEH (697—639).

639. JOSIAH (639—608).

c. 630. Scythians begin to move.

626. Jeremiah's call.

621. Discovery of the Book of Law.

609. *Pharaoh Necho*, king of Egypt (609—594).

608. Battle of Megiddo and death of Josiah.

608. JEHOAHAZ or Shallum reigns for three months and is then taken to Egypt.

608. JEHOIAKIM or Eliakim (608—597).

c. 606. Fall of Nineveh and collapse of the Assyrian Empire.

605. Battle of Carchemish and defeat of Pharaoh Necho by the Babylonians.

604. *Nebuchadrezzar*, king of Babylon (604—561).

604. The writing of the Roll.

603. The destruction of the first Roll and the writing of the second.

c. 598. Jehoiakim rebels.

597. Death of Jehoiakim.

597. JEHOIACHIN reigns three months and is then taken to Babylon on the Fall of Jerusalem.

597. ZEDEKIAH or Mattaniah (597—586).

594. *Psammetichus II*, king of Egypt (594—588).

593. Plans for revolt against Babylon.

588. *Pharaoh Hophra*, king of Egypt (588—569).

586. Capture and destruction of Jerusalem and second deportation of the Jews.

561. *Evil-merodach*, king of Babylon (561—560). Release of Jehoiachin.

538. Fall of Babylon[1].

---

[1] Some of the dates in the above list are slightly different from those usually given; in deciding on them I have followed the notices in Canon Johns' *Ancient Babylonia*. The reign of Pharaoh Hophra is usually extended to 564 on the assumption that his conqueror and successor, Amasis, allowed him to remain on the throne, in name at least, until that date; since the article by Piehl in *Zeitschrift für Ägypt. S. u. A.* 1890, p. 9, this has generally been rejected and the reign of Amasis II dated from the victory of Momemphis.

THE BOOK OF JEREMIAH.

CHAPTER I.

The Prophet's Call.

This introductory ch. which really begins with *v.* 4 in our present arrangement of the text (*vv.* 1—3 being the title, not to the ch. but to the whole book)
gives an account of the call of Jeremiah, or of what has been fitly named his
'four-fold investiture' to the office of prophet. Some scholars look with suspicion
on this account of the call of Jeremiah and are disposed to question its
genuineness. Duhm, for example, refuses to admit that it comes from Jeremiah
himself, or even from the recollections of those who knew him. He would
bring the chapter down to the post-exilic period, mainly because it represents
the prophet as being *set over the nations* (*v.* 10), which, in his opinion, would
have been too lofty a claim for Jeremiah to have made on his own behalf;
neither could it have been attributed to him by Baruch, for to the latter he
was merely an Israelite prophet with a mission to his own people, but with
little interest in the affairs of other nations. These reasons seem to be quite
insufficient to bear the argument based upon them consisting as they do
mainly of assumptions. Even from the point of view of critics who deny the
objective reality of Jeremiah's call a treatment so drastic is not necessary.
Surely it is possible to argue that when the account was written the prophet
was looking back over the actual facts of his ministry, and in recording its
beginning he simply states its scope as afterwards revealed to him by the
progress of events and the gradual enlargement of the sphere of his activity.
To reject this account of Jeremiah's call, because it appears to magnify his importance, shews a lack of insight into the working of the prophet's mind; his
whole attitude towards his vocation makes it quite clear that it was only God's
appointment which made him undertake it and that he relied on the Divine
strength entirely for power and ability to fulfil it. The initial plea of un-
worthiness was, on Jeremiah's lips, no mere conventional utterance but came
from the very depths of the prophet's heart. To such a man to become the
messenger of God was to accept an office whose importance did not admit of
degrees of comparison; the geographical or ethnological limits of his mission
were mere details which could have had little consequence in his eyes. Another
argument in favour of the traditional position is that it would have been hard,
in view of the state of international affairs, for any prophet of Judah to avoid
being at the same time a prophet *to the nations*. When such a call came to
Jeremiah he would see in it nothing strange or unusual; Jehovah was the God
of all the earth, and his own appointment to be His messenger to the nations

was not without parallel in the lives of his predecessors; his heart must have glowed within him as he realised that he was treading in the steps of Amos and Isaiah.

In the books which bear the names of these two prophets the narrative as it has come down to us, for some reason or other, does not begin with an account of the call of the prophet. Such a record seems desirable as the opening of a prophetic book, for the office of a prophet like that of an apostle is one which no man taketh to himself but only as he is called of God: it is fitting therefore quite apart from chronological reasons that a work of this nature should begin with an account of the writer's qualifications[1].

The ch. may be analysed as follows:

(a) *Introductory title.* 1—3.

(b) *The prophet's call.* 4—6.

(c) *Jeremiah's consecration.* 7—10.

(d) *The sign of the almond tree.* 11—12.

(e) *The sign of the seething caldron.* 13—16.

(f) *Jehovah commands the prophet to be strong.* 17—19.

I. 1 The words of Jeremiah the son of Hilkiah, of the priests

I. 1—3. The ascription of the book to Jeremiah and the date of the prophet's call. The first two *vv.* are evidently the original superscription and *v.* 3 was added later so as to extend the scope of the title. It is to be noticed that the title, even in its extended form, does not include Jeremiah's prophetic activity subsequent to the fall of Jerusalem.

1. *words.* The only other prophetic book which has this heading is Amos. LXX. is fuller and has the singular τὸ ῥῆμα, which is much the more usual form. Kimchi and other Rabbinic commentators explained the plural as representing the fact that incidents as well as prophecies are included in the book—but such inclusions are not peculiar to Jeremiah. It is possible that there is a reference to xxxvi. 2.

Jeremiah. Various explanations have been given of the meaning of the prophet's name. Schmidt (*Enc. Bib.* 2366) suggests that it represents יִרְמְיָהוּ 'Jehovah hurls,' Ball and Wellhausen connect it with the root רמה 'to found,' and others think that it means 'Jehovah looseneth' (the womb). The name occurs not infrequently in OT.: e.g. xxxv. 3 ; 2 K. xxiii. 31, xxiv. 18 ; Neh. xii. 1, 12, &c.

Hilkiah. Probably not the priest mentioned in 2 K. xxii. in spite of the opinion of St Clem. Alex. and St Jerome. There is no evidence that Jeremiah belonged to the Jerusalem priesthood. In the case of seven of the prophets (viz. Amos, Obadiah, Micah, Nahum, Habakkuk, Haggai and Malachi) no table of descent is given, possibly because they were of humble origin. In the case of Zechariah the descent is traced

---

[1] Cf. Hamilton, *The People of God*, I. p. 160.

that were in Anathoth in the land of Benjamin : 2 to whom the word of the LORD came in the days of Josiah the son of Amon, king of Judah, in the thirteenth year of his reign. 3 It came also in the days of Jehoiakim the son of Josiah, king of Judah, unto the end of the eleventh year of Zedekiah the son of Josiah, king of Judah ; unto the carrying away of Jerusalem captive in the fifth month.

4 Now the word of the LORD came unto me, saying, 5 Before

back two stages, and in the case of Zephaniah further still (see J. M. P. Smith, *Zeph.* &c. p. 182).

of the priests. Heb. מן הכהנים. The wording of the phrase is strange, and Cornill accounts for it by supposing that Jeremiah, though a priest by birth, never exercised the office. A better explanation is to take the words as referring to *Anathoth* and to regard them as a post-exilic gloss which has been incorporated into the text.

Anathoth. See Introd. p. xxviii. The name is possibly connected with the goddess 'Anath, traces of whose name occur also in Anthothi-jah (1 Ch. viii. 24); Beth-anath (Josh., Jud.) and Beth-anoth (Josh. xv. 59).

land of Benjamin. The fact that Jeremiah was a member of the border tribe of *Benjamin* may account for his strong sympathy with the Northern Kingdom.

2. *the LORD.* The word LORD when printed in capitals in AV. and RV. represents the Divine Personal Name which in hymns and in popular speech is rendered Jehovah. This word is the result of a com-bination of the consonants יהוה (the Personal Name), with the vowels of Adonai (Lord) the word which the Jews generally substitute for it in reading the scriptures. The actual pronunciation has been lost, though many scholars now use the form 'Yahweh' (see further Dr McNeile on Ex. iii. 14).

king of Judah. The use of this phrase is suspicious, though not necessarily a sign of late date. Nebuchadrezzar, in his inscription, describes himself as king of Babylon ; but inscriptions were written for strangers, the prophetic books for the Jews themselves.

in the thirteenth year. This reference fixes the exact date of the call of the prophet (*c.* 636 B.C.), and there remained still forty years during which he was to exercise his ministry before the final fall of the kingdom. J. Lightfoot points out that as God sent Moses to teach the people for forty years before the entrance into Canaan, so He sent Jere-miah for forty years before they were banished from it.

3. *eleventh year.* The Hebrew for *eleventh*, עַשְׁתֵּי־עֶשְׂרֵה, is a late form found only in Jer., Ez., Dt. i. 3, the Priestly code and 'passages undoubtedly post-exilic, so that it may very well be a loan word from the Babylonian' (= *istin* or *išten*), *Ges.-K.* p. 290, note 1.

4—6. God's call and the prophet's hesitation. For a discussion

I formed thee in the belly I knew thee, and before thou camest forth out of the womb I sanctified thee ; I have appointed thee a prophet unto the nations. 6 Then said I, Ah, Lord GOD !

of the call of Jeremiah and a comparison with the call of other servants of God, see Introd. pp. xxix f., xxxviii.

4. *unto me.* A sudden introduction of the 1st person. Stade (*ZATW.* 1903, pp. 153 f.) thinks that this *v.* is a subsidiary heading.

5. *formed.* The root meaning of the word is 'to shape' (as a potter); it is used of the making of Adam (Gen. ii. 7—8); but very often the origin of the word is ignored and it is applied to the creation of light (Is. xlvii. 7), summer and winter (Ps. lxxiv. 17) and the spirit of man (Zech. xii. 1).

knew. Of God in Am. iii. 2 ; Hos. xiii. 5 ; Nah. i. 7 ; Ps. i. 6, xxxi. 8, cxliv. 3. The reference is not to intellectual knowledge but to selection for a definite piece of service. The writer of one of the Psalms acknowledged that God's eye was upon him even in his mother's womb (cxxxix. 13—16), and Job pleaded with God on this very ground, 'thine hands have formed me and fashioned me,' &c. (x. 8 ff.). This mention of the Divine foreknowledge was doubtless meant to encourage the youthful prophet; He who had begun a good work in him would surely not desert him until it was perfected (cf. Nu. vi.; Is. xlix. 1, 5 ; Lk. i. 15; Gal. i. 15). It is interesting to note that Nabonidus made a similar claim ; in one of his inscriptions he says that while he was yet 'in the bowels of his mother' Sin and Nergal gave to him 'the lot of sovereignty.' (See Ball, *Light from the Ancient East*, p. 208.)

sanctified. This word as originally used conveyed no idea of 'holiness' in the later sense of the word, but merely that the person or thing was set apart or consecrated to a particular purpose. This is the only place in OT. where the word is used of a prophet (cf. Ecclus. xlv. 4, xlix. 7), though other parts of the verb are used of priests (Ex. xxviii. 3, 41, &c.) and of the setting apart of the keepers of the ark (1 S. vii. 1). Our Lord speaks of Himself as *sanctified* by the Father (Jn. x. 36).

unto the nations. Though we may not agree with Duhm (see Introd. to the ch.), yet it is very strange that Jeremiah, whose message was mainly to the people of Judah and Israel and whose interests and affections were so markedly bound up in the nation, should be thus early designated as a prophet to *the nations*. Before even the bare mention of Judah or Jerusalem it is declared that his mission is an universal one. As early as the time of Calvin the peculiarity of this was noticed. 'It seems strange,' he says, 'that he was given a prophet to the nations...for he neither travelled to the Ninevites, as Jonah did (Jon. iii. 3), nor travelled into other countries, but spent his labours only among the tribe of Judah.' The Targum paraphrases the words so as to avoid any semblance of a promise of the *nations* sharing in the comfortable things of the prophet, 'I have appointed thee as prophet to make the Gentiles drink the cup of cursing.'

behold, I cannot speak : for I am a child.   7 But the LORD said
unto me, Say not, I am a child : for [1] to whomsoever I shall send
thee thou shalt go, and whatsoever I shall command thee thou
shalt speak.   8 Be not afraid because of them : for I am with
thee to deliver thee, saith the LORD.   9 Then the LORD put forth

---

[1] Or, *on whatsoever errand*

---

6.   *Ah, Lord GOD!*   This cry of the prophet becomes very familiar as an expression of pain and nervous dread (cf. iv. 10, xiv. 13,
xxxii. 17).

I cannot speak.   Like Moses (Ex. iv. 10), and possibly St Paul if
we can accept the statement of his detractors (2 Cor. x. 10; cf. 1 Cor.
ii. 1).   Demosthenes, according to Plutarch, had to overcome great
natural impediments before he became an orator.

child (LXX. νεώτερος, *zu jung*).   The Heb. word (נַעַר) is used of a
new-born child (1 S. iv. 21), but also of Abraham's trained servants
(Gen. xiv. 21), of a man of marriageable age (Gen. xxxiv. 19), and of
Absalom when grown up (2 S. xviii. 5, 12), so that it does not necessarily refer to anyone very young.   Calvin, who adopts the translation
puer, takes the word metaphorically and pours scorn on St Jerome for
saying that the prophet was only a boy when he began his ministry.   It
is difficult to know why Jeremiah pleaded his youth unless it was that
he doubted the form in which the Divine inspiration would work.   His
words seem to imply a conception of the prophetic office different from
that which had been normal in Israel, and which regarded the seer as
a merely passive instrument in the hands of God.

7—10.   'Whom God calls He equips.'

7.   Jeremiah was not making excuses in order to avoid his commission, and so God does not reprove him as He reproved Moses (Ex. iv.
14).   His lack of experience will not unfit him for the prophetic office,
for God Himself will direct him both as to the object and the contents
of his message.   The case of Jeremiah illustrates one of God's constant
principles ; never to entrust His servants with tasks which are beyond
their powers will they but take advantage of that Divine inspiration
which is ever at their command.   'Let him who speaks speak as the
oracles of God' (1 Pet. iv. 11 ; cf. Ex. vii. 2 ; Dt. xviii. 18 ; Matt.
xxviii. 20).

8.   *Be not afraid.*   Cf. *Life of B. F. Westcott*, II. 92 f.

them has no antecedent ; the reference is to *whomsoever.*

I am with thee.   When God sends forth His servants He goes with
them (cf. Acts xiii. 4 with *vv.* 9 and 52).

saith the LORD.   Lit. '*It is the whisper of Jehovah.*'   This phrase
almost invariably comes at *the end* of revelations to the prophets, though
in two cases it appears at the beginning (viz. Is. lvi. 8 ; Ps. cx. 1).

9.   *put forth his hand.*   The language of this *v.* is not intended to
be taken literally ; it was by anthropomorphisms such as this that the
ancients triumphed over the difficulty of a transcendent God.   'God

his hand, and touched my mouth ; and the LORD said unto me,
Behold, I have put my words in thy mouth : 10 see, I have this
day set thee over the nations and over the kingdoms, to pluck
up and to break down, and to destroy and to overthrow ; to
build, and to plant.

11 Moreover the word of the LORD came unto me, saying,
Jeremiah, what seest thou ?   And I said, I see a rod of [1] an almond

---

[1] Heb. *shaked.*

---

as God,' says Feuerbach, 'the infinite, universal, non-anthropomorphic
being of the understanding, has no more significance in religion than a
fundamental general principle has for a special science; it is merely an
ultimate point of support, as it were, the mathematical point of religion'
(quoted by Aubrey Moore, *Lux Mundi*, p. 91).   The same difficulty is
met with amongst the Greeks and is solved in very much the same
way : 'The old mythology was allied to sense, and the distinction of
matter and mind had not as yet arisen' (Jowett, Introd. to *Theaetetus*,
IV. 156).

touched.   Lit. 'caused it to touch.'   Here the object of the touch is
to inspire, in Is. vi. 7 it is to purify.

I have put my words in thy mouth.   As though they were something material.   (Cf. Ez. ii. 9, iii. 3, where the prophet eats the actual
words in the form of a book.)

10.   Cornill suggests that the best explanation of this *v.* is to be
found by comparing it with v. 14, vi. 11, xxiii. 29; and Is. lv. 10—11.

set thee.   'The word used suggests the idea of *set with authority* or
make an overseer' (Driver) (cf. Gen. xxxix. 4 f. and Jer. xl. 5, 7).   God
here appoints Jeremiah to be His viceroy on earth, 'der Statthalter des
himmlischen Grosskönigs' (Duhm).

to pluck up &c.   All the words here used imply from their sound
a certain amount of violence in the process ; they are used in several
other passages of the book in varying combinations: viz. xviii. 7, xxiv.
6, xxxi. 28, xlii. 10 and xlv. 4.   The use in xxxi. 28 is interesting, as
in that passage it is God Himself who is to perform the various acts
which are elsewhere ascribed to the prophet.

to build, and to plant.   Jeremiah's work was not to be merely one of
destruction, he was to clear the ground of ancient abuses and to sow
the seed of a brighter future.

11 f.   This section and that which follows contain narratives of
two visions or symbols from which the prophet learned the imminence
of the Divine judgement.   (For a discussion of the nature of these
and similar visions and the place which they occupied in Jeremiah's
ministry, see Introd. pp. lxxi f.)

11.   *what seest thou ?*   A similar formula is used in Am. vii. 8, viii.
2; Zech. iv. 2, &c.   Jeremiah, like the writer of the Song of Solomon
(see especially ii. 11—13), evidently had great sympathy with nature in

tree. 12 Then said the LORD unto me, Thou hast well seen : for I ¹watch over my word to perform it. 13 And the word of the LORD came unto me the second time, saying, What seest thou?

¹ Heb. *shoked*.

its various moods and welcomed the first sign of the coming spring[1]. But under the Divine tuition it bore for him a message not of hope, but of warning, such as was entirely foreign to the light-hearted and innocent singer of Canticles. In the natural world the sprouting of the almond may mean that

> 'Winter's rains and ruins are over
> And all the season of snows and sins'

but in the moral world towards which the prophet's eyes were constantly turned it suggested only a note of doom. 'As to Amos the fruits of autumn suggested the approach of wintry desolation, so to Jeremiah the almond first of all trees to flower suggested the advent of another season.' Edghill on Am. viii. 2.

rod. The word is used elsewhere of an actual rod (Gen. xxx. 37 ; Hos. iv. 12 ; Zech. xi. 7, &c.), and Kimchi and some of the older interpreters therefore looked upon it here as a 'symbol of correction.'

almond tree. In Palestine the almond tree was, and is, the 'harbinger of spring' amongst the flowers (cf. Pliny, *Hist. Nat.* XVI. 25 ; Tristram, *Nat. Hist. of the Bible*, p. 332)[2]. Its Hebrew name means 'that which is awakening,' and comes from the same root as the verb used in the next *v.*

12. *I watch* (שֹׁקֵד), *shôkêd*. The Hebrew contains a play upon the word for *almond tree* (שָׁקֵד), *shâkêd*. Similar instances are not uncommon in the prophets (e.g. Am. viii. 2)[3]. The word occurs again in xxxi. 28, xliv. 27 of God's activity, and in v. 6 of the sinister watchfulness of a wolf on the look-out for its prey.

13—16. The vision of the boiling caldron.

13. *the second time.* Evidently the two visions are to be closely con-

---

[1] For a note on 'Jeremiah and Nature,' see pp. 10 ff. Browning has used the almond blossom and the coming of spring somewhat in a similar way, possibly borrowing from this passage. As Palma in *Sordello* longs for the appearing of the unknown lover who is to share with her the task of uniting Italy she seems to see a prophecy of his coming in the approaching spring :

> 'Waits he not the waking year?
> His almond blossoms must be honey-ripe
> By this ; to welcome him, fresh runnels stripe
> The thawed ravines ; because of him, the wind
> Walks like a herald.'

[2] 'In the Phrygian cosmogony an almond figured as the father of all things, perhaps because its delicate lilac blossom is one of the first heralds of the spring,' Frazer, *Adonis*, I. pp. 263 f.: cf. Pausan. VII. xvii. 11; Hippol. *Refutatio*, v. 9; Arnob. *Adv. Nationes*, v. 6.

[3] Bishop Lightfoot has collected a number of examples of somewhat similar word-plays in his commentary on Phil. iii. 2: e.g. 'the saying of Diogenes that the school of Euclides was not σχολή but χολή and the discourse of Plato not διατριβή but κατατριβή (Diog. Laert. VI. 24).'

And I said, I see a seething caldron ; and the face thereof is
from the north. 14 Then the LORD said unto me, Out of the
north evil ¹ shall break forth upon all the inhabitants of the land.

¹ Heb. *shall be opened.*

nected ; it is quite possible that they formed a second call to Jeremiah
and so he included them in this account of his earliest experiences
with which their connexion may have been spiritual rather than chronological. A recent writer says that ' It is more probable that the two
visions of the almond-rod and the pot occurred much later than the
prophet's call. They may have been God's message to him when the
forecast of the Scythian invasion had been proved mistaken, and when
the true enemy from the North was just appearing on the scene.'
(Hölscher, *Die Profeten*, pp. 283 ff.)

a seething caldron. The word is used of a large cooking-pot
sufficient to contain a meal for several people (2 K. iv. 38 ff.), also
of a wash-pot (Ps. lx. 10, cviii. 10), and it is evidently not restricted to earthen vessels (Ex. xxxviii. 3 ; Ez. xxiv. 6). *Seething* is
lit. 'blown-upon': the fire under the pot is blown upon and therefore
it boils.

the face thereof is from the north. The exact explanation of the
symbol is difficult though the meaning, as stated in the next *v.*, is
quite plain. Two lines of explanation have been suggested by different
scholars. (*a*) The contents of the caldron represent the invading
force, 'the ominous North was once more boiling like a caldron'
(G. A. Smith, *Jerusalem*, II. 228)—so Keil and many other critics.
(*b*) Duhm, however, takes a different line ; he suggests that the
caldron was laid on a rough oven made of stones, one side, that
towards the North, being open and the fuel placed there. The idea is
then the same as that found in Ez. xxiv. 3—14 ; the caldron is Judah
and the fire beneath is blown upon from the North ; the contents of
the caldron which are made to boil will then be represented by the
inhabitants who are about to go into exile. The latter suggestion,
which requires a slight change in the Hebrew, has been adopted by
several modern scholars, and it must be admitted that it avoids the
difficulty of deciding what is meant by *the face* of a caldron.

14. *the north.* In Jeremiah *the north* is almost a synonym for the
coming invader, and so too in Joel ii. 20 'the northern army of locusts'
must be a metaphorical expression for an invading army, since locusts
come from S. and SE. (cf. Is. xiv. 31 'a smoke out of the north').
An army invading Palestine from Asia would do so by way of *n.* Syria,
and so the frequent experience of the Israelites had led them to look
upon the North as the quarter from which troubles usually arose.
There was always something mysterious and even supernatural about
this quarter to the Jews, and it may be that this feeling was derived
from their Semitic ancestors, for the gods of Assyria were said to dwell
in the *far North*. (Cf. Is. xiv. 13 with Wade's note; and Ps. xlviii. 2

15 For, lo, I will call all the families of the kingdoms of the north, saith the LORD; and they shall come, and they shall set every one his throne at the entering of the gates of Jerusalem, and against all the walls thereof round about, and against all the cities of Judah. 16 And I will [1]utter my judgements against them touching all their wickedness; in that they have forsaken me, and have burned incense unto other gods, and worshipped the works of their own hands. 17 Thou therefore gird up thy

[1] Or, *speak with them of my judgements*

with Kirkpatrick's note. See also Enoch lxxvii. 3 where the North contains 'the garden of righteousness,' i.e. Paradise[1].)

15 f. 'Viewed in one light war is the boiling caldron of human passion, upset by hazard, and bringing only ruin in its course; in the other it is God sitting in judgement, with the kings of the earth as His assessors, solemnly pronouncing sentence upon the guilty.' Payne Smith.

15. *families.* In the earlier writers this word was restricted in its use to the divisions of the people of Israel. It corresponds to a ' clan' or tribe-division rather than to what is generally understood as a 'family.' (Cf. W. Robertson Smith, *Rel. Sem.*[2] p. 258 &c.)

kingdoms. This passage would suit an invasion by the Babylonians much better than a Scythian incursion. The Great King would assemble his subject kings and all would march onward as a single army : cf. Is. xvii. 12—14.

set...his throne. As a sign of conquest and of judgement. Duhm sees in this *v.* the influence of the 'later dogmatic eschatology' which foretold the gathering of all nations to Jerusalem. Cf. *Sibyll. Orac.* III. 67 f. :

'In a ring round the city the accursed kings shall place
Each one his throne with his infidel people by him.'

16. God is to be known in the coming of vengeance, a thought often found in Ezekiel.

burned incense. Lit. to cause smoke or odour to go up. The Hebrew word (קטר : cf. Assyr. *kutru* = smoke) has no necessary connexion with the burning of *incense* which is generally considered to have been a comparatively late introduction into Hebrew ritual. See on vi. 20.

17—19. Jeremiah is encouraged to be strong and zealous in spite of the certain and constant opposition with which he will meet. God is calling him to a life-long warfare.

gird up thy loins. Girding, when used metaphorically, combines

[1] 'The North צפון is divided into three parts: one for men, one for waters (צפה an overflowing), and clouds and darkness (צפן to conceal), while one contains Paradise (צפן to reserve).' Charles.

loins, and arise, and speak unto them all that I command thee :
be not dismayed at them, lest I dismay thee before them. 18 For,
behold, I have made thee this day a defenced city, and an iron
pillar, and brasen walls, against the whole land, against the kings
of Judah, against the princes thereof, against the priests thereof,
and against the people of the land. 19 And they shall fight
against thee ; but they shall not prevail against thee : for I am
with thee, saith the LORD, to deliver thee.

the ideas of strength and preparedness : loosening of the loins, on the
other hand, means weakness and surrender (cf. Is. xlv. 1).   The *loins*
were looked upon as the seat of strength (Dt. xxxiii. 11; 1 K. xii.
10, &c.); and of keenest pain (Nah. ii. 11 ; Is. xxi. 3).

    be not dismayed &c., 'quail not, lest I let thee quail,' Streane.
Lit. means '*be shattered*,' and is so used of broken bows (li. 56).   The
word is a favourite one with Jeremiah who almost invariably uses it,
as here, in a metaphorical sense.

    18.   *iron pillar.*   Cornill omits this phrase (with LXX.) as being
inconsistent with a siege.

    iron...brasen.   A very frequent combination to represent firmness
and endurance: Dt. xxviii. 48; Mic. iv. 13; and cf. Dan. iv. 12.

    kings...princes &c.   Jeremiah's messages were for every class and
for all the people.   In the warfare which he had to carry on he would
need the strength of a fortified city, and at the same time he would
have to experience the isolation involved in a siege.

    19.   Confidence in another is the most certain refuge from fear.

ADDITIONAL NOTE ON I. 11.

Jeremiah and Nature.

    When we speak of Nature we use the word with different connotations.
We may mean by Nature the world of Natural Laws, or the world of Natural
Beauty; that is to say Nature may be regarded from a scientific or from an
aesthetic point of view.   Further still, Nature may be looked upon from a
merely utilitarian standpoint, as the power which provides man with food and
raiment; though this latter division might perhaps be included in the 'scientific'
aspect of Nature.

    Ancient writers, whether they emphasised the scientific or the aesthetic
side of Nature, were in the habit of personifying it, of giving to Nature a
separate existence over against God on the one side and man on the other.
In the prophets the Natural creation is often spoken of as though it were
possessed of conscious life, and even St Paul uses the same kind of language
(cf. Rom. viii. 19 ff.).   The Natural creation, for example, can be appealed to as
the judge between God and Israel (Is. i. 2 ff.) ; or as a witness for the prosecution
when the nation appears before the tribunal of the Most High (Mic. vi. 1 ff.).

Yet at the same time there is no small amount of sympathy between Nature and man; and man's feelings are often represented (by what Ruskin called 'the *pathetic* fallacy') as being produced into it (see note on p. 45).

In the strict sense of the word, Jeremiah, like the other prophets, had no scientific conception of the Natural world, nor indeed did he in any way approach such a conception. The prophets looked upon the ordinances of Nature as being due to the direct action of God Himself, and as their tendency was to emphasise the grandeur and impressiveness of Nature rather than its beauty, they saw the *power*, rather than the *love* of God, shining through the veil of His creation; at the same time they fully recognised the bounteous goodness of Him who gave the rain and fruitful harvests. The prophets were men of action rather than men of speculation; they were faced with problems which were intensely real and calling for solution, and these problems were not problems in the world of thought and imagination only, but in the world around them. The result was that they tended to exercise the moral powers rather than the intellectual or aesthetic, to realise the presence of God's activity in Nature, rather than to seek to know how it was exercised therein, much less to lay bare their souls to the waves of beauty and loveliness which were ever flowing through and from it.

The failure of the prophets to differentiate between God and the laws by which He acts led in some cases to a belief in doctrines which to the mind of a later and more enlightened age seem to be distinctly dangerous, as for example, the doctrine that the sins of parents might be visited on their children by a deliberate interference of God to that end (see pp. liv f. and cf. Adam, *Religious Teachers of Greece*, pp. 22 ff.). Another inadequate view of Nature which arose from the prophetic ignorance of scientific laws,—a view, however, which was not in itself dangerous,—was their conception that the earth was the centre of the universe, fixed and immovable, whilst the heavens were constantly changing. This conception, of course, lasted till the Middle Ages, it was shared in by our Lord Himself in His life here on earth, and is still reflected in phrases like 'sunrise' and 'sunset.' This same distinction between 'the heavens' and 'the earth' which regarded the latter as fixed and the former as in motion was a tenet of the Aristotelian philosophy. One of the great changes wrought by the acceptance of the Copernican theory was that it made it possible to do away with this distinction, and to look upon the earth as being of one piece with the heavens and no less divine than they (cf. C. C. J. Webb, *History of Philosophy*, p. 142).

Jeremiah himself, when compared with the other prophets, must be admitted to have had a much greater appreciation of the more tender aspects of Nature, especially of animate Nature, and he constantly draws illustrations from it[1]. He was evidently a close observer of bird life and several times refers to

---

[1] Cf. T. R. Glover, *The Jesus of History*, p. 31:—'Jeremiah is obviously country-bred. He might have been surprised, if he had been told how often he illustrates his thought from bird and beast and country life—and always with a certain life-like precision and a perfectly clear sympathy.'

the flight of birds across the heavens, he admired their wonderful instinct (viii. 7), he had watched their habits closely (xii. 9), and his interest followed them even into their captivity (v. 27); at the same time he seems to have had no ear for the music of their songs (cf. Cant. ii. 12). Nor did the wider aspects of Nature leave Jeremiah untouched, and he was ever alive to the changing march of the seasons. Yet with all this appreciation of the softer and gentler moods of Nature there went something that was grim and harsh, and the predominant impression left on our minds by the imagery of the book is one of tumult and horror. Descriptions of the sea dashing and raging against its bounds, of the mountains and hills rocking in the throes of a mighty earthquake, of the whole land desolate, seem more akin to the mind of Jeremiah than the soothing picture of the budding almond tree and the silent approach of spring.

CHAPTERS II.—VI.

FIRST COLLECTION OF JEREMIAH'S PROPHECIES.

The prophecies contained in these chh. refer most probably to the period between the prophet's call (c. 626 B.C.) and a date shortly after Josiah's reformation (c. 620 B.C.). They appear to form a single collection, though by no means confined to a single discourse, and, in spite of the fact that matter is contained in them which must come from a somewhat later time, they may be taken as typical of Jeremiah's earliest preaching. According to the account contained in ch. xxxvi. none of Jeremiah's prophecies had been collected in writing before 604 B.C. and so it need not be supposed that chh. ii.—vi. represent the exact words of the discourses as originally delivered; doubtless the prophet's recollections were influenced, more or less unconsciously, by the subsequent issue of events. At the same time it seems certain that some amount of editorial matter has been added, either by Baruch or by some other scribe.

The contents of the chh. may be conveniently divided into the following sections:

An appeal to the nation's past. ii.—iii. 5.
An invitation to the exiled Northern tribes to return. iii. 6—18.
A vision of penitence and restoration. iii. 19—iv. 4.
A description of the coming doom. iv. 5—31.
The utter moral depravity of Jerusalem. v.
The invader and his invincible might. vi.

CHAPTERS II. 1—III. 5.

An Appeal to the Nation's Past.

This passage contains a short summary of the history of Israel written from the prophetic point of view, and in it is emphasised the striking contrast between the patience and faithfulness of God on the one hand, and the continued sin and unfaithfulness of Israel on the other. Jeremiah begins his appeal by turning to the earliest days of the nation's history, the time of its ransom from Egypt, and it is to be noticed that in the prophet's eyes the period of the exodus and wandering in the wilderness was one of true and loving intercourse between Jehovah and His people; he seems to have no knowledge or no recollection of the stories of constant strife and backsliding on the part of the nation such as are portrayed in the Pentateuch (see below for a further discussion of this point). From this stage of 'faithfulness' *the fathers* soon fell away and forgetting the goodness of God plunged into all kinds of superstitions and debased forms of worship; they who had knowledge of the true God forsook Him, whereas the very heathen were faithful to their gods which were mere vanity and nothingness. It is not necessary to suppose, however, that Jeremiah is condemning actual apostasy, the entire desertion of Jehovah in favour of strange gods; it is more probable that he had in view a widespread adoption of customs of worship and ideas in regard to Jehovah which were equivalent to a virtual apostasy. The allegiance of Israel was merely nominal, the people still addressed their God as Jehovah, but in their hearts they thought of Him as having the attributes of one of the local Baalim. Another point in this passage which deserves attention is the attitude of the prophet towards the exiled members of the Northern Kingdom. Jeremiah has a deep love for all Israel, he does not limit God's favour to Jerusalem and Judah only, and the coming restoration is to include every true worshipper of Jehovah. (For the same doctrine in other prophets cf. Is. xi. 12 ff.; Ez. xxxvii. 16 ff.; &c.) In the last sub-section of which this division consists (iii. 1—5) Jeremiah likens the sinfulness of Israel to that of an erring wife. Israel is Jehovah's wife bound to Him by the covenant at Sinai, Israel has been false to her Husband and yet He longs for her return.

One question of considerable importance which is raised by this section remains to be discussed. Jeremiah, following Amos (ii. 10, v. 25) and Hosea (ii. 16 f.), regards the wilderness period as a time in which the closest union existed between Jehovah and Israel—a golden age at the beginning of the history of the nation such as the Greeks imagined for their own history. Such a conception is hard to reconcile, however, with the accounts of the wanderings contained in the Pentateuch, and also in the later prophets. Ezekiel, for example, looks upon the people as rebellious from the very first (ii. 3, xx. 13 ff.). Some passages in Hosea seem also to look upon the exodus in a less favourable light (ix. 10, xi. 1—3). Various attempts to explain and reconcile these apparently inconsistent statements have been made by different scholars. Graf, for example, thinks that the wilderness period was looked upon as a time of brightness only by contrast to the utter gloom of the last years of the monarchy; whilst Keil would limit the prophet's reference to the time which elapsed between the departure from Egypt and the covenant at Sinai, he would also draw a somewhat artificial and unnatural distinction between murmurings against Moses and apostasy from Jehovah.

The section may be divided as follows:

> (*a*) *The appeal to the exodus.* ii. 1—3.
> (*b*) *The ingratitude and folly of Judah.* 4—13.
> (*c*) *The penalty of forsaking God and trusting in man.* 14—19.
> (*d*) *Israel's incurable sin.* 20—25.
> (*e*) *The folly of idolatry.* 26—28.
> (*f*) *The reasons for Israel's misfortunes.* 29—37.
> (*g*) *The question of the divorced wife.* iii. 1—5.

II. 1 And the word of the LORD came to me, saying, 2 Go, and cry in the ears of Jerusalem, saying, Thus saith the LORD, I remember [1]for thee the kindness of thy youth, the love of thine espousals; how thou wentest after me in the wilderness, in a

[1] Or, *concerning*

II. 1—3. An appeal to the nation to return to its former love to Jehovah as shewn at the time of the exodus.

2. *Jerusalem.* As the religious as well as the political capital Jerusalem was the natural place for a prophet to make an appeal to the whole nation. It was recommended by tradition and situation alike. (Cf. Amos at Bethel.)

kindness. The Hebrew word חֶסֶד *chesed* is generally used either of the feelings (*a*) of a man towards his fellow; (*b*) of God to man in condescending to His creatures and their needs. The use as here to describe the attitude of Israel towards Jehovah is very rare, though there is possibly another example in Hos. vi. 4 'your piety is like a morning cloud.' Some commentators find themselves unable to take the expression in this way, and in spite of the context, make it refer to God's attitude towards Israel.

youth. Cf. iii. 4.

espousals. The conception of Israel as the bride of Jehovah is adopted from Hos. ii. 2—20. The Semites were in the habit of looking upon the god of the nation as wedded to the land, and upon the members of the nation as the fruit of their union. Cf. Is. liv. 5 and see W. Robertson Smith, *Prophets*[2], pp. 170 ff. The same metaphor purified of all heathen associations is found in NT. where St Paul speaks of the Church as the bride of Christ (Eph. v. 25).

wilderness...not sown. Oriental writers are fond of laying stress on

land that was not sown. 3 Israel *was* holiness unto the Lord, the firstfruits of his increase : all that devour him shall be held guilty ; evil shall come upon them, saith the Lord.

4 Hear ye the word of the Lord, O house of Jacob, and all

the distinction between the wilderness and the cultivated land : cf. Omar Khayyam, *Rubaiyat*, x. :

'some strip of herbage strown
That just divides the desert from the sown.'

The *wilderness* it should be remembered was something more than mere 'desert sand and empty air' ; it was the usual place for pasturing the flocks (cf. xxiii. 10 ; Joel ii. 22). The vegetation of the desert was such as grew of itself, hence the distinction from 'the sown' or cultivated land.

3. *holiness.* The word has no necessary moral content and its use in the present context merely lays stress on the fact that Israel was God's consecrated property and therefore entitled to His protection and separated to His service.

the firstfruits of his increase. In what sense can this term be applied to Israel ? Philo often speaks of Israel as the first-fruits of humanity. Driver explains it as meaning that the nation was Jehovah's 'first-fruits from the field of the world, sacred to Him (Ex. xxiii. 19) and consequently not to be touched with impunity.' But whilst not wishing to deny that Jeremiah cherished the hope that the other nations were destined to become the worshippers of the God of Israel, yet at the same time this interpretation seems to me to read too much into the text. The prophets in their choice of figures were, as a rule, influenced by one main idea and ignored all side issues[1]. In this case the only idea in the writer's mind is that Israel is God's possession (see above) in just the same sense as are the first-fruits ; there is no reason for attributing to him the secondary idea that Israel is therefore an earnest of the gathering in of the rest of the nations. According to the law the first-fruits had to be offered to God before the harvest could be used for the ordinary purposes of life (Lev. xxiii. 10—14). The same expression is used of the Christian Church by St James (i. 18).

guilty. The Hebrew word is used with three distinct though related meanings. It is used (*a*) of one who has committed an offence ; (*b*) of one who has been found guilty of committing an offence, even though there has been a miscarriage of justice ; (*c*) of one who bears the punishment of an offence and is therefore presumed to have committed it. The last sense is the one required here as the stress is on the punishment (cf. Lev. xxii. 10, 16).

4—13. In the previous section Jeremiah seems to linger over the picture of Israel's youth with a tender and pathetic longing : that the

---

[1] Cf. Jülicher, *Die Gleichnissreden Jesu*, I. p. 317; and J. W. Hunkin, *The Synoptic Parables* in *J.Th.S.* xvi. pp. 372 ff.

the families of the house of Israel: 5 thus saith the LORD, What unrighteousness have your fathers found in me, that they are gone far from me, and have walked after vanity, and are become vain? 6 Neither said they, Where is the LORD that brought us up out of the land of Egypt; that led us through the wilderness, through a land of deserts and of pits, through a land of drought

glories of those days should ever be restored is a wish almost beyond hope of fulfilment :—and yet the nation is still the same, it is still God's chosen people. From these bright visions the prophet now turns to the ingratitude and sin which soon blotted them out, and in the light of the great ideal of the past the actual state of the nation seems the more lamentable. Jehovah's appeal to the nation in *v.* 5 is very like Mic. vi. 3 'O my people, what have I done unto thee? and wherein have I wearied thee? testify against me.' In each case the challenge was unanswerable because God was the offended party.

4. *house of Jacob.* This expression is much less common than the parallel form the 'house of Israel.' It occurs only 17 times, apart from Gen. xlvi. 27 where it is used in the literal sense of the immediate descendants of the patriarch, and of these 7 are found in the book of Isaiah. The appeal here, as so often in this prophet (cf. Jas. i. 1), is all Israel, not merely the Southern Kingdom : one wonders if Jeremiah wished his message to be carried to the northern part of the land to the province of Samaria which at this time possibly included some who were worshippers of Jehovah. Cf. xli. 5 with notes.

5. *unrighteousness.* Cf. Dt. xxxii. 4.

vanity. Lit. *vapour, breath.* The root idea is vapour driven by the wind ; cf. Prov. xxi. 6. The word is often applied to idols and their worship and is very common in Jeremiah.

become vain. A verb from the same root. Another part of the verb is used in xxiii. 16 of the results of the labours of the 'false' prophets. Cf. Ps. lxii. 11 and Job xxvii. 12. Men may make gods in their own image, but their characters tend to become similar to those of the beings whom they worship.

6. 'The very name of Jehovah became known as a name of power only through Moses and the great deliverance' (W. R. Smith, *Prophets*[2], p. 33) and by reminding them of the deeds of mercy and wisdom in the past Jeremiah shews up their ingratitude in even darker colours. For a description of the wilderness of the exodus see E. H. Palmer, *The Desert of the Exodus*, especially pp. 284 ff. and cf. Dt. i. 19, ix. 15, xxxii. 10 ; Am. ii. 10 ; Mic. vi. 3 ff. The account is written from the point of view of one unused to the nomadic life and not unnaturally exaggerates the terrors of what was unknown to the writer. Asshurbanipal bears testimony to the difficulties of crossing the Syro-Arabian desert which he describes as 'a land of thirst and faintness where no beast of the field is and no bird builds its nest.'

and of ¹the shadow of death, through a land that none passed
through, and where no man dwelt? 7 And I brought you into a
plentiful land, to eat the fruit thereof and the goodness thereof;
but when ye entered, ye defiled my land, and made mine heritage
an abomination. 8 The priests said not, Where is the LORD? and
they that handle the law knew me not : the ²rulers also trans-

---

¹ Or, *deep darkness*   ² Heb. *shepherds.*

---

the shadow of death. Mg. *deep darkness* is to be preferred. To the
inexperienced traveller the desert with its absence of roads is as hard
to traverse as a land of darkness : cf. Ps. xxiii. 4 ; Is. xxi. 1, xxx. 6 ;
Job vi. 18. LXX. renders 'barrenness.'

7. In strong contrast to the hardships and dangers of the wilderness through which God led His ransomed people was the land of
promise into which they entered. Cf. Am. ii. 10 f.

plentiful land. Heb. *land of Carmel.* The word means garden-land,
plantation, and though it is used specifically of Mt Carmel, it may also
be applied to any very fertile spot.

defiled. The word used of ceremonial uncleanness. Hosea had
already made a very similar usage of the word to describe the effect of
heathen cults (v. 3, vi. 10).

my land. Cf. xvi 18 ; Hos. ix. 3.

mine heritage. From the parallelism it is evident that the land is
meant, a very rare use—Ps. lxxix. 1 furnishes another example. As a
rule the term is applied to the people itself (e.g. 1 S. x. 1 ; 1 K. viii.
53 ; Ps. xxxiii. 12).

abomination. Generally used in a religious sense though occasionally
with a wider meaning.

8. *The priests.* Jeremiah constantly attributes the failure of the
people to their natural leaders in both Church and State : cf. xxiii. 1 ff.

handle the law. The same phrase is used in Ecclus. xv. 1 with an
evident reference to the work of the scribes. In the present passage
the expression is a little awkward for the Heb. word תָּפַשׂ *tāphas = to
handle* is almost always used of a literal seizing especially with the idea
of wielding ; in one or two late passages it has acquired a metaphorical
sense, e.g. Prov. xxx. 9 'seize the name of my God,' Nu. xxxi. 27 (P)
'those skilled in war (lit. *handlers* of war).' The word translated *law*
is in the original תּוֹרָה *tōrāh* and its literal meaning is 'direction'; cf.
Ex. iv. 12, 15, where the verb is translated *teach.* The root underlying
tōrāh is used of *casting* or *shooting* and the word evidently goes back
to the time when 'direction' was given by means of arrows &c. (cf.
Ez. xxi. 21 f.) or the casting of a sacred lot. The discovery that the
early Israelites agreed with their neighbours in retaining much of the
outward ritual and religious mechanism of the primitive Semitic race
ought not to alarm us, for as Robertson Smith has wisely said 'the vast
difference between the revelation of Jehovah and the oracles of the

gressed against me, and the prophets prophesied by Baal, and
walked after things that do not profit. 9 Wherefore I will yet
plead with you, saith the LORD, and with your children's children
will I plead. 10 For pass over to the isles of Kittim, and see ;
and send unto Kedar, and consider diligently ; and see if there

nations lies in what Jehovah had to say rather than in the actual
manner of saying it.' *Prophets*[2], p. 57.

knew me not. Cf. Hos. iv. 6 (of the priests).

rulers (Heb. *shepherds*). Cf. iii. 15, xxiii. 1, 2, 4. The representation
of the leaders of the nation under the figure of shepherds would be
one which would readily suggest itself to a pastoral people (already in
Hos. iv. 4—10, &c.), though strangely enough it is most commonly used
by the later writers (Ez. xxxiv. ; Zech. ix.—xi.).

transgressed. Sin is here regarded from the point of view, not of
the breaking of a law, but of rebellion against a person.

prophets. Jeremiah was forced to condemn the members of his own
order; cf. Amos' indignant repudiation of the idea that he was a prophet
(vii. 14).

Baal. Singular for plural. Hosea similarly uses the word as a collective
noun (ii. 10, xiii. 1 ; cf. ii. 15, 19, xi. 2 ; and Zeph. i. 4).

do not profit. Jeremiah had a strong sense of the worthlessness of
the strange gods, cf. *v.* 11 : it is therefore mere foolishness to worship
them. 'Every religion is utilitarian in the best and noblest sense of
the word : what must I do to be saved ?' 'wie kriege ich einen gnädigen
Gott ? sind ihre eigentlichen Lebensfragen.' Cornill.

9. *plead.* The word is nearly always used with Jehovah as the
subject. It should be remembered that the Heb. original contains no
idea of entreaty and the word would be much less liable to misunder-
standing if it had been consistently translated 'contend' as in Is. xlix.
25, l. 8 (AV., RV.). It is here used with a forensic force as in Is. iii. 13.

10. *isles.* The word really means *coastlands* and was a vague
designation of the countries 'that gird the Northern and Western
Mediterranean...derived, no doubt, from the Phoenician mariners who
skirted their shores without penetrating into the interior.' It is often
used as a synonym for 'the West' as a whole ; cf. Is. xlii. 10 f.

Kittim. The word is usually derived from *Kition* the modern
Larnaka in Cyprus, though it is used with a much wider meaning and
here represents a people, evidently those who appear in Gen. x. 4 as
the descendants of Javan. W. Max Müller would connect the word
with the Hittites (*Asien u. Eur.* p. 345). In 1 Macc. i. 1, viii. 5 the
Kittim are the Macedonians. See further J. G. Frazer, *Adonis*, &c. I.
pp. 31 f.

and see. Cf. Am. ii. 10.

Kedar is here used to represent 'the East' in contradistinction
to the *isles of Kittim* representing 'the West': see fuller note on
xlix. 28.

hath been such a thing. 11 Hath a nation changed *their* gods, which yet are no gods? but my people have changed their glory for that which doth not profit. 12 Be astonished, O ye heavens, at this, and be horribly afraid, be ye very desolate, saith the

11. *nation.* The gods of the heathen were really in each several case the personification of the nation by whom they were worshipped and therefore a symbol of their 'political identity,' and religion had 'no higher moral standard and no higher aims than those of the worshippers themselves,' and so there was no reason from a 'religious' point of view why any people should give up their gods. At the same time there was a strong 'political' reason why they should not do so for 'that which gave the individuals of a nation unity and made them a people was the unity of its god.' (A. B. Davidson, *Expos.* 2nd Series, p. 257.) But in the case of Israel the God of the nation, in the minds of the prophets at any rate, was 'something more than a personification of their standards and aims,' and His worship involved moral restrictions which the body of the nation found too hard to bear. Cf. Ez. iii. 6, and see further W. Robertson Smith, *Prophets*[2], pp. 66 f.

To many of the nations surrounding Israel at this time there would be little need to *change* gods; because the existence and power of other gods being recognised, and their own gods not being, in actual experience, 'jealous gods,' all that would be necessary would be to *add* to the number of gods worshipped. Such a proceeding would be especially common in the case of an alliance between two nations when the gods themselves were also considered to enter into an alliance. This belief probably accounts for Solomon's action in building temples for the deities of his various wives, for there can be little doubt that his numerous marriages were intended to cement political alliances. In later times Ahab's attempt to carry out this custom met with strenuous opposition from Elijah. It is however possible that Jezebel wished to supplant Jehovah altogether by the Syrian Baal, or she may have attacked the prophets in revenge for their opposition; it would be a hard task to discover which party was really the aggressor. This action on the part of Elijah marks an advance in the conception of Jehovah as a 'jealous god,' and is a step towards monotheism. In commenting on this text Calvin mentions with approval Xenophon's commendation of the oracle of Apollo that those gods were rightly to be worshipped who have been received by tradition from ancestors.

which yet are no gods. The same phrase is used by Hosea of the calf-worship in Northern Israel (viii. 6).

12. *heavens.* The prophets constantly appeal to the heavens as a witness against Israel's rebellion and sin. 'When the Lord arraigns His people, the whole of nature is the appropriate audience.' (Wade on Is. i. 2.) In vi. 19 a similar appeal is made to the earth.

be horribly afraid...desolate. Horribly afraid is better translated *shudder.* The MT. of *be ye desolate* חרבו was read by LXX. as הרבה *ex-*

LORD. 13 For my people have committed two evils; they have forsaken me the fountain of living waters, and hewed them out cisterns, broken cisterns, that can hold no water. 14 Is Israel a servant? is he a homeborn *slave*? why is he become a prey?

ceedingly, so that the whole phrase should probably best be translated simply as *shudder exceedingly*.

13. An admirable description of the double folly of Judah for 'he hath twofold guilt who, knowing good rather chooseth evil.' The two sins, strictly speaking, are really different parts of one and the same act, for when men give up God and religion they invariably seek for some substitute, and so it comes about that an age of unbelief is always an age of superstition. (Cf. for example the state of the early Roman Empire as described by Tacitus and other writers.) 'The soul...dies by departing from the fountain of life, and thereupon is taken up by this transitory world, and is conformed into it.' St Aug. *Conf.* XIII. xxi.

living waters. This is possibly the earliest use of this phrase in connexion with the power of Jehovah. Apart from the context *living* when applied to water merely means running or springing, and no idea of life-giving is then to be attached to it. (Cf. xvii. 13; Is. xii. 30; Jn. iv. 14, and vii. 37 ff.) The people in their foolishness deserted Jehovah who is 'the fountain of life' (Enoch xcvi. 6) to serve other gods who were mere 'dead stone and lifeless wood[1].'

broken cisterns. 'The dead gods have no life and dispense no life, just as wells with rents or fissures hold no water.' The remains of these cisterns are still to be found in large numbers in Palestine. In addition to their liability to crack and so to allow the store of water to run off, these cisterns lose much water by evaporation and the residue is unpleasant to the eye and disagreeable to the taste. (Cf. Thomson, *The Land and the Book*, p. 287.)

14—19. The penalties of forsaking God, and trusting in man.

14—17. This small section has apparently got out of place and interrupts the natural sequence from *v.* 13 to *v.* 18. It would seem from *v.* 16 that Jeremiah uttered these *vv.* after the defeat and death of Josiah at Megiddo and the consequent oppression by Egypt.

14. This *v.* exhibits a strong contrast with the state of affairs in *v.* 3. Israel is no longer defended by Jehovah nor looked upon as His possession.

servant...homeborn slave. Slaves were of two kinds—those acquired by purchase, and those born in the house of the master and therefore his permanent possession according to Ex. xxi. 1—3. The form of the question requires an answer in the negative as in *v.* 31. (Cf. viii. 4 f., 22, xiv. 19, &c.)

prey. Used in Nu. xiv. 3 and Dt. i. 39 of the little ones in the

---

[1] In the Targum upon Cant. iv. 14 the words of the law are likened to a well of living waters.

15 The young lions have roared upon him, and [1]yelled : and they have made his land waste ; his cities are burned up, without inhabitant. 16 The children also of Noph and Tahpanhes have [2]broken the crown of thy head. 17 Hast thou not procured this unto thyself, in that thou hast forsaken the LORD thy God, when he led thee by the way ? 18 And now what hast thou to do in

[1] Heb. *given out their voice.*   [2] Or, *fed on*

wilderness : contrast xxx. 16 'all they that prey upon thee will I give for a prey.'

15. *young lions.* The same figure is used in Is. v. 29 and is frequent in Pss. Heb. has many words for *lion*; the one used here represents a lion able to hunt his prey and therefore older than a whelp. The lion is used of Assyria in Nah. ii. 12 f.

waste. A favourite word of Jeremiah who uses it more than twenty times. Cf. Is. i. 5—9.

without inhabitant. Driver thinks that the reference is to the Northern Kingdom.

16. *Noph.* Memphis (Egn. *Mĕnnŭfĕr*), the ancient capital of Lower Egypt, situated not far from the modern Cairo. At one time a city of great importance (cf. Diod. Sic. I. 51), it gradually decayed after the foundation of Alexandria.

Tahpanhes. The Daphnae Pelusii of the Greeks (Δάφναι Herod. II. 30, Τάφναι LXX.), modern *Tell Defenneh*. Both places later contained settlements of Jewish exiles (cf. xliv. 1, xlvi. 14), Tahpanhes being the place of the prophet's own residence (xliii. 7 f.).

broken. Mg. *fed on.* Driver suggests a slight alteration in the Heb. so as to read *lay bare* (cf. Is. vii. 20). Whichever reading is adopted the meaning of the phrase is quite clear and refers to some humiliation at the hands of Egypt, possibly in connexion with the siege of Ashdod (Herod. II. 157) or more probably after the defeat at Megiddo.

17. Cf. iv. 18.

18 f. These *vv.* refer apparently to some attempt to strengthen the position of the nation by political alliances either with Egypt, which from the middle of the seventh century B.C. began to recover something of its former power, or with Assyria. The exact occasion on which overtures were made is not known ; the use of Assyria suggests that it was in the days of Josiah, unless indeed Assyria is used, as so often in later writings (e.g. Zech. x. 10 f.), to represent any other predominant Eastern power. Isaiah likewise found reasons during his ministry to issue a similar condemnation of the pro-Egyptian party (xxx. 1—3). Judah was constantly turning from one power to the other, fluttering backwards and forwards like 'a silly dove' (Hos. vii. 11). The small Syrian States resembled in many ways the Balkan States of our own times, both in the uncertainty of their position and in the policy which they habitually pursued to improve or maintain it.

the way to Egypt, to drink the waters of ¹Shihor? or what hast thou to do in the way to Assyria, to drink the waters of ²the River? 19 Thine own wickedness shall correct thee, and thy backslidings shall reprove thee : know therefore and see that it is an evil thing and a bitter, that thou hast forsaken the Lord thy God, and that my fear is not in thee, saith the Lord, the Lord of hosts. 20 For of old time ³I have broken thy yoke, and burst thy bands ; and thou saidst, I will not ⁴serve ; for upon every high hill and under every green tree thou didst bow thy-

---

¹ That is, the Nile.   ² That is, the Euphrates.
³ Or, *thou hast*   ⁴ Another reading is, *transgress*.

---

18. *Shihor*, 'the muddy river' (St Jerome, *Ep.* cviii. 14), is usually taken to refer to the Nile (so in Is. xxiii. 3) though sometimes it refers merely to its Eastern arm, as in Josh. xiii. 3 (cf. 1 Ch. xiii. 5). LXX. Γῆων is the name of the second river mentioned in Gen. ii. 13 as flowing out of the Garden of Eden; some would identify this river with the Nile (e.g. Ecclus. xxiv. 27; Jub. viii. 15; Jos. *Ant.* I. i. 3). As it was upon the Nile that Egypt depended for its fertility, and so for its very life, the phrase *to drink the waters of Shihor* means to rely on the resources of Egypt.

the River, par excellence, is the Euphrates. Just as the Nile represents Egypt, so *the River* stands for the Eastern powers, Assyria, Babylon and their successors.

19. *Thine own wickedness.* It was mainly owing to the unreliability of Judah's promises and the constant plotting of her leaders that so many misfortunes befell the nation. The voices of the prophets who proclaimed with one mind that in 'quietness and confidence' lay her hope of survival were ignored in favour of the advice of political opportunists.

evil thing. Cf. Am. viii. 10; Zeph. i. 14.

20—25. God had done everything for the future of the nation, and yet it has turned out badly and has deserted Him. In a large variety of figures borrowed from pastoral, agricultural, and home life the prophet shews the depth of Judah's depravity.

20. *I have broken.* Better as marg., LXX. and Vg. *thou hast broken.* The Massoretes evidently mistook the archaic form of the 2nd fem. sing. for the 1st person. It is Israel that has become rebellious and broken the commands of Jehovah, not, as in xxx. 8; Hos. xi. 4; Jehovah who breaks the bonds of Israel and the yoke of her oppressors.

high hill. The Northern Semitic races seem to have had a preference for mountain tops as a place for offering sacrifices (cf. Gen. xxii. 2; Is. xv. 2). In like manner the dwelling place of the Deity was thought to be on a high mountain: Dt. xxxiii. 2; Ps. lxviii. 17 represent Jehovah as coming from Sinai His dwelling place. See

self, playing the harlot. 21 Yet I had planted thee a noble vine,
wholly a right seed: how then art thou turned into the degenerate plant of a strange vine unto me? 22 For though thou
wash thee with lye, and take thee much soap, yet thine iniquity

further W. Robertson Smith, *Rel. Sem.*[2] pp. 489 f.; H. P. Smith, *Rel.
of Isr.* p. 20; J. G. Frazer, *Folk-Lore in O.T.* pp. 62 ff.

green tree. The trees under which special worship was paid were
probably held to be sacred. The veneration of sacred trees was very
widespread amongst the ancient Semites: cf. W. Robertson Smith,
op. cit. pp. 185 ff.; H. P. Smith, *op. cit.* pp. 17 f.; and see also for the
whole subject of tree-worship J. G. Frazer, *The Magic Art*, II. pp. 6 ff.,
349 ff., *Folk-Lore in O.T.* pp. 40 ff.

didst bow thyself. The people are condemned for worshipping strange
gods at these sanctuaries just as in Hos. viii. 13; Am. v. 21. The
earlier Hebrew religion saw nothing wrong in an indefinite number of
local sanctuaries, many of which would be taken over from the original
inhabitants (Ex. xx. 4; Hos. viii. 11; Am. iv. 4). In later times, however, it was seen that it was impossible to free such sanctuaries from
their previous traditions and that the only way of purifying the worship
was to destroy them (Ez. xx. 28; Dt. xii. 12 f.). See Introd. pp. xxi f.

playing the harlot. A reference to the sin of the nation in worshipping other gods than Jehovah who was her true husband (cf. iii. 1—5,
iv. 13 f.). The term would receive greater force from the immoral
practices which were carried on in connexion with such worship. In
Is. i. 21 ff. the reference seems to be to sinning against Jehovah generally without any specific reference to idolatry.

21. *planted.* There are constant references throughout OT. to
Israel as the vine which Jehovah has planted and which has become
degenerate (Hos. x. 1; Ps. lxxx. 9, &c.). In Is. v. 1 ff. the nation is
figured as the vineyard itself. It is possible that when our Lord spoke
of Himself as the true vine He was not unmindful of its use as a symbol
for the nation (Jn. xv. 1 ff.)

noble. Heb. *Sorek,* a word which is used also in Is. v. 2 of the chosen
people.

right seed. An unique expression, though moral qualities are elsewhere attributed to seeds. (Cf. Ez. ix. 2; Mal. ii. 15; Matt. xiii. 44
καλὸν σπέρμα.) The genuineness and reliability of the original seed are
emphasised in contrast to the plant which has sprung from it (Gen.
xlix. 22; Dt. xxxiii. 32; Ez. xv. 1 ff., xvii. 5, xix. 10).

22. The agricultural figure of the vine is suddenly dropped for one
derived from the common household task of washing clothes.

wash. The word (כבם) is used generally of washing clothes; its
literal meaning is *to tread.* The same expression is used in iv. 14.

lye, washing-soda: a mineral alkali. Here and xiii. 23; Ps. li. 7.

soap, a vegetable alkali, made from the ashes of certain plants. Here
and Mal. iii. 2.

is marked before me, saith the Lord GOD. 23 How canst thou
say, I am not defiled, I have not gone after the Baalim? see thy
way in the valley, know what thou hast done: *thou art* a swift
[1]dromedary traversing her ways; 24 a wild ass used to the wilderness, that snuffeth up the wind in her desire; in her occasion

------

[1] Or, *young camel*

marked. Cf. *Macbeth*, Act II. Sc. 2:

> 'Will all great Neptune's ocean wash this blood
> Clean from my hand?'

23. The nation denies that it has followed after other gods, and
probably from its own point of view with justice, for doubtless the corrupt worship would generally be offered up in the name of Jehovah.
Judah's sin was not the attempt to substitute any other god for Jehovah,
but the failure to reach any worthy conception of His character; and
so the prophet could accuse them of multiplying the number of their
gods because he refused to recognise the validity of the worship which
they offered. Cf. the excuse of Adam (Gen. iii. 11—13) and of Saul
(1 S. xv. 13—15).

Baalim. Heb. plural. They were worshipped in different localities
mainly in connexion with agricultural pursuits.

the valley must refer to some well-known place. There can be no
doubt that the valley of the son of Hinnom is meant. See on vii. 31.

dromedary. 'The dromedary of Egypt and Syria is not the two-
humped animal described by that name in books of natural history, but
is in fact of the same family as the camel, standing towards his more
clumsy fellow-slave in about the same relation as a racer to a cart-horse.'
(Kinglake, *Eothen*, p. 183.)

traversing. Lit. *twisting*, a figure for aimless wandering: 'coursing
hither and thither' (Driver). Israel was as changeable and uncertain
in her religious as in her political life.

24. *wild ass*. The same Heb. consonants can be read *heifer*, and
Duhm prefers this reading as a wild ass would not be yoked (*v.* 20).
He thinks the figure in the prophet's mind is that of a heifer which has
broken loose and taken to the desert in her passion. But there is no
need to connect the statements in *v.* 20 with this *v.* in view of all that
lies between them, and the animal is one which is *used to the wilderness*. The blind eagerness of the Israelites in the pursuit of other gods
is only paralleled by the unrestrained speed of the *wild ass* in search of
her lovers. The wild ass is used in Job xxiv. 5, xxxix. 5—8, as here,
as a type of licence, and in Gen. xvi. 12 of love of freedom (of Ishmael).
The figure may have been suggested by Hos. viii. 9 [1].

------

[1] 'It is a characteristic of the wild ass to seek the highest summits of the
mountains, and there to stand cutting the blue sky with its head and ears erect....
They are swifter of foot and wilder than any beast that ranges the uplands.'
James Morier, quoted by Stanley, *The Jewish Church*, II. p. 443.

who can turn her away? all they that seek her will not weary
themselves; in her month they shall find her. 25 Withhold thy
foot from being unshod, and thy throat from thirst: but thou
saidst, There is no hope: no; for I have loved strangers, and
after them will I go. 26 As the thief is ashamed when he is
found, so is the house of Israel ashamed; they, their kings, their
princes, and their priests, and their prophets; 27 which say to
a stock, Thou art my father; and to a stone, Thou hast ¹brought
²me forth: for they have turned their back unto me, and not

¹ Or, *begotten me*   ² Another reading is, *us.*

25. The metaphor is changed slightly; the idea of the pursuit of
strange gods is still retained, but it is a human being, one who wears
sandals, who is bidden not to continue in her course.   Driver paraphrases : 'Do not run thy feet bare and thy throat dry.'   There is
probably no reference to the bare feet of those who are at the sanctuary
(cf. Moses, Ex. iii. 5), or to the dry throat of an unanswered but persistent worshipper.

There is no hope.   The Heb. נוֹאָשׁ expresses the hopelessness of one
who has lost even the desire for amendment although recognising her
own misery and wretchedness.   It is the utterance of absolute despair.
Cf. Is. lvii. 10 ; Jn. viii. 34.

strangers.   Foreign gods.   Cf. iii. 13 ; Is. xliii. 12.

after them will I go.   Cf. Is. xxx. 15 'this is your rest, but ye
would not.'

26—28. The folly of idolatry.   Israel's continuance in idolatry will
bring nothing but disappointment and disgrace.

26. *As the thief is ashamed.*   For another passage in which a thief is
regarded as an object of derision see xlviii. 27.   The idea underlying
the comparison is the confusion and disgrace in store for Israel.   This
disgrace will be realised not by a sudden awaking of the finer feelings
of the people, but simply through their discovery of the powerlessness
of the false gods and the consequent folly of their own conduct in worshipping them : cf. Hos. iv. 19 ; Is. i. 29 ff.

27. 'The dead stock and the lifeless stone' were fit symbols of the
gods whom they were supposed to represent: cf. Jub. xxii. 18.   J. G.
Frazer, however, thinks that Jeremiah 'was not using vague rhetorical
language, but denouncing real beliefs among his contemporaries'; see
his interesting suggestions in *Adonis*, I. pp. 107 ff.

father.   Duhm does not think that there is any reference here to
ancestor-worship, which was not found among the Hebrews.   The meaning
probably is that the people pay to idols the honour which is due to
Jehovah alone as the true Father of the nation.   Cf. Dt. xxxii. 18;
Job xxxviii. 29 ; 1 Cor. iv. 15 ; Gal. iv. 19.

back.   Cf. Ez. viii. 17 for a literal turning of the back upon Jehovah.
Cf. Jud. x. 9 f. ; Ps. lxxviii. 24 ; Is. xxiv. 16.

their face: but in the time of their trouble they will say, Arise, and save us. 28 But where are thy gods that thou hast made thee? let them arise, if they can save thee in the time of thy trouble: for according to the number of thy cities are thy gods, O Judah.

29 Wherefore will ye plead with me? ye all have transgressed against me, saith the LORD. 30 In vain have I smitten your children; they received no ¹correction: your own sword hath devoured your prophets, like a destroying lion. 31 O generation,

¹ Or, *instruction*

Arise, and save us. Ezekiel, writing of a somewhat later time, represents the people as adopting strange superstitions because they imagined that God had deserted them (viii. 12; and cf. Jeremiah's own experience in Egypt, xliv. 17 f.).

28. This *v.* hardly agrees with the denials of *v.* 23; cf. xi. 13, 19. For the tone of irony which runs through it cf. Elijah and the prophets of Baal on Mount Carmel (1 K. xviii. 27).

according to the number of thy cities. The reference here is evidently to the worship of the Baalim at the various local sanctuaries. When such sanctuaries were taken over from the Canaanites the traditional deity would in time be transformed into a representation of Jehovah Himself: there is a trace of one of these local representations retaining a sort of individuality in Absalom's oath by the Jehovah of Hebron (2 S. xv. 7). From the Middle Ages onwards a similar practice has arisen in Christian countries, and one may speak of our Lady of Walsingham, and so forth. (See note in J. M. P. Smith's *Zeph.* &c. p. 190.)

29—37. The reason for Israel's misfortunes. The prophet, speaking in the name of Jehovah, dismisses the real or pretended complaints of the people because trouble has come upon them. The evil has been brought about by their own persistent sinning and continued hardness of heart, and, if they would but recognise it, is intended to lead them to repentance. Cf. Prov. i. 24—31.

29. *plead.* See on *v.* 9.

30. *your children.* The children of the nations, i.e. the individuals of which they were composed, probably with no idea of the age of the victims; some commentators, however, take the expression literally.

correction. Lit. *instruction.* A common word in this book and also in Deuteronomy and Proverbs. The root means to 'chasten, discipline or admonish.'

your own sword. LXX., Vg., Syr. 'the sword,' probably more correctly.

your prophets. From the parallelism these must have been trusted leaders of the people, those prophets who are usually described as false prophets and who are so frequently condemned by Jeremiah (see Note,

see ye the word of the LORD. Have I been a wilderness unto
Israel? or a land of [1]thick darkness? wherefore say my people,
We are broken loose; we will come no more unto thee? 32 Can a
maid forget her ornaments, or a bride her attire? yet my people
have forgotten me days without number. 33 How trimmest thou
thy way to seek love! therefore even the wicked women hast
thou taught thy ways. 34 Also in thy skirts is found the blood
of the souls of the innocent poor: [2]I have not found it at [3]the

[1] Or, *darkness from Jah*   [2] Or, *thou didst not find them*   [3] See Ex. xxii. 2.

pp. 182 ff.). Their death was evidently calculated to have been a
striking and impressive sign to the people. It is God who has cut them
off, just as it is He who cut off their *children*, otherwise we should have
had 'my prophets.'

31. Has God failed to carry out His promises, He who is the living
water? and become to His people as a parched and dreary land, without
support or moisture? Cf. *vv.* 4 f.

wilderness. As a rule the wilderness means the uncultivated land
which was used as a browsing place for flocks and herds (see on *v.* 2),
but here apparently it refers to the wilderness in the modern sense of
the word: cf. ix. 1; Dt. xxxii. 10.

thick darkness. Just as the wilderness represents lack of support,
so *thick darkness* represents lack of guidance and protection. RVm.
gives the literal rendering of Heb. *darkness of Jah*, that is *darkness
from Jehovah*, and therefore very terrible (cf. 'flame of Jah' in Cant.
viii. 6).

broken loose. The root means to wander about without restraint.
Elsewhere only in Gen. xxvii. 40; Ps. lv. 3; and Hos. xii. 1.

32. *maid...bride.* A pathetic appeal once more to the covenant
days when Israel, like a pure virgin, was betrothed to Jehovah (*v.* 2):
now Israel, like an adulterous wife (iii. 1 ff.), has not only been faithless to Jehovah but has even forgotten Him: cf. Is. i. 3, xlix. 18.

ornaments. The women of the East are still fond of wearing many
and varied *ornaments*; the number of different Heb. words used to represent them shews their commonness in OT. See further on iv. 30.

33. The very harlots have been excelled in wickedness by Israel.
Some commentators see here a reference to the immoral practices in
connexion with religion: LXX. *thou hast done wickedly in corrupting
thy ways.*

34. This *v.* is given up by most commentators as 'incurably
corrupt.'

innocent poor. 'The allusion may be either to deaths due to miscarriage of justice or the result of exaction (vii. 6, xxii. 3, 17; cf. Mic.
iii. 10; Ps. xciv. 21), or to the sacrifice of children (see xix. 4; cf. Ps.
cvi. 38), or possibly to the martyrdoms under Manasseh (2 K. xxi. 16,
xxiv. 4).' Driver.

place of breaking in, but upon [1]all these. 35 Yet thou saidst, I am innocent; surely his anger is turned away from me. Behold, I will enter into judgement with thee, because thou sayest, I have not sinned. 36 Why gaddest thou about so much to change thy way? thou shalt be ashamed of Egypt also, as thou wast ashamed of Assyria. 37 From him also shalt thou go forth, with thine hands upon thine head: for the LORD hath rejected thy confidences, and thou shalt not prosper in them.

III. 1 [2]They say, [3]If a man put away his wife, and she go

[1] Some ancient authorities have, *every oak*.
[2] Heb. *Saying*.   [3] See Deut. xxiv. 1—4.

breaking in. Duhm thinks that a distinction is made between the *innocent poor* and the robber who could be slain without bloodguiltiness (Ex. xxii. 2)[1].

35. Israel relies on her restored prosperity which to her represents the turning away of God's anger and therefore the proof of her innocence. This hypocritical protestation is the deepest of all her crimes. The whole *v.* bears a marked resemblance to Is. i. 28 which should in all probability be translated 'come and let us implead one another' saith Jehovah 'if your sins be as scarlet are they to be reckoned as white as wool?'

36. *to change thy way.* תַּאְזְלִי = מֵאֹזְלִי from a root אזל a word common in Aramaic with the meaning 'to go.' Duhm derives from the root זלל giving to it the meaning 'to act lightly' (cf. LXX. κατεφρόνησας), but it is doubtful whether the root can be so interpreted.

ashamed. i.e. disappointed at the failure of the looked for help. Cf. Is. xx. 5 f., xxx. 3—5. The occasion which is alluded to is not specified and is unknown.

Egypt. Cf. xxxvii. 5.

Assyria. Cf. 2 Ch. xxviii. 21.

37. *thine hands upon thine head.* Cf. 2 S. xiii. 19.

III. 1—5. This small section has apparently got out of its context as the Hebrew requires some introduction (see on *v.* 1). According to the law of Dt. xxiv. 1—4, if a man divorced his wife and she married another he was unable to take her back again. This law evidently did not apply to the case of a man whose wife had been forcibly taken from him (cf. 2 S. iii. 14 ff. David and Michal). Similar prohibitions are found in other Semitic nations; e.g. the Babylonian Code of Hammurabi forbids a husband to have intercourse with his divorced wife (see S. A. Cook, *The Laws of Moses*, &c. p. 124). By a strange coincidence the Koran

[1] By § 21 of the Code of Hammurabi anyone making a breach in a house could be killed out of hand (see S. A. Cook, *The Laws of Moses*, &c. pp. 212 f.). Mr Cook refers to similar enactments in the legislation of Solon, Plato, and the Twelve Tables. Modern Arab custom requires an indemnity for anyone so killed (Jaussen, *Rev. Bib.* 1901, p. 600).

from him, and become another man's, shall he return unto her again? shall not that land be greatly polluted? But thou hast played the harlot with many lovers; [1]yet return again to me, saith the LORD. 2 Lift up thine eyes unto the bare heights, and see; where hast thou not been lien with? By the ways hast thou sat for them, as an Arabian in the wilderness; and thou hast polluted the land with thy whoredoms and with thy wickedness. 3 Therefore the showers have been withholden, and there hath been no latter rain; yet thou hadst a whore's forehead, thou refusedst to be ashamed. 4 Wilt thou not from this time cry unto me, My father, thou art the [2]guide of my youth? 5 Will

---

[1] Or, *and* thinkest thou *to return &c. ?*   [2] Or, *companion*

---

only allows re-marriage in cases where the woman *had* in the meantime been the wife of another. The obvious intention of all such laws was to discourage the husband from an arbitrary exercise of his undoubted right of divorcing his wife at will.

1. *They say.* Heb. *saying.* LXX. and Syr. omit, Vg. *vulgo dicitur.* It is possible that all that has fallen out is the usual prophetic formula 'The word of the LORD came unto me.'

land. LXX. *woman,* which agrees better with Dt. xxiv. 4 *a*.

played the harlot. Israel has not been divorced at all. She has committed shameless and constant adultery.

return. Mg. *thinkest thou to return?* is better.

2. *Arabian.* i.e. a nomad. The use of the word for the members of a particular race is probably later than OT. The wandering tribes of the desert have at all times been a danger to travellers ; as early as the fourteenth century B.C. Hattusil, king of the Hittites, wrote to the king of Babylon that communications had been interrupted by raids of the Bedouin : cf. Diod. Sic. II. 48 ; Pliny, *Hist. Nat.* VI. 28.

3. Cf. xiv. 22 ; Hag. i. 10 f.; and the passage in Enoch lxxx. 2 f. on the perversion of nature owing to the sin of man.

latter rain. The showers of Mar.-Apr. which refresh the ripening crops. In the plains the wheat harvest begins in early May, on the higher land in early June, and the barley is a little earlier. The *latter rain* is often used metaphorically, Prov. xvi. 15 (of king's favour); Job xxix. 23 (of his importance); Hos. vi. 3 (of God's grace) (see further on v. 24).

4. This *v.* may contain a reference to the nation's turning to Jehovah in the reign of Josiah, a repentance which was soon forgotten in continued sins; or it may be another example of that moral levity which allowed the people to call upon Jehovah by name and at the same time to persist in crime and idolatry.

My father. The metaphor of the erring wife was no doubt borrowed by Jeremiah from Hosea. The earlier prophet by his bitter experience

he retain *his anger* for ever ? will he keep it to the end ? Behold,
thou ¹hast spoken and hast done evil things, and hast ²had thy
way.

¹ Or, hast spoken thus, but hast done &c.　　² Heb. been able.

had learned that the relationship subsisting between husband and wife
was a symbol of an even greater mystery: cf. Eph. v. 22—32. But
something further is required to represent the relations of God and
Israel and so the metaphor of father and child is also employed (cf.
Forbes Robinson, *The Self-Limitation of the Word of God*, pp. 125,
156 f.; and for the conception of Jehovah as the father of Israel see
Smend, *Lehrbuch der A. T. Religionsgeschichte*², 96—101)¹.

my youth. Notice the continued favourable allusions to the earlier
history of the nation and the closeness of its walk with God. For the
phrase *companion of my youth*, cf. Prov. ii. 17.

CHAPTER III. 6—18.

An Invitation to the exiled Northern Tribes to return.

These *vv.* interrupt the sequence of thought, as *v.* 19 is apparently a direct
continuation of *v.* 5; the text also is in some confusion, and if the section
comes from Jeremiah himself it has evidently got out of its context. The
point upon which the passage lays stress is that Judah in spite of the warning
which it ought to have received from the fate of Samaria, has fallen into sins
worse even than those which disgraced the Northern Kingdom. The prophet
is bidden in God's name to address a message of comfort and hope to the exiled
nation, calling upon it to confess its sins and so to be in a position to receive
God's pardon. In the glorious future which will then be ushered in Judah and
Israel will once more be united, and Jerusalem, the capital of the newly restored
nation, will be called 'the throne of Jehovah.'

The fact that Jeremiah was a member of the tribe of Benjamin would give
him sympathy with the Northern Kingdom. It is rather strange that in this
passage Israel should be used for the ten tribes, in ii. 1—iii. 5 it is used of all
the families of Jacob. In xxiii. 13 and xxxi. 5 the Northern Kingdom is referred
to as Samaria though this is unusual.

Keil sums up the contents of the discourse in two thoughts, (1) Israel is not
to remain always rejected, as self-satisfied Judah imagined ; (2) Judah is not to
be always spared.

In the actual course of events the warning came too late ; Judah was too

---

¹ It should be noted, however, that the corresponding Babylonian word for
'father' *abū* is also used of a 'husband' (see Barton, *Semitic Origins*, p. 68, n. 5);
and that Robertson Smith has pointed out that in both North and South Semitic
dialects the husband can be called the 'father' of his wife (*Kinship and Marriage*,
pp. 117 f.).

far advanced on its path of sin to be checked by any reminder of the fate which befell Samaria. But in the working out of God's plan for the world it was that portion of the original Israel which had sinned more deeply—because it had had a clearer view of the punishment before it—that was to be restored and to enter into the position of being His people.

6 Moreover the LORD said unto me in the days of Josiah the king, Hast thou seen that which backsliding Israel hath done? she is gone up upon every high mountain and under every green tree, and there hath played the harlot. 7 [1] And I said after she had done all these things, [2] She will return unto me; but she returned not: and her treacherous sister Judah saw it. 8 And [3] I saw, when, for this very cause that backsliding Israel had committed adultery, I had put her away and given her a bill of divorcement, yet treacherous Judah her sister feared not; but she also went and played the harlot. 9 And it came to pass through the lightness of her whoredom, that the land was polluted, and she committed adultery with stones and with stocks. 10 And yet for all this her treacherous sister Judah hath not

[1] Or, *And I said, After she hath done all these things, she &c.*
[2] Or, *Let her return unto me*
[3] Some ancient authorities have, *she saw that, for &c.*

6. *in the days of Josiah.* Josiah came to the throne in 639. Jeremiah was called in 626 and the Northern Kingdom ceased to exist in 722, therefore some hundred years or more had probably elapsed since Israel had gone into exile.

Hast thou seen. Duhm somewhat unnecessarily objects to the form of this question. It is not intended to be taken literally and, if the passage is an insertion later than Jeremiah, the prophet was too well known a figure for anyone to have imagined that he was alive at the time of the fall of Samaria.

backsliding. In the Hebrew there is a play upon the word for 'turning back' which in the EVV. is lost through its being translated by different words, *backsliding* here and *return* in *v.* 7.

7. *She will return.* Jehovah's desire for Israel's return was something more than a mere wish, He sent His messengers to bring her back, though from the words *I said* (to myself), i.e. I thought, Rashi points out that no stress is intended to be laid on them.

8. Ezekiel makes a similar accusation against Judah in the allegory of Oholah and Oholibah (xxiii.).

bill of divorcement. Israel as a nation had been cast off by Jehovah and given a bill of divorcement; Judah on the other hand is said to have divorced herself (Is. l. 1).

10. The reform under Josiah did not go deep enough and, as at all

returned unto me with her whole heart, but feignedly, saith the
LORD. 11 And the LORD said unto me, Backsliding Israel hath
shewn herself more righteous than treacherous Judah. 12 Go,
and proclaim these words toward the north, and say, Return,
thou backsliding Israel, saith the LORD; I will not ¹look in anger
upon you: for I am merciful, saith the LORD, I will not keep
anger for ever. 13 Only ²acknowledge thine iniquity, that thou
hast transgressed against the LORD thy God, and hast scattered
thy ways to the strangers under every green tree, and ye have
not obeyed my voice, saith the LORD. 14 Return, O backsliding
children, saith the LORD; for I am a husband unto you: and I
will take you one of a city, and two of a family, and I will bring
you to Zion: 15 and I will give you shepherds according to mine

---

¹ Heb. *cause my countenance to fall upon you.*   ² Or, *know*

---

times when reformers are in power, many would outwardly conform to
principles which they felt to be burdensome, and would therefore be
only too glad of any opportunity for throwing them off.

11. Cf. Ez. xvi. 51 ; Lk. xviii. 14.

12. The exiles of Israel are still looked upon as preserving a separate
existence and are not yet absorbed into the surrounding nations.

look in anger. Lit. *cause my countenance to fall:* the same Hebrew
expression appears in Gen. iv. 5 (of Cain); and in Job xxix. 24.

I will not keep anger *for ever.* This statement seems intended to
be a reply to *v.* 5.

13. *Only acknowledge thine iniquity.* God 'will exclude from salvation no one who is willing to return' (Keil). The first stage of repentance
is recognition of sin, just as the last stage is amendment of life.

strangers. i.e. foreign gods. In later Judaism 'strange worship'
was a euphemism for idolatry, hence the title of the tractate of the
Mishnah called *Aboda Zara.*

14. *children...husband.* 'The confusion is only verbal, and the
twofold relationship gives a double certainty of acceptance. As children
they were sure of a father's love, as a wife they might hope for a revival
of past affection from the husband of their youth' (Payne Smith).

family. A division of a clan ; evidently a large body is meant from
the parallelism with *city.*

Zion. Those who return will be few in number, and are all to dwell
in Jerusalem. Some critics point out that this statement is inconsistent
with xxxi. 8 where 'a great company' is to return. It is possible to
reconcile the two statements by supposing that here the prophet has in
view the large number of exiles who would not return, which made those
who returned seem but few in proportion. In either prophecy there is
an anticipation of a large population of the Holy Land (cf. *v.* 16).

heart, which shall feed you with knowledge and understanding.
16 And it shall come to pass, when ye be multiplied and increased
in the land, in those days, saith the LORD, they shall say no more,
The ark of the covenant of the LORD; neither shall it come to
mind: neither shall they remember it; neither shall they [1]visit
it; neither [2]shall *that* be done any more. 17 At that time
they shall call Jerusalem the throne of the LORD; and all the
nations shall be gathered unto it, to the name of the LORD, to
Jerusalem: neither shall they walk any more after the stubborn-

---

[1] Or, *miss*   [2] Or, *shall it be made any more*

---

15. *shepherds.* A Messianic forecast: cf. xxiii. 4; Is. ix., xi.;
Ez. xxxiv. 23.

mine heart. The greatest sign of the Divine favour towards the
restored community is to be the gift of ' pastors' chosen by God Himself.

16. *The ark of the covenant of the LORD.* This is a late expression;
in the earlier days it was simply called the ark of the covenant, or the
ark of God. See Additional Note, pp. 34 f. In the days to come no
visible symbol of Jehovah's presence would be required.

come to mind (עלה על לב). A frequent expression in Jeremiah
(xliv. 21, li. 50) which is found also in NT. (e.g. Acts vii. 23; 1 Cor.
ii. 9).

17. *Jerusalem the throne of the LORD.* Cf. Is. xviii. 7 where ' the
place of Jehovah's name' is used as a synonym for the temple. This
exalted regard for Jerusalem is common in the visions of the prophets
and psalmists (e.g. Is. ii. 2—4, lvi. 7; Ps. xlviii. 1—2). Jeremiah is
looking forward to a time when Jerusalem will have been purified and
when the worship offered at the temple will be such as Jehovah could
accept (cf. vii. 21). Some critics think that if this passage is from
Jeremiah's own lips it belongs to the time after the destruction of
Jerusalem and that the prophet looks forward to its glorious restoration.
Against this view it is perhaps sufficient to say that Jeremiah seems to
have been convinced from a time quite early in his ministry that the
fate of Jerusalem could not be avoided and that therefore, believing as
he did in its final restoration, he did not need to wait for its actual
destruction in order to paint its future excellence. Our Lord further
extended Jeremiah's teaching by telling the woman of Samaria that
the day was coming when the temple itself would be unnecessary:
Jn. iv. 21.

gathered. Cf. Zech. ii. 15. The revelation of God's glory would
draw forth the homage of the heathen: cf. Josh. ix. 9 ff.

stubbornness. Heb. שרר lit. means *firmness.* The word, which is
characteristic of Jeremiah (8 times, elsewhere only Dt. xxix. 18; and
Ps. lxxxi. 13), is always used of firmness in a bad sense, obstinacy, and
is always connected with *heart.* The prophet from his own experience

ness of their evil heart. 18 In those days the house of Judah
shall walk ¹with the house of Israel, and they shall come together
out of the land of the north to the land that I gave for an inheritance unto your fathers.

¹ Or, *to*

felt that the heart of man was so fitted for communion with God that
it could be by deliberate obstinacy only that he would refuse to obey
Him.

18.   The division of the Jewish people into two parts was felt very
deeply by the later prophets and so they anticipate that in order to
make perfect the age which is coming both parts will be restored (Ez.
iv. 6 ; Is. xliii. 6 f.).   That a people worshipping one God should be
thus separated into two nations was to them an anomaly, especially in
view of the widespread use of the metaphor of God as the husband of
the people (cf. Hos. i. 11, viii. 3 f. ; Is. xi. 13 ; Ez. xxxiv. 23 f., xxxvii.
22).   At the same time there is at least a possibility that two other
nations of the Semitic stock also had their deity in common—Moab
and Ammon.   As a rule Chemosh is regarded as the god of Moab and
Milcom as that of Ammon but on the Moabite-stone the combination
Chemosh-Melech is found, and in Jud. xi. 24 the god of the Ammonites
is said to be Chemosh : cf. also Dr Barnes' note on 1 K. xi. 7 in the
Cambridge Bible.

ADDITIONAL NOTE ON III. 16.

The Ark of the Covenant.

The natural inference to be drawn from Jeremiah's attitude as described in
this *v*. is that the people of his day attached too much importance to the ark
as the visible symbol of Jehovah's presence (cf. 1 S. iv. 3 ff.).   Jeremiah
evidently found the ark hateful to him as being a part of the crude materialistic
religion, so popular with the people, against which his whole ministry was a
constant protest.   It should be remembered too, that though the ark might be
the sign of Jehovah's presence, it was at the same time likely to encourage men
in the belief that His presence was limited thereto ; such a conception seems
to underlie the action of the Israelites at Ebenezer referred to above, and when
David danced before the ark he could be described as dancing 'before the
LORD' (2 S. vi. 14).   Conceptions such as these must have been felt by the
prophet to be unworthy of the spiritual worship of Jehovah which he wished
to inculcate.

The history of the ark is very obscure and it is not mentioned after the
erection of Solomon's temple until the present passage, a gap of nearly four
hundred years.   There is one possible exception to the above statement, as
according to 2 Ch. xxxv. 3 it was restored to the temple by Josiah ; since,

however, there is no mention of such a restoration in 2 K. xxiii. critics are not disposed to acknowledge the genuineness of this tradition. The exact date of the disappearance of the ark is not known; it is not mentioned in connexion with the Fall of Jerusalem—except in the obviously legendary account in 2 Macc. ii. 4 ff.—nor did it find a place in the temple of the restoration (see Joseph. *Bell. Jud.* v. v. 5; Tacitus, *Hist.* v. 9).

Various suggestions have been put forward to account for the disappearance of the ark. It may have perished in some invasion. Perhaps it was taken from Jerusalem by Joash, King of Israel, in 785 B.C. when he carried off the temple treasures (2 K. xiv. 14). He may have felt, as Cheyne suggests (*Enc. Bib.* 306), that he was reclaiming 'the long-lost treasure of the Ephraimitish sanctuary at Shiloh.' If this suggestion is a sound one, and on the face of it there is nothing against it beyond the failure of the Biblical writers actually to mention it, it may be that the ark finally disappeared with the destruction of Shiloh referred to in vii. 12. The possession of the ark by the Southern Kingdom may have been a sore point with the men of Israel, and Calvin sees in Jeremiah's forecast a desire to remove a cause of offence which might prevent or endanger the reconciliation of the two parts of the nation. Another interesting suggestion, made by Canon Kennett, is that the ark was used as a receptacle for the brazen serpent and that it may have shared the fate of that object of worship (2 K. xviii. 4).

For fuller details of the history of the ark and for suggestions as to its fate see Dr McNeile's note in his commentary on *Exodus*, pp. 161 ff.; and *Enc. Bib.* 300 ff.

Chapters III. 19—IV. 4.

A Vision of Israel's Penitence and Restoration.

This prophecy is probably a continuation of iii. 5; as was pointed out in the introduction to iii. 6—18 that section is apparently an interpolation.

(a) *Israel's ingratitude and Jehovah's forbearance.* iii. 19 f.
(b) *Israel returns in penitence and shame.* 21—25.
(c) *Jehovah demands works worthy of repentance.* iv. 1 f.
(d) *A warning to the men of Judah.* 3 f.

19 But I said, How [1]shall I put thee among the children, and give thee a pleasant land, [2]a goodly heritage of the hosts of the nations? and I said, [3]Ye shall call me My father; and

[1] Or, *would...nations!*   [2] Or, *the goodliest heritage of the nations*
[3] Another reading is, *Thou shalt...and shalt not &c.*

19 f. Jehovah desired to shew mercy and forbearance to the House of Israel; but the fulfilment of His desire was prevented by her ingratitude.

shall not turn away from following me. 20 Surely as a wife
treacherously departeth from her husband, so have ye dealt
treacherously with me, O house of Israel, saith the LORD. 21 A
voice is heard upon the bare heights, the weeping *and* the
supplications of the children of Israel; for that they have
perverted their way, they have forgotten the LORD their God.
22 Return, ye backsliding children, I will heal your backslidings. Behold, we are come unto thee; for thou art the LORD
our God. 23 Truly in vain is *the help that is looked for* from

19. *How shall I.* Cf. Hos. xi. 8 where the same form of question
is used, but with reference not to privilege but to punishment.
children. Better *sons.* Israel though a woman—lands and cities
are feminine in Heb. as in many other languages—was to have her
share like a son. According to the most ancient Hebrew law daughters
had no share in their father's property, as the case of the daughters of
Zelophehad (Nu. xxvii. 1 ff.) evidently set a precedent; it should be
mentioned that this incident is considered by many critics to be late,
and probably shews the influence of Babylonian customs by which the
daughter was treated more kindly (see S. A. Cook, *Laws of Moses,* &c.
pp. 145 f.). The case of Job's daughters who held 'an inheritance in
the midst of their brethren' (xlii. 15) is an obvious instance of an
exception which proves a general rule.
pleasant land. Cf. Zech. vii. 14 ; Ps. cvi. 24.
20. *treacherously.* Cf. v. 11 ; Hos. v. 7, vi. 7 ; Mal. ii. 11.
Israel includes and in fact really means Judah ; for the promises
to the race, if the expression is read in the light of later history,
were narrowed down after the fall of Samaria to the elect Southern
Kingdom.
21—25. The children of Israel are pictured as returning to Jehovah
with weeping and with inarticulate supplications. Jehovah speaks
encouragingly to them and they take up the chorus of repentance,
confessing their sin and folly in trusting in vain gods : cf. Hos. v. 14—
vi. 4. The prophet's hopeful anticipations were however doomed to
wait long years for their fulfilment.
21. *A voice is heard.* The same phrase introduces the lament of
Rachel in xxxi. 15.
bare heights. A common place for mourning (cf. vii. 29). It is
also to be noted that it was on *the bare heights* that Israel had sinned
against Jehovah (cf. *v.* 2); 'the scene of her idolatry is the scene also of
her penitence.' (Peake.)
22. *Return...backslidings.* There is here a play on the same
Hebrew word as was noticed in *v.* 6. Jehovah is willing to accept
even the slightest desire for repentance and to increase it (cf. xxx.
17, xxxiii. 6); He will 'heal' the backslidings of His children (Hos.
xiv. 4).

the hills, the [1]tumult on the mountains: truly in the LORD our
God is the salvation of Israel.   24 But the [2]shameful thing hath
devoured the labour of our fathers from our youth; their flocks
and their herds, their sons and their daughters.   25 Let us lie
down in our shame, and let our confusion cover us: for we have
sinned against the LORD our God, we and our fathers, from our
youth even unto this day: and we have not obeyed the voice of
the LORD our God.

---

[1] Or, *noisy throng*   [2] Heb. *shame.* See ch. xi. 13.

---

23. *hills...mountains.* Cf. *v.* 21.   Ezekiel was commanded to
prophesy against the mountains owing to the unlawful worship which
had taken place upon them (vi. 2 ff.). The nation in its moments of
loyalty to Jehovah looked upon the hills as the place from whence His
power would come (Ps. cxxi. 1 f.).

24. *the shameful thing.* i.e. Baal. The writers of OT. not infrequently use the Hebrew word meaning shame (Bosheth) for Baal (cf.
xi. 13 ; Hos. ix. 10). In some proper names ending in Baal the second
half has been changed into Bosheth : e.g. Ishbaal the son of Saul
(1 Ch. viii. 33) is called Ishbosheth in 2 S. ii. 8 (see Driver's note *ad
loc.*). When the name had originally been given Baal was no doubt
intended as a title of Jehovah (cf. Hos. ii. 16).

their sons and their daughters. The references to human sacrifice
in OT., as it stands at present, are not very numerous and many critics
think that the humanitarian instincts of a later age caused their
omission, or even erased them from existing accounts. The writer of
2 K. iii. 27 evidently recognised the efficacy of such sacrifices even
when offered to a foreign deity[1]. It is sometimes stated that the
deaths of the two sons of Hiel the Bethelite during his rebuilding
of Jericho (1 K. xvi. 34 ; cf. Josh. vi. 26) were what are known as
'foundation sacrifices.' These sacrifices were intended to bring good
fortune to the owners of the house and the custom of offering them is
a very widespread one (see Tylor, *Primitive Culture*, I. pp. 94—7 ;
Curtiss, *Primitive Semitic Religion To-day*, p. 184, and Père Vincent,
Canaan (1907), pp. 188, 195). The loss of Hiel's sons however was
looked upon as something unusual and even if he offered them as
sacrifices the custom was sufficiently rare in Israel to excite general
notice.

from our youth. Cf. ii. 2.

25. *lie down.* Cf. 2 S. xii. 16 (David on the death of the child
of Bathsheba), xiii. 31, &c.

we and our fathers. 'In Semitic antiquity the whole ritual conception of the purging away of sin is bound up with the notion of the
solidarity of the body of worshippers—the same notion which makes

---

[1] For another explanation of this passage in Kings, see Pusey on Am. ii. 1.

IV. 1 If thou wilt return, O Israel, saith the LORD, unto me shalt thou return: and ¹if thou wilt put away thine abominations out of my sight, then shalt thou not be removed; 2 and thou shalt swear, As the LORD liveth, in truth, in judgement, and in righteousness; and the nations shall bless themselves in him, and in him shall they glory.

3 For thus saith the LORD to the men of Judah and to Jerusalem, Break up your fallow ground, and sow not among

---

¹ Or, *if thou wilt put...and wilt not wander, and wilt swear...then shall the nations &c.*
or, *then shalt thou swear...and the nations &c.*

---

the pious Hebrews confess and lament not only their own sins, but the sins of their fathers.' W. Robertson Smith, *Rel. Sem.* ² p. 429.

IV. 1 f. Jehovah's answer. Israel's penitence must exhibit itself in deeds—by a return to the worship of Himself, and by the putting away of false gods. This conduct will glorify Jehovah in the sight of the heathen.

1. *abominations.* The word which is used in Dan. xi. 31 of 'the abomination of desolation.' It represents the Divine attitude towards that which was a 'shameful thing' even in the eyes of human beings (iii. 24). The word is first found in Hos. ix. 10 and is common in Jer. and Ez. of the false gods and all the paraphernalia of their worship. LXX. followed by Ewald, Hitzig, Cheyne &c. reads *and if thou puttest away thy detestable things out of thy mouth* (cf. Zech. ix. 7) *and dost not wander from before me.*

2. The people are evidently in the habit of treating repentance as an easy thing.

swear. Cf. xii. 16 ; Is. lxv. 16 ; Ps. lxiii. 10. To swear by Jehovah means to be His worshipper.

in truth. Not the mere taking of God's name in vain by the light use of a formula, ii. 35, v. 2 ; cf. Dt. vi. 13, x. 20.

'*Judgment* is wanting in an uncautious oath ; *truth* in a lying oath ; *righteousness* in an iniquitous or unlawful oath.' St Thos. Aquinas, *Sum. Theol.* II. ii. 89.

3 f. A warning to the men of Judah couched in severer tones : cf. Ez. xviii. 30. Cornill quotes Mk. vii. 21 to illustrate these *vv.* Just as the thorns must be rooted right out of the ground before sowing, so must the evils of the heart be overcome ; no mere ceremonial purification is of any avail but only that 'spiritual circumcision' which Calvin defined as 'the denial of self.'

3. *Judah...Jerusalem.* Also named separately in Is. i. 1 ; Joel iii. 20, &c.

Break up your fallow ground. The phrase is evidently quoted from Hos. x. 12. The people are called upon to make fresh ventures in their religious life and at the same time to cast out the sins which

thorns. 4 Circumcise yourselves to the LORD, and take away
the foreskins of your heart, ye men of Judah and inhabitants of
Jerusalem: lest my fury go forth like fire, and burn that none
can quench it, because of the evil of your doings.

had rendered the past unprofitable by the use of the plough of penitence
and discipline. The new seed must have every chance given it of
bringing forth fruit (iii. 23 b, cf. Matt. xiii. 7). No man can afford to
leave part of his nature undeveloped and neglected : if he does it will
produce on its own account and the crop will be one of unsightly weeds
and thorns. The Vulgate rendering *Novate Novale* is well known from
its use as the title of a Society of Mission Priests founded by Arch-
bishop Benson when Chancellor of Lincoln.

4. *Circumcise yourselves.* Circumcision was the work of the Old
Covenant, the New Covenant demanded something deeper ; not the
outward circumcision of the flesh but the inward circumcision of the
heart. In this passage Jeremiah seems to anticipate the teaching of
St Paul (Rom. ii. 28 f. &c.) that circumcision is not merely a bodily
rite but also a change of heart. It must be 'an outward and visible
sign of an inward and spiritual grace.' This thought is still further
illustrated by ix. 25.

foreskins of your heart. Cf. the similar command in Dt. x. 16 and
also the promise that Jehovah Himself would circumcise the hearts of
the Israelites that they might love Him (Dt. xxx. 6). See further on
vi. 10.

fire. To destroy the thorns: cf. vii. 20 ; Am. v. 6 ; Ps. lxxxix. 47.

CHAPTER IV. 5—31.

A Description of the Coming Doom.

All the efforts of the prophet have been in vain, the people persist in
following after the desires of their own hearts and in despising the warnings
of the messenger of Jehovah. But now a real and threatening danger is at
hand, evil is about to break upon them from the North and once again the voice
of Jeremiah, like a trumpet, repeats its warning message. Most critics are
agreed that the prophecies in this and the following chh. were originally
written in reference to the Scythian invasion of *c.* 625 B.C. (see Introd.
pp. xix, xxx) and that they were afterwards re-written to make them refer to
the approach of the Babylonian army in 604 B.C. The chh. as they now stand
(with the exception of certain passages) might be applied to either adversary,
though it must be confessed that as a whole they suit better the Babylonians and their monarch than a horde of unknown barbarians (cf. iv. 7,
v. 15, 19).

The section may be divided up as follows:

(a) *The sounding of the alarm.* 5—8.
(b) *The helplessness of the leaders.* 9 f.
(c) *The swift coming of the invader.* 11—18.
(d) *The prophet's agony.* 19—22.
(e) *Jeremiah's vision of desolation.* 23—26.
(f) *Judah is deserted by her lovers.* 27—31.

5 Declare ye in Judah, and publish in Jerusalem; and say,
Blow ye the trumpet in the land: cry aloud and say, Assemble
yourselves, and let us go into the fenced cities. 6 Set up a
standard toward Zion: flee for safety, stay not: for I will bring
evil from the north, and a great destruction. 7 A lion is gone up
from his thicket, and a destroyer of nations; he is on his way, he
is gone forth from his place; to make thy land desolate, that thy
cities be laid waste, without inhabitant. 8 For this gird you with

5—8. Judah is bidden to make what preparations she can for the
approach of an overwhelming foe: cf. Hos. v. 15 ff.

5. *in Jerusalem.* Omitted by Giesebrecht as unnecessary and
moreover as being hard to reconcile with Zion in *v.* 6. The *v.* is evidently in some confusion and 'it is awkward' as Peake says 'that one
group of people should be told to bid a second group say to a third
group *Assemble yourselves, &c.*'

trumpet (Heb. שׁוֹפָר). The alarm signal usually sounded as a call
to battle, here to flight; and to be carefully distinguished from the
trumpet sounded in the temple services, though in later writers the
distinction is lost. The word literally means *horn* and may be connected with the Assyrian *šappar(u)* 'wild goat': cf. Driver on Am. ii. 2.

Assemble yourselves. The same advice is given to the Philistines in
Zeph. ii. 1; cf. Joel i. 4, ii. 15, iii. 11.

the fenced cities. The foe was evidently too strong to be met in
the open field: cf. viii. 14. For the phrase (lit. *cities of fortification*)
cf. Nu. xiii. 19, xxxii. 17, 36; and see Nowack, *Arch.* I. 368.

6. *standard.* Cf. Is. xxxiii. 23; Ez. xxvii. 7. Driver explains it
as a way-mark to guide the fugitives (cf. Ps. lx. 6): but the reading of
LXX. φεύγετε is probably to be preferred to the MT.; שְׂאוּ will then
refer to the snatching up of their property by the fugitives: cf. Is. x. 31.

flee. See on vi. 1.

destruction. Lit. *breaking*; cf. Zeph. i. 10.

7. *A lion* refers better to an individual like Nebuchadrezzar than
to the Scythians. The same expression is used in xlix. 19 for the enemy
who is to overthrow Edom.

he is on his way. The Heb. (נסע) means literally *to pull up* and so
from the pulling up of tent pegs *to start out.*

sackcloth, lament and howl: for the fierce anger of the LORD is not turned back from us. 9 And it shall come to pass at that day, saith the LORD, that the heart of the king shall perish, and the heart of the princes; and the priests shall be astonished, and the prophets shall wonder. 10 Then said I, Ah, Lord GOD! surely thou hast greatly deceived this people and Jerusalem, saying, Ye shall have peace; whereas the sword reacheth unto the soul. 11 At that time shall it be said to this people and to Jerusalem, A hot wind from the bare heights in the wilderness toward the

8. *sackcloth.* S. A. Cook suggests from the usage of the word that *sackcloth* was 'nothing more than a loin-cloth, similar, no doubt, to the *ihrām* of Moslem pilgrims at Mecca,' and having a religious significance: *Enc. Bib.* 4182 f.

lament. There is now no trace of any hope such as was to be found in ii.—iv. 4: God's wrath cannot be turned away: cf. Joel i. 13; Mic. i. 8; Jas. iv. 9.

9 f. The astonishment and helplessness of Jerusalem and its natural leaders. All those upon whom the people had leaned and by whom they had bolstered up their confidence prove wanting.

heart. Usually with the meaning of *intelligence*, but this context demands the meaning of *courage*: cf. Am. ii. 16. All the leaders of society are to be driven into a state of impotence by the news of the coming of the invader: cf. Is. vii. 2.

10. *Then said I.* The text as it stands is difficult to interpret. Jeremiah had never prophesied 'Peace' to the city, but always the contrary (cf. Mic. ii. 11). The best solution of the difficulty is to adopt the reading found in LXX. A and to read *And they shall say*; the words will then come from the prophets of *v.* 9 who still think that their 'comfortable' message had been inspired by the Lord: cf. vi. 14, xiv. 13, xxiii. 17; 1 K. xxii. 22; Ez. xiv. 9. It would be rather hard to imagine that Jeremiah had himself been deceived by them as the reading of MT. almost certainly requires.

11—18. In this section the invader is described under various figures; first as a sirocco from the desert, and then as the clouds brought up by the wind. The prophet's words, few though they be, are full of suggestions of horror and swiftly approaching calamity. He points to the distant and terrible North where the unknown menace is already gathering force to burst upon the people like the sudden blast of a desert wind.

11. *hot wind.* LXX. πνεῦμα πλανήσεως. The exact meaning of the word translated *hot* is not known; in Is. xviii. 4 it is rendered *clear* (of heat), and in Cant. v. 10 *white* (of complexion). It seems a strange word to apply to a wind and perhaps the best translation is *glowing* or *dazzling*; the rendering of LXX. in this and other places suggests that they too were at a loss for the meaning of the word.

daughter of my people, not to fan, nor to cleanse; 12 [1]a full wind from these shall come for me: now will I also [2]utter judgements against them. 13 Behold, he shall come up as clouds, and his chariots *shall be* as the whirlwind: his horses are swifter than eagles. Woe unto us! for we are spoiled. 14 O Jerusalem, wash thine heart from wickedness, that thou mayest be saved. How long shall thine evil thoughts lodge within thee? 15 For

---

[1] Or, *a wind too strong for this*   [2] See ch. i. 16.

not to fan, nor to cleanse. The wind which was made use of to remove the chaff will blow away the grain as well (li. 1 f.). The approaching storm is not a mere warning intended to arouse repentance, but is to be for the overwhelming of the nation. 'It is not a chastisement to purify the people, but a judgement which sweeps away the whole nation—both wheat and chaff' (Keil). Wind as a destroying agent is used in various ways: cf. Ez. xvii. 10 'a blighting east wind.'

13. Descriptive passages such as this are common in the prophetic writings (e.g. vi. 22—6; Is. v. 26—30). The Hebrews were essentially a warlike race and the prophets loved to dwell on the equipment and fierceness of even an invading army. They are evidently influenced by something more than the mere desire to draw a picture of what the people may expect as a penalty for their sins.

clouds. A very forcible figure for the swift and irresistible approach of the enemy. Just as the clouds gradually overspread the sky beginning 'like a man's hand' and then in a short time darkening the whole heaven (1 K. xviii. 44 f.), so will the alien armies overrun the guilty land. Ezekiel has a similar description of the armies of Gog (xxxviii. 16).

whirlwind. Cf. Is. v. 28 'their wheels as a whirlwind,' and lxvi. 15.

eagles. Eagles are not common in Palestine (see Nowack, *Arch.* I. p. 84) and the Hebrew word is better translated *vultures (gyps fulvus)*, the *našru* of the inscriptions, which are still found. Their piercing vision enables them to sight their prey at a distance, and their long swoop upon it provided the prophets and other writers of OT. with a simile of an invading army, the force of which would be recognised by all their hearers. See Dt. xxviii. 49; Job ix. 26; Hab. i. 8, &c.

14. *O Jerusalem.* The prophet still seems to think that Jerusalem has time to repent; or does this *v.* represent merely his heart-broken cry over the impenitent city? Cf. xiii. 27 and our Blessed Lord's lament in Lk. xiii. 34.

How long &c. Hosea makes a similar appeal to Samaria and its inhabitants: 'How long will it be ere they attain to innocency?' (viii. 5).

evil thoughts &c. Cf. Prov. xxiii. 7; Matt. xii. 35; Jas. i. 15; and the passage in the collect at the beginning of the Communion Office: 'Cleanse the thoughts of our hearts by the inspiration of thy Holy Spirit.'

15. *For* introduces the event which shews the necessity of penitence and at the same time declares its impossibility.

[1]a voice declareth from Dan, and publisheth evil from the hills of Ephraim: 16 make ye mention to the nations; behold, publish against Jerusalem, *that* watchers come from a far country, and give out their voice against the cities of Judah. 17 As keepers of a field are they against her round about; because she hath been rebellious against me, saith the LORD. 18 Thy way and thy doings have procured these things unto thee; this is thy wickedness; [2]for it is bitter, [2]for it reacheth unto thine heart.

19 My bowels, my bowels! [3]I am pained at [4]my very heart;

[1] Or, *there is a voice of one that declareth &c.*   [2] Or, *surely*
[3] Another reading is, *I will wait patiently.*   [4] Heb. *the walls of my heart.*

a voice &c. It is better to translate as Buttenwieser does:

> *Hark! a messenger from Dan,*
> *A bearer of evil news from Mt Ephraim.*

The mention of these two places, *Dan* on the northern border of the whole country and *Mt Ephraim* on the northern border of Judah, is a dramatic way of describing the rapid approach of the invaders: cf. Is. xv.; and in modern literature Macaulay, *Horatius*, XVII.—XX.

16. *watchers.* Duhm suggests the reading *leopards*; this involves only a slight change in the Heb. and suits the immediate context much better. Cf. v. 6; Hab. i. 8.

give out their voice. As the lion in *v.* 7.

cities of Judah. This phrase is not intended to lay stress on the individual cities, it is equivalent to the whole land itself. Cf. Jud. xii. 7 (Heb.).

17. *keepers of a field.* This phrase fits in better with the original reading *watchers* in the previous *v.*; it suggests that just as those who have to guard cattle in the field put up booths round about it, so the besiegers will do round about Jerusalem and keep it in on every side.

18. *wickedness.* The Hebrews did not distinguish between sin and its consequences, or even what appeared to be the consequences of sin. (Cf. Kennett, *Early Ideas of Righteousness*, pp. 6 ff.)

19—22. A vivid description of the agony of the inhabitants of the land as represented by the prophet himself. This section is of great interest as being the first of several similar revelations of Jeremiah's own feelings. The prophet from his youth up had been aware 'of the great stream of human tears falling always through the shadows of the world' and his tender soul is now torn by realising the fate which is coming upon his native land: cf. the similar feelings of St Paul as described in Rom. ix.—xi.

19. *My bowels.* The seat of the deepest emotions. Cf. xxxi. 20; Is. xvi. 11, &c. There can be little doubt that the speaker is the prophet as the Targum states in so many words.

my very heart. Heb. *the walls of my heart.*

my heart is disquieted in me; I cannot hold my peace; because
[1]thou hast heard, O my soul, the sound of the trumpet, the alarm
of war. 20 Destruction upon destruction is cried; for the whole
land is spoiled: suddenly are my tents spoiled, *and* my curtains
in a moment. 21 How long shall I see the standard, and hear
the sound of the trumpet? 22 For my people is foolish, they
know me not; they are sottish children, and they have none
understanding: they are wise to do evil, but to do good they
have no knowledge.

23 I beheld the earth, and, lo, it was [2]waste and void; and

[1] Or, as otherwise read, *my soul heareth*   [2] See Gen. i. 2.

is disquieted. In 'The Testaments of the Twelve Patriarchs' Zebulon
describes how he wept with Joseph and his 'heart sounded' (*Test.
Zeb.* ii. 5).

20 f. It has been suggested that these *vv.* would apply well to the
Scythian invasion from the sudden approach of the enemy and the
stress laid on plunder: but *speed* and *spoil* were not marks peculiar to
any one invader: cf. Maher-shalal-hash-baz (Is. viii. 1).

tents. i.e. 'home.' The word was used long after the Hebrews had
abandoned the nomadic life. The practice of the modern Arabs may
be contrasted who refer to their tents as 'houses of hair.' The same
description is used metaphorically in x. 20, and repeatedly in OT. In
xlix. 29 there is a reference to the actual spoiling of tents. Calvin
looked upon *tents* as being a derisive description of the fortified cities
which collapsed before the invading army.

curtains. i.e. tent-hangings; cf. x. 20, xlix. 29; Hab. iii. 7.

21. Cf. *vv.* 5—6.

22. Cornill rejects this *v.* as agreeing with its context in neither
sense nor metre. It is possible to explain its position quite naturally
however, the prophet turns from the calamities which are falling upon
the people to the folly and ignorance which have been their cause.

they know me not. 'They display the same temper which the people
had always shewn; they have a faith in Jehovah but no knowledge of
what Jehovah is.' Davidson on Ez. xxxiii. 24.

evil...good. 'It is part of the miserable blindness of sin, that while
the soul acquires a quick insight into evil, it becomes at last, not para-
lysed only to *do* good, but unable to perceive it.' Pusey on Am. iii. 10.

23—26. Jeremiah describes a vision of the destruction of Judah
under the form of an upheaval of nature. The description is amazingly
vivid and its force is not exceeded by anything similar in the whole
prophetic literature. In it 'inanimate nature is pictured,' as Pusey
says of another passage (Nah. i. 5), 'as endowed with the terror which
guilt feels at the presence of God.'

At first the prophet can distinguish nothing but confusion, then

the heavens, and they had no light.   24 I beheld the mountains, and, lo, they trembled, and all the hills ¹moved to and fro.

---

¹ Or, *moved lightly*

---

gradually he is able to pick out the details of the vision, he sees the mountains but they tremble, and when he looks for any sign of life he can find none: the very birds have fled away from the darkened sky: cf. ix. 9.

Many critics regard this passage as later than the time of Jeremiah (Duhm, Giesebrecht, also Cheyne, and Schmidt in *Enc. Bib.* 953 and 2390), on account of its lack of connexion with the previous section and also because they see in its language an apocalyptic tone. There is no real reason however for rejecting it, the description is obviously figurative and the *gloom* overlying the whole picture is projected from the prophet's own mind and has nothing eschatological about it (so Buttenwieser, *The Prophets of Israel*, p. 201).

23. The primitive chaos has returned upon the universe which has fallen back into the state in which it was before 'the spirit of God moved on the face of the waters' (Gen. i. 2). 'The order which had been so beautifully arranged, had now disappeared through God's wrath' (Calvin): cf. Ps. xciii. 1. Cornill thinks, however, that there is no reference to 'primitive chaos' but that the prophet sees the earth merely as a horrible waste (*and void* is omitted by LXX.) without any living thing upon it: cf. Is. xlv. 18.

24. The effect of earthquakes seems to have made a deep impression on the mind of orientals in all ages, and naturally so. The trembling of the mountains represents to them the overturning of all that is stable and trustworthy. Our Lord adopts this kind of language in speaking of the 'last things' (Mk. xiii. 8, 24 ff.) and Muhammed habitually speaks of the judgement as the day when the mountains will be set in motion (Koran, lxix. 14, lxxviii. 20, xcix. &c.)¹.

---

¹ Ruskin has a fine passage in which he makes reference to this verse. Speaking of the mountains, he says:—'We yield ourselves to the impression of their eternal, unconquerable stubbornness of strength ; their mass seems the least yielding, least to be softened, or in anywise dealt with by external force, of all earthly substance. And, behold, as we look farther into it, it is all touched and troubled, like waves by a summer breeze; rippled far more delicately than seas or lakes are rippled; *they* only undulate along their surfaces—this rock trembles through its every fibre, like the cords of an Eolian harp—like the stillest air of spring with the echoes of a child's voice. Into the heart of all those great mountains, through every tossing of their boundless crests, and deep beneath all their unfathomable defiles, flows that strange quivering of their substance....They, which at first seemed strengthened beyond the dread of any violence or change, are yet also ordained to bear upon them the symbol of perpetual Fear: the tremor which fades from the soft lake and gliding river is sealed to all eternity, upon the rock; and while things that pass visibly from birth to death may sometimes forget their feebleness, the mountains are made to possess a perpetual memorial of their infancy.' *Modern Painters*, v. ix. 6.

25 I beheld, and, lo, there was no man, and all the birds of the heavens were fled. 26 I beheld, and, lo, [1]the fruitful field was a wilderness, and all the cities thereof were broken down at the presence of the LORD, *and* before his fierce anger. 27 For thus saith the LORD, The whole land shall be a desolation; yet will I not make a full end. 28 For this shall the earth mourn, and the heavens above be black: because I have spoken it, I have purposed it, and I have not repented, neither will I turn back from it. 29 The whole city fleeth for the noise of the horsemen and bowmen; they go into the thickets, and climb up upon the rocks: every city is forsaken, and not a man dwelleth therein. 30 And thou, when thou art spoiled, what wilt thou do? Though thou clothest thyself with scarlet, though thou deckest thee with ornaments of gold, though thou [2]enlargest thine eyes with paint,

---

[1] Or, *Carmel*   [2] Heb. *rendest.*

25. *no man.* The prophet suddenly realises his loneliness amidst the scene of desolation, all created things had been destroyed or had fled: cf. Is. ii. 19, 21.

birds. Cf. Hos. iv. 3; Zeph. i. 3.

26. *fruitful field.* Heb. *Carmel,* lit. *garden-land,* a symbol of all that was fruitful or cultivated. There is probably no reference here to Mt Carmel: cf. Is. xxix. 17, xxxii. 15.

27—31. Judah in her hour of need finds herself despised by her lovers in spite of all her arts to win them back.

27. *full end.* The same expression occurs in v. 10, 18 and many critics think it is an insertion 'from a later hand to make the warning less terrible' (Smend, Cornill, &c.). In any case it is a remarkable thing that whilst all the empires of antiquity, and even Samaria, have disappeared, yet the Jewish people still exists and that in spite of the loss of country and dominion. To the non-religious man this must ever be an astounding phenomenon which can hardly be explained along the lines of ordinary historical investigation.

28. *the earth mourn.* The devastation of the earth makes her productive powers of no avail.

I have not repented. Cf. Zech. viii. 14.

29. *The whole city.* Read with LXX. *the whole land.*

horsemen. The Assyrians were noted for their cavalry and these would be taken over by the victorious Babylonians, one reason for whose speedy success was that they inherited the Assyrian military traditions.

bowmen. Cf. Jud. v. 11 'far from the noise of archers.'

thickets &c. The natural refuge of the people from the face of their enemies: cf. Jud. vi. 2; 1 S. xiii. 6; and see note on xl. 7.

30. *ornaments of gold,* to attract her lovers. There may be a refer-

in vain dost thou make thyself fair; *thy* lovers despise thee, they seek thy life. 31 For I have heard a voice as of a woman in travail, the anguish as of her that bringeth forth her first child, the voice of the daughter of Zion, that gaspeth for breath, that spreadeth her hands, *saying*, Woe is me now! for my soul fainteth before the murderers.

ence to actual efforts by the nation and its rulers to make its alliance important in the eyes of other nations: cf. Hezekiah and Merodach-Baladan, Is. xxxix.

paint. Antimony or eye paint. This was 'applied to the eyelids either dry or reduced to a paste by means of oils, with a blunt-pointed style or eye-pencil...which is drawn horizontally through between the closed eyelids....This proceeding Jeremiah sarcastically terms rending open the eyes' (Keil). The practice is as common amongst the women of the East at the present day as it was in the days of Jezebel (2 K. ix. 30; cf. Prov. vi. 25; Ecclus. xxvi. 9). According to Enoch viii. 1 it was the evil angel Azazel who taught men the use of 'metals and the art of working them, and bracelets, and ornaments, and the use of antimony and the beautifying of the eyelids': cf. Tertullian's use of the passage in *De Cultu Fem.* I. 2, II. 10; and *Testament of Reuben* v., where the daughters of men are said to have seduced the giants by their ornaments.

lovers. Cf. Ez. xxiii. 5, &c. The reference here must be to allied nations and not to 'strange gods' as in Hos. ii. 15. If this is part of the original prophecy it excludes any reference to the Scythians, who are hardly likely to have been allies of the Hebrews, or even to have been heard of by them before their incursion into Palestine.

31. *anguish* (Heb. צרה) cannot mean a cry of agony, but the pain which produces the cry. Giesebrecht, following LXX., accordingly emends to צוחה.

murderers. The metaphor of the woman in travail is suddenly dropped.

CHAPTER V.

The Utter Moral Depravity of Jerusalem.

The corruption of the nation is so complete that nothing can now turn back the instruments of the Lord's vengeance. This ch. brings to a climax the prophetic denunciations which go before it. Jeremiah seeks in vain to find a single lover of truth or doer of justice in the whole of Jerusalem. Followers of Jehovah may indeed abound, but he feels that the God whom they serve is not the God he knows although both are addressed by the same name. It is not the poor and ignorant alone who have forsaken God but the great men and the nobles in like manner; therefore the prophet despairs of his countrymen and proclaims the condemnation of the city. The wickedness and blindness of the people are all the more amazing as they had already received many warnings (cf. *v.* 3, possibly a reference to the defeat at Megiddo), but they would not hearken to them (*v.* 12) and the message of the prophets they looked upon as mere *wind* and vanity (*v.* 14).

Duhm has a rather novel idea that this ch. describes the prophet's sentiments after his first visit to Jerusalem, and that the previous chh. come from the time when he was living in Anathoth. This would account in his eyes for the greater severity of the succeeding chh. when Jeremiah has realised that the Holy City itself is in such a state that judgement is inevitable. He draws a parallel between this supposed first visit and Luther's first visit to Rome. The whole theory is condemned by Giesebrecht as 'fanciful' and when it is remembered that Anathoth was practically a suburb of Jerusalem being less than three miles from it, it seems impossible to imagine that anyone with interests such as Jeremiah had could have been ignorant of all that was passing there even in the extremely unlikely event of his never having actually visited it.

The ch. ends with a further description of the nation which threatened Jerusalem; among its terrifying attributes was that of speaking in a strange tongue. It is somewhat surprising to notice the exaggerated dread and aversion shewn towards those who spoke a foreign language, the phenomenon is constantly referred to throughout the Bible, from the early attempt to account for it in Gen. xi. 1—9 to the miracle by which it was overcome in Acts ii. 5—11. See further on *v.* 15.

    (*a*)   *Rich and poor are alike unrighteous.* 1—9.
    (*b*)   *The call to the destroyers.* 10—19.
    (*c*)   *The rebelliousness of the people.* 20—29.
    (*d*)   *The sin of the prophets.* 30 f.

V. 1 Run ye to and fro through the streets of Jerusalem, and see now, and know, and seek in the broad places thereof, if ye can find a man, if there be any that doeth justly, that seeketh

V. 1—9. The connexion with iv. 31 seems rather slight; in that passage the prophet has described Jerusalem in her death agony, here he returns to those sins which will cause punishment to fall upon her.

1. The search recommended in this *v.* brings to mind the story of Diogenes lighting a lamp in the day-time and saying, 'I am trying to *find a man*' (Diog. Laert. VI. ii. 41).

Run ye to and fro. LXX. περιδράμετε, Vg. *circuite.* The wording indicates the thoroughness of the search: cf. Zeph. i. 12; Ps. cxxxix. 7—12. The command is a general one and is not addressed to any particular person.

streets. Duhm pictures Jeremiah, a stranger from the country, as being shocked by the levity and heedlessness of the townspeople.

a man. Cf. Abraham's appeal for Sodom (Gen. xviii. 23—32); and

[1]truth; and I will pardon her. 2 And though they say, As the LORD liveth; surely they swear falsely. 3 O LORD, [2]do not thine eyes look upon [1]truth? thou hast stricken them, but they were not grieved; thou hast consumed them, but they have refused to receive [3]correction: they have made their faces harder than a rock; they have refused to return. 4 Then I said, Surely these are poor: they are foolish; for they know not the way of the LORD, nor the judgement of their God: 5 I will get me unto the great men, and will speak unto them; for they know the way of the LORD, and the judgement of their God. But these with one accord have broken the yoke, and burst the bands. 6 Wherefore a lion out of the forest shall slay them, a wolf of the [4]evenings

---

[1] Or, *faithfulness*   [2] Heb. *are not thine eyes upon.*
[3] Or, *instruction*   [4] Or, *deserts*

---

other similar complaints (Ez. xxii. 30; Mic. vii. 2). The prophets not seldom looked upon the darker side of things, and there must have been in Jerusalem many who were loyal worshippers of Jehovah: cf. Elijah at Mount Horeb (1 K. xix. 18).

truth includes faithfulness towards God and justice towards men: cf. Hos. iv. 1.

2. In spite of the most solemn oaths the men of Judah were willing to perjure themselves. It is interesting to remember in this connexion that in the earliest Greek conception of a future world the only people who were punished and tortured were those who had forsworn themselves cf. *Iliad*, III. 278 ff., XIX. 259 ff.

3. *rock* is used in OT. as a symbol of firmness, often in an evil sense as here, but also in a good sense: Is. l. 7; Ez. iii. 7—9; cf. Lk. ix. 51.

4. *they know not.* Cf. viii. 7; Hos. iv. 6.

5. The prophet's search amongst the various classes of the community finds a parallel in the life of Socrates, who describes himself as going from politician to poet, and from poet to artisan, in search of one who was truly wise (*Apol. Socr.* 21 B—22 E).

6. *lion...wolf...leopard.* These animals are all mentioned in Hos. xiii. 7, and the *wolf* and the *leopard* are used of the Chaldeans in Hab. i. 8. There can be little doubt that it was from this *v.* that Dante borrowed the three beasts which appear in Canto I of the *Inferno*: the '*leopard*...whose skin full many a dusky spot did stain,' the *lion*, and the 'she-*wolf*, with all ill greed defiled.'

wolf. The animal referred to was probably smaller than the modern species, as Herodotus tells us that the Egyptian wolf was 'scarcely larger than a fox.' It may be noticed that here as elsewhere in OT. (with the exception of Gen. xlix. 27) the wolf is referred to as an ignoble animal; this is in strong contrast with the usage of non-Semitic peoples.

shall spoil them, a leopard shall watch over their cities, every one that goeth out thence shall be torn in pieces: because their transgressions are many, *and* their backslidings are increased. 7 How can I pardon thee? thy children have forsaken me, and sworn by them that are no gods: when I had [1]fed them to the full, they committed adultery, and assembled themselves in troops at the harlots' houses. 8 They were as fed horses [2]in the morning: every one neighed after his neighbour's wife. 9 Shall I not visit for these things? saith the LORD: and shall not my soul be avenged on such a nation as this?

10 Go ye up upon her walls, and destroy; but make not a full end: take away her branches: for they are not the LORD's. 11 For the house of Israel and the house of Judah have dealt very treacherously against me, saith the LORD. 12 They have

---

[1] Or, according to another reading, *made them swear*
[2] Or, *roaming at large*

A similar difference of opinion prevailed in regard to the ass, which was highly esteemed by the Arabs for its courage, and indeed gave a title to one of the bravest of the Caliphs, Marwān II, who was called *Al Hamar* (i.e. the ass). Gibbon (*Decline and Fall*, &c. VI. p. 20, 'Standard Library' Edition) remarks that this surname 'may justify the comparison of Homer (*Iliad*, v. 557, &c.), and both will silence the moderns who consider the ass as a stupid and ignoble emblem.'

evenings. Cf. Caedmon's description of the beasts of prey around the camp of Penda, including 'the wolves' who 'sing their horrid evensong.' The best reading, however, is probably that of marg. *steppes* or *deserts*: cf. Hab. i. 8; Zeph. iii. 3[1].

7. Cf. *v.* 28; Dt. xxxii. 15. 'There is here what rhetoricians call a conference: for God seems here to seek the judgement of the adverse party, with whom he contends, on the cause between them' (Calvin).

8. The Heb. of this *v.* seems to be corrupt.

fed horses. A similar expression is used in xlvi. 21, where the Egyptians' mercenaries are called 'calves of the stall.'

10—19. The Divine instruments are called upon to carry out the Lord's sentence.

10. For the figure of Judah as a vineyard see on xii. 10.

Go ye up. A summons either to supernatural beings as in Ez. ix. 1 f., or to the enemies of Israel as in Is. v. 26, vii. 18.

her walls. The meaning of Heb. is a little doubtful. Driver suggests a slight change which would give the reading *vine-rows*.

12 f. An entirely different conception of Jehovah from that of the

---

[1] LXX. rendering ἕως τῶν οἴκων represents עַד בָּתִּים, an evident misreading of MT. עֲרָבוֹת.

denied the LORD, and said, It is not he; neither shall evil come upon us; neither shall we see sword nor famine: 13 and the prophets shall become wind, and the word is not in them: thus shall it be done unto them. 14 Wherefore thus saith the LORD, the God of hosts, Because ye speak this word, behold, I will make my words in thy mouth fire, and this people wood, and it shall devour them. 15 Lo, I will bring a nation upon you from far,

prophets underlies these *vv*. In the eyes of the people He was their covenant God and so was pledged to support them, and at the same time He was not nearly so exacting as the prophets painted Him. In a somewhat similar manner at the present time the 'man in the street' in so far as he recognises God at all looks upon Him as an easy-going Providence; those who declare His message of denunciation and condemnation are merely derided by him as 'gloomy' pessimists.

12. *It is not he.* Duhm suggests that this is a 'popular saying' (*volksthümliche Aposiopese*): cf. Zeph. i. 12; Job viii. 18. The atheism of the Hebrews, as of their descendants in the Middle Ages, was practical rather than theoretical: cf. Ps. xiv. 1, and see Introd. p. xliv. They did not deny the existence of God in so many words, but by their action they shewed that it was quite safe to ignore Him.

13. Jeremiah constantly lays stress on the unbelieving attitude of the people towards those sent to warn them: cf. Ez. xii. 22 f., xvii. 15.

the prophets. Not the 'false prophets' who foretold good things, but those who, like Jeremiah himself, foretold only disaster: cf. xxviii. 8.

14. The prophets are to be vindicated even if the fulfilment of their message involves the destruction of the people. Though the ungodly are like 'brass and iron' (vi. 28) in their opposition to God, yet they will be burned up like *wood*; the word of the prophets which they had scoffed at and called *wind* was to prove a devouring *fire*: cf. xxiii. 29; Is. i. 31, ix. 7, lv. 10 f.; Ps. cxlvii. 15.

God of hosts. This phrase is used frequently of God by several of the prophets (Amos, Haggai, Zechariah, Malachi) and especially by Isaiah. It represents the irresistible might of Him who is the leader not only of the armies of Israel (Ex. vii. 4, xii. 41), but also of the hosts of heaven (Ps. ciii. 21) and the stars (Is. xl. 26). See Dr Wade's note in his commentary on *Isaiah*, p. 12.

15. Three points are to be noted about the invader: (*a*) he comes from a distance; (*b*) he is of ancient race; (*c*) his language is unknown to the Hebrews. The two first points suit the Babylonians, and the Assyrian language, in spite of its belonging to the same family as that of the Hebrews, would hardly be understood by the common people: cf. 2 K. xviii. 26. The second point seems definitely to exclude the Scythians, who were, according to Herodotus (IV. 5), 'the most recent

4—2

O house of Israel, saith the LORD: it is ¹a mighty nation, it is
an ancient nation, a nation whose language thou knowest not,
neither understandest what they say. 16 Their quiver is an open
sepulchre, they are all mighty men. 17 And they shall eat up
thine harvest, and thy bread, *which* thy sons and thy daughters
should eat: they shall eat up thy flocks and thine herds: they
shall eat up thy vines and thy fig trees: they shall ²beat down
thy fenced cities, wherein thou trustest, with the sword. 18 But
even in those days, saith the LORD, I will not make a full end
with you. 19 And it shall come to pass, when ye shall say,
Wherefore hath the LORD our God done all these things unto us?
then shalt thou say unto them, Like as ye have forsaken me, and

¹ Or, *an enduring nation*   ² Or, *impoverish*

of all nations.' Dr Peake's argument that Jeremiah 'may well have
thought of the Scythians as a primaeval people like the Nephilim' is
simply pure conjecture.

mighty (Heb. אֵיתָן). Lit. *enduring*. The meaning of this word was
lost by the Jews; and those responsible for the various translations of
OT. (LXX. &c.) seem to depend upon the context for their rendering.
The comparative study of the Semitic languages, however, has brought
to light a cognate root in Arabic, *watana* = 'to be constant, unfailing.'
The word is very often used of a wady which is perennial or ever
flowing.

whose language thou knowest not. Difference of speech was ever a
cause of dread and uneasiness in the ancient world (cf. Is. xxviii. 11,
xxxiii. 19; Dt. xxviii. 49), and a phenomenon which could only be
accounted for by the direct interference of the Deity Himself (Gen. xi.
1—9). On the other hand, a 'pure language' which the nations could
use 'with one consent' was to be one of the blessings of the coming
age (Zeph. iii. 9).

16. *Their quiver* &c. This comparison of human weapons—taking
quiver as representing its contents—to an open grave ever ready to
swallow up fresh victims is a very striking one, which nothing but
familiarity robs of its force.

17. In Dt. xxviii. 53—57 the Israelites ate their own sons and
daughters, and it is possible to translate the Heb. with this meaning:
they shall eat thy sons and thy daughters (cf. iii. 24, x. 25, *they devour
Jacob*).

fig trees would be something of a novelty to the Babylonians, for
Herodotus tells us that they were not found in Babylon (I. 193).

18. See on iv. 27.

19. Such as was the crime, so shall be the punishment; cf. Wisd.
ii. 16.

served strange gods in your land, so shall ye serve strangers in
a land that is not yours.

20 Declare ye this in the house of Jacob, and publish it in
Judah, saying, 21 Hear now this, O foolish people, and without
¹understanding; which have eyes, and see not; which have ears,
and hear not: 22 Fear ye not me? saith the LORD : will ye not
tremble at my presence, which have placed the sand for the bound
of the sea, ²by a perpetual decree, that it cannot pass it? and
though the waves thereof toss themselves, yet can they not
prevail; though they roar, yet can they not pass over it. 23 But
this people hath a revolting and a rebellious heart; they are
revolted and gone. 24 Neither say they in their heart, Let us
now fear the LORD our God, that giveth rain, both the former

¹ Heb. *heart*.　　　　　² Or, *an everlasting ordinance, which it cannot pass*

land...not yours. This, again, cannot refer to the Scythians, who
were wandering tribes in search of plunder and not possessed of territories to which they could transplant whole nations.

20—29. The moral blindness of the people which prevents their
realising the power of Jehovah is alone responsible for the fate which
is about to befall them.

20. *Jacob...Judah.* A double address to both Israel and Judah.

21. *without understanding.* Lit. *heartless.*

eyes...ears. Cf. Mk. viii. 18 and also the saying of Heraclitus: 'Eyes
and ears are bad witnesses to those who have barbarian souls.'

22. Jeremiah is very fond of appealing to the stability of nature as
a witness to the steadfastness of God's promises (xxxii. 20—22). He
who has power to keep in check the waves of the sea is well able to
protect His people from the attacks of the Babylonians or from any
other invader. Here, however, he uses the appeal rather to remind the
nation of the majesty of Him against whom they have sinned. This
line of argument would seem to have been calculated to create a deep
impression on the prophet's contemporaries, believing as they did that the
sea was only kept within its bounds by the express command of God
(cf. Job vii. 12 'Am I a sea...that thou settest a watch over me?' and
Gen. i. 9 with Driver's note). Even in later times the constant marvel
of the tides has aroused man's admiration. 'How comes it,' says Calvin,
' that the sea does not overflow the whole earth? for it is a liquid and
cannot stand in one place except retained by some secret power of God.'
Cf. Enoch lxix. 18; 2 Esdr. iv. 18.

23. *revolting and...rebellious.* The same phrase is used in Dt. xxi.
18, 20, and Ps. lxxviii. 8; cf. also Rom. x. 21.

heart. The heart of the people raged against the bounds which God
had set for them in just the same way as the sea.

24. *that giveth rain.* To ancient peoples the rain was a perpetual

and the latter, in its season; that reserveth unto us the appointed weeks of the harvest. 25 Your iniquities have turned away these things, and your sins have withholden good from you. 26 For among my people are found wicked men: they watch, as fowlers lie in wait; they set a trap, they catch men. 27 As a cage is full of birds, so are their houses full of deceit: therefore they are become great, and waxen rich. 28 They are waxen fat, they shine: yea, they overpass in deeds of wickedness: they plead not

mystery and was looked upon as the direct gift of God Himself (Acts xiv. 17), and in its plentifulness it was a type of His all-including mercy (Matt. v. 45). None knew whence it came nor why it fell upon the desolate places of the wilderness 'where there is no man' (Job xxxviii. 25 ff.). The life of every agricultural community, such as Judah was, depends very largely on a due supply of rain; but this was especially so in the west of Palestine, where the only river, the Kishon, was in summer nothing but a small brook. 'The fertility of Palestine is dependent exclusively on the rain which falls in winter and on the dew of the summer, wherefore it is more clearly and more perceptibly than in other lands a blessing from above.' Cornill, *Hist. of People of Is.* p. 11. Cf. iii. 3; Joel ii. 23. In Zech. xiv. 17 rain is withheld because the feasts have not been duly observed: cf. *Iliad*, ix. 533 ff.

26. *they catch men.* Cf. Ez. xxii. 25 'they have devoured souls.'

27. Note the sudden change of figure, the metaphor of the previous *v.* introducing a further comparison. Hitzig suggests that the *cage* was really another form of trap, woven of willows, into which the birds were decoyed (cf. Ecclus. xi. 30) and the lid shut down upon them. However the translation *cage* suits the context better, as it requires a word describing not the *means of stealing* but a *receptacle for the things stolen*. The Heb. word occurs elsewhere in Am. viii. 1 where it is translated *basket*.

deceit. i.e. the gains of deceit.

28. *waxen fat.* The Hebrews judged ill of fatness deeming it a mark of self-indulgence (Dt. xxxii. 15, of Israel as a nation; Is. vi. 10), if not of actual impiety (Job xv. 27; Ps. lxxiii. 7). Julius Caesar, if Shakespeare is to be trusted, held a very different opinion:

> 'Let me have men about me that are fat;
> Sleek-headed men, and such as sleep o' nights.'

shine. Cf. F. D. Maurice's condemnation of the upper classes in England in 1842 as being 'sleekly devout, for the sake of good order, avowedly believing that one must make the best of the world without God.'

they plead not the cause. Judgement is to come upon men for their neglect of doing what is right, as well as for doing wrong: cf. the General Confession in the Prayer Book.

the cause, the cause of the fatherless, that they should prosper; and the right of the needy do they not judge. 29 Shall I not visit for these things? saith the LORD: shall not my soul be avenged on such a nation as this?

30 ¹A wonderful and horrible thing is come to pass in the land; 31 the prophets prophesy falsely, and the priests bear rule ²by their means; and my people love to have it so: and what will ye do in the end thereof?

¹ Or, *Astonishment and horror*   ² Or, *at their hands*

30 f.   The corruption of the nation is due to the religious leaders and those who support them. Jeremiah is constantly making similar complaints; vi. 13, xiv. 18, xxiii. 11.

31.   *prophets...priests.* As a general rule the prophetic class and the priestly in any religion are at variance; in Israel at this time the regular orders of prophets were evidently under the direction of the priests and both were united in defending the accepted customs of the day, the vested interests of their class. Doubtless this instance amongst others was in the mind of St Jerome when he wrote that 'on searching diligently ancient histories I could not find that any divided the church, or seduced people from the house of the Lord, except those who have been sent by God as priests and prophets.'

my people love to have it so. Populus vult decipi, decipiatur. 'Evil acquires a sort of authority by time. The popular error of one generation becomes the axiom of the next' (Pusey). No doubt the people acquiesced in the teaching of the false prophets because they foretold pleasant things: cf. Mic. ii. 11; Rom. i. 24—32.

CHAPTER VI.

The Invader and his Invincible Might.

This ch. simply continues the prophet's warnings as narrated in the previous chh. but with a note of greater urgency. In iv. 5 ff., for example, the people were advised to betake themselves to the various walled cities for safety from the foe; in this passage, on the contrary, even Jerusalem itself will not provide any certainty of adequate protection, and Jeremiah warns his fellow tribesmen to flee from the city whilst there is still an opportunity for so doing (vi. 1 ff.). The difference in tone between these passages must be due to the progress of events and may be explained in one of two ways; either by taking both passages to refer to the same invasion, in which case some little time must be allowed to have elapsed during which the enemy have gradually overrun the outlying parts of the country; or else to take the warning in iv. 5 ff. as being called forth by the approach of the Scythians against whose fierce but transitory attacks the smaller strongholds might afford sufficient power of resistance (cf. the 'peels' erected in the N. of England as places of refuge from the Scottish raiders), and that in vi. 1 ff. the reference is to the later and more serious Babylonian invasion.

The following are convenient divisions of the ch.:

(a) *The call to escape.* 1—8.
(b) *The ruin which is surely coming.* 9—15.
(c) *Judah has not been ignorant of the penalty for her sins.* 16—21.
(d) *A further description of the invader.* 22—26.
(e) *The rejection of the people.* 27—30.

VI. 1 Flee for safety, ye children of Benjamin, out of the midst of Jerusalem, and blow the trumpet in Tekoa, and raise up a signal on Beth-haccherem: for evil looketh forth from the north,

VI. 1—8. A call to the children of Benjamin to leave the doomed city, the threatened evil is about to break forth from the North. Vigour and reality are lent to the warning by a description of the conversation of the besiegers and the methods which they will adopt against Jerusalem, and at the same time stress is laid on the intense wickedness which is bringing all this to come to pass.

1. *Flee:* העזו Hiph. of עוז. The idea underlying the Heb. is that of gathering up one's possessions for flight: so in iv. 6; Ex. ix. 19, &c.

children of Benjamin. This may be an address to those members of the tribe, possibly friends and relatives of the prophet, who were dwelling in the midst of the guilty city; or it may be merely another way of describing the whole population of Jerusalem as being situated mainly in Benjamite territory: cf. Josh. xv. 8, xviii. 16 f.; Ez. xvi. 3. Duhm accounts for the prophet's despair over the safety of Jerusalem as being due to his suddenly becoming acquainted with the awful depths of sin to which it had sunk: see Introd. to ch. v.

Tekoa. This village was famous as the home of the prophet Amos; it was situated on the top of a hill of considerable area some 12 miles S. of Jerusalem and overlooking the Dead Sea; the site is covered with ruins to an extent of nearly 5 acres, though these probably come from a later time. In 1 Ch. ii. 24 *Tekoa* is the name of an individual. In the Heb. of this *v.* there is a play on the word *blow* (lit. *strike*) which has the same root letters as *Tekoa.* The prophets often enforced their messages by the use of such devices. The most noteworthy instance of this is to be found in the long list of villages in Mic. i. each one of which furnishes the prophet with 'a symbol of the curse that is coming upon his country, and of the sins that have earned the curse.' G. A. Smith, *ad loc.* Cf. also i. 11 f.; Am. iii. 6, &c.

signal. This probably took the form of a beacon: cf. Jud. xx. 38, 40; Is. xxx. 27.

Beth-haccherem. Here and Neh. iii. 14. It is usually identified with a hill called the Frank Mountain—from its connexion with the Crusaders—which stands between Bethlehem and Tekoa and forms a conspicuous

and a great destruction. 2 The comely and delicate one, the daughter of Zion, will I cut off. 3 Shepherds with their flocks shall come unto her; they shall pitch their tents against her round about; they shall feed every one in his place. 4 [1]Prepare ye war against her; arise, and let us go up at noon. Woe unto us! for the day declineth, for the shadows of the evening are stretched out. 5 Arise, and let us go up by night, and let us destroy her palaces. 6 For thus hath the LORD of hosts said, Hew ye down [2]trees, and cast up a mount against Jerusalem: this is

---

[1] Heb. *Sanctify*. [2] Or, as otherwise read, *her trees*

---

eminence such as would be a suitable position for a beacon: see Buhl, *Pal.* pp. 157 f. In the time of St Jerome it was known as Bethacharma.

evil looketh forth. The prophet seems to feel the sinister eyes of Destruction looking down on its prey.

2. *comely and delicate one.* The phrase is here applied to the community personified, similar phrases are elsewhere used of the individuals composing it: Am. vi. 1; Is. xxxii. 9 ff. &c. As it stands however the text is suspicious.

3. Just as flocks eat up the grass so shall Judah and Jerusalem be devoured by the invader from the North: cf. Mic. v. 6 (RVm.).

4. The prophet suddenly drops the pastoral metaphor in favour of an imaginary description of a conversation between the besiegers.

Prepare. Lit. *sanctify.* Cf. the Homeric phrase ἱερὸς στρατός and see W. Robertson Smith, *Rel. Sem.*[2] pp. 402, 455; Frazer, *Taboo*, pp. 157 ff. The expression is not an uncommon one in OT.: cf. xxii. 7, li. 27 f.; Mic. iii. 5; Zeph. i. 7; Is. xiii. 3; Dt. xx. 3; Jud. iv. 9.

noon was the time of the siesta (cf. xv. 8, xx. 16; Zeph. ii. 4), and therefore a fit opportunity for a surprise attack.

shadows of the evening. This may be a lament of the inhabitants of the city inserted between the shouts of the invaders; or it may be made by the attacking forces who think that their opportunity has gone (so Driver).

stretched out. Cf. Nu. xxiv. 6 (Heb.).

5. *night.* The prophet mentions various times during the day to remind the people that they will have no peace nor security when once the city is invested.

palaces. The large and stately buildings in which the people took such pride would be the first resort of the plunderers. It is possible that Jeremiah looked with disfavour on the luxury of which they were both the scene and the representatives.

6. A vivid description of the various processes of the siege preliminary to the final assault.

trees were cut down in ancient warfare for the construction of siege-works: cf. Dt. xx. 19 f. where an exception is made in the case

the city to be visited; she is wholly oppression in the midst of
her. 7 As a well [1]casteth forth her waters, so she [1]casteth forth
her wickedness: violence and spoil is heard in her; before me
continually is sickness and wounds. 8 Be thou instructed, O
Jerusalem, lest my soul be alienated from thee; lest I make thee
a desolation, a land not inhabited.

9 Thus saith the LORD of hosts, They shall throughly glean

[1] Or, *keepeth fresh*

of fruit-trees. This *v.*, which is rejected by Cornill on metrical grounds,
can hardly apply to the Scythians who would not be willing to spend
time over the siege of fortified towns.

this is the city to be visited. The MT. is suspicious and LXX. *Ah!
false city* is to be preferred, unless indeed the whole phrase be rejected
as a marginal gloss.

7. *well, v.l. cistern.* The difference between a *well* and a *cistern* is
that the one is self-originating and self-fed, whilst the other requires
filling and the water in it is an alien element introduced from without.
Cornill prefers the reading *cistern* as he does not think that Jeremiah
looked upon sin as 'original': cf. xiii. 23.

casteth forth. Mg. *keepeth fresh.*

Adopting the readings *cistern* and *keepeth fresh* the meaning of the
v. will be that just as a cistern keeps cool its waters and so prevents any
reduction in their quantity by evaporation, so Jerusalem keeps un-
diminished the sum of her wickednesses: see on ii. 13; and for the use
of similar figures cf. Is. lvii. 20; Jas. iii. 11.

violence and spoil (Heb. חָמָס וָשֹׁד) This phrase which has a sinister
and threatening sound in the original is used twice by Jeremiah (here
and xx. 8): it was probably borrowed from Am. iii. 10.

8. At the end of his dramatic sketch of the horrors which are to
come upon the beloved city, the prophet turns to it in anxiety and
tenderness and makes yet another appeal for repentance and amendment.

9—15. The ruin which is coming upon the city is only exceeded
by the corruption and impenitence of its inhabitants. 'Keine Hoffnung,
keine Aussicht: alles verloren, alles umsonst' (Cornill).

9. Driver translates *Turn back thine hand as a grape-gatherer upon
the tendrils* and supposes the words to be 'dramatically addressed by
Jahweh to the chief of the grape-gatherers (i.e. the leader of the foe)':
cf. xlix. 9 f.; Dt. xxiv. 21; Is. xlvi. 3. The reference is a little uncertain, it may be that Samaria represents the main part of the vine
and Judah the remnant which Jehovah wishes to preserve: but more
probably it is a picture of the small number of Judah itself who will
escape the overflowing invasion.

Duhm and Cornill omit several words of the original, and look upon
the *v.* as a command to Jeremiah to search for any who are faithful

the remnant of Israel as a vine: turn again thine hand as a
grapegatherer ¹into the baskets. 10 To whom shall I speak and
testify, that they may hear? behold, their ear is uncircumcised,
and they cannot hearken: behold, the word of the LORD is become
unto them a reproach; they have no delight in it. 11 Therefore
I am full of the fury of the LORD; I am weary with holding in:
pour it out upon the children in the street, and upon the assembly
of young men together: for even the husband with the wife shall
be taken, the aged with him that is full of days. 12 And their
houses shall be turned unto others, their fields and their wives

¹ Or, upon the shoots

and true of heart in the city: cf. v. 1 ff. This omission which they
base upon metrical grounds certainly helps to bring *vv.* 9 and 10 into
closer connexion with one another.

remnant. See on xi. 23.

10. *uncircumcised.* The idea underlying the metaphor is a certain
dulness and unfitness for the highest employments: cf. iv. 4, xx. 8;
Ex. vi. 12 (of the lips); Acts vii. 51.

they cannot hearken. Those who resist God's will become in time
incapable of obeying or even of comprehending it.

no delight in it. There are times even in the lives of the greatest
saints when the service of God seems to lose all delight and the soul
seems to be left in loneliness and darkness; often enough the cause
is sin, as here, but this is by no means always the case. The literature of mysticism furnishes countless examples of this feeling which
in the lives of humbler Christians must be looked upon as a call
to walk by faith and not by sight and to render to God that adoration
and worship which is His due quite apart from the feelings of the
worshipper.

11. The contrast between the prophet and the people is complete;
they have despised the word of God and have lost all joy in it and
therefore it no longer exerts any influence over their lives: he, on the
other hand, is full of the Divine indignation which breaks forth in
scathing denunciation of those who have provoked God's anger and
upon whom its consequences must inevitably descend: cf. Ez. iii. 14.

pour it out. A slight alteration in the Heb. gives the much better
reading *I will pour it out*, LXX. ἐκχεῶ, and so AV. As the text stands
the imperative is a command from Jehovah to the prophet.

children &c. War is no respecter of persons and neither age nor
sex will be spared in the coming destruction, even the little innocent
children playing in the streets will not escape: cf. ix. 20.

12—15. These *vv.* are very similar to viii. 10—12 into which ch.
they have probably been inserted.

12. *houses...fields...wives.* The evils which are to come upon the

together: for I will stretch out my hand upon the inhabitants of the land, saith the LORD. 13 For from the least of them even unto the greatest of them every one is given to covetousness; and from the prophet even unto the priest every one dealeth falsely. 14 They have healed also the [1]hurt of [2]my people lightly, saying, Peace, peace; when there is no peace. 15 [3]Were they ashamed when they had committed abomination? nay, they were not at all ashamed, neither could they blush: therefore they shall fall among them that fall: at the time that I visit them they shall [4]be cast down, saith the LORD.

[1] Or, *breach*
[2] Another reading is, *the daughter of my people*, as in ch. viii. 11, 21.
[3] Or, *They shall be put to shame because they have committed abomination: yea, they are not &c.*　　[4] Or, *stumble*

people are very similar to those threatened in Deuteronomy, see especially Dt. xxviii. 30 'wife...house...vineyard' to be given to another; also Am. v. 11 *b* 'vineyard'; Zeph. i. 13 'houses...vineyards'; in Is. lxv. 21 f. the people are promised immunity from such evils, 'they shall not build and another inhabit; they shall not plant and another eat.' It is interesting to notice the order in which a man's possessions are arranged in these and other passages of OT.: e.g. the tenth commandment in its different versions, Ex. xx. 17 'house...wife' and Dt. v. 21 'wife...house ...field.' Commenting on the former passage Dr McNeile says that 'it is not improbable that this command originally ended at "house," all the remainder being an enlargement detailing the contents of the house. Dt., in a more humane spirit, places the wife first...and governed by a different verb.'

13. Cf. Is. lvi. 10 ff. where the rulers are compared to blind watchmen, greedy dogs, and shepherds without understanding, whose one idea is gain and pleasure. See on v. 30 f.

14. *lightly*. LXX. ἐξουθενοῦντες. Like faithless physicians they dismissed their patient without going to the trouble of examining him properly; soothing him with the medicine of pleasant-sounding phrases when what was wanted was the deep-cutting knife of a thorough-going repentance.

Peace, peace. To the comfortable words of the false prophets Jeremiah replied with the ominous message 'violence and spoil, violence and spoil': see on *v.* 7.

15. *they were not at all ashamed.* The nation had 'a whore's forehead' (iii. 3) and so remorse was impossible; cf. Zeph. iii. 5. Such a people as this made even shame itself avoid them. There is something Homeric in this condemnation of those who are impervious to the promptings of αἰδώς.

that I visit them. LXX. reads *at the time of visitation* (ἐν καιρῷ ἐπισκοπῆς): cf. Lk. xix. 44.

16 Thus saith the LORD, Stand ye in the ways and see, and ask for the old paths, where is the good way, and walk therein, and ye shall find rest for your souls: but they said, We will not walk *therein*. 17 And I set watchmen over you, *saying*, Hearken to the sound of the trumpet; but they said, We will not hearken. 18 Therefore hear, ye nations, and know, O congregation, what

16—21. The fate of Judah will not come upon it unannounced, nor is the Lord about to punish a people which is ignorant of the consequences of its misdeeds. The nation, in spite of the continuous and repeated warnings of God's watchmen, the prophets, has always been bent on leaving the old paths and following a new made way of its own.

16. *saith.* Better *said.*

in the ways. At the cross-roads, the point at which a deliberate choice has to be made.

the old paths. Jeremiah based all his appeals on the experience of the past, and in doing so he was setting an example for prophets and teachers in all ages, for 'true reformers do not claim to be heard on the ground of the new things they proclaim, but rather because they alone give due weight to old truths which the mass of their contemporaries cannot formally deny, but practically ignore' (W. Robertson Smith, *Prophets*[2], p. 83). Even the *old paths* are not without their dangers and men may be made to stumble therein (xviii. 15).

rest for your souls. There can be little doubt that our Blessed Lord had this *v.* in mind when He made the promise of Matt. xi. 29. In fulfilling the longings of OT. our Lord very often gave to them a more spiritual meaning than they had had for the original hearers; and in referring to this *v.* He is thinking of something higher than mere material safety. The pragmatic character of Israelite religion was first pointed out by Hosea (ix. 10, x. 9, xi. 1 ff., xii., xiii. 1, 6).

This *v.* forms the text for the sermon in *The Canterbury Tales.* The sermon has been well described as 'unmercifully long.'

17. *I set.* Better to translate with Driver *I ever raised up.*

watchmen. 'A title of the prophets as espying, by God's enabling, things beyond human ken' (Pusey). By a common and easily understood figure, it describes the prophetic office as one of warning: cf. Is. xxi. 6, lii. 8; Hab. ii. 1; and Ez. iii. 17.

18 f. God justifies His treatment of the nation in the eyes of the earth and its inhabitants: cf. Is. iii. 10.

18. The latter part of this *v.* seems to be corrupt, as *congregation* cannot be applied to heathen *nations* and even if it could the meaning would still be obscure. Several critics have adopted Ewald's suggestions and translate *take good knowledge of that which is coming.* Peake prefers Rothstein's proposed emendation *wherefore hear ye heavens and bear witness against them.*

is among them. 19 Hear, O earth: behold, I will bring evil upon
this people, even the fruit of their thoughts, because they have
not hearkened unto my words; and as for my law, they have
rejected it. 20 To what purpose cometh there to me frankincense
from Sheba, and the sweet ¹cane from a far country? your burnt
offerings are not acceptable, nor your sacrifices pleasing unto me.
21 Therefore thus saith the LORD, Behold, I will lay stumblingblocks before this people: and the fathers and the sons together
shall stumble against them; the neighbour and his friend shall
perish.

¹ Or, *calamus*

19. *law.* The context here seems to require something more
definite than 'direction' and almost points to the existence of an
accepted code: cf. Is. v. 24, xxx. 9; and see on ii. 8.

20. *frankincense.* In the opinion of many scholars this is the first
mention of incense in OT.; the parts of the Pentateuch in which it
occurs are by them considered late. Wellhausen, for example, considers that it was 'an innovation from a more luxuriously-developed
foreign cultus' (*Hist. Israel*, pp. 64 f., 74 n.). It is not mentioned by
the earlier prophets in their condemnations of innovations and here it
is referred to as something strange and new.

Sheba. In SW. Arabia, a country noted for the export of incense;
cf. Is. lx. 6, &c. and Virgil's *tus Sabaeum, Aen.* I. 416 f.: Milton also
speaks of 'Sabaean odours from the spicy shore of Araby the blest,'
Par. Lost, IV. 162 f.

cane. Mg. *calamus.* It formed one of the ingredients of the
'holy anointing oil' (Ex. xxx. 23—25).

far country. Pliny says that calamus came from Arabia, India and
Syria (*Hist. Nat.* XII. 48). It is no longer obtained from Arabia Felix,
but is brought to Mecca by pilgrims from the Malay islands (Doughty,
Arab. Deserta, I. 97). Probably India is here meant.

burnt offerings are not acceptable. See note on vii. 21 f.

Jeremy Taylor sums up the teaching of this *v.* in a single sentence.
'It is but a poor return' he says 'which men make to God, who gives
them all things, when they offer Him "a piece of gum or the fat of
a cheap lamb"' (Dedication to *Holy Living*).

21. *I will lay stumblingblocks.* It is God Himself who will make
the people to stumble: cf. our Lord's use of Is. vi. 9 f. On the thought
of God as the cause of the offences which bring punishment upon the
people see 2 S. xxiv. 1 (cf. 1 Ch. i. 21); Ez. iii. 20. It was the opinion
of some of the later Rabbis that God had created in man an 'evil
tendency' and so was Himself the cause of sin: cf. Tal. Bab. *Qiddushin*
30*b*, and *Bereshith Rabba* on Gen. vi. 6. This opinion was never accepted
universally and Ben Sira protests strongly against those who say 'From

22 Thus saith the LORD, Behold, a people cometh from the north country; and a great nation shall be stirred up from the uttermost parts of the earth. 23 They lay hold on bow and spear; they are cruel, and have no mercy; their voice roareth like the sea, and they ride upon horses; every one set in array, as a man to the battle, against thee, O daughter of Zion. 24 We have heard the fame thereof; our hands wax feeble: anguish hath taken hold of us, *and* pangs as of a woman in travail. 25 Go not forth into the field, nor walk by the way; for *there is* the sword of the enemy, *and* terror on every side. 26 O daughter of my people, gird thee with sackcloth, and wallow thyself in ashes: make thee mourning, as for an only son, most bitter lamentation; for the spoiler shall suddenly come upon us. 27 I have

God is my transgression' (Ecclus. xv. 11 ; cf. Wisd. i. 12—16 ; Philo, *De Mut.* 4, and *De Conf. Ling.* 35 f.; Jas. i. 13). In this passage *stumbling* refers probably to misfortunes in the material rather than in the moral sphere.

22—26. The invader is once more described in all the glory and terror of his advance.

22. Ezekiel foretells the coming of Gomer and the house of Togarmah 'from the uttermost parts of the North' (xxxviii. 6, 15 ; also Gog, xxxix. 2).

23. Every feature of the hostile army which could serve to alarm the men of Judah is emphasised by Jeremiah in order to restore them to their allegiance to Jehovah; cf. Is. xvii. 12. In times of peril nothing is gained by half-measures and by concealing the seriousness of the situation. The account was probably at first intended to apply to the Scythians but it would equally well serve to describe the Babylonian cavalry.

cruel, 'frightful.' History gives innumerable instances of this characteristic of the Assyrians and Babylonians: cf. for example Sennacherib's attempt to 'obliterate' Babylon in 689 B.C. 'The whole city was sacked, fortifications and walls, temples and palaces, as well as private houses, were levelled with the ground, the people massacred or deported, and the waters of the Arakhtu canal turned over the site.' C. W. H. Johns, *Ancient Bab.* p. 122.

25. *terror on every side.* Cf. xx. 3.

26. The death of an only son meant the extinction of the family, a terrible misfortune in the eyes of a people like the Hebrews who had but a vague and uncertain hold upon the doctrine of a future life ; cf. Gen. xxii. 2, 12, 16 ; Am. viii. 10 ; Zech. xii. 10. In all three places LXX. renders a *beloved* son and many commentators think that they read יָדִיד for יָחִיד. This explanation is as old as St Jerome, but it should be remembered that the usage of ὁ ἀγαπητός for an *only* son is an idiom

made thee a [1]tower *and* a fortress among my people; that thou mayest know and try their way. 28 They are all grievous revolters, going about with slanders; they are brass and iron: they all of them deal corruptly. 29 The bellows [2]blow fiercely; the lead is consumed of the fire: in vain do they go on refining; for the wicked are not plucked away. 30 Refuse silver shall men call them, because the LORD hath rejected them.

<hr>

[1] Or, *trier*   [2] Or, *are burned*

<hr>

found in classical Greek from the time of Homer (e.g. *Od.* II. 365, IV. 727, 817, &c.), and by the time of Aristotle it had become so common that he was able to extend the usage and employ it in speaking of depriving a one-eyed man of 'his *only* organ of vision'; ἀγαπητὸν γὰρ ἀφῄρηται. In Jud. xi. 34 LXX. (i.e. LXX. A) reads both μονογενής and ἀγαπητή.

27—30. The people are likened to metal which the refiner casts away as being useless for his purpose.

28. *brass and iron.* i.e. containing no precious metal. 'Their impudence resembles brass, and their obstinacy may be compared to iron.' Lowth.

29. *lead.* 'In refining the alloy containing the gold or silver is mixed with lead and fused in a furnace...a current of air is turned upon the molten mass...the lead oxidizes and carries away the alloy (J. Napier, *The Ancient Workers in Metal,* pp. 20, 23). In the case here imagined, so inextricably is the alloy mixed with the silver, that, though the bellows blow, and the lead is oxidized in the heat, no purification is effected: only impure silver remains.' (Driver.)

The process of purging dross from gold or other precious metal is almost invariably used of a successful effort in which the impurities are purged from out the nation; here the whole nation is dross. In just the same way St Peter talks of a faith purified by fire, but he is silent as to the man whose faith is unable to stand the test. Many notions as to the purifying effects of suffering and pain, whether in this present life or in a future state, are based on a misleading use of this metaphor. In any case gold is passive and has to endure the test: man, within certain limits, has liberty and may refuse to meet it.

30. *Refuse silver.* Cf. Ez. xxii. 18 'the dross of silver.'

CHAPTERS VII.—X.

A GROUP OF PROPHECIES DELIVERED AT THE TEMPLE GATE.

Scholars are not agreed as to the date to which these chh. belong, two periods seeming to have good claims upon them; the reign of Josiah and that of Jehoiakim. If the discourse in vii. 1—28 could be proved beyond all doubt to refer to the same incident as ch. xxvi. the question of date would be settled, as the latter ch. is definitely headed 'In the beginning of the reign of Jehoiakim' (see below for a discussion of this reference). Dean Stanley, who regarded chh. vii.—ix. as a single discourse, has pointed out the wide scope and representative character of this section containing as it does 'almost every element' of Jeremiah's constant teaching. 'It struck the successive chords of invective, irony, bitter grief, and passionate lamentation. It touched on all the topics on which his countrymen would be most sensitive—not only the idolatrous charms by which they hoped to win the favour of the Phœnician deities,...but on the uselessness and impending fall of the ancient institutions, which seemed to contain a promise of eternal duration—the Temple of Solomon, the Mosaic ritual, the Holy Sepulchres, the Holy City, the Chosen People, the sacred rite of Circumcision' (*The Jewish Church*, II. 449).

The chh. fall naturally into five main divisions which can themselves be broken up into smaller sections :

A denunciation of excessive regard for the temple. vii. 1—viii. 3.
The penalty of national sin is national ruin. viii. 4—ix. 1.
The treachery of the people is the forerunner of destruction. ix. 2—26.
The vanity of idols. x. 1—16.
The nearness of the exile. x. 17—25.

Chapters VII. 1—VIII. 3.

A Denunciation of Excessive Regard for the Temple.

There seems to be a great probability that this section gives a fuller report of Jeremiah's warning to the people as narrated in xxvi. 1—9; the message and the place of its delivery are the same; and the date prefixed to the latter narrative suits the present context most excellently. In the one case the stress is laid on the sermon itself ; and in the other on the effect which it had upon those who heard it. In view of the state of the text of Jeremiah and the absence of anything like chronological order in the book no surprise need be occasioned by the wide separation of these two complementary accounts of the same incident. The importance of the message—and of the results which followed its delivery—is sufficient justification for its two-fold record, for as Buttenwieser truly says 'The Temple-sermon...formed the decisive event in the prophet's career. It marked the parting of the ways. In it Jeremiah mercilessly attacked what the people felt to be their holiest beliefs and institutions, and mocked at the hollowness of their worship' (*The Prophets of Israel*, p. 44). The section may be sub-divided as follows:

(a) *The temple is no guarantee of national salvation, but will itself share the fate of Shiloh.* 1—15.
(b) *The prophet is no longer to intercede for the people.* 16—20.
(c) *Obedience is better than sacrifice.* 21—28.
(d) *The rejection of Judah.* 29—34.
(e) *The desecration of the graves of the kings and people.* viii. 1—3.

VII. 1 The word that came to Jeremiah from the LORD, saying, 2 Stand in the gate of the LORD's house, and proclaim there this word, and say, Hear the word of the LORD, all ye of Judah, that enter in at these gates to worship the LORD. 3 Thus saith the LORD of hosts, the God of Israel, Amend your ways and your doings, and I will cause you to dwell in this place. 4 Trust ye not in lying words, saying, The temple of the LORD, the temple

VII. 1—15. This sub-section consists of an attack on those who held the temple to be the guarantee of the safety of the nation and made worship a substitute for holiness of life; and this in spite of the warning contained in the fate of Shiloh and the Northern Kingdom.

1—2. These *vv.* form the heading of the section and it is probable, as Cornill suggests, that they represent an attempt to fix the circumstances of the sermon for the benefit of a later age (cf. xxvi. 1 f.). LXX. has 'Hear the words of Jehovah, all Judah.'

2. *gate* (xxvi. 2 *court*). Probably the prophet stood at the gate between the outer and the inner court.

3—7. The sermon is undoubtedly compressed even in the larger form contained in this ch., hence, in part, the appearance of tautology and repetition. The words which would remain most firmly fixed in the mind of the people would be those which carried the burden of the message. Jeremiah's utterance has an especial interest because of the connexion between it and our Lord's action in cleansing the temple (cf. Mk. xi. 15—18).

3. *your ways and your doings.* A favourite expression with Jeremiah: cf. Zech. i. 6. The word for *doings* has usually a bad sense though in Ps. lxxvii. 12 and lxxviii. 7 it is used of the works of God.

4. Jeremiah's condemnation of the message of those who were the accepted teachers of the day was nothing less than a declaration of war. The feeling of trust which the nation had in the inviolate city had stood the test of history and in addition had the sanction of prophetic utterances. Moreover since the centralisation of the cultus in the days of Josiah it was the only remaining sanctuary of Jehovah, and so He was, as it were, bound to defend the city which was identified with His worship. Another less worthy motive which would arouse the fury of the priests and prophets would be the danger threatening 'vested interests' if teaching such as that of Jeremiah became at all popular. See Introd. p. xxxi.

lying words. Heb. *words of deception, disappointment.* The word is often used by Jeremiah to describe the vanity and falsehood of hopes founded on the message of the teachers who opposed him.

The temple of the LORD. For other examples of this three-fold repetition cf. xxii. 29; Is. vi. 3. Dante probably had this passage in mind when he made St Peter say:

of the LORD, the temple of the LORD, are these. 5 For if ye throughly amend your ways and your doings; if ye throughly execute judgement between a man and his neighbour; 6 if ye oppress not the stranger, the fatherless, and the widow, and shed not innocent blood in this place, neither walk after other gods to your own hurt: 7 then will I cause you to dwell in this place, in the land that I gave to your fathers, from of old even for evermore. 8 Behold, ye trust in lying words, that cannot profit. 9 Will ye steal, murder, and commit adultery, and swear falsely,

'my seat,
My seat, my seat, I say, which to the eye
Of God's dear Son is vacant at His feet.'
Parad. XXVII. 22—24.

The Targum suggests that the repetition is on account of the three great acts of worship, viz. service, sacrifice, and prayer, which were offered in the temple. (For a collection of similar explanations, see Payne Smith, *ad loc.*) Probably the phrase was constantly on the lips of the people and the prophet was trying to reproduce the effect of its constant recital; cf. Is. xxviii. 10 'line upon line.' Wade in commenting on Is. vi. 3 compares τρισμέγιστος, τρίλλιστος, and *ter felix* (Ovid, *Metamorph.* VIII. 51).

temple. The Heb. word (הֵיכָל) is probably derived from the Accadian *e-gal*, i.e. great house.

these. The temple and the buildings which surrounded it: cf. Mk. xiii. 1.

5—7. These *vv.* are Deuteronomic in spirit and in language. The continued security of the people is dependent on the practice of social virtues and on the service of Jehovah to the exclusion of every other object of worship. The prohibition in *v.* 6 of walking 'after other gods' seems hardly to fit the context and it is best to omit it. The whole object of Jeremiah's sermon is to condemn an excessive and superstitious zeal for the service of Jehovah, and this being so it would hardly seem necessary for him to go out of his way to declare to the people the reward which would follow their avoidance of false gods; cf. *v.* 9 also.

6. *the stranger, the fatherless, and the widow.* These various classes were without power in the administration of affairs and therefore specially liable to be oppressed. The *stranger* was the alien, resident for the time being in Judah.

7. *to dwell...in the land.* This promise would best refer to a time when there was actual danger of the people being taken into exile.

8. *that cannot profit.* Better *in order not to profit*—the effect of the action of the people is stated as though it were the motive.

9. *steal, murder, and commit adultery.* The prophet is probably referring to the prohibitions of the Decalogue which the people were in

and burn incense unto Baal, and walk after other gods whom ye
have not known, 10 and come and stand before me in this house,
¹which is called by my name, and say, We are delivered; that ye
may do all these abominations? 11 Is this house, which is called
by my name, become a den of robbers in your eyes? Behold, I,
even I, have seen it, saith the LORD. 12 But go ye now unto my
place which was in Shiloh, where I caused my name to dwell at the

---

¹ Heb. *whereupon my name is called.*

---

the habit of breaking. The order differs slightly from that in MT. of
Ex. xx. and Dt. v. and also from that in Rom. xiii. 9; Jas. ii. 11 and
Lk. xviii. 20. (See list of variations in McNeile, *Exodus*, p. 119.)

burn incense unto Baal. See on ii. 8 and vi. 20.

10. *stand before.* To worship and to serve.

which is called by my name. 'The calling of a name *upon* an object
(or person) designates it as the property of the bearer of the name.'
Cornill.

We are delivered &c. Driver continues *in order* (forsooth) *to do
all these abominations,* a possible translation of the Heb. If all these
words are spoken by the people the meaning must be that God has
set the stamp of His approval upon their way of life by the deliverance
which they are celebrating. It is perhaps better to follow RV. and
to restrict the people's speech to *We are delivered,* i.e. we are in a
state of safety because of the merit of our religious observances (cf.
Gen. xxxvii. 22).

11. *den of robbers.* The limestone caves of Palestine were much
used as a refuge for brigands between the carrying out of their various
deeds of violence. This *v.* is quoted by our Blessed Lord in Mk. xi.
17; and is borrowed by Dante:

> 'The walls which once were as an Abbey's shrine
> Are made as dens of robbers.'
> *Parad.* XXII. 76—77.

Behold, I, even I, have seen it. The meaning of the RV. is rather
vague and Buttenwieser's suggested translation is an improvement,
Verily I do look upon it as such (*The Prophets of Israel,* p. 12).

12—15. The appeal to history. The sanctity of Shiloh did not
protect it in time past, and so in the present Jerusalem will not be
spared if the people do not repent.

12. *my place.* Heb. מָקוֹם. The related Arabic word *maḳām* is
used in a similar way of a sacred place (cf. *ZATW.* 1914, p. 73, and a
note by Dr Cowley in *J. Th. S.* 1916, pp. 174 ff.). In the Mishnah and
other later literature the word was used as a substitute for the name
of God Himself.

Shiloh. The modern *Seilūn* on the road from Bethel to Shechem
is generally accepted as the site of Shiloh. It was the place where the

first, and see what I did to it for the wickedness of my people
Israel. 13 And now, because ye have done all these works, saith
the LORD, and I spake unto you, rising up early and speaking,
but ye heard not; and I called you, but ye answered not: 14 therefore will I do unto the house, which is called by my name, wherein
ye trust, and unto the place which I gave to you and to your
fathers, as I have done to Shiloh. 15 And I will cast you out of
my sight, as I have cast out all your brethren, even the whole
seed of Ephraim.

sanctuary containing the ark was situated (1 S. iii. 3, 15), and according to the priestly writer owed its importance to the action of Joshua
himself (Josh. xviii. 1). This sanctuary was very probably destroyed
when the ark was carried off after the Battle of Ebenezer (1 S. iv. 11);
though there is some uncertainty as to whether Jeremiah is referring
to this destruction, or to some more recent catastrophe (see Additional
Note below).

    at the first. Better perhaps *formerly*: cf. G. B. Gray on Nu. x. 12
(*I.C.C.*).

    13. *rising up early and speaking.* The phrase occurs only in
Jeremiah with the exception of 2 Ch. xxxvi. 15. Its meaning is that
God imparts His revelation 'insistently and continuously' (cf. Wade
on Is. l. 4); a similar tradition exists among the followers of Muhammed. (See D. B. Macdonald, *Aspects of Islam*, p. 218.)

    14. *wherein ye trust.* The people trusted in a formula about God
or His temple and had lost faith in the living God Himself: cf. Am.
iii. 14, v. 4 f. The greatest obstacle in the way of the progress of the
Kingdom of Heaven is the large mass of 'conventional' religion which
takes God's name upon its lips and yet avoids any attempt to carry
out His commands. This state of affairs is always partly due to the
professed teachers of the people, whether it be in the time of Jeremiah
or in our own. Cf. the striking warning of F. D. Maurice, 'we have been
dosing our people with religion, when what they want is not this but
the living God; and we are threatened now, not with the loss of
religious feeling, so-called, or of religious notions or of religious observances, but with atheism.'

    15. *all your brethren.* Omit *all* with LXX.
    Ephraim. i.e. the whole of the Northern tribes.

ADDITIONAL NOTE ON VII. 12.

The Destruction of Shiloh.

    The destruction of Jehovah's place at Shiloh which was used by Jeremiah as
a warning of the coming fate of Jerusalem is nowhere described in OT. as we
have it at present, though Wellhausen has suggested that such a description

originally stood in the place of 1 S. vii. From the absence of any mention of Shiloh as a sanctuary after the time of the Judges and from the subsequent establishment of the priests of the house of Eli at Nob it is generally held that Shiloh was destroyed at the time of the capture of the ark by the Philistines at the Battle of Ebenezer (1 S. iv. 11); so for example Wellhausen says, 'The old sanctuary at Shiloh was destroyed by them (the Philistines); its temple of Jehovah thenceforward lay in ruins[1].' According to Jud. xviii. 30 f. Jonathan and his sons 'were priests to the tribe of the Danites until the day of the captivity of the land,' and Micah's image remained at the sanctuary 'all the time that the house of God was in Shiloh.' These statements suggest that the priesthood of Jonathan's sons and the existence of the shrine at Shiloh were both continued until the 'captivity of the land,' and accordingly older writers referred the words to the Philistine war (see references in Moore, *Judges*, p. 400 note); recent critics, however, attribute the two statements to different versions of the story of Micah's image[2]. The reference of 'the captivity of the land' to the Philistine aggression is obviously strained, and a much more natural explanation is to refer it to the deportation of 734 or 722 B.C. A destruction of Shiloh at such a date would fit in well with Jeremiah's reference, as apparently the ruins were still visible, and the event itself was connected in some way with the fall of Ephraim (see vii. 15). At the same time if Shiloh was destroyed by the Assyrians it is strange that there is no mention of the fact in 2 K. It is true that the Northern sanctuaries were regarded as schismatic by the later writers, but that would not prevent their including an account of the destruction of one of them, especially if accompanied with circumstances of peculiar horror.

At first sight it seems strange that Shiloh should be thought worthy of comparison with Jerusalem, but the parallel is a fairly close one, as in the early days of the nation Shiloh was the central sanctuary. Dr Kennett thinks that Shiloh, in strong contradistinction to most of the other sacred sites of the Hebrews which were almost certainly taken over from the Canaanites, was a genuinely Israelitish sanctuary. 'It is noteworthy that no theophany is related in connexion with it; no patriarch is buried there; its foundation is associated with no great name; while on the other hand, a tradition which, though perhaps considerably modified, cannot be very late ascribes to it the possession of the ark[3].'

It seems probable that Shiloh whether destroyed by the Philistines or not, lost its importance with the loss of the ark. The town was in existence in the time of Jeroboam I (1 K. xiv. 2), but he evidently attached no special value to it as the site for a new national sanctuary, though his neglect of it might be on account of its somewhat retired situation. It is not at all unlikely that the town was still in existence in the time of Jeremiah (xli. 5; but see note *ad loc.*), but the rebuilding of the town after its destruction would not necessarily interfere

---

[1] *Hist. Israel*, p. 448; see also Wade, *O.T. Hist.* p. 211.
[2] E.g. Moore, *op. cit.* p. 399.
[3] *HDRE.* VII. p. 441. Dr Kennett suggests that Shiloh was originally the sanctuary of Levi when that tribe held territory of its own (*op. cit.* p. 440).

with the ruins of the sanctuary. When Jud. xxi. 12, 19 was written the site
was evidently little known, hence the minute and detailed description contained
in the text; it may however be as Moore suggests 'merely the archaeological
style of a late author, or an indication that he wrote for readers in foreign lands,
perhaps himself lived in exile' (*op. cit.* pp. 447 f.).

Objection has been taken to the fact that since the sanctuary at Shiloh was
only a tent or tabernacle no ruins would survive its destruction. The account
in 1 S. i.—iv. seems however to suggest some more permanent structure, and
according to a Rabbinic tradition the temple at Shiloh had stone walls with a
tent stretched over the top. Traces of a suitable site have been described by
Sir Charles Wilson as situated at Seilûn[1]. The identification of Shiloh with
Seilûn was well known to the Moslem geographers[2], but was only rediscovered
in modern times by Robinson in 1838. According to Colonel Conder there is no
site in the country fixed with greater certainty than that of Shiloh[3].

16 Therefore pray not thou for this people, neither lift up

16—20. The continued idolatry of the people makes it impossible
for God to receive intercessions on their behalf. Several critics are
disposed to look upon this section as being out of its context, owing to
a supposed difference in situation from what has gone before. Duhm,
for example, points out that Jeremiah is no longer in the temple before
'all Judah' but alone with Jehovah. But even if such a supposition
be correct and it be admitted that the prophet is alone with his God,
it by no means follows that he has left the temple; the withdrawal
may well have been spiritual and mental rather than physical. Many
parallels to this can be found in the life of our Lord, when turning
aside from those who opposed Him, He addressed His Father and
received from Him a definite reply according to His needs (e.g. Jn. xii.
27 ff.). A further objection is urged that idolatrous worship of the
kind here described did not take place in the temple during the reign
of Jehoiakim, and that the section is therefore but 'an embellished
account' (Ausschmückung) of xliv. 17—19. In reply to this it is
enough to say that the cult of the queen of heaven was, according
to most critics, introduced in the reign of Manasseh, it was prevalent
in the exilic period (as xliv. 17—19 itself shews), and that in the
meantime many other superstitious practices were in vogue (Ez. viii.).
It is, of course, possible that the effects of Josiah's reformation had
not at this time yet worn off, but the onus of proof would seem to lie

---

[1] 'The ruins of Seilûn (Shiloh) cover the surface of a "tell," or mound, on a
spur which lies between two valleys, that unite about a quarter of a mile above
Khan Lubban, and thence run to the sea....Northwards, the tell slopes down to a
broad shoulder across which a sort of level court, 77 feet wide and 412 feet long,
has been cut out. The rock is in places scarped to a height of five feet....It is not
improbable that the place was thus prepared to receive the Tabernacle.' *PEFQS.*
1873, pp. 37 f.

[2] Le Strange, *Palestine under the Moslems*, pp. 477, 527; referred to by Moore.

[3] *Tent Life in Palestine*, I. pp. 81 f.

cry nor prayer for them, neither make intercession to me: for I
will not hear thee. 17 Seest thou not what they do in the cities
of Judah and in the streets of Jerusalem? 18 The children
gather wood, and the fathers kindle the fire, and the women
knead the dough, to make cakes to the queen of heaven, and to

on those who deny the existence of such worship, rather than on those
who affirm it.

16. *pray not.* The state of the people was worse than at the time
of the exodus when according to Ex. xxxii. 10—14 Moses persisted
in his intercessions until ' the Lord repented of the evil which he said
he would do.' Even such powerful intercessors as Moses and Samuel
would avail nothing at the present crisis (xv. 1), and the repeated
attempts of Jeremiah are equally in vain (cf. xi. 14, xiv. 11). It would
seem that it is possible for a nation or individual to fall so deeply into
sin as to be beyond the help of the prayers of others (cf. 1 Jn. v. 16;
Test. xii. Patr. *Issach.* vii. 1), but it is not for man to decide when such
a state has been reached, nor is the sinner necessarily beyond God's
mercy. In spite of this *v.* Jewish tradition persisted in regarding
Jeremiah as the intercessor *par excellence* of the nation; cf. 2 Macc.
xv. 14; 4 Bar. ii. 3; 2 Bar. ii. 2.

18. *children...fathers...women.* The worship of the queen of
heaven drew in all the members of the family. It is hardly necessary
to suppose that the prophet is laying stress on the poverty of those
who engaged in this cult; he wishes to point out that all ages and both
sexes were alike infected by it.

cakes. Probably in the shape of the moon—like the σελῆναι of the
Athenians—or in that of a star; or it may be that they were intended
to be substitutes for animals and so were made in their shape. Similar
cakes were offered to Artemis in the Μουνυχία. (For fuller details
see Preller, *Griechische Mythologie*[2], I. 236; Zimmern, *KAT.*[3] II.
440 ff.)

queen of heaven (LXX. τῇ στρατιᾷ τοῦ οὐρανοῦ). Called Ishtar by
the Babylonians and 'Ashtoroth of the glorious heavens' in Zidonian
inscriptions[1]. The worship of this deity—the national god of Syria
according to Tertullian, *Apol.* xxiv.—was especially cultivated by
women. Cf. Milton, *Parad. Lost*, I. 438—441:

> 'Ashtoreth whom the Phoenicians called
> Astarte, queen of heaven, with crescent Horns;
> To whose bright Image nightly by the Moon
> Sidonian virgins paid their Vows and Songs.'

Ishtar was the planet Venus, and not the moon (see Cornill, *ad loc.*),
and the worship here described was probably paid to that planet. Euse-

---

[1] She was called the Heavenly Goddess or the Heavenly Aphrodite by the
Greeks (Herod. I. 105, III. 8; Pausan. I. xiv. 7). Tertullian (*Apol.* xxiii.) and
St Augustine (*De Civ. Dei*, II. 4) refer to her as the Heavenly Virgin.

pour out drink offerings unto other gods, that they may provoke me to anger. 19 Do they provoke me to anger? saith the LORD; *do they* not *provoke* themselves, to the confusion of their own faces? 20 Therefore thus saith the Lord GOD: Behold, mine anger and my fury shall be poured out upon this place, upon man, and upon beast, and upon the trees of the field, and upon the fruit of the ground; and it shall burn, and shall not be quenched.

21 Thus saith the LORD of hosts, the God of Israel: Add your

bius identifies Astarte with Venus (*Praep. Evang.* I. 10); cf. also Suidas' statement Ἀστάρτη ἡ παρ᾽ Ἕλλησιν Ἀφροδίτη λεγομένη, θεὸς Σιδωνίων; and Cicero, *De natura deorum*, III. xxiii. 59.

pour out drink offerings. The libation was a common form of offering and there are traces of its having formed part of the worship of Jehovah (Gen. xxxv. 14; Nu. xv. 5; 1 S. i. 24, x. 3; Hos. ix. 4; cf. also 1 S. vii. 6; 2 S. xxiii. 16).

anger. Better *chagrin*, a word which occurs very frequently in Jeremiah.

20. The effects of man's sin are seen even in the world of natural things, 'the whole creation groaneth and travaileth together.' Further illustrations of this can be found in the traditions concerning the Fall and the Flood where the curse which came upon man came also upon man's humbler companions. At the same time in some mysterious way the effect of Christ's atoning and reconciling work is not limited merely to the human part of creation: Eph. i. 10; Col. i. 20. It can hardly be, however, that the beasts are punished for their own sins, as is the case in the quatrain of Archilochus, 'O father Zeus, thine is the dominion of heaven: thou seest men's deeds of wickedness and right: thou regardest the insolence and justice of beasts[1].'

21—28. 'Obedience is better than sacrifice.' In this section Jeremiah is once more back amongst the people in the temple area and his utterance in the name of God would fall on their startled ears with all the shock of blasphemy and impiety. The whole system of the popular religion was founded on the due performance of the established ritual, and to neglect or to despise it, was, in their eyes, a much more serious offence against God than failure to fulfil the requirements of the moral law. To speak of their burnt-offerings and sacrifices as mere *flesh*—'so much butcher's meat' as we might say—which had no sanctity and could therefore be eaten by anybody, was a crime and an outrage of the utmost gravity. But when the prophet went on to deny not only the utility of their customs in the present, but also the sanction which they had received from the past, the fury of his hearers was increased to the utmost. Jeremiah had thus committed the double offence which

---

[1] Quoted by J. Adam, *Religious Teachers of Greece*, p. 86.

burnt offerings unto your sacrifices, and eat ye flesh. 22 For I
spake not unto your fathers, nor commanded them in the day
that I brought them out of the land of Egypt, concerning burnt
offerings or sacrifices: 23 but this thing I commanded them,
saying, Hearken unto my voice, and I will be your God, and ye
shall be my people: and walk ye in all the way that I command
you, that it may be well with you. 24 But they hearkened not,
nor inclined their ear, but walked in *their own* counsels *and* in
the stubbornness of their evil heart, and went backward and not
forward. 25 Since the day that your fathers came forth out of
the land of Egypt unto this day, I have sent unto you all my
servants the prophets, daily rising up early and sending them:
26 yet they hearkened not unto me, nor inclined their ear, but
made their neck stiff: they did worse than their fathers.

27 And thou shalt speak all these words unto them; but they
will not hearken to thee: thou shalt also call unto them; but
they will not answer thee. 28 And thou shalt say unto them,
This is the nation that hath not hearkened to the voice of the

in later times cost St Stephen his life, he spoke both against the *holy
place* and against *the law* (Acts vi. 13).

21. *burnt offerings...sacrifices.* The very sacrifices specified in Dt.
xii. 6; the former were burned entire; of the latter the kidney fat was
burned, the priests had their portion, and the rest was cooked and eaten
in the sanctuary. (For further details see McNeile, *Exodus*, p. 124.) In
God's sight there was no distinction between sacrifices and mere flesh
when offered by unworthy worshippers.

22. *I spake not.* Cf. similar statements in vi. 20, xi. 15, xiv. 12;
Am. v. 21—24; Hos. vi. 6, viii. 13; Is. i. 10—12, and Mic. vi. 6—8, and
see Additional Note below.

the day. The reference cannot be limited to the period actually
following the exodus from Egypt, but includes the wandering in the
wilderness.

23. The relation between Israel and Jehovah was one of mutual
benefit, the Divine aid and guidance was conditional, and depended on
the obedience of the people. In a similar way the Christian at his
baptism receives certain privileges from God and in return certain vows
are made on his behalf.

24. *they hearkened not.* Cornill points out that this *v.* is hard to
reconcile with the statement in ii. 2; cf. also xxii. 21.

stubbornness. See on iii. 17.

25 f. Very similar to xi. 7 f. and cf. Am. ii. 10, iii. 7 f.; Hos. xii. 13.

26. *worse than their fathers.* Cf. Hor. *Odes*, III. 6.

LORD their God, nor received [1]instruction: [2]truth is perished, and is cut off from their mouth.

[1] Or, *correction*   [2] Or, *faithfulness*

28. *This is the nation.* The history of Israel has been one continuous record of stubbornness and rebellion, and in his innermost heart the prophet knows that the future holds no prospect of improvement: cf. Ps. xii. 4, and Zeph. iii. 2 which is almost identical.

ADDITIONAL NOTE ON VII. 22.

Sacrifice in the Wilderness.

At first sight Jeremiah's statement, as we have it in EVV., that God gave no commands as to sacrifices and burnt offerings during the wilderness period is exceedingly startling and unexpected. Even the most drastic critic considers that some, at any rate, of the sacrifices went back to the exodus. What is the explanation? Before going on to consider the various answers to the enquiry, a somewhat similar statement in Am. v. 25 should be noticed. Amos, speaking in God's name, challenged the men of Israel 'Did ye bring unto me sacrifices and offerings in the wilderness?' obviously expecting an answer in the negative. 'Amos means that during the whole of the wilderness wanderings the Israelites did not bring Jahveh sacrifice or offering; from which it follows that sacrificial worship cannot be the indispensable condition of maintaining Jahveh's gracious relation toward Israel[1].' This passage therefore supports Jeremiah's contention. It should, however, be pointed out that the suggestion has been made that the passage is merely a statement that it was not sacrifices *only* that were offered, but also 'true worship of the heart and righteousness, public and private[2]'; and this explanation has been accepted by no less a critic than W. R. Harper, who says 'This rendering places the emphasis in its proper place and does not compel Amos to say that there were no sacrifices or offerings in the wilderness[3].'

The explanation of the meaning of Jeremiah's words which is current in the predominant school of criticism may be given in the words of Driver. 'When Jeremiah wrote, the priestly parts of the Pentateuch had in all probability not yet been combined with the rest of the Pentateuch, and the reference here is to the latter. Sacrifices are indeed enjoined in JE (Ex. xxiii. 14—19), and Deuteronomy, but little stress is laid upon them; and the *promises* (as here "in order that it may be well with you") are annexed more generally to loyalty

---

[1] E. A. Edghill, *Westminster Commentary ad loc.*

[2] Macdonald, *JBL.* XVIII. pp. 214 f.

[3] *Amos and Hosea* (*ICC.*), p. 136. Dr Harper here goes against the great majority of critics, amongst others Ewald, Wellhausen, G. A. Smith, Driver, Marti.

to Yahweh and the refusal to follow after other gods.' Against this explanation it may be urged that, in spite of Driver's distinction, Deuteronomy would be equally excluded by Jeremiah's statement, for it contains even in its oldest parts recognitions of the origin of sacrifice in the wilderness period (e.g. xii. 5 ff., 13, xv. 19 ff., xvi. 2, 5 ff., xvii. 1, &c.). For those who agree with Dr Kennett in placing the composition of Deuteronomy in the exilic period this argument of course raises no difficulty, but to the follower of the Wellhausen school it is distinctly inconvenient. Further, the very sacrifices mentioned by Jeremiah, 'burnt offerings or peace offerings' are named in the Book of the Covenant (Ex. xxiii. 14 ff.) as essential to the ritual of worship even in the earliest times. The present writer finds himself unable to agree with Driver that the less frequent commands in regard to sacrifice contained in Dt. and JE exclude them from the scope of Jeremiah's statement. The command to sacrifice is admittedly contained in them; and therefore it follows that either the books were unknown to the prophet; or else that he did not recognise their authority. It is quite possible to argue that Jeremiah, carried away by his hatred of the sacrificial system as he found it in his own day, refused to believe that it could have had a Divine origin; his accusations of forgery against the scribes (viii. 8) may have been called forth by their producing commands in the Book of the Covenant, for example, upholding the official cultus. Some such explanation as this seems necessary to the present writer if the *vv.* are to be translated as in EVV.

The question, however, of the meaning of the passage is by no means clear, and an alternative translation is grammatically possible; furthermore this translation avoids the difficulties involved in any explanation which may be suggested on behalf of the more usual rendering. The variation turns on the use of the Hebrew expression על־דבר which EVV., following LXX., translate *concerning*. Another meaning of the phrase is *because of, for the sake of*, which is the rendering in Gen. xii. 17 'the LORD plagued Pharaoh...*because of* (על־דבר) Sarai Abram's wife'; and in Dt. iv. 21 'the LORD was angry with me *for your sakes*' (על־דבריכם). In 2 S. xviii. 5 EVV. translate 'the king gave... charge *concerning* Absalom' (על־דבר), but the context supports the rendering '*for the sake of* Absalom' equally well, and is indeed the translation adopted by Kautzsch. In Jer. xiv. 1 the same phrase is used and translated '*concerning* the drought' (על־דברי הבצרות), but it would be quite in keeping with the context to render it '*on account of* the drought.' If this meaning is attached to the phrase in the present passage, Jeremiah's statement would then be rendered 'I spake not unto your fathers...*for the sake of* or *on account of* burnt offerings.' In other words the prophet is emphasising the fact that God did not reveal Himself to the people in order to obtain their sacrifices, a rendering which obtains support from *v.* 21; the two *vv.* might be paraphrased 'eat your own meat yourselves, God doesn't want it.' The same lesson exactly is taught in Ps. l. 12 f. 'If I were hungry, I would not tell thee: for the world is mine and all the fulness thereof.' God wanted the hearts of His people not their offerings. This is the reality underlying all sacrifice, and where the thing symbolised is lacking, the symbol is but a mockery and intrinsically valueless. That it seems to me was Jeremiah's meaning in this passage; he was not denying the cherished belief of the people that the sacrificial system was of Divine origin, but he was trying to restore to them a worthy notion of the meaning of that system. 'In the writings of Jeremiah, on the eve of the long exile, when the sacrificial ritual became impossible, it was natural in the order of divine Providence that the realities symbolised by sacrifices should be brought into prominence[1].'

29 Cut off [1]thine hair, *O Jerusalem*, and cast it away, and take up a lamentation on the bare heights; for the LORD hath rejected and forsaken the generation of his wrath. 30 For the children of Judah have done that which is evil in my sight, saith the LORD: they have set their abominations in the house which is called by my name, to defile it. 31 And they have built the

[1] Heb. *thy crown.*

29—31. Jerusalem is called upon to lament because God has forsaken her.

29. No person is named in the text but the verbs are fem. sing. in the Hebrew and there can be little doubt that the section is an appeal directed to Jerusalem (as EVV. take it) or to some personification of the nation.

hair. Heb. *crown.* Cf. Job i. 20; Mic. i. 16. Keil sees in this command a reference to the Nazirite's vow (Nu. vi. 7). Jerusalem has broken her vows and so, like a faithless Nazirite, she may also cut off the hair which was their symbol.

take up. Cf. Nu. xxiii. 7, &c., and the word משׂא=burden used of a discourse (xxiii. 33 ff.).

lamentation. Heb. *Qinah*: the special form of verse used in Hebrew elegies (see E. G. King, *Early Religious Poetry of the Hebrews*, pp. 39 ff.). Jeremiah often adopts it as a medium for his prophecies but it hardly seems necessary, with Duhm, to reject those prophecies which are not written in this metre.

bare heights. See on iii. 31.

generation of his wrath. The generation upon whom the accumulated anger of God is about to fall—a strange phrase[2].

30. *abominations.* See on iv. 1. Giesebrecht thinks that there is here a reference to the doings of Manasseh (2 K. xxi. 5, 7). This may well be so, but it would be easier to imagine that Jeremiah had in mind the evils of his own day. In the time between the two captures of Jerusalem evils were practised which seem exactly to fit the terms of this condemnation; cf. Ez. viii. and for similar language v. 11, vii. 20.

[1] Westcott on Hebrews viii. 12.
[2] LXX. τὴν ποιοῦσαν ταῦτα evidently read עָשָׂה זֹאת.

high places of Topheth, which is in the valley of the son of Hinnom, to burn their sons and their daughters in the fire; which I commanded not, neither came it into my [1]mind. 32 Therefore, behold, the days come, saith the LORD, that it shall no more be called Topheth, nor The valley of the son of Hinnom, but The valley of Slaughter: for they shall bury in Topheth, [2]till there

[1] Heb. *heart*.   [2] Or, *because there shall be no place else*

31. *Topheth.* LXX. Ταφέθ seems to point to a different vocalisation and it is very probable that the word was read as *Bosheth* and that the Massoretes retained the consonants of the original word but pointed them with the vowels of בֹּשֶׁת. It is to be noticed that in xxxii. 35 *Baal* is read in a similar phrase instead of *Topheth*, and *Bosheth* is often used as being equivalent to *Baal* (see on iii. 24). Many scholars connect the word with an Aramaic root meaning 'fire-place'; cf. Is. xxx. 33 and Wade's note.

valley of the son of Hinnom. The meaning and origin of the name are lost though various attempts have been made to recover them; cf. Rashi, 'the son of *sobbing.*' Graf also would derive it from the Arabic *hanna* 'to whimper.' A similar disagreement exists as to the site of the valley; some experts identify it with the Tyropoeon, the central of the three valleys which meet at the pool of Siloam (so Robertson Smith, *Enc. Brit.*[9] and Sayce, *PEFQS.* 1883, p. 213); others prefer the Kidron which runs parallel to it to the East (so Warren, *HDB.* II. 287); the greater number of modern scholars however are in favour of its identification with the *Wâdy er-Rabâbî* which runs below the SW. corner of Jerusalem (Wilson, Smith's *DB.*[2]; Buhl, *Pal.* 132). For the arguments in support of the various views see *HDB.* and *Enc. Bib.* ('Hinnom' and 'Jerusalem'). Many legends have clustered round this valley, amongst them being that of a subterranean fire which lay below Gehenna and which was to be the scene of the punishment of apostate Jews: cf. Enoch xlvii. 6, xlviii. 9; Matt. v. 29 f., and see Weber, *Jüd. Theol.* pp. 341 ff.

burn their sons and their daughters. See on iii. 24; Wade's note on Is. lvii. 5; and W. R. Smith, *Rel. Sem.*[2] p. 464.

32—34. The recital of the sins of Israel is an introduction to the statement of the terrible punishment which is about to overtake them. The scene of the slaughter of their innocent children is to be the scene of their own slaughter. This is an instance of 'the principle of compensation' in punishment which the writer of Wisdom is so fond of declaring: 'by what things a man sinneth by these he is punished' (xi. 16; cf. xii. 23, xvi. 1; also Philo, *Vit. Mos.* I. 17).

32. *bury in Topheth.* Driver explains that 'the land will be so full of corpses that they will have to be buried even in the unclean place of Topheth.' (Following the reading of mg. which represents the original better than does the text.) Against this it may be argued that

be no place *to bury*. 33 And the carcases of this people shall
be meat for the fowls of the heaven, and for the beasts of the
earth; and none shall fray them away. 34 Then will I cause to
cease from the cities of Judah, and from the streets of Jerusalem,
the voice of mirth and the voice of gladness, the voice of the
bridegroom and the voice of the bride: for the land shall become
a waste.

VIII. 1 At that time, saith the LORD, they shall bring out the
bones of the kings of Judah, and the bones of his princes, and
the bones of the priests, and the bones of the prophets, and the
bones of the inhabitants of Jerusalem, out of their graves: 2 and
they shall spread them before the sun, and the moon, and all the
host of heaven, whom they have loved, and whom they have served,

those who had offered sacrifice there would hardly look upon the place
as unclean. The real meaning of the *v.* is obscure and the text possibly
corrupt. Duhm rejects the *v.* as an *ex post facto* explanation of the
custom of burying in Topheth.

33. *fray.* Old English = frighten away: cf. the action of Rizpah
(2 S. xxi. 10). The word occurs also in Dt. xxviii. 26; Zech. i. 21;
1 Macc. xiv. 12, &c.

34. Jeremiah had a deep appreciation of the joys which life affords;
he was no mere pessimist and harbinger of woe whose only desire was
to make others as miserable as himself.

VIII. 1—3. The graves of the princes and of the people are to be
desecrated and their corpses spread out before the heavenly bodies whom
they had vainly worshipped.

1. All classes of the population had sinned and therefore punishment would fall upon all, even the dead were not exempt. The exposing
of a dead body was considered to entail dreadful consequences on the
spirit to whom it belonged. The desecration here spoken of may have
been deliberate and intended as a further insult to the defeated who
were thus shewn to be incapable of defending either 'the ashes of
their fathers' or 'the temple of their God'; or it may have occurred in
the search for buried treasure. Asshurbanipal warned his enemies that
his enmity would follow them even into the grave ; *KB.* II. 193.

2. *spread.* Cf. Aeschylus, *Choephorae*, 980 ff. where Orestes lays
the instruments of guilt beside the dead bodies of his father's murderers
in the sight of 'the all-seeing-sun.'

before the sun. Cf. Nu. xxv. 4; 2 S. xii. 12.

sun. Sun worship according to H. P. Smith, *Religion of Israel*,
p. 68, is not a Syrian custom though traces of it are found in place
names (e.g. Beth-shemesh), because the sun is hostile to the crops rather
than favourable.

host of heaven. Cf. xix. 13. This worship is usually held to be a

and after whom they have walked, and whom they have sought, and whom they have worshipped: they shall not be gathered, nor be buried; they shall be for dung upon the face of the earth. 3 And death shall be chosen rather than life by all the residue that remain of this evil family, which remain in all the places whither I have driven them, saith the LORD of hosts.

late innovation though it soon became popular and appears to have been much in favour with the later kings of Judah: cf. Zeph. i. 5; Ez. viii. 16. The very means by which men were intended to be led to worship the Creator became a snare to drag them down into idolatry: cf. St Athanasius, *de Inc.* XII. 3 Ἐξὸν οὖν ἦν ἀναβλέψαντας αὐτοὺς εἰς τὸ μέγεθος τοῦ οὐρανοῦ...γνῶναι τὸν ταύτης ἡγεμόνα. The worship of the *host of heaven* was not altogether an unprofitable piece of superstition; through their worship men began to take an intense interest in the movements of the divine beings by whom they imagined their lives were influenced, and so arose the first attempts at a scientific study of the stars. The superstitions of the astrologer laid the foundation for the discoveries of the astronomer, and at the same time provided him with material—in the shape of early observations—by which his calculations could be tested and verified.

whom they have loved &c. The prophet in bitter irony enumerates these witnesses of the future dishonour of the nation—the very powers upon whose aid the people were relying for their safety. The heaping up of verbs describing the foolishness of the people adds to the irony.

dung. Always used of unburied corpses; cf. ix. 2, xvi. 4, &c.

3. This *v.* presents a picture of the absolute and utter despair into which the nation will fall. They will long for death as for 'hid treasures' (Job iii. 21; cf. vii. 15), and death itself 'will flee from them' (Rev. ix. 6).

CHAPTERS VIII. 4—IX. 1.

The Penalty of National Sin is National Ruin.

This section relates apparently to the same situation as the former one; Cornill, indeed, thinks that it must be looked upon as a variant account of the preceding temple-sermon, though he does not deny that it comes from Jeremiah himself. In the last few *vv.* of the previous section (vii. 29—viii. 3) the prophet had given a description of the doom which will come upon the nation; in the opening *vv.* of this section he describes once again the sins of the people which are bringing it about. In doing so he lays stress in the manner of Isaiah (cf. Is. i. 3), on the faithfulness of the members of the animal creation to the instincts which govern them; in contrast to this the faithlessness of Judah becomes all the more unnatural. The section ends with a picture of hopeless ruin and incurable sin such as to call forth the tears of the speaker himself as he condemns it.

(a) *The contrast between man and the fowls of the air.* 4—9.
(b) *The benumbing terror of the invasion.* 10—17.
(c) *The prophet's distress.* 18—ix. 1.

4 Moreover thou shalt say unto them, Thus saith the LORD: Shall men fall, and not rise up again? shall one turn away, and not return? 5 Why then is this people of Jerusalem slidden back by a perpetual backsliding? they hold fast deceit, they refuse to return. 6 I hearkened and heard, but they spake not aright: no man repenteth him of his wickedness, saying, What have I done? every one ¹turneth to his course, as a horse that rusheth headlong in the battle. 7 Yea, the stork in the heaven knoweth

¹ Or, *turneth away in his course*

4—9. Jehovah complains of the heedlessness of the men of Judah who rely on their privileges and refuse to repent and to seek after Him; the bitter contrast with the birds of the heaven.

4. *Shall men fall* &c. In the ordinary affairs of life if a man makes a mistake or follows a course of conduct which turns out to be unprofitable he retraces his steps as best he can; so it was to have been expected that Judah would have already given heed to the warnings which had come to her. The comparison is between the conduct of an individual in his practical life and of a nation in its religious life. St Chrysostom argued from this *v.* that no sinner need ever despair of repentance.

5. *of Jerusalem.* LXX. omits.

deceit. Israel not only refuses to *rise up again*; she will not even admit the possibility of a *fall*. It was this self-deceit which made repentance impossible: cf. v. 3, vii. 28, ix. 6.

6. *I hearkened and heard.* God Himself is waiting to hear the first cry of penitence—and He waits in vain. The men of Judah counted His 'longsuffering' as mere 'slackness' and refused to return; cf. 2 Pet. iii. 9.

as a horse. A very forcible picture of men continuing in sin: cf. ii. 23 f. for the use of a somewhat similar figure; and for a description of the glory of the war-horse see Job xxxix. 21—25.

7. The failure of Judah to return to God reminds Jeremiah by contrast of the sudden, yet regular, return of the various migratory birds in response to the voice of instinct within them; 'they remain faithful to their land, Israel...returns not to Jehovah' (Duhm). This obedience on the part of the animal creation further suggests to him that Judah, with all the privilege, not of an implanted instinct, but of an open ordinance, fails to practise a like obedience to God. The prophet

her appointed times; and the turtle and the swallow and the crane observe the time of their coming; but my people know not the [1]ordinance of the LORD. 8 How do ye say, We are wise,

[1] Or, *judgement*

does not, however, intend to teach that sinning and repentance are both part of the natural relation between man and God, and therefore to be accepted as inevitable, like the flight and return of the birds. Dante, too, has noticed the obedience of birds to their instincts:

> 'doves, when love its call has given,
> With open steady wings to their sweet nest
> Fly.'   *Inf.* v. 82 ff.

stork. Two species of stork are found in Palestine, the White which is a passing visitor 'usually met with during the month of April,' and the Black which though a native is little known from its habit of living in the desert away from human habitations.

turtle. Seven species of dove are found in Palestine. Dr Shipley thinks that the reference here is to the *Turtur communis* or *auritus*, the most common dove in Palestine to which it begins to return in April (*Enc. Bib.* 1130). Its coming marks the approach of spring (Cant. ii. 12).

swallow. This bird returns to Palestine about the same time as the stork and the turtle.

crane. Noted for the 'loud and trumpet-like sounds' to which it gives utterance.

8.   This *v.* is a difficult one to explain; there is no doubt however, if the true meaning of the original text is still preserved, that in it Jeremiah repudiates the authority of *the law of the Lord* which was recognised by the leaders of the people, and even accuses the scribes of deliberate forgery. The word for *law* as explained above (see on ii. 8) means 'direction' and the reference here must be to some written body of such traditional 'direction.' It is possible that the prophet had in mind 'the book of direction' found in the temple by Hilkiah (2 K. xxii. 8); this is the opinion of Marti, Wellhausen, Duhm, Cornill and other critics who identify the book, at any rate in part, with Deuteronomy. If their theories are correct the traditions thus condemned now form part of our Canonical Scriptures. On the other hand the reference may be to a deliberate attempt on the part of opposing prophets to falsify the law (so Klamroth, *Die jüdischen Exulanten in Babylonien*). Driver suggests that the scribes brought this accusation upon themselves 'by claiming to have Yahweh's sanction for practices or ceremonial usages, of which in reality He did not approve' (cf. vii. 22). In a somewhat similar way the early Christians accused each other of altering the words of Scripture and even of inventing new gospels, though the extent to which these accusations were made has probably been exaggerated (cf. Origen, *c. Cels.* ii. 27).

We are wise. Cf. Is. v. 21; Prov. iii. 7 'Be not wise in thine own eyes.'

and the law of the LORD is with us? But, behold,'the false pen of the scribes hath [1]wrought falsely. 9 The wise men are ashamed, they are dismayed and taken: lo, they have rejected the word of the LORD; and what manner of wisdom is in them? 10 Therefore will I give their wives unto others, and their fields to them that shall possess them: for every one from the least even unto the greatest is given to covetousness, from the prophet even unto the priest every one dealeth falsely. 11 [2]And they have healed the hurt of the daughter of my people lightly, saying, Peace, peace; when there is no peace. 12 Were they ashamed when they had committed abomination? nay, they were not at all ashamed, neither could they blush: therefore shall they fall among them that fall: in the time of their visitation they shall be cast down, saith the LORD. 13 I will utterly consume them, saith the LORD: there shall be no grapes on the vine, nor figs on the fig tree, and the leaf shall fade; and [3]*the things that* I have given them shall pass away from them. 14 Why do we sit

---

[1] Or, *made* of it *falsehood*   [2] See ch. vi. 14, 15.
[3] Or, *I have appointed them those that shall pass over them*

scribes. This is the first occasion on which the scribes are referred to as a professional class in OT. For further particulars as to their functions and the part which they played in the development of Hebrew religion see Lightley, *Les Scribes*; Schürer, *The Jewish People* &c. (ET.), II. i. 306—379; Oesterley, *The Books of the Apocrypha*, pp. 113 ff.

9. The best commentary on this *v.* is Prov. i. 7 'The fear of the Lord is the beginning of wisdom'; but to despise or reject His counsel soon leads to misfortune.

10—17. This section gives a picture of the utter despair into which the people have fallen; they are resigned to their fate and are simply waiting for the invader to come upon them without any hope of being able to resist him.

10—12. These *vv.* are not found in LXX. and are closely parallel to vi. 12—15.

13. *no grapes.* The vine and fig-tree are here, as in Joel i. 7 (cf. Matt. xxi. 19), emblems of that prosperity and ease to which they contributed. There does not seem to be in this *v.*, as in some passages (e.g. Is. v. 7; Mic. vii. 1), any reference to the religious state of the nation.

I have given. Taking RV. as it stands the sense of the *v.* is that of Hos. ii. 12 'I will lay waste her vines and her fig-trees, whereof she hath said, These are my hire that my lovers have given me.' The source of God's gifts will be recognised only by their withdrawal. The

still? assemble yourselves, and let us enter into the defenced
cities, and let us [1]be silent there: for the LORD our God hath
[2]put us to silence, and given us water of [3]gall to drink, because
we have sinned against the LORD. 15 We looked for peace, but
no good came; *and* for a time of healing, and behold dismay!
16 The snorting of his horses is heard from Dan: at the sound
of the neighing of his strong ones the whole land trembleth;
for they are come, and have devoured the land and all that is in
it; the city and those that dwell therein. 17 For, behold, I will
send serpents, [4]basilisks, among you, which will not be charmed;
and they shall bite you, saith the LORD.

[1] Or, *perish*   [2] Or, *caused us to perish*
[3] See Deut. xxix. 18.   [4] Or, *adders*

MT. is however very obscure and Dr Streane thinks that ' it is perhaps
the corruption of an interpolation.'
14 f. The doomed people are suddenly introduced, and the prophet
represents them as addressing one another in terms which shew that
they are prepared to meet the punishment which they now recognise
as being brought upon them by their own sins. The expectation of
peace which had been fostered amongst them by the false prophets is
seen to be vain, no peace was possible to a guilty people.
14.   *assemble yourselves* &c. Cf. iv. 5.
silent...silence. The mg. *perish...caused us to perish* is to be preferred. The horrors and sufferings of a besieged city would be a subject
of common knowledge.
gall. The same threat is used in ix. 15, where see note, and in
xxiii. 15; the latter passage represents *gall* as the portion of the
prophets themselves.
15. = xiv. 19 *b*.
16.   *Dan.* Dan in the far North has already been reached by the
foe and so certain is their approach that the land is already as good as
destroyed: cf. iv. 15. Irenaeus, v. xxx. 2 takes this *v.* to mean that
Dan is Anti-Christ, an old idea—founded possibly on the evil reputation
of the tribe—which finds expression in Rev. vii. 5—8 where Dan is
missing from the tribes in heaven. The connexion is first declared in
Test. Dan. v. 6 (where see Charles' note).
strong ones. i.e. war-horses as the parallelism shews; cf. Job xxxix.
19, &c.
17.   *basilisks.* LXX. renders θανατοῦντας and connects with the
previous word, i.e. *deadly serpents.*
be charmed. Cf. Ps. lviii. 5 which represents the same idea though
the Hebrew word for ' charm ' is different.
The connexion between *v.* 16 and *v.* 17 seems to be rather slight,
and the whole section is a strange mixture of actual and figurative

18 Oh that I could comfort myself against sorrow! my heart
is faint within me. 19 Behold, the voice of the cry of the daughter
of my people ¹from a land that is very far off : Is not the LORD
in Zion? is not her King in her? Why have they provoked me
to anger with their graven images, and with strange vanities?
20 The harvest is past, the ²summer is ended, and we are not

¹ Or, *because of*　　　　² Or, *ingathering of summer fruits*

description. But such a confusion is not sufficient to impugn the
integrity of the passage; in the mind of the prophet images and figures
followed each other in so rapid a succession that he had no time to
question their literary suitability or even their connexion one with
another.

18—IX. 1 (= 18—23 Heb.). As in iv. 19 the description of the
coming invader is followed by a revelation of the prophet's own feelings.
He bewails the future disaster which he is unable to prevent, and his
agitation is shewn in the repeated questions which he piles one upon
another without waiting for an answer; cf. *vv.* 19 *b*, 22.

18. *Oh…comfort myself.* Lit. *Alas! my brightness.* The meaning of
the word had been lost by the Jews and has been restored from a cognate
root in Arabic; see further Driver's note on Amos v. 9.

sorrow. Cornill points out that Jeremiah does not say *my* sorrow;
it is not a personal, but a national, grief which is vexing the soul of the
prophet.

faint. The word occurs here and Is. i. 5; and Lam. i. 22.

19. In *v.* 14 Jeremiah introduced the lament of the people when
they discovered the invincible approach of the invader; now he carries
his dramatic depiction of the future a stage further, and in imagination
he hears the desolate cry of the exiles proclaiming that Jehovah has
forsaken Zion and that the Divine sovereign no longer defends Jerusalem.
It may well be however that the cries are uttered by the prophet himself.

land that is very far off. The Hebrew is better translated *from a
wide spreading land*; i.e. from the length and breadth of the land¹.

King. The reference is doubtless to Jehovah and not to a human
king. Jeremiah was much more of a religionist than a royalist. Cf.
Mic. iv. 9: 'Is there no king in thee?'

20. The prophet is here, it may be, quoting a popular proverb the
meaning of which is easy to understand. When the *harvest*, which
extended from April to June, was a failure there still remained hopes
from the ingathering of *summer* fruits which came later; but once this
was past there was no further possibility of recovery. Duhm thinks that
the reference is historical rather than proverbial, and that the Scythians

---

¹ The phrase (ארץ מרחקים) is the same as that used in Is. xxxiii. 17; and
contains no necessary idea of exile. The RV. represents ארץ מרחק (so read by LXX.)
which is the reading in iv. 16, vi. 20.

saved. 21 For the hurt of the daughter of my people am I hurt:
I am ¹black; astonishment hath taken hold on me. 22 Is there
no balm in Gilead? is there no physician there? why then is not
the ²health of the daughter of my people ³recovered?

IX. 1 Oh that my head were waters, and mine eyes a fountain

¹ Or, *mourning*   ² Or, *healing*   ³ Or, *perfected* Heb. *gone up.*

invaded the land in the spring and remained in possession of it until
after the ingathering.

saved. No ethical content can be given to the word in this context;
the reference is to material welfare.

21. The prophet, by reason of the sin of his people, feels compelled
to pass his days in one long mourning; cf. xv. 17.

black. The word is often used of the sky or the heavenly bodies
being darkened (as in iv. 28); here the reference is to the sad and
gloomy appearance of those in sorrow, hence mg. *mourning.*

22. *balm.* This rendering of the Hebrew word צֳרִי is found in
Coverdale's *Bible.* Cf. Shakespeare's use in *Richard II*, Act III. Sc. 2,

> 'Not all the water in the rough, rude sea
> Can wash the balm from an anointed king.'

The actual product referred to by the original is not known with
any certainty. Mr McLean following the Arabic usage suggests mastic,
the resin from the tree *Pistacia Lentiscus* (*Enc. Bib.* 465); the more
usual suggestion is that צֳרִי is balsam, but this product was apparently
not found in Gilead. The connexion of *balm* with healing occurs here,
in v. 8 and in xlvi. 11. It was evidently very highly valued, being
amongst the presents sent by Jacob to Joseph (Gen. xliii. 11). For
other references and comments see Nowack, *Arch.* I. xiv. 2; Conder,
Heth and Moab, p. 88; also Pliny, *Hist. Nat.* XII. 25, XXIV. 22: and for
the connexion between anointing and healing Dr Knowling's note on
Jas. v. 14.

Gilead. The mountainous district beyond Jordan, and amongst the
first of the Israelite territories to fall to the Assyrians (2 K. xv. 29).
See note on xxii. 6.

physician. The high opinion of *physicians* expressed in Ecclus.
xxxviii. 1 ff. was not accepted by all the later Jews; cf. 2 Chr. xvi. 12;
Tobit ii. 10 (B and א), and the Rabbinic opinion that the best of them
was worthy of Gehenna, *Kidushim*, iv. 14.

health. The Hebrew word suggests the fresh flesh gradually *lengthening* (i.e. forming) over a wound.

Gilead the home of skilled physicians and healing medicines is not
able to provide for the hurt of her own children.

IX. 1. (Heb. viii. 23.) This *v.* is the culmination of the prophet's
grief and should certainly be attached as in the Hebrew to what
goes before. Jeremiah's sorrow over Israel reads like an anticipation of
Rom. ix. 2, x. 1. This *v.* was a favourite one with the Apocalyptic

of tears, that I might weep day and night for the slain of the
daughter of my people!

writers and it is even put into the mouth of Baruch (2 Bar. xxxv. 2)
and of Enoch (En. xcv. 1).

fountain of tears. Cf. the representations on Egyptian monuments
of women weeping with long lines drawn from their eyes to suggest the
tears bursting forth from them.

weep day and night. Cf. xl. 6; Is. xxii. 4; Mic. i. 8 f.

CHAPTER IX. 2—26.

The Treachery of the People and its Sequel.

This section apparently continues the previous one, and, like it, comes from
a period when the prophet was undergoing or had undergone much opposition
and persecution. The closing *vv.* of the section have evidently become detached
from their context and consist of two unconnected fragments, *vv.* 23 f. and 25 f.
The continuation of *v.* 22 is to be found in x. 17 as the section x. 1—16 is of
late date (see Introd. to that section).

(a)   *The prophet longs to escape to a place of quiet.* 2—9.
(b)   *A lamentation over the destruction of Judah.* 10—16.
(c)   *A call for the professional mourners.* 17—22.
(d)   *The vanity of wisdom and privilege.* 23—26.

2   [1]Oh that I had in the wilderness a lodging place of way-

---

[1] Or, *Oh that I were in the wilderness, in &c.*

2—9. The treachery and deceit of the men of Judah cause the
prophet to give up all hope of the return of the people to God.

There is perhaps nothing so heart-breaking as the despair of
a sincerely religious man; the despair of one who feels that in spite
of all the resources of nature and of grace nothing further can be done
for those amongst whom he dwells, and that like Lot he himself must
flee from out of the midst of the doomed city. History furnishes
numerous examples of those who followed such a course of action and
amongst them it will perhaps be sufficient to mention the countless
numbers who found in the retirement of the convent a refuge from the
corruption of Roman society; and nearer our own time, those who
braved the dangers of the wintry sea and the unknown terrors of
a strange continent, in order that they might be alone and enjoy peace
and freedom of conscience. The motive which made Jeremiah long
for a lodge in the wilderness was the same as that which animated the
minds both of the founders of Western monasticism and of the Pilgrim
Fathers.

faring men; that I might leave my people, and go from them!
for they be all adulterers, an assembly of treacherous men.

The attractions of solitude have been well expressed by Hogg in
his poem *On the Skylark*:

> 'Bird of the wilderness
> Blythesome and cumberless
> Sweet be thy matins o'er moorland and lea!
> Emblem of happiness,
> Blest is thy dwelling-place,
> O to abide in the desert with thee.'

The treachery from which the prophet wished to flee was partly the
product partly the cause of the devious course which the leaders of the
people were following.   It is quite true to say that the foreign politics
of a nation are influenced by the national character, but these in their
turn react upon it. The rulers had lost their faith in God as the
guardian and director of the State and had come to rely on their own
plots and political stratagems for national salvation.   The necessities
of the situation made it impossible to conduct such a policy without
the employment of methods of treachery and deceit, and these methods
and ideals descended to the common people and found expression in
their dealings one with another.   International politics must have
been followed with close attention by all classes of the community and
indeed the relations of Judah with Egypt on the one hand and Babylon
on the other doubtless formed the staple of conversation with every
travelling merchant in the bazaar.

2. *in the wilderness.*   Cf. Job xxxviii. 26 'the wilderness where
there is no man'; Ps. lv. 6 f., where the metaphor of the dove is
abandoned for that of the traveller, probably, as Dr Briggs thinks, under
the influence of the present passage.

lodging place. A place of temporary shelter where travellers would
pass a night or so before going on their way, a khan or caravanserai[1].
The prophet's words however suggest that he wished to leave his
people and not to return to them : but one must not press the logic of
words which come from lips of suffering.

that I might leave &c. Jeremiah knew well the feeling which was
expressed by the Dominican monk Eckhardt when he said that 'a crowd
is often more lonely than a wilderness.'

assembly. The Hebrew word is one which is used of religious
assemblies, and its use in this context is an instance of the prophet's
irony, an irony which comes from the bitter experience of his own
heart. The later Jews used the word as a term for the Feast of
Weeks; cf. Joseph. *Ant.* III. x. 6, &c. and see the note in Driver's
Deut. p. 195.

treacherous men.   Cf. Mic. vii. 2 and see above.

---

[1] Cf. Spenser, *The Faery Queen*, Bk II. xii. 32 :
> 'This is the port of rest from troublous toil,
> The world's sweet inn from pain and wearisome turmoil.'

3 And they bend their tongue *as it were* their bow for falsehood; and they are grown strong in the land, but not for
¹truth: for they proceed from evil to evil, and they know not
me, saith the LORD.   4 Take ye heed every one of his neighbour, and trust ye not in any brother: for every brother will
utterly supplant, and every neighbour will go about with slanders.
5 And they will ²deceive every one his neighbour, and will not
speak the truth: they have taught their tongue to speak lies;
they weary themselves to commit iniquity.   6 Thine habitation
is in the midst of deceit; through deceit they refuse to know
me, saith the LORD.

¹ Or, *faithfulness*   ² Or, *mock*

3.   In this *v. falsehood*, whether in word or conduct, is denounced
because of the practical evil in which it results (cf. Mic. vi. 12; Ps.
lii. 4), not on any ground of the value of truth as such.   According to
Dr Briggs it was not until Persian influence began to be felt that the
Jews regarded lying as being ethically wrong; see his note on Ps. lii. 4
in *ICC*.

bend.   Tread with the foot: cf. Ps. lxiv. 3.

truth.   Better *faithfulness* as in margin.   See note on v. 1.

4.   *supplant.*   The Hebrew suggests a reference to Gen. xxvii. 36;
Every brother will prove a very Jacob.   It was perhaps to counteract
the impression produced by this aspect of the patriarch's character that
he is later referred to as Jeshurun, i.e. the upright one (Dt. xxxiii. 4 f.,
cf. Hos. xii. 4).

The prophet's own experience was to teach him the full meaning
of the treachery of friends and even kinsfolk (xi. 18 ff.: cf. Mic. vii. 5f.).
Peake suggests that this whole section (ix. 2—22) does not belong to
the earliest time of Jeremiah's ministry as it seems to pre-suppose
'a great deal of unhappy experience¹.'

5.   *deceive.*   Better as mg. *mock*; so Gen. xxxi. 7.

taught their tongue.   God has given to each of us our various
members to be used in His service (cf. Eph. iv. 25), any other use of
them is misuse.

6.   *Thine habitation.*   LXX. by dividing up the letters of the
Hebrew into different words includes part of this word in *v.* 5 and
accordingly gives a different translation of the *vv.* viz. *they committed
iniquity and ceased not to turn aside.*   (*v.* 6) *Oppression on oppression
and deceit on deceit* &c.

they refuse to know me.   God is the God of Truth and can only be
known and comprehended by those who are truth loving and truth

¹ יְהָלֹךְ is the Qal impft. fuller form for the more usual יֵלֵךְ as so often in
Job (xiv. 20, &c.).

7 Therefore thus saith the LORD of hosts, Behold, I will melt them, and try them; for how *else* should I do, because of the daughter of my people? 8 Their tongue is a deadly arrow; it speaketh deceit: one speaketh peaceably to his neighbour with his mouth, but in his heart he layeth wait for him. 9 Shall I not visit them for these things? saith the LORD: shall not my soul be avenged on such a nation as this?

10 For the mountains will I take up a weeping and wailing, and for the pastures of the wilderness a lamentation, because they are burned up, so that none passeth through; neither can

seeking. They who love deceit and darkness by their very preference thrust the knowledge of God away from them.

7. *melt* (Driver, *smelt*). Assaying includes besides the idea of purifying, that of fusing the scattered metal contained in the ore, and the rejection of the useless fragments. What was useful was purified and amalgamated, what was useless was thrown away (cf. Is. i. 25). Jeremiah, like Michaelangelo in his poems, is very fond of this metaphor of the refining fire of the goldsmith: see further on vi. 29.

8. *arrow*. Cf. *v.* 4 where the tongue is compared to a bent bow which shoots out the arrow of *falsehood*, here the tongue itself is the arrow as being the source of the mischief which is done. The metaphor is very common in Pss. (xii. 2, xxviii. 3, lv. 21, &c.).

peaceably (Heb. שָׁלוֹם). Dr Briggs in a note on Ps. xxviii. 3 points out that this word is used in several different ways each of which requires a different translation in English: (1) soundness, health; (2) welfare, prosperity; (3) quiet, peacefulness, tranquillity, security; (4) peace, alliance, friendship between man and man; (5) peace with God; (6) peace from war.

9. The refrain is repeated from v. 9, 29; cf. Is. i. 24.

10—16. This section has striking similarities to iv. 23—26 both in matter and diction: in the present passage Judah and Jerusalem are definitely named, and the reason is given for the utter ruin which is to overtake them.

10. *mountains*. Jeremiah mourns for the mountains because of their destruction; Ezekiel denounces them because of the profane rites of which they were the scene (vi. 2 f.).

lamentation. See note on vii. 29.

burned up. Not necessarily to be taken literally, means *to be desolate, laid waste*; cf. ii. 15, where it is used of the cities of Israel and *v.* 12 where the land is said to be 'burned up like a wilderness.' However it is to be remembered that the dry grass which clothed the pastures of the wilderness was very inflammable and that a fire once started would often cover whole tracts of country. The Arabs are said to put to death even the innocent originator of such a fire (cf. Burckhardt, *Travels in Syria*, pp. 331 f.).

men hear the voice of the cattle; both the fowl of the heavens
and the beast are fled, they are gone. 11 And I will make
Jerusalem heaps, a dwelling place of jackals; and I will make
the cities of Judah a desolation, without inhabitant. 12 Who is
the wise man, that may understand this? and *who is* he to whom
the mouth of the LORD hath spoken, that he may declare it?
wherefore is the land perished and burned up like a wilderness,
so that none passeth through?

13 And the LORD saith, Because they have forsaken my law
which I set before them, and have not obeyed my voice, neither
walked therein; 14 but have walked after the stubbornness of
their own heart, and after the Baalim, which their fathers taught
them: 15 therefore thus saith the LORD of hosts, the God of

11. *jackals.* There are constant references to jackals in OT.
especially in connexion with deserted sites; e.g. Is. xiii. 22, xxv. 2,
xxxiv. 13, &c. Kinglake makes some interesting observations on their
habits: 'These brutes,' he says, 'swarm in every part of Syria; and
there were many of them even in the midst of those void sands which
would seem to give such poor promise of food. I can hardly tell what
prey they could be hoping for, unless it were that they might find now
and then the carcass of some camel that had died on the journey.
They do not marshal themselves into great packs like the wild dogs of
Eastern cities, but follow their prey in families like the place-hunters
of Europe.' *Eothen*, p. 150. See also the articles in *Enc. Bib.* and
HDB.

12—16. This passage is rejected as a whole by Duhm and Giesebrecht and as to parts by Cornill and Rothstein; it is a prose section
embedded in a piece of verse. It may be that the passage is a gloss
intended to point the moral, or it may be that it is here introduced
into a wrong context on account of the similarity of wording between
v. 12 and *v.* 10. *vv.* 13—16 especially are objected to as an editorial
addition giving a conventional answer to the question of *v.* 12 and
consisting of a string of quotations in the style and manner of Deuteronomy.

12. *Who is the wise man.* Is this a challenge to those who boasted
that their 'lips still possessed knowledge'? The land was evidently
suffering from drought and the recognised teachers were unable, or
unwilling, to give any satisfactory reason for it. It is a call to consider the works of the Lord in which alone is wisdom to be found;
Ps. cvii. 43; Hos. xiv. 9.

14. *their fathers.* Cornill points out that by this phrase Jeremiah
usually means the generation of the exile, here the reference must be
to those who settled in the Promised Land.

Israel, Behold, I will feed them, even this people, with wormwood, and give them water of ¹gall to drink. 16 I will scatter them also among the nations, whom neither they nor their fathers have known: and I will send the sword after them, till I have consumed them.

17 Thus saith the LORD of hosts, Consider ye, and call for the mourning women, that they may come; and send for the cunning women, that they may come: 18 and let them make haste, and take up a wailing for us, that our eyes may run down with tears, and our eyelids gush out with waters. 19 For a voice of wailing is heard out of Zion, How are we spoiled! we are greatly confounded, because we have forsaken the land, because ²they have cast down our dwellings. 20 Yet hear the word of

---

¹ See ch. viii. 14.   ² Or, *our dwellings have cast* us *out*

---

15. *feed...to drink.* Cf. Ps. lxxx. 5 'Thou hast fed them with the bread of tears, And given them tears to drink.' The same punishment is promised to the false prophets (xxiii. 15).

wormwood...water of gall. These two words appear constantly together as a metaphor for some disagreeable experience; indeed what is said of *wormwood* is true of both. 'The references to it in OT. are so purely symbolical, that we learn nothing but that it was an edible substance of extreme bitterness.' *Enc. Bib.* 5355.

17—22. The call for the mourning women, and the contents of the dirges which they are bidden to chant.

17. *the mourning women.* Professional mourners are one of the most ancient institutions in the East and survive to the present day. They consisted generally speaking of women, though men also took part in these lamentations (2 Ch. xxxv. 25; Eccles. xii. 5; cf. Am. v. 16), and their object was to arouse the relatives of the deceased and those who attended the funeral to an outward manifestation of their sorrow. Their methods consisted of singing songs which dealt with the virtues of the dead person and playing upon flutes or pipes. (Cf. Lane, *Modern Egyptians*, II. p. 252; Thomson, *The Land and the Book*, p. 287.)

18. This *v.* exposes the artificial character of the grief which needed all the efforts of *cunning women* to arouse it (cf. Ecclus. xxxviii. 16 ff.); possibly the prophet wished to suggest that the penitence of the men of Judah was of a like nature, in so far as it could only be aroused by a narration of the horrors which were coming upon them.

20. The Lord Himself will teach the women the subject matter for their songs of lamentation, and the desolation which they are to foretell will be so great that it will require the services of them all to

the LORD, O ye women, and let your ear receive the word of
his mouth, and teach your daughters wailing, and every one
her neighbour lamentation. 21 For death is come up into our
windows, it is entered into our palaces; to cut off the children
from without, *and* the young men from the streets. 22 Speak,
Thus saith the LORD, The carcases of men shall fall as dung upon
the open field, and as the handful after the harvestman, and
none shall gather *them.*

23 Thus saith the LORD, Let not the wise man glory in his
wisdom, neither let the mighty man glory in his might, let not

describe it. In 2 S. i. 18 there is another example of the teaching of
a song of mourning, in this case by an earthly monarch.

21. *windows.* A mark of the suddenness with which death will
approach, like a thief, or like locusts which 'climb up into the houses
and enter in at the windows' (Joel ii. 9).

palaces. The rich suffer as well as the poor; cf. Ex. xi. 5, xii. 29.

children...young men. The fate of the innocent child at play in
the streets (cf. Zech. viii. 5), and that of the young man who fought
to defend his country will be one and the same; both will be cut off.

streets. Better *open spaces, squares.*

22. *Speak...LORD.* To be omitted with LXX. as they interrupt the
sequence.

dung. See on viii. 2.

handful. Better *swathe, row of fallen grain*; elsewhere Am. ii. 13
(on a cart); Mic. iv. 12; Zech. xii. 6. The point of the comparison is
not that the *carcases of men* shall be few, which *handful* would imply,
but rather the contrary; the dead will lie on the open field like rows
of fallen grain but with no hope of being gathered up and garnered.

23 f. A short utterance inserted here possibly because of some
verbal connexion with *v.* 12 (*wise man*). The object of the passage is
to exalt moral over intellectual or martial qualities. The knowledge
of God and actions suitable to one who has this great privilege are the
true basis of glorying. Both *vv.* are quoted in Clem. *ad Cor.* xii. 7,
and *v.* 24 is referred to in Rom. ii. 17; 1 Cor. i. 31; 2 Cor. x. 17; and
possibly in Phil. iii. 3.

23. *wisdom...might...riches.* The three great sources of worldly
pride and satisfaction then as now. The scholar, the athlete and the
man of wealth each tends to find a substitute for God in his particular
pursuit. No doubt the prophets had to put up with much opposition
from these various classes on account of their fearless condemnation of
existing abuses and 'vested interests.' It is interesting to compare
this exposure of the folly of those who trust in mere material things
with that in Eccles. ix. 11 where the condemnation is based on grounds
which are purely utilitarian, the happenings of 'time and chance.'

the rich man glory in his riches: 24 but let him that glorieth
glory in this, that he understandeth, and knoweth me, that I am
the LORD which exercise lovingkindness, judgement, and righteousness, in the earth: for in these things I delight, saith the
LORD. 25 Behold, the days come, saith the LORD, that I will
punish all them which are circumcised in *their* uncircumcision;
26 Egypt, and Judah, and Edom, and the children of Ammon,
and Moab, and all that have the corners *of their hair* polled,
that dwell in the wilderness: for all the nations are uncircumcised, and all the house of Israel are uncircumcised in heart.

     24. To know God is the truest happiness on earth and is indeed
the beginning in time of that Life whose quality is Eternal (Jn. xvii. 4).
This stress on the value of knowing God is reminiscent of Hosea
(e.g. v. 4, vi. 4, viii. 2); just as the insistence on the importance of
doing the things in which God delights is characteristic of Micah
(e.g. vi. 8, vii. 18).

     25 f. These *vv.* are regarded by almost all critics as a detached
fragment, but it is possible to trace out a connexion with the previous
fragment; there Jeremiah condemned those who trusted in human
attainments, here he condemns those who trust in religious privileges.
The passage is interesting as an anticipation of the teaching of St Paul
and of the distinction which he made between the circumcision which
is merely that of the flesh and the deeper circumcision of the heart
(see also on iv. 4)[1].

     26. *Judah* comes in a strange position between Egypt and Edom,
and its presence is hard to explain.

     all...uncircumcised. The exact force of this statement is not quite
clear, does it mean that the rite was not practised by these nations?
if so it conflicts with *v.* 25; or does it mean that their circumcision
was merely an outward symbol with no deeper meaning? in which case
it would not differ from that of Israel. Keil doubts whether circumcision was customary amongst the other nations, but there is a large
amount of evidence for it (see Driver's note on Gen. xvii. 23 ff.); the
fact that the Philistines are so constantly referred to as 'the uncircumcised' seems alone sufficient to prove it. On the contrary it might
be inferred from the story in Gen. xxxiv that the Canaanites did not
observe the rite. Circumcision was certainly known amongst the
Egyptians (cf. Josh. v. 9), and indeed Herodotus claims that they,
with the Colchians and Ethiopians, were the originators of it; and that
from them it spread into Phoenicia (II. 36, 37, 104). In later times

    [1] Philo in his treatise *de Circum.* II. p. 211 M discusses the moral significance
of the rite.

the Edomites were not in the habit of circumcising (Joseph. *Ant.* XII.
ix. 1, xv. vii. 9), but this may well have been through their becoming ashamed of the rite owing to the spread of Greek influence
amongst them (cf. 1 Macc. i. 15; Herod. II. 104), or through fear of
persecution (cf. Assumpt. Moses viii. 1: 'the king... shall crucify those
who confess to their circumcision'). St Jerome avoids the difficulty
mentioned above by taking the phrase to refer to *nations* not previously
enumerated.

  corners...polled. See also xxv. 23, xlix. 32. The reference is to
the custom of certain Arab tribes who cut their hair in 'a circular
form' in honour of 'Bacchus' (Herod. III. 8). The habit is forbidden
in Lev. xix. 27, evidently on the ground of its religious significance;
the priests were even forbidden to shave off the corners of their beards
(Lev. xxi. 5).

CHAPTER X. 1—16.

The Vanity of Idols.

  This passage is evidently inserted out of its proper context, and indeed
it shews signs of belonging to a period later than that of Jeremiah. In the
first place the people here addressed are sincere followers of Jehovah who
are apparently in danger of being led away by heathen forms of worship,
especially idolatry; in Jeremiah's time such habits of worship were already only
too common and indeed the prophet's condemnation had gone forth (cf. vii. 17ff.,
30ff., &c.). 'Jeremiah's contemporaries looked for *help* from unreal gods, and
are told by the prophet that they cannot *save* them (ii. 28, xi. 12); the Israelites
here addressed are in a different situation altogether and are told not to *dread*
unreal gods for they cannot harm them.' Driver, *LOT.*[8] p. 254. Further this
passage ridicules the idols and casts scorn on those who worship them, whereas
Jeremiah did not make use of ridicule, but only of fiery indignation. Secondly
the people referred to in this ch. appear to be living in close touch with heathen
nations and even to be under their power. If by *nations* the Chaldean invaders
are to be understood the attitude taken up towards them is hardly consistent
with that usually adopted by Jeremiah (see especially *vv.* 8 and 10). In any
case this section (as was pointed out above) interrupts the sequence of thought
between ix. 22 and x. 17, and if LXX. is a trustworthy authority the text itself
is in some confusion, for that version omits *vv.* 6—8 and 10, and places *v.* 9 in
the middle of *v.* 5.

  The impression given by the passage as a whole is that it fits in much better
with the situation of the Hebrews when in exile in Babylon. During that period
many of them must have been strongly attracted to the worship of idols by the
elaborate ritual which was there practised, as well as by the fact that the gods
of Babylon were the gods of their conquerors. The line of attack pursued by
the writer is to all intents and purposes identical with that of 2 Isaiah, and

Movers goes so far as to attribute the *vv.* to his authorship (cf. Is. xl. 19—22, xli. 7, 29, xliv. 9—20, lxiv. 5—7). The section may be conveniently divided up into two portions:

(a) *A warning against putting trust in the works of men's hands.* 1—5.
(b) *A declaration of God's omnipotence and omniscience.* 6—16.

X. 1 Hear ye the word which the LORD speaketh unto you, O house of Israel: 2 thus saith the LORD, Learn not the way of the nations, and be not dismayed at the signs of heaven; for the nations are dismayed at them. 3 For the [1]customs of the peoples are vanity: for [2]one cutteth a tree out of the forest, the work of the hands of the workman with the axe. 4 They deck it with silver and with gold; they fasten it with nails and with hammers, that

---

[1] Heb. *statutes.*   [2] Or, it is but *a tree which one cutteth*

X. 1—5. A warning against the foolishness of behaving like the heathen, and putting trust in mere senseless idols which have themselves to be moved from place to place.

2. *Learn not the way.* The Heb. of this phrase is very awkward and a slight change in the pointing gives the translation *Be not impelled* (into the way of the heathen)[1].

signs of heaven. The religion of the people amongst whom the Israelites were dwelling evidently laid great stress on the movements of the heavenly bodies; this was a characteristic of the Babylonian religion especially in its later developments (cf. L. W. King, *Babylonian Religion*, pp. 25 f.). Even in Christian countries comets and similar phenomena have been looked upon as portents; and so it is not hard to imagine what effect they must have had upon a population of which the vulgar, at any rate, identified the heavenly bodies with the gods whom they worshipped (see on viii. 2). According to the Book of Jubilees (xii. 16 f.) it is foolish even to gaze at the stars because they are 'all in the hands of the LORD'; at the same time there is another aspect of the matter, and Joel tells us that 'wonders in the heavens' are amongst the signs which are to accompany the approach of 'the great and terrible day of the LORD' (ii. 30 f.; cf. Am. viii. 9; Lk. xxi. 25).

3. Idols were probably first set apart to be the dwelling of the deity; then they were carved to be a rough representation of him; and so in course of time they acquired an intrinsic sanctity of their own: cf. W. Robertson Smith, *Rel. Sem.*[2] pp. 211 f.

tree. Cf. Wisd. xiii. 11; and Hor. *Sat.* i. viii. 1.

4. The wooden idol is decorated in various ways and is then

---

[1] MT. reading is אֶל־דֶּרֶךְ...אַל־תִּלְמָדוּ. Perles suggests pointing תְּלַמְּדוּ and compares מַלְמֵד = ox-goad and the Heb. of xxxi. 18 (see *JQR.* N.S. II. p. 104).

it move not. 5 They are like a ¹palm tree, of turned work, and
speak not: they must needs be borne, because they cannot go.
Be not afraid of them; for they cannot do evil, neither is it in
them to do good. 6 There is none like unto thee, O LORD; thou
art great, and thy name is great in might. 7 Who would not
fear thee, O King of the nations? for ²to thee doth it appertain:
forasmuch as among all the wise men of the nations, and in all
their royal estate, there is none like unto thee. 8 But they are
³together brutish and foolish: ⁴the instruction of idols, it is but
a stock. 9 There is silver beaten into plates which is brought
from Tarshish, and gold from ⁵Uphaz, the work of the artificer

¹ Or, *pillar in a garden of cucumbers* See Baruch vi. 70.
² Or, *it beseemeth thee*   ³ Or, *through one thing*
⁴ Or, it is *a doctrine of vanities*
⁵ According to some ancient versions, *Ophir*.

secured to the place prepared for it, in order, either that it shall not
fall down, which would be an ominous event (cf. 1 S. v. 3), or that it
may not be stolen (cf. Bar. vi. 18).

   move. Lit. *totter.* Cf. Wisd. xiii. 16 'he taketh thought for it
that it may not fall down, knowing that it is unable to help itself.'

   5. *palm tree, of turned work.* The rendering of RVm. is to be
preferred—*pillar in a garden of cucumbers,* in other words a *scarecrow*
(Bar. vi. 70).

   evil...good. That is they can do nothing at all. Cf. Gen. ii. 17.
'The knowledge of good and evil' means not a supreme judgement in
ethical matters, but omniscience; because everything comes within the
two categories of good and evil. The same jeer is made against
Jehovah by the dwellers of Jerusalem who are 'settled on their lees'
(Zeph. i. 12).

   6—16. The great might and wisdom of God, especially as manifested
in creation, places Him far above the idols of the heathen.

   6—8 are omitted by LXX., and the omission is supported by Streane
(see *The Double Text* &c. p. 123).

   7. *King of the nations.* The idea that Jehovah is King of the
nations is usually regarded as late (cf. Ps. xliii., xlvi., xlviii. &c.).

   8. Ex nihilo nihil fit; a stream cannot flow above its source, and
from a material idol no moral or spiritual counsel is to be expected.

   9. *Tarshish* was the extreme western limit of the ancient world.
It is probably to be identified with the Phoenician colony Tartessus on
the Guadalquivir (i.e. Wady-el-Kebir, the great river). *Tarshish* gave
its name to a special type of ocean-going vessel (1 K. xxii. 48, &c.) just
as according to the Egyptian monuments ships engaged in traffic with
Keftiu (Crete) were called 'Keftiu' ships. Ezekiel tells us that it was
noted for its *silver* (xxvii. 12, so also Diod. Sic. v. xxxv. 1).

   Uphaz. Here and Dan. x. 5. It is better to read Ophir, which was

and of the hands of the goldsmith; blue and purple for their clothing; they are all the work of cunning men. 10 But the LORD is ¹the true God; he is the living God, and an everlasting king: at his wrath the earth trembleth, and the nations are not able to abide his indignation.

11 ²Thus shall ye say unto them, The gods that have not made the heavens and the earth, ³these shall perish from the earth, and from under the heavens.

¹ Or, *God in truth*   ² This verse is in Aramaic.
³ Or, *they shall...under these heavens*

proverbial for its gold (cf. Ps. xlv. 10, &c.). On Ophir and the various suggestions which have been made as to its situation see Driver on Gen. x. 29 (with the important matter in the Addenda); it was probably in Arabia and perhaps the port from which the gold was embarked rather than the region which produced it.

blue and purple. These two words often occur in conjunction. The former was the colour of the covering for the temple vessels (Nu. iv. 6, &c.), also of the hangings of the palace at Shushan (Est. i. 6). Both words are applied to the hangings of the tabernacle (Ex. xxv. 4, &c.); in one passage the latter word is used of a woman's hair (Cant. vii. 5), a very vivid touch which is in keeping with the other striking similes of the writer. The dye was obtained from a certain sea-shell (*murex trunculus*), hence the name applied to it in 1 Macc. iv. 23 (אV) πορφύραν θαλασσίαν.

cunning men. The manufacture of idols was a 'skilled trade.' The idol consisted of a core of wood or some inferior metal which was plated over with gold or silver: cf. Is. xl. 19 and see G. A. Cooke, *North Sem. Inscript.* p. 75.

10. Cf. 1 Thes. i. 9 'Turned from idols to serve the living and true God'; Jn. v. 26.

God is contrasted with the idols in three respects. They are false, He is true or as the margin says *God in truth*¹; they are inanimate, He is living; they are liable to destruction and the decay of all material things, He is eternal.

LXX. omits the *v.*

11. This *v.* is in Aramaic and interrupts the sequence of *vv.* 10 and 12. Driver thinks that it was probably originally a marginal note suggested by the argument of the text, and intended as a reply which might be used by Jews living in heathen countries, when invited to take part in idol-worship. Giesebrecht says the Aramaic is of the Western dialect not of the Eastern which was spoken in Babylon; it is to be noticed that two distinct words are used for *earth* in the *v.* and that both have been

¹ Cf. the Jewish Prayer for the New Year: 'Purify our hearts to serve thee in truth. Thou, O God, art Truth, and thy word is Truth and standeth for ever.'

12 He hath made the earth by his power, he hath established the world by his wisdom, and by his understanding hath he stretched out the heavens: 13 [1]when he uttereth his voice, there is a tumult of waters in the heavens, and he causeth the vapours to ascend from the ends of the earth; he maketh lightnings for the rain, and bringeth forth the wind out of his treasuries. 14 Every man [2]is become brutish *and is* without knowledge; every goldsmith is put to shame by his graven image: for his molten image is falsehood, and there is no breath in them. 15 They are vanity, a work of [3]delusion: in the time of their visitation they shall perish. 16 The portion of Jacob is not like these;

---

[1] Or, *at the sound of his giving an abundance of waters...when he causeth &c.* or, *he causeth &c.*

[2] Or, *is too brutish to know*   [3] Or, *mockery*

---

found in the Assuan papyri. (For further information as to the Aramaic dialects see E. Kautzsch, *Gram. des Biblisch-Aram.* §§ 6 f., *Enc. Bib.* 280 ff., and on this passage in particular Driver, *LOT.*[8] p. 255.)

12—16 (= li. 15—19). The power of God is revealed in the wonders of the natural world. The thought contained in these *vv.* is one which occurs frequently in OT. and Driver has collected together a number of passages of Scripture 'containing thoughts or lessons suggested by the religious contemplation of nature'; see his note on Gen. ii 1—4 *a*.

13. *uttereth his voice.* Thunder is a favourite accompaniment of a theophany, often ending in lightning and rain. 'The Lord also thundered in the heavens, and the Most High uttered his voice; hailstones and coals of fire'; Ps. xviii. 13; Ecclus. xliii. 14.

the vapours to ascend. There is here no reference to the doctrine of evaporation; it is the actual, visible motions of the clouds moving up from the distant horizon which the prophet has in mind; cf. 1 K. xviii. 44; Ps. cxxxv. 7; and see W. Robertson Smith, *Rel. Sem.*[2] p. 106.

lightnings for the rain. Pusey suggests *into rain*, the lightning disappearing in the rain which follows it.

treasuries. Cf. Dt. xxviii. 12 (of the rain); Job xxviii. 22 (of the snow and hail); and also the parallel in the well known passage in Virgil, *Aen.* i. 52—63

'Hic vasto rex Æolus antro
Luctantes ventos tempestatesque sonoras
Imperio premit, ac vinclis et carcere frenat,' &c.

14. A description of the powerlessness of the idols and the despair of their makers in the presence of the powers of nature.

graven image. Lit. *carved*: the generic name for an idol without reference to the substance or process of manufacture.

16. *portion of Jacob.* Here only and in the parallel passage li. 19; cf. Ps. xvi. 5, lxxiii. 26; and in a more material sense Nu. xviii. 20.

for he is the former of all things; and Israel is the tribe of his inheritance: the LORD of hosts is his name.

the tribe of his inheritance. Cf. li. 19; Ps. lxxiv. 2 where Dr Briggs thinks it is inserted from the present passage.

CHAPTER X. 17—25.

The Nearness of the Exile.

This section resumes the discourse which was interrupted after ix. 22. Its genuineness has been questioned by many critics; the text as it stands is certainly corrupt in places (cf. LXX.), and there is great probability that more than one marginal gloss has found its way into the body of the passage.

(a) *The prophet's vision of Jerusalem besieged.* 17—22.
(b) *An appeal to God for mercy.* 23—25.

17 Gather up [1]thy wares out of the land, [2]O thou that abidest in the siege. 18 For thus saith the LORD, Behold, I will sling out the inhabitants of the land at this time, and will distress them, that they may [3]feel *it.* 19 Woe is me for my hurt! my wound is

[1] Or, *thy bundle from the ground*
[2] Or, *O inhabitant* (Heb. *inhabitress*) *of the fortress*   [3] Heb. *find.*

17—22. The prophet tells of the vision which he has seen of Jerusalem besieged and of the consternation which the event itself will occasion.

17. *Gather up thy wares:* i.e. prepare for flight; cf. mg. *Gather up thy bundle from the ground.* The meaning of the word translated *wares* is somewhat doubtful, but it appears to be connected with the root underlying 'Canaanite.' This latter word is often used as a synonym for trader (cf. Prov. xxxi. 24; Job xli. 5). The mg. *bundle* derives the word from a root similar to one found in Arabic meaning 'to bind up,' 'contract.' It is to be noted that at a later time the exiles in Babylon were warned of the second fall of Jerusalem by Ezekiel gathering together his possessions as if to fly from a besieged city (Ez. xii. 3—7).

thou. Fem. in Heb. and therefore to be applied to the community.

18. *sling out.* This is the only place where the expression means to drive a people into exile, though Abigail uses the metaphor in a somewhat similar sense when she speaks of Jehovah slinging out the souls of David's enemies (1 S. xxv. 29; and cf. Is. xxii. 18 of the punishment of Shebna).

19 f. These *vv.* bear a strong resemblance to iv. 19—21, and in them, as in the earlier passage, the prophet is speaking in the name of the community whose griefs he shares.

grievous: but I said, Truly this is *my* [1]grief, and I must bear it.
20 My tent is spoiled, and all my cords are broken: my children
are gone forth of me, and they are not: there is none to stretch
forth my tent any more, and to set up my curtains. 21 For the
shepherds are become brutish, and have not inquired of the
LORD: therefore they have not [2]prospered, and all their flocks
are scattered. 22 The voice of a rumour, behold it cometh, and
a great commotion out of the north country, to make the cities
of Judah a desolation, a dwelling place of jackals. 23 O LORD,
I know that the way of man is not in himself: it is not in man

[1] Or, *sickness*   [2] Or, *dealt wisely*

20. *tent*. The use of the figure of the *tent* to describe the whole
nation is frequent, especially in the later writers. In Is. liv. 2 the en-
larging of the tent and the lengthening of the cords is a sign of the
increased prosperity and populousness of the land; and the Divine
promise that Zion shall be 'a quiet habitation' is couched in terms of
the same figure, she is to be 'a tent which shall not be removed'
(Is. xxxiii. 20).

21. In this *v.* the image used to portray the desolation of the city
is changed from that of an Arab whose tent has been broken down and
his children destroyed, to that of a flock which has been scattered through
the foolishness of its shepherds. This last figure seems to contain a
reference to the folly of the rulers of Judah; cf. ii. 8, iii. 15, xxiii. 1,
&c.

22. *jackals*. See on ix. 11.

23—25. Jeremiah pleads the ignorance and feebleness of his
countrymen as an excuse for their sin, and prays that Jehovah will
have mercy upon His worshippers and avenge them upon their heathen
oppressors. These *vv.* are rejected by Duhm and Erbt, as well as by
Giesebrecht. There does not, however, seem to be any insuperable
difficulty in regarding *vv.* 23—24 as genuine; and there is much to
recommend Cornill's suggestion that Jeremiah is here making 'one
last appeal to the unfathomable mercy of Jehovah' not for a reversal
of the judgement, for that is forbidden him (vii. 16, xi. 14, xiv. 11),
but for clemency in carrying it out. *v.* 25 is almost identical with
Ps. lxxix. 6 f. and comes unnaturally from the lips of one who habitually
regarded the nations as God's own appointed instruments for the very
purpose of punishing Jacob; in any case it reflects the time after the
second fall of Jerusalem and therefore is out of place here. Possibly
Jeremiah looking back on the fallen city felt that the nations had
exceeded their commission and that they had rendered to Jerusalem
'double' for her sins.

23. An acknowledgement of man's dependence on the Divine will
which taken alone would amount to fatalism; cf. Rom. ix. 16. A similar

that walketh to direct his steps. 24 O LORD, correct me, but with judgement; not in thine anger, lest thou [1]bring me to nothing. 25 [2]Pour out thy fury upon the heathen that know thee not, and upon the families that call not on thy name: for they have devoured Jacob, yea, they have devoured him and consumed him, and have laid waste his [3]habitation.

[1] Heb. *diminish me.*   [2] See Ps. lxxix. 6, 7.   [3] Or, *pasture*

sentiment is expressed in Ps. xxxvii. 23; Prov. xvi. 9; but with the idea of a man's choice being overruled by God.

24. An admission of sin and an appeal for mercy. In the office for Morning and Evening Prayer this *v.* is used, as here, for the confession of common sin.

25. The genuineness of this *v.* is very doubtful (though see Introd. to the section); it suggests that a godly nation had been overcome and desolated by the ungodly, not that the wickedness of Judah was being punished.

CHAPTERS XI. 1—XII. 6.

Jeremiah's Proclamation of the Covenant and its Results.

Jeremiah shews his sympathy with the legal side of religion by proclaiming the 'words of the covenant'; by which is meant some sort of code of Divine requirements. It is difficult however to know what exactly the phrase implies, the usual interpretation is that it represents the contents of the 'book of the law' found in the temple in the days of Josiah (2 K. xxii. 8); which 'book' according to most critics formed the nucleus of Dt. In the account of Josiah's reformation in 2 K. xxii.—xxiii. no mention is made of Jeremiah, and the prophet seems to have had little sympathy with the king's methods and actions (see Introd. pp. xxii f.). The covenant into which Josiah entered was accepted by 'all the people' (2 K. xxiii. 2) and at first sight there would seem to have been no need for its subsequent 'proclamation'; the words however can hardly be taken literally, and in any case even when the covenant had been accepted the need for explanation and comment would still be present.

(*a*)   *The conditions of the covenant.* 1—8.
(*b*)   *The failure of the prophet's warnings.* 9—14.
(*c*)   *The prayer of hypocrites will be in vain.* 15—17.
(*d*)   *The plots of the men of Anathoth.* 18—23.
(*e*)   *Why do the wicked prosper?* xii. 1—6.

XI. 1 The word that came to Jeremiah from the LORD, saying,

XI. 1—8. Jeremiah is commanded to bring back to the minds of the men of Judah the conditions upon which they hold their land, viz.: that they keep the covenant which God made with their fathers at the

2 Hear ye the words of this covenant, and speak unto the men
of Judah, and to the inhabitants of Jerusalem; 3 and say thou
unto them, Thus saith the LORD, the God of Israel: Cursed be
the man that heareth not the words of this covenant, 4 which
I commanded your fathers in the day that I brought them forth
out of the land of Egypt, out of the iron furnace, saying, Obey
my voice, and do them, according to all which I command you:
so shall ye be my people, and I will be your God: 5 that I may
establish the oath which I sware unto your fathers, to give them
a land flowing with milk and honey, as at this day. Then answered I, and said, Amen, O LORD.

time of the exodus. It is rather a remarkable fact that the earlier
prophets do not seem to look back to the legislation at Sinai as the
beginning of the covenant relation between Israel and Jehovah, but to
the deliverance from Egypt (cf. Am. ii. 10; Hos. ii. 15, xi. 1, xii. 9, 13).
The passage contains a double command, couched in very similar language, to proclaim the covenant. Cheyne rejects the whole section as
'poor in diction and in metre and quite out of harmony with what Jeremiah says elsewhere' (*Decline and Fall of Kingdom of Judah*, p. 32).

2. *Hear ye...speak.* The plural is awkward as there is no clue
to the persons addressed; read the singular with LXX.

this covenant. The phrase has no antecedent. The reference may
be to the covenant made by Josiah and the people which was to them
but a renewal of the ancient covenant made during the exodus; or it
may be a direct reference to the Deuteronomic covenant. The two
references are not necessarily exclusive, in fact most critics consider
that it was the Deuteronomic covenant which Josiah renewed, though
there is a difficulty in referring to it as made when God brought the
people out of Egypt, for such a reference suggests that Dt. was the
content of the revelation at Sinai[1].

4. Taking the Pentateuch as we now have it this *v.* would better
refer to the covenant at Sinai than to the later one in Moab (see previous
note). The whole of *vv.* 3—5 is, however, full of Dt. phrases and in
fact forms a summary of the Dt. teaching. It seems more than doubtful
whether this passage is not the addition of a Dt. scribe, though such a
theory has its difficulties in view of the apparent confusion of the legislation of Sinai with that of Moab.

iron furnace. Cf. Dt. iv. 20; Ez. xxii. 18 ff.

5. *milk and honey.* A common phrase in J and D, once in H

---

[1] This difficulty is pointed out by Chapman, *Int. to the Pent.* p. 129, 'the
reference,' he says, 'seems to be to the *beginning* rather than to the *end* of the
journeyings. If the prophet knew the law as a part of the complete Book of
Deut., would it not have been represented as proclaimed in the land of Moab
(Deut. xxix. 1).'

6 And the LORD said unto me, Proclaim all these words in the cities of Judah, and in the streets of Jerusalem, saying, Hear ye the words of this covenant, and do them. 7 For I earnestly protested unto your fathers in the day that I brought them up out of the land of Egypt, even unto this day, rising early and protesting, saying, Obey my voice. 8 Yet they obeyed not, nor inclined their ear, but walked every one in the stubbornness of their evil heart: therefore I brought upon them all the words of this covenant, which I commanded them to do, but they did them not.

9 And the LORD said unto me, A conspiracy is found among the men of Judah, and among the inhabitants of Jerusalem. 10 They are turned back to the iniquities of their forefathers,

(Lev. xx. 24), outside the Pentateuch it occurs here, xxxii. 22, and Ez. xx. 6, 15 only.

Amen. For the different uses of *Amen* in the Bible see an article in *JQR.* Oct. 1896.

6. Cf. Rom. ii. 13.

7 f. These *vv.* are omitted by LXX.; they are closely parallel to vii. 23 f. and also to *vv.* 4 f. of this same chapter.

protested. God's protest is a solemn declaration of His requirements in spite of man's disobedience and neglect; cf. the note in Driver's *Deut.* pp. 80 f.

8. *the words of this covenant.* i.e. the punishments threatened for refusal to obey the law.

9—14. In the previous section Jeremiah is represented as proclaiming the covenant and warning the people of the consequences of refusal to fulfil its requirements; in this section the warnings have proved vain and the people have already fallen away from their obedience. The reformation has been a failure and the state of Judah is as bad as ever. This 'word from the Lord' probably came to the prophet in the early days of Jehoiakim's reign when the pathetic death of Josiah had crushed out any sparks of a true and living faith in Jehovah which the king had succeeded in kindling by his example. In the presence of all the iniquities and idolatries of the nation the prophet's denunciation once more rings out.

9. *conspiracy.* It is not necessary to find in this word any organised intrigue (such as a plot by the pro-Egyptian party), but merely a vivid description of the effect of the conduct of the men of Judah; by following false gods they had shewn themselves to be bound together in an agreement, although it was an implied and not a deliberate one. The same expression is used by Ezekiel of the prophets (xxii. 25; cf. Hos. vi. 9).

10. *forefathers.* Is this a reference to their immediate ancestors

which refused to hear my words; and they are gone after other gods to serve them: the house of Israel and the house of Judah have broken my covenant which I made with their fathers. 11 Therefore thus saith the LORD, Behold, I will bring evil upon them, which they shall not be able to escape; and they shall cry unto me, but I will not hearken unto them. 12 Then shall the cities of Judah and the inhabitants of Jerusalem go and cry unto the gods unto whom they offer incense: but they shall not save them at all in the time of their [1]trouble. 13 For according to the number of thy cities are thy gods, O Judah; and according to the number of the streets of Jerusalem have ye set up altars to the [2]shameful thing, even altars to burn incense unto Baal. 14 Therefore pray not thou for this people, neither lift up cry nor prayer for them: for I will not hear them in the time that they cry unto me [3]for their [1]trouble.

15 [4]What hath my beloved to do in mine house, seeing she

[1] Heb. *evil*.   [2] Heb. *shame*.   See ch. iii. 24.
[3] Many ancient authorities have, *in the time of*.
[4] The text is obscure.   The Sept. renders thus: *Why hath the beloved wrought abomination in my house?   Shall vows and holy flesh take away from thee thy wickednesses, or shalt thou escape by these?*

of the pre-reformation period or to the generation of the exodus? Cf. ii. 2 f.

12.   To the men of Judah the test of the power of a god was a practical one, his ability to help his worshippers. Josiah had received no help from Jehovah against Egypt, but, so the prophet warns them, neither will they receive any help from their newly adopted objects of worship; cf. ii. 28, which is evidently in the writer's mind though he drops the irony of the former passage and speaks in all earnestness.

13.   The decay of the national religion is followed by the springing up of a huge crop of superstitions. Faith in the established worship having been shaken men feel left to their own devices and each city and every street makes its own choice of the deity under whose protection it will place itself. 'The soul that is not unified and harmonised by the fear of the one God, is torn and distracted by a thousand contending passions, and vainly seeks peace and deliverance by worshipping at a thousand unholy shrines.'   (Ball, *ad loc.*)

14.   The first half of the *v.* should probably be omitted, having been introduced from vii. 16; the whole section then refers to the vain attempts of the people to obtain the help of God whilst not running the risk of giving up any of their superstitious practices.

15—17.   The prayer of hypocrites will be in vain; and the fair

hath wrought lewdness *with* many, and the holy flesh is passed
from thee? ¹when thou doest evil, then thou rejoicest. 16 The
Lord called thy name, A green olive tree, fair with goodly fruit:
with the noise of a great tumult he hath kindled fire upon it,
and the branches of it are broken. 17 For the Lord of hosts,
that planted thee, hath pronounced evil against thee, because of
the evil of the house of Israel and of the house of Judah, which
they have wrought for themselves in provoking me to anger by
offering incense unto Baal.

18 And the Lord gave me knowledge of it, and I knew it:

---

¹ Or, *when thine evil* cometh

---

olive tree which gave a deceitful promise of goodly fruit will be blasted
(cf. Matt. xxi. 19).

15.   It is impossible to get any meaning out of MT. as it stands
and most critics follow the LXX. which is represented in the margin.

my beloved. Here applied to the whole nation as in Ps. lx. 5
(= cviii. 6); in Dt. xxxiii. 12 it is used of the tribe of Benjamin only;
and in 2 S. xii. 24 f. of an individual, Solomon or Jedidiah (cf. also
Ps. cxxvii. 2 'so he giveth his beloved sleep').

holy flesh. Cf. Hag. ii. 12.

16.   *olive tree.* This tree was a fit symbol for prosperity on account
of its great beauty and value (cf. Hos. xiv. 6; Ps. lii. 8, cxxviii. 3).
Israel is more frequently depicted as a vine though in the famous allegory in Rom. xi. the olive is selected by St Paul.

tumult. The same Heb. word as that used for the noise of the
wings of the living creatures in Ez. i. 24. Perhaps the writer wished
to make use of the picture of a smouldering fire being fanned into flame
by a stormy wind.

17.   Judah is to suffer for the sins of the house of Israel as well as
for its own: a thought which is found in Dan. ix. 7 and Ass. Moses
iii. 5.

18—23.   The Lord reveals to Jeremiah a plot which has been formed
against him by his fellow-townsmen. The prophet's judgement upon
them.

This section has no obvious connexion with the two that go before
and they may have been grouped together because in *v.* 9 there is
mention of a *conspiracy* and here an account is given of an actual plot,
not, it is true against Jehovah, but against His prophet and spokesman.
At the same time it is evident that some introductory matter has been
omitted at the beginning of the section, as the names of the offenders
are only given at the end and then almost by chance. It has been suggested that the reason for the deadly hatred exhibited by the men of
Anathoth against Jeremiah was the part which he took in carrying out
the reforms of Josiah including the centralisation of all worship at

then thou shewedst me their doings. 19 But I was like a gentle
lamb that is led to the slaughter; and I knew not that they had
devised devices against me, *saying*, Let us destroy the tree with
the [1]fruit thereof, and let us cut him off from the land of the
living, that his name may be no more remembered. 20 But, O

[1] Heb. *bread*.

Jerusalem. This reform would have the effect of 'disestablishing' the
local sanctuaries, including that at Anathoth, and in the latter case the
bitterness would be the greater as the priests there were descendants
of Abiathar, who was displaced in Solomon's reign by Zadok (1 K. ii. 27)
from whom the Jerusalem priests claimed their succession. The sons
of Abiathar felt that the priesthood at the temple was theirs by right
and now they were to be deprived of even their own sanctuary and only
to be allowed to minister at all by becoming subordinates to their hated
and triumphant rivals. That a member of their own family and possibly
of the priestly guild itself should support such a movement must have
seemed to them an intolerable wrong. In any case the secrecy with
which the plots were made would only be necessary in the reign of
Josiah.

18. This *v.* seems to take for granted that the reader is in full
possession of the facts of the attempt upon Jeremiah's life. Cornill
suggests that this section should be transposed so as to follow xii. 6.

19. *gentle.* AV. *an ox* is a possible translation of MT. (cf. Hesiod,
Op. 403), but RV. gives a better meaning to the comparison. The idea
is that of a lamb which has been brought up 'as one of the family'
(cf. 2 S. xii. 3) without suspicion of the fate in store for it. The word
used here for *lamb* is almost always applied to lambs for sacrifices[1]; cf.
Is. liii. 7 which is possibly founded on this passage.

the tree with the fruit. Heb. *bread* which is an unusual phrase
though it is defended by Keil on the grounds of there being a similar
Arabic usage. It seems better however to adopt the slight emendation
suggested by Hitzig and to read *sap*. The figure then represents a
strong young tree in the fulness of life, and the reference is to the
youth and vigour of the prophet. The *v.* is quoted by Tertullian, *adv.
Marc.* iii. 19 and also by St Athanasius in such a manner as to make it
a forecast of the crucifixion, δεῦτε καὶ ἐμβάλωμεν ξύλον εἰς τὸν ἄρτον αὐτοῦ
(*De Inc.* xxxv. 3). In Ecclus. vi. 3 f. a dried-up tree (i.e. a tree without
fruit) is an expression for a childless man: but it is practically certain
that Jeremiah was unmarried (xvi. 2).

land of the living. A phrase common in Ezekiel (xxvi. 20, &c.)
and in the Psalms (xxvii. 13, &c.).

---

[1] In many systems of worship the victim is supposed to offer itself spontaneously
(cf. Gen. xxii. 13), and if it struggles on the way to the altar it is considered
to be a bad omen (see Livy, xxi. 63, and cf. Robertson Smith's note in *Rel. Sem.*[2]
p. 309).

LORD of hosts, that judgest righteously, that triest the reins and the heart, let me see thy vengeance on them: for unto thee have I revealed my cause. 21 Therefore thus saith the LORD concerning the men of Anathoth, that seek thy life, saying, Thou shalt not prophesy in the name of the LORD, that thou die not by our hand: 22 therefore thus saith the LORD of hosts, Behold, I will ¹punish them: the young men shall die by the sword; their sons and their daughters shall die by famine; 23 and there shall be no remnant unto them: for I will bring evil upon the men of Anathoth, ²even the year of their visitation.

XII. 1 Righteous art thou, O LORD, when I plead with thee:

¹ Heb. *visit upon.*   ² Or, *in the year*

20. *the reins and the heart.* The *reins* (or *kidneys*) to the Hebrews were the seat of the emotions and the *heart* the seat of the reasoning faculty. God sees both, for to Him 'all hearts are open and all desires known' and therefore He has all the material at His disposal for forming a perfectly just judgement.

unto thee have I revealed. This statement seems out of place in view of God's admitted omniscience and some critics by deriving the Hebrew word from another root translate *upon thee have I rolled my cause.*

21. *Thou shalt not prophesy.* Cf. the similar command in Am. ii. 12, v. 10; Micah was also bidden to keep silence (ii. 6), as was Isaiah (xxviii. 9 f.).

in the name of the LORD. Cf. note on xxvi. 16.

die not by our hand. The men of Anathoth evidently intended to take the law into their own hands.

22 f. In these *vv.* Jeremiah declares that the sin of the men of Anathoth cannot fail to bring its due punishment: there is nothing vindictive in the prophet's utterance. (Cf. xiv. 15, xliv. 12.) No doubt Anathoth from its close proximity to Jerusalem would suffer severely during the siege.

23. *no remnant.* This expression is not to be taken literally, as according to Ezra ii. 23; Neh. vii. 27 the number of the men of Anathoth who returned from exile was 128. The Heb. word for *remnant* in this *v.* (שְׁאֵרִית) is used with a variety of meanings, as Dr Briggs has pointed out, all of which can be illustrated from the book of Jeremiah: (*a*) *posterity* as here and in 2 S. xiv. 7; (*b*) *remainder* of a thing, vi. 9, xxxix. 3; Ps. lxxvi. 10; (*c*) *remnant* of a people, xxxi. 7; Ez. ix. 8, &c.

XII. 1—6. This section contains one of the earliest extant passages in Hebrew literature, if not the earliest, in which there is a discussion of the eternal problem of the prosperity of the wicked[1].

---

[1] Cf. H. W. Robinson, 'the problem of individual suffering finds expression first of all in the prophet who is most individual in his thought and experience,' *Relig. Ideas of OT.* p. 171.

Jeremiah is God's servant and yet he is in a perilous state, his life is constantly threatened and made a misery to him; his enemies on the other hand are godless and evil and yet they prosper and live in security and ease. It is to be noted that the prophet in spite of the urgency of the problem and its intimate relation to his own sufferings does not for a moment lose his confidence in God's justice. He 'sets down,' as Pusey said of Habakkuk, 'at the very beginning his entire trust in God... teaching us that the only safe way of inquiry into God's ways is by setting out with a living conviction that they are mercy and truth.'

The passage, in whole or in part, is accepted as genuine by nearly all critics (Duhm would reject it as post-exilic, but the reasons which he gives seem insufficient).   Cornill looks upon vv. 1—2 at any rate as being genuine beyond all dispute; he would place the passage before xi. 18—23 and thinks that the utterance comes from a time immediately after the tragedy of Megiddo when the fate of Josiah had attracted universal attention to the problem.

To a cursory reading the passage seems to offer no solution of the difficulty but on going deeper there are to be found what seem to be clear traces of Jeremiah's having reached the only true and worthy answer to the question. The two contrasted statements in vv. 2 b, 3 a thou art near in their mouth, and far from their reins and But thou, O Lord, knowest me; thou seest me, and triest mine heart toward thee, are generally interpreted as being evidence of the hypocrisy and sin of his enemies when compared with the innocence and sincerity of the prophet himself; but may they not be read as a statement of the great fact which consoles the suffering man of God in his affliction—that though his enemies live and are mighty yet he has in his constant access to God a 'prosperity' which as far as real happiness is concerned goes infinitely beyond any which they can possibly enjoy? 'He says, in effect, that in spite of the material prosperity of the wicked, he knows that no relation exists between them and God, whereas he feels that he has entered with God into such an intimate relation that nothing further can be desired; in this at-oneness with God he possesses the supreme good. In other words, he recognises that not material prosperity constitutes man's happiness, but that peace and strength of soul which is enjoyed only by him who lives a life of righteousness and feels himself at one with God.' Buttenwieser, op. cit. p. 18. If this interpretation be adopted it seems almost necessary to reject v. 3 b which has already been done upon other grounds by Duhm and even by Cornill. The section ends with a rebuke to the prophet for his impatience; if he complains at the beginning of his trials how will he be able to endure those greater hardships which are yet to come upon him? The problem of the prosperity of the wicked is often referred to in OT., notably in Ps. xxxvii., xlix., lxxiii., and in the book of Job where the question is approached from the side of the suffering of the righteous.

1. when I plead. Plead has a forensic application; the prophet is willing to allow that if he were to bring an action against God, God would gain the verdict. Cf. Theognis, 373 ff. 'Dear Zeus, I wonder at

yet would I ¹reason the cause with thee: wherefore doth the
way of the wicked prosper? wherefore are all they at ease that
deal very treacherously? 2 Thou hast planted them, yea, they
have taken root; they grow, yea, they bring forth fruit: thou
art near in their mouth, and far from their reins. 3 But thou,
O LORD, knowest me; thou seest me, and triest mine heart toward thee: pull them out like sheep for the slaughter, and
²prepare them for the day of slaughter. 4 How long shall the
land mourn, and the herbs of the whole country wither? for the
wickedness of them that dwell therein, the beasts are consumed,
and the birds; because they said, He shall not see our latter end.
5 If thou hast run with the footmen, and they have wearied thee,

---

¹ Heb. *speak judgements*. ² Heb. *sanctify*.

---

thee: thou art the lord of all; thou hast great power and honour and
knowest well the thoughts of each man's heart. How then, son of
Cronus, dost thou think fit to deal the same measure to sinful and just,
careless whether their hearts are turned to moderation or to insolence?'
Quoted by James Adam, *Relig. Teachers of Greece*, p. 87.

2. *in their mouth.* The wicked have God's name on their lips but
their deeds are not in agreement with their words.

3. *triest mine heart.* The prophet's heart was tried by the bitter
test of suffering.

sheep. Cf. xi. 19, a somewhat vindictive reversal of the metaphor.
Cheyne says of this passage, 'There is the dross of human frailty in
this...to be excused, not to be justified. And whenever we read such
words even in the Scripture...let us mentally correct them in accordance with the words, "Father, forgive them; for they know not what
they do."' (*Life and Times of Jer.* p. 111.)

day of slaughter. Cf. xxv. 34; Jas. v. 5; and in extra-canonical
literature, Ps. Sol. viii. 1; En. xciv. 9.

4. In the eyes of the prophets the dumb creation and even the land
itself are involved in the sufferings of the human race (cf. Ps. cvii. 34),
but they also share in its rejoicings (Is. xliii. 20, &c.).

mourn. Cf. Am. i. 2; Hos. iv. 3; Joel i. 10, &c.

our latter end. The meaning is that even if the prophet's predic-
tions are fulfilled he will not have the satisfaction of knowing this for
means will have been found to bring his life to a sudden close in the
mean time. Probably, however, the reading of LXX. is to be preferred,
He (i.e. *God*) *seeth not our ways*.

5 f. These *vv.* seem a little out of place though it is hardly necessary to suppose that anything has fallen out after *v.* 4. God makes His
reply to Jeremiah, and, as it were, forecloses the discussion by rebuking
the prophet's impatience, just as in the drama of Job He overwhelms

then how canst thou contend with horses? and though in a land
of peace thou art secure, yet how wilt thou do in the [1]pride of
Jordan? 6 For even thy brethren, and the house of thy father,
even they have dealt treacherously with thee; even they have
cried aloud after thee : believe them not, though they speak
[2]fair words unto thee.

[1] Or, *swelling*   [2] Heb. *good things.*

the patriarch from the midst of the whirlwind (xxxviii. 1 ff.). Two
striking figures are used to warn Jeremiah of the hardships which lie
before him; his past endurance has been only that of one who runs
against men, he will yet have to run against horses, and even the dangers
through which he has come have been those of a civilised land, those
of the future will be like the perils of the jungle.

5. *contend.* The Hebrew word gives the idea of hotly striving to
excel and is used again in xxii. 15 of Jehoiakim's building operations.

pride of Jordan. Lit. *swelling,* the Ἰάρδην δρυμός of Josephus (*Bell.
Jud.* VII. vi. 5), the luxuriant undergrowth of the Jordan valley which
formed the home of wild beasts (cf. xlix. 19 = 1. 44; Zech. xi. 3). The
great heat caused the trees and shrubs to grow to an immense height.
Travellers of the present day record temperatures of 109° F. in the
shade during the month of May and 95° F. even after sunset. The valley
is still the haunt of wild animals.

Chapter XII. 7—17.

God's Lament over the Desolation of His Heritage.

This prophecy is usually held to refer to the invasion of Judah by the
neighbouring peoples after the revolt of Jehoiakim against Nebuchadrezzar
(see 2 K. xxiv. 1, 2). The opening *v.* however suggests a calamity of even greater
magnitude; the forsaking by Jehovah of His house can hardly refer to anything
less than the fall of Jerusalem itself. If the whole passage is a unity it seems
most likely that it comes from the time immediately after the first capture of
Jerusalem in 597 B.C. when indignation was still felt against the surrounding
nations for their share in the desolation of the land. There is a good deal however to be said for Duhm's distinction between *vv.* 7—13 and *vv.* 14—17. In
the earlier section there is no clear reference to attacks from Judah's neighbours,
v. 9 is merely a description of the besiegers, and in the same way the *many
shepherds* of *v.* 10 are the various leaders of the Babylonian army as in vi. 3.
Duhm's further suggestion that *vv.* 14—17 come from the time of John Hyrcanus
has little to recommend it and is open to serious objections (cf. Cornill,
ad loc.).

7 I have forsaken mine house, I have cast off mine heritage; I have given the dearly beloved of my soul into the hand of her enemies. 8 Mine heritage is become unto me as a lion in the forest: she hath uttered her voice against me; therefore I have hated her. 9 Is mine heritage unto me as a speckled bird of prey? are the birds of prey against her round about? go ye, assemble all the beasts of the field, bring them to devour. 10 Many shepherds have destroyed my vineyard, they have trodden my portion under foot, they have made my pleasant portion a desolate wilderness. 11 They have made it a desolation; it mourneth unto me, being desolate; the whole land is made desolate, because no man layeth it to heart. 12 Spoilers are come upon all the bare heights in the wilderness: for the sword

7—13. This section is generally accepted as being the work of Jeremiah; the main point upon which critics are at variance in regard to it is as to whether it is a forecast of events about to come to pass, or whether it looks back on a devastation already accomplished, the latter view being that supported by Graf and Hitzig.

7. This *v.* seems connected with xi. 15 and is the sequel to it; because the *beloved* of Jehovah has polluted His *house*, therefore He has forsaken it and she herself has been given over to her enemies.

mine house. Probably here used in the wider sense of land (as in Hos. viii. 1, ix. 15) rather than temple.

8. *as a lion.* Judah has roared against the Lord like *a lion* and has taken up a position of hostility to Him. This simile is a good example of Hebrew usage which lays stress on one point only of the comparison and ignores the rest; here, for example, there is no question of the action of Judah inspiring fear in the Lord, such as the roar of the lion brings to the wayfarer. For a similar reason, Duhm's suggestion, that the use of *a lion* as a symbol of the nation implies that it was still powerful, may be put on one side.

9. *unto me...bird of prey* &c. Graf suggests that כִּי, *that*, should be read for לִי, *unto me*; the two questions then become one and may be translated *Is mine heritage as a speckled bird of prey, that the birds of prey* &c. The figure is based on the habit of birds attacking any other bird of unfamiliar plumage; this habit was noted and commented on by classical writers (cf. Pliny, *Hist. Nat.* x. 19; Tacitus, *Ann.* VI. 28; Suetonius, *Caes.* 81).

all the beasts. Cf. Is. lvi. 9.

11. *unto me.* Cf. Gen. xxxiii. 13 and xlviii. 7 (RVm.).

no man layeth it to heart. i.e. no one has considered what will be the result of Judah's policy; cf. *v.* 13; Is. lvii. 1.

12. *bare heights.* A favourite word in Jeremiah where six out of the ten instances of its use occur.

of the LORD devoureth from the one end of the land even to the
other end of the land: no flesh hath peace. 13 They have sown
wheat, and have reaped thorns; they have put themselves to
pain, and profit nothing : and ¹ye shall be ashamed of your fruits,
because of the fierce anger of the LORD.

14 Thus saith the LORD against all mine evil neighbours, that
touch the inheritance which I have caused my people Israel to
inherit: Behold, I will pluck them up from off their land, and
will pluck up the house of Judah from among them. 15 And it
shall come to pass, after that I have plucked them up, I will
return and have compassion on them; and I will bring them
again, every man to his heritage, and every man to his land.
16 And it shall come to pass, if they will diligently learn the
ways of my people, to swear by my name, As the LORD liveth;
even as they taught my people to swear by Baal; then shall they
be built up in the midst of my people. 17 But if they will not

¹ Or, *be ye ashamed* Or, *they shall be ashamed*

flesh. This expression is used to represent humanity in its weakness and transitoriness (cf. Is. xl. 5 f. &c.). In xxxii. 27 the stress is
on the close connexion between the natural man and the lower world.

13. The crop is not merely to be a failure (as in Hag. i. 6), or to
become the property of foemen (as in Mic. vi. 15), but it will produce
deadly evil (cf. Is. lix. 5). The exact reference is obscure, the subject
of the sentence, whether it be taken to be *the spoilers* of *v.* 12 or the
people of Judah, is equally difficult in the present context of the verse.

14–17. Judah is after all the Lord's inheritance, although He
appears to have forsaken it, and those who ravage it will themselves
be turned away into perpetual exile unless indeed they adopt the
worship of Jehovah. The attitude of this prophecy is not that which
is usually found in Jeremiah: here it is the nations who have caused
Judah to sin (*v.* 16), she herself is hardly responsible and in due time
Jehovah will restore her. There is no condemnation of the sin which
brought upon Judah her punishment and it is Jehovah who will turn
to Judah, not Judah who will turn to Him. Such an attitude of mind
is, however, quite possible in Jeremiah, especially after the destruction
of the kingdom, and the expectation of the exile of the other nations
is clearly stated in ch. xxv.

14. *evil neighbours.* The destruction is not to be due to Babylon
alone: cf. Ez. xxv. 3, 8, xxviii. 24, &c.; Zech. ii. 8.

15. Cf. Am. ix. 14; Ez. xxviii. 25.

16. For a similar anticipation of the nations turning to worship
Jehovah see xvi. 19 f.

be built up. Cf. Job xxii. 23 'If thou return unto the Almighty

hear, then will I pluck up that nation, plucking up and destroying it, saith the LORD.

thou shalt be built up.' The idea of the spiritual society as a building is further developed in many well-known passages in NT. (e.g. Eph. ii. 20 f.; 1 Pet. ii. 5, &c.).

17. The opportunity of hearing the word of the Lord is also an opportunity of refusing to accept it, and so of reaping the consequences: cf. Is. lx. 12; Zech. xiv. 17.

CHAPTER XIII.

Warnings and Lamentation.

This ch. consists of a series of warnings, some in the form of acted parables, ending with a lamentation over the fate of Jerusalem. There is no apparent connexion between the various sections except a similarity in subject matter, which is doubtless the reason for their being grouped together. The following are the natural divisions of the ch.; (*a*) and (*b*) are written in the elevated prose style so often adopted by the prophets, the rest in the Qinah measure.

(*a*) *The parable of the buried waist-cloth.* 1—11.
(*b*) *The parable of the wine-bottles.* 12—14.
(*c*) *A warning to the pride of Judah.* 15—17.
(*d*) *A warning to the pride of the ruling house.* 18 f.
(*e*) *A lamentation over 'the beautiful flock.'* 20—27.

XIII. 1 Thus said the LORD unto me, Go, and buy thee a

XIII. 1—11. The prophet in accordance with God's instructions buys a linen waist-cloth, and after wearing it for a short time receives a second command to hide it in a hole in the rock on the Euphrates. After some time a third message from God orders him to recover it, and on so doing he finds that the waist-cloth has become marred and useless. The section closes with an explanation of the parable.

Several questions are raised by this parable. (i) Is it intended to be taken as literal fact, and if so what does the prophet mean by *Euphrates*? (ii) What is the teaching intended to be conveyed? (iii) From what period of the prophet's activity does the parable come? (i) Parables such as this invariably cause disagreement amongst critics as to whether the prophet is recording events which actually took place or whether he merely employs a vivid form of narrative. In the case of many of Ezekiel's parables it is almost certain that some of the actions were performed by the prophet in imagination only, and the same probably applies to Jeremiah also. In the present instance the mention of a specific place as the scene of the action does not by any means preclude discussion as to the reality of what took place—the imagination of

linen girdle, and put it upon thy loins, and put it not in water.
2 So I bought a girdle according to the word of the LORD, and
put it upon my loins. 3 And the word of the LORD came unto
me the second time, saying, 4 Take the girdle that thou hast
bought, which is upon thy loins, and arise, go to Euphrates, and

the prophets was exceedingly vivid, and Jeremiah would quite naturally
fix upon some place as being suitable in his own mind for hiding the
girdle. If the Heb. word פְּרָת (*Perāth*) rendered *Euphrates* be taken to
refer to the town of Parah, not many miles from the prophet's home at
Anathoth, there is a sufficient reason for his choice (see further on *v.* 4).
The question, however, is not one of great importance; the teaching for
which the incident forms the vehicle is quite independent of any question of whether it actually happened or not. (ii) Critics agree that the
waist-cloth represents Judah, which has been brought near to God, but
they disagree as to the interpretation of the details. Graf, followed by
Cornill, looks upon the spoiling of the girdle as representing the moral
corruption of the people through Babylonian influences (cf. ii. 18),
which was the cause of the exile; Keil and the older critics say that it
'signifies not the moral but the physical decay of the covenant people,'
which was to take place after God had thrown them off from Himself. The second line of explanation seems to fit the time sequence of
the parable better than the former. (iii) Cornill, who sees in the corruption of the girdle the influence of Babylon, places the incident early
in the ministry of Jeremiah. There is, however, very little clue to the
period from which it comes.

1. *linen* was the material for priestly wear (Lev. vi. 10, &c.).
girdle. The garment here meant is not a *girdle* but rather a *waist-
cloth*. See W. Robertson Smith in *JQR.* 1892, pp. 289 ff.
put it not in water. The girdle was to be kept from the water which
was afterwards to cause its decay: commentators see in this a reference
to the early purity of Israel and Judah.

4. *Euphrates*. The English name for this river is derived, through
the Greek, from the Old Persian *Ufrātū*; whilst the Heb. פְּרָת (*Perāth*)
represents the Assyrian *Purātū*. In this passage there is some dispute
regarding the correctness of translation of the Heb., because in other
places when it represents the *Euphrates* it usually has the word for
'river' written before it; but as examples occur without any such addition (e.g. li. 63; Gen. ii. 4) this objection is not insuperable. As the
future scene of the exile of Judah, the *Euphrates* would be a suitable
place for burying the waist-cloth; but against it there are two further
objections. The first is geographical; the river in the neighbourhood
of Babylon is not rocky, though above Carchemish steep banks are
to be found which would suit the requirements of the *v.* The other
objection is more serious; it has been pointed out that the decay of the
waist-cloth takes place after the burying in the rock, and therefore that
Jeremiah intended to imply by the parable that the captivity would

hide it there in a hole of the rock. 5 So I went, and hid it by
Euphrates, as the LORD commanded me. 6 And it came to pass
after many days, that the LORD said unto me, Arise, go to
Euphrates, and take the girdle from thence, which I commanded
thee to hide there. 7 Then I went to Euphrates, and digged,
and took the girdle from the place where I had hid it: and,
behold, the girdle was marred, it was profitable for nothing.
8 Then the word of the LORD came unto me, saying, 9 Thus
saith the LORD, After this manner will I mar the pride of Judah,
and the great pride of Jerusalem. 10 This evil people, which
refuse to hear my words, which walk in the stubbornness of their
heart, and are gone after other gods to serve them, and to worship
them, shall even be as this girdle, which is profitable for nothing.

end in the ruin of the nation, a view which is quite opposed to his
teaching elsewhere. As long ago as 1880 Birch, in *PEFQS*. pp. 236 ff.,
suggested that the Heb. should be read as פָּרָה (Parah), and that the
reference is to the small town mentioned in Josh. xviii. 23. This place
is only a few miles from Anathoth and would therefore be very familiar
to the prophet, and its insignificance might easily cause a post-exilic
scribe to 'correct' it into the present reading which in his eyes would
then contain a forecast of the captivity.

6. *after many days*. According to Keil's interpretation of the
parable these represent the seventy years of the exile. If the double
journey to the River Euphrates is taken literally much time must have
been spent on it, and there is no trace of Jeremiah's having been to
Babylon or its neighbourhood.

7. *marred*. The waist-cloth had been spoiled by water penetrating
to it. If the suggestion in the note on *v.* 4 be accepted the damage would
most likely have been caused by the waters of the *Wady Fāra*.

8—11. The explanation of the symbolical act. Just as the waist-
cloth has been spoiled by the water, so will the pride of Judah and
Jerusalem be broken down by the disasters which will come upon them.
The passage as it stands seems to contain statements which are not,
strictly speaking, consistent the one with the other. In *v.* 9, for
example, the *marring* has yet to take place, presumably during the
exile when the nation's pride will be reduced to helpless shame; but in
v. 11 there is the statement that it is on account of the marred condition of the waist-cloth that God is going to cast it away from Him;
that is, presumably, the nation is to be sent into exile. Cornill would
restore consistency by making large omissions; but such drastic treatment seems really unnecessary. We must not expect to find logical and
balanced utterances coming from the lips of a prophet like Jeremiah,
of one who was struggling to express by every means that he knew the
dangerous state into which the nation had fallen and the near approach

11 For as the girdle cleaveth to the loins of a man, so have I caused to cleave unto me the whole house of Israel and the whole house of Judah, saith the LORD; that they might be unto me for a people, and for a name, and for a praise, and for a glory: but they would not hear. 12 Therefore thou shalt speak unto them this word: Thus saith the LORD, the God of Israel, Every ¹bottle shall be filled with wine: and they shall say unto thee, Do we not know that every ¹bottle shall be filled with wine? 13 Then shalt thou say unto them, Thus saith the LORD, Behold, I will fill all the inhabitants of this land, even the kings that sit ²upon David's throne, and the priests, and the prophets, and all the inhabitants of Jerusalem, with drunkenness. 14 And I will dash them one against another, even the fathers and the sons together,

---

¹ Or, *jar*   ² Heb. *for David upon his throne.*

---

of punishment. The inconsistency, which is really only verbal, is probably original.

11. Cf. Dt. xxvi. 19; Is. lxiii. 12 ff.

praise…glory. Cf. Eph. i. 14 'to the praise of his glory.'

12—14. The parable of the wine-bottles. In this passage the prophet is evidently combating the influence of some popular proverb or saying which tended to lull the people into a false sense of security. In his usual vigorous and almost ruthless manner Jeremiah shews that this saying, like so many others, is capable of bearing several interpretations. On the lips of the people no doubt it meant that just as bottles are made to be filled with wine and in due course the wine is poured into them, so the men of Judah will receive the reward of being God's chosen people: Jeremiah, on the other hand, shews that the proverb, far from representing the certainty of Judah's triumph, is a guarantee of its punishment.

12. *bottle.* The Heb. word is used for a vessel for wine in 1 S. i. 24, x. 3; 2 S. xvi. 1, and may quite easily be used of a wine-skin (the root meaning of the word is unknown); in this passage, however, *jar* seems to be required (cf. *v.* 14), and this use can be established from xlviii. 12; Is. xxii. 24, xxx. 14, &c.

13. Having got the people to acknowledge the truth of the maxim, the prophet, speaking in God's name, turns it against them. Just as a jar is filled with wine so will the men of Judah be filled with the wine of God's wrath and made 'drunken.'

drunkenness is also used to express the results of God's wrath in xxv. 15 f.; Is. li. 17, 21, &c.

14. *dash them.* The people in their drunken fury will destroy one another.

the fathers and the sons. Cf. ix. 21 'young man and child.'

saith the LORD: I will not pity, nor spare, nor have compassion, that I should not destroy them.

15 Hear ye, and give ear; be not proud: for the LORD hath spoken. 16 Give glory to the LORD your God, before ¹he cause darkness, and before your feet stumble upon the ²dark mountains; and, while ye look for light, he turn it into ³the shadow of death, and make it gross darkness. 17 But if ye will not hear it, my soul shall weep in secret for *your* pride; and mine eye shall weep sore, and run down with tears, because the LORD's flock is taken captive. 18 Say thou unto the king and to the queen-mother,

¹ Or, *it grow dark*   ² Heb. *mountains of twilight.*
³ Or, *deep darkness*

15—17. To the wicked who continue in sin light becomes darkness because they are blinded by their overweening pride.

15. *proud.* The unbending pride of the men of Judah made it impossible for them to realise their own shortcomings or to accept the prophet's warnings: cf. Jn. ix. 39—41, xiii. 35.

16. In this *v.* Jeremiah compares the situation of the nation to that of men overtaken by sudden darkness and seeking vainly for their lost way.

light...darkness. Cf. Jn. xii. 35. For the contrast between light and darkness used symbolically see Westcott's note on 1 Jn. i. 5. *Light* here means salvation and deliverance, as in Is. lix. 9 ¹.

17. The fate of the people made constant drafts on the sympathy of Jeremiah. A rather curious Jewish tradition quoted by Edersheim (*Life and Times* &c. II. 16) applies the *v.* to God Himself, who after the fall of Jerusalem 'no longer laughs, but weeps...in a secret place of His own': cf. *Chagigah,* 56.

weep in secret. Duhm sees in this a reference to the time when Jeremiah was in hiding during the reign of Jehoiakim. But surely the usual habit of the sorrowful is to choose out a place of retirement away from the ordinary flow of life; and in Jeremiah's case the need for solitude would be infinitely greater because of the lack of sympathy of the men of Judah. He himself has told us that on account of the burden which was upon him he 'sat alone' and 'did not join the assembly of them that were merry' (xv. 17; cf. xx. 8, &c.).

the LORD's flock. Israel is represented under the figure of a flock in *v.* 20, xxiii. 2; Is. xl. 11; and frequently 2 in Psalms.

18 f. Having warned the people of Judah on account of their pride, Jeremiah goes on to attack the royal house on the same grounds. The address is evidently delivered against Jehoiachin and the queen-mother Nehushta: cf. xxii. 26 and 2 K. xxiv. 8, &c.

---

¹ Cf. Pindar, *fr.* 142, 'It is in the power of God...to shroud the day's pure gleam in cloudy darkness.'

[1]Humble yourselves, sit down: for your headtires are come down, even [2]the crown of your glory. 19 The cities of the South are shut up, and there is none to open them: Judah is carried away captive all of it; it is wholly carried away captive.

20 Lift up your eyes, and behold them that come from the north: where is the flock that was given thee, thy beautiful flock? 21 [3]What wilt thou say, when he shall set *thy* friends over thee as head, seeing thou thyself hast instructed them against thee?

[1] Or, *Sit ye down low*   [2] Or, *your beautiful crown*
[3] Or, *What wilt thou say, when he shall visit thee, seeing thou thyself hast instructed them against thee, even* thy *friends to be head* over thee?

18. *the queen-mother.* The office of *queen-mother* was one of great importance in an oriental court (cf. 1 K. ii. 19)[1]; she was one, and the wives of the king were many, and moreover the harem was under her rule. It is true that the king had the power to remove his mother from her official position (cf. 1 K. xv. 13), but this power does not seem often to have been exercised. From the comparatively frequent mention of Nehushta it would seem that she was looked upon as exercising a predominant influence over her son during his short reign.

headtires. This *v.* is better rendered by the LXX. (slightly changing the Heb., which is somewhat obscure), *come down from your head is the crown of your glory.*

19. *The cities of the South.* Heb. *Negeb*; a district in the S. of Judah, which evidently bore this name from very early times as the oldest Egyptian name for it, *pa-nagbu*, clearly shews. *Negeb* originally meant *dry, parched*, and the meaning *South* is only a secondary one: see Gray on Nu. xiii. 17. It seems strange that *the cities of the South* should be picked out for special mention; the choice is evidently intended to shew that the invaders from the N. will penetrate throughout the whole country.

20—27. A repeated lamentation over 'the beautiful flock.' From the certainty of captivity in the distant future the prophet comes back to the imminence of the actual invasion which is to lead up to it (*v.* 20); he describes the horrors which will accompany the change of rule, and goes on to drive home the lesson that they are all due to the ingrained sin of the nation (*vv.* 21—23); therefore a long period of exile will be necessary, and only after much suffering will Jerusalem be cleansed (*vv.* 24—27).

20. *thy beautiful flock.* The lamentation is addressed to Jerusalem (cf. LXX.), the fold of *the flock* and the home of its shepherds (cf. iii. 15, vi. 3, &c.). The term used points back to *v.* 17.

21. The Hebrew text of this *v.* is difficult and its meaning is ex-

[1] Naqia the mother of Esar-haddon, king of Assyria 680—688 B.C., acted as regent during her son's frequent absences on campaigns; see Johns, *Anct. Bab.* p. 123.

shall not sorrows take hold of thee, as of a woman in travail?
22 And if thou say in thine heart, Wherefore are these things
come upon me? for the [1]greatness of thine iniquity are thy skirts
discovered, and thy heels suffer violence. 23 Can the Ethiopian
change his skin, or the leopard his spots? then may ye also do
good, that are [2]accustomed to do evil. 24 Therefore will I scatter
them, as the stubble that passeth away, [3]by the wind of the
wilderness. 25 This is thy lot, the portion measured unto thee
from me, saith the LORD; because thou hast forgotten me, and
trusted in falsehood. 26 Therefore will I also discover thy skirts
[4]upon thy face, and thy shame shall appear. 27 I have seen
thine abominations, even thine adulteries, and thy neighings, the
lewdness of thy whoredom, on the hills in the field. Woe unto

[1] Or, *multitude*   [2] Heb. *taught*.
[3] Or, *unto*   [4] Or, *before*

ceedingly obscure. There is probably a reference to Hezekiah's friendship with Merodach-baladan (Is. xxxix.) and to the days of the
Assyrian supremacy when Judah and Babylon were natural allies.
Driver's rendering brings out the force of the *v.* 'what wilt thou say,
when he shall set over thee as head those whom thou hast thyself
taught to be friends unto thee?' cf. Ez. xxiii. 22 ff.

22. The metaphors used to describe the fate of Jerusalem are
themselves employed in Is. xlvii. 2 f. in reference to Babylon.

23. In considering this and similar *vv.* it is to be remembered
that the scope of the reference is not to be limited to individuals, or
even to be applied primarily to them. W. Robertson Smith remarks
in connexion with this subject that 'the prophets were not primarily
concerned with the amendment of individual sinners; it was the
nation that they desired to see following righteousness and the knowledge of Jehovah, and they were too practical not to know that the
path of national amendment is to get rid of evil-doers and put better
men in their place.' *The Prophets* &c.[2] p. 107.

the Ethiopian. i.e. *Cush*, the only non-white or non-Caucasian race
mentioned in Gen. x. The Cushites inhabited what is now called the
Sudan (from Arabic *aswād* = black). At one time they were despised
by the Hebrews (cf. Am. ix. 7), but later became very powerful: cf. Is.
xviii.; and Herodotus, III. 20. Ebed-melech was a member of this
race (xxxviii. 7, &c.).

leopard. See on iv. 11.

24. *the wind of the wilderness.* Cf. Is. xxi. 1 'whirlwinds...from
the desert, from a terrible land.'

25. *the portion...from me.* So in Job xx. 29; Ps. xi. 6.

27. *neighings.* Cf. v. 8.

thee, O Jerusalem! thou wilt not be made clean; how long shall
it yet be?

thou wilt not &c. The text is better taken as a question, *How
long will it be ere thou be made clean?* Cf. the similar question of
Hosea, 'How long ere they attain to innocency?' (viii. 5).

CHAPTERS XIV.—XV

The Drought and what came of it.

These chh. are in the form of a dialogue between the prophet and his God
in regard to a severe drought which had distressed both man and beast.
Jeremiah recognises in it a sign that Jehovah is displeased with Judah and
implores Him to have mercy. God rejects his petition, and he again renews it
pleading that the nation has been led astray by those whom they had every
reason for trusting as God's messengers. God replies that the prophets who
misled the people spoke lies in His Name and that they shall accordingly be
punished, but the doom of the nation cannot be averted. Jeremiah again replies
and reminds God of His covenant with Israel. The prophet's supplication is
once more rejected, nothing can save the people. Jeremiah thereupon breaks
into a lament regretting the day of his birth. God comforts him and at the
same time reproves him for his want of faith.

Critics are much at variance on the question of the contents of these chh.
and of the integrity of the section as a whole; most of them separate xv. 10—21
from the earlier part of the ch. and doubt whether it has any connexion with it
apart from chance arrangement. It would, however, seem quite natural for the
prophet to burst out into a wild outcry against his bitter lot, when he realised
that God would not have mercy upon the people, and that his own message
must still be one of denunciation with all the hatred and opposition which such
a message would continue to arouse.

    (*a*)   *A description of sufferings during a drought.* 1—6.
    (*b*)   *The people's prayer and God's reply.* 7—10.
    (*c*)   *Deceivers and deceived will alike be punished.* 11—18.
    (*d*)   *A further plea from the people.* 19—22.
    (*e*)   *God rejects their plea and proclaims their punishment.* xv. 1—9.
    (*f*)   *The despair of the prophet and God's promise of strength.* 10—18.
    (*g*)   *Further complaints are cut short and endurance is commanded.*
        19—21.

XIV. 1 The word of the LORD that came to Jeremiah concerning the drought.

XIV. 1—6. A vivid picture of the severity and extent of the
drought. Such a visitation was an event of great moment to an Eastern

2 Judah mourneth, and the gates thereof languish, they sit in black upon the ground; and the cry of Jerusalem is gone up. 3 And their nobles send their [1]little ones [2]to the waters: they come to the pits, and find no water; they return with their vessels empty: they are ashamed and confounded, and cover their heads. 4 Because of the ground which is [3]chapt, for that no rain hath been in the land, the plowmen are ashamed, they cover their heads. 5 Yea, the hind also in the field calveth, and forsaketh *her young*, because there is no grass. 6 And the wild asses stand on the bare heights, they pant for air like [4]jackals; their eyes fail, because there is no herbage.

[1] Or, *inferiors*   [2] Or, *for water*
[3] Or, *dismayed*   [4] Or, *the crocodile*

people, threatening as it did the means of their very existence, and no true prophet of God could have been expected to keep silence at such a crisis (cf. Dean Stanley on Elijah in *The Jewish Church*, II. 249).

1. This *v.* is evidently editorial and lays more stress on the actual *drought* than is perhaps justified by the text. Hitzig, followed by Cornill and others, sees in the passage, xiv. 2—xv. 9, a combination of two distinct accounts, one describing a *drought* (xiv. 2—10, xiv. 19—xv. 1), and the other threatening *sword, famine and pestilence* (xiv. 12—18, xv. 2—9). There seems no decisive argument in favour of this analysis, the section is concerned with the various ways in which God has punished or will punish His rebellious people, and *drought* and *famine* are intimately connected[1].

2. *gates.* i.e. cities, the part representing the whole, an expression very common in Deuteronomy. The representation is carried a stage further and the *gates* are personified and appear as sitting *upon the ground* in the garb of mourners; cf. Job ii. 13; Lam. ii. 10; Is. iii. 26.

3. *little ones.* Better as mg. *inferiors* or servants.

cover their heads. The confusion and grief of the servants are emphasised; cf. 2 S. xv. 30, xix. 5.

4. Those engaged in agriculture share the dismay of the townspeople.

5 f. Two companion pictures are drawn of the situations of the tame and the wild animals respectively; cf. Job xxxix. 1—8.

5. *hind.* The hind is noted for its care of its young; see Prov. v. 19.

6. *pant.* Cf. ii. 24, iv. 31.

jackals. The reading of mg. *crocodile* involves a slight change in Heb.; the thought suggested is the panting of the crocodiles when they come out of the water to get air.

---

[1] Cf. Flinders Petrie, *Egypt and Israel*, p. 26, 'The recent studies in Central Asia have led to the view that there are recurring periods of dryness, which…cause frequent famines (Huntingdon, *Roy. Geog. Soc.*, 1910).'

7 Though our iniquities testify against us, work thou for thy name's sake, O LORD: for our backslidings are many; we have sinned against thee. 8 O thou hope of Israel, the saviour thereof in the time of trouble, why shouldest thou be as a sojourner in the land, and as a wayfaring man that ¹turneth aside to tarry for a night? 9 Why shouldest thou be as a man astonied, as a mighty man that cannot save? yet thou, O LORD, art in the midst of us, and we are called by thy name; leave us not.

10 Thus saith the LORD unto this people, Even so have they loved to wander; they have not refrained their feet: therefore the LORD doth not accept them; now will he remember their iniquity, and visit their sins. 11 And the LORD said unto me,

¹ Or, *spreadeth* his tent

7—10. The people confess their repeated fallings away from Jehovah and yet they call upon Him not to forsake them. Jehovah replies that His forsaking them and His refusal to abide with them are on account of their own similar behaviour towards Himself. The intercession is evidently spoken by the people or put into their mouth by Jeremiah (cf. *v.* 10, *unto this people*), the drought has apparently made more impression on them than the prophetic warnings. Duhm thinks that the prophet is speaking ironically in view of the popular conception of God as a 'good-natured' Deity; cf. Hos. v. 14—vi. 4; Mic. iii. 9—11.

7. *for thy name's sake.* This phrase has usually the idea of preserving God's honour in the sight of the nations, but here the reference is perhaps to His covenant promises; cf. *vv.* 8 f.

our backslidings are many. God alone can restore His people; behind the confession of this *v.* one seems to discern the sad story of many vain attempts at amendment of life.

8. *hope of Israel.* Cf. xvii. 13.

sojourner &c. i.e. one who has no permanent interest in the nation.

to tarry for a night. Cf. Hos. vi. 1 f.; Lk. xxiv. 29; and the phrase in Wisd. v. 14 'the remembrance of a guest that tarrieth but a day,' where the stress is on the speed with which the wayfarer is himself forgotten.

9. *astonied.* Read with LXX. *asleep* which requires only very slight changes in two Hebrew letters: cf. Ps. xliv. 23 f.; Mk. iv. 38, &c.

in the midst of us. The same phrase is used by the unrighteous and blood-stained rulers of Israel in Mic. iii. 11.

10. *Even so.* God does but follow the example of His people, and make the estrangement mutual.

therefore...sins. Quoted from Hos. viii. 13 *b*.

11—18. The prophet is bidden to cease from prayer on behalf of the people and he pleads that they are deceived by their spiritual

Pray not for this people for *their* good. 12 When they fast, I will not hear their cry; and when they offer burnt offering and [1]oblation, I will not accept them: but I will consume them by the sword, and by the famine, and by the pestilence. 13 Then said I, Ah, Lord GOD! behold, the prophets say unto them, Ye shall not see the sword, neither shall ye have famine; but I will give you [2]assured peace in this place. 14 Then the LORD said unto me, The prophets prophesy lies in my name: I sent them not, neither have I commanded them, neither spake I unto them: they prophesy unto you a lying vision, and divination, and a thing of nought, and the deceit of their own heart. 15 Therefore thus saith the LORD concerning the prophets that prophesy in my name, and I sent them not, yet they say, Sword and famine shall not be in this land: By sword and famine shall those prophets be consumed. 16 And the people to whom they prophesy shall be cast out in the streets of Jerusalem because of the famine and the sword; and they shall have

---

[1] Or, *meal offering*   [2] Heb. *peace of truth.*

guides (cf. ii. 6); but Jehovah though punishing the prophets will not spare those who allow themselves to be deceived.

11. *Pray not for this people.* See on vii. 16. It is difficult to imagine that Jeremiah took God's command literally and refrained from interceding for his nation, for 'never to a people came there a true prophet who had not first prayed for them'; though doubtless the form of his intercession was altered by the constant deepening of their sin. Hitzig and other critics consider that this and the following *v.* (as far as *accept them*) are an insertion to link up *v.* 10 and *vv.* 12 *b* ff.

12. *sword...famine...pestilence.* The combination appears seven times elsewhere in Jeremiah. It is interesting to notice that the Jews still pray during the ten days of Penitence to be rid 'of pestilence, and the sword, of famine, captivity and destruction.' All three forms of suffering are the natural accompaniments of war like King Sweyn Forkbeard's 'three wonted comrades, fire, pillage and slaughter' (Henry of Huntingdon).

13 f. For the relation of the false and the true prophets see Additional Note, pp. 182 ff.

in this place. i.e. they will not go into exile.

14. The false prophets derived their message from three sources: *vision* which was legitimate; *divination* which was forbidden at any rate by Dt. xviii. 10; 2 K. xvii. 17; and their *own hearts*, a self-constituted and therefore deceitful means of seeking inspiration. Cf. Note, pp. and note on xxiii. 16.

15. Cf. xliv. 12.

none to bury them, them, their wives, nor their sons, nor their daughters: for I will pour their wickedness upon them. 17 And thou shalt say this word unto them, Let mine eyes run down with tears night and day, and let them not cease; for the virgin daughter of my people is broken with a great breach, with a very grievous wound. 18 If I go forth into the field, then behold the slain with the sword! and if I enter into the city, then behold ¹them that are sick with famine! for both the prophet and the priest ²go about ³in the land and have no knowledge.

19 Hast thou utterly rejected Judah? hath thy soul loathed Zion? why hast thou smitten us, and there is no healing for us? We looked for peace, but no good came; and for a time of healing, and behold dismay! 20 We ⁴acknowledge, O LORD, our wickedness, and the iniquity of our fathers: for we have sinned against thee. 21 Do not ⁵abhor *us*, for thy name's sake; do not disgrace the throne of thy glory: remember, break not thy

---

¹ Heb. *the sicknesses of famine.*   ² Or, *traffick*
³ Or, *into a land that they know not*   ⁴ Or, *know*   ⁵ Or, *contemn*

16. *none to bury them.* The same phrase is used in Ps. lxxix. 3 of the fate of persecuted saints.
  pour. Cf. Hos. v. 10.
18. The prophet speaks of the future as already realised when the army of Judah will have been driven into the city, leaving many fallen in the open field, there to be at the mercy of famine¹.
  go about. i.e. 'as merchantmen' (so mg. *traffic*), or if a meaning occasionally found in Syriac may be adopted 'as beggars.' Giesebrecht proposes to substitute ש for ס and reads *are bowed in mourning to the earth.*
19—22. The people renew their prayer 'acknowledging their wretchedness' and their despair of any succour apart from the God whose covenant they have broken. Duhm, followed by Cornill, rejects this passage together with xv. 1—4.
19. The only way of accounting for the distress of Zion is by concluding that it has been forsaken by God, its natural protector.
  no healing for us. Cf. Nah. iii. 19; Wisd. ii. 1.
20. *acknowledge.* Heb. *know* as in Ps. li. 3.
21. *the throne of thy glory.* Cf. 1 S. ii. 8; Ecclus. xlvii. 11. The reference is to Jerusalem and especially to the temple. If the temple fell into the hands of the invaders God's honour would be disgraced.

---

¹ The word in the original for *them that are sick* תַּחֲלֻאֵי is an Aramaism for חֳלִי, it also occurs in xvi. 4; Dt. xxix. 21; Ps. ciii. 3; 2 Ch. xxi. 19.

covenant with us. 22 Are there any among the vanities of the
heathen that can cause rain? or can the heavens give showers?
art not thou he, O LORD our God? therefore we will wait upon
thee; for thou hast [1]made all these things.

XV. 1 Then said the LORD unto me, Though Moses and
Samuel stood before me, yet my mind could not be toward this
people: cast them out of my sight, and let them go forth. 2 And
it shall come to pass, when they say unto thee, Whither shall we

[1] Or, *done*

Similar phrases are found in NT. (e.g. Matt. xix. 28 'the throne of his
glory'; Heb. iv. 16 'the throne of grace').

22. This *v.* seems to refer back to the drought described in *vv.*
2—5.

cause rain. Cf. v. 24 and see note there. Ability to produce rain
is here made a test of Divine power as it was by Elijah (1 K. xvii. 1).
The Rabbis said that there were four keys which God never trusted
to the angels, and the chief of these is that of rain. Agricultural
peoples always have a strong sense of God as one who provides for
their crops: so warlike people tend to think of God as a warrior.
God is infinite, and to each nation or individual it is given to catch
but a part of His character; and it will only be when every nation
has been won to Him and has made the contribution of its own vision
that anything like fulness of knowledge will be possible.

made all these things. This *v.* was perhaps in the mind of the
writer of Jubilees xii. 4 'worship the God of heaven, who causes the
rain...and has created everything.'

XV. 1—9. God again refuses to listen to the pleadings of the
nation. The destiny of the men of Judah is fixed and no intercessions
will make God change His attitude towards them; henceforth 'Famine
waits and War with greedy eyes.'

1. *Moses and Samuel.* Cf. Ps. xcix. 6 'Moses and Aaron and
Samuel'; and Ez. xiv. 14 'Noah, Daniel and Job.' The present passage
seems to refer to the value which the intercessions of these men would
have had, had they been alive, but in later Judaism the doctrine of the
'Intercession of Saints' was fully developed. (See Note, pp. 129 f.)

Moses constantly interceded for Israel in his lifetime (Ex. xvii. 11,
xxxii. 11 f.; Nu. xiv. 13 ff.), and later writers attributed the success
of the nation to his prayers (cf. Ass. Moses xi. 14). *Samuel* also was
noted in the same way (1 S. vii. 9 f. &c.) and his last thought at the
end of his active leadership of the people was that he still might intercede for them (1 S. xii. 17, 23). It is rather strange that neither in
this passage nor in the similar one in Ezekiel is there any mention of
Abraham or the patriarchs. *Moses* is referred to elsewhere in the
prophets in Is. lxiii. 12 and Mal. iv. 4, *Samuel* not at all. .

'Moses and Samuel and the blest St John' are taken by Dante as

go forth? then thou shalt tell them, Thus saith the LORD: Such as are for death, to death; and such as are for the sword, to the sword; and such as are for the famine, to the famine; and such as are for captivity, to captivity. 3 And I will appoint over them four [1]kinds, saith the LORD: the sword to slay, and the dogs to [2]tear, and the fowls of the heaven, and the beasts of the earth, to devour and to destroy. 4 And I will cause them to be tossed to and fro among all the kingdoms of the earth, because of Manasseh the son of Hezekiah king of Judah, for that which he did in Jerusalem.

[1] Heb. *families*.   [2] Heb. *drag*.

types of souls in the highest state of bliss (*Parad.* IV. 29) probably owing to the influence of this passage, otherwise *Moses and Elias* would have seemed a more natural choice.

2. *death.* Pestilence is more usual in these combinations (e.g. xviii. 21 and Ez. v. 12, &c.) and very probably such is here the meaning of *death*, cf. 'the Black Death.' A natural death rather than one by violence or misadventure is meant; cf. θάνατος in Rev. vi. 8, xviii. 8; and in 2 S. xxiv. 15 (LXX.).

3. *four kinds.* i.e. of destruction. Cf. the Babylonian idea of the four great plagues, Delitzsch, *Parad.* p. 146.

dogs. Orientals regard dogs as ignoble creatures, being acquainted with them only as the 'fierce prowlers of the night and scavengers of the street.' The references in OT. are constantly unfavourable and often in connexion with devouring corpses, e.g. 1 K. xiv. 11, xvi. 4; Ps. lxviii. 34; Ex. xxii. 30, &c., and cf. Homer, *Iliad*, I. 4 f.

> 'Whose limbs unburied on the naked shore,
> Devouring dogs and hungry vultures tore.'

to tear. Lit. *to drag* (as mg.). The word is used here and in xxii. 19 of corpses being dragged along the ground, and in xlix. 20 and l. 45 of captives being dragged away like sheep. It is found elsewhere only in 2 S. xvii. 13.

4. *to be tossed.* The root of the Heb. word means *to shake* and so either *to cause fear* or *to tremble.* Driver suggests the translation *I will make them a consternation* which includes both meanings.

Manasseh the son of Hezekiah. Later writers looked upon Manasseh almost as a counterpart of Jeroboam, the son of Nebat, who made Israel to sin. It is rather difficult to imagine that the second half of this *v.* comes from Jeremiah who looks upon the coming judgement as being a punishment for the sins of the whole nation and of the contemporary generation especially; also it teaches that the sins of the fathers were being avenged on the children, a doctrine with which Jeremiah did not agree (cf. xxxi. 30 and see Charles, *Eschatology*[2], p. 59). As Cornill says, 'if he really believed that the sins of Manasseh were unpardonable his whole prophetic activity would have been meaning-

5 For who shall have pity upon thee, O Jerusalem? or who shall
bemoan thee? or who shall turn aside to ask of thy welfare?
6 Thou hast rejected me, saith the LORD, thou art gone backward: therefore have I stretched out my hand against thee, and
destroyed thee; I am weary with repenting. 7 And I have
fanned them with a fan in the gates of the land; I have bereaved
them of children, I have destroyed my people; they have not
returned from their ways. 8 Their widows are increased to me
above the sand of the seas: I have brought upon them ¹against
the mother of the young men a spoiler at noonday: I have caused

---

¹ Or, *against the mother* and *the young men*

less.' The Hebrew form of Hezekiah used is that which is common in
Chronicles and this supports the suggestion that *v.* 4 *b* is a gloss, though
on the other hand it can hardly be a very late one as 2 Ch. xxxiii. 11 ff.
takes it for granted that Manasseh's sins were forgiven him. Cf. Wellhausen, *Hist. Israel*, p. 207.

5 f. The desolation of Jerusalem has come upon her of her own
free will; she has deserted God and therefore her own friends and
lovers have deserted her. The *vv.* might be paraphrased in the words
of a modern poet 'all things betray thee, who betrayest Me.'

5. Cf. Is. li. 19; Nah. iii. 7 (of Nineveh).

6. Cf. Hos. xiii. 14 'repentance shall be hid from mine eyes.'

7. *fan.* i.e. a *winnowing-fork*, such as is intended in Matt. iii. 12
'whose fan is in his hand.' For fuller particulars see *Enc. Bib.* 84;
Driver, *Jeremiah*, p. 360; and for the process cf. note on iv. 11.

the gates of the land. i.e. the entrances, hardly the cities which is
the meaning of *gates* in some passages. There is possibly a reference
to the disaster at Megiddo.

they have not returned. The men of Judah continue to carry out
their own plans in spite of the disasters which fall upon them. The
losses inflicted by the plundering bands before Jerusalem itself was
finally invested were examples of God's warnings.

8. *mother of the young men.* This phrase has caused much trouble
to most critics mainly because they have insisted on taking אֵם as a
construct before בָּחוּר (except Duhm who emends the text). LXX. as
Buttenwieser points out (*op. cit.* p. 192), in reading μητέρα νεανίσκους
took the words as being co-ordinate. אֵם probably refers to Jerusalem,
the mother-city (cf. 2 S. xx. 19 'a city and a mother in Israel'), as
Rashi already saw, and בָּחוּר to the picked or chosen warriors (cf. 2 S.
vi. 1, &c.). The phrase can then be paraphrased *I have brought* [*upon
them*] *against the metropolis yea against the picked troops which garrison
it one who will destroy them.*

noonday. Noonday is the time of rest (see on vi. 4). The attack is
therefore to come suddenly. The expression may almost be taken as

anguish and terrors to fall upon her suddenly. 9 She that hath borne seven languisheth; she hath given up the ghost; her sun is gone down while it was yet day; she hath been ashamed and confounded: and the residue of them will I deliver to the sword before their enemies, saith the LORD.

referring not to the exact time when the city was to fall, but to the brief period of its resistance[1].

anguish. Heb. עִיר the usual meaning of which is 'city'; Driver (*op. cit.* pp. 360 f.) suggests a derivation from עוּר 'to be stirred up.' It is possible that the word is an Aramaism (cf. עָר = *adversary* Dan. iv. 16; and see Driver's note on 1 S. xxviii. 16).

9. The magnitude of the coming slaughter can be conceived from the fact that even the mother of seven has lost all her children and the hope of her household is extinguished.

She that hath borne seven. A figure for perfect happiness in a woman: cf. 1 S. ii. 5 'the barren hath borne seven'; and Job i. 2, xlii. 13; Ruth iv. 15.

given up the ghost. Heb. *breathed out her soul*; cf. Job xxxi. 39.

sun...day. The figure of the sun going down while it was yet day suggests that the loss was unnecessary as well as unexpected. There may be a reference to the eclipse of Sept. 30, 610 B.C. (cf. Payne Smith, *ad loc.*).

ADDITIONAL NOTE ON XV. 1.

The 'Intercession of Saints' in Jewish Literature.

In the comment on the *v.* it was said that the reference was probably to the value which the intercessions of Moses and Samuel would have had in case they had been alive at the time and had interceded for the men of Judah. Later Jewish thought would have found no difficulty in extending the effective operation of their prayers beyond the time when they ceased to live on the earth. Even in OT. itself there are a number of passages which recognise the value and the possibility of intercession by beings in another sphere.

Job v. 1 :　　Call now; is there any that will answer thee?
　　　　　　　And to which of the holy ones wilt thou turn?
Job xxxiii. 24:　Then he (an angel) is gracious unto him and saith,
　　　　　　　Deliver him from going down to the pit.

Zech. i. 12: Then the angel...said, O Lord of hosts, how long wilt thou not have mercy on Jerusalem?

2 Macc. xv. 14: This...is the lover of the brethren who prayeth fervently for the people and the holy city, Jeremiah the prophet of God.

Tob. xii. 12: I (Raphael) did bring the memorial of your prayer before the glory of the Lord. (Cf. Rev. viii. 3 f.)

---

[1] Cf. G. A. Smith, *Twelve Prophets*, II. 62.

The Jewish Pseudepigraphal works contain many references to this doctrine, especially the book of Enoch, two of which are as follows:

ix. 3: To you the holy ones of heaven the souls of men make their suit.

xv. 2: Say to the watchers of heaven...you should intercede for men and not men for you.

(For a fuller investigation into the subject see Charles' Note on *Test. Levi* iii. 5 in his commentary on *The Testaments of the Twelve Patriarchs*; Weber, *Altsyn. Theol.* pp. 287 ff.[1])

10 Woe is me, my mother, that thou hast borne me a man of strife and a man of contention to the whole earth! I have not lent on usury, neither have men lent to me on usury; *yet* every one of them doth curse me. 11 The LORD said, Verily [1]I will

[1] The Vulgate has, *thy remnant shall be for good.*

10—18. Jeremiah is prepared to sink under the weight of oppression and persecution which has come upon him owing to the ill-will of his enemies; his life is too hard to be borne and as in xx. 14 he curses the day of his birth. In his despair he likens his isolation to that of a money-lender whom his debtors avoid, or to a debtor who will not pay his debts. The word of the Lord burning in his bones forbade him to mingle with the company of those who were making merry, and in his deep loneliness the prophet even despairs of God Himself. Longing and aching to draw his countrymen from their ruinous courses Jeremiah is, by the very efforts that he makes for them, cut off and set apart to be a mark for derision and an object of rejection.

It is interesting to notice that the message which the prophet had to deliver was so often one which made him shrink back from his task. He was impelled by no mere flood of emotion, but by the clear and calm realisation of the will of God, and of his own duty in connexion with the declaration of it.

10. *strife.* Here used of one attacked, 'an object of contention' as in Ps. lxxx. 6, usually of the aggressors: cf. Is. xli. 11; Job xxxi. 35.

whole earth. An exaggeration if taken literally, but at the same time an evidence of Jeremiah's realisation of the universal scope of his mission.

lent. The statements in the second half of the *v.* give a glimpse into the state of the nation, usury is evidently very common and the money-lenders rapacious. To lend, or to borrow, has the same effect apparently of arousing the mutual ill-will of those concerned in the transaction. 'The effect of money relations upon friendship seems to be part of the worldly wisdom of all ages.'

curse. The belief in the efficacy of a *curse* in ancient times made it something to be dreaded: cf. Nu. xxii. 6; 2 S. iii. 35.

11. A *v.* of great difficulty which is rejected by many critics and

[1] Cf. also Philo, *de Excer.* IX.; Ass. Moses xi. 11, 17, xii. 6; Apoc. Bar. ii. 2.

[1]strengthen thee for good; verily [2]I will cause the enemy to make supplication unto thee in the time of evil and in the time of affliction.

12 [3]Can one break iron, even iron from the north, and brass? 13 Thy substance and thy treasures will I give for a spoil without price, and that for all thy sins, even in all thy borders. 14 And [4]I will make *them* to pass with thine enemies into a land which thou knowest not: for a fire is kindled in mine anger, which shall burn upon you.

15 O LORD, thou knowest: remember me, and visit me, and avenge me of my persecutors; take me not away in thy long-suffering: know that for thy sake I have suffered reproach. 16 Thy words were found, and I did eat them; and thy words were unto me a joy and the rejoicing of mine heart: for I am

---

[1] Another reading is, *release*.   [2] Or, *I will intercede for thee with the enemy*
[3] Or, *Can iron break iron from &c.*
[4] Or, *I will make thine enemies to pass into &c.* According to some ancient authorities, *I will make thee to serve thine enemies in a land &c.*   See ch. xvii. 4.

---

largely emended by others. LXX. differs considerably from MT. which contains a word that is probably Aramaic. Buttenwieser (*op. cit.* p. 95) rejects *vv.* 11—14, and thinks that *v.* 15 is the natural continuation of *v.* 10. It certainly seems likely that *vv.* 13 f., at any rate, have been inserted here from their proper context after xvii. 2 (where they re-appear). *vv.* 11 f. seem to contain a reminiscence of the Divine promise in i. 18 which the prophet is endeavouring to recall.

12. This *v.* also has caused great perplexity amongst commentators; perhaps the best way of taking it is to follow the margin *Can iron break iron from the North,* and to read it as a complaint of Jeremiah that though God has made him iron, his enemies are iron of even harder substance. The alternative is to put the words into the mouth of God and to apply *iron* to the Babylonians, as Ewald does, 'Can anything avail to resist the power of the Chaldeans, the Northern Colossus?'

13 f. = xvii. 3 f. These *vv.* interrupt the dialogue between God and the prophet and are rejected by nearly all critics.

15. Jeremiah's appeal for vengeance on his enemies is based on the fact that it was for God's sake that the prophet suffered; the sin against the servant demands the intervention of the Master; cf. Ps. viii. 5, lxix. 7.

16. *I did eat them.* This phrase probably suggested Ez. ii. 8—iii. 3. The later writer, however, has worked out the thought in a way which is slightly too materialistic and literal.

rejoicing. The prophet at the outset of his ministry rejoiced to be God's servant; in the first flush of enthusiasm when his earlier shrinking had been overcome he was conscious only of the strength of Him who

called by thy name, O LORD God of hosts.   17 I sat not in the
assembly of them that make merry, nor rejoiced: I sat alone
because of thy hand; for thou hast filled me with indignation.
18 Why is my pain perpetual, and my wound incurable, which
refuseth to be healed? wilt thou indeed be unto me as a deceitful
brook, as waters that [1]fail?

19 Therefore thus saith the LORD, If thou return, then will I
bring thee again, that thou mayest stand before me; and if thou
take forth the precious from the vile, thou shalt be as my mouth:
they shall return unto thee, but thou shalt not return unto them.

---

[1] Heb. *are not sure.*

---

had called him.   He had first learned that strength in the 'eagle
flight' of a Divine revelation, he had yet to learn its sustaining power
in the 'walk' of common life; cf. Is. xl. 31.

17.   The prophet could take no joy in the ordinary pleasures of life
because all the while he was filled with a divine *indignation* (the word
is always used of God except here and in Hos. vii. 16), and could see
beneath the outward rejoicing the inward corruption and rottenness
which were eating away the life of the nation; cf. xvi. 5—9.

thy hand.   Cf. 2 K. iii. 15 (of Elisha); Is. viii. 11; Ez. i. 3, &c.

18.   Jeremiah's task was one which could never be finished—the
people would persist in their sinful ways and their sins would call
forth his continual rebuke.

incurable.   Like the hurt of the people (x. 19, xxx. 12).

deceitful.   Job makes use of the same metaphor in his complaint
about the treatment of his brethren (vi. 15). For a use of the metaphor
in an opposite sense see xxxi. 12; Is. lviii. 11.   The prophet was going
through sufferings which foreshadowed in some slight degree that experience of our Blessed Lord which called forth the great cry of
dereliction (Mk. xv. 34).

19—21.   God's answer to the prophet's complaint.   He reassures
and strengthens him, and yet at the same time points out that his
distrust and lack of courage unfit him for the life-work which he has
undertaken.   If he is to continue to be God's prophet Jeremiah must
put away his uncertainty and despair (cf. i. 17).

19.   *If thou return.*   Jeremiah had fallen away from God by his
despair and needed to repent on his own behalf; cf. Zech. iii. 7.

stand before me.   i.e. be my servant.   (See on xxxv. 19.)

the precious from the vile.   Driver paraphrases 'if thou separatest,
like a refiner, what is pure and divine in thee from the slag of earthly
passion and weakness with which it is mixed.'

mouth.   Cf. Ex. iv. 16, vii. 1.

they shall return...them.   Jeremiah had evidently fallen into the

20 And I will make thee unto this people a fenced brasen wall;
and they shall fight against thee, but they shall not prevail against
thee: for I am with thee to save thee and to deliver thee, saith
the LORD. 21 And I will deliver thee out of the hand of the
wicked, and I will redeem thee out of the hand of the terrible.

error which threatens God's servants in every age of attempting to
conform too much to the wishes of his contemporaries[1].

20. The renewal of the call is accompanied by a renewal of the
promises.

CHAPTERS XVI.—XVII. 18.

Messages of Ruin and Comfort both to Individuals and to the State.

These chh. are usually grouped together as a single narrative but the various
elements composing them have probably been collected and arranged by one
or more editors. In spite of Duhm's remark that though this passage is 'very
interesting' it is not genuine, there does not seem to be any real reason for
attributing it to any other than the prophet; at the same time it is impossible
to assign it to any particular date with any certainty. The following principal
divisions may be adopted for purposes of analysis (*vv.* xvi. 14 f. recur in xxiii. 7 f.
and are not included).

(*a*)   *The fate of those who marry and of their offspring.*   1—13.

(*b*)   *The sin of Judah will be punished by exile.*   16—xvii. 4.

(*c*)   *The contrast between those who trust in man and those who put
their trust in the Lord.*   5—13.

(*d*)   *The prophet's appeal.*   14—18.

XVI. 1 The word of the LORD came also unto me, saying,

XVI. 1—13. The prophet is forbidden to take a wife, for the
times are evil, and the offspring of those who marry will not survive,
parents and children will alike perish (*vv.* 1—4); moreover the prophet
must not take part in feasts of joy or of mourning for in the wave of
universal calamity which is coming all such feasts, with those who
partake of them, will be submerged (*vv.* 5—9); all these evils are the
result of the idolatry of the people and the prophet is commanded to
announce their true nature (*vv.* 10—13).

---

[1] The phrase is so taken by St Thomas Aquinas who says that 'we love sinners
in charity, not that we should wish what they wish, or rejoice at what they rejoice
in, but to make them wish what we wish and rejoice in what is matter of joy to
us.' *Summa II.* II. xxv. 6[4].

2 Thou shalt not take thee a wife, neither shalt thou have sons or daughters in this place. 3 For thus saith the LORD concerning the sons and concerning the daughters that are born in this place, and concerning their mothers that bare them, and concerning their fathers that begat them in this land: 4 They shall die [1]of grievous deaths; they shall not be lamented, neither shall they be buried; they shall be as dung upon the face of the ground: and they shall be consumed by the sword, and by famine; and their carcases shall be meat for the fowls of heaven, and for the beasts of the earth. 5 For thus saith the LORD, Enter not into the house of mourning, neither go to lament, neither bemoan them: for I have taken away my peace from this people, saith the LORD, even lovingkindness and tender mercies. 6 Both great and

---

[1] Heb. *deaths of sicknesses.*

---

2. *Thou shalt not take thee a wife.* Jeremiah's conduct would mark him out as a standing witness to the Jews (see Introd. p. xlii), though for one who was, as Cornill says, 'the friend of the children and who saw in *the voice of the bridegroom and the voice of the bride* the type of the purest and deepest joy,' it would be none the less difficult to abstain from marriage. Cf. the advice of St Paul in 1 Cor. vii. 25 ff.; notice especially *v.* 29 'the time is short'; the prophet had in view temporary distress, the apostle the end of all things.

in this place. Cf. vii. 3.

4. *grievous deaths.* Heb. *deaths of sicknesses.* For a state of affairs similar to that described here, cf. vii. 33, xxii. 18 f.; Ps. lxxix. 2, &c.[1] and for the use of the Aramaic word see footnote to xiv. 18.

5—9. The prophet is forbidden to shew his sympathy with either mourning or rejoicing : both alike will soon be forgotten in the troubles which are coming upon the nation.

5. *mourning.* Lit. *shrill crying*: cf. Am. vi. 7. Driver quotes Mk. v. 38 ἀλαλάζοντας πολλά.

peace. Contrast Ps. lxxxv. 8 'he will speak peace unto his people.'

lovingkindness &c. The Lord has withdrawn the marks of His interest in His people, and so Jeremiah as the Divine representative must not shew himself at such ceremonies.

6. Death is to come upon them at a time of such disturbance that the rites owing to the dead by the living will be neglected. The various signs of mourning here mentioned are forbidden by Dt. xiv. 1 and

---

[1] Cf. the description of the effects of the plague at Athens in the second year of the Peloponnesian War: 'The bodies of dying men lay one upon another, and half-dead creatures reeled about the streets:…men…became utterly careless of everything whether sacred or profane. All the burial rites before in use were entirely upset, and they buried the bodies as best they could.' Thucydides, Bk. II. ch. vii.

small shall die in this land: they shall not be buried, neither shall men lament for them, nor cut themselves, nor make themselves bald for them: 7 neither shall men ¹break *bread* for them in mourning, to comfort them for the dead; neither shall men give them the cup of consolation to drink for their father or for their mother. 8 And thou shalt not go into the house of feasting to sit with them, to eat and to drink. 9 For thus saith the LORD of hosts, the God of Israel: Behold, I will cause to cease out of this place, before your eyes and in your days, the voice of mirth and the voice of gladness, the voice of the bridegroom and the voice of the bride. 10 And it shall come to pass, when thou shalt shew this people all these words, and they shall say unto thee,

¹ See Is. lviii. 7.

Lev. xix. 28, xxi. 5; similar practices were forbidden by Muhammed, but in neither case do the prohibitions seem to have been observed.

cut themselves. Probably as a mark of 'enduring affection' as among the Australian bushmen of the present day. The custom was found among the Greeks and other ancient peoples: cf. W. Robertson Smith, *Rel. Sem.*² pp. 322 f.; Frazer, *The Dying God*, pp. 92 f., *Folk-Lore in O.T.* pp. 273 ff.

make themselves bald. This also was an ancient custom found amongst the Greeks (cf. Aesch. *Choephorae*, 167 f.; Eurip. *Alcestis*, 429, &c.) and other nations (cf. Herod. II. 36 and IX. 24, of the Persians; and IV. 71, of the Scythians). The Hebrews shaved the front of the head only (see W. Robertson Smith, *op. cit.* p. 324) and it is not stated that the hair was laid on the tomb as was the case with the Arabs (see H. P. Smith, *Rel. of Isr.* p. 27; Goldziher, *Muhammedan. Studien*, I. p. 248; and Jaussen, *Coutumes des Arabes*, p. 94).

7. *break* bread *for them.* Probably at a funeral feast which was originally perhaps a communion with the dead (see W. Robertson Smith, *op. cit.* p. 322, Note 3, and Tylor, *Primitive Culture*, II. pp. 26 ff.): cf. Hos. ix. 4; Is. viii. 19; Ecclus. vii. 23 and Tob. iv. 17.

cup of consolation. Cf. Prov. xxxi. 6 f. A somewhat similar custom still exists amongst the Arabs who slaughter 'a sheep at the death of a member of the tribe, and another seven days later. This latter is called the sacrifice of consolation.' (H. P. Smith, *op. cit.* p. 27.)

8 f. These *vv.* are an elaboration of xv. 15—18.

9. All the common festivals and simple ceremonies of everyday life are to be brought to an end as in Hos. ii. 11.

10—13. The people will profess surprise at the hard message of the prophet: the answer which he is bidden to give them. The whole section is Deuteronomic in style and teaching, and so is the method of providing a ready answer for a possible enquiry.

Wherefore hath the Lord pronounced all this great evil against us? or what is our iniquity? or what is our sin that we have committed against the Lord our God? 11 then shalt thou say unto them, Because your fathers have forsaken me, saith the Lord, and have walked after other gods, and have served them, and have worshipped them, and have forsaken me, and have not kept my law; 12 and ye have done evil more than your fathers; for, behold, ye walk every one after the stubbornness of his evil heart, so that ye hearken not unto me: 13 therefore will I cast you forth out of this land into the land that ye have not known, neither ye nor your fathers; and there shall ye serve other gods day and night; [1]for I will shew you no favour.

14 Therefore, behold, the days come, saith the Lord, that it shall no more be said, As the Lord liveth, that brought up the children of Israel out of the land of Egypt; 15 but, As the Lord liveth, that brought up the children of Israel from the land of the north, and from all the countries whither he had driven them: and I will bring them again into their land that I gave unto their fathers. 16 Behold, I will send for many fishers, saith the Lord,

---

[1] Or, *where*

10. *Wherefore.* The people apparently claim to have had no previous warnings and are full of virtuous indignation at the sudden onslaught upon their habits of worship.

13. *cast you forth.* Cf. Zech. vii. 14 'by a whirlwind.'

other gods. The change of country would be followed by a change of the objects of worship.

day and night. The reverse order *night and day* is often used as the Jews began their reckoning from sunset, so also did the Athenians (Pliny, *Hist. Nat.* II. 79). In NT. St John always adopts the order *day and night*, whilst St Paul invariably speaks of *night and day*.

no favour. *Favour* in Heb. is *chaninah*, which suggested one of the names of the later Jews for the Messiah; 'The Gracious One' as we might say. (Cf. Edersheim, *Life and Times* &c. I. 155 n.)

14 f. These *vv.* recur in xxiii. 7 f. where they appear to be original.

16—18. The great sin of Judah will bring upon it a complete and terrible punishment.

16. Neither the depths of the sea nor the heights of the mountains will serve as a refuge from the fury of the Lord. The fishers will 'net' the inhabitants, while the hunters track down the few who have escaped from the cities.

fishers. Cf. a similar use of the metaphor in Am. iv. 2; Hab. i. 15; Ez. xii. 13, xxix. 4, 8 and also in Herod. III. 149, IV. 9, VI. 31 (σαγηνεύειν).

and they shall fish them; and afterward I will send for many hunters, and they shall hunt them from every mountain, and from every hill, and out of the holes of the rocks. 17 For mine eyes are upon all their ways : they are not hid from my face, neither is their iniquity concealed from mine eyes. 18 And first I will recompense their iniquity and their sin double; [1]because they have polluted my land with the carcases of their detestable things, and have filled mine inheritance with their abominations. 19 O LORD, my strength, and my strong hold, and my refuge in the day of affliction, unto thee shall the nations come from the ends of the earth, and shall say, Our fathers have inherited nought but lies, *even* vanity and things wherein there is no profit. 20 Shall a man make unto himself gods, which yet are no gods? 21 Therefore, behold, I will cause them to know, this once will I cause them to know mine hand and my might; and they shall know that my name is Jehovah.

[1] Or, *because they have polluted my land: they have filled mine inheritance with the carcases of their detestable things and their abominations*

The metaphor is used by our Blessed Lord with a gracious reversal of application (cf. Mk. i. 17, &c.)[1].

17. Cf. Am. ix. 8; Job xxxiv. 21; Prov. v. 21, xv. 3.

18. *double.* Cf. Is. xl. 2 for the fulfilment of the threat. *Double* means ample, the idea that God's punishment has been too great cannot as Skinner says 'be pressed theologically.'

carcases of their detestable things. The idols whom the people worshipped are merely so much carrion.

19—21. The heathen will one day recognise the folly of their fathers and turn to the service of Jehovah, a thought which is common in the later half of Isaiah.

19. *vanity,* 'denotes figuratively what is evanescent, unsubstantial, worthless.' Driver.

20. The god which a man makes for himself has no more power than its maker.

21. A single exhibition of Jehovah's great power will convince the nations of His unique position amongst the gods. The connexion with the previous *vv.* is awkward owing to the sudden introduction of God as the speaker. The *v.* is in the manner of the second Is. and reads like an exilic promise of restoration.

---

[1] Cf. Clem. Alex. *hymn. in Chr.* where our Lord Himself is the fisher (quoted in Dr Swete's commentary on *St Mark*).

XVII. 1 The sin of Judah is written with a pen of iron, *and* with the point of a diamond: it is graven upon the table of their heart, and upon the horns of [1]your altars; 2 whilst their children remember their altars and their [2]Asherim by the green

---

[1] Another reading is, *their*.　　[2] See Ex. xxxiv. 13.

XVII. 1—4. Judah's sin is so deeply engraven that it is impossible to pass it over.

These *vv.* are omitted from LXX. perhaps, as Cornill thinks, because the translator's eye wandered from יהוה in xvi. 21 to יהוה in xvii. 5. St Jerome suggests that the Greek translators omitted the passage in order not to hand down to posterity words of such strong condemnation[1]. It is possible that this suggestion gives the correct reason for the omission, though strictly speaking it applies to *vv.* 1 f. only.

1. *pen of iron.* Cf. Job xix. 24 (of graving in the hard rock).

diamond. The diamond was probably unknown to the ancient Hebrews (cf. *Enc. Bib.* 63 and 1097) as it was to the Greeks before the time of Alexander; probably the hard mineral corundum is meant, it is still used for polishing steel and cutting gems. The same Heb. word is used in Ez. iii. 9 for the firmness of the prophet and in Zech. vii. 12 as a figure for a hard heart.

table of their heart. The phrase recurs in Prov. iii. 3, vii. 3, the word for *table* is that used of the tablet on which the Decalogue was written.

2 f. The text is almost certainly corrupt as it stands or at any rate it has been glossed. Duhm and Cornill following the Syriac version omit *whilst their...Asherim.* Driver renders *vv.* 1—3 *a* as follows:

'The sin of Judah is written with a pen of iron,
　With the point of a diamond is it graven
　　Upon the table of their heart,
　Upon the horns of their altars, upon every spreading tree,
　Upon the high hills, the mountains in the field.'

Keil, following the Rabbinic commentators, takes *children* as the object and translates כ *when* by *as*: as (they) think of their children, (so they think of) their altars.

Asherim. These were wooden posts in all probability worshipped as representing sacred trees[2]. Such posts would form part of the furniture of the Canaanite shrines which were taken over by the Israelites.

---

[1] 'Ne scilicet aeterna in eos sententia permaneret' (quoted by Dr Streane, *The Double Text* &c. p. 150).

[2] The Mishnah strangely enough looks upon Asheras as actual trees: cf. *Aboda Zara*, iii. 7 f. and the notes in the edition by W. A. L. Elmslie in *Texts and Studies*. G. F. Moore doubts the connexion of the Ashera with a living tree: *Enc. Bib.* 331.

trees upon the high hills. 3 O my mountain in the field, I will give thy substance and all thy treasures for a spoil, *and* thy high places, because of sin, throughout all thy borders. 4 And thou, even of thyself, shalt discontinue from thine heritage that I gave thee; and I will cause thee to serve thine enemies in the land which thou knowest not: for ye have kindled a fire in mine anger which shall burn for ever.

5 Thus saith the LORD: Cursed is the man that trusteth in man, and maketh flesh his arm, and whose heart departeth

---

The reformation under Josiah had abolished the high places, and yet so strong was the attraction of the sacred spots that the hearts of the men of Judah still yearned towards them. In the same way some of the earliest followers of Muhammed asked the prophet to appoint them certain sacred trees (quoted by Cheyne, *Life and Times* &c. p. 103), and even Christianity itself was unable to eradicate the tendency to tree-worship of some of the Syrians (see W. Robertson Smith, *Rel. Sem.*² p. 186)[1].

3. *mountain in the field.* Cf. xiii. 27 'hills in the field,' and xxi. 13 'rock of the plain'; also Is. ii. 3 'mountain of the LORD.' Evidently Jerusalem is meant, though the figure is an awkward one (see further on xxi. 13), and perhaps the words are best attached to the previous *v.* as Driver suggests (see above).

4. *of thyself.* Heb. ובך should probably be read ידך as suggested by J. D. Michaelis: the *v.* will then run *and thou shalt withdraw thine hand from thine heritage* &c. (cf. Dt. xv. 3).

5 f. In this section Jeremiah goes to the very root of Judah's failure and shews the cause of her continual sin. Though the worship of God was still carried on and His name was constantly on the lips of the people yet any real trust or belief in Him had long departed from among them. The men of Jerusalem were so convinced of their own skill and cleverness that they ignored the need of Divine aid, and like 'the drunkards of Ephraim' they might have said 'we have made a covenant with death and with hell are we at agreement' (Is. xxviii. 1, 15).

5. This *v.* is used in the Commination Service.

the man. Cornill sees in the passage a reference to Zedekiah in person.

flesh his arm. 'Judah sought man's help, not only apart from God, but against God. God was bringing them down, and they, by man's aid, would lift themselves up.' Pusey on Hos. v. 13.

---

[1] Cf. the letter of Gregory the Great to the Bishop of Terracina ordering him to punish certain tree-worshippers (Greg. *Reg. Ep.* VIII. 19; quoted by Ed. Spearing in *The Patrimony of the Roman Church*, p. 12).

from the LORD. 6 For he shall be like ¹the heath in the desert,
and shall not see when good cometh; but shall inhabit the parched
places in the wilderness, a salt land and not inhabited. 7 Blessed
is the man that trusteth in the LORD, and whose ²hope the LORD
is. 8 For he shall be as a tree planted by the waters, and that
spreadeth out his roots by the river, and shall not ³fear when
heat cometh, but his leaf shall be green; and shall not be careful
in the year of drought, neither shall cease from yielding fruit.
9 The heart is deceitful above all things, and it is desperately

¹ Or, *a tamarisk*   ² Heb. *trust*.   ³ According to another reading, *see*.

from the LORD. Whatever a man trusts in becomes his god, whether
it be the net of the poor fisherman described in Habakkuk (i. 16), or
the armies of great powers like Egypt (as here) or Assyria (Is. x.
13 ff.).

6.   *the heath*. The reference is to the juniper tree (cf. Tristram,
Nat. Hist. of Bible, p. 358) which is a symbol of desolation owing
to its being cropped by the wild goats.

a salt land and not inhabited. Cf. Dt. xxix. 23; Ps. cvii. 34.
The imagery is suggested by the land round the Dead Sea (cf. Zeph.
ii. 9), which has been well described by a recent traveller as follows :
'Before us lay a sheet of hard mud on which no green thing grows.
It is of a yellow colour, blotched with a venomous grey-white salt :
almost unconsciously the eye appreciates its enmity to life' (G. Lowthian Bell, *The Desert and the Sown*, p. 12).

7 f. In strong contrast with the man who relies on mere human
aid is the true worshipper of God. The prophet describes him in
language very like that of Ps. i. 3 f.¹ as having a constant supply
of nourishment and refreshment even in the time of heat and drought.

8.   *planted*. Better perhaps *transplanted*, the word is always used
with some reference to the choice of situation.

in the year of drought. The righteous man abides in God and can
safely endure the misfortunes of life ; the evil man, on the contrary, is
in distress even in the time of plenty and is liable to sudden destruction
(cf. Prov. xi. 28; Ez. xvii. 5—10).

yielding fruit. Like 'the tree of life' in Rev. xxii. 2.

9—11. The heart of man is no sure ground of confidence, nor
will anyone but a fool place reliance on riches acquired by unlawful
means.

9. No man ever knows fully his neighbour's thoughts and motives,
nor whether he will remain faithful to his engagements.

¹ That there is a close connexion between the two passages is generally admitted, but commentators are not agreed as to which is the original. Kirkpatrick
in *Camb. Bib.* says that Jeremiah paraphrases and expands the passage from
the Ps.; on the other hand Briggs in *Int. Crit. Comm.* says that the *v.* is based
on Jer. xvii. 5—8 and Ez. xlvii. 12.

sick: who can know it? 10 I the LORD search the heart, I try
the reins, even to give every man according to his ways, according
to the fruit of his doings. 11 As the partridge ¹that gathereth
young which she hath not brought forth, so is he that getteth
riches, and not by right; in the midst of his days ²they shall
leave him, and at his end he shall be a fool.

12 A glorious throne, *set* on high from the beginning, is the
place of our sanctuary. 13 O LORD, the hope of Israel, all that
forsake thee shall be ashamed; they that depart from me shall
be written in the earth, because they have forsaken the LORD,

---

¹ Or, *sitteth on* eggs *which she hath not laid*	² Or, *he shall leave them*

---

deceitful. Buttenwieser (*Prophets*, p. 106) suggests the translation
intricate and compares Is. xl. 4; and Ecclus. xx. 6.
10. God alone can search the hearts of men and reward them according to their merits. If this *v.* is in its proper context the meaning must
be that God who is ' greater than our hearts' and who alone can know
them is a safer ground of confidence than they are.
I the LORD search. The attributes of God here set out are applied
to our Blessed Lord in the letter to the church of Thyatira (Rev. ii. 23;
cf. also Jn. ii. 25; Acts i. 24, xv. 8; Rom. viii. 27; Ps. vii. 10).
11. This *v.* reads like an extract from the book of Proverbs and
seems hardly in a suitable context here.
partridge. The *partridge* is the most common game-bird in
Palestine, though it is only referred to three times in OT. (here;
1 S. xxvi. 20; and Ecclus. xi. 30). The *partridge* lays so many eggs
that she was popularly thought to steal eggs from other birds. The
meaning of the figure is plain, though the application of it is difficult:
wealth is compared to the young birds who soon desert their foster-
mother (following mg.); or as Driver, who proposes the rendering
that heapeth together eggs, *but doth not bring forth* young, suggests
'with allusion to the large number of eggs laid...which are eagerly
sought for by the Arabs as food, so that the bird often hatches no
young.'
12 f. A description, in the manner of the Psalms, of the enduring
might of God.
12. *on high.* Cf. Is. vi. 1.
13. *written in the earth.* Cf. the expression 'written on the sand,'
a figure for that which is unenduring, and also the epitaph on Keats'
tomb, chosen by the poet himself to represent the shortness of his life,
'Here lies one whose name was writ in water.' The opposite of this
phrase is used in Lk. x. 20 'your names are written in heaven.' The
Heb. word for *earth* hardly means 'ground' or 'soil' and so the phrase
is difficult; perhaps Giesebrecht's emendation יכרתו *they shall be cut off*
for יכתבו *they shall be written* gives the best solution of the difficulty.

the fountain of living waters. 14 Heal me, O LORD, and I shall
be healed; save me, and I shall be saved: for thou art my praise.
15 Behold, they say unto me, Where is the word of the LORD?
let it come now. 16 As for me, I have not hastened from being
a shepherd after thee; neither have I desired ¹the woeful day;
thou knowest: that which came out of my lips was before thy
face. 17 Be not a terror unto me: thou art my refuge in the
day of evil. 18 Let them be ashamed that persecute me, but
let not me be ashamed; let them be dismayed, but let not me be

¹ Some ancient versions read, *the judgement day of man.*

14—18. The prophet is in deep distress because of the reproaches
of his countrymen, evidently they accuse him of delighting in condemnations and forecasts of woe. In the anguish of his soul he turns
to his only source of comfort, and cries out to God for strength and
courage. With pathetic entreaty he prays God to be not a *terror* to
him, such as were his familiar friends (xx. 10); nor to send him forth
once more with a message of reproof; but to be a refuge and a shelter
to hide in.

15. These words must have been written before the approach of the
Babylonian armies, and certainly before the first fall of Jerusalem. If
the earlier chh. of Jeremiah refer to the Scythian invasion, whose
terrors passed harmlessly by the men of Jerusalem, this *v.* may be a
taunt over their non-fulfilment. Such mistakes in detail do not
discredit the prophets, who, after all, are dealing with great principles
which are bound to fulfil themselves sooner or later, though the time
may be more distant than the prophet himself imagines (cf. W.
Robertson Smith, *Prophets²*, pp. 268 f.; Buttenwieser, *op. cit.* p. 153).

Where. This is a not unusual way of beginning a taunt in both
OT. and NT., e.g. Ps. xlii. 3 'where is now thy God?' 2 Pet. iii. 4
'where is the promise of his coming?'

16. *from being a shepherd.* These words are represented by one
word only in the Heb., and this word can be read, without any change
in the consonantal text, *because of the evil,* the translation adopted by
Aq. and Symm. The meaning would then be in the words of Dr Streane,
who approves of the alteration, 'I have not pursued thee with persistent
supplication to bring calamity upon my foes.' The meaning of the
v. as it stands in RV., however, is quite consistent and hardly needs
'much improvement to the parallelism'; Jeremiah did not refuse to
bear God's message and to act as a prophet, but on the other hand, he
certainly did not *desire the woeful day.* The title *shepherd* is nowhere
else applied to a prophet, though it is used of one entrusted with the
care of a nation.

dismayed: bring upon them the day of evil, and [1]destroy them
with double destruction.

---

[1] Heb. *break them with a double breach.*

---

18. *double destruction.* Rothstein in order to make this reading
possible emends the Heb. and reads the construct state[1]. Is it not
possible to take מִשְׁנֶה as an accusative of time and to translate *destroy*
them with a second destruction? According to Buttenwieser who puts
forward the above suggestion (*op. cit.* 110 f.), the first destruction which
the prophet has in mind is the fall of Samaria. If *double* is retained
it may mean *complete* (cf. xvi. 18 and note there); it can hardly refer,
as some commentators used to think, to a punishment which will be
effective in this life and also in that which is to come.

CHAPTER XVII. 19—27.

The Sabbath is to be hallowed by the Cessation of all Labour.

The genuineness of this section has been denied by the majority of critics
mainly on two grounds, viz.: that (1) it bears signs of belonging to a later date;
and (2) the attitude towards ceremonies is inconsistent with Jeremiah's usual
teaching.

(1) Jeremiah does not elsewhere refer to the Sabbath, and indeed the pre-
exilic prophets had apparently little interest in it except as a day of rest for
the common people (cf. Am. viii. 5). It was during the exile that the importance
of the Sabbath as a mark of the religion of Jehovah first came to be realised;
when the Jews, cut off as they were from the temple, had a hard struggle to
preserve their national and religious life in the midst of heathen institutions
(Ez. xx. 12). As Peake remarks 'the detachment of the Jews from sacred places
by the exile gave a wholly new value to sacred times.' In this passage such
stress is laid on the keeping of the Sabbath that the very existence of the State
is made to depend upon it. Such an attitude seems to be post-exilic and to
reflect the situation of Haggai and Zechariah, especially as *v.* 25 seems to imply
that at the time when it was written no king sat on the throne of David, and
v. 26 tacitly excludes Samaria from those offering worship at Jerusalem. Most
critics, for these reasons, connect the section with such a passage as Neh.
xiii. 15—22 (so Kuenen, *Einleitung*, II. 167 ff.; Duhm; Cornill &c.), and indeed
some find traces in it of actual dependence on that passage (Siegfried, *Ezra,*
Neh. u. Esth. on Neh. xiii. 15; and Buttenwieser, *op. cit.* 49 ff.).

(2) In this section not only is stress laid on the importance of keeping the
Sabbath holy, but in *v.* 26 there is also a high regard expressed for incense and
sacrifices. This seems at first sight quite inconsistent with Jeremiah's usual

---

[1] מִשְׁנֶה for מִשְׁנָה.

teaching. It should, however, be remembered that the Sabbath was an ancient custom and that it had not only a ritual but also a humanitarian significance; and also it is quite possible that in the prophet's mind the ideal future would be a time when worthy sacrifices might be offered out of pure and sincere hearts (cf. Driver, *LOT.*[8] p. 258). A similar sentiment seems to have moved some later writer to add *vv.* 18 f. to Ps. li. (cf. *vv.* 16 f.).

In conclusion it must be admitted that the passage bears resemblances, possibly due to imitation, to the style of Jeremiah, and that it may belong, as Orelli thinks, to the early years of his ministry (it is certainly out of its context here); but on the whole the point of view displayed in it is post-exilic and closely akin to that of Nehemiah.

In considering the question of Sabbath observance, especially in the present day, the two aspects of the institution should both be borne in mind. The Sabbath has a religious and a social aspect; in other words, it is to be regarded as the day upon which special worship is offered to Almighty God, and as the day on which men deny themselves in order that their neighbours may also have an opportunity for rest and worship, 'The enemies of the sabbath are the enemies of the poor.' The late Edward King, Bishop of Lincoln, in one of his pastoral letters recommended three names to be used for Sunday. (1) *The Lord's Day.* 'The day for special worship in every best way we can; the day for the special Christian service, the Eucharist.' (2) *The Day of Rest.* 'We should rest from our bodily labours that our minds and hearts may have leisure to learn more of God.' (3) *The Home Day.* 'All the members of the family are at home on Sunday; it is a day for cultivating Brotherly Love; a day for rekindling the love in our own households.'

19 Thus said the LORD unto me: Go, and stand in the gate of [1]the children of the people, whereby the kings of Judah come in, and by the which they go out, and in all the gates of Jerusalem; 20 and say unto them, Hear ye the word of the LORD, ye kings of Judah, and all Judah, and all the inhabitants of Jerusalem, that enter in by these gates; 21 thus saith the LORD: Take heed [2]to yourselves, and bear no burden on the sabbath day, nor bring

[1] Or, *the common people* See ch. xxvi. 23.   [2] Or, *for your life's sake*

19. *gate of the children of the people.* As the gate is also used by the kings in some peculiar way the expression is difficult, and no satisfactory suggestion has been made as to its locality or special use.

20. *kings.* Again no satisfactory explanation has been offered for the plural, though it is possible that it is a scribal error perhaps due to the influence of *v.* 25 (cf. xxii. 2).

21. *burden.* In the passage Neh. xiii. 15—21 the word *burden* seems to refer to merchandise and possibly the same reference is to be supposed here, in which case Sunday trading is especially condemned.

it in by the gates of Jerusalem; 22 neither carry forth a burden out of your houses on the sabbath day, neither do ye any work: but hallow ye the sabbath day, as I commanded your fathers; 23 but they hearkened not, neither inclined their ear, but made their neck stiff, that they might not hear, and might not receive instruction. 24 And it shall come to pass, if ye diligently hearken unto me, saith the LORD, to bring in no burden through the gates of this city on the sabbath day, but to hallow the sabbath day, to do no work therein; 25 then shall there enter in by the gates of this city kings and princes sitting upon the throne of David, riding in chariots and on horses, they, and their princes, the men of Judah, and the inhabitants of Jerusalem: and this city shall ¹remain for ever. 26 And they shall come from the cities of Judah, and from the places round about Jerusalem, and from the land of Benjamin, and from the lowland, and from the mountains, and from the South, bringing burnt offerings, and sacrifices, and ²oblations, and frankincense, and bringing *sacrifices of* thanksgiving, unto the house of the LORD. 27 But if ye will not hearken unto me to hallow the sabbath day, and not to bear a burden and enter in at the gates of Jerusalem on the sabbath day; then will I kindle a fire in the gates thereof, and it shall devour the palaces of Jerusalem, and it shall not be quenched.

¹ Or, *be inhabited*   ² Or, *meal offerings*

22. *out of your houses.* This law was avoided by the later Jews by merging 'several private precincts into one' by which means food or vessels would not be moved *out of the houses,* and so could be carried to any distance (see Herford's note in *Oxford Apoc.* II. p. 827).

25. *and princes.* Evidently an insertion (cf. *their princes*) and so to be omitted.

26. The restored kingdom is evidently to be limited to the tribes of Judah and Benjamin, i.e. Samaria is not included in it. This seems to reflect a post-exilic standpoint and is as much opposed to the usual teaching of Jeremiah (cf. iii. 11 ff., xxiii. 6, &c.) as is the value attached to incense.

lowland...mountains...the South. Every part of Judah is to be represented, the Shephelah (including the foothills on the Philistine border), the hill country round Jerusalem, and the Negeb or land to the South (cf. Josh. xv. 21—60 where the same districts are referred to but in different order).

27. *will I kindle...palaces.* This expression is borrowed from Am. i. 4, &c. (where see E. A. Edghill's note) and is used frequently by

B.   10

Jeremiah (cf. xxi. 14, xlix. 27, l. 32, also xliii. 12) and by other prophets (Hos. viii. 14; Ez. xx. 47).

CHAPTER XVIII.

The Visit to the Potter's House and what came of it.

Chh. xviii.—xx. all deal with subjects connected with the potter's art, hence probably their being placed together in the collection of Jeremiah's prophecies. The earlier *vv.* of ch. xviii. have met with much criticism—Duhm rejects everything up to *v.* 12 as too trivial, and Cornill rejects *vv.* 5—12 as an insertion which misses the point of the story. It is quite true that the teaching of *vv.* 7—12 is not in agreement with that of *v.* 4; the former *vv.* imply that God will reject His agents entirely if they fail, whereas the meaning of the original figure is that God's plans cannot be baffled by the failure of His agents, they can be remoulded and, as it were, given a fresh start.

(*a*) *Jeremiah is commanded to go down to the potter's house.* 1—4.
(*b*) *God's dealings with the nations.* 5—12.
(*c*) *Judah's horrible crime shall receive a punishment of horror.*
     13—17.
(*d*) *The people's plot and the prophet's prayer.* 18—23.

XVIII. 1 The word which came to Jeremiah from the LORD, saying, 2 Arise, and go down to the potter's house, and there I

XVIII. 1—4. God commands the prophet to go down to the house of the potter. This section is interesting as furnishing what is perhaps the first recorded instance of the use of a symbol found in many languages and literatures[1]. For other instances of its use in biblical and cognate literature in addition to those referred to below, see Is. xlv. 9, lxiv. 8; Wisd. xv. 7; Ecclus. xxxiii. 13; also Test. XII. Patriarchs, *Napht.* ii. 2—4. For non-biblical uses cf. the saying of Heraclitus 'the clay out of which things are made is for ever being moulded into new forms' (Zeller, *Pre-Soc. Phil.* II. p. 17); Omar Khayyam, *Rubaiyat*, XXXVI., LIII., LIX. ff.; and in our own day Browning's *Rabbi Ben Ezra*, XXV.—XXXII.

2. *the potter's house.* Probably some well known place where Jeremiah had often watched the potter at work (though Hebrew idiom does not demand this). The potters of Judah formed a guild (1 Ch. iv. 23) and probably occupied a quarter of their own, perhaps on the lower slopes of Hinnom (cf. *go down*).

---

[1] Is. xxix. 16 is possibly earlier but its genuineness is questionable. The Egyptians also believed that the god Khnoumou moulded gods and men on a potter's wheel: cf. J. G. Frazer, *Magic Art*, II. p. 132.

will cause thee to hear my words. 3 Then I went down to the
potter's house, and, behold, he wrought his work on the wheels.
4 And when the vessel that he made of the clay was marred in
the hand of the potter, he made it again another vessel, as seemed
good to the potter to make it.

5 Then the word of the LORD came to me, saying, 6 O house
of Israel, cannot I do with you as this potter? saith the LORD.
Behold, as the clay in the potter's hand, so are ye in mine hand,
O house of Israel. 7 At what instant I shall speak concerning
a nation, and concerning a kingdom, to pluck up and to break
down and to destroy it; 8 if that nation, concerning which I

3. *the wheels.* The potter made use of two wheels, the smaller resting
on the larger, which was driven by the feet of the potter (Ecclus. xxxviii.
29 f.). For a full description see *Enc. Bib.* 3820 and Thomson, *The
Land and the Book*, pp. 520 f.

4. *the clay was marred* &c. The potter is not dependent on his
material but can mould it according to his own ideas, and he is free to
change his plans for any particular portion of it during the process of
manufacture. Jeremiah's use of the symbol of the potter's clay is quite
different from that of St Paul in Rom. ix.—xi., where the Apostle uses
it to shew man's powerlessness in God's hands and the Creator's absolute
right over His creatures. This interpretation of the figure, which may
be called the pessimistic interpretation, has made the deeper impression
on men's minds, but it is not the one which is uppermost in the mind
of Jeremiah: his interpretation of the symbol is on the contrary opti-
mistic, God can remould His creatures if they fail and does not need
to cast them utterly away.

5—12. Just as the potter re-moulds his material when it proves
unsuitable for a particular vessel, so God deals with the nations. In *vv.*
11 f. the general principle is applied to the specific case of Judah (cf.
Am. ii. 6 ff.).

7 ff. God's threats, like His promises, are conditional. If the nation
continues in its sin then will the effects of His anger fall upon it; if
however it accepts His warning then it will be spared. God's unlimited
power, as Keil says, 'is exercised according to man's conduct, not according to a *decretum absolutum* or unchangeable determination.' This
passage contains no application to individuals (contrast Ez. xviii. 21 ff.,
xxxiii. 12 ff.) and no thought of predestination in the popular sense, for
vv. 8 f. shew that Jeremiah is not thinking of men's hearts but of their
external circumstances.

7. *a nation.* The statement of the principles which regulate God's
dealings with nations is quite general and 'perhaps implies that the
prophet hoped his teaching might bear fruit beyond the border of Israel
proper.' Kennett, *Servt. of the Lord*, p. 24.

have spoken, turn from their evil, I will repent of the evil that I thought to do unto them. 9 And at what instant I shall speak concerning a nation, and concerning a kingdom, to build and to plant it; 10 if it do evil in my sight, that it obey not my voice, then I will repent of the good, wherewith I said I would benefit them. 11 Now therefore go to, speak to the men of Judah, and to the inhabitants of Jerusalem, saying, Thus saith the Lord: Behold, I frame evil against you, and devise a device against you: return ye now every one from his evil way, and amend your ways and your doings. 12 But they say, There is no hope: for we will walk after our own devices, and we will do every one after the stubbornness of his evil heart.

13 Therefore thus saith the Lord: Ask ye now among the nations, who hath heard such things; the virgin of Israel hath done a very horrible thing. 14 Shall the snow of Lebanon fail from the rock of the field? *or* shall the cold waters [1] that flow

---

[1] Or, *of strange lands that flow down be &c.*

8. *I will repent.* 'The necessities of human thought require that sometimes, through man's failure or change, God, who is unchangeable, should be said to repent. The temporary interruption of the accomplishment of His counsel of love must appear in this light under the conditions of time to those "who see but part."' Westcott on Heb. vii. 21. Cheyne rejects *vv.* 5—10 on the ground that Jeremiah was quite certain of the destruction of Jerusalem, *Enc. Bib.* 3878.

11. *frame.* The Heb. word for *potter* is derived from this verb.

12. The people are self-condemned; cf. Is. xxviii. 15, xxx. 10 f.

13—17. Judah's horrible crime will soon be followed by a punishment of equal horror.

13. *Ask ye...among the nations.* Cf. ii. 10 f., v. 30; and 1 Cor. v. 1.

virgin. The use of this term in its present context adds to the horror of the description.

14. *rock of the field.* The meaning of this phrase is obscure; in xvii. 3 Jerusalem is apparently called 'my mountain in the field' (cf. xxi. 13), but such an interpretation would throw no light on the present context. Various attempts have accordingly been made to find an explanation by means of emendations. (1) Giesebrecht suggests that *sâdeh* (field) should be pointed *Shaddai* (Almighty); (2) Duhm would emend so as to read Sirion (the Phoenician name for Mt Hermon, cf. Dt. iii. 9; Ps. xxix. 6)[1] and he translates 'Does the hoar frost leave Sirion, the

---

[1] It is interesting in view of Duhm's suggestion to notice that the Arabs call Hermon *Towil eth-Thalj* 'the height of snow.'

down from afar be ¹dried up? 15 For my people hath forgotten me, they have burned incense to vanity; and they have caused them to stumble in their ways, in the ancient paths, to walk in bypaths, in a way not cast up; 16 to make their land an astonishment, and a perpetual hissing; every one that passeth thereby shall be astonished, and shake his head. 17 I will scatter them as with an east wind before the enemy; I will ²look upon their back, and not their face, in the day of their calamity.

18 Then said they, Come, and let us devise devices against

¹ Or, *plucked up*   ² Or, *shew them the back, and not the face*

snow Lebanon?'; (3) Cornill's suggestion is very similar to the last, he would read (substituting *white* for *Lebanon*, the root meaning of which is *white*) 'Does the white snow melt away from the rock of Sirion?' In support of this suggestion it has been pointed out that Lebanon, unlike Hermon, does not retain its snow throughout the summer.

cold waters...dried up. The second half of the *v.* is equally obscure and certainly requires some emendation even if it be only the slight one adopted by RV., i.e. the transposition of one letter in order to read *dried up* for *plucked up* (mg.) which term can hardly be applied to waters. The Heb. translated literally then reads *shall the strange, cold, flowing waters be dried up.* *Strange* should probably be omitted as an accidental repetition of *cold* (the words are very similar in the original) though Duhm by a rather elaborate and ingenious emendation retains it. He, however, divides up the Heb. consonants differently and reads *waters of the scatterers* instead of *strange waters.* By a reference to an obscure passage in Job xxxvii. 9 he explains the *scatterers* as the rainbringing Northern stars. This explanation seems much too involved and it is perhaps best to adopt Rothstein's suggestion and read *are the cold flowing waters of the hills dried up?* The meaning is quite clear in spite of the apparent corruption of the text: the waters of Lebanon are constant (cf. Cant. iv. 15) but the conduct of Judah is fickle and unnatural; cf. viii. 7 where the birds who obey their instincts are contrasted with the disobedience of Judah.

15.   *For.* This may continue *v.* 13 or on the other hand it may draw out a different thought from *v.* 14: Judah's faithlessness is the cause of her coming punishment, she has given up God and so will become like a stream separated from its source (cf. ii. 13).

ancient paths. Cf. vi. 16. The difficulties of travel in ancient times are well illustrated by passages such as these.

16.   *hissing.* A sound expressing not contempt but surprise; cf. Jud. v. 16.

17.   *east wind.* For a description of this wind see *Enc. Bib.* 5304 f. and Driver on Am. iv. 9.

18—23.   The people form a plot against Jeremiah, who gives himself

Jeremiah; for the law shall not perish from the priest, nor counsel from the wise, nor the word from the prophet. Come, and let us smite him with the tongue, and let us not give heed to any of his words.

19 Give heed to me, O LORD, and hearken to the voice of them that contend with me. 20 Shall evil be recompensed for good? for they have digged a pit for my soul. Remember how I stood before thee to speak good for them, to turn away thy fury from them. 21 Therefore deliver up their children to the famine, and give them over to the power of the sword; and let their wives become childless, and widows; and let their men be slain of death, *and* their young men smitten of the sword in battle. 22 Let a cry be heard from their houses, when thou shalt bring a troop suddenly upon them: for they have digged a pit to take me, and hid snares for my feet. 23 Yet, LORD, thou knowest all their counsel against me to slay me; forgive not their iniquity, neither blot out their sin from thy sight: but let

up to prayer (cf. xi. 18—23, xii. 1—6, xv. 10 f., 15—21). There is no clue to the date of this passage which appears here as a fragment; it probably comes from a time after Jeremiah's attack on the temple.

18. Note the three classes of recognised teachers, the *priest* who gave answers to enquirers by means of the sacred lot, or by the traditions of his sanctuary; the *wise man* who gave advice to those who consulted him; the *prophet* to whom the message of the Lord came in order that he might deliver it to the people: cf. viii. 8; Ez. vii. 26. If God really turned His back on the nation, as Jeremiah foretold, these three sources of counsel would be dried up.

19. Jeremiah brings himself and his adversaries before God's tribunal.

20. Jeremiah brings to God's recollection his own prayers on the nation's behalf and in the bitterness of his soul repents that they were ever made.

stood. The usual attitude for prayer, cf. xv. 1; Neh. ix. 4, &c., though at times of special urgency kneeling was resorted to (1 K. viii. 54; Ezra ix. 5; Dan. vi. 10, &c.).

21—23. These *vv.* are in such strong contrast to Jeremiah's habitual attitude towards the people of Judah that many critics look upon them as a later addition.

21. The expression of the desire for vengeance upon the wife and family of the offender is very similar to Ps. cix. 9 ff.

22. *a troop suddenly.* The punishment is evidently to be caused by raiders rather than by a regular invasion.

digged a pit &c. As in Ps. lvii. 6.

them be ¹overthrown before thee; deal thou with them in the time of thine anger.

¹ Heb. *made to stumble.*

CHAPTERS XIX.—XX. 6.

The Symbol of the Broken Vessel.

The connexion between this section and ch. xviii. is probably literary rather than chronological. The account evidently refers to a time when Babylon had become prominent (xx. 4), and should therefore be dated sometime after the Battle of Carchemish which took place in the third year of the reign of Jehoiakim, 605 B.C. Duhm considers the whole passage to be late, but there are no reasonable grounds for such a sweeping treatment though there can be little doubt that later insertions have been included, e.g. xix. 3—9.

(a) *The prophet's instructions.* 1 f.
(b) *The prophet's message.* 3—9.
(c) *The symbolical action.* 10—13.
(d) *The vengeance of the authorities.* 14—xx. 6.

XIX. 1 Thus said the LORD, Go, and buy a potter's earthen bottle, and *take* of the elders of the people, and of the elders of the priests; 2 and go forth unto the valley of the son of Hinnom, which is by the entry of ¹the gate Harsith, and proclaim there the words that I shall tell thee: 3 and say, Hear ye the word of

¹ Or, *the gate of potsherds*

XIX. 1 f. Jeremiah is bidden to go to the valley of Hinnom carrying with him an earthen vessel and accompanied by some of the elders: he will there receive God's message.

1. *elders of the priests.* Cf. 2 K. xix. 2. The command does not allow of any hesitation or refusal on the part of the elders, Jeremiah evidently still had great influence and was recognised as God's spokesman.

2. *valley...of Hinnom.* See on vii. 31.

the gate Harsith. Better with mg. *the gate of potsherds*, perhaps from the broken vessels lying near it or because potsherds were there ground down in order to make cement (*PEFQS.* 1904, p. 136). AV. renders *the east gate*, deriving *Harsith* from *ḥeres* 'sun.' The reference is probably to the gate called the Dung-gate in Neh. ii. 13, &c. which led into the valley of Hinnom.

3—9. These *vv.* are generally rejected as an editorial insertion by most critics since Giesebrecht, the contents of the section being very similar to other parts of the book; and also because it seems strange

the LORD, O kings of Judah, and inhabitants of Jerusalem; thus saith the LORD of hosts, the God of Israel, Behold, I will bring evil upon this place, the which whosoever heareth, his ears shall tingle. 4 Because they have forsaken me, and have estranged this place, and have burned incense in it unto other gods, whom they knew not, they and their fathers and the kings of Judah; and have filled this place with the blood of innocents; 5 and have built the high places of Baal, to burn their sons in the fire for burnt offerings unto Baal; which I commanded not, nor spake it, neither came it into my ¹mind: 6 therefore, behold, the days come, saith the LORD, that this place shall no more be called Topheth, nor The valley of the son of Hinnom, but The valley of Slaughter. 7 And I will ²make void the counsel of Judah and Jerusalem in this place; and I will cause them to fall by the sword before their enemies, and by the hand of them that seek their life: and their carcases will I give to be meat for the fowls

---

¹ Heb. *heart.*   ² Heb. *empty out.*

---

that when Jeremiah has been told to go to the valley of Hinnom to hear God's message he should be represented as receiving it immediately. A further argument advanced by Giesebrecht is that the Greek of this passage is different in style from the rest of the book, which suggests that the original translators did not find these *vv.* in their Heb. text and so it was added later. There is nothing remarkable in the subject matter of the section which, as was pointed out above, is apparently derived from other passages: terrible punishments are to come upon Jerusalem on account of the evil rites practised by her, and so straitened will the city become that the inhabitants will be reduced to cannibalism.

3. *kings.* The use of the plural seems to point to a time when the monarchy was only a memory (cf. xvii. 20), though it may be merely a scribal mistake due to dittography. At the same time the prophet may be addressing the shade of the monarchs whose wickednesses had some share in causing the coming distress (cf. *v.* 4 LXX.).

ears shall tingle. Cf. 1 S. iii. 11; 2 K. xxi. 12.

4.   *estranged.* By worshipping foreign gods in it.

their fathers and the kings of Judah; and have filled. LXX. places the division at *fathers* and continues *and the kings of Judah have filled* &c.

blood of innocents. Cf. ii. 34; 2 K. xxi. 16, xxiv. 4; the reference however should not be confined to child-sacrifice.

5 f.   Almost identical with vii. 31 f.

7.   *make void.* Heb. *empty out* with a play on the word for *earthen bottle*; used in Is. xix. 3 of 'courage.' The latter part of *v.* is similar to vii. 33.

of the heaven, and for the beasts of the earth. 8 And I will make this city an astonishment, and an hissing; every one that passeth thereby shall be astonished and hiss because of all the plagues thereof. 9 And I will cause them to eat the flesh of their sons and the flesh of their daughters, and they shall eat every one the flesh of his friend, in the siege and in the straitness, wherewith their enemies, and they that seek their life, shall straiten them. 10 Then shalt thou break the bottle in the sight of the men that go with thee, 11 and shalt say unto them, Thus saith the LORD of hosts: Even so will I break this people and this city, as one breaketh a potter's vessel, that cannot be made whole again: and they shall bury in Topheth, ¹till there be no place to bury. 12 Thus will I do unto this place, saith the LORD, and to the inhabitants thereof, even making this city as Topheth: 13 and the houses of Jerusalem, and the houses of the kings of Judah, which are defiled, shall be as the place of Topheth, even all the houses upon whose roofs they have burned incense unto all the host of heaven, and have poured out drink offerings unto other gods.

¹ Or, *because there shall be no place else*

8.   This *v.* is very similar to xviii. 16.

9.   *eat the flesh.* A worse fate than for the body to be left unburied (cf. Lev. xxvi. 29; Ez. v. 10; and Lam. iv. 10); the *v.* is derived from Dt. xxviii. 53, commenting on which Driver says, 'The thought...is dwelt upon for the purpose of illustrating, in two vivid pictures, the ghastly reversal of natural affection to which the severity of the siege will give rise.'

10—13.   In ch. xviii. Jeremiah taught that God could remould the potter's clay and that a nation if only it would repent might be spared; the potter's art is here used to shew the fate of the nation which refuses to hear God's warnings. The prophet, if *vv.* 3—9 are genuine, first gave the teaching and then enforced it by his dramatic action; if however the *vv.* be omitted Jeremiah first performed the action and then interpreted it to the elders.

11.   *and they...bury.* Omitted by LXX. and almost certainly an insertion from vii. 32.

13.   See on viii. 2 and cf. xxxii. 29, xxxiii. 4; 2 K. xxiii. 11 f.; Zeph. i. 5; and Ez. xxiii. 7.

roofs. The flat roofs of oriental houses were and are used for a variety of purposes (see Dr Swete on Mk. xiii. 15 f.).

14 Then came Jeremiah from Topheth, whither the LORD had
sent him to prophesy; and he stood in the court of the LORD's
house, and said to all the people: 15 Thus saith the LORD of
hosts, the God of Israel, Behold, I will bring upon this city and
upon all her towns all the evil that I have pronounced against
it; because they have made their neck stiff, that they might not
hear my words.

XX. 1 Now Pashhur the son of Immer the priest, who was
chief officer in the house of the LORD, heard Jeremiah prophesying these things. 2 Then Pashhur smote Jeremiah the prophet,
and put him in the stocks that were in the upper gate of Benjamin, which was in the house of the LORD. 3 And it came to pass

14—**XX.** 6. The prophet returns to Jerusalem and repeats the
substance of his message in the temple court to the people there assembled. He is arrested by Pashhur and imprisoned in the stocks. Jeremiah
denounces Pashhur and foretells his fate.

14. Doubtless the news of Jeremiah's action had preceded his return
and the people would wait with much curiosity for his message: the
temple crowds would differ but little from those of our Lord's day when
His deeds and sayings were eagerly discussed amongst them.

XX. 1. *Pashhur the son of Immer*. Both *Pashhur* and *Immer* appear
in post-exilic times as names of priestly families (see Ezra ii. 37 f., x. 20;
Neh. vii. 40, &c.) and this fact has caused some doubt to be thrown on
the genuineness of their reference here to persons. *Pashhur* however is
common in this book, appearing in xxi. 1 and xxxviii. 1 (of two different persons). According to *v.* 6 Jeremiah's opponent was himself a
prophet, this fact need not cause surprise as the majority of the prophets
were apparently firm allies of the priests and it was only when individual
prophets rose above the spiritual level of their order that conflicts ensued.

chief officer, lit. *ruler, overseer*. The office seems to have carried
with it functions similar to those exercised by Zephaniah 'the second
priest' (xxix. 26, cf. lii. 24), though there is nothing to shew that the
two offices were identical (cf. Erbt, *Jeremia*, pp. 15—17).

2 f. The Bible records three other instances of similar treatment;
Micaiah (1 K. xxii. 24 f.), St Paul (Acts xxiii. 2 f.) and our Blessed
Lord Himself (Matt. xxvi. 67 f.). In every instance except the last the
undeserved insult brought forth a fierce reply from the victim.

2. *the stocks*, according to Ecclus. xxxiii. 26, were much used to
punish unfaithful servants.

gate of Benjamin. The northern gate of the temple (cf. 2 K. xv. 35);
one of the city gates bore the same name and is referred to in xxxvii. 13
and xxxviii. 7.

3. The Hebrew prophets whilst they denounced the sins of the
nation at large were also concerned with the offences of individuals. Cf.

on the morrow, that Pashhur brought forth Jeremiah out of the stocks. Then said Jeremiah unto him, The LORD hath not called thy name Pashhur, but ¹Magor-missabib. 4 For thus saith the LORD, Behold, I will make thee a terror to thyself, and to all thy friends: and they shall fall by the sword of their enemies, and thine eyes shall behold it: and I will give all Judah into the hand of the king of Babylon, and he shall carry them captive to Babylon, and shall slay them with the sword. 5 Moreover I will give all the riches of this city, and all the gains thereof, and all the precious things thereof, yea, all the treasures of the kings of Judah will I give into the hand of their enemies, which shall spoil them, and take them, and carry them to Babylon. 6 And thou, Pashhur, and all that dwell in thine house shall go into captivity: and thou shalt come to Babylon, and there thou shalt die, and there shalt thou be buried, thou, and all thy friends, to whom thou hast prophesied falsely.

¹ That is, *Terror on every side.*

Amos' denunciation of Amaziah, the priest of Bethel (Am. vii. 10—17); and Isaiah's condemnation of Shebna (Is. xxii. 15 ff.).

Magor-missabib meaning as the mg. says *terror on every side.* The expression is also used in *v.* 10, vi. 25, xlvi. 5, xlix. 29; Lam. ii. 22.

4. In this case the fate of the survivor is worse than that of the slain (cf. xxii. 10); the death of Pashhur's friends seems to be connected with him in some way; possibly he was a traitor, or more probably he represented a policy which resulted in the overthrow of Jerusalem and his friends with it.

6. *all thy friends.* In *v.* 4 the *friends* were to be slain.

CHAPTER XX. 7—18.

The Prophet's Complaints.

This section quite evidently contains two distinct complaints by the prophet, and the connexion between them, in spite of the opinion of Rothstein, can hardly be more than external and accidental. The tremendous importance of *vv.* 7—10 as a revelation of the working of the prophetic mind has already been commented upon in the Introduction (pp. xiii, xv) and the burst of praise which follows it (*vv.* 11—13) comes quite naturally upon the lips of one who has surrendered himself to God's inspiration. The difficulty arises when the attempt is made to read *vv.* 14—18 as an immediate sequel, for as Buttenwieser says, 'It would be psychologically impossible...for such faith, such surrender, such spiritual exultation...to be followed immediately by such utter dejection and bitterness of spirit.' Ewald tried to avoid this difficulty by transposing the two sections and it is possible that such a change represents the true order, it is best however to treat the two passages as quite independent expressions of the prophet's agony.

Most critics look upon *vv.* 7—13 as coming from a time in Jeremiah's ministry when his words were merely received with derision (*v.* 7 *b*) because the danger which he foretold was still very remote and indeed not yet apparent. The rest of the passage, however, seems to shew that the prophet has suffered violence and that he has had many internal struggles to overcome; *v.* 10 also suggests the later part of his ministry when he suffered much from those who spied upon him. The burst of praise (*vv.* 11—13) may have been the natural result of Jeremiah's trust in God, but if any external event called it forth none would seem more suitable than the prophet's rescue from the dungeon (xxxviii. 10—13).

> (*a*)　*Jeremiah's complaint.*　7—10.
> (*b*)　*The outburst of praise.*　11—13.
> (*c*)　*Jeremiah curses the day of his birth.*　14—18.

7　O Lord, thou hast ¹deceived me, and I was deceived: thou art stronger than I, and hast prevailed: I am become a laughing-stock all the day, every one mocketh me.　8 For as often as I speak, I cry out; I cry, Violence and spoil: because the word of

---

¹ Or, *enticed*

7—10. Jeremiah complains that God has seized upon him and forced him, against his own will, to become the vehicle of the Divine utterance regarding Judah and Jerusalem. The circumstances of the prophet's life are too strong for him and he lives in an atmosphere of perpetual danger and suspicion. There is a rather interesting parallel to this protest of Jeremiah in the *Sibylline Oracles,* III. 1 ff. ' O thou who thunderest from on high...I pray thee give me a short respite from mine unerring oracle, for my soul within me is weary. Nay why did my heart again flutter, and why is my soul lashed with a spur from within, compelled to announce my message ? '

7. *deceived*: mg. *enticed.* The underlying idea is that the prophet has been drawn into an undertaking which was dangerous beyond anything which he had anticipated. Savonarola had exactly the same feeling, as he told the people of Florence in Advent 1494: 'I was in a safe haven, the life of a friar; I looked at the waves of the world and saw therein much fish; with my hook I caught some, that is by my preaching I led a few into the way of salvation. As I took pleasure therein the Lord drave my bark into the open sea. Before me on the vast ocean I see terrible tempests brewing. Behind I have lost sight of my haven: the wind drives me forward, and the Lord forbids my return.' Quoted by Creighton, *Hist. of the Papacy,* IV. 252 f.

8.　*Violence and spoil.* The monotony of Jeremiah's message was

the LORD is made a reproach unto me, and a derision, all the day.
9 And if I say, I will not make mention of him, nor speak any
more in his name, then there is in mine heart as it were a burning fire shut up in my bones, and I am weary with forbearing,
and I cannot *contain*. 10 For I have heard the defaming of
many, terror on every side. Denounce, and we will denounce
him, *say* all my familiar friends, they that watch for my halting;
peradventure he will be enticed, and we shall prevail against
him, and we shall take our revenge on him. 11 But the LORD
is with me as a mighty one *and* a terrible: therefore my persecutors shall stumble, and they shall not prevail: they shall be
greatly ashamed, because they have not [1]dealt wisely, even with
an everlasting dishonour which shall never be forgotten. 12 But,

---

[1] Or, *prospered*

---

apparent even to himself, and yet it was the only one possible in view
of the state of the nation (cf. xxiii. 33 ff. and the similar experience of
Isaiah, xxviii. 9 ff.).   Some critics, however, take the reference to be to
the prophet's own experience whenever he speaks in God's name,
Buttenwieser, for example, translates *As often as I speak I have to cry
out, have to complain of violence and abuse.*

unto me. Not a reproach and derision to Jeremiah himself, but
the cause of his being a reproach and derision (cf. xv. 15).

9. *burning fire.* If the messengers of the old dispensation, which
was one of condemnation, thus burned to deliver their message how
much more should the preacher of the glad tidings of salvation long
'to burn out for God.' Qui non ardet non incendit. The metaphor of
fire is often used for the effect of the prophet's message; see Ecclus.
xlviii. 1 where it is said of Elijah that he 'arose a prophet like fire
whose word was like a burning furnace.' Cf. Mal. iv. 1, 5.

10. *familiar friends.* Cf. xxxviii. 22; Ps. xli. 9.

enticed. The plan of these false friends was probably similar to
that of the Pharisees who endeavoured to entrap our Lord into making
incriminating statements by means of which they could denounce Him
to the authorities.   The experiences of the servants are gathered up in
the experiences of the Master.

11—13. The prophet's confidence is fixed on the infinite might
and knowledge of God and therefore he can be certain of ultimate
triumph.

11.   *as a mighty one* &c. Kimchi suggested the possibility of
applying these words to Jeremiah himself which improves the sense of
the *v.*   *Since the LORD is with me I am as a mighty one...therefore my
persecutors shall stumble.*

12.   This *v.* is probably a gloss here from xi. 20.

O LORD of hosts, that triest the righteous, that seest the reins and the heart, let me see thy vengeance on them; for unto thee have I revealed my cause. 13 Sing unto the LORD, praise ye the LORD: for he hath delivered the soul of the needy from the hand of evil-doers.

14 Cursed be the day wherein I was born : let not the day wherein my mother bare me be blessed. 15 Cursed be the man who brought tidings to my father, saying, A man child is born unto thee; making him very glad. 16 And let that man be as the cities which the LORD overthrew, and repented not: and let him hear a cry in the morning, and ¹shouting at noontide; 17 because he slew me not from the womb; and so my mother should have been my grave, and her womb always great. 18 Wherefore came I forth out of the womb to see labour and sorrow, that my days should be consumed with shame?

¹ Or, *an alarm*

13.   When the prophet's heart is strengthened he feels that the victory is won, for his worst enemy is his own weakness of spirit.

14—18.   Jeremiah bewails the hour in which he was born, the beginning of a life of pain and sorrow.   A similar passage is to be found in Job iii. 3—12 and in the opinion of most critics it is based on the present one.   Peake, for example, says, 'Jeremiah's is a natural outburst, springing from a soul stirred to its depths; Job's curse is much more artificial and literary' (see however Bishop Gibson, *Job*, p. xx).

14.   *the day.*   An anniversary of woe not of joy and therefore to be cursed and not to be blessed.   Cf. Euripides, *Cresph.* fr. 452 (quoted by Westcott, *Relig. Thought in the West*, p. 123).

> ''Twere well that men in solemn conclave met,
> Should mourn each birth as prelude of great woes.'

15.   Jeremiah recollects all the circumstances which aroused joy and turns them into occasions of misery.   He goes further than Job who merely curses the day itself—he does not however curse those directly responsible for his coming into the world.

man child.   The birth of a daughter was not considered to be a matter for rejoicing (cf. *Menachoth*, 43*b*).   Ecclus. xxii. 3 states that a daughter is born to the loss of her father.

16.   *the cities.*   Gen. xix. 25; cf. Is. xiii. 19.

17.   *from.*   LXX., Syr. *in* as required by the context.

CHAPTERS XXI.—XXIV.

These chapters deal with a series of messages delivered in response to an enquiry by Zedekiah as to the issue of Nebuchadrezzar's warlike approach, for this reason Ewald gave them the name of 'The Roll of Zedekiah.' In his reply Jeremiah depicts, in the darkest colours, the ultimate fate of Jerusalem; and at the same time he proceeds to shew upon whose shoulders the blame for it must lie. The state of desperate peril to which the nation has been brought is due primarily to the failure of the natural leaders of the people both in Church and State.

> The prophet's warning. xxi.
> Denunciations of the royal house. xxii.
> The ideal king. xxiii. 1—8.
> Denunciations of the false prophets. xxiii. 9—40.
> The symbol of the basket of figs. xxiv.

CHAPTER XXI.

Jerusalem will fall before the Babylonians.

The beginning of this ch. is placed in the reign of Zedekiah and in the midst of the siege; a truly extraordinary change of date and situation from the last one. No really satisfactory explanation can be given for the sudden transition and for the juxtaposition of the two chh.—possibly the occurrence of the name Pashhur in each section, though the reference is to different persons, may account for it. There are close similarities between the present narrative and that recorded in xxxvii. 3—10, and some critics would accordingly refer the two passages to the same incident. It is quite likely, however, that Zedekiah sent to Jeremiah for advice on more than one occasion and there are differences in the situations pre-supposed by the two narratives which suggest that they belong to different stages of the siege. The ch. may be analysed as follows:

> (a) *Zedekiah's enquiry and Jeremiah's answer.* 1—7.
> (b) *In submission alone lies the way of escape.* 8—10.
> (c) *A warning to the house of David.* 11 f.
> (d) *A fragment of condemnation.* 13 f.

XXI. 1 The word which came unto Jeremiah from the LORD,

XXI. 1—7. Jeremiah's reply to the deputation which Zedekiah sent to enquire as to the result of the siege:—God will fight for the enemies of Jerusalem until the city falls into their hands. The deputation which consisted of men of high rank (cf. Balak's embassy to Balaam; Nu. xxii. 15) was sent in all probability shortly after the beginning of the siege (cf. *v.* 4).

1. *The word...LORD.* The same introduction occurs in vii. 1, xi. 1, &c.

when king Zedekiah sent unto him Pashhur the son of Malchijah, and Zephaniah the son of Maaseiah the priest, saying, 2 Inquire, I pray thee, of the LORD for us; for Nebuchadrezzar king of Babylon maketh war against us: peradventure the LORD will deal with us according to all his wondrous works, that he may go up from us.

3 Then said Jeremiah unto them, Thus shall ye say to Zedekiah: 4 Thus saith the LORD, the God of Israel, Behold, I will turn back the weapons of war that are in your hands, wherewith ye fight against the king of Babylon, and against the Chaldeans which besiege you, without the walls, and I will gather them into the midst of this city. 5 And I myself will fight against

Pashhur. In xx. 1 the name also occurs of another Pashhur, the son of Immer the priest. Pashhur the son of Malchijah, who is mentioned here and xxxviii. 1, was probably not a priest as the title does not appear after his name (contrast Zephaniah).

Zephaniah. It has been suggested that *Zephaniah* was the father of Josiah (see Zech. vi. 10, cf. 14). He is mentioned also in xxix. 25 and xxxvii. 3. In the latter passage he appears as being sent to Jeremiah on a similar errand; some critics therefore think that the recurrence of the name makes it probable that two different accounts have been preserved of the same interview.

2. *Nebuchadrezzar.* The original of the name is *Nabu kuduruzur,* i.e. Nebo protect the crown; the form here used is therefore the correct one (see Schrader, *KAT.*² pp. 361 ff.).

wondrous works. Zedekiah evidently expected a miraculous intervention of the Divine Power similar to that which had occurred in the time of Hezekiah (Is. xxxvii. 6). The king and his advisers failed entirely to realise that the possibility of Jehovah's intervention depended on the moral condition of those who besought it. This state of affairs must have made the position of Jeremiah exceedingly difficult. Why did he not come forward like a second Isaiah and save the nation and the holy city? At the very least he ought to strengthen the defenders by encouraging words.

4. From the evidence of this *v.* the siege was only in its early stages as fighting was still taking place outside the walls (cf. Is. xxviii. 6). Jeremiah, however, foretells that the defenders will be driven in, and the city closely invested; contrast the very different answer of Isaiah under similar circumstances (xxxvii. 29).

5. The language of this *v.* is similar to that of Dt. xxix. 28. Duhm points out that the strong phrases elsewhere used of Jehovah fighting against the enemies of Israel, are here used of His fighting against Israel itself.

you with an outstretched hand and with a strong arm, even in anger, and in fury, and in great wrath. 6 And I will smite the inhabitants of this city, both man and beast: they shall die of a great pestilence. 7 And afterward, saith the LORD, I will deliver Zedekiah king of Judah, and his servants, and the people, even such as are left in this city from the pestilence, from the sword, and from the famine, into the hand of Nebuchadrezzar king of Babylon, and into the hand of their enemies, and into the hand of those that seek their life: and he shall smite them with the edge of the sword; he shall not spare them, neither have pity, nor have mercy. 8 And unto this people thou shalt say, Thus

outstretched hand. The figure is here used of punishment, and not, as is more common, of salvation (cf. Dt. iv. 34, v. 15, xxvi. 8 and see on *v.* 5).

anger...fury...great wrath. Notice the threefold repetition of synonyms in this and the following *v. Anger* (אף), lit. *nostril*, represents the heavy breathing caused by strong emotion, the word is generally used, by an anthropomorphism, of the Divine anger; *fury* (חמה) comes from a root meaning to be hot, and therefore means burning anger, rage; *great wrath* (קצף) is always used of God except in late passages.

6. *man and beast.* The city would be crowded with refugees who had fled from the surrounding country driving their cattle before them.

pestilence. The outbreak of epidemics was an especial danger during a siege, and sometimes played a decisive part in ancient warfare. See further on xvi. 4.

7. *edge of the sword.* Lit. *according to the mouth of the sword* i.e. as the sword devours, ruthlessly, without mercy or quarter.

spare...pity...have mercy. These three words represent the contemplative, the negative, and the active sides of benevolence respectively. The last word is generally used of God's loving-kindness.

8—10. Submission alone can bring escape from death: the people are bidden to make their choice. The message to the king is followed by a message to the people; but though these two passages are placed together, it is by no means necessary to suppose that they were spoken on the same occasion. The prophet puts to his hearers the same pitiable alternative as in the answer to the king—life, on the one hand, by desertion to the enemy; on the other, death, by remaining in the city.

8. The figure of the Two Ways is, according to Cornill, of Jeremiah's coinage. It also occurs in Dt. xxx. 15, and became very popular with later writers of an allegorical turn of mind (e.g. Ecclus. xv. 17; Mt. vii. 13 f.; 2 Pet. ii. 2; *The Didache* i. 1; Ep. Barn. 17; Clem. Alex. *Strom.* v. 5).

B.

saith the LORD: Behold, I set before you the way of life and the way of death. 9 He that abideth in this city shall die by the sword, and by the famine, and by the pestilence: but he that goeth out, and falleth away to the Chaldeans that besiege you, he shall live, and his life shall be unto him for a prey. 10 For I have set my face upon this city for evil, and not for good, saith the LORD: it shall be given into the hand of the king of Babylon, and he shall burn it with fire.

11 And touching the house of the king of Judah, hear ye the word of the LORD: 12 O house of David, thus saith the LORD, Execute judgement in the morning, and deliver the spoiled out

the way of life. The way, that is, which leads to life; that policy which will ultimately result in the salvation of the State, or in the personal safety of the individual, as the case may be.

9. *for a prey.* i.e. escape with his bare life. The figure is of one who goes out in search of spoil, and in the end is glad to return without the loss of his life. Jeremiah is the only writer who makes use of the metaphor (xxxviii. 2, xxxix. 18, xlv. 5), and this is the first occasion of his so doing. It is possible that our Lord's picture of the man who gained the whole world and yet lost his own life ($\psi v \chi \acute{\eta}$), was suggested by this usage of Jeremiah (Mk. viii. 36). Cf. Ea's warning to Utnapishtim in the Babylonian flood story:—

> 'Forsake thy possessions, seek to save life
> Abandon thy goods and cause thy soul to live.'

10. *set my face.* The same expression is found in Arabic; and cf. Lk. ix. 51.

11 f. These *vv.* have no apparent connexion either with what precedes or with what follows. They evidently come from an earlier period when national repentance was still possible. No really satisfactory reason can be suggested for their presence here unless the reference to *fire* in *vv.* 10 and 14 seemed to provide a context for *fire* in *v.* 12.

12. *O house of David.* The mention of *David* was doubtless intended as a reminder to the king of his noble ancestry, and all that it involved of service to God and uprightness towards man.

judgement. To administer justice was the primary duty of the oriental ruler, and was recognised as such by the popular conscience; hence the success of Absalom's specious arguments against his father (2 S. xv. 4).

morning. The early morning was the usual time for the administration of justice, so as to avoid the heat of the later part of the day (cf. 2 S. iv. 5). The reference, however, need not be taken literally; the prophet's demand is that the king should make justice his first concern

of the hand of the oppressor, lest my fury go forth like fire, and
burn that none can quench it, because of the evil of ¹your doings.
13 Behold, I am against thee, O ²inhabitant of the valley, ³*and*
of the rock of the plain, saith the LORD; ye which say, Who shall
come down against us? or who shall enter into our habitations?
14 and I will punish you according to the fruit of your doings,
saith the LORD: and I will kindle a fire in her forest, and it shall
devour all that is round about her.

¹ Another reading is, *their*.   ² Heb. *inhabitress*.   ³ Or, *and rock*

(cf. Zeph. iii. 5, and the constantly recurring phrase 'rising up early
and sending').

spoiled...oppressor. These words are often found in the same
context. The Heb. word for *spoiled* is used in Job xxiv. 9 of a child
snatched from its mother's breast. *Oppressor* may be used of tyranny
over a nation or an individual (cf. vii. 6, xxii. 3).

13 f. These *vv.* have been described as 'very obscure and difficult,'
and it is indeed hard to explain them in their present context with any
satisfaction. *Inhabitant* (*v.* 13) is feminine and would naturally be
applied to Jerusalem; but the holy city was situated neither in a
valley, nor yet upon a *rock* rising from a *plain* (cf. Ps. cxxv. 2).
Possibly the passage as originally composed referred to some other
nation or city (cf. xlviii. 8, 45 on Moab) and having been detached
from its context was inserted here by a compiler; so Driver.

13. *I am against thee.* Cf. Ez. xiii. 8.

plain. The Heb. word used here (מִישׁוֹר) is generally applied to the
elevated table-land east of the Jordan (cf. xvii. 3).

come down. This phrase is never used of approaching Jerusalem.

habitations. Driver suggests the translation *lairs,* and adds the
following note: ' In which we are secure, like lions in their forest homes.
The word, as Ps. civ. 22; Nah. ii. 12 ("dens").'

14. *forest.* Cf. xlvi. 23. Jerusalem is compared to a *forest* by
Ezekiel (xxi. 1—4), and Israel by Isaiah (ix. 18, x. 18). Keil suggests
that the figure was chosen because a city was a *forest* of houses (cf.
xx. 6).

CHAPTER XXII.

A Series of Denunciations of the Kings of the Period.

This ch. contains a number of oracles on the kings of Judah who succeeded
Josiah; it is not probable that they were all uttered on the same occasion, and
therefore it is necessary to suppose that they have been brought together by

Jeremiah himself, or by Baruch, or some other editor. Many critics think that the original oracles have received later additions.

(a) *Jeremiah's mission of warning.* 1—5.
(b) *Forecast of the overthrow of the house of David.* 6—9.
(c) *The oracle on Jehoahaz.* 10—12.
(d) *The contrast between Josiah and Jehoiakim.* 13—19.
(e) *The fate of Coniah.* 20—30.

XXII. 1 Thus said the LORD: Go down to the house of the king of Judah, and speak there this word, 2 and say, Hear the word of the LORD, O king of Judah, that sittest upon the throne of David, thou, and thy servants, and thy people that enter in by these gates. 3 Thus saith the LORD: Execute ye judgement and righteousness, and deliver the spoiled out of the hand of the oppressor: and do no wrong, do no violence, to the stranger, the fatherless, nor the widow, neither shed innocent blood in this

XXII. 1—5. This section, with that which follows, forms an introduction or setting to the oracles as a whole and is to a large extent the work of an editor. In *vv.* 1—5 the rulers are exhorted to do justice in the land if they desire God's favour (cf. the similar stress on justice in xxi. 11 f.).

1. For the opening formula *Thus said the LORD* followed by a command, cf. xiii. 1, xxvi. 2, xxvii. 2.

Go down. The temple, where Jeremiah evidently received God's commands, was higher than the palace; cf. xxvi. 10, xxxvi. 12; 2 Ch. xxiii. 20.

2. The phraseology of this *v.* is rather unusual, but has some similarity to vii. 2, xvii. 20.

throne of David. The men of Judah were undoubtedly proud that their reigning family could claim direct descent from *David*, especially in contrast with the short lived dynasties of the ill-fated Northern Kingdom. The unbroken succession had also its significance as a mark of God's favour.

that enter in by these gates. Cf. the use of the same phrase in Gen. xxiii. 10, 18, xxxiv. 24, for the citizens of a town.

3. This *v.* from its tone might be an utterance by Micah, or Isaiah, or one of the earlier prophets: cf. xxi. 12, xxiii. 5, and Introd. p. lxi.

do no violence. The Heb. word is always used of internal oppression (except in Is. xlix. 26), and especially of tyranny over the *stranger* (Ex. xxii. 20; Lev. xix. 33, xxv. 14, &c.).

stranger. 'The foreigner temporarily resident in Israel who had no legal status of his own and who is repeatedly commended to the regard of Israel in Deuteronomy.' Cf. vii. 6.

place. 4 For if ye do this thing indeed, then shall there enter
in by the gates of this house kings sitting ¹upon the throne of
David, riding in chariots and on horses, he, and his servants, and
his people. 5 But if ye will not hear these words, I swear by
myself, saith the LORD, that this house shall become a desolation.
6 For thus saith the LORD ²concerning the house of the king of
Judah: Thou art Gilead unto me, *and* the head of Lebanon:
yet surely I will make thee a wilderness, *and* cities which are
not inhabited. 7 And I will ³prepare destroyers against thee,
every one with his weapons: and they shall cut down thy choice

---

¹ Heb. *for David upon his throne.*   ² Or, *unto*   ³ Heb. *sanctify.*

4. Cf. xvii. 25.
this house. The palace not the temple.
upon the throne of David. The mg. gives the literal translation
for David upon his throne.
5. *I swear by myself.* Cf. xlix. 13, li. 14; Gen. xxii. 16; Dt. xxxii.
40—42; Am. vi. 8; Is. xlv. 23.
6—9. A lament over the king's house under the figure of the
destruction of the forests of Gilead and Lebanon. In strong contrast
to the previous section the doom of the nation is here held to be
inevitable. The change of outlook would in itself be sufficient to make
it probable that this section has no vital connexion with its predecessor,
and the probability is made almost certain by the change of metre,
vv. 6 f. being in the Qinah measure (cf. Budde, *ZATW.* II. 29, III.
303). As Giesebrecht says, the previous section was a sermon, this
one is an elegy.
6. *house of the king of Judah.* This is rather a strange phrase,
and may refer either to the House of David, or to the actual palace
taken as a symbol of the nation and its government.
Gilead...Lebanon. Doughty was especially struck by *Gilead*: 'How
fresh,' he says, ' to the sight and sweet to every sense are those wood-
land limestone hills, full of the balm-smelling pines...in all paths are
blissful fountains; the valley heads flow down healing to the eyes with
veins of purest water.' *Arabia Deserta,* I. 17. (Cf. Is. ii. 13, xxxiii.
9; Nah. i. 4; Zech. xi. 2.) *Lebanon* is similarly used in Is. xxxvii. 24;
Ps. lxxii. 16; and Cant. iv. 15. It is interesting to notice that in the
Talmudic Tractate *Yoma* 39 *b Lebanon* is used as a synonym for
Jerusalem.
cities...not inhabited. The metaphor is suddenly abandoned, and the
climax of the warning is reached by the swift introduction of the literal
fact.
7. *prepare,* mg. *sanctify*: see on vi. 4.
thy choice cedars. The prophet again returns to his metaphor.
Lebanon was noted from the earliest times for its wonderful cedars,

cedars, and cast them into the fire. 8 And many nations shall pass by this city, and they shall say every man to his neighbour, Wherefore hath the Lord done thus unto this great city? 9 Then they shall answer, Because they forsook the covenant of the Lord their God, and worshipped other gods, and served them.

10 Weep ye not for the dead, neither bemoan him: but weep sore for him that goeth away; for he shall return no more, nor see his native country. 11 For thus saith the Lord touching ¹Shallum the son of Josiah, king of Judah, which reigned instead

---

¹ In 2 Kings xxiii. 30, *Jehoahaz*. Compare 1 Chr. iii. 15.

---

which are mentioned in the inscriptions of Gudea of Sirgurla (*c.* 2800 B.C.), and even in the present are held in reverence[1]. In this passage the *cedars* represent the leaders of the nation.

8—9. These *vv.* are an addition in Deuteronomic style made by a prosaic scribe who wished to point the moral. *vv.* 6—7 in the Hebrew are in a poetic form and the sudden descent into prose though not uncommon is suspicious; cf. v. 19; Dt. xxix. 24 f.; 1 K. ix. 8 f.; Mal. i. 4.

10—12. A lament over Shallum. Cf. Ez. xix. 2 ff. and see Introd. p. xxiii.

10. This *v.* is in metrical form and serves, as it were, for the text of what follows.

the dead. i.e. Josiah, who fell in the battle of Megiddo. Captivity in Egypt is looked upon as a worse fate than death in battle. According to 2 Ch. xxxv. 25 there were annual lamentations for Josiah.

he shall return no more. Jehoahaz was the first ruler of the Southern Kingdom to die in exile.

11. *Shallum.* i.e. Jehoahaz: so called in 1 Ch. iii. 15, according to which passage he was the youngest son of Josiah. *Jehoahaz* was evidently chosen by the people to succeed his father on account of the similarity of their policy; at any rate he was unacceptable to Pharaoh Necho who deposed him after a reign of only three months. Why Jehoahaz was called Shallum is not certain; it was apparently no unusual thing for kings of Judah to change their names on coming to the throne, and such a change may have taken place in his case. Another explanation is that the name was given to him by the prophet, or the people, because the shortness of his reign was a punishment for his misdeeds (*Shallum* in Hebrew means *requited*). Graf suggests that just as Jezebel called Jehu a Zimri on account of the similarity of their conduct (2 K. xi. 31), so the shortness of his reign may have suggested a com-

---

¹ Kinglake, writing early in the last century, says, 'The group of cedars remaining on this part of the Lebanon is held sacred by the Greek Church, on account of the prevailing notion that the trees were standing at the time when the Temple of Jerusalem was built.' *Eothen*, p. 229.

of Josiah his father, which went forth out of this place: He shall
not return thither any more; 12 but in the place whither they
have led him captive, there shall he die, and he shall see this land
no more.

13 Woe unto him that buildeth his house by unrighteousness,
and his chambers by injustice; that useth his neighbour's service
without wages, and giveth him not his hire; 14 that saith, I will
build me a wide house and spacious chambers, and cutteth him
out windows; and it is cieled with cedar, and painted with vermilion. 15 Shalt thou reign, because thou [1]strivest to excel in

------

¹ Or, *viest with the cedar*

------

parison with Shallum of Israel (2 K. xv. 13). In any case *Shallum* was
a common enough name, and was borne by fourteen different people in
OT. including the uncle of Jeremiah himself (xxxii. 7); the husband of
the prophetess Huldah (2 K. xxii. 14); as well as by the father of Jeremiah's contemporary Maaseiah (xxxv. 4)¹.

13—19. A condemnation of Jehoiakim on account of his extravagant
and oppressive building operations. No doubt Josiah's long and peaceful
reign had enabled the people to amass a certain amount of wealth and
the tribute to Egypt was not an excessively heavy one (2 K. xxiii. 33),
so possibly the prophet's judgement is a little harsh in this instance.
At the same time Jehoiakim's desire for luxurious buildings, which were
of no use for purposes of defence, must have aroused much opposition
and murmuring amongst the people (see Introd. pp. xxiii f.).

13. The prophets as a whole seem to have been opposed to anything
which savoured of luxury, probably because it was alien to the earlier
spirit of the nation (cf. Am. i. 4 with Edghill's note).

chambers. Better *roof-chambers*, so Driver. Cf. 1 K. xvii. 19; 2 K.
i. 2, &c. and see Thomson, *The Land and the Book*, II. p. 634.

without wages. An Eastern monarch thought little of exacting forced
labour from his subjects, though the excessive indulgence of the supposed
right was often the cause of rebellion and trouble (cf. 2 Ch. ii. 17 f.).
The parallelism suggests that in this case the wages were withheld by
injustice (cf. Job vii. 2; Ecclus. xxxiv. 22; Jas. v. 4). The right to the
due payment of his wages was the only one which the hireling had by
law (Dt. xxiv. 14 ff.; Lev. xix. 13) and unlike the slave he had no one
to protect his interests. In the so-called 'Sumerian farming-laws' provision is made for the prompt payment of the hired labourer; see
S. A. Cook, *Laws of Moses* &c. pp. 171, 189 f.

14. *vermilion*. A favourite colour with the ancients, which can still

------

¹ It is perhaps not out of place to compare the Japanese custom of referring to
a dead emperor by a name different from that which he bore during his lifetime,
e.g. the late Emperor Mutsu Hito (Gentle Piety) who died on June 30th, 1912, is
now known as Meiji (Enlightened Government).

cedar? did not thy father eat and drink, and do judgement and
justice? then it was well with him. 16 He judged the cause of
the poor and needy; then it was well. Was not this to know
me? saith the LORD. 17 But thine eyes and thine heart are not
but for thy ¹covetousness, and for to shed innocent blood, and for
oppression, and for violence, to do it. 18 Therefore thus saith
the LORD concerning Jehoiakim the son of Josiah, king of Judah:
They shall not lament for him, *saying*, Ah my brother! or, Ah
sister! they shall not lament for him, *saying*, Ah lord! or, Ah

¹ Or, *dishonest gain*

be found on excavated buildings. According to Pliny, *Hist. Nat.* xxxv.
13, the dye came from Sinope.

15. *in cedar.* LXX. (and Arabic) reads *with Ahaz*; LXX. A reads
Ahab (cf. 1 K. xxii. 39). Cornill thinks that a personal name is wanted
here and accepts the LXX. reading as the original (*SBOT.* p. 62); but
it is hard to see why Ahaz or Ahab should have been chosen rather
than Solomon.

thy father. The last section contained a comparison between Josiah
and one of his sons as to his fate; this section contains a comparison
between Josiah and another son as to his rule and character. That
Jeremiah should feel himself able to hold up Josiah as an example, after
his tragic fate, is a wonderful testimony to the strength of his convictions,
and reveals his ability to go against popular standards of judgement.

18 f. There is some doubt as to the fate of Jehoiakim's body; a
similar prophecy in xxxvi. 30 says that 'his dead body shall be cast out
in the day to the heat and in the night to the frost.' But according to
the account in 2 K. xxiv. 6 Jehoiakim 'slept with his fathers,' which
would presumably mean that he was buried with the kings of Judah.
It is hardly likely that these utterances would both have been preserved
if later generations knew them to be inconsistent with the facts; possibly
Jehoiakim received a hurried and unceremonious burial during the first
siege (but cf. note on *v.* 19), and when the Chaldeans entered Jerusalem
his body was exhumed and then 'cast out'; cf. Cambyses' treatment
of the body of Amasis (Herod. III. 16)¹, and the fate of the bodies of
Cromwell and the other regicides at the Restoration; and see also
Joseph. *Antiq.* XVI. vii. 1 ff. for the horrors involved in desecrating a
tomb.

18. *Jehoiakim.* Jeremiah does not shrink from denouncing the
king by name.

not lament for him. See Gen. xxiii. 2 (with Driver's note); Am.

¹ For other examples of the mutilation of dead bodies in ancient times see
Frazer, *Adonis* &c. II. pp. 103 f.

his glory!   19 He shall be buried with the burial of an ass,
drawn and cast forth beyond the gates of Jerusalem.

20 Go up to Lebanon, and cry; and lift up thy voice in Bashan:
and cry from Abarim; for all thy lovers are destroyed.   21 I spake
unto thee in thy prosperity; but thou saidst, I will not hear.
This hath been thy manner from thy youth, that thou obeyedst

v. 16; and cf. Spenser's lines on the death of the Earl of Leicester in
The Ruins of Time:

> 'I saw him die, I saw him die, as one
> Of the meane people, and brought forth on beare;
> I saw him die and no man left to mone
> His doleful fate.'

19.   *burial of an ass.*   This probably means that his body was simply
dragged aside and left for the dogs or vultures to devour, like that of
Jezebel (cf. Jud. xv. 15 where the jaw-bone of an ass is found lying
about).   To the ancients the fate which befell the body had an important
influence on the future life and the position which would be given to
the deceased in the nether world.   (According to *Bel and the Dragon*
32 one of the great horrors of the fate provided for Daniel was that his
body would be unburied and cf. Ez. xxxii. 23; Is. xiv. 15; Enoch xcviii.
13 f.; for the same belief amongst the ancient Egyptians see Ebers,
Aegypten, p. 324; and for the Babylonians, Jastrow, *Relig. Belief in Bab.
and Ass.* p. 359).   It was therefore an act of great piety and merit to
bury the dead (Tob. i. 18, ii. 8) and, especially amongst the Greeks, one
which was to be performed at all costs (cf. the *Antigone* of Sophocles;
Xenophon, *Anab.* IV. i. 19, and the punishment inflicted on the
Athenian admirals after the battle of Arginusae).

20—30.   This section consists of three distinct passages; *vv.* 20—23
addressed to the people calling upon them to lament; *vv.* 24—27
threatening Jehoiachin with captivity; and *vv.* 28—30 adding the
further punishment of childlessness.

20—23.   These *vv.* are apparently a fragment inserted here because of the reference in *v.* 22 to the rulers under the figure of
shepherds.

20.   *Lebanon...Bashan...Abarim.*   These mountains overlooked
Israel and Judah beginning from the North and working down the
Eastern boundary.   The people are bidden to assemble on the outposts
of the land and to lift up their voices (cf. iii. 21; Is. xv. 2).   The
mountains of *Abarim* lie to SE. of Judah across the Dead Sea and it
was from Nebo, the summit of this range, that Moses looked upon the
promised land (Nu. xxvii. 12; Dt. xxxii. 49).

lovers.   The term here probably refers to allied nations, as in liv. 30.

21.   This *v.* describes Judah's 'forgetfulness' of God 'in the time
of her wealth.'

not my voice. 22 The wind shall ¹feed all thy shepherds, and thy lovers shall go into captivity: surely then shalt thou be ashamed and confounded for all thy wickedness. 23 O ²inhabitant of Lebanon, that makest thy nest in the cedars, ³how greatly to be pitied shalt thou be when pangs come upon thee, the pain as of a woman in travail! 24 As I live, saith the LORD, though ⁴Coniah the son of Jehoiakim king of Judah were the signet upon my right hand, yet would I pluck thee thence; 25 and I will give thee into the hand of them that seek thy life, and into the hand of them of whom thou art afraid, even into the hand of Nebuchadrezzar king of Babylon, and into the hand of the Chaldeans. 26 And I will cast thee out, and thy mother that bare thee, into another country, where ye were not born; and there shall ye die. 27 But to the land whereunto ⁵their soul longeth to return, thither shall they not return. 28 Is this man Coniah a despised broken ⁶vessel? is he a vessel wherein is no

¹ Or, *feed upon*   ² Heb. *inhabitress.*
³ Some ancient versions have, *how wilt thou groan.*
⁴ In ch. xxiv. 1, and 1 Chr. iii. 16, *Jeconiah.* In 2 Kings xxiv. 6, 8, *Jehoiachin.*
⁵ Heb. *they lift up their soul.*   ⁶ Or, *pot*

22. *feed.* The mg. *feed upon* is better; it contains a play on the word *shepherds,* 'depasture thy pastors.'
23. Cf. Is. xxxvii. 24; Hab. ii. 9.
24—27. These *vv.* refer to the fate which is to befall Jehoiachin in the future.
24. *Coniah.* Also called *Jehoiachin,* lii. 31; 2 K. xxiv. 6, &c. and *Jeconiah,* xxiv. 1, &c. His brief reign of only three months was long enough to give cause for the prophet's indignation.
signet. Perhaps the badge of royal power; cf. Gen. xli. 42; Est. iii. 10; Tob. i. 22; 1 Macc. vi. 15. The same metaphor is used for the restoration of Judah in Hag. ii. 23 evidently with this passage in mind. Cf. the value of a *signet-ring* or seal in Gen. xxxviii. 18; and Cant. viii. 6. For a description see Benzinger, *Archäol.* 106; *Enc. Bib.* 4113.
26. *thy mother.* See on xiii. 18.
28—30. The fate which threatened Coniah and the nation has now been accomplished and the vessel which no longer served God's purpose has been shattered and thrown away (cf. xix. 11).
28. *vessel.* This word is different from that similarly translated in the next clause; it occurs here only but the root meaning is to *mould* or *fashion,* hence it could be used of a *pot* (as mg.) or of a carved image (cf. *Enc. Bib.* 3818).
vessel wherein is no pleasure. Cf. xlviii. 38; Hos. viii. 8 where the

pleasure? wherefore are they cast out, he and his seed, and are
cast into the land which they know not? 29 O ¹earth, earth,
earth, hear the word of the LORD. 30 Thus saith the LORD, Write
ye this man childless, a man that shall not prosper in his days:
for no man of his seed shall prosper, sitting upon the throne of
David, and ruling any more in Judah.

XXIII. 1 Woe unto the shepherds that destroy and scatter

¹ Or, *land*

same phrase is used. LXX. translates *wherein is no use* (χρεία), contrast
2 Tim. ii. 21.

29. *earth, earth, earth.* The translation of mg. *land* is perhaps
more suitable. See note on vii. 4 for the three-fold repetition; and cf.
'Oh! earth, earth, earth, thou yet shalt bow' in Christina Rossetti's
poem *To what Purpose is this Waste*.

30. *Write ye.* Cf. Ps. lxix. 28, lxxxvii. 6; Ez. xiii. 9. Driver paraphrases 'Register him so in the roll of citizens.'
childless. Cf. *v.* 28 'and his seed.' Jehoiachin was *childless* in
the sense that no son of his sat upon the throne of Judah. According
to 1 Ch. iii. 17 f. he had children and his name is included in the
genealogical list in Matt. i. 11 f. The LXX. rendering ἐκκήρυκτον *banished*
is purely arbitrary and in the endeavour to avoid any appearance of
disagreement with other passages of Scripture it sacrifices accuracy of
translation.

XXIII. 1—8. A denunciation of the evil shepherds who have
scattered the flock, and a promise of a righteous ruler (cf. Ps. lxxii.).
This passage, after condemning those who have led the nation astray,
takes for granted the accomplishment of God's purpose of judgement
and looks forward to a time when the nation will be restored. The
shepherds are to be punished, but the remnant of the flock will be
gathered and led back to the fold; the Lord will also appoint over them
true shepherds (cf. Ez. xxxiv. where David himself is to be the shepherd
of the people). Many critics look upon this section as a continuation
of the previous judgements on the successors of Josiah, and though
Zedekiah is not named there is much to be said for this view. The name
of the ideal king *Jehovah is our righteousness* may well be taken as a
play on Zedekiah (Jah is righteous), and as a sign that the name which
was given by a heathen sovereign to the last legitimate king of Judah
(2 K. xxiv. 17) would be fulfilled in all its meaning by the Messianic
ruler. The fact that Zedekiah is not actually condemned or even named
may be due to his having been merely a tool in the hands of the unworthy princes (the shepherds of *v.* 1). Cornill points out that Jeremiah,
unlike Ezekiel, nowhere makes a direct personal attack on Zedekiah.
The whole passage is rejected as late by Duhm and Erbt; other scholars,
however, are content to reject parts of it only (see on *vv.* 5 f. and 7 f.).

1. *the shepherds.* i.e. the rulers as in ii. 8 and so often in Jer.

the sheep of my pasture! saith the Lord. 2 Therefore thus saith the Lord, the God of Israel, against the shepherds that feed my people: Ye have scattered my flock, and driven them away, and have not visited them; behold, I will visit upon you the evil of your doings, saith the Lord. 3 And I will gather the remnant of my flock out of all the countries whither I have driven them, and will bring them again to their folds; and they shall be fruitful and multiply. 4 And I will set up shepherds over them which shall feed them: and they shall fear no more, nor be dismayed, neither shall any be lacking, saith the Lord.

5 Behold, the days come, saith the Lord, that I will raise

and Ezek. These were the upstart nobles who took the places of those removed in the deportation of 597 (cf. 2 K. xxiv. 14 'he carried away ...all the princes'). The use of the figure of the *shepherd* as a description of a ruler has ever been a favourite one with poets, and very often, it may be noticed, as a figure of condemnation. Cf. Dante's denunciation of corrupt Popes—'Fierce wolves in shepherd's garb with greedy eyes' (*Parad.* XXVII. 55); and also Milton, *Lycidas*, 114 ff.

my pasture. God is the chief shepherd; earthly rulers are only deputies and must ever remember 'that strict and solemn account which they must one day give before the judgement-seat of Christ'; cf. 1 Pet. v. 4; and our Lord's claim in Jn. xxi. 15; and for the phrase itself Ez. xxxiv. 31; Ps. lxxiv. 1, lxxix. 13, c. 3.

2. This *v.* was probably in our Lord's mind before the feeding of the five thousand (Matt. ix. 16).

scattered. The rulers are held responsible for the exile.

visited...visit. The play on words here made is reproduced from the original.

3. *my flock*. This description seems to identify the true flock with the exiles. For Jeremiah's anticipations as to the fate of *the Lord's flock* see xiii. 17; and for his judgement on the comparative merits of the exiles and those left in the land see the allegory in xxiv. 1 ff.

I have driven them. Cf. v. 2.

folds. The Heb. word נָוֶה is used in a variety of ways, both of the abode of the shepherd himself and of his sheep (usually in a figurative sense); in poetry it has the wider sense of 'habitation.'

4. *set up*. Evidently the rulers are not to be hereditary princes.

5 f. These *vv.* are rejected by Duhm, Marti and other critics[1] but their objections are over-ruled by Cornill after a very full discussion. The way in which Zechariah makes use of *the Branch* as a Messianic title (Zech. iii. 8, vi. 12) shews that by his day it had become a technical term and this requires that some interval of time should have elapsed.

---

[1] E.g. by Stade, *Geschichte des Volkes Isr.* II. 125.

unto David a righteous [1]Branch, and he shall reign as king and
[2]deal wisely, and shall execute judgement and justice in the land.
6 In his days Judah shall be saved, and Israel shall dwell safely :
and this is his name whereby he shall be called, [3]The LORD is
our righteousness.   7 [4]Therefore, behold, the days come, saith
the LORD, that they shall no more say, As the LORD liveth, which

[1] Or, *Shoot* Or, *Bud*   [2] Or, *prosper*   [3] Or, *the LORD our righteousness*
[4] See ch. xvi. 14, 15.

Kennett thinks that this utterance and the similar one in xxxiii. 14 ff.
are variant forms of a prophecy composed by Jeremiah or one of his
disciples during the governorship of Gedaliah (*Schweich Lectures*,
p. 26 n.).

5. *the days come.* This phrase occurs sixteen times in Jeremiah,
and but five times elsewhere; viz. Am. iv. 2, viii. 11, ix. 13; 1 S. ii. 31;
and 2 K. xx. 17 (= Is. xxxix. 6). It almost invariably occurs before an
announcement, usually in a short and striking form, of special importance (cf. *v.* 7).

Branch. The mg. *Shoot* more nearly represents the meaning of the
Heb., which refers to that which sprouts from the roots, and not from
the trunk. The figure suggested is that of the stump of a tree, which
has been felled, suddenly shewing fresh life, and it is therefore well suited
for the description of the ruler of a restored community.

king. Cf. Is. xxxii. 1; Zech. ix. 9.

deal wisely. Or *prosper*. A mark of the Servant of the Lord in
Is. lii. 13.

6. *Judah...Israel.* The *righteous Branch* is to have a mission to
both parts of the Hebrew nation, viz. to all the descendants of the
original kingdom over which David ruled.

dwell safely. Cf. Lev. xxvi. 5; Dt. xxxiii. 12; Hos. ii. 18.

The LORD is our righteousness. The king's name is ideal, and represents the longings of the prophet and his friends (see Introd. pp.
lxv f.). It is interesting to compare the phrase in Enoch xlvi. 3 'the Son
of man who hath righteousness' (cf. Pss. Sol. xvii. 23 ff.). Driver points
out that ' in xxxiii. 16 exactly the same name is given to the ideal
Jerusalem of the future.'

7 f. These *vv.* are very similar to xvi. 14 f. and LXX. omits them
here, inserting them quite inappropriately after *v.* 40. There is no
real reason for their rejection as they fit quite well into their present
context, though, if the *vv.* are in their original place, the displacement
in the LXX. is hard to explain.

7. *they shall no more say.* In times past the exodus had been the
outstanding marvel in the nation's history, and the event above all
others in which God's power and favour had been shewn to His chosen
people (cf. Mic. vii. 15); but so great will be His dealings in restoring
the exiles to Zion that even the wonders of the exodus will sink into

brought up the children of Israel out of the land of Egypt;
8 but, As the LORD liveth, which brought up and which led the
seed of the house of Israel out of the north country, and from
all the countries whither I had driven them; and they shall
dwell in their own land.

the background.   The exodus loomed large in the minds of the prophets
as being the beginning of the nation, but the restoration from captivity
was to be a still more glorious re-birth.

CHAPTER XXIII. 9—40.

The Denunciation of the Prophets.

Having denounced those who had led the people astray in the political
sphere, Jeremiah now deals with the faithless shepherds whose messages had
likewise led them astray in the sphere of religion (for a discussion of the position
of the 'false' prophets see Additional Note, pp. 182 ff.).   The passage has received drastic treatment at the hands of critics, much of which is probably
altogether too severe, for whilst there can be little doubt of the presence of
editorial or other additions, yet the greater part of the passage reads like the
genuine utterance of the prophet himself.   Duhm is here, as elsewhere, the most
extreme critic and rejects *vv.* 16—40; Cornill rejects *vv.* 24—40.   Giesebrecht
vv. 30—40.   It may be worthy of mention that Duhm places the date of the
composition of *vv.* 16—40 as late as the second century B.C., looking upon it as a
protest against the 'enthusiasm' of the apocalyptists.

> (a)   *The effect of the profanity of the prophets upon Jeremiah: the
>   prophets of Jerusalem are worse than those of Samaria.*   9—15.
> (b)   *The ignorance and presumption of the prophets call forth God's
>   wrath.*   16—20.
> (c)   *The self-commissioned prophets do not escape God's notice.*   21—32.
> (d)   *What is the burden of the Lord?*   33—40.

9 Concerning the prophets.   Mine heart within me is broken,
all my bones shake; I am like a drunken man, and like a man

9—15.   Jeremiah's distress because of the falsehood and adultery
of the prophets of Jerusalem who are worse than those who caused
Samaria to err.

9.   *Concerning the prophets.*   For the heading cf. xlvi. 2, xlviii. 1, &c.
Mine heart...broken.   Cf. Ps. lxix. 20 'reproach hath broken my heart.'
shake.   Cf. Ps. xxii. 14 'all my bones are out of joint.'

drunken man.   Jeremiah applies to himself the metaphor used of
the nations in xxv. 15.   The text suggests that the prophet suffers
thus on account of the message which he has to deliver.

whom wine hath overcome; because of the LORD, and because
of his holy words. 10 For the land is full of adulterers; for
because of ¹swearing the land mourneth; the pastures of the
wilderness are dried up; and their course is evil, and their force
is not right. 11 For both prophet and priest are profane; yea,
in my house have I found their wickedness, saith the LORD.
12 Wherefore their way shall be unto them as slippery places
in the darkness: they shall be driven on, and fall therein: for I
will bring evil upon them, ²even the year of their visitation, saith
the LORD. 13 And I have seen folly in the prophets of Samaria;
they prophesied by Baal, and caused my people Israel to err.

¹ Or, *the curse*   ² Or, *in the year*

holy words. The stress on *holy* contains an implied reproof of the
unholy prophets.
10. *adulterers.* The word may be taken in its literal sense, or it
may be a reference to those who worship false gods: this latter use
is generally if not invariably confined to the nation, and the former
meaning is probably the correct one here (cf. xxix. 23).
swearing. Better as mg. *the curse*; cf. Dt. xxviii. 15, xxix. 27.
the pastures of the wilderness. As was pointed out above (see on
ii. 2) *the wilderness* or desert was not an utter waste. It has been well
described by Kinglake in *Eothen*, p. 94. 'From those grey hills right
away to the gates of Bagdad stretched forth the mysterious "desert"
—not a pale, void, sandy track, but a land abounding in rich pastures—
a land without cities or towns, without any "respectable" people or any
"respectable" things, yet yielding its eighty thousand cavalry to the
beck of a few old men.'
11. *in my house.* God's house, as well as His name, has been desecrated. The abominations in the house of God are described in Ez. viii.;
they consisted amongst other things of an image of Asherah (*v.* 6),
totemistic animals (*v.* 10), weeping for Tammuz (*v.* 14) and sun worship
(*v.* 16).
12. *slippery places...darkness.* The combination of *slipperiness* and
darkness (i.e. the failure of the sight as an effective instrument of vision)
sums up the horrors and anxieties of the situation of men who, having
chosen their own way, are now being forced along it by circumstances,
to certain calamity. The punishment is long drawn out and constant
stumbles precede the final plunge to destruction. For the metaphor
cf. xiii. 16; Mic. iii. 6; Is. viii. 22; Ps. xxxv. 6, lxxiii. 18. In Nah. i. 8
darkness itself pursues the enemies of God.
13. *folly.* The meaning of the Heb. word is that which is unsavoury;
cf. Job vi. 6. Is this implied in the context here?
by Baal. The error which the prophets of Israel promulgated was

14 In the prophets of Jerusalem also I have seen an horrible thing; they commit adultery, and walk in lies, and they strengthen the hands of evil-doers, that none doth return from his wickedness: they are all of them become unto me as Sodom, and the inhabitants thereof as Gomorrah.

15 Therefore thus saith the LORD of hosts concerning the prophets: Behold, I will feed them with wormwood, and make them drink the water of ¹gall: for from the prophets of Jerusalem is profaneness gone forth into all the land. 16 Thus saith the LORD of hosts, Hearken not unto the words of the prophets that prophesy unto you; they teach you vanity: they speak a vision of their own heart, and not out of the mouth of the LORD. 17 They say continually unto them ²that despise me, The LORD hath said, Ye shall have peace; and unto every one that walketh

¹ See ch. viii. 14.
² According to the Sept., *that despise the word of the Lord*, Ye &c.

doctrinal; that of the prophets of Judah, as *v.* 14 shews, was also ethical and moral.

14. The prophets led the people astray in the matter of worship, and added immorality to their false teaching; so that their sin was as bad as that of the cities of the plain. Tauler condemned the false mystics of his day by the selfsame test: 'No one can be free from the observance of the law of God and the practice of virtue.'

strengthen...evil-doers. Negatively by their neglect, and positively by their example; cf. Ez. xiii. 22; Rom. i. 32.

15. See notes on ix. 14.

16—20. The people are warned not to give any heed to the utterances of the prophets who foretell pleasant things: their message comes from their own hearts, and God's wrath is about to break forth upon them.

16. The immoral lives of the false prophets should have been enough to shew the nation that they were no messengers of a righteous and holy God. History, however, shews that people are always anxious to recognise those who condone their sins, and who, at the same time, bring fair promises.

teach...vanity. Heb. *make you vain*, i.e. support you by false hopes.

of their own heart. Moses protested that his works had not been done of his 'own mind' (Nu. xvi. 28); and Balaam was unable 'to do either good or bad' of his 'own mind' (Nu. xxiv. 13). It is not necessary to look upon the prophets denounced by Jeremiah as conscious deceivers, they probably imagined that they were inspired by God, and that they stood for the traditional teaching of the older prophets which, according to their view of things, Jeremiah was contradicting.

17. Cf. vi. 14; and Mic. iii. 11.

in the stubbornness of his own heart they say, No evil shall come upon you. 18 For who hath stood in the council of the LORD, that he should perceive and hear his word? who hath marked [1]my word, and heard it? 19 Behold, the tempest of the LORD, *even his* fury, is gone forth, yea, a whirling tempest: it shall burst upon the head of the wicked. 20 The anger of the LORD shall not return, until he have [2]executed, and till he have performed the intents of his heart: in the latter days ye shall [3]understand it perfectly. 21 I sent not these prophets, yet they ran: I spake not unto them, yet they prophesied. 22 But if they had stood in my council, then had they caused my people to hear my words, and had turned them from their evil way, and from the evil of their doings. 23 Am I a God at hand, saith the LORD,

---

[1] Another reading is, *his*.   [2] Or, *done* it   [3] Or, *consider*

18. *who hath stood* &c. Eliphaz asked Job the same question, obviously expecting an answer in the negative (Job xv. 8). Jeremiah can hardly here intend to deny that he himself had stood in God's council (cf. Am. iii. 7), the fulfilment of his warnings would in due season shew that he had done so; if the other prophets had known the mind of the Lord they too would have warned Jerusalem against the disasters which were coming upon her (cf. *v.* 22).

19 f. These *vv.* recur in xxx. 23 f. where they are probably original.

21—32. The prophets have no commission from God, and are ignorant of His purposes; the lying dreams which they proclaim to the people are not worthy to be placed beside the true message of God.

21. *they ran.* Cf. 2 S. xviii. 22.

22. *my council.* See on *v.* 18 and cf. 2 Tim. iii. 16 f. for a similar practical test of the true message of God.

23 f. Various attempts have been made to interpret these *vv.* and with results which differ widely from each other. (1) Taking the text as it stands Jeremiah's question emphasises the fact that God is *far off* and not *at hand*; in other words it lays stress on the transcendence of God. This doctrine was much in favour with later Judaism, and often finds expression in OT. itself (cf. 1 K. viii. 27); Is. xlv. 15 seems at first sight also to support it and to be an utterance similar to these *vv.*; but the words 'thou art a God that hidest thyself' were almost certainly spoken by the heathen nations who 'had never suspected that the God of an insignificant people like Israel was an incomparable Deliverer' (Wade). It is however hard to see on the surface why Jeremiah should have made use of this doctrine in his controversy with false prophets, and why therefore the *vv.* stand in their present context. Cornill suggests that Jeremiah is insisting upon God's dignity, and declaring that He is a Being Who chooses His servants with care, and until anyone is

B.   12

and not a God afar off? 24 Can any hide himself in secret places that I shall not see him? saith the LORD. Do not I fill heaven

called to the office of a prophet he cannot presume to enter into God's presence as he might enter into his neighbour's house. The weakness of this explanation is that, if it be accepted, v. 24 must mean that the prophet when called cannot refuse the office or hide himself from God's sight (cf. Jon. i. 3 ff.), a warning which Jeremiah himself might once have needed, but which would sound strange to the self-confident prophets who were only too willing to undertake the office. (2) Keil also follows MT. as it stands, but he manages to read into it more than can perhaps be justified: 'A God near at hand is one whose domain and whose knowledge do not extend far; a God afar off is one who sees and works into the far distance.' This explanation is only valid if *a God at hand* means a purely localised God Who has no knowledge of what is happening except in His own immediate neighbourhood, a conception which would hardly be entertained even by the false prophets. (3) The only really satisfactory way of arriving at Jeremiah's meaning is to follow Giesebrecht, and to regard LXX. as having preserved the original text; this involves reading v. 23 not as a question but as an affirmation: *I am a present God and not a far-off God: Can any hide himself from me?* Cf. Dt. iv. 7[1]. The *vv.* when read thus connect quite smoothly with what goes before, the evil deeds of the prophets are known to God and they cannot be hidden. The true prophet 'knew that God was present in man...and it is out of the fulness of this experience that Jeremiah declares that God is not a far-off God, but a near God filling heaven and earth[2].' (Buttenwieser, *op. cit.* p. 147.) This view seems to be in direct opposition to the later orthodox opinion (see above); and there can be little doubt that, as Giesebrecht suggests, it was for this reason that v. 23 was turned into a question, and its teaching thus made to agree with the current Jewish conceptions.

24. The express declaration of the immanence of God is rare in OT. (instances of it are to be found in 1 K. viii. 27; Is. lxvi. 1; Ps. cxxxix. 7 ff.), and God is sometimes looked upon as so far separated from the world that He has 'to come down' from heaven to see what is happening (cf. Gen. xi. 1 ff., xviii. 20 f.). Jeremiah himself had outgrown the conception of a God dwelling far away in the height of heaven, and had come to look upon Him as an omnipresent spiritual Being (cf. Giesebrecht). It is, however, very doubtful whether more than a few of the prophet's contemporaries had even risen to the idea of Jehovah as the God of the whole universe.

Do not I fill &c. Cf. Eph. iv. 10 'that he might fill all things'; Acts xvii. 24.

---

[1] Dr Lock suggests that the question may be an indignant way of stating the fact; cf. the question in xxii. 28.

[2] Cf. St Cyprian, *On the Lord's Prayer*, IV. 'God is everywhere present, hearing and seeing everyone, and, in the plenitude of His Majesty, penetrating even into secluded and hidden places.'

and earth? saith the LORD. 25 I have heard what the prophets have said, that prophesy lies in my name, saying, I have dreamed, I have dreamed. 26 How long shall this be in the heart of the prophets that prophesy lies; even the prophets of the deceit of their own heart? 27 which think to cause my people to forget my name by their dreams which they tell every man to his neighbour, as their fathers forgat my name for Baal. 28 The prophet that hath a dream, let him tell a dream; and he that hath my

25. *I have dreamed, I have dreamed.* That the Deity communicated His wishes and plans by means of dreams was a widespread belief amongst all ancient peoples. Homer looked upon 'mystic dreams from Zeus' as a channel of prophetic inspiration (*Iliad*, I. 63), and Aeschylus puts dreams first amongst such channels:

'I taught the various modes of prophecy,
What truth the dream portends,'

Prom. Vinct. 485 f.

whilst the confidence which even Socrates placed in their guidance is well known (cf. *Apol.* 33 C; *Crito*, 44 A; *Phaedo*, 60 E, &c.). According to the various writers of OT. dreams were frequently sent from God both for guidance and for warning (such accounts are especially common in the document E of the Pent.; see also Joel ii. 28; Job xxxiii. 14 ff. and the book of Daniel). In the later literature, in spite of the warning of Ecclus. xxxiv. 1—8 that they were 'vanity,' dreams and visions form a not uncommon vehicle for revelation (cf. Enoch lxxxiii.—xc.; 4 Ezra x. 59). In NT. they are also found, and are especially used by the writer of the Infancy narratives in the first gospel (see Matt. i. 20, ii. 12, 13 and 19: and cf. Lk. i. 11, 26 ff.). For a fuller discussion of the whole question of the Jewish belief in dreams see *Jew. Enc.* IV. 837. It is interesting to notice that amongst Moslems dreams are recognised as being channels of revelation though other channels may be more important; cf. the traditional utterance of Muhammed himself that 'dreaming is one six-and-fortieth part of prophecy.' (See D. B. Macdonald, *Aspects of Islam*, p. 188.)

26. Two emendations have been suggested in this *v.*, the opening of which in the Heb. is evidently corrupt. By the first Duhm would read a third *I have dreamed* (cf. vii. 4, xxii. 29) for *How long*; and secondly Giesebrecht by dividing up the Heb. consonants differently reads *Will the heart of the prophets turn?*

27. *fathers.* Not Samaria as in *v.* 13, but the people of the exodus (cf. ii. 5).

Baal. Cf. note on ii. 23.

28. *he that hath...faithfully.* Declaring 'the whole counsel of God,' Acts xx. 27.

word, let him speak my word faithfully. What is the straw to
the wheat? saith the LORD. 29 Is not my word like as fire?
saith the LORD; and like a hammer that breaketh the rock in
pieces?

30 Therefore, behold, I am against the prophets, saith the
LORD, that steal my words every one from his neighbour. 31 Behold, I am against the prophets, saith the LORD, that [1]use their
tongues, and say, He saith. 32 Behold, I am against them that
prophesy lying dreams, saith the LORD, and do tell them, and
cause my people to err by their lies, and by their vain boasting:
yet I sent them not, nor commanded them; neither shall they
profit this people at all, saith the LORD. 33 And when this

---

[1] Heb. *take.*

---

straw...to wheat. God's word is food for those who will take it;
the word of the false prophets only chaff fit for burning.

29. *fire...hammer.* Cf. v. 14. God's word will burn up and destroy
all opposing messages. The comparison of the tongue, and that which
is spoken by it, to *fire* is common in Jewish literature, usually with the
idea of the harm which it may do: Ps. cxx. 4; Prov. xvi. 27; Ecclus.
xxviii. 10 ff.; Ps. Sol. xii. 2 ff.; and Jas. iii. 6.

30 ff. A condemnation of merely conventional utterances and
phrases, and of those who utter them. Such exponents of religion
merely weaken their own cause, and by accustoming their hearers to
the contents of the message tend to harden them against those who
preach it in all sincerity.

30. *from his neighbour.* Repeating the maxims or oracles put
forth by one another (cf. the prophets in 1 K. xxii. 6 ff.); or, possibly,
stealing the message of the true prophets and turning it in such a way
as to express peaceable tidings (cf. Hananiah, xxviii. 10).

31. *tongues.* The message of the false prophets was like 'a tale of
little meaning though the words were strong.' Buttenwieser makes the
interesting suggestion that there is here an early reference to the phenomenon of 'speaking with tongues' which caused trouble at Corinth
(1 Cor. xiv.). LXX. gives some amount of support to this theory, especially the reading of A, γλώσσῃ ἐκβάλλειν being the equivalent of γλώσσῃ
λαλεῖν.

He saith. Evidently a prophetic formula placing the responsibility
for the utterances on God Himself.

33—40. The *burden* of the Lord is the nation itself and it will be
thrown off; the very word *burden* is no longer to be used in Judah
since the people have profaned it by their mockery. This passage
teaches the lesson of reverence, and the sin of taking the Lord's name
or any word of sacred meaning in a vain and light sense.

people, or the prophet, or a priest, shall ask thee, saying, What is the burden of the LORD? then shalt thou ¹say unto them, ²What burden! I will cast you off, saith the LORD. 34 And as for the prophet, and the priest, and the people, that shall say, The burden of the LORD, I will even punish that man and his house. 35 Thus shall ye say every one to his neighbour, and every one to his brother, What hath the LORD answered? and, What hath the LORD spoken? 36 And the burden of the LORD shall ye mention no more: for every man's own word ³shall be his burden; for ye have perverted the words of the living God, of the LORD of hosts our God. 37 Thus shalt thou say to the prophet, What hath the LORD answered thee? and, What hath the LORD spoken? 38 But if ye say, The burden of the LORD; therefore thus saith the LORD: Because ye say this word, The

¹ Or, *tell them what the burden is*
² The Sept. and Vulgate have, *Ye are the burden.*
³ Or, *is his burden, and ye pervert &c.*

33. *burden.* The Heb. word מַשָּׂא, *massa*, may mean either a *burden* or an oracle (as in Nah. i. 1 'the burden of Nineveh'; Hab. i. 1, &c.). The latter meaning probably arose by derivation from the former, and represents something 'taken up' by the prophet (see on vii. 19; and RVm. of 2 K. ix. 26 where 'uttered' is literally 'took up'). Cf. the explanation offered by St Jerome in his comment on Mal. i. 1 'The word of the Lord is heavy, therefore it is a burden.'

What burden? Read with LXX. and Vg. *Ye are the burden.* The message of the pre-exilic prophets was constantly one of woe and condemnation (cf. xxviii. 8 f.), and that of Jeremiah was no exception. The people tired out by his repeated prophecies of disaster, and in their blindness refusing to believe him, looked upon his denunciations as a fit subject for a play upon words. Hence God's indignation and the turning of the pun against those who had made it.

34. 'The rigorous prohibition of the word "burden" is not quite easy to understand, but apparently the people had by a trivial witticism, imported into the derived sense of the word something of its primary meaning: one may call the prophetic utterance a "burden" for it is both heavy and wearisome. Hence the use of the word is forbidden, that such profane misuse may be rendered impossible.' Peake.

35. *answered...spoken.* This *v.* includes requests for answers to enquiries made by the priests, and for voluntary utterances such as came to the prophets.

36. *living God.* Cf. x. 10.

37. Omitted by LXX. The *v.* is the same as *v.* 35 with the exception of the substitution of *prophet* for *neighbour.*

burden of the LORD, and I have sent unto you, saying, Ye shall not
say, The burden of the LORD; 39 therefore, behold, I will ¹utterly
forget you, and I will cast you off, and the city that I gave unto
you and to your fathers, away from my presence: 40 and I will
bring an everlasting reproach upon you, and a perpetual shame,
which shall not be forgotten.

¹ Or, according to some ancient authorities, *lift you up*

39. *forget*. The mg. *lift you up* is a better rendering as it preserves
the pun; the Heb. for the verbs *forget* and *lift up* is practically identical
in an unpointed text.

ADDITIONAL NOTE ON XXIII. 9.

The False Prophets.

In considering the question of the '*false* prophets' it is necessary first to
remember that in OT. the epithet is unknown, the true and the false are alike
designated by the same title of prophet. This refusal to distinguish between
the two classes almost certainly represents the views of those who were the
contemporaries of each canonical prophet, and the men of Jeremiah's day looked
upon that prophet and those who opposed him as equally accredited as the
messengers of Jehovah; similarly the Athenians regarded Socrates as a 'sophist'
just as much as the false claimants to knowledge whom he denounced. It must
indeed have been a hard task to discriminate between the true and false spokes-
men of the God of Israel; all alike spoke in the name of Jehovah and used the
same formulas (cf. xxiii. 31, xxviii. 2 ff.; 1 K. xxii. 11); all alike bore the name
of prophet—though Amos disclaimed the name for himself (Am. vii. 14; but cf.
v. 15 and iii. 7); they made use of very similar methods, though the false prophets, both those who prophesied in Judah (xxiii. 27 f.) and those in Babylon
(xxix. 8), seem to have placed too high a reliance on dreams and visions. How
then were men to know the true messengers from the false? The task was not
easy and even the elect must often have been deceived (cf. Matt. xxiv. 25), at
any rate for a time. The tests which Jeremiah himself proposed appear to a
modern mind to be inadequate. (*a*) The first mark of the genuine word of the
Lord was that it was like 'fire' or 'a hammer that breaketh the rock in pieces'
(xxiii. 29), that is the true prophet will be one who is full of a divine energy.
But the energy exhibited by men like Zedekiah the son of Chenaanah (1 K.
xxii. 24), and Hananiah the son of Azzur must have seemed to the simple-minded
nothing less than inspired, and even Jeremiah was on one occasion apparently
silenced by his opponent (xxix. 11). (*b*) The second test was that of fulfilment
'when the word of the prophet shall come to pass, then shall the prophet be
known, that the Lord hath truly sent him' (xxviii. 9; cf. Dt. xviii. 21 f.).
This test however required the lapse of time and was an appeal to posterity

rather than to the living generation. (c) Jeremiah's third test was really an argument in a circle and begged the whole question; if these prophets had really stood in God's council they would have turned the people from their evil doings, i.e. their teaching would have agreed with that of Jeremiah, the very question which was in dispute. It is rather interesting to notice that neither side makes any appeal to the working of signs and wonders (contrast Matt. xxiv. 25), and that records of the performances of miracles are almost completely absent from the pages of the written prophets; this is a point which has not received nearly as much attention as it deserves, and anticipates our Lord's teaching that the working of miracles is no test of truth.

Later ages always tend to pass a harsh judgement upon the sincerity of the defeated party in any religious dispute and by branding them as heretics and false teachers to suggest that they were inspired by selfish and perverse motives. There have been, of course, many persons who have made claims to divine inspiration as a means of obtaining power or notoriety, and sometimes such men are detected and receive a worthy punishment[1]; there are also those who begin their careers with a genuine belief that they are being used as God's messengers but who afterwards use their influence for their own private ends—the prophet Muhammed is a striking instance of one who thus degenerated; but it seems probable that the majority of these so-called false prophets really believed in the words they uttered and in the Divine authority which they claimed for them. It is true that Jeremiah condemned their message as lies and vain boasting (xxiii. 32), and declared that they had no commission from Jehovah (xxiii. 21), but on the other hand they were equally ready to return the accusation. Nor does it follow that Jeremiah was denouncing their sincerity, rather he looked upon them as self-deceived (xxiii. 26). In another passage where it is said that Jehovah had sent a lying vision into the hearts of the prophets (1 K. xxii. 22)[2], as Christians we can hardly take the phrase literally, the writer in accordance with the Hebrew habit of thought is describing the cause in terms of the effect; it is the self-deception of the prophets which has laid them open to such visions. And here we have I think the clue to the understanding of these men; they had a strong belief in their message: they really held themselves to be divinely inspired and yet they were self-deceived.

Jeremiah differed from the prophets of his day mainly on three grounds,

---

[1] There is a story told by Lord Macaulay 'about one of the French prophets of the 17th century, who came into the Court of King's Bench, and announced that the Holy Ghost had sent him to command Lord Holt to enter a *nolle prosequi*. "If," said Lord Holt, "the Holy Ghost had wanted a *nolle prosequi* he would have bade you apply to the Attorney-General. The Holy Ghost knows that I cannot enter a *nolle prosequi*. But there is one thing which I can do, I can lay a lying knave by the heels"; and thereupon he committed him to prison.' *Life and Letters*, II. p. 178.

[2] Cf. Jas. i. 13; Plato, *Rep.* II. 380 D—383 C. The belief of earlier ages of course regarded such visions as deliberately and directly sent from the Deity : cf. Homer, *Iliad*, XXII. 296 ff. and see Adam, *Rel. Teachers of Greece*, p. 40. The gradual spread of a purer idea of God's action in this regard can be seen by comparing 2 S. xxiv. 1 and 1 Ch. xxi. 1.

those of political policy, moral teaching, and personal experience[1], and it was because the 'false' prophets held preconceived ideas on these subjects and refused to surrender them that they allowed themselves to be deceived. It must be remembered that the effect of religious feeling is always to deepen and strengthen the belief in any cause or idea to which it lends its support, and history shews quite plainly that the causes and ideas which have been taken up by religion in the past have not always been such as have contributed to national or social well-being, or even to the advancement of justice and righteousness[2]. In the political sphere the false prophets were closely attached to the ruling house and desired only to prophesy smooth things (cf. 1 K. xxii. 6 ff.); they were a professional ministry and like the poets whom Plato condemned were of the number of those who are 'the friends of the tyrant and bask in the sunshine of his patronage.' In the sphere of morals the false prophets, if Jeremiah is to be believed, were distinctly culpable and indeed the leaders in sin and wickedness (xxiii. 11 ff., xxix. 23); by their deeds they 'had closed their minds against the deepening of the idea of God to an unconditionally ethical conception, and were thus no longer able to penetrate into the depths of his counsel[3].' In the sphere of psychological experience it would be interesting to know how the two classes of prophets differed, but such knowledge is beyond our reach; there is no reason for doubting that the false prophets had religious experiences of a very deep and compelling character and Jeremiah would not have denied the fact, but at the same time he would have insisted that they were not inspired by Jehovah[4].

When a prophet or a teacher feels that his message comes to him from some external, supra-normal source he becomes intolerant of any opposition and even of any rivalry, and it may be supposed with good reason that even amongst those prophets who were banded together against Jeremiah's teaching there would be a large measure of disagreement. One who believes himself to be the accredited messenger of God—and especially if he is self-deceived—looks with little sympathy on those making similar claims even when such claimants support him and agree with his teaching. Sir Auckland Colvin in his book *The Making of Modern Egypt* relates an incident which well illustrates this attitude of mind. Soon after the death of the Mahdi there arose one who claimed to be the Prophet Jesus and in view of the Muhammedan belief that Jesus is to re-appear after the coming of the Mahdi his arrival was a testimony to the claims of the Mahdi's successor, the Khalifa. But Abdullah judged otherwise, he declared the claimant to be a false prophet and quickly disposed of him. Even then the Khalifa was not satisfied and he announced that in a vision he had seen the pretender and his followers at 'an unseen depth of Hell'; 'all were under the charge of black persons who tortured them in various degrees....They are still falling down into the depths of Hell, nor have they yet reached the bottom.'

---

[1] Cf. Davidson in Camb. Bible on *Ezekiel*, pp. 85 f.

[2] The same thing is true of the petitionary side of prayer in the life of the individual, prayer may in this way do much harm to the characters of those who use it unwisely.

[3] Budde, *Rel. of Is.* p. 131.　　　　[4] Cf. Hamilton, *The People of God*, i. p. 141.

CHAPTER XXIV.

The Two Baskets of Figs.

In 597 Nebuchadrezzar carried Jehoiachin and the best of the nation into captivity in Babylon. Those who remained behind attributed their escape to their superior virtue and merit. In this ch. Jeremiah gives a very different estimate of the two communities in the sight of God, and in this judgement he is supported by Ezekiel (cf. xii., xx. 37 ff. &c.). There is an ancient Jewish tradition, that at the time of the return from exile the best of the people stayed behind in Babylon. 'The flour remained at Babylon, the chaff came to Palestine.' The choice of the figure was probably suggested by Jeremiah's usage. For further details of the relations between the exiles and those who remained behind see Additional Note, pp. 222 f.

(a) *The prophet describes his vision.* 1—3.
(b) *The meaning of the vision.* 4—10.

XXIV. 1 The LORD shewed me, and, behold, two baskets of figs set before the temple of the LORD; after that Nebuchadrezzar king of Babylon had carried away captive Jeconiah the son of Jehoiakim, king of Judah, and the princes of Judah, with the craftsmen and smiths, from Jerusalem, and had brought them to Babylon. 2 One basket had very good figs, like the figs that are first ripe: and the other basket had very bad figs, which could not be eaten, they were so bad. 3 Then said the LORD unto me, What seest thou, Jeremiah? And I said, Figs; the good figs, very good; and the bad, very bad, that cannot be eaten,

XXIV. 1—3. The vision of the figs.
1. *before the temple.* The mention of the exact spot suggests that Jeremiah actually saw the baskets, though Cornill rejects the clause on the ground that Jeremiah does not elsewhere use הֵיכָל for *temple*, and if the figs were intended as an offering, none but those fruits which were first-ripe were in accordance with the law (Dt. xxvi. 2). The somewhat similar vision of 'the summer-fruit' in Am. viii. 1 may have influenced the choice of the symbol (see further, Introd. pp. lxx f.).

smiths. The exact meaning of the Heb. is not known.

2. *figs that are first ripe.* The *first ripe figs* can be gathered in June, and they are valued not only on account of their early appearing (the normal time for gathering figs being August), but for their superior flavour. The Heb. word בְּכוּרָה occurs elsewhere only in Hos. ix. 10; Mic. vii. 4; Is. xxviii. 4; the same root is found in the Spanish *alba-cora* which is evidently borrowed from the Moors.

3. *What seest thou?* Cf. note on i. 11.

they are so bad. 4 And the word of the LORD came unto me, saying, 5 Thus saith the LORD, the God of Israel; Like these good figs, so will I regard the captives of Judah, whom I have sent out of this place into the land of the Chaldeans, for good. 6 For I will set mine eyes upon them for good, and I will bring them again to this land: and I will build them, and not pull them down; and I will plant them, and not pluck them up. 7 And I will give them an heart to know me, that I am the LORD: and they shall be my people, and I will be their God: for they shall return unto me with their whole heart. 8 And as the bad figs, which cannot be eaten, they are so bad; surely thus saith the LORD, So will I give up Zedekiah the king of Judah, and his princes, and the residue of Jerusalem, that remain in this land, and them that dwell in the land of Egypt: 9 I will even give them up to be ¹tossed to and fro among all the kingdoms of the earth for evil; to be a reproach and a proverb, a taunt and a curse, in all places whither I shall drive them. 10 And I will send the sword, the famine, and the pestilence, among them, till they be consumed from off the land that I gave unto them and to their fathers.

¹ Or, *a terror unto*

4—10. The interpretation of the vision.

5. *for good.* Cf. xiv. 11. The state of those who had been carried away during the first deportation would be enviable when contrasted with all the horrors which the remnant would have to endure.

7. *heart to know me.* Cf. xxxi. 33, xxxii. 39 f.; Ez. ii. 19.

8. *Egypt.* The mention of *Egypt* is rather strange because no Jewish colony is known to have settled there until a much later date¹. At the same time Egypt was always a convenient place of refuge for any who wished to escape from the Babylonian rule, and very probably other Jews were taken into exile along with Jehoahaz (2 K. xxiii. 34). Hosea had already threatened those who went down to Egypt that it would be their grave (ix. 9).

9. *to be…a proverb.* A common phrase in OT. (Dt. xxviii. 37; Job xvii. 6, &c.); cf. Wisd. v. 3 and see on xxvi. 6.

---

¹ See Additional Note, pp. 315 f.

Chapter XXV.

The Punishment of the Nations.

At first sight this ch. as it is contained in EVV. looks straightforward enough; the section called by Ewald the Roll of Zedekiah ended with xxiv., and a new section is opened which returns once more to the reign of Jehoiakim. Jeremiah recapitulates his prophecies against the people, and to add vividness to his warnings he is permitted to state the actual length of the captivity and of the supremacy of Babylon. He then goes on, by the use of the figure of the cup of God's fury, to amplify the warning to the nations round about Judah, returning at the close of the ch. to his own people and the fate which will befall them together with all flesh. On turning to LXX. however the ch. is seen to be full of difficult problems, and its unity and simplicity are destroyed. The most striking change which the LXX. has made is the insertion, immediately after *v.* 13, of the chh. numbered xlvi.—li. in the Heb. and EVV. That a close connexion exists between xxv. and xlvi.—li. is obvious to even a casual reader; both deal with the same peoples though in a somewhat different order[1], in xlvi.—li. the Heb. is nearer than the LXX. to the summary in xxv. 19 ff. Again *vv.* 1—13 form a suitable introduction to a series of oracles on foreign nations, and *v.* 13 actually mentions a book of *words pronounced against Babylon* which seems to be a reference to l.—li. Duhm considers that the *book* to which these *vv.* (so far as they are genuine) were attached was the original form of the roll dictated to Baruch (xxxvi.). Cornill finds traces of a revision which these *vv.* have undergone in order to make them suitable for an introduction (following Schwally, *ZATW.* 1888, pp. 177 ff.); and he further points out, with much insight, that the only appropriate place for the insertion of xlvi.—li. is *after* the figure of the cup and not before it. In his opinion this was the original position of the chh., and he thinks that when Jeremiah's prophecy of the wrath of God was not fulfilled by events, the oracles were banished to the end of the collection, and their crude historical forecasts were given a vaguer and more apocalyptic tinge. It seems almost certain therefore that the arrangement of LXX. is not the original one, as in addition to the arguments mentioned above, the effect of it is to divide up xxv. (which has every appearance of being a unity) into two distinct sections.

---

[1] The following is the order of the nations in the different lists:

xxv.	xlvi.—li. Heb.	xlvi.—li. LXX.
1. Egypt	Egypt	Elam
2. (Uz)	Philistines	Egypt
3. Philistines	Tyre and Sidon	Babylon
4. Edom	Moab	Philistines
5. Moab	Ammon	Edom
6. Ammon	Edom	Ammon
7. Tyre, &c.	Damascus	Kedar and Hazor
8. Dedan, Tema, &c.	Kedar and Hazor	Damascus
9. Elam and the Medes	Elam	Moab
10. Babylon	Babylon	

The question then remains—Is xxv. the genuine work of Jeremiah at all ? and naturally enough it has received a variety of answers. Schwally rejects *vv.* 1—13 as being too general and abstract in tone, and also because there is no mention in them of Jeremiah's constant teaching of the possibility of repentance. In reply to this Cornill points out that in this passage the prophet is dealing, not with Judah alone, but with the surrounding nations also, and that therefore the preaching of penitence is not so appropriate; Jeremiah evidently shared in what must have been the common opinion that Nebuchadrezzar would make full use of his victory to the subjugation of the whole of Syria. Schwally also rejects *vv.* 15—31 on the somewhat arbitrary ground that Jeremiah was not a prophet to the nations (cf. pp. 1 f.). Most other critics are not so sweeping in the application of their methods, and it is best to conclude with Giesebrecht and Cornill that the ch. as a whole is the genuine work of Jeremiah although it has received various later additions.

(a) *Judah's obstinacy is about to be punished.* 1—7.
(b) *The coming triumph and overthrow of Babylon.* 8—14.
(c) *The nations shall be made to drink of the wine of God's fury.* 15—29.
(d) *God will come like a lion against Judah and all the peoples of the earth.* 30—38.

XXV. 1 The word that came to Jeremiah concerning all the people of Judah in the fourth year of Jehoiakim the son of Josiah, king of Judah; the same was the first year of Nebuchadrezzar king of Babylon; 2 the which Jeremiah the prophet spake unto all the people of Judah, and to all the inhabitants of Jerusalem, saying: 3 From the thirteenth year of Josiah the son of Amon, king of Judah, even unto this day, these three and twenty years, the word of the LORD hath come unto me, and I have spoken unto you, rising up early and speaking; but ye have not hearkened. 4 And the LORD hath sent unto you all his servants the prophets,

XXV. 1—14. After the battle of Carchemish in 605 the Chaldeans became supreme in Western Asia, and Jeremiah accordingly advises Judah and the surrounding nations that they too will have to submit to the same power. At the end of seventy years Babylon herself shall be made desolate.

1. *fourth year* &c. The somewhat elaborate synchronism in the second half of the *v.* is not found in LXX. and is therefore open to suspicion; moreover it apparently conflicts with the statement in xlvi. 2 that Carchemish was fought in this very year, and therefore before Nebuchadrezzar had actually succeeded to the throne of Babylon.

3. *the thirteenth year of Josiah.* The year of Jeremiah's call.

4. This *v.* should almost certainly be rejected on account of the sudden change of speaker, together with the unsuitability of the sub-

rising up early and sending them; but ye have not hearkened, nor inclined your ear to hear; 5 saying, Return ye now every one from his evil way, and from the evil of your doings, and dwell in the land that the LORD hath given unto you and to your fathers, from of old and even for evermore: 6 and go not after other gods to serve them, and to worship them, and provoke me not to anger with the work of your hands; and I will do you no hurt. 7 Yet ye have not hearkened unto me, saith the LORD; that ye might provoke me to anger with the work of your hands to your own hurt. 8 Therefore thus saith the LORD of hosts: Because ye have not heard my words, 9 behold, I will send and take all the families of the north, saith the LORD, and *I will send* unto Nebuchadrezzar the king of Babylon, my servant, and will bring them against this land, and against the inhabitants thereof, and against all these nations round about; and I will [1]utterly destroy them, and make them an astonishment, and an hissing, and perpetual desolations. 10 Moreover I will [2]take from them the voice of mirth and the voice of gladness, the voice of the

---

[1] Heb. *devote*.   [2] Heb. *cause to perish from them.*

---

ject matter—as Cornill says, the real offence was not ignoring the warnings of the earlier prophets but of Jeremiah himself—and the awkwardness of the grammar.

rising up early. He who 'neither slumbers nor sleeps' can hardly be said to rise early; the expression means as in Ps. lxiii. 1 to make the action in question the chief object of His attention.

7. *to your own hurt.* God plans good things for His children, evil comes upon them as a consequence of their own folly (cf. vii. 6, xxiv. 6).

8—14. The triumph and destruction of Babylon.

9. *my servant.* The conception of a heathen monarch as the *servant* of Jehovah, and that in order to destroy His own people, presented a hard problem to the pious Jew (cf. Hab. i. 6 ff.; Am. vi. 14). LXX. omits the title here and elsewhere, doubtless because it was felt that it could not rightly be applied to an idolater. The same designation was also applied to Cyrus (Is. xliv. 28, xlviii. 14, &c.) who not only was not a worshipper of Jehovah, but one who attributed his victories, possibly for reasons of policy, to Bel and to Marduk 'his friend and companion' (see Sayce, *Higher Criticism* &c. p. 505).

10. The first part of this *v.* is similar to vii. 34; the later half makes a sinister addition, 'not merely every sound of joyfulness, but even every sign of life' is to be cut off.

bridegroom and the voice of the bride, the sound of the millstones, and the light of the candle. 11 And this whole land shall be a desolation, and an astonishment; and these nations shall serve the king of Babylon seventy years. 12 And it shall come to pass,

millstones. The sound of the mill is 'heard daily in an eastern village, and is a sign of the presence of life in it (cf. Rev. xviii. 22). The hand-mill…consists of two circular stones, eighteen inches or two feet in diameter, the lower one being fixed to the ground, while the upper one is turned round by a woman…kneeling or sitting beside it.' Driver[1].

11. *these nations…Babylon.* LXX. omits *these* and *the king of Babylon* and inserts *among* before *nations*: thus reading *they shall serve among the nations.* This reading probably represents the original Heb. text, though *serve* when it is used with a preposition usually means *make to serve,* i.e. enslave.

seventy years. This number need not be taken as an exact estimate of the length of the captivity as the same period is used in a prophecy from the reign of Zedekiah (xxix. 10), nor would it agree exactly with the actual history. Jeremiah's desire was to impress upon the people that no immediate return was to be looked for and so he makes use of an approximate figure which had a symbolical significance; Keil points out that 7 according to the Jews represents the perfection of God's work and 10 the perfection of human work. The writer of Chronicles regarded the *seventy years* as a punishment for the neglect of the sabbatic years (2 Ch. xxxvi. 21). Many critics reject the Jeremianic authorship of the prediction, Duhm, for example, considering that it was based on Zech. i. 12 'how long wilt thou not have mercy on Jerusalem and the cities of Judah, against whom thou hast had indignation these threescore and ten years?'

12—14. These *vv.* seem out of place in their present context as there is no point in making a warning to Babylon part of the prophecy on the surrounding nations; the oracle in l.—li. 58 is almost certainly not from Jeremiah and it seems to be pre-supposed by the writer of these *vv.* The sudden change into the third person in the middle of an utterance is very suspicious (*v.* 13 *which Jeremiah hath prophesied*). Most scholars have rejected the passage in whole or in part as a later insertion. It must be confessed that *vv.* 15 ff. follow quite smoothly on *v.* 11 though possibly *v.* 13 *a* is genuine and ought to be included. In LXX. the oracles on the nations come immediately after *v.* 13.

---

[1] The reading of LXX. ὀσμὴν μύρου *the smell of ointment* for קוֹל רֵחַיִם *the sound* (lit. *voice*) *of the millstones* is interesting. The usual explanation is that a double corruption has taken place, μύλου has become μύρου and רֵחַיִם has been divided up into רֵיחַ, which is elsewhere translated by ὀσμή when it bears this meaning, and מֹר (see Cornill however on this suggestion). At the same time it is possible that ὀσμήν is a corruption of ᾆσμα.

when seventy years are accomplished, that I will punish the king of Babylon, and that nation, saith the LORD, for their iniquity, and the land of the Chaldeans; and I will make it ¹desolate for ever. 13 And I will bring upon that land all my words which I have pronounced against it, even all that is written in this book, which Jeremiah hath prophesied against all the nations. 14 For many nations and great kings ²shall serve themselves of them, even of them: and I will recompense them according to their deeds, and according to the work of their hands.

15 For thus saith the LORD, the God of Israel, unto me: Take the cup of the wine of this fury at my hand, and cause all the

---

¹ Heb. *everlasting desolations.*　　² Or, *have served themselves* or, *made bondmen*

12. *I will punish...Babylon.* The lesson of these *vv.*, whoever may have written them, is that no amount of service in the past can save a nation or an individual from the consequences of sin in the present. Even those who can claim to have cast out devils in our Lord's name may find themselves outside His kingdom (cf. Matt. vii. 22 f.).

14. This *v.* is absent from LXX.; it seems to be derived from xxvii. 7, and l. 29, li. 24.

15—29. The nations are to drink of the wine-cup of the fury of the Lord. The passage has been rejected by some scholars (see Introd. to the section), but there can be but little doubt that, though it may contain later additions, as a whole it comes from the prophet himself. LXX. gives the clue to some of these later insertions (see on *v.* 18).

15. *cup.* The use of the symbol of the *cup* to represent a bitter and trying experience is common in OT. (cf. Ps. xi. 6, lxxv. 8; Is. li. 17; Ez. xxiii. 31 f. &c.), though in some passages the *cup* is not actually mentioned (Job xxi. 20; Ps. lx. 3; Obad. 16). In NT. the use is sanctified by our blessed Lord Himself in the agony in the garden (Mk. xiv. 36); and it also appears in Rev. xiv. 8, xvii. 2, 4, xviii. 3. Dr Wade in commenting on Is. li. 17 suggests a comparison to Homer, *Iliad*, XXIV. 527 δοιοὶ γάρ τε πίθοι κατακείαται ἐν Διὸς οὔδει δώρων οἷα δίδωσι κακῶν, ἕτερος δὲ ἐάων¹.

this fury. The *wine* is the wrath of God which is poured out upon the nations. Intoxication is a very apt 'figure for the bewilderment and helplessness produced...by an overwhelming calamity.'

---

¹ An interesting use of the same figure is to be found in the vision of Friar James of La Massa (*The Little Flowers of St Francis*, ch. XLVIII.), though it is there used as a symbol, not of the fury of the Lord, but of His grace. 'And thereafter he beheld Christ seated on a pure white throne exceeding great, whereunto Christ called St Francis and gave him a cup, full of the spirit of life, and sent him forth, saying, "Go and visit thy friars and give them to drink of this cup of the spirit of life."'

nations, to whom I send thee, to drink it. 16 And they shall
drink, and reel to and fro, and be mad, because of the sword that
I will send among them. 17 Then took I the cup at the LORD's
hand, and made all the nations to drink, unto whom the LORD
had sent me: 18 *to wit*, Jerusalem, and the cities of Judah, and
the kings thereof, and the princes thereof, to make them a desolation, an astonishment, an hissing, and a curse; as it is this day;
19 Pharaoh king of Egypt, and his servants, and his princes, and
all his people; 20 and all the mingled people, and all the kings
of the land of Uz, and all the kings of the land of the Philistines,

16.   *the sword* &c. Duhm would omit these words as a piece of
literalism.

17.   *Then took I the cup.* It has been suggested by commentators
who strive to preserve the literal meaning of the prophetic writings at
any cost, that Jeremiah actually handed *the cup* to representatives of
the various nations enumerated in the passage; such a conception is
quite unnecessary and indeed entirely unworthy. Cf. Keil 'as the
wrath of God is no essence which may be drunk by the bodily act, so
manifestly *the cup* is no material one.'

18—26.   If the text of LXX. can here be relied on, additions were
evidently made to the list of nations at a comparatively late date, and
indeed there must have been a great temptation to a scribe to add
a present enemy to an ancient list of nations who were to be punished.
LXX. omits *all the kings of the land of Uz* (*v.* 20), either *all the kings
of Arabia* or *all the kings of the mingled people* (*v.* 24), and *all the
kings of Zimri* (*v.* 25). It is noticeable that all these omissions by LXX.
contain the phrase ' all the kings of' and Giesebrecht followed by Cornill
would exclude the other nations so introduced.

18.   *as it is this day.* Omitted by LXX., and evidently an exilic
gloss. Cornill thinks that Pharaoh originally headed the list as being
the first to suffer from the might of Babylon.

20.   *mingled people.* Foreigners resident in Egypt for purposes of
trade &c. In later times the word became a synonym for the Gentiles—
cf. Ps. Sol. xvii. 17 'the child of the covenant in the midst of *the
mingled peoples.*'

land of Uz. Cf. Gen. x. 23, xxii. 21, &c. In Lam. iv. 21 there is
a possible reference to this *v.* The exact content of the phrase is somewhat doubtful, cf. W. Robertson Smith's note in *Kinship* &c. p. 260 f.,
and Bishop Gibson's note on Job i. 1.

kings of...the Philistines. The use is strange because the *Philistines*
were ruled by 'lords'—cf. however 1 S. xxi. 10 'Achish, *king* of
Gath,' and parallel expressions in the Assyrian inscriptions. It is
probable that the whole phrase ought to be omitted with Giesebrecht
(see above), as the cities themselves are mentioned in detail, with the

and Ashkelon, and Gaza, and Ekron, and the remnant of Ashdod;
21 Edom, and Moab, and the children of Ammon; 22 and all
the kings of Tyre, and all the kings of Zidon, and the kings of
the ¹isle which is beyond the sea; 23 Dedan, and Tema, and
Buz, and all that have the corners *of their hair* polled; 24 and
all the kings of Arabia, and all the kings of the mingled people
that dwell in the wilderness; 25 and all the kings of Zimri, and
all the kings of Elam, and all the kings of the Medes; 26 and
all the kings of the north, far and near, one with another; and
all the kingdoms of the world, which are upon the face of the

¹ Or, *coastland*

exception of Gath (cf. Am. i. 6—8; Zeph. ii. 4; Zech. ix. 5 f.; and see
Bliss and Macalister, *Excavations in Palestine*, pp. 63—65). *Ekron*
(modern 'Akir) was, until the recent war, the site of a flourishing
Jewish colony; no trace of the old town now exists.

the remnant of Ashdod. Ashdod is probably spoken of as a *remnant*
because of its sufferings during the long siege by Psammetichus I
(reigned 666—610 B.C.) which lasted for twenty-nine years (Herodotus
II. 157, cf. however Zeph. ii. 4).

22. *the isle which is beyond the sea.* Better (cf. mg.) *coastland*, with
a possible reference to the Phoenician colonies. In some of the inscriptions on the older Egyptian tombs there are references to certain
Mediterranean rulers who are styled 'princes of the Isles in the midst
of the Great Green Sea.'

23. *Dedan.* A north Arabian tribe descended from Abraham.
See Driver's note on Gen. x. 7.

Tema. Mentioned with Dedan in Is. xxi. 13 f.

Buz. See Gen. xxii. 21 (with Driver's note); Job xxxii. 2; and cf.
Delitzsch, *Parad.* p. 307.

corners...polled. See on ix. 26.

24. In the unpointed Heb. text *Arabia* and *mingled people* are
the same, and probably one of them should be omitted (so LXX.). It
must be remembered that in OT. the term *Arabia* represents a much
more restricted area than in later usage: cf. *Enc. Bib.* 272.

25. *Zimri.* This name is not found elsewhere as the name of a
people and LXX. omits. It has sometimes been identified with Zimran
in Gen. xxv. 2, which Driver thinks may be Ζαβραμ, 'the capital of an
Arabian tribe, W. of Mecca'; or again it may be Σεμβρῖται in Ethiopia
mentioned by Strabo XVII. i. 786. Duhm thinks that the word
conceals a reference to the Romans and that it is therefore a very late
insertion. See also *ZATW.* 1914, p. 64.

Elam. See on xlix. 34. Elam lay to the E. of Babylon and NE.
of the Persian Gulf.

the Medes. See on li. 11. Media lay to the N. of Elam.

earth: and the king of ¹Sheshach shall drink after them. 27 And
thou shalt say unto them, Thus saith the LORD of hosts, the God
of Israel: Drink ye, and be drunken, and spue, and fall, and rise
no more, because of the sword which I will send among you.
28 And it shall be, if they refuse to take the cup at thine hand
to drink, then shalt thou say unto them, Thus saith the LORD of
hosts: Ye shall surely drink. 29 For, lo, I begin to work evil
at the city which is called by my name, and should ye be utterly
unpunished? Ye shall not be unpunished: for I will call for a
sword upon all the inhabitants of the earth, saith the LORD of
hosts. 30 Therefore prophesy thou against them all these words,
and say unto them, The LORD shall roar from on high, and utter
his voice from his holy habitation; he shall mightily roar against
his ²fold; he shall give a shout, as they that tread *the grapes*,

¹ According to ancient tradition, a cypher for *Babel*. See ch. li. 41.
² Or, *pasture*

26. *Sheshach*. The consonants of this word in Heb. are S S K and
by the system of cypher-writing known as Atbash—in which the last
letter of the alphabet is substituted for the first, the next to the last
for the second, and so on—they correspond to the letters B B L; i.e.
Babel (see however an article in *ZATW*. 1914, p. 64). The use of
this method of writing is probably late (other instances of it occur in
li. 1, 41) and the clause is absent from LXX.

27—29. These *vv.* are evidently out of their context as the Lord
is suddenly introduced as the speaker without any warning and the
'drinking' by the nations has apparently not yet taken place.

29. Judgement must begin at the house of God (cf. Ez. ix. 6);
but this is a pledge that others will not escape.

called by my name. See on vii. 10; and cf. 1 Pet. iv. 17.

30—38. God will come like a lion against all the peoples of the
earth. This passage resumes a more poetic style but at the same time
its genuineness is more than doubtful owing to its eschatological outlook
and lack of originality.

30. *The LORD shall roar*. Cf. Am. i. 2; Joel iii. 16. He will come
as a lion against His own people (cf. Hos. v. 14) as well as against the
rest of the world.

on high. From heaven, not, as in the passages quoted above, from
Jerusalem. Cf. Dante, *Parad.* XXVII. 143 'these heavenly spheres shall
roar so loud.'

holy habitation. Cf. Dt. xxvi. 15; Ps. lxviii. 5.

fold. The same Heb. word is translated 'habitation' in x. 25. In
this context it represents the place or *pasture* (cf. mg.) where the Lord's
own flock is feeding (cf. xxiii. 3).

shout. The word may be used of the 'battle-cry' as well as of the

against all the inhabitants of the earth.   31 A noise shall come even to the end of the earth; for the LORD hath a controversy with the nations, he will plead with all flesh; as for the wicked, he will give them to the sword, saith the LORD.

32 Thus saith the LORD of hosts, Behold, evil shall go forth from nation to nation, and a great tempest shall be raised up from the uttermost parts of the earth.   33 And the slain of the LORD shall be at that day from one end of the earth even unto the other end of the earth: they shall not be lamented, neither gathered, nor buried; they shall be dung upon the face of the ground.   34 Howl, ye shepherds, and cry; and wallow yourselves *in ashes*, ye principal of the flock: for the days of your slaughter are fully come, [1]and I will break you in pieces, and ye shall fall like a pleasant vessel.   35 And [2]the shepherds shall have no way to flee, nor the principal of the flock to escape.   36 A voice of the cry of the shepherds, and the howling of the principal of the flock! for the LORD layeth waste their pasture.   37 And the

---

[1] Or, *and I will disperse you* Many ancient versions read, *and your dispersions*.
[2] Heb. *flight shall perish from the shepherds, and escape from &c.*

---

shout of those who gather the grapes, hence the play on the word in xlviii. 33. The same metaphor of the vintage to represent the slaughter of God's enemies is used in Is. lxiii. 1—6.

31.   Cf. Is. iii. 13 f., lxvi. 6.

plead.   i.e. contend; cf. Joel iii. 2.

all flesh.   This term is generally used with the idea of laying stress on the frailty of mankind in comparison with God (cf. xvii. 5).

32.   Judgement shall come suddenly, like a storm rising from the sea (cf. 1 K. xviii. 44 f.), which gradually sweeps over all nations.

33.   *the slain of the LORD.*   The same phrase is used in Is. lxvi. 16.

34.   The first half of the *v.* preserves the figure of the flock suggested by *v.* 30; in the second half the simile of the broken vessel—of which Jeremiah was very fond—is suddenly introduced, only to be dropped in the following *v.* LXX. by a slightly different reading of the Heb. substitutes *rams* for *vessel*, and Duhm adopts the rendering, and by another slight change reads *of slaughter* for *pleasant* (cf. Zech. xi. 4).

wallow.   Better *sprinkle* as in vi. 26.

principal.   Heb. *majestic ones*; the chief citizens.

fall.   Cf. li. 7 f.

35.   Cf. Am. ii. 14.

36 ff.   Cf. Zech. xi. 3 'A voice of the howling of the shepherds! for their glory is spoiled: a voice of the roaring of young lions! for the pride of Jordan is spoiled.'

peaceable folds are brought to silence because of the fierce anger of the LORD. 38 He hath forsaken his covert, as the lion: for their land is become an astonishment because of ¹the fierceness of the oppressing *sword*, and because of his fierce anger.

¹ Or, according to some ancient authorities, *the oppressing sword* See ch. xlvi. 16.

38. This *v.* returns to the figure with which the passage began— the Lord will come up like a lion disturbed from its lair.

the fierceness of the oppressing sword. There is probably no need to supply *sword* in the text as by a small emendation the Heb. for *fierceness* חרון may be read as חרב *sword* (so mg. following LXX.; cf. xlvi. 16).

CHAPTER XXVI.

Jeremiah's Warning and its Consequences.

In this ch. the prophet warns the people, with solemn force, that unless they amend their ways and their doings the fate which befell Shiloh will come upon Jerusalem. The occasion of the sermon is probably the same as that of vii. (see Introd. to that ch.); there the contents of the sermon are preserved, here the results which followed upon the prophet's boldness. The earlier record may be part of the roll read to Jehoiakim, and for this reason it contained only the main facts. The present ch. is written more from Jeremiah's own point of view and therefore goes into greater detail; its great value lies in its being an instance of that opposition against which the prophet was ever contending, and which weighed upon his sensitive soul until his life became a burden to him. The record probably comes from Baruch and its genuineness can hardly be questioned.

(*a*) *The warning.* 1—6.
(*b*) *The indignation of priests and prophets.* 7—9.
(*c*) *The intervention of the princes and the people.* 10—16.
(*d*) *The appeal to history.* 17—19.
(*e*) *The fate of Uriah.* 20—24.

XXVI. 1 In the beginning of the reign of Jehoiakim the son of Josiah, king of Judah, came this word from the LORD, saying,

XXVI. 1—6. Jeremiah's public warning from the temple court.
1. *beginning.* The dating of events is characteristic of those parts of the book which are generally attributed to Baruch. Duhm thinks that the warning may have been given at Jehoiakim's coronation, but such an occasion would surely have received special mention, and Jeremiah would hardly have declared his message in terms so uncompromising before events had had time to develop.

2 Thus saith the LORD: Stand in the court of the LORD's house, and speak unto all the cities of Judah, which come to worship in the LORD's house, all the words that I command thee to speak unto them; keep not back a word. 3 It may be they will hearken, and turn every man from his evil way; that I may repent me of the evil, which I purpose to do unto them because of the evil of their doings. 4 And thou shalt say unto them, Thus saith the LORD: If ye will not hearken to me, to walk in my law, which I have set before you, 5 to hearken to the words of my servants the prophets, whom I send unto you, even rising up early and sending them, but ye have not hearkened; 6 then will I make this house like Shiloh, and will make this city a curse to all the nations of the earth. 7 And the priests and the prophets and

2. *the court* &c. The outer court where the people would be gathered together, so in xix. 14.

keep not back a word. Heb. *diminish*, the word used in Ex. v. 8, 19 of the tale of bricks. Jeremiah, in view of the danger of his task, needed the renewal of the warning which had accompanied his call 'speak to them all that I shall command you' (i. 17). The idea is the same as that which underlies Rev. xxii. 19, where a curse is pronounced against anyone who 'shall take away from the words of the book of this prophecy.'

3. *every man.* The stress on the individual is characteristic of Jeremiah.

repent. God's condemnations are always conditional, if the guilty repent God will forbear. See on xviii. 8 (cf. *v.* 13); Ez. xviii. 21 ff.; 'and its most beautiful expression in the Book of Jonah' (Peake).

purpose. The failure to repent will be followed by a speedy judgement; cf. Rev. ii. 5.

4—6. These *vv.* are rejected by Duhm as being too 'legal'; cf. ix. 12 f. Peake, however, defends their genuineness on the ground that Jeremiah would distinguish between the ceremonial and the moral requirements of the law.

6. *Shiloh.* See note on vii. 12.

a curse. The city will become a by-word for ill-fortune, just as Abraham was a by-word for good (Gen. xii. 3). Judah is not to remain *a curse* for ever: 'It shall come to pass that as ye were a curse among the nations, O house of Judah and house of Israel, so will I save you and ye shall be a blessing' (Zech. viii. 13).

7—9. The indignation of priests and prophets.

7. *the prophets.* That is those prophets who discredited all forecasts of coming evil; LXX. makes a clear distinction between them and Jeremiah by inserting 'false' here and in *vv.* 8, 11, and 16.

all the people heard Jeremiah speaking these words in the house
of the LORD. 8 And it came to pass, when Jeremiah had made
an end of speaking all that the LORD had commanded him to
speak unto all the people, that the priests and the prophets and
all the people laid hold on him, saying, Thou shalt surely die.
9 Why hast thou prophesied in the name of the LORD, saying,
This house shall be like Shiloh, and this city shall be desolate,
without inhabitant? And all the people were gathered unto
Jeremiah in the house of the LORD.

10 And when the princes of Judah heard these things, they
came up from the king's house unto the house of the LORD; and
they sat in the entry of the new gate of the LORD's *house*. 11 Then
spake the priests and the prophets unto the princes and to all the
people, saying, This man is worthy of death; for he hath prophesied against this city, as ye have heard with your ears. 12 Then

8. *made an end.* Jeremiah was allowed to finish his discourse, not
because men were cut to the heart by his words, but simply because,
until the end, he was following the conventional lines of denunciation
laid down by his predecessors; when however he began to attack the
temple worship, as he did at the close of his sermon, the indignation of
the priests and their allies broke forth (cf. Introd. pp. xxxi f.).

all the people. These words should probably be omitted as a mistaken repetition from the previous *v.*, in *vv.* 11 ff. the people are looked
upon as being in some sense judges between the prophet and his accusers.
At the same time the ease with which a crowd will change sides must
not be forgotten, the people may have been carried away, by what they
thought to be blasphemy, to make an onslaught on Jeremiah, in much
the same way as their descendants attacked St Stephen (Acts vii. 54 ff.);
later on, finding that the princes were disposed to look upon the case
as by no means so obvious and clear an offence as did the priests, their
sympathies may have veered round in the prophet's favour.

9. *in the name of the LORD.* The prophet's utterances were a direct
contradiction of the popular conception of Jehovah in whose name he
claimed to speak, hence the gravity of his offence (see on *v.* 16).

10—16. The intervention of the princes and the people.

10. *the princes of Judah.* The intervention of the princes probably
saved Jeremiah's life and rescued him from a situation in which there
was every prospect of his anticipating the fate of St Stephen.

the new gate. So called in xxxvi. 10; it may be that this gate was
the one made by Jotham some hundred years before (2 K. xv. 35); it
is generally identified with 'the upper gate' mentioned in xx. 2.

12—15. The simplicity and noble courage which Jeremiah shewed
when brought face to face with his accusers are strikingly similar to the

spake Jeremiah unto all the princes and to all the people, saying,
The LORD sent me to prophesy against this house and against
this city all the words that ye have heard. 13 Therefore now
amend your ways and your doings, and obey the voice of the
LORD your God; and the LORD will repent him of the evil that
he hath pronounced against you. 14 But as for me, behold, I
am in your hand: do with me as is good and right in your eyes.
15 Only know ye for certain that, if ye put me to death, ye shall
bring innocent blood upon yourselves, and upon this city, and
upon the inhabitants thereof : for of a truth the LORD hath sent
me unto you to speak all these words in your ears. 16 Then
said the princes and all the people unto the priests and to the
prophets: This man is not worthy of death; for he hath spoken

conduct of Socrates on a like occasion. Cf. especially his fear that the
consequences of the crime which they are committing unwittingly may
fall upon them, with a like anxiety on the part of Socrates (*Apol. Socr.*
30 D ff.). Jeremiah's *apologia* is a straightforward reply to the charge
made against him; he does not shirk the consequences of his own acts,
nor wish to tone down the denunciations which he had levelled at the
heads of the people. 'In a sentence he reaffirms his claim to have been
charged by God with the message he has just delivered. He renews his
exhortation to amendment, and promises that judgement will then be
averted. Of his own case he speaks neither with heroics nor unmanly
entreaty. He recognises the legal right of the tribunal to execute him,
and confronts the prospect without theatrical defiance on the one hand
or abject cowardice on the other, but with a serene expression of willing-
ness to accept the verdict his judges pronounce. Only he would be doing
less than his duty were he so proudly to refuse all comment on his own
case, that he failed to point out what a crime they would commit in
slaying one, whose only fault had been his faithfulness in executing the
commission his God and theirs had given him. It is a great scene which
here passes before us, in which the prophet's bearing is wholly worthy
of himself, and in which we do well to observe his unshaken conviction
that his message had been entrusted to him by God Himself.' Peake.

13. *amend your ways.* The accused, as Giesebrecht points out,
here becomes the accuser.

14. *as for me.* Jeremiah derives courage from the greatness of his
cause; his is only a single life; the contest is not really between himself
and his accusers, but between good and evil, right and wrong, God and
the powers of darkness. He forgets himself in realising God.

15. *innocent blood.* Cf. Matt. xxvii. 24 f.

16. *This man is not worthy of death.* According to RV. the princes
and the people recognise the justice of Jeremiah's plea, and the authority
of his message. Dr Buttenwieser, however, thinks that the result of the

to us in the name of the LORD our God.   17 Then rose up certain
of the elders of the land, and spake to all the assembly of the
people, saying,   18 ¹Micaiah the Morashtite prophesied in the

¹ Another reading is, *Micah*.   See Micah i. 1.

trial was not the acquittal, but the condemnation of the prophet; hence
the attempt of the elders (otherwise quite unnecessary) to secure his
escape; and also the statement that but for the protection of Ahikam
Jeremiah would have met the fate of Uriah (*v.* 24).   He thinks that
Jeremiah was condemned because he had broken the law of Dt. xviii.
15—22 by delivering what was obviously a false message *in the name
of the LORD*; he would therefore translate this *v.* 'Verily this man
deserves the death-penalty because he hath spoken unto us in the name
of YHWH our God.'   He justifies his translation by claiming that it
requires no change in the consonantal text¹.   The suggestion is an interesting one and helps to explain some of the difficulties of the passage,
but it must be remembered that some scholars are of the opinion that
this law is of a later date than Jeremiah (see Introd. p. lxxxvi; and
cf. Marti on Dt. xviii. 15—22, and A. F. Puukko, *Das Deuteronomium*
(1910), pp. 254 ff.), and it seems somewhat strange that the prophet
should have put forth as his defence what he must have known to be
the very grounds upon which he was accused.   I have further criticised
this theory elsewhere².

17—19.   The appeal to history.   The comparison of Jerusalem to
Shiloh made by Jeremiah is now imitated by the elders in comparing
the prophet himself to Micah.

17.   *elders of the land.*   The elders were an important body in ancient
Israel (see *Enc. Bib.* 1906 ff., 2717 f.; Benzinger, *Arch.* §§ 41 ff.; Nowack,
Arch. I. pp. 300 ff.) though it is not possible to distinguish between the
various classes of elders or even to know whether titles such as that
used here represent any distinction (cf. xix. 1, &c.).   Dr Peake suggests
that the phrase merely refers to the age of the speakers, that they were
aged country folk who 'related the story of Micah's drastic prediction
as it had come down to them in their traditions.'

18.   *Micaiah.*   Mg. *Micah* the spelling of the canonical book.   The
shorter form is probably a contraction of the longer which means 'Who
is like Yahweh?' (cf. Michael), though Dr G. B. Gray thinks that it may
mean simply 'Who is like (this child)?' and is complete in itself; see
Hebr. Proper Names, p. 157.

---

¹ 'The only change required in verse 16 to restore what according to this conclusion must have been the original text is to change the vocalisation of *'en* (אֵין)
to *'in* (אִין).   We should then have here another example of the particle, *'in*, which
occurs in 1 Sam. xxi. 9, and which has baffled ancient and modern exegetes alike,
but which on closer examination proves to be a by-form of the emphatic particle,
hen, hinne.'   *The Prophets of Israel*, p. 36; see also pp. 24—37 and Supplementary
Note, pp. 327 ff.
² See *J. Th. S.* XVI. p. 134.

days of Hezekiah king of Judah; and he spake to all the people of Judah, saying, Thus saith the Lord of hosts: [1]Zion shall be plowed as a field, and Jerusalem shall become heaps, and the mountain of the house as the high places of a forest. 19 Did Hezekiah king of Judah and all Judah put him at all to death? did he not fear the Lord, and intreat the favour of the Lord, and the Lord repented him of the evil which he had pronounced against them? Thus should we commit great evil against our

[1] See Micah iii. 12.

Morashtite. The same title is prefixed to the Book, in order to distinguish the prophet from the many others who bore the same name; it is derived from the village of Moresheth (cf. Mic. i. 14) which was probably Micah's birth-place.

Zion shall be plowed &c. Quoted from Mic. iii. 12, and of unique interest as the only direct quotation in one prophet of another in OT. It should be remembered that Micah's denunciation, though it reads as severely as that of Jeremiah, was uttered before the doctrine of the inviolability of Jerusalem had been vindicated by the destruction of Sennacherib's army; and that the temple was now the only place where Jehovah could be worshipped, and therefore a shrine which He was bound to defend at all costs.

mountain of the house. The hill on which the temple is built will become like a wooded height (LXX. both here and in Mic. iii. 12 reads the singular). The phrase is preserved in 1 Macc. iv. 46 where Judas takes down the defiled altar and hides the stones in *the mountain of the house* until a prophet should arise to give instruction concerning them.

19. *Did Hezekiah* &c. This passage suggests that the influence of Micah's preaching was much greater than is usually imagined, and that he should be placed alongside Isaiah as inaugurating the reforms of Hezekiah. Possibly the elders were exaggerating the influence of a countryman like themselves, and in any case as J. M. P. Smith has pointed out (*Micah* in *ICC.* p. 26) the prophet's teaching, as far as it has been preserved, is much more concerned with social wrongs, especially the wrongs of the poor, than with idolatry and the cultus.

intreat the favour. Lit. *make sweet the face.* Many critics look upon this as an anthropomorphic expression and give as its literal meaning *smooth the face* or even *stroke the face* (e.g. of an idol); without denying the possibility of this derivation there is nothing in the Heb. itself to suggest it[1]. The expression may be used of one man's act towards another (Ps. xlv. 12; Prov. xix. 6; Job xi. 19 only); as well as of man's act towards God.

Thus should we commit great evil. Heb. *But we are committing,* an

[1] For an examination into the meaning of the root חלה in Heb. and cognate languages see Dr Pusey's note on Zech. vii. 2 and cf. *BDB.* p. 318.

own souls. 20 And there was also a man that prophesied in the name of the LORD, Uriah the son of Shemaiah of Kiriath-jearim; and he prophesied against this city and against this land according to all the words of Jeremiah: 21 and when Jehoiakim the king, with all his mighty men, and all the princes, heard his words, the king sought to put him to death; but when Uriah heard it, he was afraid, and fled, and went into Egypt: 22 and Jehoiakim the king sent men into Egypt, *namely*, Elnathan the son of Achbor, and certain men with him, into Egypt: 23 and they fetched forth Uriah out of Egypt, and brought him unto Jehoiakim

instance of what Dr Buttenwieser has named the 'potential participle,' i.e. its use to express 'the disposition or tendency, or predetermination of the subject to, or its qualification for the action.' Dr Buttenwieser sees in this statement by the elders further proof that Jeremiah had been condemned (*op. cit.* p. 26).

20—24. The fate of Uriah. Jeremiah owed his life to the protection of powerful friends, other prophets were not so fortunate. These *vv.* are almost certainly not part of the speech of the elders; and the incident must have taken place after the escape of Jeremiah, as the temple sermon was at the beginning of the reign of Jehoiakim (xxvi. 1), and time would be needed for the flight of Uriah to Egypt, and for his apprehension, which would probably be no very speedy process.

20. *Uriah the son of Shemaiah.* Nothing further is known of this prophet though the suggestion has been made that he was the unknown author of Zech. xii.—xiv. (see Stanley, *The Jewish Church*, II. 449).

Kiriath-jearim. Usually identified with *Kirjat el-inab* which lies some seven miles WNW. of Jerusalem on the road to Jaffa.

21. *Egypt.* Uriah thus followed the example of Jeroboam the son of Nebat (1 K. xi.), but with less success.

22. *Elnathan...Egypt.* These words are wanting in LXX. From the account of him in xxxvi. 12, 25 it is unlikely that *Elnathan* would be employed on such an errand and LXX. is probably right in its omission. It may be that Jehoiakim's agent was his father-in-law Elnathan of Jerusalem (2 K. xxiv. 8), who was perhaps a different person from *the son of Achbor*; if the latter words got into the text by mistake, some scribe may have omitted the whole phrase as inconsistent with xxxvi. 12, 25; it seems to me to be easier to account for the omission than for the subsequent insertion of the words.

23. In the first years of his reign Jehoiakim was under the over-lordship of Pharaoh, and so it would be easy for him to get the extradition of a fugitive from Egypt, especially of one who was guilty of attacks on his rule. At the same time extradition treaties are no new thing, Ramses II, for example, in the fourteenth century B.C. had one with a Syrian king named Chetta.

the king; who slew him with the sword, and cast his dead body into the graves of the ¹common people. 24 But the hand of Ahikam the son of Shaphan was with Jeremiah, that they should not give him into the hand of the people to put him to death.

¹ Heb. *sons of the people.*

slew him. Mr R. B. Rackham in his *Commentary on Acts,* p. 101, has pointed out that though there 'were many traditions as to the fates of the prophets; and the persecuting and slaying of the righteous was recognized as a feature of the history of Israel' yet in OT. itself 'we read of but few martyrdoms of the prophets.' See 1 K. xviii. 13; and 2 Ch. xxiv. 20—22.

24. *Ahikam the son of Shaphan.* The brother of Gemariah (xxxvi. 12), and the father of Gedaliah (xxxix. 14, xl. 5). He, like Achbor (*v.* 22), had been one of the deputation which Josiah sent to the prophetess Huldah (2 K. xxii. 12).

CHAPTERS XXVII.—XXIX.

These three chh. are closely connected both in their contents and in the circumstances which they pre-suppose. They come from an early period in the reign of Zedekiah; they contain the messages which Jeremiah delivered against the prophets who opposed him; constant exhortations to accept the rule of the Babylonian conquerors are found in them. In addition to these similarities of subject matter the chh. are distinguished from the rest of the book by certain literary characteristics. (*a*) Those proper names which end in -iah (in the English versions) are usually spelt in Heb. יָהוּ (-iahū), but in these chh. the predominant form is יָה (-iah); for example the name Jeremiah is not found with the shorter spelling in the rest of the book though it appears several times in this form in xxvii.—xxix. (*b*) The name Nebuchadrezzar is always (and correctly) so spelt in the rest of the book (leaving out xxxiv. 1 and xxxix. 5 which come from 2 K.); in this section it occurs once only (in xxix. 21), while the less accurate form Nebuchadnezzar is found eight times. (*c*) The title of 'the prophet' is added to Jeremiah's name much more frequently than elsewhere. (*d*) The difference of text between MT. and LXX. is much greater than usual, the latter being the shorter text.

These phenomena all point towards the probability of this section's having had a separate existence before being incorporated in the larger collection. Giesebrecht tries to account for the differences by supposing that copies of these chh. were sent to Babylon for the benefit of the exiles (an event which is very probable, and in view of xxix. 1 almost certain), and that additions were there made to them as well as changes in spelling, &c. This theory seems to involve the disappearance of the originals which presumably did not come under the same influences. Cornill and Duhm see traces of later writers in these chh. though they allow that parts of them are due to Baruch. Graf has tried to explain away the peculiarities but not with complete success.

Warnings against opposition to Babylon. xxvii.
The case of Hananiah. xxviii.
Jeremiah's letter to the exiles. xxix.

CHAPTER XXVII.

Warnings against Opposition to Babylon.

The fourth year of the reign of Zedekiah (594—593 B.C.) was evidently one of much unsettlement in Palestine; the rule of Babylon, in spite of Nebuchad-rezzar's successes, had not yet come to be recognised as a fact which had to be submitted to; and the small states were plotting amongst themselves for the recovery of their independence (see Introd. p. xxvi). In Judah, and in the other states also (cf. *v.* 9), these national aspirations received the active support of those who were the recognised leaders of religion. In this ch. Jeremiah utters a solemn warning to all who have been in any way influenced by the forecasts of these 'false' prophets; the Babylonian supremacy has still many years to run, and meanwhile the only wise and right policy is to submit to it; at the same time he does his best to prevent the carrying out of what C. J. Ball has aptly termed 'the suicidal policy of combination with heathenish and treacherous allies, most of whom were the heirs of innumerable feuds with Judah.'

(*a*) *Warning to the ambassadors.* 1—11.
(*b*) *Warning to the king.* 12—15.
(*c*) *Warning to the priests and people.* 16—22.

XXVII. 1 In the beginning of the reign of [1]Jehoiakim the son of Josiah, king of Judah, came this word unto Jeremiah from the LORD, saying, 2 Thus saith the LORD to me: Make thee

---

[1] Properly, *Zedekiah*, as in some ancient authorities. See vv. 3, 12, 20, ch. xxviii. 1.

XXVII. 1—11. God, to whom the earth belongs, has given it into the hands of the Babylonians for a certain season, any nation therefore which rebels against them will be punished by Him.

1. *reign of Jehoiakim.* By a scribal error *Jehoiakim* has been written for *Zedekiah* (so mg. and cf. *vv.* 3, 12 and 20). The *v.* is omitted by LXX. and probably the heading of xxviii. 1 should be transferred to this place (see note *ad loc.*).

2. *to me.* LXX. rightly omits.

bands and ¹bars, and put them upon thy neck; 3 and send them
to the king of Edom, and to the king of Moab, and to the king
of the children of Ammon, and to the king of Tyre, and to the
king of Zidon, by the hand of the messengers which come to
Jerusalem unto Zedekiah king of Judah; 4 and give them a
charge unto their masters, saying, Thus saith the LORD of hosts,
the God of Israel: Thus shall ye say unto your masters; 5 I
have made the earth, the man and the beast that are upon the
face of the earth, by my great power and by my outstretched
arm; and I give it unto whom it seemeth right unto me. 6 And
now have I given all these lands into the hand of Nebuchadnezzar

¹ See Lev. xxvi. 13.

bands and bars. These together formed a yoke, the wooden bars
being fastened together by thongs (see *Enc. Bib.* 78). The yoke was
an easily understood symbol for submission, either to an earthly or to
a heavenly sovereign; the metaphor is often used by Jeremiah in one
or other of these senses, cf. ii. 20, v. 5, xxx. 8. For the employment
of similar means of warning cf. Is. xx. (the prophet goes 'naked and
barefoot'); in 1 K. xxii. 11 'horns of iron' are used by the 'false'
prophet Zedekiah.

3. *them.* In the previous *v.* there is no mention of any yoke
beyond the one which the prophet himself was to wear, it seems best
therefore to omit *them* (so Lucian).

the messengers. Isaiah made a similar use of the presence of
ambassadors from Ethiopia (Is. xviii. 1 ff.). Duhm has collected other
instances of foreign nations giving heed to the prophets of Jehovah
(e.g. Jud. iii. 20; 1 K. xix. 15 ff. &c.).

5 f. The God of Israel is proclaimed as the God of the whole
earth, a declaration which must have required tremendous faith in the
prophet in view of the political insignificance of Judah. It would be
interesting to know if the representatives of the other national gods
accepted Jeremiah's statement without protest, involving as it did the
subordination of their own deities. The action of the prophet was in
itself sufficient to render impossible any alliance between Judah and
these nations, because alliances carried with them the mutual recognition of the gods of the contracting parties.

5. The wording of this *v.* probably suggested that of Dan. ii. 37 f.

my outstretched arm. This expression is more often used of acts
of deliverance (Ps. cxxxvi. 12 and frequently in Dt.), or of punishment
(cf. xxi. 5). In the later chh. of Is. the 'arm of the Lord' is a constant metaphor for God's operations in history (cf. Is. li. 9, lii. 10,
liii. 1, &c.); the use of the term, as here, in connexion with creation is
rare, though it also occurs in xxxii. 17.

6. *have I given.* Cf. Is. xlv. 3; Jud. xi. 24, &c. and the various
similar expressions on the Moabite stone.

the king of Babylon, my servant; and the beasts of the field also
have I given him to serve him. 7 And all the nations shall serve
him, and his son, and his son's son, until the time of his own land
come: and then many nations and great kings shall serve themselves of him. 8 And it shall come to pass, that the nation and
the kingdom which will not serve the same Nebuchadnezzar king
of Babylon, and that will not put their neck under the yoke of
the king of Babylon, that nation will I punish, saith the LORD,
with the sword, and with the famine, and with the pestilence,
until I have consumed them by his hand. 9 But as for you,
hearken ye not to your prophets, nor to your diviners, nor to
your dreams, nor to your soothsayers, nor to your sorcerers, which
speak unto you, saying, Ye shall not serve the king of Babylon:
10 for they prophesy a lie unto you, to remove you far from your
land; and that I should drive you out and ye should perish.
11 But the nation that shall bring their neck under the yoke of
the king of Babylon, and serve him, that *nation* will I let remain
in their own land, saith the LORD; and they shall till it, and
dwell therein.

my servant. See on xxv. 9.
the beasts of the field. Man's dominion includes *the beasts of the
field*, see Gen. i. 26 with Driver's note; Judith xi. 7.
7. This *v.* is not found in LXX. probably because it is a late
addition and somewhat unsuited to its context. At the same time it
is quite possible that the forecast of the overthrow of Babylon might
be included in a warning not to resist her rule, if, as here, a clear
statement was made that such an overthrow would not happen for two
generations.
son, and his son's son. This prophecy will not bear a literal interpretation as more than two rulers occupied the throne of Babylon
after Nebuchadrezzar; possibly this failure to correspond with actual
facts caused the omission of the latter part of the *v.* by LXX. If the
words are from Jeremiah it is not necessary to read into them anything
more than a statement that the Babylonian supremacy had still a long
period during which to flourish (cf. the more detailed forecast of
'seventy years' in xxv. 11 and Ep. Jer. 3 'seven generations').
9. The attitude of the party who wished to rebel against Babylon
in each of the nations was supported, as in Judah, by the hopeful
forecasts of the official teachers of religion. For the meaning of the
different terms used here see Driver on Dt. xviii. 10.
10. *to remove you.* The consequences of following the advice of
the 'false' prophets are given as though they were the deliberate
purpose which inspired them.

12 And I spake to Zedekiah king of Judah according to all these words, saying, Bring your necks under the yoke of the king of Babylon, and serve him and his people, and live. 13 Why will ye die, thou and thy people, by the sword, by the famine, and by the pestilence, as the LORD hath spoken concerning the nation that will not serve the king of Babylon? 14 And hearken not unto the words of the prophets that speak unto you, saying, Ye shall not serve the king of Babylon: for they prophesy a lie unto you. 15 For I have not sent them, saith the LORD, but they prophesy falsely in my name; that I might drive you out, and that ye might perish, ye, and the prophets that prophesy unto you. 16 Also I spake to the priests and to all this people,

12—15. The warning to Zedekiah.

12. *I spake.* Evidently this section was dictated by Jeremiah himself.

Bring your necks under the yoke. The policy which Jeremiah recommends is well described in Matthew Arnold's lines:

> 'The East bow'd low before the blast,
> In patient, deep disdain.
> She let the legions thunder past,
> And plunged in thought again[1].'

13—15. These *vv.* are very similar to *vv.* 8 ff.

13. *Why will ye die?* So Ez. xviii. 31.

16—22. The warning is repeated for the benefit of the priests and the residue of the people. It should be noticed that LXX. and MT. differ very considerably in this section, *vv.* 17 and 18 *b* being omitted by the former, and *vv.* 19—22 appearing in a much shorter form. LXX. is probably right in leaving out *v.* 17 which seems to be an insertion based on other similar statements[2].

16. The prophets of 'Peace' evidently chose something concrete as the basis of their forecasts; a definite prophecy, such as this of the restoration of the temple vessels, must have been much more impressive than merely general promises of good things to come.

the priests. Jeremiah met with constant opposition from *the priests* and in the actual question in dispute their prejudices as the official guardians of the temple and its contents would naturally be with those who promised a speedy return of the stolen vessels.

---

[1] *Obermann once more*, 109 ff.

[2] In *v.* 18 יִפְגְּעוּ נָא is rendered ἀπαντησάτωσάν μοι (evidently reading בִּי for נָא unless indeed it represents a contracted form of בִיהוה), and Cornill thinks that the eye of the translator then wandered on from בִי to כִי at the beginning of *v.* 19 and that *v.* 18 *b* is therefore part of the original text, which has been mistakenly omitted.

saying, Thus saith the LORD: Hearken not to the words of your prophets that prophesy unto you, saying, Behold, the vessels of the LORD's house shall now shortly be brought again from Babylon: for they prophesy a lie unto you. 17 Hearken not unto them; serve the king of Babylon, and live: wherefore should this city become a desolation? 18 But if they be prophets, and if the word of the LORD be with them, let them now make intercession to the LORD of hosts, that the vessels which are left in the house of the LORD, and in the house of the king of Judah, and at Jerusalem, go not to Babylon. 19 For thus saith the LORD of hosts concerning the pillars, and concerning the sea, and

18.   Jeremiah is just as willing to be definite as his rivals. For the sarcasm which underlies his answer cf. Elijah and the prophets of Baal (1 K. xviii. 27)[1].

19—22.   In LXX. these *vv.* appear as follows (the spaces represent words found in MT.): ' *For thus saith the Lord…concerning the residue of the vessels…which…the king of Babylon took not, when he carried away captive Jeconiah…from Jerusalem….They shall be carried to Babylon…saith the Lord.*' The two texts agree in foretelling the removal of the vessels to Babylon, the MT. alone speaks of their return. It is possible that the Heb. represents the original and that LXX. omitted part of it on account of the statement in lii. 17 (= 2 K. xxv. 13) that certain of the vessels were broken up by the conquerors of Jerusalem and taken away as scrap metal.

19.   *the pillars.* The manufacture of these pillars is described in 1 K. vii. 15—22 (2 Chr. iii. 15—17) where see Dr Barnes' notes. They were two in number and probably stood at a little distance from the front of the temple. It is generally thought that these *pillars* are representations of the sacred trees so typical of Semitic altars[2].

the sea. Cf. 1 K. vii. 23—26. The molten sea was a large basin supported, until the time of Ahaz (see 2 K. xvi. 17), upon the backs of twelve oxen. The meaning of it has been lost, Josephus, for example, could only account for its name 'because of its great size' (*Antiq.*

---

1 The form בֹּאוּ really stands for בָּאוּ 3 m.p. Qal; cf. זֹרוּ in Ps. lviii. 4.

2 Robertson Smith points out that ' the details of the capitals…are those of huge candles or cressets. They had bowls (1 Kgs. vii. 41) like those of the golden candlestick (Zech. iv. 3), and gratings like those of an altar hearth. They seem therefore to have been built on the model of those altar candlesticks which we find represented on Phoenician monuments; see *CIS.* Pt. I. pl. 29, and Perrot and Chipiez, *Hist. de l'Art*, vol. III. figs. 81 *sqq.* The similarity to a candlestick, which strikes us in the description of the Hebrew pillars, is also notable in the twin detached pillars which are represented on coins as standing before the temple at Paphos.' *Rel. Sem.*[2] p. 488. This suggestion is interesting in view of Grotius' idea that the Heb. word חַמָּנִים ('glowing ones') translated ' sun images ' in Is. xvii. 10, xxvii. 9, &c. actually represents πυρεῖα.

concerning the bases, and concerning the residue of the vessels that are left in this city, 20 which Nebuchadnezzar king of Babylon took not, when he carried away captive Jeconiah the son of Jehoiakim, king of Judah, from Jerusalem to Babylon, and all the nobles of Judah and Jerusalem; 21 yea, thus saith the LORD of hosts, the God of Israel, concerning the vessels that are left in the house of the LORD, and in the house of the king of Judah, and at Jerusalem: 22 They shall be carried to Babylon, and there shall they be, until the day that I visit them, saith the LORD; then will I bring them up, and restore them to this place.

VIII. iii. 5); it is possible that it corresponded to the sacred lake found in front of some Egyptian temples.

the bases. The ten carriages for holding the lavers are called *bases.* For a description of them see 1 K. vii. 27—37, with Dr Barnes' notes, and also Stade, *ZATW.* 1901, pp. 145—190.

20. *nobles.* The word here used in MT. חֹרִים is late and of Aramaic origin. It occurs in 1 K. xxi. 8, 11, but its presence there is due, according to Cornill, to the North Israelite origin of the narrative.

22. Jewish speculation was never tired of inventing legends connected with the fate of the temple vessels. According to 2 K. xxiv. 13 all the *golden* vessels made by Solomon were cut up when Jerusalem was taken during the reign of Jehoiachin. These were replaced by silver ones, according to Baruch i. 8 f., and these latter vessels, which Nebuchadrezzar had captured in 587, were restored to Jerusalem whilst Jehoiachin was still alive (cf. *v.* 3). This tradition seems to contradict Jeremiah's forecast, and to be in conflict with Ezra i. 7—11 which states that Cyrus restored to the returning exiles the vessels of the house of the Lord which Nebuchadrezzar had taken away; however as Jehoiachin was born in 615 it is possible that he was still alive in 536. In the inventory of *vv.* 9—11 the presence of so many articles of gold is hard to reconcile with 2 K. xxiv. 13 (quoted above) and with Hag. ii. 6—8 from which 'it is a fair inference that in the second year of Darius there was little or no gold or silver in the Temple at Jerusalem.' Kennett, *Schweich Lectures*, p. 33. According to 2 Macc. ii. 4—8 Jeremiah himself hid the tabernacle, the ark and the altar of incense in a cavern; whilst another tradition says that angels descended and rescued all the vessels from the temple and at their command the earth opened her mouth and received them (2 Baruch vi. 7 ff.).

CHAPTER XXVIII.

The case of Hananiah.

In the previous ch. Jeremiah warned various classes of people both Jew and Gentile against trusting in the promises of the prophets who foretold a speedy delivery from the yoke of Babylon; this ch. exhibits the prophet himself in active contest with one of these 'false' prophets. The two chh. have other connexions besides that of subject matter, and probably in their original form composed a single account. As xxvii. now stands it is written mainly in a somewhat diffuse style, it seems best, however, following the guide of LXX. to cut out certain parts of the ch. and to transpose the heading of xxviii. 1 to xxvii. 1. The events recorded in the complete narrative may quite well have occurred on the same day.

(a) *Hananiah contradicts Jeremiah and breaks the yoke from off his neck.* 1—11.

(b) *The yoke of wood is to be replaced by one of iron.* 12—17.

XXVIII. 1 And it came to pass the same year, in the beginning of the reign of Zedekiah king of Judah, in the fourth year, in the fifth month, that Hananiah the son of Azzur the prophet, which was of Gibeon, spake unto me in the house of the LORD, in the presence of the priests and of all the people, saying, 2 Thus speaketh the LORD of hosts, the God of Israel, saying, I have broken the yoke of the king of Babylon. 3 Within two

XXVIII. 1—11. Hananiah publicly announces that the yoke of Babylon has already been broken and that the vessels will be returned in two years.

1. *in the beginning...fifth month.* In LXX. this statement of time appears at the head of ch. xxvii. which seems to be its obvious place.

Hananiah was 'one of the religious fanatics of the national party' as Cornill describes him, and apart from his bold and determined acceptance of the challenge which Jeremiah had flung down, nothing is known of him. In spite of the life-like skill with which he is here portrayed, he is really nothing but a specimen of the prophets who opposed Jeremiah (see Additional Note, pp. 182 ff., for a discussion of the relation of the various claimants to divine inspiration); he is not so much a 'false' prophet as a 'fallen' prophet; one who in Cheyne's words 'with a light heart made promises in Jehovah's name inconsistent with the moral condition of the people, and therefore not to be realised.'

Gibeon. Probably *el-Jib* some five miles NW. of Jerusalem, in the territory of Benjamin; and the scene of Solomon's dream.

3. *two full years.* The exact statement of time added force to the prophecy.

full years will I bring again into this place all the vessels of the
LORD's house, that Nebuchadnezzar king of Babylon took away
from this place, and carried them to Babylon: 4 and I will bring
again to this place Jeconiah the son of Jehoiakim, king of Judah,
with all the captives of Judah, that went to Babylon, saith the
LORD: for I will break the yoke of the king of Babylon. 5 Then
the prophet Jeremiah said unto the prophet Hananiah in the
presence of the priests, and in the presence of all the people
that stood in the house of the LORD, 6 even the prophet Jeremiah said, Amen: the LORD do so: the LORD perform thy words
which thou hast prophesied, to bring again the vessels of the
LORD's house, and all them of the captivity, from Babylon unto
this place. 7 Nevertheless hear thou now this word that I speak
in thine ears, and in the ears of all the people: 8 The prophets
that have been before me and before thee of old prophesied
against many countries, and against great kingdoms, of war, and
of evil, and of pestilence. 9 The prophet which prophesieth of
peace, when the word of the prophet shall come to pass, then
shall the prophet be known, ¹that the LORD hath truly sent him.

¹ Or, *whom the LORD hath truly sent*

4.   *Jeconiah.*   The restoration of *Jeconiah* would of course have
involved the deposition of Zedekiah: it seems strange that any prophet
should have thus dared to flout Zedekiah in his own capital city; the
king was, however, no Jehoiakim, and Hananiah ran no danger of
sharing the fate of Uriah (xxvi. 20 ff.).   In *v.* 6 when Jeremiah takes
up the words of Hananiah he makes no mention of Jeconiah.

6.   *Amen: the LORD do so.*   Probably Jeremiah uttered these words
with regret; not with the sarcasm or mockery which Micaiah shewed
on a similar occasion (1 K. xxii. 15).   Hananiah's forecast differed
from his own mainly in its omission of the need for repentance before
it could be fulfilled.

7—9.   The great importance of these *vv.* for the light which they
throw on the nature of OT. prophecy has been recognised on all sides;
two great principles are set forth in them:—(*a*) that the true prophet
was not one who spoke smooth things, such messages might be delivered
by anyone, but he was one who felt compelled to condemn the nation's sin,
even at the risk of his own life; (*b*) the prophet of peace can only be
accepted as genuine when his forecast is confirmed by the event itself;
it is to be noted that the same test is given in Dt. xviii. 20 ff.   (See
further, Additional Note, pp. 182 ff.)

9.   *of peace.*   In Micah's time the prophets *of peace* were subsidised
(iii. 5).

10 Then Hananiah the prophet took the bar from off the prophet
Jeremiah's neck, and brake it. 11 And Hananiah spake in the
presence of all the people, saying, Thus saith the LORD: Even so
will I break the yoke of Nebuchadnezzar king of Babylon within
two full years from off the neck of all the nations. And the
prophet Jeremiah went his way. 12 Then the word of the LORD

11. *Jeremiah went his way.* The fact that as far as can be gathered
from the account Jeremiah made no reply to Hananiah has troubled
many critics; Cornill and others would reject the above clause as a
gloss suggested by the command in *v.* 13 'go and tell.' It must be
acknowledged that the account as it stands is full of difficulty, and
that it is hard to account for the action of Jeremiah. To the onlooker
his silence could have but one meaning—that he was unable to defend
himself, and if he did this voluntarily it would mean, as Cornill says,
that 'he had denied his God and given up his people to a lie.' Various
reasons have been put forward to account for the prophet's conduct;
it has been suggested that he lost his confidence in the reality of his
own message in face of the certainty and confidence of Hananiah; but
such an idea can hardly be considered in a man of Jeremiah's experience; that he had to wait for a direct message from God in reply
to Hananiah, and this explanation seems to fit in with *v.* 12 in which
the contest is renewed at the command of God; but surely Jeremiah
would not need any 'special' revelation before he opposed teaching
which was in such violent contradiction to his own, and which he had
already, as it were, condemned by anticipation. In the opinion of the
present writer the last fact supplies a clue to the right solution. It is
a sufficient answer to Cornill's arguments to point out that Jeremiah
had so often and so strongly expressed his opinion on the teaching of
the prophets of peace, that no one would for a moment imagine that
he had been at last convinced by them; probably in sheer weariness,
and hopeless of making any impression on minds so utterly perverted,
he turned away in sorrow and disgust (cf. similar actions by our
Blessed Lord, Jn. viii. 25); and one may be sure that his attitude
towards the matter in dispute would not have been misunderstood by
any of those present, for doubtless he expressed his own feelings in his
face, if not by an outward gesture; his attitude it seems to me is that
of Hos. iv. 17 'Ephraim is joined to idols; let him alone.' There is
another possible explanation which, though it is not immediately
suggested by the text, is in agreement with the sequence of events
there related, and that is, that the emotional act of Hananiah inspired
the crowd to such an extent, and they were evidently sympathetic,
that the life of Jeremiah was in danger, or at any rate they were in
such a mood that any further protest on the prophet's part could have
done no possible good. It is only necessary to think of the conduct of
an English crowd towards an unpopular speaker to realise the likelihood

came unto Jeremiah, after that Hananiah the prophet had broken the bar from off the neck of the prophet Jeremiah, saying, 13 Go, and tell Hananiah, saying, Thus saith the LORD: Thou hast broken the bars of wood; but thou shalt make in their stead bars of iron. 14 For thus saith the LORD of hosts, the God of Israel: I have put a yoke of iron upon the neck of all these nations, that they may serve Nebuchadnezzar king of Babylon; and they shall serve him: and I have given him the beasts of the field also. 15 Then said the prophet Jeremiah unto Hananiah the prophet, Hear now, Hananiah; the LORD hath not sent thee; but thou makest this people to trust in a lie. 16 Therefore thus saith the LORD, Behold, I will send thee away from off the face of the earth: this year thou shalt die, because thou hast spoken rebellion against the LORD. 17 So Hananiah the prophet died the same year in the seventh month.

of this explanation, and the fact that the men of Judah were much less highly civilised adds probability to it (cf. Mk. xv. 5; Lk. iv. 30).

12—17.   The yoke of wood is replaced by one of iron.

13.   *tell Hananiah.*   Cf. the reply of Rehoboam 'My father chastised you with whips, but I will chastise you with scorpions.' (1 K. xii. 14; cf. Am. v. 19).

thou shalt make.   Read with LXX. *I will make* (cf. *v.* 14).

14.   The last part of this *v.* from *and they shall serve* is not found in LXX.

16.   *I will send thee away.*   The Lord had not *sent* him (*v.* 15) but He will *send him away.*   Hitzig.

because...the LORD.   LXX. omits.   The phrase has possibly been interpolated from Dt. xiii. 5, where, however, it refers to the crime of idolatry.   Zedekiah would be guilty of *rebellion* if he followed Hananiah's guidance on two grounds: (*a*) Nebuchadrezzar was God's servant (xxvii. 6); (*b*) Zedekiah had sworn a solemn oath to obey him (Ez. xvii. 13 f.).

17.   *the seventh month.*   Jeremiah's forecast was uttered not earlier than the *fifth* month (*v.* 1), the fulfilment of it was therefore very speedy.   The fact of Hananiah's death is accepted by Giesebrecht, Duhm and Cornill; Cheyne doubted the truth of the narrative in *The Decline and Fall of the Kingdom of Judah*, p. 77, but in *The Two Religions of Israel*, p. 58, he treats it as a possible case of second sight and compares a somewhat similar incident in Adamnan's *Life of St Columba* (quoted by Peake).   In many cases where the Divine judgement is declared against some notable offender there is no record, as there is here, of its having been carried out; this is not a sign that God's word was not fulfilled, rather the contrary, for as Pusey says (*Joel and Amos*, p. 39), 'At times, as in the case of Hananiah, Scripture records the individual fulfilment of God's judgments. Mostly, it passes by unnoticed the execution of God's sentence. The sentence of the criminal, unless reprieved, in itself implies the execution. The fact impressed those who witnessed it; the record of the judgment suffices for us.'

CHAPTER XXIX.

The Letter to the Exiles.

The contest with Hananiah and his brethren in Judah did not exhaust Jeremiah's efforts against those whom he considered to be unworthy representatives of Jehovah. The vain hopes which were fostered amongst the people in Palestine by the 'false prophets' were also to be found amongst that part of the nation which had gone into captivity after the first fall of Jerusalem. Accordingly, Jeremiah took advantage of an embassy from the king to Nebuchadrezzar to send a letter on his own account to the exiles in Babylon, warning them against the teaching of those who foretold a speedy return to their own land. The date of this letter (the genuineness of which, apart from some later additions, is admitted by most critics) is probably to be sought in the early part of the reign of Zedekiah before his visit to Babylon (li. 59), and soon after the arrival of the exiles in their new country. This ch. must therefore be considered to be earlier than the two which go before it, and with which it has close similarities (see Introd. to the three chh.). The ch. is interesting, in view of the great use made of epistles in NT. times, as containing the first recorded example of an epistle in the Bible. For other instances in OT. see 2 Ch. xxi. 12, xxx. 1, xxxii. 17.

(a) *Introduction.* 1—3.
(b) *The exiles are told to settle down and not to be deceived by the prophets of lies.* 4—9.
(c) *Babylon will be supreme for seventy years.* 10—14.
(d) *The punishment of those left behind in Jerusalem.* 15—19.
(e) *Condemnation of Ahab and Zedekiah the false prophets.* 20—23.
(f) *Condemnation of Shemaiah.* 24—32.

XXIX. 1 Now these are the words of the letter that Jeremiah the prophet sent from Jerusalem unto the residue of the elders

XXIX. 1. *the residue of the elders.* The meaning of this phrase is obscure, and several critics would follow the reading of LXX. which has *the elders* only. The objection to this course is that it is easier to explain the omission of *the residue*, granting that it formed part of the original text, than it would be to explain its insertion. It is possible that some of the elders had been removed from their posts and even put to death by the Babylonians, and that Jeremiah's letter is a warning to the remainder. For the condition of the exiles see note, pp. 222 f.

of the captivity, and to the priests, and to the prophets, and to all the people, whom Nebuchadnezzar had carried away captive from Jerusalem to Babylon : 2 (after that Jeconiah the king, and the queen-mother, and the eunuchs, *and* the princes of Judah and Jerusalem, and the craftsmen, and the smiths, were departed from Jerusalem;) 3 by the hand of Elasah the son of Shaphan, and Gemariah the son of Hilkiah, (whom Zedekiah king of Judah sent unto Babylon to Nebuchadnezzar king of Babylon,) saying, 4 Thus saith the LORD of hosts, the God of Israel, unto all the captivity, whom I have caused to be carried away captive from Jerusalem unto Babylon: 5 Build ye houses, and dwell in them; and plant gardens, and eat the fruit of them; 6 take ye wives, and beget sons and daughters; and

2. This *v.* which is evidently dependent on xxiv. 1, and 2 K. xxiv. 12 ff. reads like an interpolation.

queen-mother. See on xiii. 18 f.

smiths. See on xxiv. 1.

3. *Elasah.* Probably the brother of Ahikam the son of Shaphan who befriended Jeremiah (xxvi. 24); the ambassadors must have been well disposed to the prophet to be entrusted with his message.

Gemariah. Possibly the son of that *Hilkiah* who discovered the roll in the temple (2 K. xxii. 8).

sent unto Babylon. Perhaps bearing the annual tribute.

4—9. The exiles are advised to make Babylon their home and to identify themselves with its fortunes. Some of the people and their descendants took the prophet's advice so much to heart that they refused to return even at the end of the exile; and it was probably to influence such that the apocryphal *Epistle of Jeremiah* was written (see Oxford Apocr. I. pp. 596 ff.).

5. *gardens.* When Alexander the Great occupied Babylon, he and his servants 'were drawn to experiment in the acclimatizing of the plants of their native land. In this they had been anticipated to some extent by the old Eastern kings, who were zealous to collect fauna and flora of remote countries in their gardens.' Edwyn Bevan, *The House of Seleucus*, I. p. 246; cf. Tiele, *Babyl.-assyr. Gesch.* p. 603. According to Strabo xv. 731 the vine was one of the trees so experimented with; possibly its cultivation had already been tried by some of the Jewish exiles.

6. Not only were the exiles to build and to plant but they were also to marry and 'to settle down.' Cornill has suggested that this was a command to take wives of the Babylonian women, but the double form of the phrase *take wives for your sons, and give your daughters to husbands* seems to contradict his supposition that there would not be enough Jewish wives for all the exiles (cf. Dt. vii. 3).

take wives for your sons, and give your daughters to husbands, that they may bear sons and daughters; and multiply ye there, and be not diminished. 7 And seek the peace of the city whither I have caused you to be carried away captive, and pray unto the LORD for it: for in the peace thereof shall ye have peace. 8 For thus saith the LORD of hosts, the God of Israel: Let not your prophets that be in the midst of you, and your diviners, deceive you, neither hearken ye to your dreams which ye [1]cause to be dreamed. 9 For they prophesy falsely unto you in my name: I have not sent them, saith the LORD. 10 For thus saith the

[1] Or, dream

multiply. God's promise to Abraham was also a command.

7. *seek the peace of the city.* Both the Old and the New Testament recognise the duty of loyalty to the existing form of political government, provided it really carries out its responsibilities (Matt. xxii. 31; 1 Tim. ii. 2; 1 Pet. ii. 13—17)[1]. *The city* need not be limited to Babylon, the exiles were probably divided up into a number of bodies to prevent treachery, and scattered in different places. LXX. reading *land* has much to recommend it.

I have caused. Notice the stress here and in *v.* 4 which the prophet lays upon the ultimate cause of the captivity being Jehovah Himself; this teaching is the real basis of his advice to dwell in Babylon as being the place in which God has put them.

8. *dreams.* See on xxiii. 25.

ye cause to be dreamed. The MT. as it stands is not good Hebrew and possibly owes its form to dittography; by striking out the initial letter of the verb, *ye dream* is read (so LXX., Syr. and Vg.). The original text suggests that the people asked the prophets to make them the subjects of their dreams so as to be able to give them the advice they needed. Cornill would read *they dream*, making the dream refer to the false prophets as in xxiii. 25 ff., cf. also Dt. xiii. 2 ff.

10—14. The seventy years of the Babylonian supremacy must be fulfilled. Jeremiah's message to the captives must have been very disappointing to many of them, who were doubtless living in almost daily expectation of some event which would bring their captivity to an end, and vindicate Jehovah's power by the annihilation of His enemies.

---

[1] Many instances could be cited to shew the way in which the later Jews fulfilled the spirit of Jeremiah's command. In Ezra vi. 10 Cyrus is represented as asking for the prayers of the people, and according to 1 Macc. vii. 33 offerings were made for the Syrian monarchs (so in *Ep. Arist.* 45). The writer of Bar. ii. 21 ff. was probably thinking of the above command when he denounced rebellion against the heathen king as rebellion against God (cf. also i. 10 ff.). Later instances of the same attitude can be found in Joseph. *de Bell. Jud.* II. xvii. 2, and *Contra Ap.* II. 6; and in the Mishnah: 'Pray for the welfare of the government, since but for the fear thereof men would swallow each other alive,' *Aboth*, III. 2.

LORD, After seventy years be accomplished for Babylon, I will visit you, and perform my good word toward you, in causing you to return to this place. 11 For I know the thoughts that I think toward you, saith the LORD, thoughts of peace, and not of evil, to give you [1]hope in your latter end. 12 And ye shall call upon me, and ye shall go and pray unto me, and I will hearken unto you. 13 And ye shall seek me, and find me, when ye shall search for me with all your heart. 14 And I will be found of you, saith the LORD, and I will [2]turn again your captivity, and I will gather you from all the nations, and from all the places whither I have

---

[1] Heb. *a latter end and hope.*   [2] Or, *return to*

---

10. *seventy years.* In xxv. 11 the same period is mentioned as the length of time to be fulfilled before the Babylonian dominion would come to an end. The prophet is therefore using round numbers. In point of fact the Babylonian supremacy lasted roughly from 607, the date of the Fall of Nineveh (or from the battle of Carchemish in 605) till 538. The captivity lasted either sixty-one years, that is from the first capture of Jerusalem in 597 to the approximate date of the first return in 536; or if the date of the second capture be taken as the starting point, fifty years only.

11. God's purposes for Israel are for their well being, and at the latter end the misfortunes of the nation will be seen to have been part of its necessary training. Cf. Dt. viii. 16.

hope...end. Dr Streane compares mg. *a latter end and hope* with Prov. xxiii. 18, xxiv. 14, 20.

12—14. LXX. text for these *vv.* is much shorter, omitting *v.* 12 up to *go* and the whole of *v.* 14 after *I will be found of you.*

13. There is much pathos in this *v.* when one thinks of the prophet's condemnation of the Israelite worship, and their half-heartedness, or as St James would call it 'double-mindedness' (cf. i. 5—8), in seeking God. Cf. Hos. v. 15 'in their affliction they will seek me earnestly' and contrast Is. lxvi. 1.

14. *turn...captivity.* The Heb. of this expression was generally understood in this sense by the older writers; Ewald, however, questioned it, and suggested that the literal meaning was *turn a turn*, that is to say *restore the fortune.* Since his time most critics have accepted the rendering he proposed, Driver, for example, in commenting on Dt. xxx. 3 says, 'Whether שְׁבוּת be derived from שָׁבָה or שׁוּב the expression does not mean '*bring back* thy captives': it is used commonly with reference to a decisive *turn*, or change, in a people's fortune. Here, as also Jer. xxix. 14, xxx. 3; Ez. xxix. 14, the return from captivity is mentioned separately afterwards.' In some passages the old rendering is only possible when taken in a metaphorical sense (as Ez. xvi. 53; Job xlii. 10).

driven you, saith the LORD; and I will bring you again unto the
place whence I caused you to be carried away captive. 15 For
ye have said, The LORD hath raised us up prophets in Babylon.
16 For thus saith the LORD concerning the king that sitteth upon
the throne of David, and concerning all the people that dwell in
this city, your brethren that are not gone forth with you into
captivity; 17 thus saith the LORD of hosts: Behold, I will send
upon them the sword, the famine, and the pestilence, and will
make them like vile figs, that cannot be eaten, they are so bad.
18 And I will pursue after them with the sword, with the famine,
and with the pestilence, and will deliver them to be ¹tossed to
and fro among all the kingdoms of the earth, to be an execration,
and an astonishment, and an hissing, and a reproach, among all
the nations whither I have driven them: 19 because they have
not hearkened to my words, saith the LORD, wherewith I sent
unto them my servants the prophets, rising up early and sending
them; but ye would not hear, saith the LORD. 20 Hear ye there-

¹ Or, *a terror unto*

15—19. The punishment of those left behind in Jerusalem. Cf.
xxiv. 8—10. These *vv.* seem to have got out of their context and can
hardly be retained as part of the genuine text. LXX. omits *vv.* 16—19
and also *v.* 20, *v.* 15 then connects quite smoothly with *vv.* 21 ff.¹; in
Lucian's recension *vv.* 16—20 are found before *v.* 15. Driver looks
upon the *vv.* as of Babylonian origin, and thinks that they were incorporated into the book from an exilic version of the letter.

16. *the king:* i.e. Zedekiah.

17. *vile figs.* The way in which this figure is referred to seems to
presuppose a knowledge of xxiv. 2—8; there is however no insuperable
difficulty in the way of admitting such knowledge on the part of the
exiles.

18. *I have driven them.* The writer seems to see things from the
point of view of one who could look back on the second deportation.

19. *ye would not hear.* The words must be addressed to those
who remained behind and are therefore unsuitable in a letter sent to
Babylon. In this and the previous *v.* the interpolator, as Cornill says,
has forgotten his assumed situation.

20—23. The condemnation of Ahab and Zedekiah. These *vv.* are
probably a response to the boast on the part of the exiles that the Lord
had raised up prophets amongst them (see Introd. to *vv.* 15—19).

---

¹ It should not be overlooked, however, that LXX. omission can be accounted for
by the scribe's eye having wandered from *Babylon* in *v.* 15 to *Babylon* in *v.* 20.

fore the word of the LORD, all ye of the captivity, whom I have
sent away from Jerusalem to Babylon.

21 Thus saith the LORD of hosts, the God of Israel, concerning
Ahab the son of Kolaiah, and concerning Zedekiah the son of
Maaseiah, which prophesy a lie unto you in my name: Behold,
I will deliver them into the hand of Nebuchadrezzar king of
Babylon; and he shall slay them before your eyes; 22 and of
them shall be taken up a curse by all the captives of Judah which
are in Babylon, saying, The LORD make thee like Zedekiah and
like Ahab, whom the king of Babylon roasted in the fire:
23 because they have wrought folly in Israel, and have committed
adultery with their neighbours' wives, and have spoken words in
my name falsely, which I commanded them not; and I am he
that knoweth, and am witness, saith the LORD.

20. This *v.* is best explained as being a link to connect the interpolation with what follows; it is missing from LXX.

21. *Ahab...Zedekiah.* These two prophets are but names and
symbols of punishment; nothing is known about them and in LXX.
even the names of their fathers are omitted. The punishment which
they underwent was not, apparently, a Jewish one, as the appropriate
punishment under the law, except in certain unusual cases (cf. Lev. xx.
14, xxi. 9) was stoning (Ez. xvi. 38, &c.)[1]. In any case Nebuchadrezzar
would hardly be likely to put these men to death for such an offence;
they must have incurred his wrath for some political crime such as
stirring up the people against the Babylonian rule. The event seems
to have made a great impression on the mind of the Jews and later
tradition gave the names of *Ahab* and *Zedekiah* to the two elders in
Susanna, probably on account of the similarity of their fate.

22. *a curse.* As the Heb. for *curse* is kĕlālāh a play on Kolaiah
is perhaps intended, and also on kālāh = *roasted.*

roasted. Cf. the fate of the seven brethren (2 Macc. vii. 3 ff.).

23. The combination of immorality with a presumptuous claim to
speak in the name of God was also a mark of the prophets condemned
by Jeremiah in xxiii. 14.

folly, in Heb. has not quite the same meaning as in English; the
fool is not merely one who lacks wisdom, but also one whose moral
faculties are blunted (cf. Ps. xiv. 1).

he that knoweth. This phrase is absent from LXX. and may be an
interpolation; the idea underlying it is not uncommon (cf. Ex. ii. 25;
Hos. v. 3; Nah. i. 7).

---

[1] Burning was also an exceptional punishment under the Code of Hammurabi
(see § 157). In Jubilees xx. 4 burning is stated to be the normal punishment for
fornication.

24 And ¹concerning Shemaiah the Nehelamite thou shalt speak, saying, 25 Thus speaketh the LORD of hosts, the God of Israel, saying, Because thou hast sent letters in thine own name unto all the people that are at Jerusalem, and to Zephaniah the son of Maaseiah the priest, and to all the priests, saying, 26 The LORD hath made thee priest in the stead of Jehoiada the priest, that ye should be officers in the house of the LORD, for every man

¹ Or, *unto*

24—32. The condemnation of Shemaiah. The letter which Jeremiah sent to the exiles naturally caused much consternation amongst the prophets who were condemned by it, and one of them, Shemaiah the Nehelamite, attempted to have Jeremiah arrested and punished.

The section as it stands is in a state of great confusion and can hardly be original. Four strata, as it were, of speech are represented; (*a*) the Lord speaks, (*b*) Jeremiah is to hand on what He says, (*c*) this includes what Shemaiah wrote, (*d*) which repeats Jeremiah's words. The first part of *v.* 25, which is addressed to Shemaiah, is not consistent with *v.* 29, in which the letter from him is read to Jeremiah, apparently for the first time. The best solution of the difficulty is perhaps to strike out *v.* 25 *a* and to turn the rest of the *v.* into the third person, retaining the words *concerning Shemaiah the Nehelamite* (*v.* 24) as a heading to the section. LXX. has the matter of this passage arranged in a different order from MT., but it gives no help towards making the confusion any less.

24. *Shemaiah the Nehelamite.* Nothing is known of this man, and it is uncertain whether his designation is a family or a geographical one.

25. *in thine own name.* Not in the name of God; perhaps this statement is not intended to be taken literally, Shemaiah would doubtless have claimed that he was acting quite as much as was Jeremiah under the guidance of God.

unto all....Jerusalem. This phrase together with *and to all the priests* is omitted by LXX., and rightly so as the actual contents of the letter shew.

Zephaniah. Also mentioned in xxi. 1 (where see note) and xxxvii. 3 as being sent to ask for an oracle from Jeremiah; and in lii. 24 ff. (= 2 K. xxv. 18 ff.) as being put to death by Nebuchadrezzar. In this latter passage he is called 'the second priest.'

Maaseiah. Also the name of the father of Zedekiah the prophet (*v.* 21), though in that context he is not called *the priest.*

26. *Jehoiada the priest.* Probably the high priest of the reign of Joash is meant (cf. 2 K. xi. 18).

officers. There is little doubt that the singular should here be read with LXX., Targ., Syr., &c. The Heb. word used, פקים, is the same as that applied to Pashhur in xx. 1, though in his case the word נגיד (translated 'chief' in RV.) is added; probably the offices were the same, in view

that is mad, and maketh himself a prophet, that thou shouldest put him in the stocks and in [1]shackles. 27 Now therefore, why hast thou not rebuked Jeremiah of Anathoth, which maketh himself a prophet to you, 28 forasmuch as he hath sent unto us in Babylon, saying, *The captivity* is long: build ye houses, and dwell in them; and plant gardens, and eat the fruit of them? 29 And Zephaniah the priest read this letter in the ears of Jeremiah the prophet. 30 Then came the word of the LORD unto Jeremiah, saying, 31 Send to all them of the captivity, saying, Thus saith the LORD concerning Shemaiah the Nehelamite:

[1] Or, *the collar*

of the similarity of their functions, but the matter is by no means certain.

mad. Cf. the question in 2 K. ix. 11 'wherefore came this *mad* fellow to thee?' Eastern peoples, even to the present day, look upon madmen as in some sense inspired, and the same thought evidently underlies the use of μάντις (from μαίνομαι *to rage furiously, be mad*) for a soothsayer or prophet amongst the Greeks.

stocks. See note on xx. 2.

shackles. The exact meaning of the Heb. is not certain and the word is not found elsewhere; mg. *collar* is from a cognate Arabic word and probably better represents the original.

27.   *maketh himself a prophet.* Better *behaves like a prophet.* The temple authorities quite evidently had no sympathy with the 'dervish-like' excesses of the prophets (cf. 1 S. x. 10, 12 f., xvii. 10, xix. 20 ff.). The priests as a body despised the prophets—that is those of them who were not subservient to themselves—and looked upon them as mad enthusiasts. In just the same way the philosophers and poets of ancient Greece were in constant antagonism (cf. Plato, *Repub.* x. 607 B)[1]. The poets, for their part, mostly attacked the 'sophistical' upholders of systems and in doing so exhibited remarkable affinities to the prophets of Israel. The guardians of the established order, and especially of religious order, are at all times suspicious of the unusual; or as a modern writer has well said 'are so [much] afraid of religious vagaries and so little afraid of religious stagnation[2].' At the same time there is another side of the case, and so fervent an evangelist as St Paul had to warn his converts that 'the spirits of the prophets are subject to the prophets' (1 Cor. xiv. 32).

---

[1] See the first of Mr James Adam's Gifford Lectures on *The Religious Teachers of Greece* entitled 'The place of Poetry and Philosophy in the Development of Greek Religious Thought.'

[2] Walter Rauschenbusch, *Christianity and the Social Crisis*, p. 339.

Because that Shemaiah hath prophesied unto you, and I sent him not, and he hath caused you to trust in a lie; 32 therefore thus saith the LORD, Behold, I will punish Shemaiah the Nehelamite, and his seed; he shall not have a man to dwell among this people, neither shall he behold the good that I will do unto my people, saith the LORD: because he hath spoken rebellion against the LORD.

32. *he shall not...the good.* It is hard to understand this statement as it stands. What is meant by *the good* which God will do to His people? It can hardly refer to the restoration, which was according to Jeremiah's own teaching to be delayed for seventy years, for Shemaiah would have no reasonable expectation of living to see that event. The punishment should therefore be applied to the *seed* as is done by LXX. which reads *there shall not be a man of them in the midst of you to see the good.*

ADDITIONAL NOTE ON XXIX. 1.

The Condition of the Exiles.

The Babylonians in their foreign policy were not so rigorous or so cruel as the Assyrians, they did not sweep away entire populations and substitute strangers for them. Their object after the fall of Jerusalem was to render Judah powerless by the removal of the nation's leaders and its warriors. The number of captives was therefore comparatively small, according to 2 K. xxiv. 16 eight thousand men (*v.* 14 gives the number as ten thousand), and according to Jer. lii. 28 three thousand and twenty-three Jews only. In some cases the captives were allowed to take their families with them (which probably accounts for the difference in the above figures), but this was not so in every instance (cf. Ez. xxiv. 21). It should be noticed in passing that the policy of Babylon was not successful; the remnant prospered in an amazing way and the nation soon recovered its strength. When the yoke of Babylon was eventually thrown off in 588 Jerusalem offered a more determined resistance, though defended by a remnant only, than it had done during the first siege.

The land to which the Hebrews were taken was noted for its fertility and wealth. 'It was...to the very centre of the world—the most populous and busy part of His earth—to which God sent His people for their exile.' If the treatment of Jehoiachin is any guide it is probable that the exiles of the first deportation were well treated. They were not looked upon as slaves and distributed amongst a number of private masters, but were allowed to retain some form of self-government, living probably in fairly large communities under the rule of elders (xxix. 1; Ez. iii. 15, viii. 1, xiv. 1) as in the early days of the nation before the establishment of the monarchy. Their life would be very little different from that of the ordinary villager though probably somewhat strange to the aristocratic Jews who formed the bulk of the exiles. Many of them were doubtless employed on the large building and irrigating schemes which were then being carried on in Babylon; many of them seem to have taken to trade on their own account; and some of them, perhaps in rather later times, had sufficient leisure to lay the foundation of the literary activity which made the exile period of so much value in the religious development of the nation.

The religious life of the exiles was rendered difficult by reason of their separation from Jerusalem and their dwelling in 'an unclean land.' The faith of many of them must have been severely tried by the fall of Jerusalem, and by what seemed to them the evident inability of Jehovah to protect His worshippers when confronted by the servants of Bel and Marduk; the elaborate and stately ritual must have tempted many into disloyalty; and the whole system of deportation, whether deliberately planned or not, must have tended to make the old worship impossible, and so to undermine the very existence of the nation. Many nations did, indeed, entirely disappear when subjected to this fate.

One effect of the first deportation was to divide the nation into two halves between whom there was apparently much ill-feeling. That the relations of the exiles and the remnant should be unfriendly is not really surprising. On the one side those who had been carried away were the pick of the nation, the nobles, the craftsmen and the priests, and they would naturally look down on their low-born and inexperienced successors. This feeling of antagonism would be reinforced by the events preceding the deportation when the exiles were forced to get rid of their property, almost certainly at very low prices. The remnant, on their side, looked upon their survival in the land as due to their greater holiness and despised the exiles accordingly (cf. xxiv. and the prophet's own opinion). In spite of these differences there was much that was similar in the two communities; they both hoped for speedy deliverance; the temple at Jerusalem in spite of its having been looted was still held to be the guarantee of God's protection and of national restoration (cf. xxvii. 16). Hopes such as these were fostered and perhaps originated, in both Babylon and Palestine, by the false prophets; and in each case these prophets were opposed by a single true prophet, by Ezekiel in Babylon and by Jeremiah in Jerusalem.

CHAPTERS XXX.—XXXIII.

Critics of an older generation considered that these four chh. formed a united whole, and at first sight there is much to be said for this view. The prevailing gloom, which overspreads the authentic prophecies of Jeremiah in the previous portion of the book, seems here to lift for a while, and these utterances are marked by a spirit of hope and expectancy, and by the promise of coming good. A closer examination of the passages, however, soon reveals the fact that much of the matter contained in them cannot readily be attributed to Jeremiah, nor to anyone living in his day, and that whatever unity they possess is editorial rather than original. It is, however, convenient to group the chh. together for the purpose of analysis. Payne Smith divides them up as follows:

'A triumphal hymn of Israel's salvation.' xxx., xxxi.

The purchase of the field at Anathoth. xxxii.

A direct promise of the return of the nation and of the restoration of the Davidic throne. xxxiii.

CHAPTERS XXX., XXXI.

The Glories of the Future.

These two chh. form a literary unity and are so treated by all critics; they shew one side of the picture of which xlvi.—li. gives the other, here blessings are promised to the oppressed people, there punishment is to fall on the surrounding nations. Their position immediately after xxix. 32 is almost certainly due, as Cornill says, to the fact that they describe 'the good' which Shemaiah, or more probably his descendants, was to forfeit (see above). As they break the continuous series of narratives which stretch from xxiv. to xliv. and themselves consist entirely of prophecies or spoken words some such explanation of their position is necessary.

The hopeful tone of these chh., the evident fact that they come from a time when Jerusalem had fallen (xxx. 18, xxxi. 40), and that if they are a unity they presuppose a Palestinian origin (xxxi. 8, 21), has led many critics to reject them *in toto*. Stade, and Smend, and more recently, H. P. Smith are amongst this class; the latter says 'in the book of Jeremiah, we have the complete Messianic programme set forth in language that we cannot possibly suppose to have been used by that preacher (Jer. 30 and 31),' *The Religion of Israel*, pp. 245 f. This manner of dealing with the passage has seemed to many critics too sweeping, and they would retain part at any rate of the chh., especially the poetic portions, as coming from the prophet. Movers noticing the similarity of some of the utterances to the later chh. of Isaiah, separated them and attributed them to the writer of those chh.; Graf however thought that the indebtedness was the other way, and that the passages in Jeremiah are the original and were copied by later writers. It must be confessed that a great deal of uncertainty exists as to the authenticity of much of the section; there is little doubt that it contains later additions, but it is also probable that much which has been rejected by some critics is genuine; the fact, for example, that the chh. come from some writer living in Palestine subsequent to the fall of Jerusalem does not absolutely preclude Jeremianic authorship, as the prophet did not go down to Egypt at once. The only conclusion that can be safely put forward is that each part of the section must be examined on its own merits; in other words that the chh. are a literary unity and not a single utterance.

(a) *The heading of the prophecies.* xxx. 1—4.
(b) *Troubles are to come upon all peoples.* 5—11.
(c) *The restoration of Zion.* 12—22.
(d) *The storm of God's anger.* 23 f.
(e) *The restoration of Ephraim.* xxxi. 1—9.
(f) *The Lord's purpose is proclaimed to the nations.* 10—14.
(g) *The sorrows of Rachel.* 15—22.
(h) *The coming blessings on both Israel and Judah.* 23—30.
(i) *The New Covenant with the house of Israel.* 31—34.
(j) *The stability of Israel.* 35—40.

XXX. 1 The word that came to Jeremiah from the LORD, saying, 2 Thus speaketh the LORD, the God of Israel, saying, Write thee all the words that I have spoken unto thee in a book. 3 For, lo, the days come, saith the LORD, that I will [1]turn again the captivity of my people Israel and Judah, saith the LORD: and I will cause them to return to the land that I gave to their fathers, and they shall possess it.

4 And these are the words that the LORD spake concerning Israel and concerning Judah. 5 For thus saith the LORD: We have heard a voice of trembling, [2]of fear, and not of peace.

---

[1] Or, *return to*   [2] Or, there is *fear, and no peace*

XXX. 1—4. The heading of the prophecies. This heading is probably late and intended to be an introduction to the two chh. Graf thought that the glorious picture of Israel's future contained in these chh. was intended to form the ending of Jeremiah's roll as issued for the second time (xxxvi. 32); it seems as if this introduction was written for an utterance put forth after the fall of Jerusalem and in view of the return.

4. *these are the words.* The *vv.* following seem to be the contents of the book referred to in *v.* 2.

5—11. This section deals with the judgements coming upon all peoples; upon Jacob in order that he may be delivered; upon the nations that their yoke may be burst from off his neck. For this double function of the judgement Driver compares Is. xiii. 6—15 (the fall of Babylon), and Is. xiv. 1 f. (the salvation of Israel).

5. *thus saith the LORD.* As the statement which follows is in the 1st person plural and obviously unfitted to be a divine utterance, the words should be deleted as the addition of a careless scribe, unless indeed 'Ye say' should be inserted after them.

B.   15

6 Ask ye now, and see whether a man doth travail with child:
wherefore do I see every man with his hands on his loins, as a
woman in travail, and all faces are turned into paleness? 7 Alas!
for that day is great, so that none is like it: it is even the time
of Jacob's trouble; but he shall be saved out of it. 8 And it
shall come to pass in that day, saith the LORD of hosts, that I will
break his yoke from off thy neck, and will burst thy bands; and
strangers shall no more serve themselves of him: 9 but they
shall serve the LORD their God, and David their king, whom I will

6.   'Men do not suffer the pains of child-bearing; what, then, is
the cause of the terror and agony which they are all displaying?'
Driver.   For child-bearing as a type of great pain and terror cf. Is.
xiii. 8, where it is said that 'their faces shall be faces of flame'; xxi. 3;
and frequently in Ps. and elsewhere[1].

paleness.   The word here used is usually applied to mildew; cf.
Joel ii. 6; Nah. ii. 10.

7.   *that day.*   The day of the Lord; i.e. the time when, in the
popular imagination, the foes of Israel were to be crushed by the sudden
intervention of Jehovah Himself.   See Edghill's note on Am. v. 18
(where the phrase is first used); and cf. Mk. xiii. 7 f., 17—20, 24.

Jacob.   A favourite term for Israel in the later chh. of Is. and
other writings which are usually considered to be of a late date.   In
Is. ii. 5, viii. 17, x. 20 the name is used for Judah only; in Is. ix. 8
for Ephraim only; the usage in this ch. is a little uncertain, probably
it includes both branches of the nation (cf. *v.* 4).

8.   The early part of the *v.* is strongly reminiscent of Is. x. 27;
cf. also Nah. i. 13.   Driver thinks that the sudden and awkward change
from the 3rd to the 2nd person is due to the influence of the former
passage.   LXX. reads the 3rd person which looks like a correction.

bands.   See on xxvii. 2.

9.   *the LORD their God, and David their king.*   This phrase is also
found in Hos. iii. 5; Cheyne considers that in each case it is an insertion (Introd. to Robertson Smith's *Prophets*[2], p. xviii.).   *David
their king* refers to an ideal king of the house of David and not to
David risen from the dead; the Targum paraphrases 'Messiah the son
of David, their king.'   At the same time, in view of similar legends,
it is probable that many of the common people liked to think that
David himself was to return, just as Orthodox Jews, even to the present
day, look for a literal return of Elijah.   It is a remarkable, though

[1] Herodotus records that the Scythians were punished by having birth-pangs
inflicted upon them for their crime in plundering the temple of Venus at Ascalon
(I. 105).   Prof. R. A. S. Macalister compares the Irish legend of the Tain Bo Cuailuge
in which the same punishment is brought on the men of Ulster by the curse of
Macha.   *Schweich Lectures*, p. 94 n.

raise up unto them. 10 Therefore fear thou not, O Jacob my servant, saith the LORD; neither be dismayed, O Israel: for, lo, I will save thee from afar, and thy seed from the land of their captivity; and Jacob shall return, and shall be quiet and at ease, and none shall make him afraid. 11 For I am with thee, saith the LORD, to save thee: for I will make a full end of all the nations whither I have scattered thee, but I will not make a full end of thee; but I will correct thee with judgement, and will in no wise [1]leave thee unpunished.

12 For thus saith the LORD, Thy hurt is incurable, and thy wound grievous. 13 There is none to plead [2]thy cause, [3]that

[1] Or, *hold thee guiltless*
[2] Or, *thy cause: for thy wound thou hast no medicines* nor *plaister*
[3] Heb. *for closing up*, or, *pressing*.

perhaps not an unnatural, fact that constant and widespread traditions exist that certain great rulers and kings are to come back to be the saviours of their people, as, for example, our own king Arthur, Frederick Barbarossa, and also the Moslem belief that the Mahdi will return[1].

10 f. These *vv.* are missing from LXX. though they are found in xlvi. 27 f. where they recur in the Heb. Driver thinks that they are a detached fragment added in both places by the compiler; other critics disagree as to which of the places of occurrence is the original, but agree in rejecting the Jeremianic authorship.

Jacob my servant. The phrase is very common in Deutero Isaiah, though as Canon Kennett warns us 'we must be on our guard against the too common assumption that phrases in the Bible have always exactly the same *nuance.*' *The Servant of the Lord*, p. 8.

afraid. Cf. Is. xvii. 2.

11. *with judgement.* Cf. x. 24.

unpunished. Literally as mg. *hold thee guiltless.*

12—22. The restoration of Zion. Judah cannot heal her own wounds and as all capacity for repentance seems gone there is no hope that she will appeal to the only wise physician; God Himself will however interfere on her behalf because of the taunts of the enemy.

12. Cf. xv. 18 where the prophet uses the same language to describe his own sufferings.

13. *to plead thy cause.* A forensic metaphor which seems a little

---

[1] Cf. Miss Gertrude Lowthian Bell's description of the Mosque at Samarra (on the Tigris to the north of Baghdad). 'Inside under the dome of priceless tiles are the tombs of the tenth and eleventh Shi'ah Imams, while the smaller dome of gold covers the cleft into which vanished the Mahdi, who will appear again when the time is ripe. Therefore when you see black ensigns, black ensigns coming out of the East, then go forth and join them; for the Imam of God will be with those standards, and he will fill the world with equity and justice.' *Amurath to Amurath*, p. 212.

15—2

thou mayest be bound up: thou hast no healing medicines.
14 All thy lovers have forgotten thee; they seek thee not: for
I have wounded thee with the wound of an enemy, with the
chastisement of a cruel one; for the [1]greatness of thine iniquity,
because thy sins were increased. 15 Why criest thou [2]for thy
hurt? thy pain is incurable: for the [1]greatness of thine iniquity,
because thy sins were increased, I have done these things unto
thee. 16 Therefore all they that devour thee shall be devoured;
and all thine adversaries, every one of them, shall go into captivity; and they that spoil thee shall be a spoil, and all that prey
upon thee will I give for a prey. 17 For I will restore [3]health
unto thee, and I will heal thee of thy wounds, saith the LORD;
because they have called thee an outcast, *saying*, It is Zion,
whom no man [4]seeketh after. 18 Thus saith the LORD: Behold,
I will [5]turn again the captivity of Jacob's tents, and have compassion on his dwelling places; and the city shall be builded
upon her own [6]heap, and the palace shall [7]remain after the

---

[1] Or, *multitude*   [2] Or, *for thy hurt, because thy pain is incurable?*
[3] See ch. viii. 22.   [4] Or, *careth for*   [5] Or, *return to*
[6] Or, *mound* Heb. *tel.*   [7] Or, *be inhabited*

---

out of place as the rest of the *v.* continues the medical language of
v. 12.   Duhm omits, probably correctly.

The exact meaning of the latter part of the *v.* is a little uncertain,
and the mg. seems to give the best translation: *for* thy *wound thou hast
no medicines* nor *plaister*.

14.   *thy lovers.* This may mean either the Baalim or Judah's
allies, probably the latter.

16.   *Therefore.* The connexion is rather difficult because the sins
of Zion are apparently made the reason for her restoration. It may be,
however, that the meaning intended is 'Because of thy great need' &c.

shall go into captivity. LXX. *shall eat their own flesh*; this rendering
which involves only a slight change in Heb. is accepted by Cornill who
compares Is. xlix. 26; cf. also Is. ix. 20; Hag. ii. 22.

17.   *restore health.* See on viii. 22.

18.   *tents.* The corresponding Arabic word is used of households.

heap. Heb. *tel.* The city was to be rebuilt on its old site. 'A "tell"'
is in appearance an ordinary hill; but it is in reality, at least in its
upper part, a mass of ruins. In the East, from the earliest times,
buildings have been constructed of sun-dried bricks, blocks of mud
held together by chopped straw. A city was built of houses made in
this way; and after a while, either from war or from decay, the mud
houses fell to pieces; streets and rooms were filled with the remains of

manner thereof. 19 And out of them shall proceed thanksgiving
and the voice of them that make merry: and I will multiply them,
and they shall not be few; I will also glorify them, and they
shall not be small. 20 Their children also shall be as aforetime,
and their congregation shall be established before me, and I will
punish all that oppress them. 21 And their prince shall be of
themselves, and their ruler shall proceed from the midst of them;
and I will cause him to draw near, and he shall approach unto
me: for who is he that [1]hath had boldness to approach unto me?
saith the LORD. 22 And ye shall be my people, and I will be your
God.

23 [2]Behold, the tempest of the LORD, *even his* fury, is gone
forth, a [3]sweeping tempest: it shall burst upon the head of the
wicked. 24 The fierce anger of the LORD shall not return, until

---

[1] Heb. *hath been surety for his heart.*   [2] See ch. xxiii. 19, 20.
[3] Or, *gathering*

---

the fallen walls; the level of the streets also was often raised independently by the accumulation of refuse in them; and when, as
often happened, the city was rebuilt on its former site, it naturally
stood some feet above the original city. This process might naturally
be repeated; and the excavation of Tell el-Hesy showed that it had
actually been repeated there ten times.' Driver, *Schweich Lectures,*
p. 41. The city, however, was sometimes rebuilt in the neighbourhood
in order to avoid the labour of preparing the old site; see Bliss and
Macalister, *Excavations in Palestine,* 1898—1900, pp. 67 f.

palace. See note on vi. 5, and cf. Prov. xviii. 19 'citadel.'
19. *not be few.* Cf. xxix. 6.
20. *congregation.* The use of this word suggests a post-exilic
origin for the passage, it is common in the Priestly document of the
Pentateuch and gives the idea of the people as a church rather than
a nation.
21. *their prince.* The term king seems definitely to be avoided
(contrast *v.* 9), which is also a sign of late date. The priestly functions
which he is to assume are also significant (cf. Nu. xvi. 5; Lev. xxi. 21,
23; Ez. xliv. 13), and though it seems hardly necessary to go down as
late as the time of Jason, Menelaus, and Alcimus, to find a suitable
date for the passage (as Duhm does), yet it bears clear marks of the
conditions and ideals of the later Judaism.
hath had boldness to approach. The reading of mg. is more literal
and preserves a striking metaphor: *hath been surety for his heart to
approach.*
23 f. These *vv.* contain a description of the storm of God's anger
which is almost identical with xxiii. 19 f. where see notes.

he have executed, and till he have performed the intents of his
heart: in the latter days ye shall understand it.

XXXI. 1 At that time, saith the LORD, will I be the God
of all the families of Israel, and they shall be my people. 2 Thus
saith the LORD, The people which were left of the sword ¹found
grace in the wilderness; even Israel, ²when I went to cause him
to rest. 3 The LORD appeared ³of old unto me, *saying*, Yea, I
have loved thee with an everlasting love: therefore ⁴with lovingkindness have I drawn thee. 4 Again will I build thee, and thou
shalt be built, O virgin of Israel: again shalt thou be adorned
with thy tabrets, and shalt go forth in the dances of them that

¹ Or, *have found…when I go*   ² Or, *when he went to find him rest*
³ Or, *from afar*   ⁴ Or, *have I continued lovingkindness unto thee*

XXXI. 1—9. The restoration of Ephraim. In iii. 12, spoken
in the early part of his ministry, Jeremiah shewed his concern for the
lost Northern tribes, here again his old interest is to the fore.

1. *all the families of Israel.* Here and ii. 4, &c.

2. The exact meaning of this *v.* is somewhat hard to discover. It
is perhaps best to interpret the past tenses as 'prophetic' (i.e. they
look upon that which is Jehovah's will as if it had already been carried
out), as is done in mg., *have found…when I go.* The *wilderness* then
means not the historic exodus but the symbolic wilderness of exile
(cf. Hos. ii. 14), and those *left of the sword* are not the fugitives from
Egypt, but those who escaped with their lives when Samaria fell, or
rather their descendants.

when I went &c. Driver's emendation (which involvest he omission
of a letter in the Heb.) gives the best reading *I will go that I may
cause Israel to rest.*

3. *of old.* Better as mg. *from afar* (cf. xxx. 10). The prophet is
represented as speaking amongst the exiles and Jehovah appears from
Mount Zion.

with lovingkindness. The text *have I drawn thee* is based on
Hos. xi. 4, 'I drew them with cords of a man, with bands of love';
cf. Jn. vi. 44: the mg. *have I continued…unto thee* follows the rendering
of Ps. xxxvi. 11. The former is to be preferred.

4. Jeremiah contemplates with sympathy the manifestations of
joy exhibited by the restored exiles. This *v.* gives the other side of
the picture presented in Ps. cxxxvii. 'By the rivers of Babylon.'

tabrets. The nation is personified as one of its own daughters
going forth with 'timbrels and dances': cf. Ex. xv. 20 f. (Miriam);
Jud. xi. 34 (Jephthah's daughter). The *tabret*, or timbrel, was very
much like the present day tambourine, and its use was not confined to
women (see 1 S. x. 5; 2 S. vi. 5; 1 Ch. xiii. 8).

dances. Dancing in ancient times was often a religious exercise;

make merry. 5 Again shalt thou plant vineyards upon the mountains of Samaria: the planters shall plant, and shall [1]enjoy *the fruit thereof.* 6 For there shall be a day, that the watchmen upon the hills of Ephraim shall cry, Arise ye, and let us go up to Zion unto the LORD our God. 7 For thus saith the LORD, Sing with gladness for Jacob, and shout [2]for the chief of the nations: publish ye, praise ye, and say, O LORD, save thy people, the remnant of Israel. 8 Behold, I will bring them from the north country, and gather them from the uttermost parts of the earth,

[1] Heb. *profane,* or, *make common.* See Lev. xix. 23—25; Deut. xx. 6, xxviii. 30.
[2] Or, *at the head*

such was David's dancing before the ark (2 S. vi. 14); and the dances at the vintage and other agricultural festivals no doubt had a religious significance (see J. C. Murray-Aynsley in *Folklore Journal,* v. pp. 253 ff.). For the art as an expression of religious emotions in later times see Franz Delitzsch, *Iris,* pp. 189—204 (referred to by Peake); and an article in *The Interpreter,* I. 505 ff. 'Church-dancing in many lands.'

5. The picture here given is one of settled peace and security; for since the vine does not yield fruit for several years after it has been planted, those who own vineyards depend on a secure holding of their property in order that they may enjoy its increase. Later writers were much more definite in their promises (cf. Enoch x. 18 f.).

enjoy. Lit. as mg. *profane, make common.* Cf. Lev. xix. 23 ff. The owner did not *enjoy* the fruits until the fifth year, the fourth being sacred to Jehovah and the first three remaining ungathered.

6. *watchmen.* The same word is used in Job xxvii. 18; Is. xxvii. 3 of the keepers of the vineyard.

let us go up to Zion. The long quarrel between Israel and Judah is now over, and the Northern Kingdom is represented as returning to worship at the ecclesiastical capital of the religion of Jehovah (cf. xli. 4 ff.). Cornill denies the genuineness of this *v.* as, in his opinion, it could not have been spoken by one who had a conception of religion so spiritual as was Jeremiah's; he points out the different attitude towards Jerusalem adopted in vii. 1—15. This view seems to over-emphasise Jeremiah's opposition to the temple and Jerusalem.

7. *Sing.* The word is used of any shrill cry, whether of joy, as here and generally, or of sorrow, as in Is. x. 30.

the chief of the nations. Duhm's suggested emendation *on the tops of the mountains* has much to recommend it; cf. Is. xlii. 11.

O LORD, save thy people. The reading of LXX. and Targ. *The LORD hath saved His people* is to be preferred.

8. *the uttermost parts of the earth.* This phrase is in the manner of 2 Is. (e.g. xliii. 6), whose influence is to be seen in *vv.* 7—14. It is just possible that Jeremiah might have written the words (cf. vi. 22), but not at all likely.

and with them the blind and the lame, the woman with child and
her that travaileth with child together: a great company shall
they return hither. 9 They shall come with weeping, and with
supplications will I lead them: I will ¹cause them to walk by
rivers of waters, in a straight way wherein they shall not stumble:
for I am a father to Israel, and Ephraim is my firstborn.

10 Hear the word of the LORD, O ye nations, and declare it

¹ Or, *bring them unto*

the blind and the lame. These two classes of afflicted people are
often grouped together (Ex. iv. 11; Lev. xxi. 18; Dt. xv. 21; Mal. i.
8; Job xxix. 15, &c.); probably because both are unable to travel;
cf. the words which Socrates puts into the mouths of his critics, 'You
have been less out of Athens than the blind and the lame.' *Crito* 53 A.

hither. That is to Palestine, the writer's real or assumed location.

9. *with weeping.* The text is rather hard to understand. Why
should the people come with weeping? It may be that their tears
were tears of penitence for the past¹, or possibly tears of joy. LXX.
gives here, I think, the better text *They went forth with weeping but
with consolation will I bring them back.* Peake, who looks upon this
reading as likely to be correct, points out its similarity in tone to
various passages in 2 Is. (xl. 1 f., xliii. 1 ff., xliv. 21 ff., &c.).

rivers of water...straight way. Both these means by which the
return of the exiles was to be facilitated are common in 2 Is. *Straight*
is better rendered *level* as it refers to the quality of the surface of the
road, rather than to its directness. The phrase *straight way* occurs in
Ps. cvii. 7.

father to Israel. OT. never seems to get beyond the idea of God
as the *father* of the nation (cf. Dt. xxxii. 6; Is. lxiii. 16; also Jub. i.
24), or of some particular class within it: see Sanday and Headlam on
Romans i. 7.

firstborn. That Ephraim should be exalted over Judah is very
strange, and the later the passage is brought down the stranger it
becomes. There are other slight traces that Ephraim (i.e. the ten
tribes) claimed to be older than Judah (cf. 2 S. xix. 43, LXX.); and in
1 Ch. v. 1—3 the birthright of Reuben falls to the sons of Joseph.
According to Ex. iv. 22 Israel is God's *firstborn* (see Dr McNeile's note)
and so Jub. ii. 20. Dr Peake would transfer this clause to the end of
v. 20 in view of the difficulty of taking it as post-exilic on the one
hand, and of attributing it to Jeremiah in its present context on the
other. Cornill looks upon it as a connecting link between *v.* 5 and *vv.*
15 ff.

¹ So *Tanchuma* on Gen. xlv. 2 which puts forward the 'beautiful thought, that,
when God redeems Israel, it will be amidst their weeping.' See Edersheim, *Life
and Times,* &c. i. p. 169.

in the isles afar off; and say, He that scattered Israel will gather
him, and keep him, as a shepherd doth his flock. 11 For the
LORD hath ransomed Jacob, and redeemed him from the hand of
him that was stronger than he. 12 And they shall come and
sing in the height of Zion, and shall flow together unto the goodness of the LORD, to the corn, and to the wine, and to the oil, and
to the young of the flock and of the herd: and their soul shall
be as a watered garden; and they shall not sorrow any more at
all. 13 Then shall the virgin rejoice in the dance, and the young
men and the old together: for I will turn their mourning into

10—14. Jehovah proclaims His purposes to the nations. The
whole passage is written in the manner of 2 Is., notice the mention of
the isles, redeemed, &c.

10. *isles*. See on xxv. 22.

He that scattered. God was the author of their exile, and He will
be their restorer. The honour of Jehovah demanded that the heathen
should become aware that it was through no weakness or want of power
on His part that the people had been overcome by their enemies (cf.
Is. lii. 5 f.).

scattered. Cf. Jn. vii. 35; Jas. i. 1; 1 Pet. i. 1.

shepherd. The image of the shepherd was particularly dear at the
time of the exile (cf. Ez. xxxiv., xxxvii.; Is. xl. 11, &c.).

12. The catalogue of 'goodness' shews the great importance of
the agricultural and pastoral life of the community; goodness being
of course not spiritual, but material blessings, though the latter were
a sign of spiritual well-being.

in the height of Zion. So Is. li. 11. For the phrase cf. Ez. xvii. 23
(height of Israel), xx. 40.

flow together. The meaning of the Heb. is not quite clear. If the
translation of R.V. be retained, the returning tribes are likened to an
overflowing river which streams from Jerusalem, after the thanksgiving,
to cover the whole land (i.e. as the people go to their separate holdings
to enjoy there the bounty of the Lord). The word rendered *flow* is
elsewhere translated *be lightened* (Ps. xxxiv. 5; Is. lx. 5), and Cornill
would take it with some such meaning in this passage, 'be radiant over.'

corn...wine...oil. Better *corn, must* and *fresh oil*; it is the raw
materials that are meant. The same combination occurs in Hos. ii. 8,
22, &c., and represents the three principal products of the country.

a watered garden. The same figure is used in Is. lviii. 11. The
meaning is that every wish or desire will be abundantly fulfilled—the
word is a strong one and *saturated* or *soaked* would better represent
the original. The metaphor would have much force in the minds of
dwellers in a thirsty land. The same figure is used in Ecclus. xxiv. 31
of a man taught by wisdom.

joy, and will comfort them, and make them rejoice from their
sorrow. 14 And I will satiate the soul of the priests with fatness,
and my people shall be satisfied with my goodness, saith the
LORD.

15 Thus saith the LORD: A voice is heard in Ramah, lamenta-

14. *satiate...the priests.* The verb comes from the same root as
watered in the note above. The people are to be so prosperous that
the claims of religion and the dues of the priests will receive full
attention.

15—22. Rachel the ancestress of the tribes of Joseph and Benjamin
weeps over the fate of her children. This poem is certainly a genuine
and typical production of Jeremiah, and one which exhibits his deep
sensitiveness and tender sympathies. Delitzsch connects this passage
with xl. 1 seeing in it that 'word which came to Jeremiah from the
LORD after that Nebuzaradan the captain of the guard had let him go
from Ramah,' a word which the compiler for some reason unknown has
omitted to record in its proper context. This suggestion has met with
favourable notice from several critics (e.g. Hitzig and Orelli), but the
connexion between the two passages is at the best precarious, and it is
difficult to suppose that Jeremiah in the hour of his nation's downfall
would be greatly concerned over the return of the ten tribes.

15. *Ramah.* Ramah is situated five miles to the north of Jerusalem and was the scene of the collecting of the Jewish prisoners for
deportation to Babylon (xl. 1). The grave of Rachel was somewhere
in the near neighbourhood for according to 1 S. x. 2 f. she was buried
on the northern border of Benjamin (i.e. between the two tribes who
claimed her as their common mother) and not far from Bethel which is
ten miles north of Jerusalem. The traditional site of Rachel's tomb,
however, is south of Jerusalem and not far from Bethlehem. This
tradition is doubtless influenced by the quotation of this passage of
Jeremiah in connexion with the murder of the Innocents in Matt. ii.
17 f. The writer of the first gospel takes the weeping of Rachel as
a type of the weeping of the mothers of the massacred children. In
Gen. xxxv. 19 Rachel is said to have been buried 'in the way to
Ephrath' and the statement is added, 'the same is Bethlehem'; this
statement is almost certainly, as Driver says, 'an incorrect gloss' and
the Ephrath referred to must be somewhere to the north in order to
agree with the requirements of 1 S. x. 2 and the present passage. See
further Driver's note on Gen. xxxv. 19, and the thorough discussion in
PEFQS. 1912, pp. 74 ff.[1]

---

[1] The modern site of Rachel's tomb is marked by a shrine *Kubbet Rāḥēl*, just as
in earlier days it was marked by a sacred stone or pillar (Gen. xxxv. 19). In this
passage there is no actual mention of the tomb and it may be that Rachel is pictured
as standing on the heights of Ramah and looking down on the captives. More
probably the reference is to the widespread idea of spirits mourning round their
tombs.

tion, and bitter weeping, Rachel weeping for her children; she refuseth to be comforted for her children, because they are not. 16 Thus saith the LORD: Refrain thy voice from weeping, and thine eyes from tears: for thy work shall be rewarded, saith the LORD; and they shall come again from the land of the enemy. 17 And there is hope for thy latter end, saith the LORD; and *thy* children shall come again to their own border. 18 I have surely heard Ephraim bemoaning himself *thus*, Thou hast chastised me, and I was chastised, as a calf unaccustomed *to the yoke*: turn thou me, and I shall be turned; for thou art the LORD my God. 19 Surely after that I was turned, I repented; and after that I

for her children. Cf. Mic. i. 16; Is. xlix. 21 (Jerusalem bereaved of her children), lxiii. 16 (the expected interest of the ancestor in his descendants).

refuseth to be comforted. So Jacob when told of the supposed death of Joseph (Gen. xxxvii. 35).

16. *Refrain.* 'Rachel's hundred years of weeping are almost at an end' (Duhm) so the prophet dares to think; but his tender message sent to the mother in the hopeless abandon of her grief was not destined to be fulfilled.

thy work. Rachel like any other mother had laboured for her children and all her care and watchfulness seemed lost, she had laboured in vain and 'brought forth for calamity' (Is. lxv. 23); but now they are to return and her work will be rewarded (cf. 2 Ch. xv. 7).

18. *I have...heard.* Cf. iii. 21. The words are spoken by Jehovah, but the *v.* represents another hopeful anticipation, by the prophet, of Ephraim's repentance. Jeremiah, in his earlier days, lived in the constant expectation of seeing his dreams fulfilled and both parts of the nation aroused to a sense of their sin.

calf. The metaphor is derived from agriculture; if the calf submits the yoke is easy, if it resists the yoke is hard, but must still be borne, cf. Hos. iv. 16. *Calf* is better translated *young bullock* (see Dr McNeile's note on Ex. xxxii. 4). According to Duhm, Jeremiah looked upon the Northern Kingdom as having perished in its youth before it had yet had time to learn.

turn thou me. Ephraim recognises the purpose of the chastisement and prays to be delivered.

19. *Surely...repented.* According to this translation Ephraim's repentance was the result, and not the cause, of his return. This process is a reversal of what is usual 'Pain first, and then the joy of health restored'; and some scholars take *turned* here as referring to turning *away* from God; others get rid of the difficulty by omitting the words, Duhm renders *Surely I repented after I was chastised, I*

was instructed, I smote upon my thigh: I was ashamed, yea, even confounded, because I did bear the reproach of my youth. 20 Is Ephraim my dear son? is he a pleasant child? for as often as I speak against him, I do earnestly remember him still: therefore my bowels ¹are troubled for him; I will surely have mercy upon him, saith the LORD. 21 Set thee up waymarks, make thee guide-posts: set thine heart toward the high way, even the way by which thou wentest: turn again, O virgin of Israel, turn again to these thy cities. 22 How long wilt thou go hither and thither, O thou backsliding daughter? for the LORD hath created a new thing in the earth, A woman shall encompass a man.

¹ Heb. *sound.*

smote upon my thigh. This reading gives a good sense but it does not account for the Heb.

smote upon my thigh. So Ez. xxi. 12.

20. This *v.* is one of the Lessons for the New Year service of the Jewish synagogue (see *J. Th. S.* 1915, p. 182). In it the prophet represents Jehovah as a human father thinking with tenderness of the son whom he has had to punish, and now that the punishment is over he longs for the son's return. David's longing for the return of Absalom from his banishment gives a good instance of the feelings which are here attributed to God (2 S. xiii. 37—39).

21. *waymarks...guide-posts.* The Israelites are immediately to begin to prepare for the return by sending out pioneers to mark out the way back to Palestine. The word for *guide-posts* occurs here only and the translation depends on the parallelism.

22. The Israelites are called upon to make up their minds, and to abandon their want of faith; in order to encourage them a sign is promised. Cf. Jud. vi. 36 ff. (Gideon); Is. vii. 11 ff. (Ahaz).

go hither and thither. Here and Cant. v. 6.

created. 'The root signifies *to cut...*so probably the proper meaning is *to fashion by cutting, to shape.* In the simple conjugation, however, it is used exclusively of God, to denote viz. the production of some-thing fundamentally new, by the exercise of a sovereign power ori-ginative, altogether transcending that possessed by man.' Driver on Gen. i. 1. The word is used in a figurative sense in Is. xliii. 1, 15, xlv. 8, lxv. 17, &c.; cf. also Nu. xvi. 30 'if the LORD creates a creation' (so Heb.).

A woman, &c. No satisfactory explanation of this 'created sign' has ever been discovered by critics; something quite outside the natural order of human experience is obviously foretold, but whether it has any direct connexion with the actual event of the return or not, is impossible to say (cf. the sign in Is. vii. 14 'a virgin shall conceive').

23 Thus saith the LORD of hosts, the God of Israel: Yet again
shall they use this speech in the land of Judah and in the cities
thereof, when I shall ¹ bring again their captivity: The LORD bless
thee, O habitation of justice, O mountain of holiness. 24 And
Judah and all the cities thereof shall dwell therein together; the
husbandmen, and they that go about with flocks. 25 For I have
satiated the weary soul, and every sorrowful soul have I re-
plenished. 26 Upon this I awaked, and beheld; and my sleep

¹ Or, *return to*

It is perhaps not uninteresting to record the attempts which have been
made at various times to explain the phrase; no doubt it had its
meaning for those for whom it was written, and indeed may be a reference to a popular proverb, but all clue to it has now been lost. (*a*) The
woman shall woo the man, i.e. Israel shall court Jehovah (Cheyne; but
cf. *Critica Biblica*, pp. 70 f. for his later ideas); (*b*) the woman shall
protect the man, i.e. Israel shall protect Jehovah (that is the temple);
or taking the phrase literally, a time of peace is coming in which the
protection of the man will be unnecessary; (*c*) a woman shall be turned
into a man¹. This suggestion, which involves a slight change in the
Heb., alone seems to satisfy the need for a 'portent'; it was first suggested by Ewald and is explained as a promise that the woman Israel
shall be endowed with manly courage; (*d*) Pearson *On the Creed* takes
the sign as being a forecast of the miraculous conception of our Lord, and
quotes passages from Jewish writers which definitely apply the prophecy
to the Messiah.

23—30. The promise of restoration to Ephraim is also to be made
to Judah. This passage is similar in many ways to *vv.* 12—14, and, as
it presupposes the fall of Jerusalem, is probably later than Jeremiah;
nor would the prophet have been likely to refer to the capital as the
mountain of holiness.

23. *habitation of justice...mountain of holiness*. Cf. l. 7; Zech. viii. 3
'a city of truth...the holy mountain'; Ps. ii. 6; Is. lxvi. 20.

25. This *v.* recalls the promises of *vv.* 12 and 14. Cf. Matt. xi. 28 ff.;
Jn. vii. 37.

26. *my sleep*. It is not quite clear who is the speaker in this *v.*
The consensus of opinion is against attributing the words to either
God or the exiles, and the most suitable speaker is the prophet himself.
The words just uttered have come to him in a vision, and the nature
of its contents are of a sufficiently pleasant character to justify the
epithet *sweet*. It is hardly likely that the passage can be from Jeremiah as his estimate of the value of the revelations which come through
dreams is too well known (see xxiii. 25).

¹ Hippocrates and Pliny found no difficulty in believing accounts of such trans-
formations; and in later times Casaubon accepted them as did Bishop Burnet (see
Mark Pattison, *Isaac Casaubon*, pp. 497 f.).

was sweet unto me.   27 Behold, the days come, saith the LORD,
that I will sow the house of Israel and the house of Judah with
the seed of man, and with the seed of beast.   28 And it shall
come to pass, that like as I have watched over them to pluck up
and to break down, and to overthrow and to destroy, and to
afflict; so will I watch over them to build and to plant, saith the
LORD.   29 In those days they shall say no more, The fathers have
eaten sour grapes, and the children's teeth are set on edge.
30 But every one shall die for his own iniquity: every man that
eateth the sour grapes, his teeth shall be set on edge.

31 Behold, the days come, saith the LORD, that I will make a

27 f. These *vv.* may well come from Jeremiah. The land to which
the exiles will return will be only thinly populated and like an unsown
field; God will till it and sow it (Ez. xxxvi. 9) with the seeds of men
and of beasts, and so make it populous. Cf. the legend of Cadmus,
who sowed the teeth of the dragon which he had slain, and from them
there sprang up armed men who became the first inhabitants of his
city, Cadmeia, afterwards called Thebes. The threat that Israel should
be greatly reduced in number is constantly held out (Ez. xxxvi. 12, &c.),
and it was substantially fulfilled, for even in the time of Nehemiah
the people—or at any rate those of them who had returned to Palestine—
were few in number (Neh. vii. 4). The promise of restoration and
multiplication is however still remembered (Is. xxvi. 16—19: Ez. xxxvi.
36; Hos. i. 10; Zech. ii. 4).
    28. Cf. i. 10, and 11 f.
    30 f. This passage attacks a doctrine, which, based as it was on the
primitive idea of the solidarity of the tribe or nation, was widely prevalent. If any member of the body corporate sinned his relatives were
involved in his guilt, and, if his offence were against the tribe law or
custom they were liable to punishment; if the offence were against
another tribe or one of its members, the whole body might be involved
in a blood feud (see, further, Introd. pp. liv f.). The same proverbial
expression of the doctrine is found in Ez. xviii. 2. The genuineness of
the passage here has been denied as it seems to regard the doctrine 'as
justifiable under the present conditions, but as inapplicable and un-
called for in the time to which he looks forward,' and that 'such a
judgement we cannot easily reconcile with what we know of Jeremiah'
(Dr Peake). But surely the writer is attacking a popular saying, and
his meaning is that God's action in restoring the innocent descendants
of the original exiles will take away any justification that there was,
even to the popular mind, for the ideas underlying the proverb. Cf. a
similar proverb derived from agricultural life in Hos. viii. 7.
    31—34. In the age of the restoration the people will have God's
laws written on their hearts, and will not be dependent for their know-

new covenant with the house of Israel, and with the house of Judah: 32 not according to the covenant that I made with their fathers in the day that I took them by the hand to bring them out of the land of Egypt; ¹which my covenant they brake, although I was ²an husband unto them, saith the LORD. 33 But this is the covenant that I will make with the house of Israel after those days, saith the LORD; I will put my law in their inward parts, and in their heart will I write it; and I will be their God, and they shall be my people: 34 and they shall teach no more every man his neighbour, and every man his brother, saying, Know the LORD: for they shall all know me, from the least of them unto the greatest of them, saith the LORD: for I will forgive

¹ Or, *forasmuch as they brake my covenant*   ² Or, *lord over them*

ledge of His will upon an external code. All will know God. This passage is one of the most important in the Old Dispensation and a forecast of that New Covenant which our Blessed Lord sealed with His own blood (Matt. xxvi. 28). For an estimate of the teaching of the doctrine see Introd. pp. li ff., and for a discussion of its authorship see note pp. 241 ff.

31. *covenant.* For the meaning and use of the term see note, pp. 243 f.

and with the house of Judah. This phrase is almost certainly a gloss (cf. *v.* 33) and its removal brings the *v.* into the Qinah rhythm.

32. The negative description of the covenant; it is not to be like the one made at Sinai which has proved ineffective.

in the day. See on vii. 22.

by the hand. Cf. Hos. xi. 1—4; Dt. i. 31.

husband unto them. The Heb. word Baal may mean either *lord* or *husband* (cf. Hos. ii. 16 where the nation is told no more to use the ambiguous word in addressing Jehovah, but to call him *Ishi*, i.e. *vir*), hence mg. reading *lord over them*. Recent scholars adopting an emendation proposed by Giesebrecht, an emendation which involves the change of a single letter only in the Heb., read *and I abhorred them*; this reading is supported by LXX. (cf. the quotation in Heb. viii. 9) and Syr.

33. *I will put my law.* 'God's word, not in a book but in the heart and mouth of His servants, is the ultimate ideal as well as the first postulate of prophetic theology.' W. Robertson Smith, *O.T. in Jewish Church*, p. 300. Mr C. J. Ball compares the prayer of Nabopolassar 'O Sin...the Fear of thy Great Godhead in the heart of their people do Thou implant.'

34. In this *v.* the knowledge of God is closely connected with forgiveness and the removal of that sin which is the great hindrance to its attainment. Cf. St Augustine 'Man being renewed in his mind, and able to discern and understand the truth, needs no more any direction of man.' *Conf.* XIII. 22. This *v.* is apparently referred to by

their iniquity, and their sin will I remember no more. 35 Thus saith the LORD, which giveth the sun for a light by day, and the ordinances of the moon and of the stars for a light by night, which ¹stirreth up the sea, that the waves thereof roar; the LORD of hosts is his name: 36 If these ordinances depart from before me, saith the LORD, then the seed of Israel also shall cease from being a nation for ever. 37 Thus saith the LORD: If heaven above can be measured, and the foundations of the earth searched out beneath, then will I also cast off all the seed of Israel for all that

¹ Or, *stilleth the sea*, *when &c*. See Is. li. 15.

NT. and patristic writers (e.g. Jn. vi. 45; 1 Cor. ii. 13; 1 Thes. iv. 9; and Ep. Barn. § 21; Athenag. *Leg.* § 11, &c.), though possibly the reference in these cases is rather to Is. liv. 13 'all thy sons shall be taught of God.'

35—40. The survival of Israel is as certain as the eternity of the ordinances which control the world of nature: Jerusalem is not only to be preserved, but to be greatly enlarged. These *vv.* with their strongly national tone come somewhat strangely after the passage recording the promise of the New Covenant, and it is hard to imagine that Jeremiah is responsible for them, or, at any rate, for their position. The last part of the section (*vv.* 38—40) is almost certainly late and bears marked similarities to Zech. xiv. (cf. Is. liv. 2); the mind of Jeremiah was too wide in its outlook to stoop to details such as the future topography of the Holy City. The earlier part (*vv.* 35—37) if it is a genuine utterance must be a fragment. Critics are not agreed as to the authorship, some condemning the passage for the extreme nationalism exhibited, as well as for its prosaic style. Giesebrecht finds parallels to the later chh. of Isaiah (see especially xl. 12, 26, xlii. 5, xliv. 24 ff., xlv. 7, 18).

35. *ordinances.* In Gen. i. 16 ff. God is said to have given the two great luminaries to divide the light from the darkness, and it is to this belief that the present passage points; a similar statement is found in Ps. cxxxvi. 7—9, and one which is indeed nearer to this in form. Cf. Ps. Sol. xviii. 13 f.

the LORD of hosts. So in Am. iv. 13, v. 8, ix. 6 (all passages dealing with the creation).

36. *If these* &c. Our Lord used still stronger language 'Heaven and earth shall pass away, but my words shall not pass away' Mk. xiii. 31.

a nation. The preservation of the Jews as a separate people is one of the greatest miracles of history; probably the writer of these words thought not so much of the national existence in itself as of the peculiar privileges which the people enjoyed in being the chosen of God; cf. next *v.*

37. In order to deepen the impression of Israel's stability a further comparison is made, not this time to the eternity of the heavens, but

they have done, saith the LORD.   38 Behold, the days come, saith
the LORD, that the city shall be built to the LORD from the tower
of Hananel unto the gate of the corner.   39 And the measuring
line shall yet go out straight onward unto the hill Gareb, and
shall turn about unto Goah.   40 And the whole valley of the dead
bodies, and of the ashes, and all the fields unto the brook Kidron,
unto the corner of the horse gate toward the east, shall be holy
unto the LORD; it shall not be plucked up, nor thrown down any
more for ever.

to their immensity.   (Cf. Job xi. 8; Enoch xciii. 14.)   In LXX. this *v.*
comes before *v.* 35; it is possibly a marginal gloss which has been
incorporated into the text.

38.   *the city.*   The various places named in this account are intended
to shew the boundaries of the Jerusalem of the return; not much, however, is known of them, and so it is not possible to say how much larger
the new city was than the old one (see *PEFQS.* Jan. 1912, p. 28, for a
discussion of the places named).

the tower of Hananel.   Mentioned also in Zech. xiv. 10; and Neh.
iii. 1, xii. 39; the latter passages locate it at the NE. corner of the
city wall.

gate of the corner.   See also Zech. xiv. 10; 2 K. xiv. 13; 2 Ch. xxvi. 9.
The *corner gate* seems to have been at the NW. end of the wall.

39.   *Gareb...Goah.*   Nothing further is known of these places, they
are evidently on the W. and S. of the wall.

40.   *the...valley of the dead bodies.*   The valley of Hinnom to S. of
Jerusalem (see on vii. 31).

horse gate.   Mentioned in Neh. iii. 27 f.; it was on SE. of Jerusalem.

holy.   Every place included within the boundaries of the city, even
those which were before held to be unclean like Hinnom, was to be
considered *holy*, the city itself was to be a vast sanctuary; hence perhaps the omission of any mention of the temple.

ADDITIONAL NOTE ON THE AUTHORSHIP OF XXXI. 31—34.

These *vv.* have been described by Cornill as 'the climax and crown of
Jeremiah's prophetic activity,' and with certain exceptions, to be considered
later, critics have concluded that the passage as a whole is the work of the
prophet himself.   Those who do not accept the accuracy of Cornill's statement,
at any rate as regards authorship, may be divided into two classes; writers who
reject xxx. and xxxi. as a whole and this passage with them, e.g. Smend (in
A. T. Religionsgesch. pp. 239 ff.), Stade (*Gesch. d. Volk. Isr.* I. p. 643), and
Schmidt (*Enc. Bib.* 934, 2391); and those who reject the *vv.* on their own
merits, amongst which class the outstanding name is Duhm.   The first class of

critics has been dealt with in the Introd. to xxx., xxxi., though it is interesting to notice that Hitzig, who sees much in the chh. which comes from 2 Is. (following Movers), is firmly convinced of the genuineness of this oracle. The arguments of Duhm, as the representative of the latter class, must now be considered.

It should be stated first of all that Duhm only rejected these *vv.* after much consideration and with obvious reluctance, which needless to say makes his condemnation all the more weighty. His arguments are arranged under two main heads: style and contents. The style of the prophecy is condemned as bad, cumbersome, and inexact, neither has it any of those figures of speech which distinguish even the shorter poems of Jeremiah, whilst it contains phrases which are typical of the supplementer. It will perhaps simplify the discussion if these criticisms are dealt with immediately before going on to state Duhm's objections to the matter of the prophecy which are of a much more serious nature. The objections to the style of the passage are easily met, so it seems to the present writer; in the first place no one would deny that the prophecy as it is preserved in the text has received small and unimportant additions from a later hand, but after laying aside such words and phrases, so careful a critic as Cornill is able to say of the passage that it is a 'rhythmic, elevated and articulate discourse.' The truth of the matter is that Duhm, in considering questions of style, is prejudiced by his own somewhat arbitrary notions of what is Jeremiah's workmanship and what is not; he is unable to apply to any particular passage a sufficiently wide standard of comparison, since for him what is genuine and typical of the prophet is limited to a small number of poems written in one particular metre.

Duhm's arguments against the contents of the prophecy must now be stated. He sees in the passage not an attempt to put into words a highly spiritual doctrine, but the efforts of a legalistic scribe to defend and enforce the law; the promise that was needed was not that the 'law' should be written on men's hearts, but that an entirely new law should be given; as it stands the New Covenant is no advance on the teaching of such passages as Dt. vi. 6—8 and xxx. 11 ff. which recognise the necessity of the law being ever 'on the heart' and emphasise its 'nearness'; the knowledge of God and the knowledge of the law are not the same thing. Duhm makes the further objection that the interpretation of the passage which sees in it a promise of a spiritual bond between God and the individual must face the question why the original covenant had no such provision. This last objection can be dismissed with a few words ignoring as it does the progressive nature of God's revelation. Why, it might equally well be asked, did not our Lord appear on earth at the creation? why was not man made capable of receiving the full knowledge of God from the very first? To state such questions is to answer them, or rather is sufficient to shew that no answer is possible; these matters of times and seasons are in the hands of God Himself and it is not for man to know them. The course and development of history, alike in religion and politics, we can indeed trace out, but the deeper questions of ultimate origin and control are beyond the grasp of finite minds.

Duhm's main argument, then, is that the doctrine of the New Covenant is not a spiritualising of the Old, not a step forward in the evolution of religion, but a desire to rivet still firmer upon the Jewish Church the fetters of a formal law. He protests against the danger of being led away by phrases which have at different times quite different meanings; in his eyes the doctrine is not worthy of a prophet whose ideas of religion were those of Jeremiah. There is not a sufficient antithesis between the passage and Deuteronomy. All these arguments to an unprejudiced mind seem purely arbitrary; Duhm first of all reads into the *vv.* his own meaning, and then proceeds to shew that from the standpoint of his interpretation they could not have come from Jeremiah ; he is sufficiently candid to admit that if the genuineness of the passage could be proved its importance would be very great, because it would then present that antithesis to the teaching of Deuteronomy which in his opinion would be found in a genuine utterance of Jeremiah. It is hard to sympathise with special pleading of this nature, and, as in the question of style, Duhm seems to have been led away by his preconceived notions.

Cornill, in his admirable refutation of the arguments of Duhm, begins by making clear what Jeremiah meant by the Old Covenant which the new teaching was to replace, and from this basis he proceeds to demonstrate the true spirituality of the conception of the New Covenant and its fitness to be the crown of the prophet's preaching.

Before enquiring what Jeremiah meant by the Old Covenant, however, it will be well to ask ourselves what is the real meaning of the Hebrew word בְּרִית (*berīth*) which is rendered *covenant* in EVV. In ordinary usage a covenant is an agreement, but such a meaning is too narrow for the original word. Dr McNeile in the note in his commentary on Exodus gives as its nearest English equivalent *obligation*, and he points out further that an obligation may be imposed upon another or upon oneself, or that mutual obligations may be incurred[1]. The covenant which Jeremiah has in mind is the series of mutual obligations incurred between Jehovah and Israel when He led them out of Egypt and brought them to Sinai. In his teaching Jeremiah laid very great stress on that part of the Covenant of Sinai which is called the Ten Words or the Decalogue (see especially ch. vii.). These commandments had been delivered to Israel by Moses and though written by the finger of Jehovah, they had been written upon tables of stone (Ex. xxxi. 18) and not upon the living heart of the people. It is this law therefore that Duhm regards as obsolete and requiring

---

[1] *Exodus*, pp. 150 ff., see also *Enc. Bib.* 928 ff., and the elaborate enquiry by Valeton in *ZATW.* 1892, pp. 1 ff., 224 ff., 1893, pp. 245 ff. In the opinion of the present writer there is still room for further investigation into the early use of the word when it was employed in a very vague way and apparently without any technical or theological meaning at all (cf. Am. i. 9; Hos. ii. 20). Driver is ready to admit that in Amos and Isaiah it has no technical meaning, but he cites Hos. vi. 7 and viii. 1 as instances of such a use in early times. But Hos. viii. 1 is almost certainly late (so Wellhausen, Nowack, Harper, &c.) and vi. 7 does not require any 'theological' content, as the translation 'like men who break covenants' gives a perfectly satisfactory sense.

to be done away with, but it will surely be admitted that the Decalogue is still the basis of morality, and One greater than Jeremiah was not ashamed to confess that He came not to destroy the law but to fulfil it (Matt. v. 17). The New Covenant was indeed the promise of this 'fulfilment' of the Covenant at Sinai, because it was to spiritualise that Covenant and to enable men to carry it out[1]. The law was to be written no longer on tables of stone, that is it was not to consist of mere outward ordinances, but it was to be written on the heart (cf. Is. l. 13; Joel ii. 28 f.; Jn. vi. 15). Teaching such as this is quite what might reasonably be expected from the lips of Jeremiah, for following the example of his predecessor Hosea, he laid constant stress on the importance of 'knowing' God (ii. 8, iv. 22, ix. 3, 5, 24, xxii. 16, xxiv. 7; cf. Hos. iv. 1, v. 4, vi. 6); further he had already made the attempt of spiritualising the legal requirement of circumcision (iv. 4)[2]. In addition, as was pointed out above[3], the experiences of the prophet's own life were such as to make him realise the necessity for personal communion with God such as is the real basis of the New Covenant. It may also be allowable to see in Jeremiah's strong conviction that the religion of Jehovah would survive the downfall of the nation a further argument in favour of the authenticity of this passage, postulating as it did a new and more spiritual conception of the bond subsisting between Jehovah and His worshippers[4].

In conclusion the present writer, after much thought and a fresh review of all the available evidence, feels in complete agreement with Dr W. J. Moulton when he says that 'Every conception of the passage becomes transparent and easy if we attribute it to Jeremiah; all the difficulties arise if it is of late date and unknown authorship[5].'

CHAPTER XXXII.

The Purchase of the Field at Anathoth.

This ch., like that which follows it, comes from a time when Jeremiah was imprisoned in the court of the guard (*v.* 2; cf. xxxiii. 1). Incidents such as that which it relates, the request that the next of kin should exercise the right or duty of buying the family possessions in order that they should not pass into alien hands, must have been no uncommon thing in Judah; what made it so

---

[1] Cf. Vatke, *Bibl. Theol.* p. 526.

[2] Duhm's own note on this passage is interesting in view of his rejection of xxxi. 31 ff.

[3] Introd. pp. lii f.

[4] The following references to special covenants between Jehovah and His people contained in later writers are interesting, though of course no certain arguments can be based upon them: 'I will make an everlasting covenant with you' (Is. lv. 3, cf. lxi. 8; Ez. xvi. 60, xxxvii. 26); 'this is my covenant, &c.' (Is. lix. 21); 'people in whose heart is my law' (Is. li. 7); 'I will make with them a covenant of peace' (Ez. xxxiv. 25, cf. xxxvii. 26).

[5] See his article in *The Expositor*, 1906, pp. 370 ff.

striking on this occasion was that the actual property sold was at the time occupied by the Chaldean armies who were besieging Jerusalem. The offer which Hanamel made to Jeremiah seemed to the prophet a divinely sent opportunity of shewing his faith in the restoration of the nation, and his belief in the over-ruling hand of God (cf. Introd. p. lxv). The incident itself is described in quite a brief manner, though full details are given (*vv.* 6—15), and it seems probable that the rest of the ch. consists mainly of editorial additions. The discussion of these additions will be dealt with in the introduction to each section. The following are the divisions of the ch.:

(*a*) *The prophet's circumstances at the time of the purchase.* 1—5.

(*b*) *The description of the transaction.* 6—15.

(*c*) *The prophet's doubts and the Divine reply.* 16—27.

(*d*) *The fate of Jerusalem and the sins which have made it inevitable.* 28—35.

(*e*) *The promise of restoration.* 36—44.

XXXII. 1 The word that came to Jeremiah from the LORD in the tenth year of Zedekiah king of Judah, which was the eighteenth year of Nebuchadrezzar. 2 Now at that time the king of Babylon's army besieged Jerusalem: and Jeremiah the prophet was shut up in the court of the guard, which was in the king of Judah's house. 3 For Zedekiah king of Judah had shut him up, saying, Wherefore dost thou prophesy, and say, Thus saith the LORD, Behold, I will give this city into the hand of the king of Babylon, and he shall take it; 4 and Zedekiah king of

XXXII. 1—5. A description of the exact date of the purchase and of the situation in which the prophet found himself at the time. The *vv.* are almost certainly the work of an editor supplied in order to acquaint the reader with the desperate position both of the prophet himself and also of the state.

1. *the tenth year.* As the siege began in Zedekiah's ninth year (xxxix. 1) affairs were probably getting very desperate.

2. *was shut up.* Jeremiah had been arrested on attempting to leave the city during the short interval which elapsed between the Chaldean withdrawal from Jerusalem on the approach of an Egyptian army and their return to continue the siege (xxxvii. 5, 11—15). Duhm and Cornill were both of the opinion that the incident took place before the resumption of the siege, but the latter in the Introduction to his Commentary (p. xxxvi) withdraws his statement to this effect contained in the body of the work (p. 248).

the court of the guard. This was near to the king's palace (Neh. iii. 25), and was evidently used as a place of detention for political or other prisoners who were not to be imprisoned with the common folk.

3—5. These *vv.* explain why Jeremiah was imprisoned.

Judah shall not escape out of the hand of the Chaldeans, but shall surely be delivered into the hand of the king of Babylon, and shall speak with him mouth to mouth, and his eyes shall behold his eyes; 5 and he shall lead Zedekiah to Babylon, and there shall he be until I visit him, saith the LORD: though ye fight with the Chaldeans, ye shall not prosper?

6 And Jeremiah said, The word of the LORD came unto me, saying, 7 Behold, Hanamel the son of Shallum thine uncle shall come unto thee, saying, Buy thee my field that is in Anathoth: for the right of redemption is thine to buy it. 8 So Hanamel mine uncle's son came to me in the court of the guard according to the word of the LORD, and said unto me, Buy my field, I pray thee, that is in Anathoth, which is in the land of Benjamin: for the right of inheritance is thine, and the redemption is thine; buy it for thyself. Then I knew that this was the word of the LORD. 9 And I bought the field that was in Anathoth of Hanamel mine uncle's son, and weighed him the money, even seventeen

5. *visit him.* Visitation, as St Jerome says, may mean either consolation or punishment. In this case it probably meant death.

6—15. The visit of Hanamel and the sale of the field to Jeremiah in the presence of witnesses and with all the necessary legal formalities.

6. *And Jeremiah said* &c. LXX. has a simpler text reading *The word of the LORD came to Jeremiah saying.*

7. *Hanamel the son of Shallum thine uncle.* It is clear from *vv.* 8 and 9 that it was *Shallum* who was the prophet's *uncle.*

Anathoth. See Introd. p. xxviii.

the right of redemption. Amongst the Hebrews, as amongst other Semitic peoples, every effort was made to prevent land from passing out of the possession of a family and going to strangers (cf. Lev. xxv. 24 f.; Ruth iv. 6; and, for the custom with the Arabs, see Doughty, *Arabia Deserta,* II. p. 116). The right of the next-of-kin included the power of buying back the land even if it had been sold, but there is no reason for supposing that Hanamel had already disposed of the field. He was evidently a refugee in Jerusalem and perhaps in financial difficulties owing to his position, and therefore he came to his kinsman to raise money by the sale of his property.

8. *which...Benjamin.* Jeremiah hardly needed to be told the situation of his own home; LXX. rightly omits.

9. The prophet buys the field for the normal price in spite of its being in the possession of the besiegers; cf. Livy XXVI. 11 where the actual ground on which Hannibal's army was encamped was sold by public auction in Rome.

seventeen shekels. The shekel was worth about 2*s.* 9*d.* of English

shekels of silver. 10 And I subscribed the deed, and sealed it, and called witnesses, and weighed him the money in the balances. 11 So I took the deed of the purchase, both that which was sealed, [1]*according to* the law and custom, and that which was open: 12 and I delivered the deed of the purchase unto Baruch the son of Neriah, the son of Mahseiah, in the presence of Hanamel mine uncle's *son*, and in the presence of the witnesses that subscribed the deed of the purchase, before all the Jews that sat in the court of the guard. 13 And I charged Baruch before them, saying, 14 Thus saith the LORD of hosts, the God of Israel: Take these deeds, this deed of the purchase, both that which is sealed, and this deed which is open, and put them in an earthen vessel; that they may continue many days. 15 For thus saith the LORD of hosts, the God of Israel: Houses and fields and vineyards shall yet again be bought in this land.

16 Now after I had delivered the deed of the purchase unto

---

[1] Or, containing *the terms and conditions*

---

money though its purchasing power was much greater. It is interesting to compare the prices paid in other similar transactions: Abraham paid for the field of Ephron and the cave of Machpelah four hundred shekels (Gen. xxiii. 16); David paid fifty shekels for the threshing-floor of Araunah together with the oxen (2 S. xxiv. 24).

10. *witnesses.* As in Gen. xxiii. 16. *Witnesses* were customary in Babylonian land transactions (*KB*. iv. p. 109 ff.), and in the Assuan papyri eight are apparently necessary. In Jeremiah's case the witnesses served a double purpose, they made the purchase binding, and also they bore testimony to future ages of the prophet's trust in God (cf. Is. viii. 1 ff.).

11. The details of the legal customs described in this *v.* at one time caused some amount of difficulty; the discovery of similar deeds in Babylonia and Assyria has, however, removed them. It was apparently the usual thing to enclose the actual deed in an outer wrapper which itself bore a copy of the deed (cf. Jeremias, *O.T. in the Light of the Ancient East*, ii. p. 281; Johns, *Bab. and Ass. Laws*, &c. pp. 10 f.). Commercial customs in the East go back to the remotest antiquity, an article in the *Asiatic Quarterly Rev.* Oct. 1901, describes the system in use in Susa before 4000 B.C. Contract tablets from Gezer from times earlier than Jeremiah shew the influence of Assyrian customs.

12. *Baruch.* This is the first mention of Jeremiah's faithful friend and secretary, and the man to whom we probably owe most of the book of Jeremiah. In the apocryphal epistle of Baruch the genealogy is carried several stages further back. See Introd. pp. lxxiv f.

16—27. The prophet's doubts. In spite of the far-seeing faith

Baruch the son of Neriah, I prayed unto the LORD, saying,
17 Ah Lord GOD! behold, thou hast made the heaven and the
earth by thy great power and by thy stretched out arm; there
is nothing too ¹hard for thee: 18 which shewest mercy unto
thousands, and recompensest the iniquity of the fathers into the
bosom of their children after them: the great, the mighty God,
the LORD of hosts is his name: 19 great in counsel, and mighty
in work: whose eyes are open upon all the ways of the sons of
men; to give every one according to his ways, and according to
the fruit of his doings: 20 which didst set signs and wonders

¹ Or, *wonderful*

which Jeremiah exhibited in buying the field of Hanamel, and buying
it in so striking a manner, his heart began to fail him; according to
the account in this section he despaired because the fall of Jerusalem
seemed imminent. It is of course possible that a mind such as that
of Jeremiah might thus by a single bound travel from lively hope to
the deepest pessimism, but the best explanation of the passage is that
it comes from an interpolator. Jeremiah had too frequently faced the
certainty of the fall of the city, deeming it a necessary preliminary to
the ultimate recovery of the nation, to be dismayed because it was about
to come to pass. The actual contents of the section, consisting as they
do of a collection of phrases found elsewhere in the prophet's writings
and the book of Deuteronomy, are not such as to restore confidence in
its genuineness. The long and elaborate introduction leading up to
a prayer which consists of two *vv.* only, is unlike Jeremiah, and indeed
finds a close parallel in Neh. ix. 5—38. Many critics look upon the
prayer itself (*vv.* 24 f.) as genuine, but in this case it seems best to
follow Duhm, and, in view of the difficulties named above, to reject it.
Although the introductory passage is out of proportion to the matter
which it introduces it is in itself no unskilful composition; it begins
by reciting the power and the mercy of God (*vv.* 17—19), especially
as shewn in the history of the chosen people (*vv.* 20—22), and ends
with a statement of their ingratitude (*v.* 23).

17. *stretched out arm.* This phrase as a rule refers to Jehovah's
interventions in history and not to His creative activity: cf. *v.* 21;
Ps. cxxxvi. 12; and see on xxvii. 5.

there is...hard for thee. Quoted in Enoch lxxxiv. 3. LXX. reads
hidden for *hard*.

18. *unto thousands.* There is here a reference to the Decalogue
(Ex. xx. 5; Dt. v. 9).

the bosom. In the robe of an Eastern the folds at the *bosom* were
used as a pocket (cf. Ruth iii. 15; Is. xl. 11, &c.). The figurative
use of the phrase is also found in Is. lxv. 6; Ps. lxxix. 12.

19. *all the ways.* Cf. Jn. ii. 25.

20. *didst set.* Cf. Dt. vi. 22; Neh. ix. 10.

in the land of Egypt, even unto this day, [1]both in Israel and among *other* men; and madest thee a name, as at this day; 21 and didst bring forth thy people Israel out of the land of Egypt with signs, and with wonders, and with a strong hand, and with a stretched out arm, and with great terror; 22 and gavest them this land, which thou didst swear to their fathers to give them, a land flowing with milk and honey; 23 and they came in, and possessed it; but they obeyed not thy voice, neither walked in thy law; they have done nothing of all that thou commandedst them to do: therefore thou hast caused all this evil to come upon them: 24 behold the mounts, they are come unto the city to take it; and the city is given into the hand of the Chaldeans that fight against it, because of the sword, and of the famine, and of the pestilence: and what thou hast spoken is come to pass; and, behold, thou seest it. 25 And thou hast said unto me, O Lord GOD, Buy thee the field for money, and call witnesses; whereas the city is given into the hand of the Chaldeans.

26 Then came the word of the LORD unto Jeremiah, saying, 27 Behold, I am the LORD, the God of all flesh: is there any thing too hard for me?

28 Therefore thus saith the LORD: Behold, I will give this

[1] Or, *and*

unto this day. The expression is hard to explain, perhaps *in the land of Egypt* is a gloss as Cornill thinks; or it may be that the memory of the wonders was still maintained, and it was thus possible to speak of them by a slight exaggeration as continuing to *this day.*

Israel...men. For a similar contrast see Jud. xvi. 7; Ps. lxxiii. 5.

madest thee a name. Cf. Gen. xi. 4; Is. lxiii. 12, 14.

21. This *v.* is very similar to Dt. xxvi. 8; cf. also Ex. xv. 14; Dt. ii. 25, iv. 34; Josh. ii. 9 ff., &c.

22. Cf. xi. 5; and see Neh. ix. 22—35.

23. Cf. xi. 8.

24. *the mounts.* Cf. vi. 6.

is given. The city is as good as lost already so far have the siege works of the Chaldeans progressed.

26 f. In these two *vv.* God reassures the prophet by emphasising His omnipotence.

27. *of all flesh.* Cf. Nu. xvi. 22, xxvii. 16; Job xii. 10; Am. ix. 7.

too hard. Cf. the positive statement in *v.* 17.

28—35. This section in its attitude is quite in accordance with

city into the hand of the Chaldeans, and into the hand of Nebuchadrezzar king of Babylon, and he shall take it: 29 and the Chaldeans, that fight against this city, shall come and set this city on fire, and burn it, with the houses, upon whose roofs they have offered incense unto Baal, and poured out drink offerings unto other gods, to provoke me to anger. 30 For the children of Israel and the children of Judah have only done that which was evil in my sight from their youth: for the children of Israel have only provoked me to anger with the work of their hands, saith the LORD. 31 For this city hath been to me a provocation of mine anger and of my fury from the day that they built it even unto this day; that I should remove it from before my face: 32 because of all the evil of the children of Israel and of the children of Judah, which they have done to provoke me to anger, they, their kings, their princes, their priests, and their prophets, and the men of Judah, and the inhabitants of Jerusalem. 33 And they have turned unto me the back, and not the face: and though I taught them, rising up early and teaching them, yet they have not hearkened to receive instruction. 34 But they set their abominations in the house which is called by my name, to defile

the usual teaching of Jeremiah—the fate of the nation will be the fruit of its own sin and folly—but as a reply from God to the prophet's doubts it is most unsuitable.

29. *upon whose roofs.* Is this a reference to the worship of the heavenly bodies? (cf. Zeph. i. 5).

30. This *v.* contains two difficulties; Jeremiah has elsewhere spoken in quite a different tone of the *youth* of Israel (ii. 2; cf. Hos. xi. 1); and the sins of *the children of Israel* are hardly a reason for the destruction of Jerusalem. The latter half of the *v.* is missing from LXX. probably correctly as the phrase *children of Israel* is used in two quite different senses in the two halves of the *v.*

31. Ezekiel takes the same view of the sin of Jerusalem but attributes it to the heathen origin of the city (xvi. 3—6). This present *v.* suggests that the city had been built by the Israelites, but the reference is perhaps to its rebuilding when it became the chief city of Israel (2 S. v. 9).

33. For the figure of God as the Teacher of His people, cf. Is. xlviii. 17; Ps. lxxi. 17.

34 f. These *vv.* are very similar to vii. 30 f. where see notes.

34. *their abominations.* For a description of the illegal objects of worship which were introduced by the last generation of the men of Judah into the house of God, see Ez. v. 11, viii. 6 ff.

it. 35 And they built the high places of Baal, which are in the valley of the son of Hinnom, to cause their sons and their daughters to pass through *the fire* unto Molech; which I commanded them not, neither came it into my [1]mind, that they should do this abomination ; to cause Judah to sin.

36 And now therefore thus saith the LORD, the God of Israel,

[1] Heb. *heart*.

35. *Baal...Molech.* The two deities are apparently identified. As was pointed out above (see on vii. 31), *Molech* is probably intended for *Melech*, the Heb. for *king*, and the title king was applied to various gods by the Phoenicians (see Dr Barnes' note in the Camb. Bible on 1 K. xi. 5).   A Phoenician deity named Melechbaal (מלכבעל) is mentioned in *CIS*. 147, 194, 380.   At the same time the later part of the *v.* seems to regard the sacrifices as offered to Jehovah Himself, as it is He who protests that He never commanded them (cf. vii. 22); it should not be forgotten that the titles both of *Baal* and *Melech* are applied to Jehovah (Hos. ii. 16; Lev. xviii. 21, xx. 2—5)[1].

to pass through the fire.   The exact meaning or manner of the rite has been lost.   It is not absolutely necessary to look upon it as a sacrifice, it may have been merely a ceremony of purification, though the destruction of the children is almost certain: cf. Nu. xxxi. 23, and see *Enc. Bib.* 3184; Frazer, *Magic Art*, II. p. 232; *Adonis*, II. p. 219.

36—44.   The promise of restoration.   The fate of the city is certain, it is to be given up to the sword, the pestilence and the famine, the three invariable accompaniments of every prolonged siege.   But none the less the future contains a hope which is equally certain, the nation will be restored once more to its own land, and at the same time a closer relationship will be made possible between Jehovah and the individual Israelite.   The genuineness of this section has been much more readily recognised than that of the previous *vv.* though the majority of scholars reject it (e.g. Duhm, Cornill, and Giesebrecht). There are considerable difficulties to be faced by those who regard the *vv.* as coming from Jeremiah himself; *v.* 37, for example, looks upon the dispersion as already accomplished, and *v.* 43 must be from a time subsequent to the desolation of Judah.   There is, however, in this passage some originality, it is not merely a string of quotations, and it is well suited to the position of the prophet as revealed in *vv.* 6—15; the present writer is therefore disposed to follow Dr Peake in accepting the section as 'substantially Jeremianic, but committed to writing in its present form after the destruction of Jerusalem and the deportation of the captives had taken place.   Even the reference to the deportation is not necessarily impossible on Jeremiah's lips: cf. xxiii. 3, 7, 8, xxiv. 9.'

36.   *therefore.* This word seems to look back to *v.* 27.

[1] Dr Kennett has made the interesting suggestion that the children may have been offered originally to the reigning king regarded as an incarnation of the deity. This suggestion has been worked out by Frazer, *Adonis*, II. pp. 219 ff.

concerning this city, whereof ye say, It is given into the hand of the king of Babylon by the sword, and by the famine, and by the pestilence: 37 Behold, I will gather them out of all the countries, whither I have driven them in mine anger, and in my fury, and in great wrath; and I will bring them again unto this place, and I will cause them to dwell safely: 38 and they shall be my people, and I will be their God: 39 and I will give them one heart and one way, that they may fear me for ever; for the good of them, and of their children after them: 40 and I will make an everlasting covenant with them, that I will not turn away [1]from them, to do them good; and I will put my fear in their hearts, that they shall not depart from me. 41 Yea, I will rejoice over them to do them good, and I will plant them in this land [2]assuredly with my whole heart and with my whole soul. 42 For thus saith the LORD: Like as I have brought all this great evil upon this people, so will I bring upon them all the good that I have promised them. 43 And fields shall be bought in this land, whereof ye say, It is desolate, without man or beast; it is given into the hand of the Chaldeans. 44 Men shall buy fields for money, and subscribe the deeds, and seal them, and call witnesses, in the land of Benjamin, and in the places about Jerusalem, and in the cities of Judah, and in the cities of the hill country, and in the cities of the lowland, and in the cities of the South: for I will cause their captivity to return, saith the LORD.

[1] Heb. *from after them.*   [2] Heb. *in truth.*

37.   Cf. xxiii. 3, 6; Hos. xi. 11.
38.   Cf. xxxi. 33.
39.   *they may fear...after them.*   Cf. Dt. iv. 10, vi. 24.
40.   The *everlasting covenant* of this *v.* is evidently the same as the New Covenant of xxxi. 31 ff.   Cf. Is. lv. 3; Ez. xvi. 60.
41.   *plant them.*   Cf. xxiv. 6, xxxi. 27 f.
   my whole heart...soul.   The phrase is Deuteronomic and is not used elsewhere of God.
44.   Cf. xvii. 26 for the meaning of the various geographical divisions of the country.

CHAPTER XXXIII.

Further Promises of Return and Restoration.

This ch. is connected with xxxi., as was pointed out above, and involves some of the same problems. The first half of the passage (*vv.* 1—13) is as a whole probably genuine, in spite of the contrary opinion of Duhm and Cornill; it is necessary however to allow for the presence in it of later interpolations. The latter part (*vv.* 14—26) has been rejected by nearly all recent scholars and the fact that it is entirely missing from LXX. condemns it as late. It is replete with phrases apparently borrowed from other parts of the book, and also contains expressions which can hardly have been used in the time of Jeremiah. The contents may be divided as follows:

(*a*) *Jehovah's invitation to the prophet.* 1—3.
(*b*) *Jerusalem will fall but her latter days will be glorious.* 4—9.
(*c*) *The restoration of the desolate land.* 10—13.
(*d*) *God will give kings and priests in due succession.* 14—18.
(*e*) *The ordinances of nature are no surer than the future of Israel* 19—26.

XXXIII. 1 Moreover the word of the LORD came unto Jeremiah the second time, while he was yet shut up in the court of the guard, saying, 2 Thus saith the LORD that doeth it, the LORD that formeth it to establish it; the LORD is his name: 3 Call unto me, and I will answer thee, and will shew thee great things, and [1]difficult, which thou knowest not. 4 For thus saith the

[1] Heb. *fenced in.*

XXXIII. 1—3. Jehovah calls upon Jeremiah when in the court of the guard to share in His secret plans.

1. *the second time.* See xxxii. 2 for the previous occasion, and for the expression cf. i. 13.

the court of the guard. See note on xxxii. 2.

2 f. These *vv.* are rejected by nearly all scholars as a later insertion probably influenced by 2 Is. (e.g. xlv. 18, xlvii. 4, xlviii. 6). The last part of *v.* 3 is strange, as the contents of the promised revelation merely repeat what had already been declared in xxxi., xxxii.

2. *that doeth it.* The reading of LXX. is to be preferred *who made the earth and formed it to establish it.*

3. *Call unto me.* Prophecy and prayer are here connected; cf. Prov. ii. 1—6 (the search for wisdom). The *v.* is very interesting and important as shewing the need for human cooperation if the Divine revelation, which God is willing and anxious to unfold, is to become possible.

difficult. Lit. *cut off, inaccessible;* cf. mg. *fenced in*[1].

---

[1] Certain MSS. read וּנְצֻרוֹת *hidden* for וּבְצֻרוֹת *fenced in*; possibly this is the correct reading; cf. Is. xlviii. 6.

LORD, the God of Israel, concerning the houses of this city, and concerning the houses of the kings of Judah, which are broken down *to make a defence* against the mounts, and against the sword: 5 They come to fight with the Chaldeans, but it is to fill them with the dead bodies of men, whom I have slain in mine anger and in my fury, and for all whose wickedness I have hid my face from this city. 6 Behold, I will bring it ¹health and cure, and I will cure them; and I will reveal unto them abundance of peace and truth. 7 And I will cause the captivity of Judah and the captivity of Israel to return, and will build them, as at the first. 8 And I will cleanse them from all their iniquity, whereby they have sinned against me; and I will pardon all their iniquities, whereby they have sinned against me, and whereby they have transgressed against me. 9 And *this city* shall be to

¹ Or, *healing*

4—9. The resistance to the Chaldeans will only result in useless bloodshed; but Jehovah Himself will bring salvation by the turning back of the captivity of Judah and Israel.

4 f. These *vv.* give a vivid picture, which bears every mark of being original, of the state of the besieged city, the breaking down of houses to strengthen the defences, the terrible slaughter of the defenders.

4. *mounts.* See on vi. 6, and cf. xxxii. 24, lii. 4; Ez. iv. 2.

5. *They come.* This *v.* as it stands is quite evidently corrupt, for the antecedent of *they* must be *houses* which does not make sense. Various suggestions involving changes of a somewhat violent nature have been put forward to simplify the *v.*, taking, as a rule, the Chaldeans as the subject. Cornill's reconstruction is perhaps the best, *The houses ...which are broken down, against which the Chaldeans come with mounds and swords to fight and to fill them with the dead bodies of men whom* &c.

hid my face. God hides His face in anger and displeasure; cf. Ez. xxxix. 23; and contrast Nu. vi. 26.

6. *health.* Mg. *healing*; literally *fresh flesh*; see on viii. 22. The object of God's compassion is probably the city regarded as a person.

abundance. The Heb. word occurs here only and from the evidence of the versions the text is probably corrupt. Duhm would read by a slight emendation *treasures* (cf. Is. x. 13).

peace and truth. It is perhaps better to read as in xiv. 13 *peace of truth;* the true peace founded on God's faithfulness and contrasted with the vain peace of the false prophets.

7. *as at the first.* Cf. Hos. ii. 15; Is. i. 26.

8. *cleanse them...pardon.* The forgiveness of the past and its obliteration from God's sight; cf. xxxi. 24; Ez. xxxvi. 25.

9. Cf. xiii. 11; Mic. vii. 15 ff.; Is. lx. 5. In the latter passage the emotion referred to is one of pleasure, see Wade *ad loc.*

me for a name of joy, for a praise and for a glory, before all the
nations of the earth, which shall hear all the good that I do unto
them, and shall fear and tremble for all the good and for all the
peace that I procure unto it. 10 Thus saith the LORD: Yet
again there shall be heard in this place, whereof ye say, It is
waste, without man and without beast, even in the cities of Judah,
and in the streets of Jerusalem, that are desolate, without man
and without inhabitant and without beast, 11 the voice of joy
and the voice of gladness, the voice of the bridegroom and the
voice of the bride, the voice of them that say, Give thanks to the
LORD of hosts, for the LORD is good, for his mercy *endureth* for
ever: *and of them* that bring *sacrifices of* thanksgiving into the
house of the LORD. For I will cause the captivity of the land to
return as at the first, saith the LORD. 12 Thus saith the LORD
of hosts: Yet again shall there be in this place, which is waste,
without man and without beast, and in all the cities thereof, an
habitation of shepherds causing their flocks to lie down. 13 In
the cities of the hill country, in the cities of the lowland, and in
the cities of the South, and in the land of Benjamin, and in the
places about Jerusalem, and in the cities of Judah, shall the
flocks again pass under the hands of him that telleth them, saith
the LORD.

14 Behold, the days come, saith the LORD, that I will perform

10—13. The desolate land shall once more be inhabited and flocks
shall lie down in safety.

10 f. These *vv.* form the basis of the closing part of the benediction
in the Jewish Marriage Service at the present day.

11. *Give thanks to the LORD* &c. The people in their rejoicing do
not forget the source from which it springs. The actual form in which
they express their thanksgivings is very similar to some of the later
psalms; e.g. Ps. cvi. 1, cvii. 1, 22, &c.; cf. also 1 Ch. xvi. 34; Ezra
iii. 11.

12. The picture of the misery and desolation of the present throws
into stronger light the joy and plenteousness of the future.

13. *that telleth them. Tell*, i.e. to count; cf. Milton, *L'Allegro*, **67**,
'every shepherd tells his tale'; and Dryden's translation of Virgil,
Eclogue, III. 34 'she takes the tale of all the lambs.' There is perhaps
a reference to Lev. xxvii. 32.

14—18. In the future age there shall be an unfailing succession of
kings upon the throne of David; the priests also shall never be cut
short.

that good word which I have spoken concerning the house of Israel and concerning the house of Judah. 15 In those days, and at that time, will I cause a ¹Branch of righteousness to grow up unto David; and he shall execute judgement and righteousness in the land. 16 In those days shall Judah be saved, and Jerusalem shall dwell safely: and this is *the name* whereby she shall be called, ²The LORD is our righteousness. 17 For thus saith the LORD: ³David shall never want a man to sit upon the throne of the house of Israel; 18 neither shall the priests the Levites want a man before me to offer burnt offerings, and to burn ⁴oblations, and to do sacrifice continually. 19 And the word of the LORD came unto Jeremiah, saying, 20 Thus saith the LORD: If ye can break my covenant of the day, and my covenant of the night, so that there should not be day and night in their season; 21 then may also my covenant be broken with David my servant, that he should not have a son to reign upon his throne; and with the Levites the priests, my ministers. 22 As the host of heaven cannot be numbered, neither the sand of the sea measured; so will I multiply the seed of David my servant, and the Levites that minister unto me. 23 And the word of the LORD came to Jeremiah, saying, 24 Considerest thou not

---

¹ See ch. xxiii. 5.
² See ch. xxiii. 6.
³ Heb. *There shall not be cut off from David.*
⁴ Or, *meal offerings*

15 f.   These *vv.* are closely parallel to xxiii. 5 f., xxix. 10.

16.   *she shall be called.* In this place the title *The LORD is our righteousness* is given to the city and not to the ideal king as in xxiii. 6 (cf. Ez. xlviii. 35; and the name which Gideon gave to the altar in his city 'Jehovah-shalom'—the LORD is peace; Jud. vi. 24).

18.   *the priests the Levites.* Before the return from exile the terms *priest* and *Levite* were synonymous (see Dr McNeile, *Numbers*, pp. xivff., in the Camb. Bible). Afterwards the *Levites* were degraded into temple-servants and were not allowed to *offer burnt offerings,* to *burn oblations* or to *sacrifice* (cf. Ez. xliv. 10—16; Nu. xvi. 9 f.).

19—26.   In this passage the argument from the fixity of the natural laws is again used to prove the certainty of God's promises (cf. xxxi. 35 f.), this time with special reference to the assured continuity of the kings and the priests. In the later *vv.* the same argument is used of the restoration of both branches of the family of Israel.

21.   *with David.* See 2 S. vii. 12—16; 1 K. ii. 4; and cf. Ps. lxxxix. 3, cxxxii. 11, for other notices of the Davidic covenant.

24.   This *v.* as it stands is difficult, as it is impossible to say

what this people have spoken, saying, The two families which the LORD did choose, he hath cast them off? thus do they despise my people, that they should be no more a nation before them. 25 Thus saith the LORD: If my covenant of day and night *stand* not, if I have not appointed the ordinances of heaven and earth; 26 then will I also cast away the seed of Jacob, and of David my servant, so that I will not take of his seed to be rulers over the seed of Abraham, Isaac, and Jacob: for I will [1]cause their captivity to return, and will have mercy on them.

[1] Or, *return to their captivity*

whether *this people* refers to Israel or to the heathen. Duhm's emendation restores the meaning *he hath cast them off, and despised his people, that it should be no more a nation before him.*

The two families. Israel and Judah (cf. *v.* 26), not Levi and David.

did choose. This is the only reference to the choice of Israel in the whole book; in Ez. also there is but one reference, xx. 5. The idea of the choice is found in Am. iii. 2; Ex. xix. 5 f. and is common in Dt.

25. *If my covenant.* A slight change in the Heb. gives the reading *If I have not created* (Duhm), and it is then unnecessary to supply a verb as is done by EVV.

26. *Isaac.* The spelling of the original[1] is unusual and found elsewhere only in Am. vii. 9, 16; Ps. cv. 9.

CHAPTERS XXXIV.—XXXIX.

In these chapters the personal history of the prophet, which was interrupted after xxix. 32, is once more resumed. The general subject of the division is Jeremiah's life during the siege. Some of the events narrated in it can be paralleled from the earlier chapters of the book and in the arrangement of his matter the compiler has not been influenced by a strict regard for chronological sequence. The contents may be grouped under the following heads:

The message to Zedekiah. xxxiv. 1—7.
The release of the slaves. xxxiv. 8—22.
The incident of the Rechabites. xxxv.
Jeremiah's roll and its fate. xxxvi.
Warnings and persecutions. xxxvii., xxxviii. 28 *a*.
The fall of Jerusalem. xxxviii. 28 *b*—xxxix. 14.
The message to Ebed-Melech. xxxix. 15—18.

---

[1] יִצְחָק for יִשְׂחָק.

CHAPTER XXXIV. 1—7.

The Message to Zedekiah.

The prophecy recorded in this passage was evidently delivered in the early part of the siege and before the temporary relief brought by the approach of the Egyptian army; Jeremiah is still at liberty (*v.* 6) and two other cities besides Jerusalem are still holding out against the Babylonians (*v.* 7).

XXXIV. 1 The word which came unto Jeremiah from the LORD, when Nebuchadnezzar king of Babylon, and all his army, and all the kingdoms of the earth that were under his dominion, and all the peoples, fought against Jerusalem, and against all the cities thereof, saying: 2 Thus saith the LORD, the God of Israel, Go, and speak to Zedekiah king of Judah, and tell him, Thus saith the LORD, Behold, I will give this city into the hand of the king of Babylon, and he shall burn it with fire: 3 and thou shalt not escape out of his hand, but shalt surely be taken, and delivered into his hand; and thine eyes shall behold the eyes of the king of Babylon, and he shall speak with thee mouth to mouth, and thou shalt go to Babylon. 4 Yet hear the word of the LORD, O Zedekiah king of Judah: thus saith the LORD concerning thee, Thou shalt not die by the sword; 5 thou shalt

XXXIV. 1. The form of this *v.* is very elaborate and resembles the opening of an Assyrian inscription rather than a Hebrew prophecy; the simpler text preserved in LXX., which omits *the kingdoms of* and *and all the peoples*, is probably original.

kingdoms. These would be the contingents sent from subject states (cf. 2 K. xxiv. 2).

3. *thine eyes* &c. Cf. xxxii. 3 f. Zedekiah was in an unenviable position, and the consciousness of his broken pledges (cf. Ez. xvii.) must have weighed heavily on his mind. There is no mention here of the putting out of Zedekiah's eyes, which leads Duhm to question the account contained in lii. 11 and 2 K. xxvii. 7; Ez. xii. 13, however, seems conclusive on the point.

mouth to mouth. Lit. *his mouth shall speak with thy mouth.*

4 f. These *vv.* come rather strangely in a threatening prophecy, Jeremiah would hardly be likely at this juncture to foretell smooth things to Zedekiah; possibly some clause has fallen out which made the promises conditional.

4. *Yet.* God reveals His plans gradually whether they be plans of punishment or of reward.

die in peace; and with the burnings of thy fathers, the former kings which were before thee, so shall they ¹make a burning for thee; and they shall lament thee, *saying*, Ah lord! for I have spoken the word, saith the LORD. 6 Then Jeremiah the prophet spake all these words unto Zedekiah king of Judah in Jerusalem, 7 when the king of Babylon's army fought against Jerusalem, and against all the cities of Judah that were left, against Lachish and against Azekah; for these *alone* remained of the cities of Judah *as* fenced cities.

¹ See 2 Chr. xvi. 14, xxi. 19.

5. *the burnings of thy fathers.* Cf. 2 Ch. xvi. 14, xxi. 19, and see Joseph. *De Bell. Jud.* I. xxxiii. 19 (at the funeral of Herod). It has been suggested that these burnings for the kings were a heathen survival, Renan, *Hist. du peuple d'Israel*, III. p. 121; cf. also Frazer, *Adonis*, I. pp. 177 f.

7. *Lachish...Azekah.* Both these towns had been fortified by Rehoboam (2 Ch. xi. 9). *Lachish* was some 35 miles SW. of Jerusalem on the site of the modern *Tell el-Hesy* (see F. J. Bliss, *A Mound of Many Cities*). It had been the headquarters of Sennacherib (Is. xxxvi. 2), though the Assyrian monarch only captured the town with difficulty and after very elaborate preparations (see Layard, *Nineveh and Babylon*, p. 149). The site of *Azekah* is unknown but it probably lay some 15 miles SW. of Jerusalem. Cf. Josh. xv. 35; 1 S. xvii. 1; Neh. xi. 30 (with *Lachish*).

CHAPTER XXXIV. 8—22.

The Release of the Slaves.

In the early part of the siege of Jerusalem the men of the city released their Hebrew slaves, perhaps in accordance with the requirements of the law (see on *vv.* 8 and 14), and as a bribe to Jehovah to gain His help against Babylon; perhaps also, as Duhm thinks, to provide more defenders for the city, for the newly emancipated slaves would have more interest in keeping out the besiegers. The former and religious motive was evidently the more prominent, the release being guaranteed by a solemn covenant. In the eyes of the men of Jerusalem their piety was speedily rewarded; for the Egyptians exhibited an unusual measure of activity and advanced to the relief of the city. Their efforts were successful and the Babylonians were compelled to abandon the siege. Ignoring their solemn oath to God, ignoring the claims of brotherly love, or even of common justice, the Hebrews immediately re-enslaved their brethren. The prophet's condemnation followed swiftly on this unrighteous conduct. Just as release had been given to the slaves, so would Jehovah give the men of Jerusalem

17—2

release from His service, and, what followed as a consequence, from His protection. On the other hand just as they had made their slaves to return, so would Jehovah make the besiegers to return upon the faithless city.

(a)   *The covenant of liberty.*   8—11.
(b)   *Law and perjury.*   12—16.
(c)   *The punishment of broken obligations.*   17—22.

8 The word that came unto Jeremiah from the LORD, after that the king Zedekiah had made a covenant with all the people which were at Jerusalem, to proclaim liberty unto them; 9 that every man should let his manservant, and every man his maidservant, being an Hebrew or an Hebrewess, go free; that none should serve himself of them, *to wit,* of a Jew his brother: 10 and all the princes and all the people obeyed, which had entered into the covenant, that every one should let his manservant, and every one his maidservant, go free, that none should serve themselves of them any more; they obeyed, and let them go: 11 but afterwards they turned, and caused the servants and the handmaids, whom they had let go free, to return, and brought them

8—11.   Zedekiah and the people made a covenant to release all native slaves of either sex.   Cf. Neh. v. 8—12 for a similar action on the part of Nehemiah.

8.   *had made a covenant.*   The release of the male slave at the end of six years from the beginning of servitude is provided for in Ex. xxi. 2 (E) and of the female in Dt. xv. 2.   If this law had ever been accepted before the days of Jeremiah, it had by his time fallen into neglect, and instead of its provisions a covering measure compelling the release of all slaves was agreed to by the people.   The number of slaves must have been very great as the frequent invasions had ruined the small landowners, who were also oppressed by the greed of the great proprietors (cf. Am. ii. 7; Mic. ii. 2, 9; Is. v. 8, &c.) and in their poverty reduced to servitude (see Introd. p. lix).

all...at Jerusalem.   As the rest of the inhabitants of Judah were cut off by the besiegers the covenant related to Jerusalem only.

liberty.   Heb. דְּרוֹר; *dĕrōr*, lit. *flowing,* and therefore *free* (cf. the Babylonian *durāru,* and see S. A. Cook, *Laws of Moses,* &c., pp. 159 note 1, 229 note 1).   The word is used in a similar connexion in Lev. xxv. 10; Ez. xlvi. 17; Is. lxi. 1: it also gives her name to the swallow.

9.   *that none...his brother.*   So Lev. xxv. 39—46.   LXX. reads *so that no one of Judah should any more be a slave.*

11.   *afterwards they turned.*   'A death-bed repentance, with the usual sequel on recovery,' Peake.   Cf. Dean Church, *St Anselm,* pp. 226 f.

into subjection for servants and for handmaids: 12 therefore the
word of the LORD came to Jeremiah from the LORD, saying, 13 Thus
saith the LORD, the God of Israel: I made a covenant with your
fathers in the day that I brought them forth out of the land of
Egypt, out of the house of ¹bondage, saying, 14 At the end of
seven years ye shall let go every man his brother that is an
Hebrew, which ²hath been sold unto thee, and hath served thee
six years, thou shalt let him go free from thee: but your fathers
hearkened not unto me, neither inclined their ear. 15 And ye
were now turned, and had done that which is right in mine eyes,
in proclaiming liberty every man to his neighbour; and ye had
made a covenant before me in the house which is called by my
name: 16 but ye turned and profaned my name, and caused
every man his servant, and every man his handmaid, whom ye
had let go free at their pleasure, to return; and ye brought them
into subjection, to be unto you for servants and for handmaids.
17 Therefore thus saith the LORD: Ye have not hearkened unto
me, to proclaim liberty, every man to his brother, and every man
to his neighbour: behold, I proclaim unto you a liberty, saith
the LORD, to the sword, to the pestilence, and to the famine; and
I will make you to be ³tossed to and fro among all the kingdoms
of the earth. 18 And I will give the men that have transgressed
my covenant, which have not performed the words of the covenant which they made before me, ⁴when they cut the calf in

---

¹ Heb. *bondmen*.   ² Or, *hath sold himself*
³ Or, *a terror unto*   ⁴ Heb. *the calf which they cut &c.*

12—16.   The prophet tells the people that they have not only
broken the law, but also the special covenant which they had made
with God; perjury has been added to treachery.

14.   *At the end of seven years.* LXX. reads *six* which is the period
really contemplated; the Hebrews in making a calculation of this kind
included both the first term and the last in their reckoning (cf. 'after
three days' Mk. viii. 31; contrast ix. 31, x. 34). According to the
Code of Hammurabi, § 117, if a man sold his wife or children for a debt
they were to be returned at the end of three years.

16.   *at their pleasure.* Lit. *according to their soul*; cf. xxii. 27.

17—22.   The sentence is proclaimed. Because the people have
neglected to carry out the law of emancipation they are to be emancipated from Jehovah's service and protection. 'The punishment is to
be according to the *jus talionis*' (Giesebrecht). Cf. Matt. vii. 2.

18.   *when they cut the calf in twain.* Cf. Gen. xv. 9—11, 17 (with

twain and passed between the parts thereof; 19 the princes of
Judah, and the princes of Jerusalem, the eunuchs, and the priests,
and all the people of the land, which passed between the parts
of the calf; 20 I will even give them into the hand of their
enemies, and into the hand of them that seek their life: and
their dead bodies shall be for meat unto the fowls of the heaven,
and to the beasts of the earth. 21 And Zedekiah king of Judah
and his princes will I give into the hand of their enemies, and
into the hand of them that seek their life, and into the hand of
the king of Babylon's army, which are gone up from you. 22 Behold, I will command, saith the LORD, and cause them to return
to this city; and they shall fight against it, and take it, and burn
it with fire: and I will make the cities of Judah a desolation,
without inhabitant.

Driver's note). The animal was slain and its carcase divided up; each
of the parties to the agreement then passed between them, invoking
a similar fate upon himself if he failed to keep his contract. Dr Bennett
(*Expos. Bible, ad loc.*) compares the case of the agreement made by the
leaders of the contending factions of the Macedonian army after the
death of Alexander, when the compromise was ratified by the contracting
parties going between the two halves of a dog (cf. also *Iliad*, III. 298).
The Chinese, even in the present day, take an oath by kneeling down
and smashing a saucer, saying meanwhile 'I shall tell the truth, the
whole truth. The saucer is broken and if I tell not the truth my soul
will be broken like the saucer.' See further McNeile, *Exodus*, p. 154
note 1. Robertson Smith, however, is not satisfied with the above
explanation as it fails to account for 'the characteristic feature in the
ceremony—the passing between the pieces; and, on the other hand,
we see from Ex. xxiv. 8...that the dividing of the sacrifice and the
application of the blood to both parties go together. The sacrifice
presumably was divided into two parts, when both parties joined in
eating it: and when it ceased to be eaten, the parties stood between
the pieces as a symbol that they were taken within the mystical life of
the victim.' *Rel. Sem.*[2] p. 481[1].

20. Cf. vii. 33, xvi. 4.

21. *Zedekiah*. Contrast *v.* 5 where the judgement passed on
Zedekiah is comparatively favourable.

---

[1] For other instances of the rite in both ancient and modern times see J. G. Frazer,
The Magic Art, I. p. 289, and the authorities there quoted.

CHAPTER XXXV.

The Incident of the Rechabites.

Towards the end of the reign of Jehoiakim (*v.* 1; see note however) Judah was overrun by bands of Syrians and Chaldeans (2 K. xxiv. 2) who drove the inhabitants of the open country and of the smaller towns to seek refuge in Jerusalem. Amongst these fugitives was the family or clan of the Rechabites who had hitherto avoided living in towns or even in houses, preserving the simpler conditions of life as handed down to them by their forefathers.

According to 1 Ch. ii. 55 the Rechabites were a branch of the Kenites, a tribe which had been associated with the Israelites from the earliest times, and who had finally settled in the south of Judah (Jud. i. 16; 1 S. xv. 6)[1]. Their avoidance of wine was not primarily a protest against drunkenness and luxury, but was part of the general religious policy of 'their father' Jonadab, the son of Rechab. This policy was probably based on the conception of Jehovah as the God of a wilderness people, and those who supported it were upholders of the 'primitive severe and unimaginative' religion of the Israelite nation against the later eclecticism with its sanction of heathen rites[2]. When the nomad Israelites settled in Canaan they were bound to take up the cultivation of the soil in order to support themselves and their families; in doing so they would be dependent on their Canaanite neighbours for instruction in the arts of agriculture, and these arts would involve the learning of religious rites intended to propitiate the Baalim who were responsible for the fertility of the ground. In adopting such practices the Israelites had no intention of abandoning, or even of compromising, their allegiance to Jehovah as the supreme God of Israel, they looked upon the local Baalim as so many demigods or guardian spirits. In course of time, however, as the conception of Jehovah as the only God to be worshipped by Israel became more general, the rites paid to these local deities, with all their underlying superstitions, would be transferred to Him. The policy of Jonadab was a protest against the nation's having anything to do with agricultural life, involving as it did the performance of these degrading rites, and this protest was carried so far as to make his followers avoid wine, at any rate, amongst the products of the soil. It should be remembered that Jeremiah had strong sympathies with the nomadic life (ii. 2; cf. Hos. ii. 14 f.), and these sympathies were no doubt intensified in the face of the growing luxury of the court (xxii. 14 f.).

---

[1] G. F. Moore thinks that the Kenites were a branch of the Amalekites and that their connexion with the Rechabites is very doubtful; *Judges*, p. 34 n.

[2] Canon Kennett in *HD Rel. and E.* vii. pp. 440 f. says 'It is not improbable that the Rechabites may be regarded as the representatives of the true Israelite as distinct from the Canaanite element in Israel. Presumably before the conquest of Canaan the Israelites lived mainly on milk, as do the Bahima and the Todas in modern times, though the eating of game may also have been allowed.' On the other hand Eardmans does not look upon the Rechabites as good evidence for early Israelite religion; he thinks that they were travelling 'smiths' who came in the train of the Babylonians; cf. their connexion with the Kenites (= smiths). *Expositor*, vii. vi. 126 ff.

The narrative of the encounter with the Rechabites bears on the face of it the marks of genuineness, and accordingly few critics have ventured to question it. Schmidt, however, rejects the account as he thinks that the very presence of the Rechabites within the walls of Jerusalem was a breach of the command of their ancestor. But there is no evidence of their living in houses during the siege, doubtless the number of houses within the city walls would not in any case have been sufficient to accommodate the mass of fugitives, and the events of the later siege make it probable that the number of houses available was reduced still further and that some of them were broken down to strengthen the defences (xxxiii. 4). If the Rechabites dwelt in tents within the walls, and there is no reason for doubting that they did so, they would not be the only people who were thus housed. Schmidt also thinks that, even if the Rechabites entered Jerusalem, it is unlikely that Jeremiah would have subjected them to so questionable and public a test as the one related here (*Enc. Bib.* 2387). This criticism like the last one is purely arbitrary and in view of the other evidence in favour of the genuineness of the ch. of little value[1].

    (*a*)   *The prophet's invitation and its sequel.* 1—11.
    (*b*)   *The lesson from the incident.* 12—19.

XXXV. 1 The word which came unto Jeremiah from the LORD in the days of Jehoiakim the son of Josiah, king of Judah, saying, 2 Go unto the house of the Rechabites, and speak unto them, and bring them into the house of the LORD, into one of the chambers, and give them wine to drink. 3 Then I took

XXXV. 1—11. Jeremiah invites the Rechabites to drink wine in one of the chambers of the temple; they refuse to do so because of their traditional avoidance of all customs inconsistent with the nomadic life.

1. *the days of Jehoiakim.* This chapter, with that which follows it, returns to the reign of Jehoiakim, and so causes a break in the account contained in chh. xxxii.—xliv. The correctness of the date has been challenged on the ground that Nebuchadrezzar, from whose approach the Rechabites had fled (*v.* 11), did not enter Judah till after the days of Jehoiakim, cf. Buttenwieser, *Prophets*, p. 45. It is not necessary to take the approach of Nebuchadrezzar to be in person, the phrase would be quite well represented by the approach of his armies (cf. 2 K. xxiv. 2).

2. *Go unto the house.* i.e. the family or clan. Jeremiah is evidently once more at liberty (cf. xxxvi. 19, 26).

the chambers. There seem to have been many rooms in the temple

---

[1] In view of the suggestion made above that the Rechabites avoided wine from religious motives it is interesting to remember that the Greeks regarded intoxication as due to a divine influence dwelling in the grape, hence their worship of Dionysus, 'the spirit of fire and dew, alive and leaping in a thousand vines' as Walter Pater described him.

Jaazaniah the son of Jeremiah, the son of Habazziniah, and his
brethren, and all his sons, and the whole house of the Rechabites;
4 and I brought them into the house of the LORD, into the chamber of the sons of Hanan the son of Igdaliah, the man of God,
which was by the chamber of the princes, which was above the
chamber of Maaseiah the son of Shallum, the keeper of the [1]door:
5 and I set before the sons of the house of the Rechabites bowls
full of wine, and cups, and I said unto them, Drink ye wine.
6 But they said, We will drink no wine: for Jonadab the son of
Rechab our father commanded us, saying, Ye shall drink no

[1] Heb. *threshold*.

courts and they were the scenes of several incidents in Jeremiah's
ministry (xxxvi. 12, 20 f.). Giesebrecht points out that it was evidently
possible for those outside to see and hear what was going on in the
chamber. In 1 S. ix. 22 the same Heb. word *lishka* is used of ' a ban-
queting hall for the communal sacrifice' and W. Robertson Smith
thinks that it is identical with the Greek λέσχη (*Rel. Sem.*[2] p. 254).

3. The names of the Rechabites as given in MT. all end in *-iah*;
LXX. seems to have had a different text or else it deliberately omitted
the ending in the case of the two last names. It is possible that the
-iah was added by a later scribe in view of *v.* 19.

4. *Hanan*. Nothing is known of *Hanan* except in this passage.
The phrase *man of God* is used in 1 S. ii. 27, ix. 6; 1 K. xiii. 1, &c. of
a prophet, and perhaps *Hanan* was himself a prophet; in which case
his *sons* were most probably his disciples (cf. 2 K. ii. 3, &c.), hence
their sympathy with Jeremiah.

Maaseiah. Probably father of Zephaniah, xxi. 1, xxix. 25, &c.

keeper of the door. Better *threshold*. Three such officers are specified in lii. 24 and they were men of great importance ranking after the
chief priest and second priest. Ps. lxxxiv. 10 suggests that the *door-
keeper* (the same root is used) was a person of low rank; the reference
however is probably not to an office at all but to an attitude, and the
line is best translated 'I had rather stand at the threshold of the house
of my God[1].'

5. *bowls*. The same word is used of Joseph's divining cup (Gen.
xliv. 2, &c.), and of the bowls of the golden candlestick (Ex. xxv. 21, &c.).

6. *Jonadab the son of Rechab*. Jonadab is mentioned in 2 K. x.
15—27 as one of Jehu's sympathisers in the strong measures which
were taken by that monarch against the worshippers of the Tyrian
Baal. Cheyne, however, identifies him with Hobab the father-in-law
of Moses (*Enc. Bib.* 2101 f.).

our father. This expression need not be taken literally (see

[1] Cf. Frazer, *Folk-Lore in O.T.* III. pp. 1 ff.

wine, neither ye, nor your sons, for ever: 7 neither shall ye build
house, nor sow seed, nor plant vineyard, nor have any: but all
your days ye shall dwell in tents; that ye may live many days
in the land wherein ye sojourn. 8 And we have obeyed the voice
of Jonadab the son of Rechab our father in all that he charged
us, to drink no wine all our days, we, our wives, our sons, nor
our daughters; 9 nor to build houses for us to dwell in: neither
have we vineyard, nor field, nor seed: 10 but we have dwelt in
tents, and have obeyed, and done according to all that Jonadab
our father commanded us. 11 But it came to pass, when Nebuchadrezzar king of Babylon came up into the land, that we said,
Come, and let us go to Jerusalem for fear of the army of the
Chaldeans, and for fear of the army of the Syrians; so we dwell
at Jerusalem.

on *v.* 4). The head or founder of any society or group amongst the
Arabs is still called its *father* (see W. Robertson Smith, *Kinship*, &c.
p. 15).

7. Prohibitions almost identical with those mentioned in this
v. were laid upon the Nabataeans, not in their case from religious
motives, but in order that their poverty might free them from fear of
the covetousness of powerful neighbours (Diod. Siculus XIX. 94; for
other instances of a similar *taboo* see W. Robertson Smith, *Rel. Sem.*[2]
pp. 484 ff.). The Bedouin of the present day consider it an unworthy
thing to engage in agriculture or handicrafts, and this feeling may date
from similar ancestral prohibitions. The instinct which prompts nomads
to be suspicious of higher types of civilisation is a true one and inspired, consciously or unconsciously, by the desire for self-preservation
(cf. R. A. Nicholson, *Literary Hist. of the Arabs*, pp. 439 ff.).

dwell in tents. Cf. Gen. iv. 20.

8. Dean Stanley quotes a very striking parallel to this instance,
illustrating the way in which the Bedouin adhere to their traditions:
'We passed a cairn, said to be the grave of the horse of Abû Zenneh, his
horse killed in battle. Who Abû Zenneh was—when he lived—what
the battle was—is quite unknown, but he left an ordinance that every
Arab should throw sand on the cairn as if it were barley, and say,
'Eat, eat, O horse of Abû Zenneh,' as if the dead creature were still
alive. So said our Bedouin, and accordingly each Arab muttered the
words and pushed the sand twice or thrice with his foot as he passed.
I could not help thinking of the Rechabites, as described by Jeremiah.'
Sinai and Pal.[23] p. 54.

11. *Syrians.* Cf. xii. 7—17; 2 K. xxiv. 2. Nöldeke thinks that
the great mass of the Chaldean army consisted of Arameans (*Enc. Bib.*
280); on the other hand Necho's army at Carchemish had its contingent
of Phoenicians (see Müller-Didot, *Fragmenta Hist. Graecae*, II. p. 506).

12 Then came the word of the LORD unto Jeremiah, saying,
13 Thus saith the LORD of hosts, the God of Israel: Go, and say
to the men of Judah and the inhabitants of Jerusalem, Will ye
not receive instruction to hearken to my words? saith the LORD.
14 The words of Jonadab the son of Rechab, that he commanded
his sons, not to drink wine, are performed, and unto this day
they drink none, for they obey their father's commandment: but
I have spoken unto you, rising up early and speaking; and ye
have not hearkened unto me. 15 I have sent also unto you all
my servants the prophets, rising up early and sending them,
saying, Return ye now every man from his evil way, and amend
your doings, and go not after other gods to serve them, and ye
shall dwell in the land which I have given to you and to your
fathers: but ye have not inclined your ear, nor hearkened unto
me. 16 Forasmuch as the sons of Jonadab the son of Rechab
have performed the commandment of their father which he commanded them, but this people hath not hearkened unto me;
17 therefore thus saith the LORD, the God of hosts, the God of
Israel: Behold, I will bring upon Judah and upon all the inhabitants of Jerusalem all the evil that I have pronounced against
them: because I have spoken unto them, but they have not

There is, however, nothing contradictory in the two statements, the
peoples of the ancient East had to provide troops for their overlord for
the time being without any regard for their own wishes or sentiments.

12—19. The fidelity of the Rechabites is to be rewarded. This
section unlike that which precedes it is in the third person (see *vv.* 12
and 18 but cf. LXX.) and consists mainly of strings of phrases apparently
borrowed from other passages of Jeremiah. Erbt thinks that *vv.* 16, 19
alone are genuine, and in any case, the substance of the passage is
contained in these *vv.* viz.: the fruit of obedience to parents is worldly
stability, a maxim which is well illustrated by the history of the
Chinese (cf. Ex. xx. 12; Eph. vi. 2 f.).

14 f. In ii. 11 the Almighty tried to arouse in Israel a sense of
shame by the example of the faithfulness of the heathen to their objects
of worship; here by the faithfulness of the Rechabites to mere human
commands. The harsh and stringent prohibitions which Jonadab had
laid on his followers were obeyed, but the requirements of Jehovah
were disregarded. The prophet holds up these men, who were non-
Israelites, as an example to the chosen people (cf. Matt. viii. 10 'I
have not found so great faith, no not in Israel').

15. 'A summary in Jeremiah's phraseology of the teaching of the
former prophets.' Driver.

heard; and I have called unto them, but they have not answered. 18 And Jeremiah said unto the house of the Rechabites, Thus saith the LORD of hosts, the God of Israel: Because ye have obeyed the commandment of Jonadab your father, and kept all his precepts, and done according unto all that he commanded you; 19 therefore thus saith the LORD of hosts, the God of Israel: Jonadab the son of Rechab shall not want a man to stand before me for ever.

18. *And Jeremiah said...Rechabites.* Omit with LXX.

19. *to stand before.* The phrase is used of attendance on a king (1 K. i. 2, x. 8, &c.), of Elijah and Elisha as ministers of Jehovah (1 K. xvii. 1, &c.), and of Jeremiah himself (xv. 19). It is usually employed as a description of the priests, and some scholars would so interpret it here. There are various traces, it is true, of a connexion between the Rechabites and the priesthood but these come from a later time, and may be a consequence of this passage. See Neh. iii. 14, the LXX. heading to Ps. lxxi. υἱῶν Ἰωναδάβ, and Hegesippus' account of the stoning of James the Just where he speaks of 'one of the priests the sons of Rechab, a son of the Rechabites spoken of by Jeremiah the prophet' (quoted by Eusebius, *Hist. Eccles.* II. p. 23). For later theories see *The Jewish Quarterly Review*, N.S. I. p. 253; *Enc. Bib.* 4019 ff.

CHAPTER XXXVI.

Jeremiah's Roll and its Fate.

This ch. like the one previous to it comes from the reign of Jehoiakim, though from a somewhat earlier period. It contains an account of what is perhaps the most striking and dramatic incident in the whole book. But the action of Jehoiakim in destroying the roll, striking and dramatic though that incident may be, does not by any means exhaust the interest and still more the importance of the ch.; on the contrary it would surely be no exaggeration to say that the composition of the roll itself, from the light which it throws on the origin of the book, outweighs in importance and even in interest the conduct of the king.

The fourth year of Jehoiakim, in which the incident took place, synchronised with one of the most momentous epochs in the history of Israel, and indeed of the world—it was the year most probably of the battle of Carchemish, the battle in which was decided the fate of Syria and the sovereignty of the known world. It may be that it was the result of this conflict which impelled Jeremiah to commit his prophecies to writing, emphasising as they did the coming of the foe from the North; it was a not unnatural temptation to him after all the years of scoffing and mockery to point out to the people that the words which God had spoken by his mouth were not so impossible of fulfilment, and that part of the prophecies having been brought to pass the remainder was surely worthy of deep consideration. He was no longer the discredited herald of woes that never came—the Babylonian triumph had vindicated his forecasts and shewn him to be the true prophet of Jehovah (cf. p. 182).

The chapter may be analysed as follows:

(*a*)	*The dictation of the roll.* 1—8.
(*b*)	*The first reading—to the people.* 9 f.
(*c*)	*The second reading—to the princes.* 11—15.
(*d*)	*The princes' warning.* 16—20.
(*e*)	*The third reading—to the king, who destroys the roll.* 21—26
(*f*)	*The roll re-written.* 27—32.

XXXVI. 1 And it came to pass in the fourth year of Jehoiakim the son of Josiah, king of Judah, that this word came unto Jeremiah from the LORD, saying, 2 Take thee a roll of a book, and write therein all the words that I have spoken unto thee against Israel, and against Judah, and against all the nations, from the day I spake unto thee, from the days of Josiah, even unto this day. 3 It may be that the house of Judah will hear

XXXVI. 1—8. Jeremiah at the command of God dictates his prophecies to Baruch; and because he is not free to go into the temple he instructs Baruch to read them to the people there assembled. It has recently been suggested by Dr Buttenwieser (*Prophets*, pp. 133 ff.) that the reason for Jeremiah's dictation of his prophecies was that he himself could not write. As so little is known of the extent to which writing was practised amongst the ancient Hebrews there is no present possibility either of proving or disproving this theory: for a discussion of the question see *J. Th. S.* XVI. pp. 135 f. Some difficulty has been felt as to the exact manner in which Jeremiah reproduced his prophecies, were they written down just as he had uttered them during a period of twenty-three years? If so how did the prophet remember them, unless he had indeed, as Stade suggests (*ZATW.* 1903, pp. 157 ff.), a repetition of the original ecstasy? In reply it may be taken as almost certain that the roll, which was only of moderate dimensions—it was read three times in one day—contained merely the bare outline and substance of Jeremiah's constantly repeated message. At the same time he may have preserved written copies of some of his discourses or they may have been retained in the minds of the hearers. Many of the passages which are contained in the earlier chh. of the canonical book shew traces of the time in which they claim to have been delivered.

2. *Israel.* LXX. reading *Jerusalem* is much to be preferred.
3. Cf. *v.* 7, xxvi. 3.

all the evil which I purpose to do unto them; that they may
return every man from his evil way; that I may forgive their
iniquity and their sin. 4 Then Jeremiah called Baruch the son
of Neriah; and Baruch wrote from the mouth of Jeremiah all
the words of the LORD, which he had spoken unto him, upon a
roll of a book. 5 And Jeremiah commanded Baruch, saying, I
am ¹shut up; I cannot go into the house of the LORD: 6 therefore go thou, and read in the roll, which thou hast written from
my mouth, the words of the LORD in the ears of the people in
the LORD'S house upon ²the fast day: and also thou shalt read
them in the ears of all Judah that come out of their cities. 7 It
may be ³they will present their supplication before the LORD,
and will return every one from his evil way: for great is the
anger and the fury that the LORD hath pronounced against this

¹ Or, *restrained*   ² Or, *a fast day*   ³ Heb. *their supplication will fall.*

4. *Baruch.* See on xxxii. 12 f.
mouth of Jeremiah. The prophet dictated to his scribe possibly
reading from earlier documents (see above).
5. *shut up.* The exact meaning of the phrase in this connexion
has greatly puzzled commentators; the fact is obvious, Jeremiah, for
some reason or other, was not allowed to enter the temple and address
the people, possibly he had been 'inhibited' from preaching there after
the incidents related in xxvi. (cf. Giesebrecht). Other critics suggest
that he was ceremonially unclean; but it is not certain that such uncleanness would have prevented his having access to the outer courts
of the temple. In a similar case Doeg the Edomite saw and heard all
that went on in the sanctuary at Nob (1 S. xxi. 8), though it is perhaps
somewhat hazardous to cite customs from this simpler tabernacle as a
precedent for the temple itself (cf. Preuschen, *ZATW*. 1903, pp. 141 ff.).
A more effective argument against the suggestion of ceremonial uncleanness is to be found in the fact that Jeremiah's inability to enter
the temple area lasted for a longer period than would be explained
on such grounds. On the other hand it is hardly likely that we are
intended to understand that the prophet was in prison at the time—
though the same expression is used with this connotation in xxxiii. 1,
xxxix. 15—for in this case he would not have had sufficient liberty of
action to carry out the advice of the princes to hide himself (*vv.* 19
and 26). Buttenwieser (*op. cit.* pp. 40 f.) thinks that Jeremiah was
prevented from entering the temple or appearing openly because he
was under sentence of death (see note on xxvi. 16).
6. *fast day.* The prophets habitually took advantage of large
gatherings of the people to deliver their message; see xxvi. 2; Is. xxviii.
7 f., xxix. 1—14 (but cf. *v.* 11).

people. 8 And Baruch the son of Neriah did according to all
that Jeremiah the prophet commanded him, reading in the book
the words of the LORD in the LORD's house.

9 Now it came to pass in the fifth year of Jehoiakim the son
of Josiah, king of Judah, in the ninth month, that all the people
in Jerusalem, and all the people that came from the cities of
Judah unto Jerusalem, proclaimed a fast before the LORD.
10 Then read Baruch in the book the words of Jeremiah in
the house of the LORD, in the chamber of Gemariah the son of
Shaphan the scribe, in the upper court, at the entry of the new
gate of the LORD's house, in the ears of all the people. 11 And
when Micaiah the son of Gemariah, the son of Shaphan, had

8. This *v.* is merely a summary of what follows.

9 f. Baruch reads the roll in the ears of the people.

9. *fifth year...ninth month.* There was evidently some little delay
between the composition of the roll and its publication. This delay
cannot be accounted for by supposing that it was occupied in copying
out the roll, its size was too small for any such a length of time to be
required. As the *ninth month* occurs in winter time (cf. *v.* 22) the
writer of the account is evidently using the Babylonian system of
reckoning; by this system the year is considered to begin in April.
The usage is not necessarily a sign of late date as it is found in Ezekiel.

a fast. Before the exile fasting was a private custom, after the
return regular days were appointed (cf. Zech. vii. 3 ff., viii. 19; Lev.
xvi. 29, xxiii. 27; and see Wade, *Isaiah*, pp. 368 f.). This special fast
may have been *proclaimed* because of the threatening approach of the
Chaldeans.

10. Duhm thinks that this exact and detailed account, in spite of
its being written in the third person, can come from none other than
Baruch himself.

in the chamber. Baruch evidently despaired of attempting to gain
the attention of all the people, they would be intent on the numerous
sacrifices which were doubtless offered up on the occasion of the fast.

Gemariah the son of Shaphan. Probably *Shaphan* is to be identified
with Josiah's officer (2 K. xxii. 3). *Gemariah,* who must not be confused with the son of Hilkiah mentioned in xxix. 3, was most probably
the brother of Ahikam, Jeremiah's protector (xxvi. 24) and the uncle
of Gedaliah (xxxix. 14). Another son of *Shaphan* seems to have been
a leader of the reactionary party (Ez. viii. 11), though it is by no
means certain that Jaazaniah is the brother of *Gemariah.* The owner
of the chamber was himself away at the time, being with the other
princes in the palace (*v.* 12), but his son Micaiah was present (*v.* 11).

11—15. Micaiah reports the contents of the roll to the princes,
and Baruch at their request reads the roll before them. Micaiah's

heard out of the book all the words of the LORD, 12 he went
down into the king's house, into the scribe's chamber: and, lo,
all the princes sat there, even Elishama the scribe, and Delaiah
the son of Shemaiah, and Elnathan the son of Achbor, and
Gemariah the son of Shaphan, and Zedekiah the son of Hananiah,
and all the princes. 13 Then Micaiah declared unto them all
the words that he had heard, when Baruch read the book in the
ears of the people. 14 Therefore all the princes sent Jehudi the
son of Nethaniah, the son of Shelemiah, the son of Cushi, unto
Baruch, saying, Take in thine hand the roll wherein thou hast
read in the ears of the people, and come. So Baruch the son of
Neriah took the roll in his hand, and came unto them. 15 And
they said unto him, Sit down now, and read it in our ears. So

action may have been inspired by unfriendly motives, he may have felt
that the contents of the roll ought to be reported to the authorities;
his relationship to Gemariah, however, makes it probable that he was
friendly to the prophet, and it was natural that he should give some
kind of report to his father of the use made of the chamber.

12. *Elishama.* The name also occurs in Nu. i. 10; 2 S. v. 16.

14. *Jehudi...Cushi.* Cushi is the ordinary Heb. word for an Ethiopian and it is hard to decide in most of the cases where it is used,
whether a proper name or a gentilic is meant. In the ancestry of the
prophet Zephaniah (i. 1) the word is certainly used of an individual,
and in an inscription from Ipsambul it is also used with a personal
reference (*CIS.* 112). Duhm thinks that a name of this kind might
be given to a child in remembrance of some incident connected with its
birth, for example *Cushi* might have been born during a visit to Ethiopia
on the part of one or both parents; this suggestion recalls the case of
St Francis of Assisi who was brought into the world whilst his father
was absent in France and baptised Giovanni, but on his parent's return
received the name of Francesco. The name *Cushi* is here probably one
of the ancestors of Jehudi though it is only usual for the ancestry of
really important people to be traced back beyond the father, and Jehudi
seems to have been only some kind of subordinate official. In consequence of this custom Cornill and other scholars would divide up
the names into two groups reading *Jehudi the son of Nethaniah and
Shelemiah the son of Cushi.*

15. *Sit down.* The princes behave in a courteous manner towards
Baruch, perhaps because he was of high social rank, or they may have
recognised his right to adopt the proper attitude of an Oriental teacher
(cf. Lk. iv. 20). On the whole they appear to have been friendly;
notice the warning in *v.* 19, and their leaving the roll behind them
when they reported its contents to the king. When in Jehoiakim's

Baruch read it in their ears. 16 Now it came to pass, when they had heard all the words, they turned in fear one toward another, and said unto Baruch, We will surely tell the king of all these words. 17 And they asked Baruch, saying, Tell us now, How didst thou write all these words at his mouth? 18 Then Baruch answered them, He pronounced all these words unto me with his mouth, and I wrote them with ink in the book. 19 Then said the princes unto Baruch, Go, hide thee, thou and Jeremiah; and let no man know where ye be. 20 And they went in to the king into the court; but they had laid up the roll in the chamber of Elishama the scribe; and they told all the words in the ears of the king. 21 So the king sent Jehudi to fetch the roll: and he took it out of the chamber of Elishama the scribe. And Jehudi read it in the ears of the king, and in the ears of all the princes which stood beside the king. 22 Now the king sat in the winter

presence, however, their better instincts seem to have been stifled by their fears.

16—20. The princes make close enquiries as to the origin of the roll and then advise Baruch to join Jeremiah in his hiding-place.

16. *unto Baruch.* LXX. rightly omits.

17. The princes are anxious to know all the facts of the case before reporting it to the king; they knew that Jeremiah was the person ultimately responsible for the prophecy, but evidently wished to discover whether he had composed the actual words.

at his mouth. Ewald follows LXX. and omits this expression.

18. *ink.* This is the only place where *ink* is mentioned in OT.; cf. 2 Jn. 12[1]. For the use of *ink* amongst the ancient Jews see W. Robertson Smith's note in *O. T. in Jew. Church*[2], p. 71.

19. *Go, hide thee.* It has been suggested that the hiding-place of the prophet and his companion was 'the Grotto of Jeremiah' outside the Damascus Gate (see *PEFQS.* 1912, p. 27).

20. *they had laid up the roll.* Perhaps they did not want the king to learn the actual words of the prophecy, but wished to preserve peace by giving him a general idea of its contents in a somewhat milder form.

21—26. Jehoiakim insists upon hearing the contents of the roll; and on his command being carried out he cuts the roll to pieces and burns it in the grate.

22. *winter house.* This was not as a rule a separate building but a part of the house used in the cold season, the interior or possibly the lower storey (see Harper on Am. iii. 15; and G. F. Moore on Jud. iii. 20).

---

[1] LXX. omits, possibly because the translators were ignorant of the meaning of the word.

B.   18

house in the ninth month: and *there was a fire in* the brasier burning before him. 23 And it came to pass, when Jehudi had read three or four ¹leaves, that *the king* cut it with the penknife, and cast it into the fire that was in the brasier, until all the roll was consumed in the fire that was in the brasier. 24 And they were not afraid, nor rent their garments, neither the king, nor any of his servants that heard all these words. 25 Moreover Elnathan and Delaiah and Gemariah had made intercession to the king that he would not burn the roll: but he would not hear them. 26 And the king commanded Jerahmeel ²the king's son,

¹ Or, *columns*   ² Or, *the son of Hammelech*

ninth month. The *ninth month* was one of piercing cold and wet (cf. Ezra x. 9).

the brasier. The Heb. text is incomplete, as the words supplied in italics shew. Brasiers of charcoal were placed in the houses of the wealthy, and the fire here was doubtless very like the one mentioned in Jn. xviii. 18, in connexion with St Peter's denial of our Lord. The temperature of Jerusalem varied very greatly, and owing to its height the nights were extremely cold.

23. *when...read.* Driver has suggested that in order to give full force to the imperfect of the original the translation should read *as often as Jehudi read three or four columns, he cut them.* This translation agrees with the statement that all the roll was consumed and also with the use of the knife. The action of the king exhibits the climax of rebellion against God, his cool contempt in destroying the prophecy, portion by portion, is more horrible than would have been a burst of fierce anger ending in his throwing the whole roll on the brasier.

leaves. The mg. *columns* is better; the word literally means doors and Cornill compares the similar use of the Arabic *bâb.*

penknife. Lit. *knife of a scribe*; it was used for making and mending the pen and perhaps also for erasures.

24. Cf. *v.* 16 and 2 K. xxii. 11. The latter passage is probably in the mind of the writer, as suggesting a contrast.

25. *Elnathan...not burn the roll.* According to the present text some of the princes overcame their lack of courage and endeavoured to bring the king to a better mind. LXX., however, omits the *not* and states that these princes *urged the king to burn the roll,* the words following *he would not hear them* are also omitted. This reading fits in better with *v.* 24 and is perhaps the original. For Elnathan's attitude on a previous occasion see xxvi. 22.

26. *the king's son.* i.e. a prince of the royal house. As Jehoiakim was only some thirty years old at the time *Jerahmeel* would scarcely be his offspring; moreover the natural way of representing the idea in

and Seraiah the son of Azriel, and Shelemiah the son of Abdeel, to take Baruch the scribe and Jeremiah the prophet: but the LORD hid them.

27 Then the word of the LORD came to Jeremiah, after that the king had burned the roll, and the words which Baruch wrote at the mouth of Jeremiah, saying, 28 Take thee again another roll, and write in it all the former words that were in the first roll, which Jehoiakim the king of Judah hath burned. 29 And concerning Jehoiakim king of Judah thou shalt say, Thus saith the LORD: Thou hast burned this roll, saying, Why hast thou written therein, saying, The king of Babylon shall certainly come and destroy this land, and shall cause to cease from thence man and beast? 30 Therefore thus saith the LORD concerning Jehoiakim king of Judah: He shall have none to sit upon the throne of David: and his dead body shall be cast out in the day to the heat, and in the night to the frost. 31 And I will punish him

Heb. would be simply to write *his son*. The mg. *Hammelech* is merely a transliteration of the Heb.

27—32. The prophet by God's command accepts the challenge implied in the burning of the roll, and re-writes it with the addition of fresh matter, including the announcement of the fate of the king and the destruction of the dynasty. Dean Stanley characteristically remarks that 'In this record...is contained the germ of the "Liberty of unlicensed Printing," the inexhaustible vitality of the written word[1].' Some critics see traces in this passage of later additions; and objection has been raised against the non-fulfilment, at any rate in the letter, of the prophecy in *v.* 30. But the fact that the forecast was not literally fulfilled is evidence in favour of the genuineness of the prophecy; a manufactured prophecy, we may be quite sure, would fit all the details of the actual event in the most exact manner.

30. *He shall have none.* The same threat has already been found in xxii. 19. Jehoiakim was in actual fact succeeded by his son Jehoiachin to whom the threat was also made (xxii. 30).

heat...frost. Cf. Gen. xxxi. 40 where Jacob says 'in the day the drought consumed me and the frost by night.' The climate of Palestine is noted for its great changes of temperature (see G. A. Smith, *Hist. Geog.* pp. 69 ff.). Dean Stanley quotes the Jewish legend that 'on the skin of the dead corpse, as it thus lay exposed, there appeared in distinct Hebrew characters the name of the demon Codonazer, to whom he had sold himself[2].'

---

[1] *The Jewish Church*, II. p. 456.   [2] *Op. cit.* II. p. 457.

and his seed and his servants for their iniquity; and I will bring
upon them, and upon the inhabitants of Jerusalem, and upon the
men of Judah, all the evil that I have pronounced against them,
but they hearkened not.   32 Then took Jeremiah another roll,
and gave it to Baruch the scribe, the son of Neriah; who wrote
therein from the mouth of Jeremiah all the words of the book
which Jehoiakim king of Judah had burned in the fire: and there
were added besides unto them many like words.

32.   *there were added* &c. God's punishments grow more severe
as His warnings are neglected and His messengers despised.   Dr Lock
points out to me the resemblance in teaching between this incident
and the legend of the Sibylline Books. In the classical story the books
are burnt by the Sibyl herself because their value is not recognised
by Tarquin who in the end has to pay for the three remaining volumes
the same price as for the original nine; the message of the Deity being
despised the terms became more severe.

CHAPTERS XXXVII.—XXXVIII. 28 *a*.

Warnings and Persecutions.

These chh. are made up of a collection of various incidents in which Jeremiah
took part during the second siege of Jerusalem (588—586 B.C.). They are a
record of the advice which the prophet continually gave to the people and their
leaders, and of the suffering which he had to undergo in consequence of his
faithfulness and courage. The section may be divided as follows:

(*a*)   *The Chaldeans shall return.* 1—10.
(*b*)   *Jeremiah is arrested as a deserter and imprisoned.* 11—15.
(*c*)   *Zedekiah sends to consult him and regards his plea for better treat-*
        ment. 16—21.
(*d*)   *Jeremiah is cast into a dungeon.* xxxviii. 1—6.
(*e*)   *The kindness of Ebed-melech the Ethiopian.* 7—13.
(*f*)   *Jeremiah appeals to the king to surrender.* 14—18.
(*g*)   *The king's fears and the prophet's warnings.* 19—23.
(*h*)   *Zedekiah's request for secrecy.* 24—28a.

XXXVII. 1 And Zedekiah the son of Josiah reigned as

XXXVII. 1—10. After an introduction (*vv.* 1—2) an account is
given of Jeremiah's warning that although the Chaldeans had retired
from the city, yet they would surely return and not leave it until they
had captured and burnt it. There is a somewhat similar narrative in
xxi. and for the relation between the two incidents see the introduction

king, instead of ¹Coniah the son of Jehoiakim, whom Nebuchadrezzar king of Babylon made king in the land of Judah. 2 But
neither he, nor his servants, nor the people of the land, did hearken
unto the words of the LORD, which he spake by the prophet
Jeremiah.

3 And Zedekiah the king sent Jehucal the son of Shelemiah,
and Zephaniah the son of Maaseiah the priest, to the prophet
Jeremiah, saying, Pray now unto the LORD our God for us.
4 Now Jeremiah came in and went out among the people: for
they had not put him into prison. 5 And Pharaoh's army was

¹ See ch. xxii. 24.

to that ch. Cornill suggests, in *SBOT.*, that this section should be
combined with xxxiv. as follows: xxxiv. 1—7, xxxvii. 5, 3, 6—10,
xxxiv. 8—22.

1 f. These *vv.* seem rather strange introducing as they do the
accession of Zedekiah as if he had not been mentioned before. There
are two explanations either of which may account for their presence:
that (*a*) they are an editorial addition to mark the return from the
reign of Jehoiakim to that of Zedekiah, or else (*b*) chh. xxxvii.—
xxxviii. were circulated independently and the heading is original.

1. *Coniah.* See on xxii. 24.

2. *people of the land.* A common post-exilic phrase, used also in
Ez. vii. 27, xii. 19, &c.

3. *Jehucal.* In xxxviii. 1—6 a certain Jucal, son of Shelemiah, is
given as one of the princes who tried to have Jeremiah put to death:
Jehucal and Jucal are probably the same person.

Zephaniah. See on xxi. 1, xxix. 25.

Pray now &c. This action on the part of Zedekiah is hard to
explain. According to xxxiv. 11 the princes and the people were so
certain that the danger was permanently averted that they immediately
broke their covenant with the slaves and took them once more into
bondage. It seems strange therefore that a deputation should be sent
to Jeremiah asking for his prayers at this particular moment. Cornill
suggests that the king was not acting in good faith but merely wished
to taunt the prophet on the failure of his forecasts; such an act seems
hardly consistent with what is reported of Zedekiah in other passages,
and the suggestion can hardly be accepted. On the other hand it must
not be forgotten that Zedekiah was undoubtedly influenced by Jeremiah, and evidently recognised that the situation was as critical as
ever, and that the insight into the future which the prophet had shewn
himself to possess might be extremely useful in facing the problems
which were bound to arise. It is necessary to make a distinction between the people with their impulsive and unthinking optimism and
the somewhat superstitious and timid monarch.

5. *Pharaoh's army.* Hophra was the name of this Egyptian monarch

come forth out of Egypt: and when the Chaldeans that besieged Jerusalem heard tidings of them, they brake up from Jerusalem. 6 Then came the word of the LORD unto the prophet Jeremiah, saying, 7 Thus saith the LORD, the God of Israel: Thus shall ye say to the king of Judah, that sent you unto me to inquire of me; Behold, Pharaoh's army, which is come forth to help you, shall return to Egypt into their own land. 8 And the Chaldeans shall come again, and fight against this city; and they shall take it, and burn it with fire. 9 Thus saith the LORD: Deceive not [1]yourselves, saying, The Chaldeans shall surely depart from us: for they shall not depart. 10 For though ye had smitten the whole army of the Chaldeans that fight against you, and there remained but [2]wounded men among them, yet should they rise up every man in his tent, and burn this city with fire.

11 And it came to pass that when the army of the Chaldeans was broken up from Jerusalem for fear of Pharaoh's army, 12 then Jeremiah went forth out of Jerusalem to go into the land of Benjamin, to receive his portion [3]there, in the midst of the

[1] Heb. *your souls*.　　[2] Heb. *thrust through*.　　[3] Heb. *from thence*.

and he probably reigned from 588—569 B.C.; by Herodotus and Diodorus he is called, rather less accurately, Apries. See further on xliv. 30.

7. The reasons for the retreat of the Egyptian army are not known, perhaps disaffection broke out amongst them or possibly an unsuccessful action was fought (cf. Ez. xxx. 21).

9 f. The exaggerated language of these *vv.* is no argument against their genuineness.

10. *wounded.* Mg. *thrust through*; the reference is not to slightly wounded men, but to those who had been stabbed again and again (cf. Abimelech, Jud. ix. 54); the same word is used in li. 4 in parallelism with 'slain.'

An interesting parallel to this prophecy is to be found in the history of the Indian Mutiny. At a time when the British power seemed broken a native prince sent to his astrologer to enquire as to what would finally be the issue of the mutiny, and he received the startling reply 'If all the Europeans save one are slain, that one will remain and fight and reconquer.'

11—15. Jeremiah on attempting to go down to his native village is arrested as a deserter and placed in prison.

12. *to receive his portion.* The meaning of Heb. is not quite clear. Driver paraphrases *to receive an inheritance*; possibly the prophet's journey had something to do with the subsequent sale to him of the family property (xxxii. 6 ff.).

people. 13 And when he was in the gate of Benjamin, a captain
of the ward was there, whose name was Irijah, the son of Shelemiah, the son of Hananiah; and he laid hold on Jeremiah the
prophet, saying, Thou fallest away to the Chaldeans. 14 Then
said Jeremiah, It is false; I fall not away to the Chaldeans;
but he hearkened not to him: so Irijah laid hold on Jeremiah,
and brought him to the princes. 15 And the princes were wroth
with Jeremiah, and smote him, and put him in prison in the house
of Jonathan the scribe; for they had made that the prison.
16 When Jeremiah was come into the ¹dungeon house, and into
the cells, and Jeremiah had remained there many days; 17 then
Zedekiah the king sent, and fetched him: and the king asked

---

¹ Or, *house of the pit*

13. *gate of Benjamin.* On the north of the city; see xxxviii. 7
and Zech. xiv. 10.

Irijah...Hananiah. Nothing further is known of *Irijah* nor does
the name occur elsewhere. *Hananiah* is almost certainly not the false
prophet of xxviii. 1 ff. who must have been a younger man.

Thou fallest away. As the prophet advised others to seek safety
with the Babylonians (xxi. 9), and as many had done so (xxxviii. 19),
it was the natural thing for Irijah to conclude that Jeremiah was
deserting.

15. *the princes were wroth.* These princes behaved in a much more
violent and unjust manner than their predecessors under Jehoiakim,
and no doubt helped to confirm Jeremiah's opinion as to the respective
merits of the exiles and the people who remained (xxiv.).   It is very
probable that the real reason for the imprisonment and ill-treatment of
the prophet was his interfering on behalf of the re-enslaved serfs (xxxiv.);
and that the accusation of falling away to the enemy was trumped up
for the occasion, more especially as it was a charge which could be supported from his own utterances.

16—21. Zedekiah sends for Jeremiah desiring to receive from him
a message of hope; the prophet can give him no comfort, but makes
an appeal on his own behalf for milder treatment, this appeal the king
allows. The incident dealt with in this section in spite of the few words
in which it is narrated is exceedingly vivid, the anxiety of the king, on
the one hand, and the fearlessness of the prophet, on the other, are
brought out with striking force.

16. *dungeon house.* The mg. gives the literal translation of the
original *house of the pit*; cf. xxxviii. 6; Ex. xii. 29; some kind of subterranean prison is meant.

17. Zedekiah, like Saul, felt the need for some word from the Lord
and his own inability to obtain it (cf. 1 S. xxviii. 6). He seems also

him secretly in his house, and said, Is there any word from the
LORD? And Jeremiah said, There is. He said also, Thou shalt be
delivered into the hand of the king of Babylon. 18 Moreover
Jeremiah said unto king Zedekiah, Wherein have I sinned against
thee, or against thy servants, or against this people, that ye have
put me in prison? 19 Where now are your prophets which
prophesied unto you, saying, The king of Babylon shall not come
against you, nor against this land? 20 And now hear, I pray
thee, O my lord the king: let my supplication, I pray thee, ¹be
accepted before thee; that thou cause me not to return to the
house of Jonathan the scribe, lest I die there. 21 Then Zedekiah
the king commanded, and they committed Jeremiah into the
court of the guard, and they gave him daily a loaf of bread out

¹ Heb. *fall.*

to have nourished the vain hope that God's purposes might have
changed since the last message from the prophet, and that conditions
might be easier; the return of the besiegers had evidently thrown him
into a state of desperate panic.

secretly. Perhaps the king thought that in a private interview he
might obtain a more favourable message than in a public utterance.
At the same time he was afraid of the scorn and rebukes of the princes
(cf. xxxviii. 5, 24 ff.).

He said also. Omit with LXX. The prophet did not keep the king
in suspense, but his answer flashed back like a sword-thrust.

18. Jeremiah, in spite of his inability to gratify the king, now
makes an appeal on his own behalf. It is rather remarkable that the
prophet is able to make this appeal which the king could grant only at
some risk to himself, and that he should place so much reliance on
honourable treatment by Zedekiah. The reproof must have fallen
heavily on the king, extinguishing as it did his last hopes of preserving his independence, and it is hard to withhold a certain amount
of pity from him and his feeble efforts to do what was right.

19. *Where now are.* The siege has been renewed and the vain
forecasts of the false prophets have been proved to be vain.

21. *court of the guard.* See on xxxii. 2.

loaf of bread. The staple food of the Hebrews, as of Western
nations, was *bread* (the same Heb. word is used for *bread* and for *food*)
and both OT. and NT. contain many references to its manufacture both
in the household and, as in this *v.*, by tradesmen. The *loaf* here mentioned is 'a small round cake or *bannock*' and it would form but a
scanty ration for a grown man; food was evidently getting scarce in
the besieged city (cf. lii. 6).

of the bakers' street, until all the bread in the city was spent. Thus Jeremiah remained in the court of the guard.

XXXVIII. 1 And Shephatiah the son of Mattan, and Gedaliah the son of Pashhur, and Jucal the son of Shelemiah, and Pashhur the son of Malchijah, heard the words that Jeremiah spake unto all the people, saying, 2 Thus saith the LORD, He that abideth in this city shall die by the sword, by the famine, and by the pestilence: but he that goeth forth to the Chaldeans shall live, and his life shall be unto him for a prey, and he shall live. 3 Thus saith the LORD, This city shall surely be given into the hand of the army of the king of Babylon, and he shall take it. 4 Then the princes said unto the king, Let this man, we pray thee, be put to death; forasmuch as he weakeneth the hands of the men of war that remain in this city, and the hands of all the people, in speaking such words unto them: for this man seeketh not the welfare of this people, but the hurt. 5 And Zedekiah the king said, Behold, he is in your hand: for the king is not

---

the bakers' street. In the East each trade has its own street or quarter. Baking was a special trade in the cities (cf. Hos. vii. 4, 6; Joseph, *Ant.* xv. ix. 2).

XXXVIII.1—6. The prophet is cast into an underground dungeon by the command of the princes who accuse him of weakening the hands of the defenders of the city. If this section is in its right order Jeremiah did not long enjoy the comparative freedom granted to him by the king; *v.* 21 of the previous chapter seems to suggest that the dole of bread to Jeremiah continued till the end of the siege and that the prophet remained in the court of the guard.

1. *Shephatiah.* Not mentioned elsewhere.

Gedaliah the son of Pashhur. This prince may have been the son of Jeremiah's old enemy (cf. xx. 1—3).

Jucal. The same as Jehucal in xxxvii. 3.

Pashhur. See on xxi. 1.

all the people. This statement suggests that the prophet is at liberty.

2. This *v.* is almost identical with xxi. 9 and many critics think that it is derived from thence.

4. The attitude of Jeremiah during the siege must have been, to say the least of it, a great trial to those responsible for the defence, and his only justification was the consciousness that he was not expressing his own private opinion but what he felt to be the revealed will of God.

that remain. The ranks of the defenders had been thinned by death and disease as well as by desertions (cf. *v.* 19).

5. *the king* &c. Zedekiah was powerless in face of the predomi-

he that can do any thing against you. 6 Then took they Jeremiah, and cast him into the [1]dungeon of Malchijah [2]the king's son, that was in the court of the guard: and they let down Jeremiah with cords. And in the dungeon there was no water, but mire: and Jeremiah sank in the mire. 7 Now when Ebed-melech the Ethiopian, an eunuch, which was in the king's house, heard that they had put Jeremiah in the dungeon; the king then sitting in the gate of Benjamin; 8 Ebed-melech went forth out of the king's

---

[1] Or, *pit*   [2] Or, *the son of Hammelech*

---

nant war party, and handed over the prophet to them without a struggle. The text of LXX. is perhaps better which reads *for the king was not able...them.* Dr Peake remarks that Zedekiah gave no permission to inflict the death penalty; but surely the power of the princes was so great as to make such permission unnecessary, and Jeremiah owed his escape from instant execution more to his reputation as a prophet whose forecasts had been confirmed by actual events than to any half-hearted attempts at protection on the part of the king.

6. *the dungeon of Malchijah.* The place into which the unfortunate prophet was cast was probably a *pit* or *cistern* (see mg.) for storing water such as was usually to be found in an Eastern house. The intention of the princes was evidently that Jeremiah should die there either from starvation or from suffocation as the depth of mud at the bottom of the pit was considerable (cf. *v.* 10).

7—13. Jeremiah is rescued from the persecutions of his own countrymen by Ebed-Melech an Ethiopian eunuch, who with the king's permission has the prophet drawn out of the pit.

7. *Ebed-melech.* This man was an *eunuch* and his presence in the court was a sign of the spread in Judah of that degraded and luxurious civilisation which was in part responsible for the downfall of the nation. Cheyne, however, thinks that the Heb. word *saris* may also be used of a court officer or a captain (see *Enc. Bib.* 1427), so also Jensen (*Zeit. Assyr.* VII. 174) who connects it with the Assyrian *sa-resi* = he who is head. It is probable that Ebed-melech was in charge of the women's quarters and that he was actually an *eunuch.* For a note on *Ethiopia* see on xiii. 23, and for the prophet's gratitude to his deliverer see xxxix. 15 ff.[1].

gate of Benjamin. To the north of the city and therefore a point of importance and danger.

---

[1] Cheyne (*Life and Times*, p. 174) looks upon *Ebed-melech* as a title; 'His true name we know not; he passed among the Jews as "King's slave"—Ebedmelech.' עבד מלך, however, is almost certainly a proper name (so LXX. 'Αβδεμέλεχ) as the office would require the definite article עבד המלך (cf. 2 K. xxii. 12, where the office is evidently a high one; see Stade, *Gesch. Isr.* I. p. 650).

house, and spake to the king, saying, 9 My lord the king, these men have done evil in all that they have done to Jeremiah the prophet, whom they have cast into the dungeon; and [1]he is like to die in the place where he is because of the famine: for there is no more bread in the city.   10 Then the king commanded Ebed-melech the Ethiopian, saying, Take from hence thirty men with thee, and take up Jeremiah the prophet out of the dungeon, before he die.   11 So Ebed-melech took the men with him, and went into the house of the king under the treasury, and took thence old cast clouts and old rotten rags, and let them down by cords into the dungeon to Jeremiah.   12 And Ebed-melech the Ethiopian said unto Jeremiah, Put now these old cast clouts and rotten rags under thine armholes under the cords.   And Jeremiah did so.   13 So they drew up Jeremiah with the cords, and took him up out of the dungeon: and Jeremiah remained in the court of the guard.

14 Then Zedekiah the king sent, and took Jeremiah the

---

[1] Heb. *he is dead.*

9.   *because of the famine.*   Whilst it is quite true that Jeremiah from his position would be liable to miss his share of the rations yet the explanation offered in this clause is not sufficient to account for the great haste which seemed to be necessary in order to save the prophet's life.   The obvious reason was that as the prophet became weaker he would gradually sink in the mire and be smothered.

10.   *thirty.*   Ewald long ago suggested that the number should be *three*, which would be quite sufficient for the task, and indeed probably as many as could be reasonably spared for it.   The MT. as it stands is irregular as according to Heb. usage nouns following 'tens' should be in the singular.

12.   *Put now these* &c.   LXX. omits *old cast clouts...armholes*, and Duhm prefers its reading to that of MT.

14—28 *a.*   This section as a whole has been accepted as genuine by practically all critics, mainly on account of the minute and exact knowledge which is exhibited in it.   Peake says, for example, that it is 'unquestionably trustworthy. Its information is too precise to come from any but a first-hand source.'   It is quite true that exact details are given of the conversation between the king and Jeremiah and of the place where the interview took place; but there are no means left to scholars by which the details concerning the latter can be either confirmed or denied (see on *v.* 14), and the report of what happened at a secret meeting naturally enough admits of no verification, it can only be judged by the test of what was probable and what was not.   On the whole the report of the intercourse between the prophet and Zedekiah is not convincing. The following reasons against its genuineness have been advanced by Dr Buttenwieser (*op. cit.* pp. 55 ff.):—(*a*) The account is based on the similar secret interview contained in xxxvii. 17—21. This interview followed Jeremiah's imprisonment in the dungeon of Jonathan and the prophet during his conversation with the king begged not to be sent back to the dungeon (xxxvii. 20) which was quite natural under the circumstances. In xxxviii. 26 Zedekiah tells the prophet to account for his interview—that is an interview which purports to have occurred after the rescue from the cistern—by saying that he had made this very petition to the king. In the conversation recorded in xxxviii. 14 ff. there is no trace of such a request. It is possible that the writer of the account confused the two imprisonments, though, at the same time, as the statement suggested to the prophet by Zedekiah was only an excuse there is no reason why it should have been a true one (on this point see on *v.* 27). (*b*) The second objection lies against the manner in which Jeremiah is depicted. He will not reveal his message to the king until he has demanded an oath from him safeguarding his life; the king is afraid that he will not reveal the whole truth (*vv.* 14 ff.). Now it may be admitted that Jeremiah was naturally of a timid disposition, and that his terrible experiences may have undermined his courage, but Zedekiah must have known him sufficiently well to be fully aware that no fears for himself would make the prophet keep back a word of his message, and it is almost impossible to imagine that one whose faith in God was so great as that of Jeremiah needed the oath of a feeble sovereign like Zedekiah before he would declare his message; the narrative itself shews what value was to be attached to the king's protection (cf. *vv.* 24 ff.). (*c*) Although the interview is said to have been a secret one it is known to the princes immediately (as the king himself seemed to anticipate), and they are full of curiosity to know what has taken place. Such curiosity on the part of the princes is most unlikely as they regarded the prophet with a contempt which was perhaps even greater than their contempt for the king himself. (*d*) Dr Buttenwieser also condemns the description of the conduct of the harem on the occasion of the fall of the city which is put into the mouth of Jeremiah (*vv.* 22 f.). 'Is it credible,' he asks, 'that Jeremiah, whose sensitive soul suffered agonies at every thought of his people's doom, could have conceived such an unnatural and revolting scene as is this picture of the women of the King's harem coming forth to jeer at the degradation of their lord....A picture so psychologically untrue could not have suggested itself to Jeremiah. He would have known instinctively that in that hour of misery and despair those women, however frivolous, would not be in the mood for derision. Had he chosen to harrow the mind of the King with a picture of his women on that day, he would most certainly have painted the grim reality, as Amos in his prophecy to Amaziah—"Thy wife will be ravished in the city."' (*e*) Finally the advice to Zedekiah to surrender is suspicious and is not found in

prophet unto him into the third entry that is in the house of the
LORD: and the king said unto Jeremiah, I will ask thee a thing;
hide nothing from me. 15 Then Jeremiah said unto Zedekiah,
If I declare it unto thee, wilt thou not surely put me to death?
and if I give thee counsel, thou wilt not hearken unto me. 16 So
Zedekiah the king sware secretly unto Jeremiah, saying, As the
LORD liveth, that made us this soul, I will not put thee to death,
neither will I give thee into the hand of these men that seek thy
life. 17 Then said Jeremiah unto Zedekiah, Thus saith the LORD,
the God of hosts, the God of Israel: If thou wilt go forth unto
the king of Babylon's princes, then thy soul shall live, and this
city shall not be burned with fire; and thou shalt live, and thine
house: 18 but if thou wilt not go forth to the king of Babylon's
princes, then shall this city be given into the hand of the Chaldeans,

the earlier account: it is almost certain also that the king was quite
without the necessary power of adopting such a policy, and that any
attempt on his part to do so would have led to his dethronement at
the hands of the princes. His supposed excuse is too feeble even for
the lips of Zedekiah. He must have known that had he surrendered,
his fears for his dignity would not have been on account of the taunts
of his compatriots but from the indignities of the Chaldeans. To sum
up it may be said that it would be difficult for anyone who compared
the accounts of the two interviews, that in xxxvii. 17—21 and that in
the present passage, to imagine that they took place between the same
people; and if the question were asked as to which best suited the
character of the prophet, would there be any hesitation in deciding on
the authentic record?

14—18. Following upon a request by Zedekiah for counsel, Jeremiah advises the king to surrender.

14. *the third entry.* This place is unknown and such a description
is not used elsewhere. Giesebrecht suggested that it might be *the
entry of the body-guard*, a reading which can be obtained by a slight
change in the Heb. (cf. 2 K. xi. 19).

16. *secretly.* LXX. omits.

As the LORD liveth &c. To take an oath by Jehovah was not
a breach of the third commandment; cf. iv. 2; Dt. vi. 13, x. 20. The
form of the oath is strange; *that made us this soul* means *that gave us
life* (cf. Is. lvii. 16).

17. *go forth.* This can hardly have been intended as a plea that
the king should desert, the soul of even such a man as Zedekiah would
have revolted against the suggestion. The alternative is that the king
was urged to surrender; on the difficulty of so doing see above.

king of Babylon's princes. Nebuchadrezzar was not present in
person (cf. xxxix. 5).

and they shall burn it with fire, and thou shalt not escape out of their hand. 19 And Zedekiah the king said unto Jeremiah, I am afraid of the Jews that are fallen away to the Chaldeans, lest they deliver me into their hand, and they mock me. 20 But Jeremiah said, They shall not deliver thee. Obey, I beseech thee, the voice of the LORD, in that which I speak unto thee: so it shall be well with thee, and thy soul shall live. 21 But if thou refuse to go forth, this is the word that the LORD hath shewed me: 22 Behold, all the women that are left in the king of Judah's house shall be brought forth to the king of Babylon's princes, and those women shall say, ¹Thy familiar friends have ²set thee on, and have prevailed over thee: *now that* thy feet are sunk in the mire, they are turned away back. 23 And they shall bring out all thy wives and thy children to the Chaldeans: and thou shalt not escape out of their hand, but shalt be taken by the hand of the king of Babylon: and ³thou shalt cause this city to be burned with fire. 24 Then said Zedekiah unto Jeremiah, Let no man

---

¹ Heb. *The men of thy peace.*   ² Or, *deceived thee*   ³ Heb. *thou shalt burn &c.*

19—23. The king's fears are brushed aside and terrible warnings put in their place.

19. *afraid.* The Heb. word is rather uncommon, it is generally used of *anxiety*, or *worry* rather than of actual fear. The root is the same as that from which Doeg is derived (1 S. xxi. 8, &c.).

mock. Better *make a toy of me, divert themselves with me.*

22. *all the women* &c. The usual fate of the harem; cf. Sennacherib's boast that he had taken from Hezekiah 'his daughters, female inmates of his palace and female slaves.'

Thy familiar friends &c. The last part of this *v.* forms two strophes of a Qinah measure. Budde (*HDB.* 'Heb. Poetry') thinks that this measure was used by the women especially, either in lamentation for the dead, or in taunt-songs as here. The first line appears again in Obad. 7 where it is almost certainly borrowed from this passage (see Brewer, *Obad.* p. 6).

mire. Cf. *v.* 6. The connexion may only be artificial as the figure here used is that of a wayfarer who strays into a bog and is then deserted by his fellow-travellers.

23. This *v.* is rejected by Duhm as redundant.

24—28 *a.* Zedekiah warns the prophet to keep the subject matter of the interview secret and provides him with an answer to any enquiries which may be made by the princes.

24. There seems no point in Zedekiah's warning as the prophet

know of these words, and thou shalt not die. 25 But if the princes hear that I have talked with thee, and they come unto thee, and say unto thee, Declare unto us now what thou hast said unto the king; hide it not from us, and we will not put thee to death: also what the king said unto thee: 26 then thou shalt say unto them, I ¹presented my supplication before the king, that he would not cause me to return to Jonathan's house, to die there. 27 Then came all the princes unto Jeremiah, and asked him: and he told them according to all these words that the king had commanded. So they left off speaking with him; for the matter was not ²perceived. 28 So Jeremiah abode in the court of the guard until the day that Jerusalem was taken.

¹ Heb. *caused to fall.*   ² Or, *reported*

had declared from the first that the city was to fall. His persistence, however, might constitute an aggravation of his crime.

26. Critics have displayed much ingenuity in defending Jeremiah from the charge of deception, probably quite unnecessarily, as it is almost certain that the account here given of the prophet's action is not authentic. At the same time OT. furnishes many examples of actual deceit (cf. the threefold story in Gen. xii. 12, xx. 1, xxvi. 7; and the blessing of Jacob, Gen. xxvii. 19; also Rahab's treachery in Josh. i.).

27. 'They questioned Jeremiah, and Jeremiah lied quite calmly.' Duhm.

CHAPTERS XXXVIII. 28 *b*—XXXIX. 14.

The Fall of Jerusalem.

This section is full of difficulties and the greater part of it is missing from LXX. As the previous chh. dealt with the fortunes of Jeremiah during the siege, an account of what befell the prophet when the Babylonians actually entered the city would have been the natural sequel; such an account is indeed presented in this passage but it has been so overlaid by other matter that to a casual reader the fate of Zedekiah and of the people in general is the important subject of the narrative. The fate of the king and people is however dealt with at some length elsewhere in the book (see lii.), and much of the matter contained in the present ch. has the appearance of being taken from the account in that ch. Duhm, Cornill, and Giesebrecht accept only *vv.* 3 and 14 in xxxix. as genuine. This involves the rejection of three groups of *vv.*: (*a*) *vv.* 1, 2; (*b*) *vv.* 4—10; (*c*) *vv.* 11—13. The first group interrupt the sequence between xxxviii. 28 *b* and xxxix. 3 and seem to be a note of time introduced from lii. 4—7 (2 K. xxv. 1—4); there can be little doubt that they are a gloss and should be omitted.

The second group of *vv.* are missing from LXX. and they connect awkwardly with the rest of the passage : (i) *v.* 4 makes the flight of Zedekiah subsequent to the entry of the princes and their taking up a position in the middle gate, whereas lii. 7 says that the men of war fled when the first breach was made; (ii) the princes mentioned in *v.* 3 are ignored in the rest of the passage, and Nebuzaradan —who is not mentioned in the list—is apparently in charge of the fallen city. But according to lii. 12 Nebuzaradan did not arrive in Jerusalem until a month after it had been captured. The third group of *vv.* are actually concerned with Jeremiah, but it is very doubtful whether Nebuchadrezzar would be at pains to give special instructions about the prophet; further they are, with the previous group, missing from LXX.; and Nebuzaradan is likewise mentioned in them. At the same time the grounds for rejection are not so strong as in the case of *vv.* 1, 2 and 4—10 and the present writer shares Giesebrecht's hesitation in re- jecting them.

And it came to pass when Jerusalem was taken, **XXXIX.** 1 [1] (in the ninth year of Zedekiah king of Judah, in the tenth month, came Nebuchadrezzar king of Babylon and all his army against Jerusalem, and besieged it; 2 in the eleventh year of Zedekiah, in the fourth month, the ninth day of the month, a breach was made in the city:) 3 that all the princes of the king of Babylon came in, and sat in the middle gate, even Nergal-sharezer, Samgar-nebo, Sarsechim, [2] Rab-saris, Nergal-sharezer, [2] Rab-mag,

---

[1] See ch. lii. 4, &c., 2 Kings xxv. 1—12.   [2] Titles of officers.

XXXIX. 3. *sat.* The word suggests that the capture of the city was completed and that the princes met in conference to decide matters connected with its fate.

middle gate. The situation of this gate is not known.

Nergal-sharezer &c. The names in this *v.* have been the source of much trouble to critics and it is very hard to say to what extent they are personal or official designations. In *v.* 13 only two princes are mentioned and each of them has an official title after his name; Hitzig regards this shorter list as the original and looks upon the present *v.* as a corruption of it. It seems possible that by mistake *Nergal-sharezer* has got into the list twice, *Samgar* being a corruption of Sar-mag = Rab-mag, i.e. the office of Nergal-sharezer in both the other places in which he is mentioned. If *Samgar-nebo* is a proper name it is the only instance of *nebo* occurring in the second half of a name; at the same time it is possible that *Samgar* is related in some way to Shamgar (Jud. iii. 31) and possibly to the king of Gargamish named Sangar (see Tiele, *Babyl.-assyr. Gesch.* p. 175). *Sarsechim* is unknown and is probably a corruption of *shazban* (*v.* 13) and by com- bining it with the previous *nebo(u)* the reading Nebushazban is obtained. The second mention of *Nergal-sharezer*, who is perhaps the Nergal-

with all the rest of the princes of the king of Babylon. 4 And
it came to pass that when Zedekiah the king of Judah and all
the men of war saw them, then they fled, and went forth out of
the city by night, by the way of the king's garden, by the gate
betwixt the two walls: and he went out the way of the Arabah.
5 But the army of the Chaldeans pursued after them, and overtook Zedekiah in the plains of Jericho: and when they had taken
him, they brought him up to Nebuchadrezzar king of Babylon to
Riblah in the land of Hamath, and he [1]gave judgement upon him.
6 Then the king of Babylon slew the sons of Zedekiah in Riblah
before his eyes: also the king of Babylon slew all the nobles of

---

[1] Heb. *spake judgements with him.*   See ch. xii. 1.

---

shar-usar who succeeded Amil-marduk on the throne of Babylon, is due
to the effort of a scribe who missed his name from the already corrupted
text and added it in order to make the *v.* agree with *v.* 13.

Rab-saris.   The meaning of this title is either *chief of the eunuchs*
or better *of the heads* (see on xxxviii. 7).

Rab-mag.   Probably *chief of the soothsayers* or perhaps *of the
princes*; Cheyne says that in the Assyrian character *Mag = rabu =
prince.*

4.   *the king's garden.*   According to Neh. iii. 15 this was near the
wall of the pool of Siloam.

the two walls.   The same phrase is used in Is. xxii. 11 in a passage
describing the construction of a reservoir—probably the pool of Siloam
(see above)—as part of the measures which were taken to defend
Jerusalem against a siege.   The *walls* were evidently in existence
before the pool was made—unless the wording of Is. xxii. 11 is decep-
tive—and therefore the suggestion that a second wall was built to
defend the pool is probably mistaken.   The reference is almost certainly to the walls of the Tyropoeon valley, the one running along its
edge on the western side, the other running across the mouth of the
valley (see G. A. Smith, *Jerusalem*, I. pp. 220 ff.).

the Arabah.   The deep valley of the Jordan to the north of the
Dead Sea.   The name is also applied to the depression to the south
running down to the Gulf of Akaba (Dt. i. 1), and in modern times
exclusively so.   The king's object was evidently to reach the trans-
Jordanic region, perhaps hoping to find refuge there as Ish-bosheth did
from the Philistines (2 S. ii. 8 ff.), and David from Absalom (2 S. xvii.
22 ff.).

5.   *Riblah.*   The name survives in the small modern village of
Ribleh situated on the Orontes some fifty miles south of Hamath.   In
ancient times it was a position of great strategic importance as being
the ' gateway into Southern Syria from the North.'   It had been used as

Judah. 7 Moreover he put out Zedekiah's eyes, and bound him
in fetters, to carry him to Babylon. 8 And the Chaldeans burned
the king's house, and the houses of the people, with fire, and
brake down the walls of Jerusalem. 9 Then Nebuzaradan the
[1]captain of the guard carried away captive into Babylon the
residue of the people that remained in the city, the deserters
also, that fell away to him, and the residue of the people that
remained. 10 But Nebuzaradan the captain of the guard left of
the poor of the people, which had nothing, in the land of Judah,
and gave them vineyards and fields at the same time. 11 Now
Nebuchadrezzar king of Babylon gave charge concerning Jere-

[1] See Gen. xxxvii. 36.

headquarters by Pharaoh Necho (2 K. xxiii. 33) as well as by Nebuchadrezzar[1].

7. *he put out Zedekiah's eyes.* This cruel form of punishment is
found in all parts of the world and survived into the Middle Ages in
Europe. An added torture was to arrange that the victim should
witness some horrible sight before being blinded as was the case with
Zedekiah. The punishment was borrowed by the Venetians from the
East as a punishment of Doges who had shewn especial incapacity.
Ruskin describes it as 'grave in judgment; in the perfectness of it,
joined with infliction of grievous sight before the infliction of grievous
blindness; that so the last memory of this world's light might remain
a grief.' *St Mark's Rest,* § 78.

fetters. As the blinded king was incapable of making his escape,
the chains were merely a mark of indignity.

8. In ancient warfare, when the hold on conquered territory was
often very slight, the policy of unlimited plunder and damage was
generally pursued. The spoil too of the fallen city was the expected
reward of the victorious army.

9. *the guard.* The Heb. word means literally *the slaughterers,*
and is even used of the cook who had to slay the animals which he
prepared for the table (1 S. ix. 23 f.). Here and in Gen. xxxvii. it is
used of the royal bodyguard.

10. *vineyards and fields.* The representative of a foreign conqueror restored to the poor of the land the possessions which their
fathers had lost to the greed of the rich.

11. If the information given in this *v.* is correct Nebuchadrezzar

[1] Cf. Dean Stanley's description in *The Jewish Church,* ii. p. 448, 'On the banks of
a mountain stream, in the midst of a vast and fertile plain at a central point, where
across the desert the roads diverge to the Euphrates, or along the coast, or through
the vale of Coele Syria to Palestine and the South, no more advantageous place of
encampment could be imagined.'

miah to Nebuzaradan the captain of the guard, saying, 12 Take
him, and look well to him, and do him no harm; but do unto
him even as he shall say unto thee.   13 So Nebuzaradan the
captain of the guard sent, and Nebushazban, Rab-saris, and
Nergal-sharezer, Rab-mag, and all the chief officers of the king
of Babylon; 14 they sent, and took Jeremiah out of the court
of the guard, and committed him unto Gedaliah the son of Ahikam,
the son of Shaphan, that he should carry him home: so he dwelt
among the people.

recognised that Jeremiah had rendered valuable services to the Babylonians; his knowledge of the prophet may have been derived, either
directly or indirectly, from the deserters who had gone over to the
Babylonians.

13.   See on *v.* 3.

14.   *Gedaliah.*   See on xxvi. 24.

home.   To his own house probably, not to the temple as Hitzig
supposed.

Chapter XXXIX. 15—18.

The Message to Ebed-melech.

This section is evidently a supplement to the account of Jeremiah's life
during the siege, and it owes its place here to the desire of the editor to complete
the story of the siege before giving this account of the prophet's benefactor.
The authenticity of the narrative has been denied by Duhm and Cornill as well
as by other critics, but if it is not a genuine story there seems to have been
little point in inventing it.   The deed of kindness for which Ebed-melech is
rewarded, and which no doubt required much courage, was described in xxxviii.
7—13; probably this prophecy was uttered soon after the performance of the
deed to which it refers.   The teaching of it is, that acts of kindness to His
servants, whether they be small or great, do not go unnoticed by God (cf. Matt.
x. 40 ff., xxv. 31—46).   The final end of Ebed-melech is not known; he may have
gone to Babylon with the other exiles, or perhaps he was among those eunuchs
who were taken into Egypt (xli. 16).   There is a promise to eunuchs as a class
in Is. lvi. 3 ff. and in NT. they were not unblessed: cf. Acts viii. 25 ff.

15 Now the word of the Lord came unto Jeremiah, while he
was shut up in the court of the guard, saying, 16 Go, and speak
to Ebed-melech the Ethiopian, saying, Thus saith the Lord of
hosts, the God of Israel: Behold, I will bring my words upon

this city for evil, and not for good; and they ¹shall be accomplished before thee in that day. 17 But I will deliver thee in that day, saith the LORD: and thou shalt not be given into the hand of the men of whom thou art afraid. 18 For I will surely save thee, and thou shalt not fall by the sword, but thy life shall be for a prey unto thee: because thou hast put thy trust in me, saith the LORD.

¹ Or, *shall be before thee*

17. Sometimes it is the lot of the righteous to be taken away before the evil comes (cf. Is. lvii. 1).

the men...afraid. Either the invaders or the princes who were anxious to punish him for his rescue of Jeremiah from the cistern.

18. *a prey.* See on xxi. 9.

CHAPTERS XL.—XLV.

These chh. complete the history of the prophet as far as it is recorded, telling the story of his life in Palestine after the carrying away of the exiles to Babylon, and of his involuntary sojourn in Egypt where according to tradition he died.

Jeremiah decides to remain in Palestine. xl. 1—6.
The murder of Gedaliah and its sequel. xl. 7—xli. 18.
The migration to Egypt. xlii. 1—xliii. 7.
Forecast of the conquest of Egypt. xliii. 8—13.
Condemnation of the worship of the queen of heaven. xliv.
The Rebuke to Baruch. xlv.

CHAPTER XL. 1—6.

Jeremiah decides to remain in Palestine.

This passage, except *v.* 6, is rejected by Duhm and Cornill as legendary. It seems clearly inconsistent with the statement in xxxix. 14 that Jeremiah was committed to the care of Gedaliah, though it may be that there is here preserved an account of what befell the prophet between his being taken out of the court of the guard and his final release. According to *v.* 1 the prophet had got as far as Ramah before he was rescued by the captain of the guard; later Jewish tradition made him go as far as Babylon itself (2 Baruch x. 2; 4 Baruch), though *Pesikta Rabbi* § 26 states that he accompanied the exiles part of the way only.

XL. 1 The word which came to Jeremiah from the LORD,

XL. 1. *The word.* This heading is evidently out of its context no oracle follows.

after that Nebuzaradan the captain of the guard had let him go
from Ramah, when he had taken him being bound in chains among
all the captives of Jerusalem and Judah, which were carried away
captive unto Babylon. 2 And the captain of the guard took
Jeremiah, and said unto him, The LORD thy God pronounced
this evil upon this place: 3 and the LORD hath brought it, and
done according as he spake; because ye have sinned against the
LORD, and have not obeyed his voice, therefore this thing is come
upon you. 4 And now, behold, I loose thee this day from the
chains which are upon thine hand. If it seem good unto thee
to come with me into Babylon, come, and I will look well unto
thee; but if it seem ill unto thee to come with me into Babylon,
forbear: behold, all the land is before thee; whither it seemeth
good and ¹convenient unto thee to go, thither go. 5 Now while
he was not yet gone back, Go back then, *said he*, to Gedaliah the
son of Ahikam, the son of Shaphan, whom the king of Babylon
hath made governor over the cities of Judah, and dwell with him
among the people: or go wheresoever it seemeth ¹convenient
unto thee to go. So the captain of the guard gave him ²victuals

---

¹ Or, *right*　　² Or, *an allowance*

Ramah. See on xxxi. 15.

2 f. These *vv.* have been looked upon with a certain amount of
suspicion by many critics owing to the improbability of a Chaldean
official uttering the words which are here attributed to Nebuzaradan.
Keil tries to retain the *vv.* by suggesting that though 'the mode of
expression is that of Jeremiah…Nebuzaradan may have expressed the
thought.' It is possible that the Babylonians were as fond of taking
up pious phrases as was Cyrus, who attributed his success equally to
Jehovah, or to Bel-marduk, according to the beliefs of those to whom
he was writing.

3. *because ye have sinned.* The same idea occurs in xxii. 8 f.; Dt.
xxix. 24 f.

4. *all the land.* The same phrase is used in Gen. xiii. 9; strangely
enough in both cases it introduces a temptation to possible worldly
advantage at the cost of principle; Lot fell before his temptation,
Jeremiah resisted.

5. *Now while he was not yet gone back.* The Heb. text is here
difficult to understand and as these words are missing from LXX. it is
best to regard them as a gloss, and to continue *but if not depart.*

victuals. Better an *allowance* or *ration.*

and a present, and let him go. 6 Then went Jeremiah unto
Gedaliah the son of Ahikam to Mizpah, and dwelt with him among
the people that were left in the land.

6. *Then went Jeremiah* &c. Josephus waxes eloquent over the
choice made by Jeremiah[1].

Mizpah. Jerusalem had been destroyed, and in any case would
not have been fit for human habitation immediately after the pestilence
and famine and all the nameless horrors of a desperate siege (cf. 2 K.
xxv. 3). *Mizpah* was some four or five miles NW. of Jerusalem: it was
also the headquarters of the Jewish nation in the time of the Maccabees
after the temple had been desecrated in 168 B.C. (1 Macc. iii. 48).
The town is to be distinguished from other places of the same name,—
the word, which means watch-tower, was applied to several prominent
points ; the hill-town here meant was situated on the mountain called
Neby Samwil, which rises to nearly 3,000 feet above the level of
the sea.

CHAPTERS XL. 7—XLI. 18.

The Murder of Gedaliah, and its Sequel.

The vividness and lifelikeness of the narratives which follow have been
recognised by all critics, and Duhm even goes so far as to rate the series as one
of the most striking and interesting passages in OT. The recognition of the
literary value of the account and the detailed knowledge which its writer exhibits has not, however, prevented Schmidt from denying its authenticity, as
he rejects it as 'A confused memory of the first Chaldean governor and of an
abortive attempt by a side branch of the Davidic family to overthrow the new
government...in its present form it cannot well be earlier than the second
century,' *Enc. Bib.* 2386. This criticism is not supported by the opinion of
other scholars, though it must be admitted that the narrative is full of difficulties.
These difficulties may be divided into two groups, (*a*) those concerning the
murder of Gedaliah himself ; and (*b*) those concerning the subsequent massacre ;
a discussion of these points is best postponed and they will be dealt with in the
notes which follow. The narrative may be divided as follows :

    (*a*) *The gathering at Mizpah.* xl. 7—12.
    (*b*) *Johanan's warning to Gedaliah.* 13—16.
    (*c*) *The murder of Gedaliah.* xli. 1—3.
    (*d*) *The massacre of the pilgrims.* 4—10.
    (*e*) *The flight of Ishmael.* 11—18.

---

[1] *Ant.* x. ix. 1 'Ὁ δὲ προφήτης οὐδ' ἔπεσθαι ἤθελεν οὔτ' ἀλλαχόσε ποῦ μένειν, ἡδέως
δ'εἶχεν ἐπὶ τοῖς ἐρειπίοις τῆς πατρίδος καὶ τοῖς ταλαιπώροις αὐτῆς διαζῆσαι λειψάνοις.'

7 [1]Now when all the captains of the forces which were in the fields, even they and their men, heard that the king of Babylon had made Gedaliah the son of Ahikam governor in the land, and had committed unto him men, and women, and children, [2]and of the poorest of the land, of them that were not carried away captive to Babylon; 8 then they came to Gedaliah to Mizpah, even Ishmael the son of Nethaniah, and Johanan and Jonathan the sons of Kareah, and Seraiah the son of Tanhumeth, and the sons of Ephai the Netophathite, and Jezaniah the son of the Maacathite, they and their men. 9 And Gedaliah the son of Ahikam the son of Shaphan sware unto them and to their men, saying, Fear not to serve the Chaldeans: dwell in the land, and

---

[1] See 2 Kings xxv. 23, 24.   [2] Or, *even*

7—12. Gedaliah at Mizpah is joined by some of the Jews who had fled to the surrounding territories.

7—9. These *vv.* appear in an abbreviated form in 2 K. xxv. 23 f.

7. It is not certain whether these bands were part of the garrison of Jerusalem who had succeeded in escaping after the flight of Zedekiah, or whether they were guerillas who had not been driven into the capital. The country round Jerusalem offered many places of refuge and shelter for such people ; Kinglake says that ‘the destruction of the mere buildings in such a place as Jerusalem would not involve the permanent dispersion of the inhabitants, for the rocky neighbourhood in which the town is situate abounds in caves, and these would give an easy refuge to the people until they gained an opportunity of rebuilding their dwellings.’ *Eothen*, p. 129.

8. *Jonathan.* This name is omitted in 2 K. It is impossible to say whether it is inserted here through confusion with *Johanan,* or whether it is an omission by the scribe of 2 K. who overlooked it for a similar reason.

the Netophathite. Netophah is mentioned in 2 S. xxiii. 28 ; Ezra ii. 22, &c. and is usually held to be the modern village of *Beit Nettif* some dozen miles W. of Bethlehem. In 2 K. the epithet is applied to Tanhumeth, *the sons of Ephai* being absent from the account.

the Maacathite. Maacah is mentioned in Gen. xxii. 24 as being the child of Nahor, Abraham’s brother, by a concubine. The tribe which dwelt SE. of Hermon is often referred to (Dt. iii. 14 ; 2 S. x. 6, 8, &c.).

9. *to serve the Chaldeans.* In the parallel passage in 2 K. xxv. 24 MT. reads *because of the servants of the Chaldeans* with which LXX. of the present passage agrees ; Dr Skinner in his commentary on *Kings* in the Century Bible, however, prefers the reading of MT. as ren-

serve the king of Babylon, and it shall be well with you. 10 As for me, behold, I will dwell at Mizpah, to stand before the Chaldeans, which shall come unto us: but ye, gather ye wine and summer fruits and oil, and put them in your vessels, and dwell in your cities that ye have taken. 11 Likewise when all the Jews that were in Moab, and among the children of Ammon, and in Edom, and that were in all the countries, heard that the king of Babylon had left a remnant of Judah, and that he had set over them Gedaliah the son of Ahikam, the son of Shaphan; 12 then all the Jews returned out of all places whither they were driven, and came to the land of Judah, to Gedaliah, unto Mizpah, and gathered wine and summer fruits very much.

13 Moreover Johanan the son of Kareah, and all the captains of the forces that were in the fields, came to Gedaliah to Mizpah,

dered in Jeremiah[1]. Dr Peake prefers LXX. seeing in it a reference to such Babylonian officials as were left behind in the conquered territory.

dwell in the land &c. Gedaliah's instructions are very similar to the prophet's own advice to the exiles of the first siege (cf. xxix. 5).

10. *stand before the Chaldeans.* The expression *stand before* is used in Heb. with one of two meanings, either *to serve*, as in xv. 19, xxxv. 19, or *to intercede*, as in xv. 1. The latter meaning is best suited to the present context[2].

gather ye wine &c. That the people were able to gather the produce of the soil within a few months of the fall of Jerusalem shews that the Babylonians had not destroyed the trees. The practice was a widespread one in the ancient world (cf. the phrase κείρειν or τέμνειν τὴν γῆν), and amongst Arab warriors the destruction of an enemy's palm-groves was a favourite exploit (see W. R. Smith, *OTJC.*[2] p. 369); on one occasion Elisha commanded the Israelites to fell every good tree (2 K. iii. 19—25) but such barbarous methods of warfare were against the spirit of the later Jewish legislation (cf. Dt. xx. 19).

ye have taken. The people were now settling down to civilised life and reoccupying the deserted cities of Judah.

13—16. Johanan and the captains endeavour to put Gedaliah on his guard against Ishmael.

---

[1] The reading of LXX. in the passage in Kings is rather interesting and Dr Streane accepts it as being the original of both passages in Jer. MT. reads מֲעֲבוֹד but LXX. evidently took it to be מַעֲבָר and accordingly rendered it by πάροδον, *the passing through.*

[2] Cf. Driver's paraphrase which combines both meanings: 'to be a servant (1 K. x. 8) admitted to their presence, and able therefore to represent your interests with them.'

14 and said unto him, Dost thou know that Baalis the king of
the children of Ammon hath sent Ishmael the son of Nethaniah
to take thy life? But Gedaliah the son of Ahikam believed them
not. 15 Then Johanan the son of Kareah spake to Gedaliah in
Mizpah secretly, saying, Let me go, I pray thee, and I will slay
Ishmael the son of Nethaniah, and no man shall know it: wherefore should he take thy life, that all the Jews which are gathered
unto thee should be scattered, and the remnant of Judah perish?
16 But Gedaliah the son of Ahikam said unto Johanan the son
of Kareah, Thou shalt not do this thing: for thou speakest falsely
of Ishmael.

XLI. 1 [1]Now it came to pass in the seventh month, that
Ishmael the son of Nethaniah, the son of Elishama, of the seed
royal, and *one of* the chief officers of the king, and ten men with
him, came unto Gedaliah the son of Ahikam to Mizpah; and

---

[1] See 2 Kings xxv. 25.

13. *Baalis...of Ammon.* There is nothing, beyond the statement
of the captains, to shew whether Ishmael was really working as the
agent of the king of Ammon; it is rather difficult to account for such
interference on his part as he must have realised that a fresh disturbance
in Judah would bring back the Chaldeans, and that his share in the
matter would not be allowed to pass unpunished: cf. Ez. xxi. 20.
Possibly he was the king of Ammon whose ambassador, together with
those of four neighbouring states, was sent back by Jeremiah's efforts
(xxvii.); in this case he may have had a grudge against Gedaliah as a
partisan of the prophet.

15. Cornill points out that the advice which Johanan gave to
Gedaliah was substantially that of Caiaphas to the Jewish rulers that
it was expedient that one man should perish rather than the whole
nation (Jn. xi. 50).

XLI. 1—3. Ishmael treacherously murders Gedaliah and his
Chaldean guard. Ishmael was a member of the royal house and he
may have murdered Gedaliah from motives of jealousy because he
himself had not been chosen; or perhaps he looked upon Gedaliah as
a traitor in accepting a post under the Babylonians, it is even possible
that the governor was one of those Jews who deserted to the Chaldeans
before the fall of Jerusalem (xxxviii. 19). Perhaps Ishmael hoped to
found a new Jewish state under the protection of Ammon.

1. *seventh month.* According to the post-exilic tradition it was on
the third of Tisri that the crime was committed, and the yearly
recurrence of this date was marked by a solemn fast (see Zech. vii. 5,
viii. 19).

there they did eat bread together in Mizpah. 2 Then arose
Ishmael the son of Nethaniah, and the ten men that were with
him, and smote Gedaliah the son of Ahikam the son of Shaphan
with the sword, and slew him, whom the king of Babylon had
made governor over the land. 3 Ishmael also slew all the Jews
that were with him, even with Gedaliah, at Mizpah, and the
Chaldeans that were found there, even the men of war. 4 And
it came to pass the second day after he had slain Gedaliah, and
no man knew it, 5 that there came certain from Shechem, from

eat bread together. The eating together made the treachery of the
murder all the greater in the eyes of the narrator (cf. Mk. xiv. 18).

2. *ten men.* The small number of Ishmael's following would not
arouse suspicion; apparently they were men of desperate and hardy
character.

3. *men of war.* These words are missing from LXX., and the
difficulty of supposing that the governor's Chaldean guard was not
sufficiently powerful to prevent the murder is thus avoided.

4—10. Ishmael adds to his crimes by massacring a party of
pilgrims from North Israel. To account for this further outrage is
even harder than to suggest reasons for the slaying of Gedaliah.
Perhaps it was the fear of discovery, or merely the desire for plunder
that prompted the deed; though it is equally likely that Ishmael and
his accomplices were acting from deeper motives and that their
hatred of everyone who even in appearance accepted the Chaldean
supremacy led them to treat these subjects of the Babylonians
as they had treated the governor of the Southern province. Perhaps
the most natural explanation, however, is to look upon Ishmael
and his band as mere desperadoes who, once they had tasted blood,
desired to do as much mischief as possible before fleeing for safety to
the protection of Ammon.

4. *the second day.* According to Jewish reckoning the next day
would be thus described.

5. The pilgrimage from these Northern sanctuaries to Jerusalem
seems to point to some close connexion between the people of the two
provinces in religious beliefs (cf. 2 K. xvii. 24 ff.; Ezra iv. 2). Dr Kennett
has made some interesting suggestions in this connexion, see his article
The Origin of the Aaronite Priesthood in *J. Th. S.* for Jan. 1905[1].

Shechem. The site of *Shechem* is now occupied by the town of
Nāblus. The sanctuary there took the place of an earlier Canaanite
shrine to Baal-berith (Jud. ix. 4 &c.).

---

[1] Dr Kennett, however, does not lay any stress on the action of these men who
may very well have been originally refugees from Judah; cf. *v.* 8, the *stores* were
evidently close by. (*Op. cit.* p. 174, n.)

Shiloh, and from Samaria, even fourscore men, having their beards
shaven and their clothes rent, and having cut themselves, with
[1]oblations and frankincense in their hand, to bring them to the
house of the LORD. 6 And Ishmael the son of Nethaniah went
forth from Mizpah to meet them, weeping all along as he went:
and it came to pass, as he met them, he said unto them, Come
to Gedaliah the son of Ahikam. 7 And it was so, when they
came into the midst of the city, that Ishmael the son of Nethaniah
slew them, *and cast them* into the midst of the pit, he, and the
men that were with him. 8 But ten men were found among
them that said unto Ishmael, Slay us not: for we have stores
hidden in the field, of wheat, and of barley, and of oil, and of

[1] Or, *meal offerings*

Shiloh. See note on vii. 12. It seems rather strange to find the
town still in existence after the example which Jeremiah was able to
draw from its ruined condition ; it may have been re-built in the
meantime, or possibly the reading of LXX. *Salem* is the correct one.

beards shaven and...clothes rent, and having cut themselves. These
signs of mourning are evidently intended to shew the sorrow of the
pilgrims at the destruction of Jerusalem, the mention of *the house of
the* LORD does not therefore mean that it was actually standing or that
the men from Ephraim were ignorant of what had taken place ; a sacred
spot was still hallowed even if the outward sanctuary had itself been
destroyed. The practices of cutting oneself *for the dead* and shaving
off *the corners* of the beard are forbidden by Dt. xiv. 1 &c. (see on xvi.
6), but it is not quite clear that there was a breach of these prohibitions
in the present case.

oblations and frankincense. The pilgrims were evidently going up
to Jerusalem to keep the feast of ingathering (cf. xl. 12 and Ex. xxiii.
16), which took place on the fifteenth of the seventh month ; cf. *v.* 1,
and see Lev. xxii. 34, 39 (P).

6. *weeping.* If this refers to Ishmael, as according to MT. it does,
there is here another exhibition of his treacherous nature ; it is probably
best to make *weeping* a plural and refer it to the pilgrims ; this was
apparently the reading of the text used by LXX. There is perhaps a
reference to the treachery of Ishmael in Ecclus. xii. 16 'though an
enemy weep with his eyes, when he findeth opportunity he will not be
satiated with blood.'

8. *stores hidden.* See a description of such stores in Thomson,
The Land and the Book, I. pp. 89 f., II. p. 194, III. p. 485[1].

of oil. Olive oil is still a staple article of diet in the East supplying
the fat which more Northern races obtain from animal foods.

---

[1] St Thomas Aquinas quotes this *v.* as a justification for borrowing money on
usury for a good purpose: 'it is lawful for a good purpose, as for the relief of one's

honey. So he forbare, and slew them not among their brethren. 9 Now the pit wherein Ishmael cast all the dead bodies of the men whom he had slain, by the side of Gedaliah, (the same was that which Asa the king had made for fear of Baasha king of Israel,) Ishmael the son of Nethaniah filled it with them that were slain. 10 Then Ishmael carried away captive all the residue of the people that were in Mizpah, even the king's daughters, and all the people that remained in Mizpah, whom Nebuzaradan the captain of the guard had committed to Gedaliah the son of Ahikam: Ishmael the son of Nethaniah carried them away captive, and departed to go over to the children of Ammon.

11 But when Johanan the son of Kareah, and all the captains of the forces that were with him, heard of all the evil that Ishmael the son of Nethaniah had done, 12 then they took all the men, and went to fight with Ishmael the son of Nethaniah, and found him by the great waters that are in Gibeon. 13 Now it came to pass that when all the people which were with Ishmael saw Johanan the son of Kareah, and all the captains of the forces that were with him, then they were glad. 14 So all the people

9. *by the side of Gedaliah.* A slight change in MT. makes it agree with the reading of LXX. *was a great pit*[1].

Asa...had made. See 1 K. xv. 22 ; 2 Ch. xvi. 6.

10. *the king's daughters.* The phrase means princesses of the blood royal, not necessarily the daughters of Zedekiah ; see note on 'the king's son' (xxxvi. 26).

11—18. Ishmael is not allowed to escape unmolested, for Johanan and other leaders pursue him so hotly that he is compelled to leave his captives behind.

12. *Gibeon.* The *great waters* are evidently the same as 'the pool of Gibeon' mentioned in 2 S. ii. 13. 'There is still an ancient broken reservoir on the west side of the hill of Gibeon and in the wet season there is a considerable pond in the plain below the modern village.' The modern village is called *el-Jib* and is about a mile to the north of *Neby Samwil*, the hill upon which Mizpah is situated.

---

own necessity or that of another, to borrow money at usury of him who is prepared so to transact usuriously; as it is lawful for him who falls amongst robbers to declare the goods that he has to escape being slain, after the example of the ten men.' *Summa*, II. ii. 68. 4.

[1] MT. reads בְּיַד גְּדַלְיָהוּ lit. *by the hand of Gedaliah*, which hardly makes good sense, though Job xv. 23 'the day of darkness is ready *at his hand*' possibly furnishes a parallel. The reading of LXX. φρέαρ μέγα represents בּוּר גָּדוֹל.

that Ishmael had carried away captive from Mizpah cast about
and returned, and wént unto Johanan the son of Kareah. 15 But
Ishmael the son of Nethaniah escaped from Johanan with eight
men, and went to the children of Ammon. 16 Then took Johanan
the son of Kareah, and all the captains of the forces that were
with him, all the remnant of the people whom he had recovered
from Ishmael the son of Nethaniah, from Mizpah, after that he
had slain Gedaliah the son of Ahikam, even the men of war, and
the women, and the children, and the eunuchs, whom he had
brought again from Gibeon : 17 and they departed, and dwelt in
¹Geruth Chimham, which is by Beth-lehem, to go to enter into
Egypt, 18 because of the Chaldeans: for they were afraid of
them, because Ishmael the son of Nethaniah had slain Gedaliah
the son of Ahikam, whom the king of Babylon made governor
over the land.

¹ Or, *the lodging place of Chimham*

14.   *cast about.*   An archaism meaning *to turn round.*   Several
examples of the use of this phrase are quoted by commentators : John
Gower in *Confessio Amantis* (fourteenth century) writes 'Then cast I all
the worlde about,' and Sir Philip Sidney uses the same expression in
his *Arcadia* 'Musidorus could doe no more but perswade the mariners
to cast about againe.'
16.   *from Mizpah.*   There is evidently a slight confusion in MT.
here as the captives were *recovered* from near Gibeon.   Hitzig's emendation gives the correct reading *the people whom Ishmael...had carried
away captive from Mizpah.*
17.   *Geruth Chimham.*   The word *Geruth* occurs here only, and
Ewald suggests that it means *inn* or *khan,* so margin *lodging-place.*
Aq. and Josephus (*Ant.* x. ix. 5) read *Gidroth = sheepfolds,* and this
reading is accepted by Hitzig and most recent scholars.   *Chimham* is
probably the son of Barzillai mentioned in 2 S. xix. 37 &c.   It has been
suggested that it was from this khan that Joseph took the infant
Saviour into Egypt: Stanley, *Sin. and Pal.*²³ p. 129.

CHAPTERS XLII. 1—XLIII. 7.

The Migration to Egypt.

The genuineness of this passage is acknowledged by nearly all critics; Duhm,
however, rejects *vv.* 7—18, 22 as being a later addition.   The narrative seems

to come from an eye-witness, and there is every reason for supposing that Baruch is the author of the passage.

(a) *The prophet's intercession and guidance are asked for.*   xlii. 1—6.
(b) *The prophet declares God's message, but anticipates the disobedience of the people.* 7—22.
(c) *The flight into Egypt.* xliii. 1—7.

XLII. 1 Then all the captains of the forces, and Johanan the son of Kareah, and [1] Jezaniah the son of Hoshaiah, and all the people from the least even unto the greatest, came near, 2 and said unto Jeremiah the prophet, Let, we pray thee, our supplication [2] be accepted before thee, and pray for us unto the LORD thy God, even for all this remnant; for we are left but a few of many, as thine eyes do behold us: 3 that the LORD thy God may shew us the way wherein we should walk, and the thing that we should do. 4 Then Jeremiah the prophet said unto them, I have heard you; behold, I will pray unto the LORD your God according to your words; and it shall come to pass that whatsoever thing the LORD shall answer you, I will declare it

---

[1] In ch. xliii. 2, *Azariah.*   [2] Heb. *fall.*

XLII. 1—6. The captains of the various bands and all the remnant of the people ask Jeremiah for his intercession on their behalf, at the same time promising to do whatsoever God shall reveal to him.

1. Jeremiah is once more brought upon the scene after the story of Ishmael's crimes; no information is given as to whether the prophet shared in the discomforts of those who fell into the hands of the murderers of Gedaliah, or whether he was absent from Mizpah at the time of the outrage.

Jezaniah the son of Hoshaiah. A certain *Jezaniah* the Maacathite is mentioned amongst the captains in xl. 8; and in xliii. 2, as mg. points out, a *son of Hoshaiah* named Azariah occurs. The question of the identity of these persons and their number is very complicated. LXX. reads here and in xliii. 2 *Azariah the son of Maaseiah.*

2. The Jews came to Jeremiah for counsel as to the manner in which the migration was to be carried out, rather than for direction whether it was God's will or not. The unnatural servility of the request, coupled with the subsequent behaviour of the people, gives a clue to the depth of their sincerity.

the LORD thy God. The prophet is regarded as a kind of magician with means of approaching God which are denied to others.

3. *the way.* This use seems to be a reminiscence of Jeremiah's own teaching; cf. vi. 16.

unto you; I will keep nothing back from you. 5 Then they said to Jeremiah, The LORD be a true and faithful witness [1]amongst us, if we do not even according to all the word wherewith the LORD thy God shall send thee to us. 6 Whether it be good, or whether it be evil, we will obey the voice of the LORD our God, to whom we send thee; that it may be well with us, when we obey the voice of the LORD our God.

7 And it came to pass after ten days, that the word of the LORD came unto Jeremiah. 8 Then called he Johanan the son of Kareah, and all the captains of the forces which were with him, and all the people from the least even to the greatest, 9 and said unto them, Thus saith the LORD, the God of Israel, unto whom ye sent me to [2]present your supplication before him: 10 If ye will still abide in this land, then will I build you, and not pull you down, and I will plant you, and not pluck you up: for I repent me of the evil that I have done unto you. 11 Be

[1] Or, against   [2] Or, lay

5. *amongst.* Better with mg. *against.* Cf. Dt. xxxi. 28.

7—22. The word of the Lord comes to Jeremiah advising the people to remain in the land where they were and assuring them of His gracious favour if they carry out His command. The king of Babylon will shew them kindness and their fears of attack will prove to have been unfounded. On the other hand if they persist in their intention of going down to Egypt in order to escape from the things that they dread such action will have the very opposite effect.

7. *after ten days.* As the message did not come to Jeremiah immediately, the faith and patience of prophet and people alike must have been much tried. In a similar way Ezekiel had on one occasion to wait for seven days for the word of the Lord to come to him (iii. 15 f.). These experiences plainly teach that the Divine message was something quite definite, and did not depend merely on the prophet's judgement; it may be that some mechanical means were used by Jeremiah for discovering God's will, though this is very unlikely. The leaders in all probability made use of the interval to collect stores and to elaborate their plans for going down into Egypt. It is evident that the command of Dt. xvii. 16 that the people were to return to Egypt no more was unknown at this time, or that its provisions were held to be inapplicable.

9. Jeremiah reminds the people that he undertook to intercede for them at their own request.

10. *will I build* &c. In i. 10 these words are applied to heathen nations.

I repent me. See on xviii. 8. God has punished His people, He will now compensate them; cf. Is. xl. 1 f.

not afraid of the king of Babylon, of whom ye are afraid; be not afraid of him, saith the LORD: for I am with you to save you, and to deliver you from his hand. 12 And I will grant you mercy, that he may have mercy upon you, and cause you to return to your own land. 13 But if ye say, We will not dwell in this land; so that ye obey not the voice of the LORD your God; 14 saying, No; but we will go into the land of Egypt, where we shall see no war, nor hear the sound of the trumpet, nor have hunger of bread; and there will we dwell: 15 now therefore hear ye the word of the LORD, O remnant of Judah: thus saith the LORD of hosts, the God of Israel, If ye wholly set your faces to enter into Egypt, and go to sojourn there; 16 then it shall come to pass, that the sword, which ye fear, shall overtake you there in the land of Egypt, and the famine, whereof ye are afraid, ¹shall follow hard after you there in Egypt; and there ye shall die. 17 So shall it be with all the men that set their faces to go into Egypt to sojourn there; they shall die by the sword, by the famine, and by the pestilence: and none of them shall remain or escape from the evil that I will bring upon them. 18 For thus saith the LORD of hosts, the God of Israel; As mine anger and my fury hath

---

¹ Heb. *shall cleave after you.*

11. *Be not afraid.* According to lii. 30 Nebuzaradan deported a large number of people from Judah in the three and twentieth year of Nebuchadrezzar; this deportation took place some five years after the final capture of Jerusalem and may have been connected with the murder of Gedaliah. It is possible that if the loyal commanders with Jeremiah in their midst had remained where they were and trusted to the Babylonian sense of justice, this deportation would not have taken place; by their flight they confessed their guilt in the eyes of the conquerors, and probably removed from Judah all those who would have been able to give an exact and unbiassed account of what had actually taken place.

12. *to return.* Read with Syr. and Vulg. *to dwell*; the difference is one of pointing, and as the party was actually in Jewish territory at the time they could not *return* thither.

14. *we shall see no war.* Owing to its position as a 'buffer-state' between Egypt and Babylonia Palestine was the scene of perpetual warfare, and so it continued to be until Egypt and Syria—the successor of Babylon —together with Judah itself were all reduced to a common obedience under the rule of Rome. Whether the longed for peace was obtained even in Egypt is a matter of doubt: see on xliii. 8—13.

been poured forth upon the inhabitants of Jerusalem, so shall
my fury be poured forth upon you, when ye shall enter into
Egypt: and ye shall be an execration, and an astonishment, and
a curse, and a reproach; and ye shall see this place no more.
19 The LORD hath spoken concerning you, O remnant of Judah,
Go ye not into Egypt: know certainly that I have testified unto
you this day. 20 For ye have dealt deceitfully ¹against your
own souls; for ye sent me unto the LORD your God, saying, Pray
for us unto the LORD our God; and according unto all that the
LORD our God shall say, so declare unto us, and we will do it:
21 and I have this day declared it to you; but ye have not
obeyed the voice of the LORD your God in any thing for the which
he hath sent me unto you. 22 Now therefore know certainly
that ye shall die by the sword, by the famine, and by the pestilence, in the place whither ye desire to go to sojourn there.

XLIII. 1 And it came to pass that when Jeremiah had made
an end of speaking unto all the people all the words of the LORD
their God, wherewith the LORD their God had sent him to them,
even all these words, 2 then spake Azariah the son of Hoshaiah,
and Johanan the son of Kareah, and all the proud men, saying
unto Jeremiah, Thou speakest falsely: the LORD our God hath
not sent thee to say, Ye shall not go into Egypt to sojourn there:
3 but Baruch the son of Neriah setteth thee on against us, for

¹ Or, *in your souls*

19. The prophet can tell from the bearing of the people that his
message is unacceptable to them.
XLIII. 1—7. In spite of their high-sounding promises Johanan
and the people refuse to hear Jeremiah and determine to follow their
own plan; accordingly they go down to Egypt taking with them the
reluctant prophet and his scribe.
2. The word which the prophet delivers does not agree with the
policy of the leaders of the people and therefore its Divine origin is
questioned.
saying. The text as it stands is not good Hebrew, by a slight
change *defiant* should be read, i.e. *the proud and defiant men.*
3. *Baruch.* Jeremiah by this time was an old man, some sixty
years and more having passed since his call, and his hearers evidently
think that he is too much under the influence of Baruch. It is probable
that the latter had allowed his own opinion on the journey to become
known, hence the accusation. Perhaps Baruch was ambitious to succeed
Gedaliah as the head of a new Jewish state; see note on xlv. 5.

B.

20

to deliver us into the hand of the Chaldeans, that they may put us to death, and carry us away captives to Babylon. 4 So Johanan the son of Kareah, and all the captains of the forces, and all the people, obeyed not the voice of the LORD, to dwell in the land of Judah. 5 But Johanan the son of Kareah, and all the captains of the forces, took all the remnant of Judah, that were returned from all the nations whither they had been driven to sojourn in the land of Judah; 6 the men, and the women, and the children, and the king's daughters, and every person that Nebuzaradan the captain of the guard had left with Gedaliah the son of Ahikam, the son of Shaphan, and Jeremiah the prophet, and Baruch the son of Neriah; 7 and they came into the land of Egypt; for they obeyed not the voice of the LORD: and they came even to Tahpanhes.

5. *from all the nations.* It is impossible to offer any reasonable explanation for this phrase which seems an altogether unsuitable description of the fugitives. LXX. omits.

6. *the king's daughters.* Flinders Petrie thinks that these women were housed in the fortress of Tahpanhes in the royal chambers as the mound is known as *Qasr Bint el Yehudi,* "the palace of the Jew's daughters." See *Egypt and Israel,* pp. 89 f.

7. *Tahpanhes.* See on ii. 16.

CHAPTER XLIII. 8—13.

The Forecast of the Conquest of Egypt.

This passage is rejected by Duhm, but is accepted by most critics as handing down a genuine prophecy of Jeremiah. At the same time it is doubtful whether the forecast was fulfilled in the letter, as the evidence for an invasion of Egypt by Nebuchadrezzar is scanty and not at all clear (see on *v.* 12). Erbt thinks that the forecast was a reply to the accusation in *v.* 2 that he was influenced by Baruch and to shew the people that his warnings against the journey had been inspired by no mere passing whim. Whether this is so or not Jeremiah's symbolical action in burying the stones was a vivid warning to the Jews that the conquest of Egypt itself was not beyond the power of Nebuchadrezzar.

8 Then came the word of the LORD unto Jeremiah in Tahpanhes,

8. *Tahpanhes.* No information is given as to the lapse of time between the events of this section and the previous one. *Tahpanhes* was one of the fortresses on the frontier and doubtless the fugitives

saying, 9 Take great stones in thine hand, and ¹hide them in mortar in the brickwork, which is at the entry of Pharaoh's house in Tahpanhes, in the sight of the men of Judah; 10 and say unto them, Thus saith the LORD of hosts, the God of Israel: Behold, I will send and take Nebuchadrezzar the king of Babylon, my servant, and will set his throne upon these stones that I have hid; and he shall spread his ²royal pavilion over them. 11 And he shall

¹ Or, *lay them with mortar in the pavement* (or *square*)   ² Or, *glittering*

would have to wait there for some time before being allowed to enter Egyptian territory.

9. *hide them in mortar.* This phrase has caused much difficulty alike to the compilers of the ancient versions and to present day critics. LXX. translates *in the forecourt* which seems almost a guess, suggested by the context, unless indeed LXX. had a different reading of the original; the othe rgreat Greek versions—Aq., Symm., Theod.—and Vulg. translate *in secret*, a reading which can be obtained by omitting one of the consonants of the Heb. word *in mortar*. This reading is accepted by some modern scholars, and its inconsistency with the statement that the incident occurred *in the sight of the men of Judah* is only verbal (cf. Ez. xii. 1—16).

in the brickwork. In the Heb. these words are represented by one word only, and it is very similar to the word for *in the mortar*; accordingly the suggestion has been made that it has crept into the text by dittography. In any case the meaning of the word, which occurs elsewhere in Nah. iii. 14 and possibly in 2 S. xii. 31, is not very certain. It is used in post-biblical Heb. for objects of a rectangular shape as well as for brickmoulds, hence the marg. *square*¹; the other marg. reading *pavement* has the support of Flinders Petrie², and is probably to be accepted.

10. *my servant.* See on xxv. 9.

will set. LXX. reading *he shall set* is to be preferred: cf. i. 15.

his royal pavilion. The meaning of this word which occurs here

---

¹ For a discussion of the meaning of מלבן in the cognate languages see *ZATW.* 1882, pp. 53 ff. and Driver's note on 2 S. xii. 31.

² Flinders Petrie supports the rendering *pavement.* He says 'It means a place of bricks, or a space paved over with bricks. Not being accustomed to such an idea, the translators could not see the sense of it. But when I came to clear the fort at Defneh, there proved to be but one entry into Pharaoh's house; and in front of that was a wide paved area on the north of the fort. It was a place probably for the external guard, and for stacking goods, unloading camels, and such purposes of out-door life in Egypt. Much of it had been washed away in the rains and there were no stones in the part that was left. The denudation by wind and rain is extreme along the coast, as is seen by the great wall of the camp, forty feet thick, which was so completely swept away that there was no trace visible, and it could only be found beneath the surface. This platform, however, was a place exactly corresponding to Jeremiah's detailed account, and the identification of it is certain.' *Egypt and Israel*, p. 92.

come, and shall smite the land of Egypt; such as are for death *shall be given* to death, and such as are for captivity to captivity, and such as are for the sword to the sword. 12 And I will kindle a fire in the houses of the gods of Egypt; and he shall burn them, and carry them away captives: and he shall array himself with the land of Egypt, as a shepherd putteth on his garment; and he shall go forth from thence in peace. 13 He shall also break the ¹pillars of ²Beth-shemesh, that is in the land of Egypt; and the houses of the gods of Egypt shall he burn with fire.

¹ Or, *obelisks*   ² Or, *The house of the sun*   Probably *Heliopolis* or *On*.

only is somewhat obscure, its relation to Assyr. *šuparruru* which means *to spread out* suggests the rendering *carpet* or *canopy*. The connexion with the root meaning *glittering* (cf. marg.) is rather doubtful.

12.   This *v.* raises the disputed question as to whether Nebuchadrezzar actually invaded Egypt. The material for arriving at a decision is very slight, consisting as it does of a short inscription of Nebuchadrezzar which states that he invaded Egypt in his thirty-seventh year and defeated Amasis¹; and a notice in Joseph. *Ant.* x. ix. 7 merely says that a Babylonian governor went down to Egypt in 581 B.C.   As regards the inscription, W. Max Müller is doubtful whether it refers to an actual invasion or only to the threat of one (*Enc. Bib.* 1246); on the other hand L. W. King thinks that Egypt was not improbably subject to Babylon in the early years of Amasis II (569—525), though 'Nebuchadrezzar's hold on Egypt cannot have been permanent' (*Enc. Bib.* 452). Driver accepts the inscription.

I will kindle. Better with LXX. *he shall kindle.*

carry them (i.e. the images of the gods) *away captives.* Cf. 1 S. iv. 11; the whole narrative of the capture of the ark suggests that it contained some image of Jehovah.

array...garment. The figure is intended to illustrate the ease with which Nebuchadrezzar will overcome the opposition of Egypt, though the exact point of the simile is not quite clear.

13.   *break.* The monarch who was mainly responsible for the destruction of the Egyptian idols was Cambyses 'the Cromwell of Egypt' as Dean Stanley calls him (*Sinai and Palestine*²³, p. xxxii).

Beth-shemesh or as mg. translates *The house of the sun.* The reference is almost certainly to the city called by the Greeks *Heliopolis* (cf. Herod. II. 59, 63) and by the natives *On*; the sacred name was *Pe-rā* (see *Sinai and Pal.*²³, p. xxvi). *On* was situated some six miles to NE. of what is now Cairo, and its modern Arab name is '*Ain-esh-*

¹ For the text of the inscription see *Trans. Soc. Bib. Arch.* VII. p. 218, and Strassmaier, *Nabuchodonossor*, p. 194. For further details see Driver in *Authority and Archaeology*, p. 117, and Winckler, *Altorient. Forschungen*, I. p. 511.

shems, i.e. fountain of the sun. The obelisk called 'Cleopatra's Needle' (now on the Thames embankment) formed one of an avenue of similar pillars in front of the temple. For a vivid and detailed description of *Heliopolis* and its wonders see Dean Stanley, *The Jewish Church*, I. pp. 74 ff.

CHAPTER XLIV.

The Condemnation of the Worship of the Queen of Heaven.

Every reformation is in danger of being followed by a reaction; in this ch. the reaction from the reformation of Josiah is seen in its most extreme form, i.e. in the statement that the gods which were then given up were stronger than Jehovah Himself, and that the constant train of disasters which had ensued upon that event was a result of neglecting to serve them. This passage contains the last recorded prophecy of Jeremiah and like so many of his other sayings it has been largely supplemented.

(a)   *Warning against idolatry.*   1—14.
(b)   *The idolaters' defiance.*   15—19.
(c)   *Jeremiah's further warning supported by a sign.*   20—30.

XLIV. 1 The word that came to Jeremiah concerning all the Jews which dwelt in the land of Egypt, which dwelt at Migdol, and at Tahpanhes, and at Noph, and in the country of Pathros,

XLIV. 1—14. Jeremiah reminds the Jews dwelling in the various cities of Egypt that the exile and the desolate state of Judah are due to their own sin and that of their forefathers in neglecting Jehovah in favour of idols. The example of the past is not enough for the exiles who persist in following the same course, a course which can only result in their destruction.

1. As in the last section no chronological note was introduced, so in this no clue is given as to the length of time which has elapsed since the settlement in Egypt. There are good reasons for supposing that large numbers of Jews were already settled under the protection of Pharaoh when the prophet and his fellow exiles fled from Judah. See Additional Note, pp. 315 f.

Migdol. The town here mentioned is almost certainly not that referred to in Ex. xiv. 2 which was probably only a small fortress or tower. According to Ez. xxix. 10, xxx. 6, where the translation *from Migdol (to) Seveneh* (i.e. Syene) should be read, Migdol represents the northern extremity of Egypt, and doubtless the two prophets refer to the same town which lay a little to the east of Tahpanhes and not far from Pelusium, on the site of the modern *Tel es Sernut.*

Tahpanhes...Noph.   See on ii. 16.

Pathros. This represents the native word for Upper Egypt, *Pa-to-ris*—the land of the South (Ass. *paturisi*).

saying, 2 Thus saith the LORD of hosts, the God of Israel: Ye
have seen all the evil that I have brought upon Jerusalem, and
upon all the cities of Judah; and, behold, this day they are a
desolation, and no man dwelleth therein; 3 because of their
wickedness which they have committed to provoke me to anger,
in that they went to burn incense, *and* to serve other gods,
whom they knew not, neither they, nor ye, nor your fathers.
4 Howbeit I sent unto you all my servants the prophets, rising
up early and sending them, saying, Oh, do not this abominable
thing that I hate. 5 But they hearkened not, nor inclined their
ear to turn from their wickedness, to burn no incense unto other
gods. 6 Wherefore my fury and mine anger was poured forth,
and was kindled in the cities of Judah and in the streets of
Jerusalem; and they are wasted and desolate, as it is this day.
7 Therefore now thus saith the LORD, the God of hosts, the God
of Israel: Wherefore commit ye *this* great evil against your own
souls, to cut off from you man and woman, infant and suckling,
out of the midst of Judah, to leave you none remaining; 8 in
that ye provoke me unto anger with the works of your hands,
burning incense unto other gods in the land of Egypt, whither
ye be gone to sojourn; that ye may be cut off, and that ye may
be a curse and a reproach among all the nations of the earth?
9 Have ye forgotten the wickedness of your fathers, and the
wickedness of the kings of Judah, and the wickedness of their
wives, and your own wickedness, and the wickedness of your
wives, which they committed in the land of Judah, and in the
streets of Jerusalem? 10 They are not humbled even unto this

2. *no man dwelleth*.   The statements in this *v.* are not meant to
be taken literally.

3. *incense*.   See on i. 16, vi. 20.

4. Cf. vii. 25, xxxii. 35.

5. Cf. vii. 26, xxv. 4.

7. *to leave you none remaining*.   Cf. Gen. xlv. 7; 2 S. xiv. 7.

8. It is rather strange that the settlers in Egypt did not adopt the
gods of the nation under whose protection they were living, if they
doubted Jehovah's power to deliver them now that they were outside
His land.   Perhaps the queen of heaven was considered to be in a
different category from other terrestrial deities, and moreover she had
been worshipped whilst the people were still in Judah.

9. *your wives*.   Read with LXX. *your princes*.

day, neither have they feared, nor walked in my law, nor in my statutes, that I set before you and before your fathers. 11 Therefore thus saith the LORD of hosts, the God of Israel: Behold, I will set my face against you for evil, even to cut off all Judah. 12 And I will take the remnant of Judah, that have set their faces to go into the land of Egypt to sojourn there, and they shall all be consumed; in the land of Egypt shall they fall; they shall be consumed by the sword and by the famine; they shall die, from the least even unto the greatest, by the sword and by the famine: and they shall be an execration, *and* an astonishment, and a curse, and a reproach. 13 For I will punish them that dwell in the land of Egypt, as I have punished Jerusalem, by the sword, by the famine, and by the pestilence: 14 so that none of the remnant of Judah, which are gone into the land of Egypt to sojourn there, shall escape or remain, that they should return into the land of Judah, to the which they ¹have a desire to return to dwell there: for none shall return save such as shall escape.

15 Then all the men which knew that their wives burned incense unto other gods, and all the women that stood by, a great assembly, even all the people that dwelt in the land of Egypt, in Pathros, answered Jeremiah, saying, 16 As for the word that

¹ Heb. *lift up their soul.*

12.   Cf. xlii. 18.

15—19.   The Jews taunt Jeremiah with the fact that Jehovah was unable to save Jerusalem, and express their belief that had they continued the worship of the queen of heaven all would have gone well with them. Therefore they repudiated Jehovah and His prophet alike.

15.   *all the men...all the women.* According to this statement the reply came from both men and women, *v.* 19 *our husbands* makes the reply come from the women alone. Probably as the worship of the queen of heaven concerned the women most nearly they were the actual speakers whilst the men made it clear that they approved of what was said¹.

great assembly. The suggestion of Duhm which is accepted by Cornill and other critics that *loud voice* should be read is probably right; it involves but the omission of a single Heb. letter.

even...Pathros. Unless the section contains the record of the

¹ Maimonides says that the Jewish women of his time were much given to astrology and soothsaying, and that therefore members of the Sanhedrin ought to have knowledge of such matters in order to judge them. *Sanhed.* c. 2.

thou hast spoken unto us in the name of the LORD, we will not
hearken unto thee. 17 But we will certainly perform every word
that is gone forth out of our mouth, to burn incense unto the
queen of heaven, and to pour out drink offerings unto her, as
we have done, we and our fathers, our kings and our princes, in
the cities of Judah, and in the streets of Jerusalem: for then had
we plenty of ¹victuals, and were well, and saw no evil. 18 But
since we left off to burn incense to the queen of heaven, and to
pour out drink offerings unto her, we have wanted all things,
and have been consumed by the sword and by the famine.
19 And when we burned incense to the queen of heaven, and
poured out drink offerings unto her, did we make her cakes to
²worship her, and pour out drink offerings unto her, without
our husbands? 20 Then Jeremiah said unto all the people, to

---

¹ Heb. *bread.*   ² Or, *pourtray*

---

proceedings of a council to consider the whole question of worship, it
is unlikely that Jews, and more especially their wives, would have been
present from the distant south. The clause should probably be omitted
as a gloss from *v.* 1 *b.*

17.   *every word* &c. 'An intention only becomes binding when it
has been embodied in speech, and so gained an independent existence;
consequently stress is frequently laid...on the *utterance* of the vow.'
G. B. Gray on Nu. xxx. 2, 12; cf. Jud. xi. 36, &c.

queen of heaven. See on vii. 18.

then had we plenty &c. Cf. Hos. ii. 5 'I will go after my lovers that
give me my bread and my water'; see also *v.* 8.

18.   *since we left off.* Some critics think that the worship of the
queen of heaven was revived in the time of Jehoiakim, and that the
series of misfortunes here referred to dates from a subsequent cessation
of that worship (see Introd. to vii. 16—20). But even if there had
been a revival after the reformation under Josiah it was from that
king's reign that things began to go adversely. The fall of Jerusalem
seemed especially clear proof that Jehovah was not able to hold His
own against the gods of other nations. In the period of the decline of
the Roman Empire accusations were repeatedly made against the
Christians that misfortunes occurred owing to their having deserted
the old gods; see Tert. *Apol.* § 40; St August. *de Civit. Dei*, I. 36.

19.   *cakes to worship her.* For a description of the *cakes* see on
vii. 18. The rendering of mg. *pourtray* suggests that the cakes
were either models of Ishtar, or bore her image or some other symbol
of dedication.

our husbands. The approval of the husbands was necessary (cf.

the men, and to the women, even to all the people which had given him that answer, saying, 21 The incense that ye burned in the cities of Judah, and in the streets of Jerusalem, ye and your fathers, your kings and your princes, and the people of the land, did not the LORD remember them, and came it not into his mind? 22 so that the LORD could no longer bear, because of the evil of your doings, and because of the abominations which ye have committed; therefore is your land become a desolation, and an astonishment, and a curse, without inhabitant, as it is this day. 23 Because ye have burned incense, and because ye have sinned against the LORD, and have not obeyed the voice of the LORD, nor walked in his law, nor in his statutes, nor in his testimonies; therefore this evil is happened unto you, as it is this day.

24 Moreover Jeremiah said unto all the people, and to all the women, Hear the word of the LORD, all Judah that are in the land of Egypt: 25 thus saith the LORD of hosts, the God of Israel, saying: Ye and your wives have both spoken with your mouths, and with your hands have fulfilled it, saying, We will surely perform our vows that we have vowed, to burn incense to the queen of heaven, and to pour out drink offerings unto her: establish then your vows, and perform your vows.

Nu. xxx. 6 f. which though late preserves earlier traditions). According to vii. 18 not only did the husbands approve, but they also assisted in the worship.

20—30. Jeremiah again warns the exiles that the calamities which have befallen the nation are the result, not of the neglect of the queen of heaven, but of the persistent idolatry and sin of which they have been guilty. The remnant in Egypt will share the fate of their countrymen, and the very king of Egypt in whose protection they trust will become a prisoner in the hands of his enemies.

20—23. The similarity of these *vv.* to *vv.* 2—14 has caused their genuineness to be suspected; they may represent a repeated warning by the prophet.

21. *the* LORD *remember*. Cf. Hos. viii. 13; Ps. xxv. 7, &c.

22. *no longer bear*. Cf. Is. i. 13.

24. *all Judah...Egypt*. Omit with LXX.

25. *Ye and your wives*. LXX. again appears to have preserved the better text reading *Ye women*.

establish...your vows. The prophet uses irony, Make good your words and see what the effect will be.

26 Therefore hear ye the word of the LORD, all Judah that dwell
in the land of Egypt: Behold, I have sworn by my great name,
saith the LORD, that my name shall no more be named in the
mouth of any man of Judah in all the land of Egypt, saying, As
the Lord GOD liveth. 27 Behold, I watch over them for evil,
and not for good: and all the men of Judah that are in the land
of Egypt shall be consumed by the sword and by the famine,
until there be an end of them. 28 And they that escape the
sword shall return out of the land of Egypt into the land of
Judah, few in number; and all the remnant of Judah, that are
gone into the land of Egypt to sojourn there, shall know whose
word shall stand, mine, or theirs. 29 And this shall be the sign
unto you, saith the LORD, that I will punish you in this place,
that ye may know that my words shall surely stand against you
for evil: 30 thus saith the LORD: Behold, I will give Pharaoh
Hophra king of Egypt into the hand of his enemies, and into the

26 ff. These *vv.* in their present form are full of difficulty and can
hardly reproduce the original text. According to *v.* 27 all the Jews in
Egypt are to be consumed ; *v.* 28, however, anticipates not only survivors
in Egypt, but also those who will succeed in escaping back to Judah.
Duhm's explanation of the origin of the present text has been accepted
by most recent critics. He takes *v.* 28 *b* as original and thinks that
v. 26 was intended as a continuation of the ironic address of the previous
v. let my name be no more &c. *vv.* 27, 28 *a* are a later addition. Jeremiah's
forecasts were pitched on too pessimistic a note as the Jewish colony in
Egypt survived to become a factor of great importance in the religious
life of the chosen people, though, apparently, they did not immediately
throw off their tendency towards the worship of other gods, as the
Elephantine Papyri reveal the worship of two deities 'Asm-Bethel and
'Anath-Bethel being still carried on in the fifth century alongside the
worship of Jehovah[1].

29. *this shall be the sign.* It is not uncommon to find signs in OT.
given in the indefinite future as the guarantee of certain happenings;
so Moses was told that when he had brought the people out of Egypt
they should worship God 'on this mountain' (Ex. iii. 12).

30. *Hophra.* This ruler, who is referred to but not named in
xxxvii. 5 &c., was so convinced of the stability of his throne that
Herodotus reports him as saying that not even a god could move him
from it. His downfall took place after a heavy slaughter of native Egyptian
troops in an expedition to Cyrene; the remnant believed that the king

[1] See the Additional Note on 'Jewish Colonies in Egypt' and especially the
article by S. A. Cook there referred to.

hand of them that seek his life; as I gave Zedekiah king of Judah
into the hand of Nebuchadrezzar king of Babylon, his enemy,
and that sought his life.

had sent them deliberately to their death and revolted from him taking
as their leader Amasis whom Hophra had sent to appease them. Hophra
and his Greek mercenaries were outnumbered and defeated and the
dethroned monarch was eventually strangled (Herod. II. 163 ff., 169).

ADDITIONAL NOTE ON XLIV. 1.

Jewish Colonies in Egypt.

Intercourse between Egypt and the Hebrews, if the traditions contained in
Genesis are to be taken as evidence, seems to have been very close from the
earliest times. Abraham the great ancestor of the race sojourned in that country
for a time on account of famine (Gen. xii. 10 &c.), and only a direct prohibition
from Jehovah prevented Isaac from following his example (Gen. xxvi. 2).
Somewhat later the sons of Jacob and their aged father went down thither for
the same reason, and their descendants, to many generations, were compelled
to remain as slaves to the Egyptians. After the establishment of the monarchy
Solomon made an alliance with the daughter of the reigning Pharaoh (1 K. iii. 1),
but under the succeeding rulers Egypt was apparently a ready refuge for exiles
from Israel (cf. 1 K. xi. 40). During the whole period of the Jewish monarchy
there seems to have been a party in Judah which regarded Egypt as the natural
friend and protector of the state; but, with the possible exception of Hos. ix. 9,
there are no traces of any actual settlements of Jews in Egypt. In 608 B.C.
however, Necho II deposed Jehoahaz and took him captive into Egypt and
with him possibly others; at any rate by the time of Jeremiah's residence in
the land the Jewish community seems to have been both numerous and widespread (xliv. 1 ff.). Some very interesting records of a Jewish settlement in
Upper Egypt have recently been brought to light by the discovery of the
Elephantine Papyri[1]. The people of this settlement had their own temple and
they claimed that its foundation went back beyond the time of the Persian invasion (529 B.C.). There is a tradition of a somewhat late date that Jewish
mercenaries were employed by Psammetichus against the Ethiopians[2], but
whether by this is to be understood the first Egyptian monarch of that name
(reigned 663—609 B.C.) or the second (594—588 B.C.) is not certain; it may be
that some of these mercenaries were the founders of the temple at Yeb, especially

---

[1] These papyri have been edited by A. H. Sayce and A. E. Cowley, *Aramaic
Papyri* (1906), and a much larger collection by E. Sachau, *Aramäische Papyrus u.
Ostraka* (1911). An excellent descriptive article by S. A. Cook is to be found in
AJTh. 1915, pp. 346 ff. entitled *The Significance of the Elephantine Papyri for the
History of Heb. Rel.*

[2] *Ep. Arist.* §§ 12 f.

as Elephantine was an important military station. Perhaps, however, the settlement was started by fugitives from Nebuchadrezzar when he first captured Jerusalem in 597 B.C. The personal names found in these papyri are very interesting and the large number of them which are similar to names of Jeremiah's contemporaries is very remarkable [1].

In later times the Jews were found in very large numbers in Egypt, especially at Alexandria; and at Leontopolis they had from c. 170 B.C. a temple modelled on that at Jerusalem and a true branch of the Aaronic priesthood. The great importance of these Jewish colonies in Egypt lay in their close contact with Greek thought, and it was amongst them that LXX. was produced and the school of Philo flourished [2].

CHAPTER XLV.

The Rebuke to Baruch.

Jeremiah finds it necessary to address words of reproof and warning to his faithful scribe and secretary; but to the reproofs he attaches the promise that in the disorder and ruin which are coming upon the land Baruch's life shall be spared. The genuineness of the passage as a whole is admitted by nearly all recent critics; though most of them, including Giesebrecht, reject the chronological note *in the fourth year of Jehoiakim* contained in the title, and would place the warning and the expressions which called it forth at a somewhat later period. Their main reason for so doing is that the roll was written in the hope of moving Jerusalem and Judah to sorrow and amendment of life, whereas the present passage looks upon the exile as certain, if not imminent. In reply to this it may be urged, as is done by Cornill, that Jeremiah himself had no great expectation that the people would repent and he seems to have recognised that the possibility of their returning to Jehovah was only a remote one. It is perhaps as well to retain the note of time and to look upon the warning as a kind of appendix to xxxvi.; its position at the end of Baruch's memoirs may be due to the writer's modesty, or to his wish not to interrupt the narrative with a merely personal passage. Cornill thinks that the rebuke was administered to Baruch because of his indignation over the fate of the people, but this theory hardly agrees with *v.* 5 where see note. The thought of later times busied itself over the motives which influenced Baruch and many traditions have been gathered round his name. According to some of them he is represented 'as so offended at the denial to him of the gift of prophecy and at the hard fate of Jerusalem and at the destruction of the temple that he apostatized from Judaism, and adopted the tenets of Zoroaster, with whom indeed they often identify him.' Payne Smith. See further on xxxii. 12.

---

[1] See an article in *Rev. Et. Juives*, LIV. pp. 35 ff., *La Colonie Juive d'Assouan*.
[2] For fuller details regarding these later colonies see *Enc. Bib.* 1108 ff. and the references there given.

The last two *vv.* of the ch. have been paraphrased by Keble in *The Christian Year*, Eleventh Sunday after Trinity:

> 'Then in His wrath shall GOD uproot
> The trees He set, for lack of fruit,
> And drown in rude tempestuous blaze
> The towers His hand had deign'd to raise ;
> In silence, ere that storm begin,
> Count o'er His mercies and thy sin.
>
> Pray only that thy aching heart,
> From visions vain content to part,
> Strong for Love's sake its woe to hide
> May cheerful wait the Cross beside,
> Too happy if, that dreadful day,
> Thy life be given thee for a prey.'

XLV. 1 The word that Jeremiah the prophet spake unto Baruch the son of Neriah, when he wrote these words in a book at the mouth of Jeremiah, in the fourth year of Jehoiakim the son of Josiah, king of Judah, saying, 2 Thus saith the LORD, the God of Israel, [1]unto thee, O Baruch: 3 Thou didst say, Woe is me now! for the LORD hath added sorrow to my pain; [2]I am weary with my groaning, and I find no rest. 4 Thus shalt thou say unto him, Thus saith the LORD: Behold, that which I have built will I break down, and that which I have planted I will pluck up; and this in the whole land. 5 And seekest thou great

---

[1] Or, *concerning*   [2] See Ps. vi. 6.

XLV. **3.** The complaints in this *v.* are very similar in wording to those of Jeremiah himself (cf. x. 19, xv. 18, &c. and also Ps. vi. 6).

4. *unto him.* These words do not fit into the context as in the previous *v.* Baruch himself is addressed, not Jeremiah.

Behold &c. Cornill sees in this utterance the recognition and declaration of the thought that because God made the world therefore He loves it, and that consequently His pain over the fate of Jerusalem is greater even than that of Baruch. Whilst admitting that the words might be made to bear such an interpretation it seems simpler and more in accordance with Heb. methods of thought to see in them a declaration of Jehovah's right to do what seems good in His eyes quite apart from the criticisms of feeble man.

and this in the whole land. LXX. omits and its reading should probably be accepted as correct ; the Heb. is awkward.

5. Cornill's theory that the warning was uttered to Baruch on account of his unselfish indignation over the fall of Jerusalem and not because of any personal feeling is contradicted by the plain and simple meaning of this *v.* Baruch was probably of high social rank (such is Cheyne's opinion, cf. xxxvi. 15, and see *Life and Times*, p. 146)

things for thyself? seek them not: for, behold, I will bring evil
upon all flesh, saith the LORD: but thy life will I give unto thee
for a prey in all places whither thou goest.

and he may have wished to become 'the leader of a new and better
Israel' (*Enc. Bib.* 492).

   seekest...not.   The words were written as a motto in Bishop Ken's
copy of Grotius, *De Veritate*; they were also in the mind of Henry
Martyn at a crisis in his life, see *Life* by Sargent, p. 15.

CHAPTERS XLVI.—LI.

   This important group of chapters is concerned entirely with the ultimate
fate and future prospects either of the nations surrounding Judah and Jerusalem, or of those which had been brought into close contact with them—Elam
for instance is included because of the part which it was to play in the fall of
Babylon. The intimate connexion between these chapters and the vision of the
cup of the Lord's fury in xxv. has already been pointed out in the notes dealing
with that passage, together with the fact that in LXX. the prophecies, arranged
in a somewhat different order, appear immediately after xxv. 13. This difference,
both in order and position between MT. and LXX. of these chh., suggests that
they were composed or collected at a comparatively late date, perhaps to supply
an appropriate oracle in connexion with each of the nations included in the
catalogue in xxv. 19 ff. There are also reasons for thinking that several of the
prophecies come from a time anterior to that of Jeremiah—Damascus, for
example, had long ceased to exist as an independent kingdom in his day—and
there can be no doubt that some of the other oracles include passages from
earlier prophets (e.g. xlviii. has some close connexion with Is. xv.—xvi.; and
xlix. 7—22 is largely borrowed from the work of the unknown prophet who
also influenced Obadiah). There is therefore good reason for supposing that
the group as it is contained in the canonical book is not entirely from the lips
of Jeremiah.

   Some critics, however, would go further than this and deny that any part
comes from the prophet (e.g. Schwally, Wellhausen, Duhm and Giesebrecht, the
latter indeed makes an exception in favour of xlvii. and a few *vv.* of xlix.), and
a variety of reasons have been found by them for holding this opinion. The
most prominent argument, that Jeremiah had no concern with any nation except
his own people has already been dealt with (see Introd. to ch. i.) and need not
detain us here ; nor do the arguments based on difference of style, and the fact
that the internal affairs of Judah are ignored in these prophecies on foreign
nations call for special treatment. A more serious matter is the statement
that the conception of Jehovah in the chh. is not that of Jeremiah, inasmuch
as He is represented as a God of vengeance. In reply to this argument two
points may be made, each of which is sufficient to dispose of it: (*a*) there is

in these chh., with the possible exception of xlvi. 10, no idea of the Divine vengeance on the heathen, apart from the punishment of crimes actually committed; and (*b*) it is not strictly accurate to say that Jeremiah never conceived of Jehovah as a God of vengeance, as a study of passages such as v. 9, 29, ix. 9, xi. 20, xv. 15, xx. 12 will quickly shew. Schwally also urges that no opportunity is given for the nations to repent and turn to God. But the idea of preaching repentance to the heathen is a late one, as Cornill points out, and receives its classic expression in the book of Jonah. These considerations go to prove that no real case can be made out against the section as a whole but that each several prophecy—and one might almost say each several verse—must be taken on its own merits. The general conclusion, in the opinion of the present writer, is that xlvi.—xlix. contain a genuine nucleus which comes from Jeremiah but that large and numerous additions have been made to it; l.—li. require separate treatment for which see notes *ad loc.* The chh. are easily analysed according to the headings of the various prophecies:

Prophecy against Egypt. xlvi.
Prophecy against the Philistines. xlvii.
Prophecy against Moab. xlviii.
Prophecy against Ammon. xlix. 1—6.
Prophecy against Edom. xlix. 7—22.
Prophecy against Damascus. xlix. 23—27.
Prophecy against Kedar. xlix. 28—33.
Prophecy against Elam. xlix. 34—39.
Prophecy against Babylon. l.—li. 58.
The mission of Seraiah. li. 59—64.

CHAPTER XLVI. (= LXX. XXVI.).

The Prophecy against Egypt.

This ch. really consists of two main divisions: (*a*) *vv.* 2—12; and (*b*) *vv.* 13—28. To the date of (*b*) there is no certain clue; (*a*) is stated to belong to the fourth year of Jehoiakim (see *v.* 2), that is to the year of the battle of Carchemish— with which event the prophecy claims to deal—and of the giving of the cup of fury to the nations (xxv. 15—19). The genuineness of both passages has been questioned by various critics mainly, it must be said, on literary grounds; the looseness of the connexion between the parts, the confusion between the actual battle and the preparations for it, the parallels to later writers contained in it, all these have combined to discredit the prophecy, and even so moderate a critic as Giesebrecht rejects the whole of (*b*) and parts of (*a*) as later additions. Cornill, however, after a careful re-examination of the section has been convinced of its substantial authenticity, though he feels that some slight re-

arrangement and the omission of several passages are necessary in order to restore it to its original state. The section may be analysed as follows:

> (a) *Title of the whole group.* 1.
> (b) *The fate of the army of Egypt.* 2—6.
> (c) *The downfall of Egypt's pride.* 7—12.
> (d) *The coming of Nebuchadrezzar.* 13—19.
> (e) *The ruin of Egypt.* 20—26.
> (f) *Jacob is comforted.* 27 f.

XLVI. 1 The word of the LORD which came to Jeremiah the
prophet concerning the nations.

2 Of Egypt: concerning the army of Pharaoh-neco king of
Egypt, which was by the river Euphrates in Carchemish, which
Nebuchadrezzar king of Babylon smote in the fourth year of
Jehoiakim the son of Josiah, king of Judah.

XLVI. 1. This *v.* forms the title to the whole series of prophecies
on the nations.
2—6. This section describes the preparations for the battle of
Carchemish and the actual event itself.
2. *Pharaoh-neco.* The title *Pharaoh* was an Egyptian word *Pr-'o*
'great house' which in course of time had come to be applied to the
king himself. Necho II, the monarch mentioned in this *v.*, was the
first to have the title coupled with his personal name; see Dr McNeile's
note on Exodus i. 11.
king of Babylon. It is doubtful whether Nebuchadrezzar was at
this time more than *general* as his father was still alive.
Carchemish. This city owed its pre-eminence, both as a military
and as a commercial[1] centre, to its situation, which commanded the most
important ford over the Euphrates. It appears in Assyrian inscriptions
as *Gargamish* and its modern name is *Jerablus*—which Nöldeke considers
to be the Arabic plural of *Jirbâs*—or *Jerâbis*. In addition to a village
the site is occupied by several mounds of which the northern is the
finest. Miss Gertrude Lowthian Bell has given the following description
of the present appearance of the city. 'Until you come to Babylon
there is no site on the Euphrates so imposing as the northern mound
of Carchemish. It was the acropolis, the strongly fortified dwelling-
place of king and god. At its north-eastern end it rises to a high
ridge enclosed on two sides in a majestic sweep of the river. From the
top of this ridge you may see the middle parts of the strategic line
drawn by the Euphrates from Samosata to Thapsacus, strung with
battlefields whereon the claims of Europe and Asia were fought out;
while to the west stretch the rich plains that gave wealth to Carchemish,
to Europus, and to Hierapolis' (*Amurath to Amurath*, pp. 33 f.).

---

[1] 'A strong proof of its commercial importance is afforded by the fact that by
far the most common unit of monetary value in Assyria down to the last was the
maneh of Carchemish.' *Enc. Bib.* 703.

3 Order ye the buckler and shield, and draw near to battle.
4 Harness the horses, and get up, ye horsemen, and stand forth
with your helmets; furbish the spears, put on the coats of mail.
5 Wherefore have I seen it? they are dismayed and are turned
backward; and their mighty ones are beaten down, and are fled
apace, and look not back: terror is on every side, saith the LORD.
6 Let not the swift flee away, nor the mighty man escape; in
the north by the river Euphrates have they stumbled and fallen.
7 [1]Who is this that riseth up like the Nile, whose waters toss
themselves like the rivers? 8 Egypt riseth up like the Nile, and
his waters toss themselves like the rivers: and he saith, I will

---

[1] Or, *Who is this like the Nile that riseth up, like the rivers whose waters toss
themselves? Egypt is like the Nile that riseth up &c.*

3—6. These verses consist of a number of short direct sentences
leading up to a climax. The prophet in a vision sees the various parts
of the Egyptian army and calls upon them to prepare for battle.
　3. *buckler...shield.* The defensive weapons of the light armed and
the heavy troops respectively.
　draw near. The same phrase is used in Jud. xx. 23; 2 S. x. 13.
　4. *Harness the horses.* The Egyptians always placed great reliance
on their chariots; cf. *v.* 9.
　get up, ye horsemen. Modern commentators favour the rendering
mount the steeds.
　with your helmets. The *helmets* would only be put on for the actual
fighting; cf. Ez. xxxviii. 5.
　furbish the spears. Cornill suggests the reading *arm yourselves with
spears* (cf. 2 S. xxiii. 7) as the moment immediately before the battle
was hardly the time to *furbish* weapons.
　coats of mail. For further details of these see *Enc. Bib.* 606.
　5. *Wherefore...dismayed.* Cf. Am. ii. 14 f.; Nah. ii. 8. LXX. omits
have I seen it? and makes the rest of the phrase a question. Jeremiah
quite possibly saw some of the fugitives with his own eyes.
　7—12. The Egyptians in spite of their boasting and in spite of the
strength of their auxiliaries will be overcome, and the disaster will be
of such magnitude that recovery will be impossible. The scene once
more returns to the preparation for the battle and the description is
continued in longer sentences.
　7. *Who is this?* This formula introduces a prophecy in Is. lxiii. 1;
cf. Cant. iii. 6, viii. 5. In viii. 7 Isaiah makes use of the simile of the
overflowing waters of the Euphrates as an illustration of the sweeping
conquests of Assyria.
　8. *and his waters...rivers.* This phrase is omitted by LXX. though
the parallelism seems to require it.

B.　　　　　　　　　　　　　　　　　　　　　　　　　　21

rise up, I will cover the earth; I will destroy the city and the inhabitants thereof. 9 Go up, ye horses; and rage, ye chariots; and let the mighty men go forth: Cush and Put, that handle the shield; and the Ludim, that handle and bend the bow. 10 For that day is *a day* of the Lord, the LORD of hosts, a day of vengeance, that he may avenge him of his adversaries: and the sword shall devour and be satiate, and shall drink its fill of their blood: for the Lord, the LORD of hosts, hath a sacrifice in the north country by the river Euphrates. 11 Go up into Gilead, and take balm, O virgin daughter of Egypt: in vain dost thou

the city. No specific city is intended; LXX. omits.

9. This *v.* contains another description of the various arms of the Egyptian host; in a vision the prophet sees them, together with the subject and allied nations whose duty it was to supply troops to their overlord.

Cush. See note on xiii. 23.

Put. Put supplied troops to Egypt (Nah. iii. 9; Ez. xxx. 5), to Tyre (Ez. xxvii. 10), and to Gog (Ez. xxxviii. 6). The situation of the country is not certain, some have identified it with the land of Punt— Cheyne, however, rejects this identification on the grounds that Punt never supplied troops to Egypt (*Enc. Bib.* 3985). Driver, in his note on Gen. x. 6, thinks that the Libyans are meant and points out that 'the western part of Lower Egypt (the so-called *Libya Aegypti*) is called in Coptic *Phaiat.*' LXX. here and in the passages in Ez. quoted above reads Λίβυες.

Ludim. The similarity of this name with the Lydians of Asia Minor who later sent mercenaries to Psammetichus led Sayce (*Higher Criticism* &c. pp. 134 f.) to regard them as identical. According to Gen. x. 13, however, they were descendants of Egypt and should therefore be looked upon as some tribe related to the Ethiopians and Libyans. Driver and Cornill reject the above identification on these and other grounds.

10. a day *of the Lord.* The phrase is here used in the popular sense of a day when Jehovah was to be avenged on His enemies. The writer of the passage, who may well have been Jeremiah himself, exhibits great animosity towards Egypt, an animosity which is not strange in men who had lived in the time of Josiah and who still remembered his tragic death at the hands of Pharaoh Necho. Jeremiah who saw in Babylon the instrument of Jehovah could not but rejoice at the overthrow of Babylon's chief adversary.

sword. Cf. Is. xxxiv. 5 ff. The present passage is probably the original of that.

hath a sacrifice &c. Cf. the similar phrase in Is. xxxiv. 6 'the LORD hath a sacrifice in Bozrah'; and see also Zeph. i. 7; Ez. xxxix. 17 ff.

11. *balm.* See on viii. 22, xxx. 13.

use many medicines; there is no healing for thee. 12 The nations have heard of thy shame, and the earth is full of thy cry: for the mighty man hath stumbled against the mighty, they are fallen both of them together.

13 The word that the LORD spake to Jeremiah the prophet, how that Nebuchadrezzar king of Babylon should come and smite the land of Egypt.

14 Declare ye in Egypt, and publish in Migdol, and publish in Noph and in Tahpanhes: say ye, Stand forth, and prepare thee; for the sword hath devoured round about thee. 15 ¹Why are thy strong ones swept away? they stood not, because the LORD did ²drive them. 16 He made many to stumble, yea, they fell

¹ Or, according to some ancient authorities, *Why is thy strong one swept away? he stood not &c.* ² Or, *thrust them down*

virgin daughter. It is somewhat unusual to find this phrase applied to a nation other than Israel; but cf. Is. xlvii. 1.

many medicines. The Egyptians were famous for their use of medicines; Dr Streane refers to Homer, *Od.* IV. 229 f.; Herod. III. 1, 132; Pliny XIX. 5.

no healing. The disaster which has come upon Egypt is one from which recovery is impossible.

13—19. Egypt is called upon to gather together the remnant of her powers to resist the invader who is close upon her borders; at the same time she is warned that she enters upon a hopeless struggle.

13. This *v.* forms the heading of the prophecy and probably owes its presence here to a supplementer (see on *v.* 16).

14. *Declare ye.* The address is to an unknown body of people as in Is. xl.

in Egypt, and publish. LXX. omits.

Migdol. See on xliv. 1.

Noph. See on ii. 16.

Tahpanhes. See on ii. 16. LXX. omits.

round about thee. LXX. reads by a slight change in Heb. *thy thicket* which may be correct in view of the use of the same metaphor in *vv.* 22 f.

15. *Why...swept away?* The rendering of the mg. which reads the singular for the plural follows some 65 Heb. MSS., and also agrees with the rest of the sentence which has the verb and pronouns in the singular. LXX. has an interesting rendering of the passage, which is evidently obtained by dividing up the MT. word for *swept away* into two, *Why is Apis fled? Thy mighty one stood not* &c. Apis is the sacred bull who was worshipped at Memphis as a re-incarnation of Osiris, and the idea suggested is the same as that in Is. xix. 1 &c. that a country is conquered because its gods are too weak to save it.

drive them. The same word is used of cattle in Ez. xxxiv. 21.

one upon another: and they said, Arise, and let us go again to
our own people, and to the land of our nativity, from the oppressing sword. 17 They cried there, Pharaoh king of Egypt is but
a noise; he hath let the appointed time pass by. 18 As I live,

16. *to our own people.* The speakers are evidently foreigners who
seeing that the fortunes of Egypt are in a desperate case decide to
leave her. This sudden introduction of foreigners has appeared to
various critics as unnatural. Cornill wishes to omit all mention of them
and to make the *v.* refer to Apis, *He hath stumbled grievously and is
fallen because of the oppressing sword*; Giesebrecht is much less drastic
and by a slight change in the Heb. of the first part of the *v.* he reads
Thy mingled people have stumbled and fallen. This last suggestion
should probably be adopted as it avoids the awkwardness referred to
above. These *mingled people* (see on xxv. 20) were probably traders
who fled from Egypt, as they fled from Babylon, having no interest in
their adopted country beyond that of personal profit (Is. xiii. 14).
There may also be a reference to the mercenary troops of which the
Egyptian army was so largely composed and who likewise had little
interest in their employers' cause when once it seemed to be lost[1].

the oppressing sword. LXX. renders *the sword of the Greeks* and
Vulg. *the sword of the dove*; the latter reading is due to the tradition
that the standards of Nebuchadrezzar bore that emblem, the Heb. word,
(יוֹנָה *Yonah* or *Jonah*) for *fierceness* and for *dove* being the same. The
former reading is presumably due to LXX. confusing *Jonah* with *Javan*
(Greece; cf. Is. lxvi. 19 &c.), and referring the prophecy to Alexander
the Great; if this was so the text in the possession of the translators
did not include *v.* 13.

17. *They cried...a noise.* The reading of the versions (LXX., Vulg.
and Syr.) is better, *Call ye the name of Pharaoh a Crash.* The meaning
is that a great destruction (cf. Ps. xl. 2 RVm.) is coming upon the
land over which Pharaoh ruled; for a similar prophecy cf. xx. 3 f.

the appointed time. There is a tide in the affairs of nations as of
men and those who miss it earn for themselves the contempt of their
fellows (cf. *Julius Caesar*, Act IV. Scene 3) ; and see Luke xix. 44, xxi. 24.

pass by. The Heb. word *he'ebir* is thought by some critics to
contain a play on Hophra which in Egyptian is Uah-ab-ra. For another
similar word-play on Egypt see Is. xxx. 7 'I called thee Rahab that
sitteth still.' The phrase is looked upon by many scholars as late
though Cornill accepts it as a contemporary utterance.

---

[1] Bishop Creighton relates an incident in his *History of the Papacy*, I. pp. 233 f.
which well illustrates the weakness of those who rely upon mercenaries. In 1409
Ladislas I, king of Naples, threatened to seize the States of the Church and was warned
by Florence against so doing; 'he scornfully asked with what troops they would
defend themselves, the Florentine ambassador...answered, "With yours." Ladislas
checked himself, for he knew that the wealth of the Florentine citizens could allure
his followers from his ranks.'

saith the King, whose name is the LORD of hosts, surely like
Tabor among the mountains, and like Carmel by the sea, so shall
he come. 19 [1]O thou daughter that dwellest in Egypt, [2]furnish
thyself to go into captivity: for Noph shall become a desolation,
and shall be burnt up, without inhabitant. 20 Egypt is a very
fair heifer; *but* [3]destruction out of the north is come, [4]it is

[1] Or, *O thou that dwellest with the daughter of Egypt*
[2] Heb. *make thee vessels of captivity.*   [3] Or, *the gadfly*
[4] Or, according to many ancient authorities, *upon her*

18. The coming conqueror is to be conspicuous above his enemies,
as conspicuous as would be one of the hills of Palestine amongst the
flat plains of Egypt.

Tabor. This mountain though its height is only some 1,800 feet
is yet very conspicuous from its being surrounded by a plain, from
which it rises like a sugar-loaf[1].

Carmel. Mount Carmel is a great headland standing out into the
sea above which it rises to the height of 600 feet, it is therefore a
most conspicuous object. In the Midrash *Bereshith Rabba* § 99 it is
said that '*Tabor* came from Beth-elim and *Carmel* from Aspamya to
attend the law-giving at Sinai.'

19. *furnish* &c. i.e. prepare what will be necessary for exile; cf.
Ez. xii. 3 f.

20—26. This passage seems to carry the history of disaster a stage
further; in the previous section the invasion is imminent, in this the
land is· already at the mercy of its enemies. The fate of Egypt is
described under various similes, she is like a heifer driven mad by
a gadfly, or again she is like a serpent whose hiding place is cut
down.

20. *fair heifer.* Driver proposes the translation *graceful* on the
ground that Heb. is a diminutive; cf. Is. ii. 20, lxi. 1. The personification of Egypt as a heifer may have a reference to the bull Apis (cf. *v.* 15),
the land being described as his spouse.

destruction. The mg. *gadfly* is probably to be accepted though this
meaning of the word is not found elsewhere[2]. Just as a heifer is driven
to flight by the stings of the fly, so has Egypt been made to flee before
her foes (cf. Is. vii. 18 'the fly that is in the uttermost part of the

---

[1] Cf. the description given by a traveller of the last century: '*Tabor* stands in-
sulated at the north-east extremity of the plain of Esdraelon. It rises to a great
height, and appears in the bee-hive form, just as Raphael has painted it in his im-
mortal picture of the Transfiguration.' *Life of Henry Venn Elliott,* p. 79.

[2] Cornill makes several alterations in the text, substituting בָּקָר *herdsman,* 'cow-
boy' for קָרֶץ *destruction* and בְּעָלָה *shall become her master* for בָּא בָא *is come, it is
come*; cf. Is. xxvi. 13.

come. 21 Also her hired men in the midst of her are like calves
of the stall; for they also are turned back, they are fled away
together, they did not stand: for the day of their calamity is
come upon them, the time of their visitation. 22 [1]The sound
thereof shall go like the serpent; for they shall march with an

> [1] Or, *Her sound is like that of the serpent as it goeth*

rivers of Egypt'). The *gadfly* or *breese* was apparently very common
in Egypt; cf. Aeschylus, *Suppliants*, ll. 307 f. :

> 'A winged pest, armed with a horrid sting.
> They who live by the Nile call it the breese.'

Figures derived from the flight of cattle before the *gadfly* are often
met with in ancient literature : cf. Homer, *Odyssey*, XXII. 229 ; Virgil,
Georg. III. 146 ff. Examples can also be found of the same use in more
modern literature : Shakespeare, for instance, describes Cleopatra as
flying,

> 'The breese upon her, like a cow in June.'
> *Antony and Cleopatra*, Act III. Sc. 8.

Cf. also

> 'The herd hath more annoyance by the breese
> Than by the tiger.'
> *Troilus and Cressida*, Act I. Sc. 3[1].

it is come. The reading of mg. *upon her* requires the change of one
consonant only in the Heb. and has the support of the versions.

21. *her hired men.* The Carian and Ionian mercenaries by whose
aid Psammetichus had obtained the supreme power in Egypt and who
remained in the service of his successors (cf. Herod. II. 152 ff.). It is a
strange paradox that Egypt of all nations should have been compelled
to trust to foreign mercenaries for her safety; in the earlier history of
the nation her people were noted for their dislike of foreigners (cf. Diod.
Sic. I. 67; Strabo XVII. i. 6 ; Herod. II. 41; and Gen. xxxix. 6, xlii. 32).

like calves of the stall. The mercenaries after being pampered and
spoiled in peace time, proved valueless in time of war.

22. *The sound...serpent.* The reading of mg. is to be preferred.
Her sound is like that of the serpent as it goeth. The meaning of the
figure is evidently intended as a representation of the feebleness of
Egypt; several suggestions, however, have been made as to its exact
interpretation ; the sound of Egypt in retreat is like the rustle of a
serpent compared with the noise of her advance to battle; or her voice
is like the impotent hiss of a serpent (cf. LXX.) driven from its lair by
woodcutters (cf. *v.* 23). The comparison of Egypt to a serpent received

---

[1] I am indebted for the above quotations to T. F. Royds, *The Beasts, Birds, and
Bees of Virgil*, p. 10.

army, and come against her with axes, as hewers of wood.
23 They shall cut down her forest, saith the LORD, ¹though it
cannot be searched; because they are more than the locusts,
and are innumerable. 24 The daughter of Egypt shall be put
to shame; she shall be delivered into the hand of the people of
the north. 25 The LORD of hosts, the God of Israel, saith: Behold, I will punish Amon of No, and Pharaoh, and Egypt, with
her gods, and her kings; even Pharaoh, and them that trust in
him: 26 and I will deliver them into the hand of those that
seek their lives, and into the hand of Nebuchadrezzar king of
Babylon, and into the hand of his servants: and afterwards it
shall be inhabited, as in the days of old, saith the LORD. 27 ²But
fear not thou, O Jacob my servant, neither be dismayed, O Israel:

¹ Or, *for*   ² See ch. xxx. 10, 11.

added point from the fact that certain serpents were, by the Egyptians,
held to be sacred (e.g. the asp to Neph). Other writers make even more
scathing references to the objects of Egyptian worship (see Juvenal,
Sat. xv. 1 f.; Philo, *Leg. ad Caium*, § 20).

axes. The word is never used elsewhere in OT. of a weapon of war—
it occurs in 1 S. xiii. 20 f.; Jud. ix. 48; Ps. lxxiv. 5—and even in the
present passage it may have no such reference, though the unusualness
of the weapon (see Rawlinson, *Anct. Mon.* I. 459) if it were used on this
occasion by the Babylonians may have led to the employment of the
figure.

23. *her forest.* Egypt is so densely populated and has so many cities
(Herod. II. 177) that it may be 'compared to a *forest*...so thick that the
only means of finding a way through it is by cutting it down.' Driver.
Cf. xxi. 14; Is. x. 18 f., 33 f.

25. The gods, the king, and the people of Egypt are to share in
the same punishment.

Amon of No. Amon or Ammon was the chief deity of later Egypt
and the seat of his worship was at Thebes (i.e. *No*), the modern *Karnak*
and *Luxor*. The temple was a famous oracle and the cult of Amon-Ra
under the title of Jupiter Ammon extended far beyond the borders of
Egypt itself (see Strabo XVII. i. 43).

that trust in him. A warning to those Jews who still had confidence
in Egypt.

26. This *v.* is rejected by some critics as a scribal gloss especially in
view of its absence from LXX.

afterwards it shall be inhabited. The same promise is made in
Ez. xxix. 13 f.

27 f. Words of comfort to Jacob almost exactly the same as these
are found in xxx. 10 f., where see notes.

for, lo, I will save thee from afar, and thy seed from the land of
their captivity; and Jacob shall return, and shall be quiet and
at ease, and none shall make him afraid. 28 Fear not thou, O
Jacob my servant, saith the LORD; for I am with thee: for I will
make a full end of all the nations whither I have driven thee,
but I will not make a full end of thee; but I will correct thee
with judgement, and will in no wise [1]leave thee unpunished.

[1] Or, *hold thee guiltless*

CHAPTER XLVII. (= LXX. XXIX. 1—7).

The Prophecy against the Philistines.

A terrible description of the overwhelming of the cities of the Philistines by
the flood from the North. The sword of the Lord cannot be quieted until they
are destroyed. Other prophecies against the Philistines occur in Am. i. 6—8;
Is. xiv. 29—32; Ez. xxv. 15—17; and Zeph. ii. 4—7, and as Cornill has pointed
out there is no trace of dependence on the part of the present passage upon
them, any similarity of phrasing being due to the similarity of the subject matter.
Those critics who reject the whole group of prophecies on the nations include
this section in their condemnation, but differ as to the time from which it
comes, Schmidt placing it in the reign of Alexander the Great (*Enc. Bib.* 2391),
and Duhm bringing it down as late as the second century. Erbt definitely
rejects *vv.* 3—5, but regards *vv.* 6 f. as authentic; Giesebrecht and Cornill
accept the prophecy as genuine and the present editor feels that their arguments
are convincing.

XLVII. 1 The word of the LORD that came to Jeremiah the
prophet concerning the Philistines before that Pharaoh smote
Gaza.

XLVII. 1. This *v.* is missing from LXX. which has merely the heading *On thePhilistines,* and is evidently no part of the original text. The
prophecy itself gives not the slightest hint that the danger to Philistia
is to come from Egypt, and the use of the phrases *out of the north* (*v.* 2)
and *sword of the LORD* (*v.* 6; cf. xxv. 29) makes it almost certain that
the enemy is Nebuchadrezzar and the Chaldeans.

Pharaoh smote Gaza. Hitzig in his monograph on the subject identified *Gaza* with the Kadytis captured by Necho after the battle of
Magdalos (i.e. Megiddo), an account of which is to be found in Herod. II.
159. This identification has been accepted by many recent scholars but
the difficulties involved in it are in my opinion so great as to render it
improbable[1]. In view of the fact that the notice of *Gaza* is missing from

[1] See *J. Th. S.* XVIII. pp. 44 ff.

2 Thus saith the LORD: Behold, waters rise up out of the north, and shall become an overflowing stream, and shall over-flow the land and all that is therein, the city and them that dwell therein: and the men shall cry, and all the inhabitants of the land shall howl. 3 At the noise of the stamping of the hoofs of his strong ones, at the rushing of his chariots, at the rumbling of his wheels, the fathers look not back to their children for feebleness of hands; 4 because of the day that cometh to spoil all the Philistines, to cut off from Tyre and Zidon every helper

the text used by LXX.—unless indeed they omitted it as inconsistent with the rest of the prophecy—the reference here may be to some quite late historical event, such as the capture of Gaza in 312 by Ptolemy I (Soter).

2. *out of the north.* In a prophecy against the Philistines in Is. xiv. 31 the coming foe is likened to *smoke* out of the north.

overflowing stream. A ready and forcible simile to those who were used to seeing the *wadis* suddenly changed from dry torrent beds to rushing streams; cf. Matt. vii. 26 f. The same figure is used in xlvi. 8 for the army of Egypt itself; and cf. Is. viii. 7.

the men shall cry. The flood which is coming on Egypt is, as Duhm says, to be 'but an episode in a great world-wide tempest.'

3. This *v.* contains a vivid description of the noise and tumult of the invaders which is quite in the usual style of Jeremiah; cf. iv. 13, 29, viii. 16, xlvi. 20 ff.

rushing. The word is used of an earthquake in Am. i. 1 &c.; in the present and similar passages (e.g. Is. ix. 4; Nah. ii. 2; Job xxxix. 24) the use is hyperbolical.

feebleness of hands. The same phrase is used in Ecclus. xxv. 23.

4. *the Philistines.* This people unlike nearly all the other races mentioned in OT. are non-Semitic[1] and came originally from Caphtor (Am. ix. 7). Their first settlement in Palestine was probably made about the time of Ramses III (see Moore, *Judges*, p. 80). According to Ebers (*Aegypten u. Bücher Moses*, pp. 127 ff.) and Sayce (*Races* &c. pp. 53 ff.) Caphtor was situated in the coastlands of the delta, but this view is exceedingly unlikely and nearly all scholars are agreed in identifying Caphtor with Crete[2]. Professor R. A. S. Macalister has recently made a close study of the Philistines and his conclusions are as follows: 'The Philistines were a people composed of several septs, derived from Crete and the south-west corner of Asia Minor. Their civilisation probably was derived from Crete, and though there was a large Carian element in their composition, they may fairly be said to have been the people

---

[1] Ewald and Stade (*Gesch. des Volkes Israel*, I. p. 142) are in favour of a Semitic origin, but they stand practically alone.

[2] An important exception is Professor Flinders Petrie: see *Eastern Exploration*, pp. 21 f.

that remaineth: for the LORD will spoil the Philistines, the
remnant of the ¹isle of Caphtor. 5 Baldness is come upon Gaza;
Ashkelon is brought to nought, the remnant of their valley: how
long wilt thou cut thyself? 6 O thou sword of the LORD, how

¹ Or, *sea coast*

who imported with them to Palestine the memories and traditions of
the great days of Minos.' *Schweich Lectures*, p. 28; cf. Evans, *Scripta
Minoa*, pp. 77 ff. For a history of the Philistines in their relations with
Israel see Harper, *Amos and Hosea*, pp. 23 ff.

Tyre and Zidon. The Babylonians invested Tyre in 586—5 B.C. and
the siege according to Josephus (*Ant.* x. xi. 1, and *c. Ap.* I. 21) lasted
thirteen years. There is no evidence apart from the present passage to
shew that the Philistines were important allies of Tyre and Zidon, and
the text is difficult. Cornill therefore by a slight change in Heb. suggests
the reading *all the remnant of their excellency* for the *every helper that
remaineth* of MT. According to Ez. xxix. 17—20 the siege of Tyre was
unsuccessful.

isle. See on ii. 10, and cf. mg. *sea coast.*

5. *Baldness.* See on xvi. 6, and cf. Dt. xiv. 1; Mic. i. 16.

Gaza. Gaza is the only Philistine town which retains any importance. Writing before the war Prof. Macalister says 'It is a modern
well-watered and populous town, standing on the ancient site and in
the form *Guzzeh* retaining the ancient name.' *Op. cit.* p. 71. Gaza has
always been a place of great importance from both a military and a trading
point of view on account of its position on the edge of the Egyptian
desert and at the dividing point of the caravans for Arabia and Egypt.
See further Pusey, *Zeph.* pp. 86 ff.

Ashkelon. Ashkelon is again mentioned in *v.* 7 and it seems strange
that two only of the Philistine cities should be distinguished from the
rest. Cornill thinks that we should here read Ashdod, and Perles sees
in the unsuitable expression *remnant of their valley* a reference to Ekron¹.
The four cities usually found are thus present in the text according to
these critics; Gath seems early to have fallen into obscurity and it has
been suggested that it had by this time been absorbed by Ashdod (see
Enc. Bib. 1646).

cut thyself. In sorrow; cf. xvi. 6.

6 f. These *vv.* have been rejected by some scholars, including Giesebrecht, on the somewhat uncertain ground of metre. There is however
no reason for separating them from the rest of the passage. A slight
change of person is necessary in *v.* 7 *How canst thou be quiet?* should
be read as *How can it* and the mg. *it* for *thee* should be adopted; the

¹ Perles sees in עמקם *their valley* a mistaken reading for עמקרן; this he thinks
was the original way of spelling עקרון, traces of which can be found in the Assyrian
Amkarruna (see *JQR.* II. N.S. p. 107). The reading of LXX. 'Ενακείμ requires ענקם
in the original, and may possibly be right, as according to Josh. xi. 22 there was a
traditional connexion between the Philistines and the Anakim.

long will it be ere thou be quiet? put up thyself into thy scabbard;
rest, and be still. 7 How canst thou be quiet, seeing the LORD
hath given [1]thee a charge? against Ashkelon, and against the
sea shore, there hath he appointed it.

[1] Heb. *it.*

vv. then fit well together, *v.* 6 being a cry put into the mouths of the
Philistines and *v.* 7 the prophet's response.

6. *sword of the LORD.* Cf. xii. 12 (used of spoilers); and the
striking passage in Ez. xxi. 28 ff.

7. *the sea shore.* The same phrase is used of Philistia in Ez. xxv. 16;
Zeph. ii. 5 ff.

CHAPTER XLVIII. (= LXX. XXXI.).

The Prophecy against Moab.

The Moabites, like the Ammonites and the Edomites, were closely related
to the children of Israel and their ancestors had entered Canaan together. The
ethnic relationship, however, did not prevent much bitterness of feeling between
the various tribes, and OT. is full of accounts of the continual struggles between
them, in fact the only peaceful account of the relations between Moab and
Israel is that contained in the story of Ruth[1]. For a great part of their history
the Moabites were tributary to the Northern Kingdom but in the reign of Ahab
and his successor (2 K. i. 1, iii. 5, 27) they established their independence which
they maintained, except for a short time during the reign of Jeroboam II, until
the fall of Samaria. After the return from the exile the Moabites are not
mentioned except as a general symbol for the enemies of Jehovah and they
appear to have become merged in the Arabs. Josephus states that Moab was
conquered by Nebuchadrezzar in the fifth year after the fall of Jerusalem
(*Ant.* x. ix. 7), but there is no evidence of such a conquest apart from his
statement. The Moabites are interesting as being the only people of Hebrew
stock besides the Jews from whom early literature has come down, and the
inscription of Mesha is of great value in that it shews the closeness of language
and ideas existing between the Israelites and their neighbours (see Driver's
Samuel, pp. lxxxiv—xciv, for an account of the inscription).

In view of the relationship between Israel and Moab, and of their close
proximity, it seems almost certain that any prophecy dealing with the nations

[1] Cf. Dean Stanley, *The Jewish Church*, i. p. 259. 'The story of Ruth has shed a
peaceful light over what else would be the accursed race of Moab. We strain our
gaze to know something of the long line of the purple hills of Moab, which form the
background at once of the history and of the geography of Palestine. It is a satisfaction to feel that there is one tender association which unites them with the familiar
history and scenery of Judaea—that from their recesses, across the deep gulf which
separates the two regions, came the gentle ancestress of David and of the Messiah.'

would include an oracle on Moab, and such oracles are found in Is. xv.—xvi.; Ez. xxv. 8—11; Am. ii. 1—3; Zeph. ii. 8—10. Suspicion has fallen however upon the oracle contained in this ch., partly on account of its great length, and partly because it contains close parallels both in subject matter and wording to other passages, and especially to the prophecy in Is. xv.—xvi. Most critics allow that the ch. contains a nucleus of genuine words of Jeremiah, but that large additions have been made.

Moab in the earliest times of its entry into Palestine held the country east of the Dead Sea, being bounded on the south by the 'brook of the willows' (Is. xv. 7), and on the north by the territory of Ammon, whilst the desert stretched away to the east. The region consists mainly of a high tableland broken up by a number of deep gorges or cañons, and there is evidence even to the present day of the great prosperity and large population of the land in the far past. 'Ruined villages and towns, broken walls that once enclosed gardens and vineyards, remains of ancient roads—everything in Moab tells of the immense wealth and population which the country must have once enjoyed.' Palmer, *Desert of the Exodus*, pp. 472 ff.

(a) *The overthrow of the cities of Moab.* 1—10.
(b) *The decadence of Moab is due to a false sense of security.* 11—19.
(c) *The destruction of Moab.* 20—28.
(d) *The fallen pride of Moab.* 29—39.
(e) *The terror inspired by the foe.* 40—47.

XLVIII. 1 Of Moab. Thus saith the LORD of hosts, the God of Israel: Woe unto Nebo! for it is laid waste; Kiriathaim is put to shame, it is taken: [1]Misgab is put to shame and [2]broken

[1] Or, *the high fort*   [2] Or, *dismayed*

XLVIII. 1—10. A description of the fate which is to come upon all the cities of Moab. The inhabitants, from Chemosh the god of the land to the humblest of his worshippers, are bidden to fly.

1. *Woe unto Nebo!* The prophet plunges straight into the midst of the sorrow. *Nebo* is used with three distinct meanings in OT.: of the Babylonian deity; of the mountain (Dt. xxxii. 49 *b*, xxxiv. 1, &c.); and, as here, of a city (so also Nu. xxxii. 3, 38). *Nebo* originally belonged to Reuben but Mesha claims to have captured it from Israel (Moabite Stone, *l.* 14). An Israelite city of this name is mentioned in Ezra ii. 29.

Kiriathaim. This town is mentioned in Nu. xxxii. 37 as belonging to Reuben, it appears on the Moabite Stone as one of the possessions of Mesha. The identification is somewhat uncertain but it is usually regarded as being the modern *Kureyat* some six miles east of *Mkaur*, the site of Machaerus.

Misgab. No town of this name is known and it is perhaps better to adopt the reading of mg. *the high fort*, or else to substitute Moab, according to the suggestion of Duhm.

down. 2 The praise of Moab is no more; in Heshbon they have
devised evil against her, Come, and let us cut her off from being
a nation. Thou also, O Madmen, shalt be brought to silence;
the sword shall pursue thee. 3 The sound of a cry from Horonaim,
spoiling and great destruction! 4 Moab is destroyed; her little
ones have caused a cry to be heard. 5 ¹For by the ascent of
Luhith with continual weeping shall they go up; for in the going
down of Horonaim they have heard the distress of the cry of
destruction. 6 Flee, save your lives, and be like ²the heath in

¹ See Is. xv. 5.   ² See ch. xvii. 6.

2. *Heshbon.* This town was apparently Moabite by origin (Nu.
xxi. 26), it afterwards became Amorite (Josh. xiii. 17), and then Reu-
benite, and finally Moabite again. It was built on two hills some 3,000
ft. above sea level. The modern name is *Ḥesbān*, and its site is thirteen
miles east of the northern extremity of the Dead Sea. According to
Cant. vii. 4 Heshbon was noted for its fish-pools.

they have devised. The Heb. word for *devised* contains a play on
Heshbon, and Dr Streane suggests as an English equivalent *in Devizes
they have devised.* Heshbon was evidently in the hands of the foe already,
by whom it had been made the headquarters for further advances.

Madmen. There is here another word play on *silence* and *Madmen.*
Since no place of this name is referred to elsewhere many critics adopt
the reading of LXX. which treats it as merely strengthening *silence* and
not as a proper name.

3. *Horonaim.* This town seems never to have been in the posses-
sion of Israel, it is mentioned by Mesha under the form *Horonen* (*ll.* 31 f.).
The site is disputed, some scholars putting it in the south of Moab
(Cheyne, &c.), and others to the north not far from Heshbon (G. A.
Smith).

spoiling and great destruction. Cf. Is. li. 19, lix. 7, &c.

4. *her little ones…heard.* The reading of LXX. should be adopted
they make a cry to be heard unto Zoar; as Zoar was at the south-east
end of the Dead Sea the cry of Moab went from north to south.

5. This and the previous *v.* are based on Is. xv. 5.

the ascent of Luhith. This place was called *Loueitha* in the time
of Eusebius and was situated between Zoar and Rabbath Moab (see an
article by Driver in *Expos. Times* for Aug. 1910). The reading of AV.
the enemies have heard is dependent on Vulg. and Kimchi.

6. *the heath.* See on xvii. 6. If this reading is retained the reference is to the starved and desolate condition of the fugitives for which
the stripped appearance of the juniper tree is a suitable figure. Cornill
prefers to accept the reading of the LXX. *wild ass* and most recent critics
agree with him. The point of the simile is that the wild ass is difficult
to approach as it flees from all who come near it: cf. Job xxxix. 5.

the wilderness. 7 For, because thou hast trusted in thy works and in thy treasures, thou also shalt be taken: and Chemosh shall go forth into captivity, his priests and his princes together. 8 And the spoiler shall come upon every city, and no city shall escape; the valley also shall perish, and ¹the plain shall be destroyed; as the LORD hath spoken. 9 Give wings unto Moab, ²that she may fly and get her away: and her cities shall become

---

¹ See Josh. xiii. 9, 17, 21.   ² Or, *for she must fly: and her cities &c.*

---

7. *thy works...treasures.* Moab and its population depended almost entirely on artificial means for their water supply and a wonderful system of tanks and sluices was necessary before any cultivation was possible¹. There may be in this *v.* a reference to these elaborate irrigation *works*, the destruction of which meant the ruin of the country. *Works* may, however, mean merchandise or even idols (Dt. iv. 28 &c.) LXX. read only one word and translated it *strongholds* and this text is preferred by many critics.

Chemosh. 'The obscene dread of Moab's sons' as Milton (*Parad. Lost*, I. 406) named him, was the national god of Moab, and as such shared in his people's dishonour and apparently in their deportation (cf. Is. xlvi. 1 f.).

8. *the valley...the plain. The valley* is the Jordan valley opening out towards the Dead Sea; *the plain* is the high table-land which forms the beginning of the great Arabian plateau and which is situated some 4,000 ft. above the Dead Sea. Geographical necessity makes these two portions of territory go together, as the east bank of the Jordan is entirely at the mercy of the dwellers in the mountains. 'At the present time the Arabs of the plateau have winter camps in the valley; and the 'Adwān tribe cultivate fields upon it.' G. A. Smith in *Enc. Bib.* 3171.

9. *wings.* To enable her to escape from the enemy. There may be a reference to the innumerable flocks of birds which find their homes in the clefts of the mountains of Moab.

that she may fly. Driver's rendering *for she would fain fly* is to be preferred.

---

¹ Dr Pusey in his commentary on *Zephaniah* quotes Tristram's picture of 'a ruin-covered ridge by an immense tank of solid masonry, 140 yards by 110 yards, at Ziza. From the surface of the water to the edge of the tank was 17 feet 6 inches. The masonry was simply magnificent. The whole system and artificial sluices were precisely similar to ancient works for irrigation in India and Ceylon.—Such works easily explain to us the enormous population, of which the ruined cities give evidence. Everywhere is some artificial means of retaining the occasional supplies of rain-water. So long as these precious structures remained in order, cultivation was continuous and famines remained unknown.—The Islamite invasion left the miserable remnants of a dense and thriving nation entirely dependent on the neighbouring countries for their supply of corn: a dependence which must continue till these border lands are secure from the predatory bands of the East.' (*Land of Moab*, pp. 183—186.)

a desolation, without any to dwell therein.　10 Cursed be he that doeth the work of the Lord [1]negligently, and cursed be he that keepeth back his sword from blood.　11 Moab hath been at ease from his youth, and he hath settled on his lees, and hath not been emptied from vessel to vessel, neither hath he gone into captivity: therefore his taste remaineth in him, and his scent is not changed.　12 Therefore, behold, the days come, saith the Lord, that I will send unto him them that [2]pour off, and they shall [2]pour him off; and they shall empty his vessels, and break their [3]bottles in pieces.　13 And Moab shall be ashamed of Chemosh, as the house of Israel was ashamed of Beth-el their

---

[1] Or, *deceitfully*　　　　[2] Heb. *tilt* (a vessel).　　　[3] Or, *jars*

10. The work of the Lord is here identified with the shedding of blood, a sentiment which can hardly have come from Jeremiah though it suits well the time of the later Hasmoneans. This *v.* was often on the lips of Pope Gregory VII (Hildebrand).

negligently. The rendering of the text is better than that of the mg. *deceitfully.*

11—19. The Moabites trusting in the strength of their material defences have become like wine left on its lees. But the pride which their security has engendered will receive a rude and violent blow; their land will be made desolate.

11. The metaphor suggests an intensification of national characteristics due to isolation from the peoples around; in the case of wine left undisturbed the effect may be good (cf. Is. xxv. 6) or bad (cf. Zeph. i. 17) according to the quality of the lees. The picture of Moab dwelling in the pride of her isolation and security is a fitting preparation for the tremendous contrast of her overthrow.

12. *pour off.* Better with mg. *tilt.* Moab is to be shaken up like wine changed from vessel to vessel by tilting one over the other and so roughly will the process be carried out that the *jars*—adopting the reading of mg.—will be broken. The meaning of the figure is that the national institutions of Moab are to come to an end and the people to go into exile.

13. *shall be ashamed.* The trust which the Moabites placed in their god will prove to be illusive. If these words come from Jeremiah the Moabites had what was to them an obvious and satisfactory retort —the trust which Judah had in Jehovah would prove equally illusive. The difference was that owing to the teaching of the prophets the pure religion of Jehovah survived, whilst the debased cult of Chemosh disappeared.

Beth-el. Cf. Am. v. 5. During the time of the Northern Kingdom, Beth-el, as the sanctuary of the predominant power, must have overshadowed Jerusalem itself, and yet it came to nought and was unable

confidence. 14 How say ye, We are mighty men, and valiant
men for the war? 15 Moab is laid waste, and [1]they are gone up
into her cities, and his chosen young men are gone down to the
slaughter, saith the King, whose name is the LORD of hosts.
16 The calamity of Moab is near to come, and his affliction
hasteth fast. 17 All ye that are round about him, bemoan him,
and all ye that know his name; say, How is the strong [2]staff
broken, the beautiful rod! 18 O thou daughter that [3]dwellest in
Dibon, come down from thy glory, and sit in thirst; for the

[1] Or, *her cities are gone up* in smoke   [2] Or, *sceptre*   [3] Or, *art seated*

to save Israel. The parallelism with Chemosh almost suggests that *Bethel*
is here a personal name and it is a remarkable fact that according to
the Elephantine Papyri the Jews living in Egypt worshipped alongside
Yahu (Jehovah) two deities named 'Asm-bethel and 'Anath-bethel. A
similar custom amongst the Babylonians has deified the great temple
Esagila under the name Esagil-idrimam (see S. A. Cook, *A. J. Th.* 1915,
p. 370).

14.   Cf. viii. 8; Is. xix. 11.

15.   The text of LXX. for this *v.* is markedly different from MT. which
is ungrammatical. Driver suggests a reconstruction of the *v.* on the lines
of *v.* 18 *The spoiler of Moab is come up against him, and his* &c.

gone up into her cities. This makes good sense but hardly represents
the Heb. The attempt of mg. *her cities are gone up* 'in smoke' was
perhaps suggested by Jud. xx. 38.

the King. Cf. Is. xliv. 6 &c.

16.   Cf. li. 33 *b*; Dt. xxxii. 35 *b*; Is. xiii. 22 *b*.

17.   *How.* This is a very common way of beginning a lament; cf.
David's lament over Saul and Jonathan (2 S. i. 19, 27); also Is. xiv. 4,
12; and various passages in Lam. (i. 1, ii. 1, &c.).

staff. The *staff* or *sceptre* (mg.) was the symbol of power and authority (Nu. xvii. 17 &c.; Ps. cx. 2).

rod. This word has almost the same meaning as *staff* though it is
frequently used of the actual branch of a tree (e.g. i. 11), and often with
a symbolical meaning (cf. Zech. xi. 7 &c.).

18.   *O thou daughter...come down.* Cf. Is. xlvii. 1 'Come down...
O virgin daughter of Babylon.'

Dibon. The modern *Dibān* situated some five miles north of the
Arnon and not far from Aroer (see below). It was the place where the
inscription known as the Moabite Stone was discovered in 1868. In
ancient times the great trunk road which ran across the plateau from
north to south went through *Dibon*, and even in Roman times it was
not without importance as the presence of milestones testifies; it is now
a deserted ruin and the great Haj or pilgrim road goes further to the east.

thirst. Through the destruction of the irrigation works described
above. The text however is corrupt and the exact meaning lost.

spoiler of Moab is come up against thee, he hath destroyed thy
strong holds. 19 O [1]inhabitant of Aroer, stand by the way, and
espy: ask him that fleeth, and her that escapeth; say, What hath
been done? 20 Moab is put to shame; for it is [2]broken down:
howl and cry; tell ye it in Arnon, that Moab is laid waste. 21 And
judgement is come upon [3]the plain country; upon Holon, and
upon Jahzah, and upon Mephaath; 22 and upon Dibon, and upon
Nebo, and upon Beth-diblathaim; 23 and upon Kiriathaim, and

---

[1] Heb. *inhabitress*.   [2] Or, *dismayed*   [3] See ver. 8.

---

19.   *Aroer.* Two other cities outside the territory of Moab bore
this name according to OT., one mentioned in Nu. xxxiii. 34 belonged
to Gad, and one in 1 S. xxx. 28 to Judah. The town here referred to
is the modern *'Ara'ir* (see Burckhardt, *Syria*, p. 372) and is situated on
the edge of the Wady Mojib—cf. Eusebius' description 'on the eye-brow
of the hill'—above the Arnon (cf. Josh. xii. 2). A fuller description
with a plan is to be found in *Arabia Petraea*, p. 130, by von Alois Musil.
   way. Evidently a reference to the great road upon which fugitives
were fleeing to the Jordan valley from before the invaders from the
desert or the north. In the Moabite Stone there is a record of the rebuilding of Aroer and the construction of the road over the Arnon.
   20—28. The destruction of Moab is utter and complete, not a city
has escaped from the general ruin and the few inhabitants who have
saved their lives must live in the rocky crevices like birds. As *vv.*
20 *b*—24 are in prose they are usually regarded as an insertion.
   20.   *in Arnon.* As the reference is to the river a better rendering
would be *by the Arnon*, that is on its banks and at the fords (cf. Ps.
cxxxvii. 1).
   21.   *the plain country.* See note on *v.* 8.
   Holon. This name is unknown and appears nowhere else of a city
of Moab. There is mention of a *Holon* in Josh. xv. 51 but the situation
is different as this place is a Levitical city near to Hebron.
   Jahzah. The name of this place is sometimes spelt as here, sometimes, as in Is. xv. 4 *Jahaz*. It was the scene of the defeat of Sihon
(Nu. xxi. 23). Like many of the other cities of this region it was assigned
to Reuben and captured by Mesha. The site is uncertain but it was
probably somewhere to the north-east of Dibon.
   Mephaath. This city like Jahaz was assigned to the Levites (Josh.
xxi. 37) and like it was situated in the territory of Reuben (Josh. xiii. 18).
Eusebius describes it as a 'castle on the edge of the desert.'
   22.   *Dibon.* See on *v.* 18.
   Nebo. See on *v.* 1.
   Beth-diblathaim. The name means *house of two figs*. The city is
mentioned in Mesha's inscription (*l.* 30) as having been fortified by him
but its exact situation is unknown, nor does there appear to be any

B

upon Beth-gamul, and upon Beth-meon; 24 and upon Kerioth,
and upon Bozrah, and upon all the cities of the land of Moab,
far or near. 25 The horn of Moab is cut off, and his arm is broken,
saith the LORD. 26 Make ye him drunken; for he magnified
himself against the LORD: and Moab shall wallow in his vomit,

other reference to it in OT., unless it is the same as *Almon-diblathaim*
mentioned in Nu. xxxiii. 46 in connexion with Dibon.

23.   *Kiriathaim.* See on *v.* 1.

Beth-gamul. This place is not mentioned elsewhere, nor is its site
at all certain though most scholars agree with Doughty, *Arabia Deserta*,
I. pp. 11 f. and identify it with the modern *Umm Jemâl* some distance to
the south of Bozrah. For a description of this site see Porter, *Giant
Cities of Bashan*, p. 69.

Beth-meon. This city is sometimes referred to as *Beth-baal-meon*
(Josh. xiii. 17; and Moabite Stone), sometimes as *Baal-meon* (Nu. xxxii.
38; Ez. xxv. 9). It was evidently a sacred site and the large extent of
its ruins shews that it must have been a city of some importance. Its
modern name is *Ma'in*, and it is situated some five miles to the south-
west of Medeba.

24.   *Kerioth.* This place is sometimes identified with Ar-Moab, and
sometimes with Kir-Moab (cf. Is. xv. 1), it is mentioned on the inscription of Mesha, and may have been the birth-place of Judas Iscariot
(cf. Dr Swete's note on Mk. iii. 19).

Bozrah. This city must not be confused with the *Bozrah* of xlix.
13; Is. lxiii. 1; which was in Edom. It is evidently the *Bezer* of
Mesha's inscription, where it appears between Dibon and Aroer; cf. Dt.
iv. 43; Josh. xx. 8, xxi. 36. In 1 Macc. v. 26 there is mention made
of both Bosora and Bosor; Dr Oesterley identifies *Bozrah* with the
former, and somewhat strangely makes the *Bezer* mentioned above to
be Bosor and therefore not the Bozrah of Moab. The place is usually
identified with *Kusr el Besheir*, situated a short distance to the south-
west of Dibon and to the north of Aroer, which agrees with the order in
which these towns are cited by Mesha (see above). In later times *Bozrah*
was the capital of a Roman province, and it had the unhappy distinction
of being the first city of Syria to fall to the Saracens.

25.   *horn...arm.* The *horn* is a symbol of power especially when
exerted aggressively (Dt. xxxiii. 17; Am. vi. 13, &c.); the *arm*, of might
and authority (xvii. 5).

26.   *drunken.* Cf. xxv. 15.

vomit. No details are spared in the description of Moab's helplessness and shame. The reading of LXX., however, avoids this unpleasant
realism, *Moab has clapped his hands*, and this fits in well with the context.
In addition it should be pointed out that the Heb. word for *wallow* is
elsewhere rendered *clap* and though it is possible to translate it here as
splash the translation is rather doubtful, and on the whole to make the
slight emendation in MT. demanded by LXX. is the best way of treating
the *v.*

and he also shall be in derision. 27 For was not Israel a derision
unto thee? was he found among thieves? for as often as thou
speakest of him, thou waggest the head. 28 O ye inhabitants of
Moab, leave the cities, and dwell in the rock; and be like the
dove that maketh her nest in the sides of the hole's mouth. 29 [1]We
have heard of the pride of Moab, *that* he is very proud; his lofti-
ness, and his pride, and his arrogancy, and the haughtiness of
his heart. 30 I know his wrath, saith the LORD, that it is nought;
his boastings have wrought nothing. 31 [2]Therefore will I howl
for Moab; yea, I will cry out for all Moab: for the men of Kir-

---

[1] See Is. xvi. 6.   [2] See Is. xv. 5, xvi. 7, 11.

27. *among thieves.* Cf. ii. 26.
waggest the head. A common gesture of mockery (Ps. lxiv. 8), but
one which must always have a peculiar and tragic interest for Christian
people (cf. Mk. xv. 29).
28. This *v.* is in metre, and as it is a suitable continuation of *v.* 25,
it seems probable that *vv.* 26 f. come from the hands of a supplementer.
dove. Cf. Cant. ii. 14. Tristram says that 'the wild rock-pigeon
invariably selects...deep ravines for its nesting and roosting place.' *Nat.
Hist. of Bib.* pp. 214 f. The last part of the *v.* is corrupt, though the
meaning is easy to gather.
29—39. The pride of Moab and the ruin which has come upon it.
This section is composed mainly of extracts from an earlier prophecy,
the substance of which is also contained in Is. xv.—xvi., unless indeed
those chh. are the original prophecy itself. Another example of the
incorporation of an earlier prophecy is found in the oracle on Edom
(xlix. 7—27).
29 f. These *vv.* are but Is. xvi. 6 in an expanded form.
29. *the pride of Moab.* The people of Moab were conspicuous for
their pride: cf. *v.* 42 ; Is. xxv. 11 ; Zeph. ii. 10 ; on each of these occasions pride is turned into shame and contempt.
31. This *v.* is similar to Is. xvi. 7 except that in the latter Moab
is bidden to weep for Moab (cf. *v.* 9). It is somewhat unusual to find
the prophets sympathising with the heathen nations whom they condemn, in spite of Rashi's comment that 'the prophets of Israel differ
from heathen prophets...in that they lay to heart the distresses which
they announce to the nations' (on Is. xv. 5).
men of Kir-heres. For *men* we should read *raisin-cakes* as in Is.
xvi. 7, the change required being very slight in the original[1]. This
alteration is almost certain, as not only were *raisin-cakes* as Dr Wade
says 'favourite dainties (Cant. ii. 5), but were also presented as offerings
to the national god (Chemosh).' *Kir-heres* (in Is. *Kir-hareseth*) is

---

[1] Viz.: אשׁישׁי for אנשׁי.

heres shall they mourn. 32 With more than the weeping of
Jazer will I weep for thee, ¹O vine of Sibmah: thy branches
passed over the sea, they reached even to the sea of Jazer: upon
thy summer fruits and upon thy vintage the spoiler is fallen.
33 ²And gladness and joy is taken away, from the fruitful field
and from the land of Moab; and I have caused wine to cease from
the winepresses: none shall tread with shouting; the shouting
shall be no shouting. 34 ³From the cry of Heshbon even unto
Elealeh, even unto Jahaz have they uttered their voice, from
Zoar even unto Horonaim, ⁴to Eglath-shelishiyah: for the waters

¹ See Is. xvi. 8, 9.   ² See Is. xvi. 10.
³ See Is. xv. 4, &c.   ⁴ Or, as *an heifer of three years old*

usually identified with *Kir of Moab* (Is. xv. 1), the modern *Kerak*
which is situated eight miles east of the Dead Sea and some eighteen
south of the Arnon (see the description in *PEFQS*. 1898, pp. 93 ff.)

32.   This *v.* is borrowed from Is. xvi. 8 f. with slight alterations.

more than.   LXX. omits, probably correctly (cf. Is. xvi. 9).

Jazer.   The site of this place is doubtful though most scholars accept
the modern *Khirbet Sar* which is ten miles north of Heshbon.

vine of Sibmah.   'The flowing Dale of Sibma clad with vines' as
Milton called it (*Par. Lost*, I. 410). *Sibmah* is the modern *Sūmia*, a
little to the west of Heshbon, and though the *vine* is said no longer to
be cultivated there, the ruins contain the remains of wine-presses and
vineyard towers.

the sea.   The products of the vine of Sibmah are likened to the vine
itself spreading over the adjacent country as far west as the Dead Sea,
as far north as Jazer, and according to Is. xvi. 8 out to the east into
the desert.   The second mention of *the sea of* (Jazer) is a mistake and
should be omitted.

spoiler.   Read with Is. xvi. 9 *battle-shout* (cf. next *v.*).

33.   This *v.* is based on Is. xvi. 10.

with shouting.   Read *with treading* as Is. xvi. 10.

shouting shall be no shouting.   The Heb. word is used of both the
shout of the grape gatherers (xxv. 30; Is. xvi. 10) and of the cry of
battle (li. 14); in this case the one is to become the substitute for the
other.

34.   There is here a sudden introduction in a shortened form of
Is. xv. 4 ff.   The opening of the *v.* presents an obvious case for emendation and Giesebrecht suggests *How criest thou, O Heshbon and Elealeh*
and Duhm *Crying are Heshbon* &c.

Heshbon.   See on *v.* 2.

Elealeh.   This town, the modern *el-'Āl*, was situated just outside
Heshbon.

Jahaz.   See on *v.* 32.

Zoar...Horonaim.   See on *v.* 3.

of Nimrim also shall become [1]desolate. 35 Moreover I will cause
to cease in Moab, saith the LORD, him that offereth in the high
place, and him that burneth incense to his gods. 36 Therefore
mine heart soundeth for Moab like pipes, and mine heart soundeth
like pipes for the men of Kir-heres: therefore the abundance
that he hath gotten is perished. 37 For every head is bald, and
every beard clipped: upon all the hands are cuttings, and upon
the loins sackcloth. 38 On all the housetops of Moab and in the
streets thereof there is lamentation every where: for I have
broken Moab like a vessel wherein is no pleasure, saith the LORD.
39 How is it broken down! [2]how do they howl! how hath Moab
turned the back with shame! so shall Moab become a derision
and a dismaying to all that are round about him. 40 For thus
saith the LORD: Behold, he shall fly as an eagle, and shall spread

---

[1] Heb. *desolations.*   [2] Or, *howl ye!*

Eglath-shelishiyah. Mg. as *an heifer of three years old* (so LXX.,
Vulg.). The reference, however, is probably to some town known as *the
third Eglath,* for so the Heb. can be translated. Its identity has not
been established (see further Dr Wade on Is. xv. 5).

the waters of Nimrim. Perhaps the *Wady Numēre* at the south-
east end of the Dead Sea.

35. Cf. Is. xv. 2, xvi. 12.

him that offereth in. LXX. by a slight change in MT. renders *him that
goeth up to*; in any case the rendering of RV. does not exactly represent
the original, which reads *him that bringeth up to,* though the meaning
is much the same.

36. *pipes.* Is. xvi. 11 reads *a harp.* The connexion between music
and mourning is evidently in the prophet's mind.

the abundance &c. Cf. Is. xv. 7.

37. Cf. Is. xv. 2 f. and for the mourning customs see note on xvi. 6
above.

38. *vessel.* See on xxii. 28.

40—47. The extent of the disaster which is to overtake Moab is
revealed in fuller detail.

40 f. The text of LXX. for these *vv.* is very much shorter and reads
simply *For thus saith the LORD: Kerioth is taken, and the strongholds
are surprised.* The rest of MT. is apparently borrowed from the oracle
on Edom (xlix. 22), Moabitish names being substituted for Edomite.

40. *eagle.* Cf. xlix. 22. This figure is a favourite description of a
conqueror. It is used of Nebuchadrezzar (Ez. xvii. 3, 7); of Cyrus (Is. xlvi.
11); and often of the swift approach of unnamed invaders (Hos. viii. 1;
Hab. i. 8; Dt. xxviii. 49). Payne Smith compares Hor. *Odes,* IV.
iv. 1.

out his wings against Moab. 41 ¹Kerioth is taken, and the strong
holds are surprised, and the heart of the mighty men of Moab
at that day shall be as the heart of a woman in her pangs.
42 And Moab shall be destroyed from being a people, because
he hath magnified himself against the LORD. 43 ²Fear, and the
pit, and the snare, are upon thee, O inhabitant of Moab, saith
the LORD. 44 He that fleeth from the fear shall fall into the pit;
and he that getteth up out of the pit shall be taken in the snare:
for I will bring upon her, even upon Moab, the year of their
visitation, saith the LORD. 45 ³They that fled stand without
strength under the shadow of Heshbon: ⁴for a fire is gone forth
out of Heshbon, and a flame from the midst of Sihon, and hath
devoured the corner of Moab, and the crown of the head of the
tumultuous ones. 46 Woe unto thee, O Moab! the people of
Chemosh is undone: for thy sons are taken away captive, and

¹ Or, *The cities are taken*   ² See Is. xxiv. 17, 18.
³ Or, *Fleeing because of the force they stand under*
⁴ Or, *but*   See Num. xxi. 28, 29.

41. *Kerioth.* See above on *v.* 24. It is probable, however, in view
of the parallelism that *Kerioth* is not here to be taken as a proper noun
and that the translation of mg. should be adopted, viz. *the cities.*

42. *Moab...people.* After the exile Moab practically disappeared.

43, 44 *a.* The substance of these *vv.* is contained in Is. xxiv. 17 f.
though without any special reference to Moab.

43. *Fear...pit...snare.* These three words in Heb. have a very
similar sound: *pahad, wāpahath, wāpāh.*

44. For the latter half of this *v.* cf. xi. 23, xxiii. 12.

45—47. These *vv.* are not found in LXX. which here resumes at
the *v.* numbered in the Heb. xxv. 15.

45. *They that fled...Heshbon.* A very dramatic representation of
the exhaustion and straits of the fugitives who have fled to the very
'starting-point of the conflagration which is to destroy Moab' (Driver).
For *Heshbon* see on *v.* 2.

a fire is gone forth &c. The rest of the *v.* and also that which follows
is taken from Nu. xxi. 28 f., xxiv. 17.

tumultuous ones. Lit. *sons of tumult:* cf. sons of might (1 K. xiv.
52) and sons of oil (Zech. iv. 14). H. G. Mitchell says of this latter
expression 'This expression belongs to a class of orientalisms frequent
in the Bible....In these cases the person or thing in question is conceived
as an example of the state or quality denoted by the dependent noun.'
Moab is often connected with *tumult* in OT.: see Am. ii. 2; Hos. x. 14.

46. *thy sons are taken away.* In Nu. xxi. 29 the Moabites are
described as being sons and daughters of *Chemosh* who himself has *given*
them into captivity.

thy daughters into captivity. 47 Yet will I [1]bring again the captivity of Moab in the latter days, saith the LORD. Thus far is the judgement of Moab.

[1] Or, *return to*

47. *in the latter days.* 'Whenever it is said *in the latter days* it is meant the days of the Messiah.' Kimchi on Is. ii. 2. See Driver's note on Gen. xlix. 1.

Thus far. This note is evidently the work of a compiler.

CHAPTER XLIX. 1—6 (= LXX. XXX. 1—5).

The Prophecy against Ammon.

The Ammonites had taken advantage of the misfortunes of Israel to widen their borders by the inclusion within them of the territories belonging to Gad. The prophet reproves them and foretells the disasters which are to overtake them. The events referred to in this prophecy are probably those in connexion with the deportation of 734 B.C. when Tiglath-Pileser III overran the East Jordan region, and Gad and some of the other tribes were carried away to Assyria, cf. Am. i. 13; Zeph. ii. 8—11. The Ammonites seem always to have carried on a very crooked policy; in the times of Jeremiah they appear (*a*) as the allies of Babylon (2 K. xxiv. 2); (*b*) leagued against Babylon (Jer. xxvii. 3); (*c*) offering a refuge to the fugitive Jews (Jer. xl. 14); (*d*) plotting to murder Gedaliah (Jer. xl. 14). In Ez. xxv. 1—7 there is a description of the exultation of the Ammonites over the fall of Jerusalem, and in xxi. 28 f. a further description of the punishment coming upon them.

The genuineness of the section is denied by those scholars who look with suspicion on all the prophecies against the nations, as also by Giesebrecht. The arguments of the latter lie mainly against the statement in *v.* 2 *b* that Israel was 'to possess them that possessed him' (i.e. Ammon), a statement which seems to contradict xxv. where Israel and Ammon are to be in exile together; and the promise of restoration in *v.* 6. There are reasons, however, for regarding these *vv.* as later additions, in which case the rest of the oracle is unaffected by his arguments.

XLIX. 1 Of the children of Ammon. Thus saith the LORD: Hath Israel no sons? hath he no heir? why then doth [1]Malcam

[1] Or, *their king*

XLIX. 1. *the children of Ammon.* For further particulars see *Enc. Bib.* 141 ff.

no heir. Even if Gad and Reuben have been taken into exile the right of inheritance belongs to the other tribes of Israel, or failing them to Judah.

Malcam. The mg. gives as the translation of this *their king*; it

[1]possess Gad, and his people dwell in the cities thereof? 2 Therefore, behold, the days come, saith the LORD, that I will cause an
alarm of war to be heard against Rabbah of the children of
Ammon; and it shall become a desolate [2]heap, and her daughters
shall be burned with fire: then shall Israel [1]possess them that
did [1]possess him, saith the LORD. 3 Howl, O Heshbon, for Ai is
spoiled; cry, ye daughters of Rabbah, gird you with sackcloth:
lament, and run to and fro among the fences; for [3]Malcam shall

[1] Or, *inherit*   [2] See ch. xxx. 18.   [3] Or, *their king*

should probably be looked upon as a proper name however but with a
slightly different pointing so as to read *Milcom*, the national deity of
Ammon; this reading agrees with LXX., Syr., Vulg. and cf. v. 3.

2. *Rabbah.* This city was apparently the only place of any size in
Ammon : cf. Am. i. 14 ; Ez. xxv. 5 ; xxi. 20. Ptolemy II Philadelphus
re-named it Philadelphia after himself, and it is now called '*Amman*.
The situation of the modern town is on the river Jabbok some twenty-
three miles east of Jordan.

heap. See on xxx. 18.

burned with fire. Most of the cases of the burning of captives occur
in the East Jordan territory ; cf. xlviii. 45 (=Nu. xxi. 28) ; 2 S. xii. 31 ;
Am. ii. 1.

shall Israel &c. As was pointed out above the prophet in xxv. seems
to look upon both Ammon and Israel as destined for exile at the same
time. The *v.* probably comes from a supplementer.

3. *Howl, O Heshbon* &c. The first part of this *v.* contains two
difficulties. To take the one which has the easier solution first, no such
Ammonite town as Ai is known to exist; this difficulty, if it is one, for
the mere fact of our lack of knowledge of such a city by no means proves
that it was non-existent, can be met by making a small emendation in
the original and reading the Heb. for *the city.* The other difficulty is
that Heshbon belongs, not to Ammon, but to Moab. But Heshbon is
only about fourteen miles from Rabbath Ammon in a north-easterly
direction (see on xlviii. 2) and there is no reason why Heshbon should
not fear—especially if the tide of invasion first struck Ammon—for
national boundaries were no protection against a powerful foe in ancient
warfare. Those critics who find the text suspicious resort to the usual
though very subjective method of emendation; Cornill proposes to read
children of Ammon[1] which, whilst it gives a very good sense, is not easy
to imagine as a possible original of which Heshbon is the corruption;
Duhm has a more attractive suggestion, and would read *palaces* ארמון
armon. This suits well the mention of Rabbah in the previous *v.* for
it was noted for its palaces (Am. i. 14 ; Ez. xxv. 5), and the only

[1] In *SBOT.* Cornill proposed עמון for חשבון, which is a not unlikely emendation; the fuller form בני עמון he thinks more desirable on metrical grounds.

go into captivity, his priests and his princes together. 4 ¹Wherefore gloriest thou in the valleys, thy flowing valley, O backsliding daughter? that trusted in her treasures, *saying*, Who shall come unto me? 5 Behold, I will bring a fear upon thee, saith the Lord, the LORD of hosts, from all that are round about thee; and ye shall be driven out every man right forth, and there shall be none to gather up him that wandereth. 6 But afterward I will bring again the captivity of the children of Ammon, saith the LORD.

¹ Or, *Wherefore gloriest thou in the valleys? thy valley floweth away*

objection to it, not one of a serious nature, is on the score of gender, *palace* being masculine and the verb *Howl* in the feminine.

4. *thy flowing valley.* These words may be due to a scribe copying out the previous words a second time by mistake. The phrase is in any case a strange one, though it is possible to refer it to one of the well-watered valleys of Rabbah 'the city of waters' (2 S. xii. 27). Buhl, *Pal.* p. 260, suggests that it is the *Nahr 'Ammon* which is a stream of considerable size and which flows from the site of Rabbah.

backsliding. This epithet though well applied to Ephraim (xxxi. 22) is hardly suited to the heathen Ammonites; emend with Duhm to *arrogant* (cf. Is. xlvii. 7—10). At the same time as the children of Ammon were descended from Abraham they might reasonably have been expected to preserve the faith of their forefather.

treasures. The wealth of the Ammonites was mainly collected by plundering expeditions.

5. There is no clue throughout the whole prophecy, as Giesebrecht points out, to the people who are to descend upon the Ammonites.

every man right forth. Each man will think only of his own safety and will make no attempt to rally the fugitives.

6. The prophecy ends with a message of comfort, but as it is missing from LXX. there is good reason for supposing that it is a later addition. The Ammonites survived for many centuries, they are mentioned by Justin in his dialogue with Trypho, but by the time of Origen they had disappeared (Comment. on Job i.).

CHAPTER XLIX. 7—22 (= LXX. XXIX. 8—23).

The Prophecy against Edom.

The relationship between Israel and Edom was considered to be very close as they were descended from the twin sons of Isaac—Jacob and Esau—whereas Ammon and Moab could only claim cousinship for their ancestors. This closeness of origin did not, however, promote unity between the peoples, in spite of the command of Dt. xxiii. 7 'Thou shalt not abhor an Edomite, for he is thy brother,' and no nation seems to have taken such delight in the fall of Jerusalem as the offspring of Esau (cf. Ps. cxxxvii. 7 &c.[1]) who according to a late tradition actually set the temple on fire (1 Esdr. iv. 45, 50). The people of Judah suffered greatly in later times from the attempts of the Edomites to establish themselves in the south of Palestine (cf. Mal. i. 2—5), when their own territory was being overrun by the Nabataeans[2], and a perpetual feud arose which did not end until after the defeat of Edom by Judas Maccabaeus (1 Macc. v. 65) and their final subdual by John Hyrcanus (Joseph. *Ant.* XIII. ix. 1). In the Apocryphal writings there are many expressions of the loathing which the sons of Jacob felt for their brethren : see the extracts in Sanday and Headlam, *Romans*, p. 247.

The passage has several *vv.* in common with the prophecy of Obadiah: *v.* 7 = Ob. 8; *vv.* 9—10 *a* = Ob. 5 f.; *vv.* 14—16 = Ob. 1—4. For a detailed examination of these two passages see Brewer's long note in *ICC.* on *Obadiah*, pp. 33 ff.; the conclusion that he comes to is that both passages are based on an older oracle, and that this oracle is better preserved in Jeremiah than in Obadiah. Pusey, however, thought that Jeremiah was the later, and that he 'interwove' into his own prophecy *vv.* derived from the earlier work of Obadiah (*Minor Prophets*, III. pp. 278 ff.); Nowack, *Die kleinen Proph.* pp. 178 f., also looks upon Jeremiah's as the later edition. The various theories as to the unity of Obadiah and its date together with its relation to Jeremiah will be found collected by Brewer, *op. cit.* p. 5, and by G. A. Smith, *Twelve Prophets*, II. pp. 165 ff.

    (*a*)   *The call to flight.* 7—12.
    (*b*)   *The desolation of Edom.* 13—22.

7 Of Edom. Thus saith the LORD of hosts: Is wisdom no more in Teman? is counsel perished from the prudent? is their wisdom vanished? 8 Flee ye, turn back, dwell deep, O inhabitants of Dedan; for I will bring the calamity of Esau upon him,

    7—12. The calamity coming upon Edom is so great that in flight alone lies any chance of safety.

    7. *Is wisdom no more in Teman?* Jeremiah is fond of short pointed questions such as this at the opening of his prophecies: cf. ii. 14 'Is Israel a servant?,' xiv. 19, &c. The Edomites had apparently a great reputation for wisdom (cf. Ob. 8; Bar. iii. 22 f.) and Job's friend Eliphaz the Temanite was noted as a sage (Job ii. 11). *Teman* was one of the clans or tribal divisions of Edom (Gen. xxxvi. 11, 15), and lay to the north of the Edomite territory; it is, however, sometimes used as a synonym for the whole country (Ob. 8; Hab. iii. 3).

    8. *Dedan.* See on xxv. 23. Keil thinks that caravans were going through Edom at the time of the invasion.

    Esau. For *Esau* as a synonym of Edom see Gen. xxv. 30, xxxvi. 1.

---

[1] It is not quite certain that these references are to be connected with the Chaldean invasion (see S. A. Cook in *Oxford Apoc.* I. p. 13).
[2] Diod. Sic. XIX. 94 f.; and see Kennett in *Cambridge Bib. Essays*, p. 117.

the time that I shall visit him. 9 If grapegatherers came to thee, [1]would they not leave some gleaning grapes? if thieves by night, would they not destroy till they had enough? 10 But I have made Esau bare, I have uncovered his secret places, and he shall not be able to hide himself : his seed is spoiled, and his brethren, and his neighbours, and he is not. 11 Leave thy fatherless children, I will preserve them alive; and let thy widows trust in me. 12 For thus saith the LORD: Behold, they [2]to whom it pertained not to drink of the cup shall assuredly drink; and art thou he that shall altogether go unpunished? thou shalt not go unpunished, but thou shalt surely drink. 13 For I have sworn by myself, saith the LORD, that Bozrah shall become an astonish-

---

[1] Or, *they will leave no gleaning grapes ; if thieves by night, they will destroy till they have enough. For &c.* See Obad. 5. [2] Or, *whose judgement was not*

To the later Jews *Esau* became the symbol of the heathen world: see Weber, *Jüd. Theol.* p. 401.

9. The destruction of Edom is to be complete. The imagery under which this destruction is put forward is taken from the peaceful and legitimate occupation of the vinedresser, and the terrifying though not infrequent visit of the midnight robber. The *v.* is much the same as Ob. 5 save that the two figures appear in the reverse order, and in that book the application is made in a slightly different manner, though both represent the methods of the enemy as absolutely pitiless. The figure of gleaning grapes is used in Is. xvii. 6, xxiv. 13 to comfort Israel.

10. *bare.* Mount Seir, the great mountain fastness of Edom, was well wooded, but its protection will be in vain.

his seed &c. Cornill shortens the second part of the *v.* for metrical reasons and reads simply *he is spoiled and he is not.* The rest of the *v.* may represent the bitter hatred of later years (see Introd. to the section).

11. In this *v.* the ordinary methods of waging war in the past, even amongst the Israelites themselves, are put aside as barbarous, women and innocent children are no longer to be regarded as fit objects for the Divine vengeance, as exercised through the persons of the invaders, to slake itself upon. Such a sentiment is well worthy of the mind of Jeremiah.

12. *cup.* Cf. xxv. 15 ff.; Is. lii. 1 ff.

13—22. A further description of the ruin of Bozrah and the cities of Edom against whom the nations are summoned to fight.

13. *Bozrah.* This city is usually identified with *Busaireh* 'in the district of Jebal' some twenty miles south-east of the Dead Sea; R. A. S. Macalister, however, thinks that the site has been entirely lost.

ment, a reproach, a waste, and a curse; and all the cities thereof shall be perpetual wastes. 14 ¹I have heard tidings from the LORD, and an ambassador is sent among the nations, *saying*, Gather yourselves together, and come against her, and rise up to the battle. 15 For, behold, I have made thee small among the nations, and despised among men. 16 As for thy terribleness, the pride of thine heart hath deceived thee, O thou that dwellest in the clefts of ²the rock, that holdest the height of the hill: though thou shouldest make thy nest as high as the eagle, I will bring thee down from thence, saith the LORD. 17 And Edom shall become an astonishment: every one that passeth by it shall be astonished, and shall hiss at all the plagues thereof.

¹ See Obad. 1—4.　　² Or, *Sela*　See 2 Kings xiv. 7.

14—16. These *vv.* are similar to Ob. 1—4.

14. *an ambassador.* 'The ambassador is any agent, visible or invisible, sent by God. Human powers who wish to stir up war, send human messengers. All things stand at God's command, and whatsoever or whomsoever He employs, is *a messenger* from Him.' Pusey on Ob. 1.

15. Edom finally lost its independence towards the close of the second century B.C. when it was conquered by John Hyrcanus and became part of Judah. In the persons of the Herods, however, members of the conquered race succeeded in obtaining power over the conquerors. According to Josephus the Edomites played a leading part in the rebellion against Rome (*Bell. Jud.* IV., V. and VI.).

16. *terribleness.* The Heb. for this word, which is not found in the passage in Ob. nor elsewhere, is probably corrupt. It may represent the exclamation of horror with which the fate of Edom is greeted by those who saw it.

the rock. Mg. *Sela.* Some scholars think that Sela and Petra were the same place though the identification is doubtful (see Buhl, *Gesch. der Edomiter*, pp. 34 f.) and in one passage impossible (cf. Moore on Jud. i. 36). The capital of Edom lay in the midst of a maze of hills and was accessible only by means of a narrow gorge. It was famous for its rock-dwellings many of which were simply carved out of the mountain side. No doubt some of them came from the time of the Nabataeans. The wonders of Petra aroused the admiration of ancient writers on many occasions, Strabo (XVI. iv. 21) for example says that it 'lies in a spot precipitous and abrupt without, but within possessed of abundant fountains for watering and horticulture'; cf. Pliny, *Nat. Hist.* VI. 28, and for a modern description G. A. Smith, *Twelve Prophets*, II. p. 179.

as the eagle. See on iv. 13; and cf. Enoch xcvi. 2 'higher than vultures shall be your nest'; Job xxxix. 27 f.; Prov. xxiii. 5.

17. *hiss.* In scorn; cf. Job xxvii. 23; and see xix. 8.

18 As in the overthrow of Sodom and Gomorrah and the neighbour cities thereof, saith the LORD, no man shall dwell there,
neither shall any son of man sojourn therein. 19 Behold, he
shall come up like a lion from the ¹pride of Jordan ²against the
strong habitation: ³but I will suddenly make him run away
from her; and whoso is chosen, him will I appoint over her: for
who is like me? and who will appoint me a time? and who is the
shepherd that will stand before me? 20 Therefore hear ye the
counsel of the LORD, that he hath taken against Edom; and his
purposes, that he hath purposed against the inhabitants of
Teman: Surely ⁴they shall drag them away, *even* the little ones
of the flock; surely he shall make their ⁵habitation ⁶desolate
with them. 21 The earth trembleth at the noise of their fall;
there is a cry, the noise whereof is heard in the Red Sea. 22 Be-

¹ Or, *swelling*   ² Or, *unto the permanent pastures*
³ Or, *for I will suddenly drive them away*
⁴ Or, *the little ones of the flock shall drag them away*
⁵ Or, *pastures*   ⁶ Or, *astonished at them*

18. *cities.* Admah and Zeboim (Dt. xxix. 23; cf. Gen. x. 19,
xiv. 2, 8).

no man shall dwell there. Petra was unknown to the Arabs and the
Crusaders and was only re-discovered in the last century. The whole
v. recurs in l. 40 in reference to Babylon.

19—21. These *vv.* are similarly used with some necessary adapta-
tions in the prophecy on Babylon (l. 44—46).

19. *lion.* Cf. iv. 7; and Zech. xi. 3.

pride of Jordan. See on xii. 5.

strong habitation. Better with mg. *permanent* or *enduring pastures,*
the metaphor of the lion is still maintained. Cornill suggests the
translation *pasture of sheep* which makes it clearer, and he continues
so will I suddenly drive them away, and their choice rams will I visit.

appoint me a time. Cf. Job ix. 19.

shepherd. Though a *shepherd* might defend his flock against a lion,
as did David (1 S. xvii. 34 f.) yet no ruler could save his people from
the hand of Jehovah.

20. *Teman.* See on *v.* 7.

they shall drag...flock. Cf. xv. 3.

their habitation. Which they had thought would last for ever; cf.
Ps. xlix. 11.

21. *The earth trembleth.* It is hard to know why the earth should
tremble at the fall of a comparatively unimportant nation like Edom
unless indeed it were accompanied by circumstances of peculiar horror.

the Red Sea. Heb. *sea of reeds.* W. Max Müller, *As. u. Eur.* pp.
42 f., thinks that the phrase originally referred to the upper end of the

hold, he shall come up and fly as the eagle, and spread out his
wings against Bozrah: and the heart of the mighty men of Edom
at that day shall be as the heart of a woman in her pangs.

Gulf of Suez; here the eastern arm of the Red Sea, the Aelanitic Gulf
or Gulf of Akaba is evidently meant; cf. Nu. xxi. 4; 1 K. ix. 26.

22. Cf. xlviii. 40 f. Dean Stanley elaborated this figure of the
eagle and says that Nebuchadrezzar's approach 'seemed to those who
witnessed it like the rising of a mighty eagle, spreading out his vast
wings, feathered with the innumerable colours of the variegated masses
which composed the Chaldean host.' *The Jewish Church*, II. p. 451.

CHAPTER XLIX. 23—27 (= LXX. XXX. 12—16).

The Prophecy against Damascus.

This section has been rejected by many scholars, including even Cornill,
mainly on account of the importance assigned to Hamath and Arpad. There
are difficulties and corruptions in the text, it is true, and probably additions
have been made to it, but there does not seem to be any convincing reason for
rejecting the whole prophecy.

Damascus is still the most considerable city in Syria and has perhaps the
longest record of any city in the world for prosperity and importance. This is
no doubt owing to its fertile situation in the midst of a wide plain raised some
2300 feet above the sea-level, protected on all sides by mountains and watered
by numerous rivers. So great are its fertility and beauty that it has been called
the 'earthly Paradise' of the Arab world[1]. At the same time the site of
Damascus had serious defects from a military point of view as the surrounding
hills gave undue advantages to an attacking force, and after its capture by
Tiglath-Pileser in 732 B.C. the city seems to have lapsed into comparative insignificance for some long period. Apart from this passage, there is no mention
of Damascus in the prophecies of the exile, except in Ez. xxvii. 18, xlvii. 16 ff.—
all of them incidental, and it was not until the Persian period that its prosperity
was revived (cf. Strabo, XVI. ii. 20; Joseph. *Ant.* XI. ii. 2).

23 Of Damascus. Hamath is ashamed, and Arpad; for they

23. *Hamath...Arpad.* These two towns appear frequently together
in Is. (x. 9, xxxvi. 19, &c.), also in Assyrian inscriptions (as *Amattu*
and *Arpaddu*). They were situated respectively some 115 and 210
miles north of Damascus. *Hamath* was on the Orontes and had been
an important stronghold of the Hittites whose sculptures are still found

---

[1] There is a Muhammedan legend that the prophet one day stood gazing down
on the city from an adjacent mountain and then turned away saying 'There is but
one paradise for man and mine is fixed elsewhere.'

have heard evil tidings, they are melted away: there is [1]sorrow
on the sea; it cannot be quiet. 24 Damascus is waxed feeble,
she turneth herself to flee, and trembling hath seized on her:
anguish and sorrows have taken hold of her, as of a woman in
travail. 25 How is the city of praise not forsaken, the city of
my joy? 26 Therefore her young men shall fall in her streets,
and all the men of war shall be brought to silence in that day,
saith the LORD of hosts. 27 And I will kindle a fire in the wall
of Damascus, and it shall devour the palaces of Ben-hadad.

[1] Or, *care*

there; in the Greek period it was known as Epiphaneia and it is now
called *Hamah.* The modern name of *Arpad* is *Tell-Erpād* ten miles
north of Aleppo.

melted away. Cf. Ez. vii. 17 (Heb.).

sorrow on the sea. The mention of *sea* in connexion with these
inland cities is very strange, possibly we should read *like the sea* (cf. Is.
lvii. 20), or with Cornill by a slight emendation *they are melted away
there from terror.* The mg. rendering *care* or *anxiety* is better than
sorrow.

25. *not forsaken.* The present text contradicts both the next
sentence and also the requirements of the context. Read with Duhm
Woe to her[1]. The lament is evidently uttered by one of the citizens of
the suffering city.

26. This *v.* is borrowed from l. 30, hence the unsuitable *therefore.*

27. This *v.* is derived from a combination of Am. i. 4 and 14.

Ben-hadad. Jerome and some modern scholars think that the name
Ben-hadad, like that of Pharaoh, was not a personal name but a title;
it was borne by several kings of Syria. The meaning *son of Hadad*
evidently had a religious significance[2]. See however *Enc. Bib.* p. 531
where it is stated that the original of the name was *Bir-'idri,* i.e. *Bir
is my glory.*

CHAPTER XLIX. 28—33 (= LXX. XXX. 6—11).

The Prophecy against Kedar[3].

This passage has also been rejected by Cornill. There seems however no
good reason for denying the Jeremianic authorship of the whole whilst at the

---

[1] The change required in the Heb. for this rendering is not great, אוֹי לָהּ being
substituted for אֵיךְ לֹא.

[2] See Frazer, *Adonis* &c. I. p. 15 and references there given.

[3] LXX. βασιλίσσῃ τῆς αὐλῆς, *the queen of the palace,* which is added to Kedar, merely
represents a different pointing of the Heb. for kingdoms of Hazor: לְמַלְכַּת חָצֵר instead of לְמַמְלְכוֹת חָצוֹר.

same time recognising the fact that it contains later insertions. The mention of Arab tribes in xxv. 23 naturally leads one to expect an oracle against them, and the appearance of Nebuchadrezzar in *v.* 30 suggests that the section, or part of it, is pre-exilic.

Dr Streane has pointed out that the passage may be divided into two parts, 'which closely correspond in length, sense, and structure. Each consists of three verses, and the three consecutive thoughts in each are (i) a summons to the enemy to attack, (ii) a promise of booty, (iii) an intimation that safety would be procured only by flight.'

28 Of Kedar, and of the kingdoms of Hazor, which Nebuchadrezzar king of Babylon smote.

Thus saith the LORD: Arise ye, go up to Kedar, and spoil the children of the east. 29 Their tents and their flocks shall they take; they shall carry away for themselves their curtains, and all their vessels, and their camels: and they shall cry unto them, Terror on every side. 30 Flee ye, wander far off, dwell deep, O ye inhabitants of Hazor, saith the LORD; for Nebuchad-

28. *Kedar*. *Kedar* was an Ishmaelite tribe (Gen. xxv. 13) noted for its flocks (*v.* 29) and for the skill of its archers (Is. xxi. 16 f.). In ii. 10 *Kedar* is taken as a typical representative of the east and as dwelling far away in the desert. The men of Kedar are mentioned in inscriptions as the *Ḳidrai*, and by Pliny, *Nat. Hist.* v. 65 as the *Cedrei*. In later times they became the type of 'all the wild tribes of the desert who were naturally disliked by the peace-loving Judaeans' (*Enc. Bib.* 2654); the beginning of this process can be seen in Ps. cxx. 5. The Rabbinic writers speak of Arabic as the language of Kedar (לשון קדר), making *Kedar* equivalent to the whole of Arabia.

kingdoms of Hazor. According to S. A. Cook, *Enc. Bib.* 1978 this 'is a collective term for the region of the settled Arabs in the S. or E. of Palestine' (cf. xxv. 34; Is. xlii. 11). The corresponding Arabic word *ḥādir* is used in a similar way, settled Arabs being called Ḥaḍarjeh as distinguished from the Wabarijeh who are nomadic[1].

children of the east. The Arab tribes in the east of Palestine, the term seems to be used with considerable latitude; cf. Jud. viii. 10; Job i. 3; 1 K. iv. 30.

29. *their curtains*. See on iv. 20.

Terror on every side. Cf. vi. 25, xx. 3 f. &c.

30. *dwell deep*. The same advice is given to the Edomites (*v.* 8), and with better application to those living in a mountainous country than to the Bedouin of the desert.

---

[1] Nöldeke quotes a poem written shortly before the time of Muhammed which divides the Arabs into 'the nomadic' and 'the settled.' By the latter class must be understood 'the inhabitants of small oases, who retained, on the whole, the customs of the Bedouins, and differed widely from the people of the towns.' *Enc. Bib.* 275.

rezzar king of Babylon hath taken counsel against you, and hath conceived a purpose against you. 31 Arise, get you up unto a nation that is at ease, that dwelleth without care, saith the LORD; which have neither gates nor bars, which dwell alone. 32 And their camels shall be a booty, and the multitude of their cattle a spoil: and I will scatter unto all winds them that have the corners *of their hair* polled; and I will bring their calamity from every side of them, saith the LORD. 33 And Hazor shall be a dwelling place of jackals, a desolation for ever: no man shall dwell there, neither shall any son of man sojourn therein.

31 f. These *vv.* are evidently influenced by Ez. xxxviii. 11; cf. also Jud. xviii. 7, 10; Mic. vii. 14; Zech. ii. 4, 9.

32. *corners...polled.* See on ix. 26.

33. Cf. ix. 11, x. 22.

CHAPTER XLIX. 34—39 (= LXX. XXV. 14—XXVI. 1).

The Prophecy against Elam.

This prophecy differs from the others in being dated in the beginning of the reign of Zedekiah; this is a sign of its authenticity, for a supplementer would have been careful to make its date agree with that of the vision of the cup (cf. xxv. 1, 25). The reign of Zedekiah was in itself a much more probable time for Jeremiah to utter a prophecy against Elam, as before the first deportation the men of Judah could have had little contact with the Elamites. Those critics who reject the Jeremianic authorship of the passage are not unnaturally at variance over the exact date to which to assign it, though several would place it in the Persian period regarding it as being written in view of the victorious approach of Alexander the Great (Schmidt, *Enc. Bib.* 2391).

The country of the Elamites was situated to the east of the southern portion of Babylon, corresponding approximately to the Susiana and Elymais of the Greeks, and to the country now known as Chuzistan. It is often mentioned in the cuneiform inscriptions as *Elamtu* and its history, in close connexion with that of Babylon and Assyria, goes back to the earliest times. The independence of Elam was lost to the Assyrians under Asshurbanipal, and by the time of the Median incursion they were too weak to defend themselves (see Canon Johns, *Ancient Assyria*, pp. 143 ff., 151). For further details see Driver's note on Gen. x. 22.

34 The word of the LORD that came to Jeremiah the prophet concerning Elam in the beginning of the reign of Zedekiah king

of Judah, saying, 35 Thus saith the LORD of hosts: Behold, I will break the bow of Elam, the chief of their might. 36 And upon Elam will I bring the four winds from the four quarters of heaven, and will scatter them toward all those winds; and there shall be no nation whither [1]the outcasts of Elam shall not come. 37 And I will cause Elam to be dismayed before their enemies, and before them that seek their life: and I will bring evil upon them, even my fierce anger, saith the LORD; and I will send the sword after them, till I have consumed them: 38 and I will set my throne in Elam, and will destroy from thence king and princes, saith the LORD. 39 But it shall come to pass in the latter days, that I will bring again the captivity of Elam, saith the LORD.

[1] Another reading is, *the everlasting outcasts.*

35. *bow.* The Elamites were famed for their archery (Is. xxii. 6), this gives all the more point to the metaphor which is also applied to Israel by Hosea (i. 5). For the converse see Job xxix. 20 'My glory is fresh in me and my bow is renewed in my hand.'

36. This *v.* is probably to be rejected as Cornill suggests. It seems to have been copied from Ez. v. 10, 12, xii. 14, and interrupts the sequence of the passage, for if Elam has been scattered to the four quarters of heaven it cannot be put to confusion before its enemies (*v.* 37).

38. *set my throne.* Cf. i. 15, xliii. 10.

39. Cf. xlix. 6.

CHAPTERS L.—LI. 58 (= LXX. XXVII., XXVIII.).

The Prophecy against Babylon.

This prophecy is distinguished from those that have gone before it by its much greater length, by the numerous repetitions which it contains, and by its being dated—if li. 59 refers as is generally supposed to the present prophecy —in the fourth year of Zedekiah. In view of these and other facts scholars are agreed in separating the oracle on Babylon from the rest of the prophecies on the nations, and further with the exception of Orelli, and possibly of Rothstein, they agree in regarding the passage as later than the time of Jeremiah. The main arguments against the genuineness of the prophecy are as follows: (i) The historical situation. In l. 8 the children of Israel are bidden to flee out of the midst of Babylon, the exile must therefore have already taken place; cf. also *vv.* 19, 28 &c. The temple has fallen and the prophet calls for vengeance for its violation (l. 28, li. 11, 51). It is possible that the language used refers merely to the deportation of 597 B.C., though some greater and more lasting

disaster seems needed to account for it. (ii) The point of view is different
from that of Jeremiah at the date when the prophecy was supposed to have
been written, for the prophet was then urging the exiles to accept residence in
Babylon as their fate for the next seventy years (xxv. 11, xxix. 10), whereas in
the present passage the Israelites are repeatedly bidden to flee out of the
doomed city. (iii) This prophecy has been chosen out by a recent writer[1] as a
specimen of the bitterness with which the exilic Jews regarded Babylon, and
of their exultation over the thought of vengeance upon the oppressing nation.
No such exultation is found in the genuine writings of Jeremiah, who looked
upon Babylon as the instrument of Jehovah's punishment, though at the same
time he recognised that she would eventually be cast on one side and punished
for her own sins. (iv) The style and arrangement of the passage are suspicious.
As was pointed out above the prophecy is much longer than even the oracle on
Moab, which is itself suspected on this ground; it also is full of repetitions, the
fall of Babylon, the subsequent desolation, and the return of the exiles to
Palestine, are each referred to some seven or more times; there are also close
parallels to late writings (e.g. l. 27, li. 40 and Is. xxxiv. 6 ff.; l. 39 f. and
Is. xiii. 19 ff., xxxiv. 14, &c.), and Ewald would add the use of words belonging
to the later development of the language, e.g. פֶּחָה, סָגָן, גִּלּוּלִים[2]. Many words
and phrases common in genuine writings of Jeremiah are found in these chapters
but they are generally regarded as borrowed. These arguments taken together
seem to shew conclusively that the passage is not the work of Jeremiah, and the
date usually assigned to it is the time when Cyrus was advancing against
Babylon and its destruction seemed imminent, that is somewhere about 538 B.C.
Dr Peake, however, thinks that the prophecy was written for those whose faith
was perplexed by the continued existence of Babylon after its conquest by
Cyrus[3]. 'To such perplexity our oracle seeks to give an answer.'

In view of the constant repetitions in the passage and of the fewness of the
ideas contained in it no analysis seems possible or necessary.

L. 1 The word that the LORD spake concerning Babylon,
concerning the land of the Chaldeans, by Jeremiah the prophet.

2 Declare ye among the nations and publish, and set up a
standard; publish, and conceal not: say, Babylon is taken, Bel

L. 2. The prophet speaks of events as already past, though they are
yet to come, so certain is he of the power of God to perform that which
his intuition has shewn him to be God's will.

set up a standard. This phrase probably comes from Is. xiii. 2, and
is missing from LXX.

---

[1] H. P. Smith, *Rel. of Israel*, p. 247.

[2] The argument from the use of words appearing in post-exilic books is not by
itself a strong one as the two first words quoted above are really loan words from
the Assyrian and the third occurs in Ezek.

[3] For the fate of Babylon see Additional Note, pp. 373 ff.

is put to shame, Merodach is [1]dismayed; her images are put to shame, her idols are [1]dismayed. 3 For out of the north there cometh up a nation against her, which shall make her land desolate, and none shall dwell therein: they are fled, they are gone, both man and beast. 4 In those days, and in that time, saith the LORD, the children of Israel shall come, they and the children of Judah together; they shall go on their way weeping, and shall seek the LORD their God. 5 They shall inquire concerning Zion with their faces [2]thitherward, *saying*, Come ye, and [3]join yourselves to the LORD in an everlasting covenant that shall not be forgotten.

6 My people hath been lost sheep: their shepherds have caused them to go astray, they have turned them away on the

---

[1] Or, *broken down*   [2] Heb. *hitherward*.
[3] Or, *they shall join themselves*

Bel...Merodach. Bel is really a title, like Baal, and means *lord*; one of the oldest of the Babylonian deities was worshipped under this title at Nippur, see further Wade's note on Is. xlvi. 1. *Merodach* or *Marduk* was the local god of the city of Babylon, he was exalted by Hammurabi to the supreme position in the Babylonian pantheon in the place of Nebo or Nabu the god of Borsippa who is known as his son. Marduk is often identified with *Bel*, though on the other hand hymns could be addressed to him as 'the darling of Anu and of Bel[1].'

idols. Lit. *idol-blocks*, a common phrase in Ez. where it occurs nearly forty times.

3. *out of the north.* If this is not a genuine utterance of Jeremiah it is borrowed from him; the phrase is somewhat unsuitable as a description of the Persian conquerors of Babylon, but the north was used more as a symbol for that which was unknown or hidden, and therefore threatening, than as a quarter of the heavens (see on i. 14).

they are fled &c. Cf. ix. 10.

4 f. In these two *vv.* the fall of Babylon is proclaimed as the signal for the release of Israel. Three stages are set forth which the writer foreshortens into almost a single event: the return from Babylon to Zion, the union of the divided tribes, and the establishment of the 'New Covenant.'

5. *thitherward.* The original reads *hitherward*, the standpoint of the writer is Palestine.

6. *lost sheep.* Misled by evil shepherds the people have fallen into

---

[1] See Rogers, *Rel. of Bab.* p. 175; and cf. L. W. King, *Bab. Rel.* pp. 18 ff. Cheyne (*Decline and Fall*, &c. p. 4) thinks that there was an attempted reaction against the supremacy of Marduk and quotes a late inscription which commands the reader to 'Trust in Nabū, trust not in another god.'

mountains: they have gone from mountain to hill, they have forgotten their resting place. 7 All that found them have devoured them: and their adversaries said, We offend not, because they have sinned against the LORD, the habitation of justice, even the LORD, the hope of their fathers. 8 Flee out of the midst of Babylon, and go forth out of the land of the Chaldeans, and be as the he-goats before the flocks. 9 For, lo, I will stir up and cause to come up against Babylon an assembly of great nations from the north country: and they shall set themselves in array against her; from thence she shall be taken: their arrows shall be as of [1]an expert mighty man; [2]none shall

[1] Or, according to another reading, *a mighty man that maketh childless*
[2] Or, *that returneth not*

superstitious habits and have wandered far from the ways of safety and peace; the thought is one which is frequent in those passages of Jer. which are generally accepted as authentic, cf. vi. 16, xxiii. 1 ff. &c.

mountains. The *mountains* were the scenes of some of the idolatrous rites; cf. ii. 20, iii. 6; Ez. vi. 2 f.[1] It does not follow of course that the mention of mountains is more than figurative; cf. xiii. 16.

resting place. Those who desert God may find many and varied substitutes for Him, but these are all alike in their inability to provide any permanent satisfaction; cf. St Augustine, *Conf.* I. i. 'Thou hast made us for Thyself and our heart is restless till it finds its rest in Thee.'

7. *We offend not.* Cf. Zech. xi. 5. Israel is no longer the first-fruits of the LORD (ii. 3) and therefore no guilt is incurred by those who devour them. The writer puts into the mouth of the enemies of Israel what was felt by the true worshippers of God—that the fate of the nation was due to its sins.

habitation of justice. Cf. xxxi. 23 (used of Jerusalem).

hope of their fathers. Cf. xiv. 8, xvii. 13; Ps. xxii. 4 f.

8. *Flee out.* Cf. xlviii. 17, xlix. 30; Is. xlviii. 20.

the he-goats. The *he-goats* are the first of the flock, so Israel must be the first of the flock of nations flying from the doomed city. Cf. Is. xiv. 8 where the same expression is used for the 'chief ones of the earth.'

9. *great nations.* See li. 27 f.

an expert mighty man. The Heb. text implied by the rendering of mg. differs from MT. by the change of a single vowel; the text is to be preferred.

none shall return. The reading of mg. is here to be taken, *that*

[1] The Heb. text reads *seducing* or better *apostate mountains*, the rendering of both A. and RV. follows the mg. and LXX.

return in vain. 10 And Chaldea shall be a spoil: all that spoil
her shall be satisfied, saith the LORD. 11 Because ye are glad,
because ye rejoice, O ye that plunder mine heritage, because ye
are wanton as an heifer ¹that treadeth out *the corn*, and neigh
as strong horses; 12 your mother shall be sore ashamed; she
that bare you shall be confounded: behold, she shall be the
hindermost of the nations, a wilderness, a dry land, and a desert.
13 Because of the wrath of the LORD it shall not be inhabited,
but it shall be wholly desolate: every one that goeth by Babylon
shall be astonished, and hiss at all her plagues. 14 Set yourselves
in array against Babylon round about, all ye that bend the bow;
shoot at her, spare no arrows: for she hath sinned against the
LORD. 15 Shout against her round about; she hath ²submitted
herself; her bulwarks are fallen, her walls are thrown down: for
it is the vengeance of the LORD; take vengeance upon her; as
she hath done, do unto her. 16 Cut off the sower from Babylon,
and him that handleth the sickle in the time of harvest: for fear
of the oppressing sword they shall turn every one to his people,
and they shall flee every one to his own land.

¹ Or, *at grass*   ² Heb. *given her hand.*

returneth not. As arrows do not return, but hit the mark, the reference
must be to the warrior.
    in vain. Cf. 2 S. i. 22.
    11. *ye are wanton.* Cf. Mal. iv. 2 '*gambol* as calves of the stall'
where the Heb. word used is the same.
    heifer. LXX. evidently read *calves.*
    treadeth out the corn. Mg. *at grass* = LXX. If the reading of the
text is preserved the metaphor is that of the unmuzzled cow (cf. Dt.
xxv. 4) eating of the corn which it was treading out.
    12. *your mother.* i.e. Babylon. Cf. Hos. ii. 2, 5 (of Israel).
hindermost of the nations. Cf. Nu. xxiv. 20, the curse on Amalek.
wilderness &c. Cf. ii. 6, li. 43.
    13. *it shall not be inhabited.* Cf. Is. xiii. 20, and see Additional Note,
pp. 373 ff. The second part of the *v.* is modelled on xlix. 17, it contains
several expressions which are typical of other passages in the book (cf.
xviii. 16, xix. 8, xxv. 9 *a*, 11 *a*).
    14. *bend the bow.* Cf. *v.* 42; Is. xiii. 18 (of the Medes).
    15. *submitted herself.* The mg. gives the literal rendering of the
expression which is late.
    16. All agriculture is to cease and the crowd of strangers will flee
on the destruction of the hope of their gain: cf. Ez. xvii. 4. The city of
Babylon had fields within the walls (Pliny, *Nat. Hist.* XVIII. 17) but the

17 Israel is a scattered sheep; the lions have driven him away: first the king of Assyria hath devoured him; and last this Nebuchadrezzar king of Babylon hath broken his bones. 18 Therefore thus saith the LORD of hosts, the God of Israel: Behold, I will punish the king of Babylon and his land, as I have punished the king of Assyria. 19 And I will bring Israel again to his ¹pasture, and he shall feed on Carmel and Bashan, and his soul shall be satisfied upon the hills of Ephraim and in Gilead. 20 In those days, and in that time, saith the LORD, the iniquity of Israel shall be sought for, and there shall be none; and the sins of Judah, and they shall not be found: for I will pardon them whom I leave as a remnant.

21 Go up against the land of ²Merathaim, even against it,

¹ Or, *fold*   ² That is, *Double rebellion.*

reference is probably not to be so limited. The second part of the *v.* is very similar to xlvi. 16; Is. xiii. 14.

17. Not only is the flesh devoured but even the bones of the carcase are broken up so that nothing is left which could be recognised.

18. Assyria had fallen according to the threats of earlier prophecies, it is now the turn of Babylon. The *v.* was evidently written before the fall of Babylon, unless indeed the writer is deliberately adopting an earlier standpoint, and it may well be a genuine utterance of Jeremiah, being free from the objections against his authorship which lie against the section as a whole (see above).

19. *pasture.* The lot of Babylon is to become a dry and barren land (*v.* 17), Israel by taking flight is to return to the fertile land from which it had originally been taken.

Carmel. The garden land; see on iv. 26. Carmel from the meaning of its name was a symbol for prosperity and pastoral wealth; cf. Is. xxxv. 2 &c.

Bashan. Famous for its herds of cattle; Ps. xxii. 12; Am. iv. 1; Ez. xxxix. 18, &c. For an interesting description of this region see Porter, *Giant Cities of Bashan*, especially pp. 14 ff.

hills of Ephraim. Cf. xxxiv. 13 f. 'I will feed them upon the mountains of Israel &c.'

Gilead. Carmel, Bashan, and Gilead are all mentioned in a passage in Mic. vii. 14 which may have been in the writer's mind. Gilead and Bashan were on the east side of Jordan and therefore would be the first lands to be reached by the returning fugitives, just as they had been the first to become the possession of Israel, and also the first to be ravaged by the Assyrians: see further on xxii. 6.

20. The restoration from Babylon is to be the sign of the coming in of the new age; cf. xxxi. 34.

21. *Merathaim.* This has been taken by Fred. Delitzsch and other

and against the inhabitants of ¹Pekod: slay and ²utterly destroy
after them, saith the LORD, and do according to all that I have
commanded thee. 22 A sound of battle is in the land, and of
great destruction. 23 How is the hammer of the whole earth
cut asunder and broken! how is Babylon become a desolation
among the nations! 24 I have laid a snare for thee, and thou
art also taken, O Babylon, and thou wast not aware: thou art
found, and also caught, because thou hast striven against the
LORD. 25 The LORD hath opened his armoury, and hath brought
forth the weapons of his indignation: for the Lord, the LORD of
hosts, hath a work *to do* in the land of the Chaldeans. 26 Come
against her ³from the utmost border, open her ⁴storehouses:
cast her up as heaps, and ⁵destroy her utterly: let nothing of
her be left. 27 Slay all her bullocks; let them go down to the

¹ That is, *Visitation.*   ² Heb. *devote.*   ³ Or, *from every quarter*
⁴ Or, *granaries*   ⁵ Heb. *devote her.*

scholars to be a reference to the Assyrian *māt marrātim*, the sea-country,
i.e. South Babylonia. The word in Heb. would mean *double rebellion* (so
mg.) or *double bitterness* (LXX.)

Pekod. This suggested to the Hebrews *visitation* (mg.); it was
the name of a Babylonian tribe the *Puqūdu* (cf. Ez. xxiii. 23).

utterly destroy. Mg. *devote*, place under a ban, so that the object
or person could not be used for any common purpose and very often
was destroyed; cf. the story of Achan (Jos. vi., vii.) and see Dr McNeile's
note on Ex. xxii. 20; W. R. Smith, *Rel. Sem.*² pp. 150 ff.

22. *great destruction.* A common expression in Jer. (iv. 6, vi. 1).

23. *the hammer.* In Is. xiv. 5 Babylon is called the 'staff' or 'sceptre.'
For the name *hammer* as a title for a conqueror cf. Charles *Martel*, the
victor of Tours, and our own Edward I 'the hammer of the Scots'
(Scotorum Malleus); the old interpretation of the name Maccabaeus
connected it with the Heb. word for *hammer* but there are difficulties
in the identification (see *Enc. Bib.* 2850).

24. *thou wast not aware.* Cf. Job ix. 5 'which removeth the
mountains and *they know it not.*'

25. *weapons of his indignation.* The same phrase is used in Is. xiii.
5, cf. x. 5; in Wisd. v. 17 ff. Jehovah makes the whole creation supply
Him with weapons for vengeance upon His enemies.

26. In this *v.* the fate of the material wealth of Babylon is foretold,
in the next it is the fate of her children.

destroy her utterly. See on *v.* 21, and cf. Dt. xiii. 16.

27. *her bullocks.* This expression may be taken literally (cf. Is.
xxxiv. 6); it is much better, however, to understand by *bullocks* the
young warriors or perhaps the leaders of the people (cf. Ps. lxviii. 30;
Is. xxxiv. 7).

slaughter: woe unto them! for their day is come, the time of
their visitation. 28 The voice of them that flee and escape out
of the land of Babylon, to declare in Zion the vengeance of the
LORD our God, the vengeance of his temple. 29 Call together
¹the archers against Babylon, all them that bend the bow; camp
against her round about; let none thereof escape: recompense
her according to her work; according to all that she hath done,
do unto her: for she hath been proud against the LORD, against
the Holy One of Israel. 30 Therefore shall her young men fall
in her streets, and all her men of war shall be brought to silence
in that day, saith the LORD. 31 Behold, I am against thee, ²O
thou proud one, saith the Lord, the LORD of hosts: for thy day
is come, the time that I will visit thee. 32 And ³the proud one
shall stumble and fall, and none shall raise him up: and I will
kindle a fire in his cities, and it shall devour all that are round
about him.

33 Thus saith the LORD of hosts: The children of Israel and
the children of Judah are oppressed together: and all that took
them captives hold them fast; they refuse to let them go.
34 Their redeemer is strong; the LORD of hosts is his name: he
shall throughly plead their cause, that he may give rest to the

¹ Or, *many*   ² Heb. *O Pride.*   ³ Heb. *Pride.*

their day. Cf. Ps. xxxvii. 13; Job xviii. 20.
28. *in Zion.* Cf. Is. lii. 7 ff.
the vengeance of his temple. Missing from LXX. and possibly
inserted from li. 11. The crime for which Babylon is to be punished is
that of sacrilege (cf. the story in Dan. v.).
29. *archers.* Cf. *v.* 14.
camp against. The same expression is used of Jehovah Himself
camping against Ariel (Is. xxix. 3).
she hath been proud &c. This half of the *v.* seems to shew the influence
of Is. xxxvii. 23.
30. = xlix. 26.
31 f. In each case the reading of mg. *Pride* as a proper name is to
be preferred to *thou proud one*: Babylon is the personification of pride:
cf. xxi. 13 f.
32. *fall.* Cf. Is. xiv. 12; Amos v. 2.
33. The standpoint of the author of this *v.* is still that of the exile,
the foreign oppressors of Israel like Pharaoh of old *refuse to let them go*:
cf. Is. xiv. 17.
34. *Their redeemer.* Cf. Prov. xxiii. 11; Is. xlvii. 4.
give rest...disquiet. Cf. Is. xiv. 5—8, 16; Nah. iii. 19. The

earth, and disquiet the inhabitants of Babylon. 35 A sword is upon the Chaldeans, saith the LORD, and upon the inhabitants of Babylon, and upon her princes, and upon her wise men. 36 A sword is upon the [1]boasters, and they shall dote: a sword is upon her mighty men, and they shall be dismayed. 37 A sword is upon their horses, and upon their chariots, and upon all the mingled people that are in the midst of her, and they shall become as women: a sword is upon her treasures, and they shall be robbed. 38 A drought is upon her waters, and they shall be dried up: for it is a land of graven images, and they are mad upon [2]idols. 39 [3]Therefore the wild beasts of the desert with the [4]wolves

[1] Heb. *boastings.*
[2] Heb. *terrors.*
[3] See Is. xiii. 21, 22.
[4] Heb. *howling creatures.*

experiences which befell the weaker nations at the hands of Babylon are now to be the lot of Babylon herself.

36. *boasters.* i.e. the lying prophets and diviners, as is shewn by a reference to Is. xliv. 25 mg.

37. *chariots.* The main strength of ancient armies, like the artillery of the present, the third arm of the service; cf. xlvi. 9; Is. xliii. 17; Ps. xx. 8.

mingled people. 'The all mingled crowd' as Aeschylus called them (*Pers.* 52 ff.); strangers resident in Babylon for purposes of trade (cf. xxv. 20), or perhaps foreign mercenaries (xlvi. 16).

as women. Cf. Nah. iii. 13.

her treasures. Cf. li. 13; Hab. ii. 6; and Is. xlv. 3 (with Dr Wade's note).

38. *drought.* As the Heb. for *sword* and *drought* is exactly the same in the unpointed text we should probably retain 'sword' as in the previous *vv.*

waters. The prosperity of Babylon was bound up with its water-supply; cf. Canon Johns, *Anc. Bab.* p. 5 'The very life of the land depended on irrigation. It was the supreme ambition of a good ruler to cut a new canal or clean out an old one....Such works often served to name the year.'

they are mad upon idols. The Heb. should be translated *they make themselves mad with idols,* probably it is better to follow the versions (LXX., Syr. &c.) and to read, with a slightly different vocalisation of the original, *they boast themselves of idols* (cf. Ps. xcvii. 7). The word for *idols,* as the mg. points out, literally means *terrors,* and such the heathen objects of worship must have seemed to those who worshipped a God of Whom no images were allowed.

39. This *v.* is based upon Is. xiii. 21, 22 *a,* 20 *a.*

wolves. As in Is. xiii. 22; the Heb is *howlers,* 'jackals' may be a better translation.

shall dwell there, and the ostriches shall dwell therein: and it shall be no more inhabited for ever; neither shall it be dwelt in from generation to generation. 40 As when God overthrew Sodom and Gomorrah and the neighbour cities thereof, saith the LORD; so shall no man dwell there, neither shall any son of man sojourn therein. 41 ¹Behold, a people cometh from the north; and a great nation, and many kings shall be stirred up from the uttermost parts of the earth. 42 They lay hold on bow and spear; they are cruel, and have no mercy; their voice roareth like the sea, and they ride upon horses; every one set in array, as a man to the battle, against thee, O daughter of Babylon. 43 The king of Babylon hath heard the fame of them, and his hands wax feeble: anguish hath taken hold of him, *and* pangs as of a woman in travail. 44 ²Behold, he shall come up like a lion from the pride of Jordan against the strong habitation: but I will suddenly make them run away from her; and whoso is chosen, him will I appoint over her: for who is like me? and who will appoint me a time? and who is the shepherd that will stand before me? 45 Therefore hear ye the counsel of the LORD, that he hath taken against Babylon; and his purposes, that he hath purposed against the land of the Chaldeans: Surely they shall drag them away, *even* the little ones of the flock; surely he shall make their habitation desolate with them. 46 At the noise of the taking of Babylon the earth trembleth, and the cry is heard among the nations.

LI. 1 Thus saith the LORD: Behold, I will raise up against

¹ See ch. vi. 22—24.   ² See ch. xlix. 19—21.

ostriches. LXX. translates θυγατέρες σειρήνων (i.e. *daughters of sirens*) as in Mic. i. 8 (cf. Enoch xcvi. 2). The rendering of AV. *owls* is generally abandoned though the Syrian peasants still call the owl 'the mother of ruins.'

40.   = xlix. 18; cf. Is. xiii. 19.

41—43.   These *vv.* are a repetition of vi. 22 ff. with slight alterations to fit them to Babylon instead of Jerusalem.

43—46.   = xlix. 19—21, Babylon being substituted for Edom.

44.   *a lion.* Cyrus is here meant, not Nebuchadrezzar as in xlix. 19.

46.   *the nations.* The noise of the fall of Edom penetrated only as far as the Red Sea (xlix. 21).

LI. 1. *Leb-kamai.* The mg. reading gives the meaning of the Heb.

Babylon, and against them that dwell in ¹Leb-kamai, a destroying wind. 2 And I will send unto Babylon ²strangers, that shall fan her; and they shall empty her land: for in the day of trouble they shall be against her round about. 3 ³Let not the archer bend his bow, and let him not lift himself up in his coat of mail: and spare ye not her young men; ⁴destroy ye utterly all her host. 4 And they shall fall down slain in the land of the Chaldeans, and thrust through in her streets. 5 For Israel is not forsaken, nor Judah, of his God, of the LORD of hosts; though their land is full of guilt against the Holy One of Israel. 6 Flee out of the midst of Babylon, and save every man his life; be not cut off in her iniquity: for it is the time of the LORD's vengeance; he will render unto her a recompence. 7 Babylon hath been a golden cup in the LORD's hand, that made all the earth drunken:

¹ That is, *The heart of them that rise up against me.* According to ancient tradition, a cypher for *Casdim,* that is Chaldea.   ² Or, *fanners*
³ Or, as otherwise read, *Against* him that *bendeth let the archer bend his bow, and against* him that *lifteth himself up &c.*   ⁴ Heb. *devote ye all &c.*

words. For the cypher see on xxv. 26. According to Rev. xvii. 5 Babylon is the type of all them that rise up against God.

a destroying wind. Better *the spirit of a destroyer*; cf. *v.* 11, xxii. 7; Hag. i. 14.

2. *strangers.* The subsequent verb requires the rendering of mg. *fanners,* i.e. winnowers, which differs from the text only in pointing.

empty. Cf. Is. xxiv. 1; Nah. ii. 2.

3. This *v.* is probably corrupt. As the latter half of the command is addressed to the invaders it is perhaps best to leave out the negatives and to look upon the whole as a single utterance. The rendering of mg. does little towards solving the difficulty of the MT. which evidently was an address to the Babylonians pointing out to them the futility of resistance.

5. *Israel is not forsaken.* The anger of Jehovah against His people is not to last for ever, and He will restore them; cf. Is. l. 1, liv. 4 ff. The word for *forsaken* literally means *widowed,* but by some confusion, since Jehovah is always looked upon as the husband of the land, it is in the masculine form.

though their land. The Heb. should probably be taken as *for their land* (i.e. Babylonia), and in this case Cornill's suggestion that the two halves of the *v.* should be transposed has much to recommend it.

6. *Flee out.* Those who remain behind, whether Jews or other foreign residents, will be involved in the fate of the guilty city. The address is probably to the Jews; cf. *v.* 45, l. 6; Is. xlviii. 20, lii. 12.

recompence. Cf. Is. lix. 18, lxvi. 6.

7. *a golden cup.* There is no real connexion between the use of

the nations have drunk of her wine; therefore the nations are mad. 8 Babylon is suddenly fallen and destroyed: howl for her; take balm for her pain, if so be she may be healed. 9 We would have healed Babylon, but she is not healed: forsake her, and let us go every one into his own country: for her judgement reacheth unto heaven, and is lifted up even to the skies. 10 The LORD hath brought forth our righteousness: come, and let us declare in Zion the work of the LORD our God. 11 Make ¹sharp the arrows; ²hold firm the ³shields: the LORD hath stirred up the spirit of the kings of the Medes; because his device is against

---

¹ Or, *bright* Heb. *clean.*　　² Heb. *fill.*　　³ Or, *suits of armour*

---

the image of the cup in this passage and that in xxv.; in the one it is the cup of God's wrath which is to be poured out upon all nations, in the other the cup of Babylon's luxury and sin, symbolised by the epithet *golden*¹, which has been drunk of by the other nations. In so far as Babylon was the instrument of vengeance in God's hand, so far she might be identified with the cup of His wrath. The *v.* is used in Rev. xvii. 4 together with Nah. iii. 4.

8. *Babylon is...fallen.* Cf. Is. xxi. 9; Rev. xiv. 8, xviii. 2. The metaphor of the golden cup is here dropped unless indeed the figure of the metal cup suggested the further image of the earthenware vessel and its fragility (cf. xix. 1 ff., xxii. 28).

balm. See on viii. 22.

9. This *v.* is best taken as the response of the nations, still infatuated with the past glory of Babylon, bewailing their inability to restore her broken fortunes.

10. The Jews here break forth with very different emotions upon the fall of the city.

our righteousness. That is, God has shewn our cause to be in the right, we have had the verdict given in our favour.

11. The nations and the Jews having ceased, a fresh exhortation is given to the approaching foe to make ready for the attack.

sharp. For the mg. *bright, clean,* cf. Is. xlix. 2 where the same Heb. root is used for '*polished* shaft.'

hold firm the shields. Prof. W. E. Barnes (*Expos. Times,* x. pp. 43—45) thinks that *shields* should be translated *armour, equipment.* This would suit the Heb. verb for *fill* (mg.) which does not give any satisfactory sense when applied to *shields:* cf. 2 S. xxiii. 7 with Driver's note.

kings of the Medes. Cf. *v.* 28; and Is. xiii. 17. LXX. reads the singular with evident reference to Cyrus, if this reading is not adopted the writer must be regarded as having had in view the rulers of the separate Median tribes. The office of the Medes seems always to be that of ravage and destruction (cf. Dan. vii. 4).

---

¹ Aeschylus called Babylon ἡ πολύχρυσος, *Pers.* 53.

Babylon, to destroy it: for it is the vengeance of the LORD, the vengeance of his temple. 12 Set up a standard against the walls of Babylon, make the watch strong, set the watchmen, prepare the ambushes: for the LORD hath both devised and done that which he spake concerning the inhabitants of Babylon. 13 O thou that dwellest upon many waters, abundant in treasures, thine end is come, the measure of thy ¹covetousness. 14 The LORD of hosts hath sworn by himself, *saying*, Surely I will fill thee with men, as with the cankerworm; and they shall lift up a shout against thee.

15 ²He hath made the earth by his power, he hath established the world by his wisdom, and by his understanding hath he stretched out the heavens: 16 when he uttereth his voice, there is a tumult of waters in the heavens, and he causeth the vapours to ascend from the ends of the earth; he maketh lightnings for the rain, and bringeth forth the wind out of his treasuries. 17 Every man is become brutish *and is* without knowledge; every goldsmith is put to shame by his graven image: for his molten image is falsehood, and there is no breath in them. 18 They are vanity, a work of delusion: in the time of their visitation they shall perish. 19 The portion of Jacob is not like these; for he is the former of all things; and *Israel* is the tribe of his inheritance: the LORD of hosts is his name.

---

¹ Or, *dishonest gain*　　　² See ch. x. 12—16.

temple. Cf. l. 28.

12. *make the watch strong.* That is the watch of the investing troops: cf. iv. 16.

13. *waters.* Cf. l. 38.

treasures. See on l. 37.

end is come. Cf. Am. viii. 2; Ez. vii. 2, 7.

measure of thy covetousness. Better taking the literal meaning of the Heb. words *the cubit of thy cutting off*; the metaphor is the same as that employed in Is. xxxviii. 12 'He will cut me off from the loom.'

14. Taking the translation of RV. the meaning of this *v.* is that God is going to fill Babylon with enemies as numerous and as harmful as locusts; another suggestion would render the Heb. by *though I have filled* &c. and take the figure to represent Babylon's immense population, the second part of the *v.* would then refer to the besiegers.

cankerworm. Common in Nah. and Joel; a symbol both for destruction (Ps. cv. 34 &c.) and for numbers (Nah. iii. 15).

15—19. These *vv.* = x. 12—16 where see notes.

20 Thou art my [1]battle axe and weapons of war: and with the ewill I break in pieces the nations; and with thee will I destroy kingdoms; 21 and with thee will I break in pieces the horse and his rider; and with thee will I break in pieces the chariot and him that rideth therein; 22 and with thee will I break in pieces man and woman; and with thee will I break in pieces the old man and the youth; and with thee will I break in pieces the young man and the maid; 23 and with thee will I break in pieces the shepherd and his flock; and with thee will I break in pieces the husbandman and his yoke *of oxen*; and with thee will I break in pieces [2]governors and deputies. 24 And I will render unto Babylon and to all the inhabitants of Chaldea all their evil that they have done in Zion in your sight, saith the LORD.

[1] Or, *maul*　　　　[2] Or, *lieutenants*

20—24. At first sight the rendering of EVV. makes these *vv.* refer to some coming instrument of Jehovah, perhaps Cyrus. The future tenses in the translation may however represent habitual action and in this case they should be translated by presents, and the *vv.* be applied to Babylon (cf. l. 23).

20. *battle axe.* The Heb. word means literally *a shatterer*: cf. l. 23 ; Nah. ii. 1; Ez. ix. 2.

23. *governors and deputies.* These words occur together in Ez. xxiii. 6, 12 ff. where however the translation is slightly different. Both words are found in the inscriptions and appear to be Assyrian by origin, though adopted later by the Persians &c. The word for *governor* (mg. *lieutenant*) is פֶּחָה (Pehah), i.e. *paḥāti* or in the fuller form *bel paḥāti*, it is used in Neh. ii. 7 of the satraps having rule 'beyond the river' as well as of Nehemiah himself (Neh. v. 14) and Zerubbabel (Hag. i. 1). The word for *deputy* is סָגָן (sāgān), i.e. *šaknu*, prefect or ruler; evidently some slightly inferior official (cf. Neh. ii. 12 &c.).

24. *unto Babylon.* If the previous *vv.* are taken to refer to Babylon—mentioned in the second person—this *v.* is best explained as an addition of one who looked upon them as referring to Cyrus (see above).

evil…in Zion. Cf. xxv. 29 'I begin to work evil at the city which is called by my name'; the point of view of this *v.* is quite different from that of Jeremiah and seems to reflect a later age when the remembrance of Judah's sin against Jehovah had been wiped out by the present reality of their sufferings at the hands of Babylon, Jehovah's instrument of vengeance (cf. Is. xl. 2).

in your sight. The words are to be connected not with those immediately before them but with God's promise of recompence: cf. Ps. xxxvii. 34, xci. 8; Mal. i. 5.

25 Behold, I am against thee, O destroying mountain, saith the LORD, which destroyest all the earth: and I will stretch out mine hand upon thee, and roll thee down from the rocks, and will make thee a burnt mountain. 26 And they shall not take of thee a stone for a corner, nor a stone for foundations; but thou shalt be desolate for ever, saith the LORD. 27 Set ye up a standard in the land, blow the trumpet among the nations, ¹prepare the nations against her, call together against her the kingdoms of Ararat, Minni, and Ashkenaz: appoint a marshal against

¹ Heb. *sanctify.*

25. *thee.* Babylon is once more addressed in the second person.

destroying mountain. Cf. 2 K. xxiii. 13 (RVm.). The address to Babylon as a mountain must be understood as figurative, for the city was built on a plain, and any elevation which it possessed was in the political rather than in the physical sphere. Budde thinks that the description may have been borrowed from Ezekiel's condemnation of Mount Seir (Ez. xxxv. 3 ff.).

roll thee down. Cf. Rev. viii. 8 'a great mountain burning with fire was cast into the sea.'

burnt mountain. The figure may be that of a volcano which after a period of destruction becomes extinct leaving its own sides desolate and bare (cf. Is. xiii. 3).

26. *a stone.* It is doubtful whether the figure of the burnt mountain is continued into this *v.* as some critics imagine; if so the stones must be taken as having been so damaged by the fire as to be unfit for building purposes. The literal explanation, however, is really the best, and the actual stones of Babylon are referred to, the meaning being that Babylon is never to be rebuilt.

27. *prepare* (mg. *sanctify*). See on vi. 4.

Ararat. Mentioned here; Gen. viii. 4; and 2 K. xix. 37 (=Is. xxxvii. 38). The country lying to the north-west of Lake Van known as *Urartu* in the inscriptions and now forming part of Armenia (cf. LXX. of Is. xxxvii. 38).

Minni. Here only in OT. but evidently the same as the *Mannai* of the inscriptions, a people whose land lay to the south-east of Lake Urumia.

Ashkenaz. Here and Gen. x. 3 (=1 Ch. i. 6). Many scholars identify this country with the Ashguza mentioned in the inscriptions, whose prince was an ally of the Mannai (*KB.* II. pp. 129, 147). The Jews of the Middle Ages identified *Ashkenaz* with Germany; and in the present day German Jews are called *Ashkenazim* to distinguish them from the Sephardim or Spanish Jews (cf. Ob. 20).

marshal. Here and Nah. iii. 17 only. The Heb. טִפְסָר (ṭiphsār) is a loan-word from the Assyrian *dupsarru*, registrar. It evidently signifies some high official, here perhaps the generalissimo of the forces allied

her; cause the horses to come up as the rough cankerworm. 28 [1]Prepare against her the nations, the kings of the Medes, the governors thereof, and all the deputies thereof, and all the land of his dominion. 29 And the land trembleth and is in pain: for the purposes of the LORD against Babylon do stand, to make the land of Babylon a desolation, without inhabitant. 30 The mighty men of Babylon have forborne to fight, they remain in their strong holds; their might hath failed; they are become as women: her dwelling places are set on fire; her bars are broken. 31 One post shall run to meet another, and one messenger to meet another, to shew the king of Babylon that his city is taken on every quarter: 32 and the [2]passages are surprised, and the [3]reeds they have burned with fire, and the men of war are affrighted.

33 For thus saith the LORD of hosts, the God of Israel: The daughter of Babylon is like a threshing-floor at the time when it is trodden; yet a little while, and the time of harvest shall

---

[1] Heb. *sanctify.*   [2] Or, *fords*   [3] Or, *marshes* Heb. *pools.*

---

against Babylon. Graf thinks that the word is intended to be a collective like *horse* (in sing. in Heb.) in the next clause, and that it represents some special kind of troops.

cankerworm. See on *v.* 14.

28. *kings.* Read with LXX. *king* (cf. *his dominion*).

governors...deputies. See on *v.* 23.

30. *bars.* The bars of a city as being amongst its most vital defences often symbolise its whole power of resistance; cf. Jud. xvi. 3; 1 K. iv. 13.

31. The king of Babylon was evidently in the city at the time of its fall and messenger after messenger came to him from the different points of the outer defences, but all with the same message of disaster.

post. Lit. *runner.*

32. *passages.* Mg. *fords* as in Jud. iii. 28. It is better, however, to see here a reference to the ferries across the Euphrates; cf. Herod. I. 186.

reeds. The Heb. *pools* may refer to the artificial channels which formed part of the defences of the city (Herod. I. 185).

burned. This must be taken as hyperbolic (so Calvin) or the text emended in some way or other.

33. *a threshing-floor.* The threshing-floor was trodden over in order to provide a level space for beating out the grain; a similar figure is used by Tiglath-Pileser III who speaks of 'treading down' the land of his enemies 'as in threshing.' Schrader, *COT.* I. p. 225.

harvest. The harvest as an image of destruction is somewhat rare, the usual figure being either the treading of the wine-press or of the vintage itself (see Pusey on Joel iii. 13).

B.

come for her. 34 Nebuchadrezzar the king of Babylon hath devoured ¹me, he hath crushed ¹me, he hath made ¹me an empty vessel, he hath swallowed ¹me up like a dragon, he hath filled his maw with my delicates; he hath cast ¹me out. 35 ²The violence done to me and to my flesh be upon Babylon, shall the ³inhabitant of Zion say; and, My blood be upon the inhabitants of Chaldea, shall Jerusalem say. 36 Therefore thus saith the LORD: Behold, I will plead thy cause, and take vengeance for thee; and I will dry up her sea, and make her fountain dry. 37 And Babylon shall become heaps, a dwelling place for jackals, an astonishment, and an hissing, without inhabitant. 38 They shall roar together like young lions; they shall growl as lions' whelps. 39 When they are heated, I will make their feast, and I will make them drunken, that they may rejoice, and sleep a perpetual sleep, and not wake, saith the LORD. 40 I will bring them down like lambs

---

¹ Another reading is, *us*.   ² Heb. *My wrong and my flesh*.
³ Heb. *inhabitress*.

34. In this and the following *vv.* the speaker is Israel herself, the sing. of the text should therefore be read rather than the plural of the mg.

empty vessel. A vessel turned upside down and from which the contents are quite exhausted, the figure is not an uncommon one; cf. *v.* 2, xlviii. 12; Nah. ii. 2, 10.

dragon. The Heb. word means any kind of sea or land monster. In Is. xxvii. 1 the great world powers are symbolised as monsters and no doubt the same idea underlies the allegory in the book of Jonah: cf. on *v.* 44.

35. Cf. Gen. xvi. 5.

36. *sea.* The Nile is referred to as a sea in Is. xviii. 2, xix. 5, &c. In the Semitic languages the usage of words for sea and river is somewhat vague, cf. the use of *nāru* in Assyrian and *baḥr* in Arabic.

37. Cf. ix. 10 &c.

39. The growling of lions over their meat suggests the picture of men falling into a drunken slumber over their wine.

their feast. There was an ancient tradition that Babylon was taken by Cyrus during a banquet (Herod. I. 191; Xenophon, *Cyrop.* VII. 23; and cf. Dan. v.); if this was so the figure may have a deeper significance than at first appears.

may rejoice. LXX. *may be stupefied*; this rendering, which involves the change of a single consonant in MT., is to be preferred as rejoicing does not fit well into the context.

a perpetual sleep. Cf. Job xiii. 12; Ps. xiii. 3, &c. In the Book of Jubilees xxiii. 1 Abraham is said to have 'slept the sleep of eternity.'

40. Cf. Is. xxxiv. 6 f.; Ez. xxxix. 18.

to the slaughter, like rams with he-goats. 41 How is [1]Sheshach taken! and the praise of the whole earth surprised! how is Babylon become [2]a desolation among the nations! 42 The sea is come up upon Babylon: she is covered with the [3]multitude of the waves thereof. 43 Her cities are become [2]a desolation, a dry land, and a desert, a land wherein no man dwelleth, neither doth any son of man pass thereby. 44 And I will [4]do judgement upon Bel in Babylon, and I will bring forth out of his mouth that which he hath swallowed up; and the nations shall not flow together any more unto him: yea, the wall of Babylon shall fall.

45 My people, go ye out of the midst of her, and save yourselves every man from the fierce anger of the LORD. 46 And let not your heart faint, neither fear ye for the rumour that shall be heard in the land; for a rumour shall come one year, and

[1] See ch. xxv. 26.   [2] Or, an astonishment
[3] Or, tumult   [4] Heb. visit upon.

41.   *Sheshach.* See on xxv. 26.
praise of the whole earth. Cf. xlix. 25; Is. lxii. 7 (of Jerusalem).
42.   *The sea.* The flood of invasion breaking over the city; cf. xlvi. 7 f., xlvii. 2; Is. viii. 7 f., xvii. 12.
44—49.   This passage from *yea, the wall* (v. 44 b) to *the slain…to fall* (v. 49 a) is missing from LXX. The matter in it is largely repeated in vv. 49 b—53 and Duhm thinks the latter passage is a revised draft of the present vv. for which they were afterwards substituted. The simplest explanation seems to be that the eye of the translator went from *Babylon shall fall* (v. 44 b) to the same words in v. 49 and the intervening vv. remained untranslated.
44.   *Bel.* See on l. 2.
swallowed. The spoils from the nations and the trains of captives. Cheyne connects this passage with the story of Jonah (*Theol. Rev.* XIV. *Jonah: a Study in Jewish Folk-lore and Religion*).
45.   Cf. *v.* 6, l. 8; Is. lii. 11; 1 Esdr. ii. 7.
46.   The state of mind here described must often have recurred in ancient times when news travelled slowly and authoritative statements were few. The description hardly agrees with the actual events which preceded the immediate fall of Babylon, though Nabonidus may have had to deal with many attempts at revolt on the part of those cities whose worship he tried to suppress[1]. The period to which this *v.* would

---

[1] Nabonidus, like Amenophis IV in Egypt and Hezekiah and Josiah in Judah, tried to centralise the national worship. The method he adopted, that of removing all the local deities to Babylon, was not calculated to earn the good will of the priests and worshippers of the despoiled shrines and indeed made the subsequent conquest by Cyrus a comparatively easy task.

after that in another year *shall come* a rumour, and violence in the land, ruler against ruler. 47 Therefore, behold, the days come, that I will do judgement upon the graven images of Babylon, and her whole land shall be ashamed; and all her slain shall fall in the midst of her. 48 Then the heaven and the earth, and all that is therein, shall sing for joy over Babylon; for the spoilers shall come unto her from the north, saith the LORD. 49 [1]As Babylon hath caused the slain of Israel to fall, so at Babylon shall fall the slain of all the [2]land. 50 Ye that have escaped the sword, go ye, stand not still; remember the LORD from afar, and let Jerusalem come into your mind. 51 We are ashamed, because we have heard reproach; confusion hath covered our faces: for strangers are come into the sanctuaries of the LORD's house. 52 Wherefore, behold, the days come, saith the LORD, that I will do judgement upon her graven images; and through all her land

[1] Or, *Both Babylon is to fall, O ye slain of Israel, and at &c.*   [2] Or, *earth*

seem best to apply is that following the death of Alexander during which his empire was forcibly divided up between his various generals and their successors. The varying fortunes of the long contest must have given opportunities for many rumours to arise, and as Palestine was part of the disputed territory no small interest must have been taken in the progress of events.

47. This *v.* bears a close resemblance to *v.* 52 and should probably be omitted.

Therefore. If this *v.* is retained *therefore* which does not connect easily with what has gone before should be rendered as *for*.

graven images. Cornill proposes to emend the text and to read *rulers*; he compares Is. xiv. 5, xlix. 7, lii. 5[1].

48. Babylon's fall is to be a matter for rejoicing not only to the nations but also to the powers of nature, heaven and earth are called in to witness the spoiling of the guilty city (cf. Is. xliv. 23).

49. The *v.* reads more smoothly if both the mg. renderings are adopted and one slight change is made in the Heb.—the repetition of a single consonant which may well have been omitted by error. The *v.* will then read *Babylon also is to fall for the slain of Israel, as for Babylon have fallen the slain of all the earth.*

50. Cf. l. 5.

51. Israel is ashamed to return to her desolate and despoiled sanctuary which has been desecrated by the presence therein of foreigners; cf. Lam. i. 10; Ps. lxxix. 1; and for the same feeling in later times Acts xxi. 28 ff.

[1] The change involved in the Heb. is not very great, משלי being substituted for פסילי.

the wounded shall groan. 53 Though Babylon should mount up to heaven, and though she should fortify the height of her strength, yet from me shall spoilers come unto her, saith the LORD. 54 The sound of a cry from Babylon, and of great destruction from the land of the Chaldeans! 55 for the LORD spoileth Babylon, and destroyeth out of her the great voice; and their waves roar like many waters, the noise of their voice is uttered: 56 for the spoiler is come upon her, even upon Babylon, and her mighty men are taken, their bows are broken in pieces: for the LORD is a God of recompences, he shall surely requite. 57 And I will make drunk her princes and her wise men, her governors and her deputies, and her mighty men; and they shall sleep a perpetual sleep, and not wake, saith the King, whose name is the LORD of hosts. 58 Thus saith the LORD of hosts: [1]The broad walls of Babylon shall be utterly [2]overthrown, and her high gates shall be burned with fire; [3]and the peoples shall labour for vanity, and the nations for the fire; and they shall be weary.

[1] Or, *The walls of broad Babylon*   [2] Or, *made bare*
[3] See Hab. ii. 13.

53. *mount up to heaven.* Cf. Gen. xi. 4; Is. xiv. 12 f.; Job xx. 6.
54. Cf. xlviii. 3, l. 22, 46.
55. *the great voice.* The din of the populous city.
their waves. The position of the words seems to make them refer to the noise of the inhabitants as did the previous clause, it is tempting however to attach them to the next *v.* and to apply them to the spoilers (cf. *v.* 42).
57. Cf. *v.* 39.
58. *The broad walls.* Better with LXX. *wall.* The walls of Babylon were one of the wonders of antiquity; cf. Herod. I. 178 f.; Pliny, *Nat. Hist.* VI. 26; Strabo XVI. 1.
utterly overthrown. Mg. *made bare,* the foundations discovered. Darius was the actual destroyer of the fortifications of Babylon.
and the peoples &c. = Hab. ii. 13, being probably a quotation in both instances from some earlier prophecy.

ADDITIONAL NOTE ON L. 13.

The Fate of Babylon.

The forecasts of the Hebrew prophets that Babylon was to be utterly destitute and without inhabitant have been fulfilled almost to the letter, though it was not till long after the fall of the city to the troops of Cyrus that its de-

cline really began. According to Herodotus, Babylon was left uninjured by
Cyrus and it was on its second capture by Darius that the walls and gates were
demolished[1]. Mr Bevan says that by the conquest Babylon did not 'lose its
imperial dignity. Its greatness was too well based on its old renown, its geographical position, its immense population, its commercial and industrial supremacy. It could not but be still the capital of the world, the seat of the
'King of kings,' even though that title now belonged to a foreigner. During
the hot Babylonian summer indeed the Iranian monarch used to withdraw to
his own high country, to Persepolis or Ecbatana; but for the seven cooler
months of the year the Persian court resided at Babylon[2].' The Babylonians
made several attempts to revolt and in consequence of one of these Xerxes
destroyed the great temple and took away the image of Bel[3]. When Alexander
had completed his long series of conquests it was to Babylon that he turned as
the destined capital of Asia, if not of his whole empire[4], and it was there that
the youthful conqueror breathed his last. The successors of Alexander, however, were the instruments by which the city finally lost its importance.
'Sennacherib had razed it to the soil, and it had risen again to new glory.
Cyrus and Alexander had conquered it, and it was still the capital of the world.
But Seleucus Nicator brought its doom upon Babylon at last. It had subsisted...
through all changes of empire owing to a prerogative which was founded upon
natural conditions. But the prerogative belonged to the land rather than to
the particular city. It was a natural necessity that there should be in this
alluvial region a great centre of human life, and if Babylon were merely dis-
persed, as by Sennacherib, the human swarm again gathered. There was only
one way by which Babylon could really be undone—by the creation of another
centre. This was what Seleucus did. Forty miles north of Babylon, Seleucus
marked the foundations of a new city, Seleucia-on-the-Tigris....From this
moment Babylon was doomed[5].' But though Babylon lost its importance it
has never been without inhabitants, that is if by Babylon is meant the whole
circuit of the ancient city, which as Aristotle said was 'not so much a city in
dimensions as a nation[6].' Strabo did indeed describe it in the last century B.C.
as a desert[7], and Benjamin of Tudela in the Middle Ages has preserved a
description of its ruined state, but as Dean Stanley says 'Babylon has never
ceased to be inhabited. Hillah, a town with a population of five thousand souls,
is within its walls, and the Arabs still wander through it[8].' At the same time

---

[1] III. 159. Berosus, however, says that Cyrus gave orders for the outer walls to
be pulled down (quoted in Joseph. c. Ap. I. 19).
[2] House of Seleucus, I. p. 241. The whole account there contained of Babylonia
from the earliest times is most interesting.
[3] Herod. I. 183.
[4] See Bevan, op. cit. I. p. 246.
[5] Bevan, op. cit. I. pp. 252 f.; see also Pliny, Nat. Hist. VI. 30, 122; Pausan
I. xvi. 3 &c.
[6] Pol. III. 3.
[7] xvi. i. 5 ἐρημία μεγάλη ἐστὶν ἡ μεγάλη πόλις.
[8] Jew. Church, III. p. 66.

the real Babylon and the site of the royal palace of Nebuchadrezzar are but a mass of ruinous heaps and unsightly mounds, and the haunt, as the prophet foretold, of the wolf and the jackal[1].

CHAPTER LI. 59—64.

The Mission of Seraiah.

Though the account contained in this section has been rejected by some scholars there is no real reason for so doing. The objections which have been brought against it are (*a*) it is closely connected with the foregoing prophecy on Babylon which is almost universally rejected by critics (*v.* 60); (*b*) it is improbable that Zedekiah visited Babylon in person at this time (*v.* 59); (*c*) the sinking of the message in the river is an act so theatrical as to be unworthy of Jeremiah. In reply to these objections it may be urged that the statement in *v.* 60 is in all probability the addition of a later writer and that the rejection of l. 1—li. 58 need not imply the rejection of li. 59—64; further there is no real improbability in a visit from Zedekiah to his overlord in Babylon in connexion with the recent attempts at revolt (xxvii.), the personal attendance of the Judean monarch may have been the only way of lulling the suspicions of the Chaldeans ; finally, the sinking of the stone in the Euphrates can be matched by many other similar acts both by Jeremiah himself (e.g. xix. 1—10, xliii. 9, &c.) and also by other prophets. Positive arguments in favour of the authenticity of the passage are not lacking. The messenger to whom Jeremiah entrusted the scroll was apparently a brother of Baruch himself (cf. *v.* 59 with xxxii. 12) and the fact that this relationship is not actually stated in so many words, as it would have been by a later writer, is strong proof of the reliability and good faith of the author. Moreover the sentiments expressed in the message are very different from those of the previous section, and quite in keeping with those utterances of the prophet which are generally accepted; Jeremiah never concealed the fact that the Babylonian supremacy was limited in time, and that when the period of punishment was over Israel would be restored.

59 The word which Jeremiah the prophet commanded Seraiah the son of Neriah, the son of Mahseiah, when he went with Zedekiah the king of Judah to Babylon in the fourth year of his reign. Now Seraiah was [1]chief chamberlain. 60 And Jeremiah wrote

[1] Or, *quartermaster*

59. Cf. xxxii. 12 and see above.

chief chamberlain. Mg. *quartermaster.* The latter rendering is probably to be preferred. Seraiah was evidently in charge of the

---

[1] For a description of the appearance of Babylon at the present day see Miss G. Lowthian Bell, *Amurath to Amurath,* pp. 167 ff.

in ¹a book all the evil that should come upon Babylon, even all these words that are written concerning Babylon. 61 And Jeremiah said to Seraiah, When thou comest to Babylon, ²then see that thou read all these words, 62 and say, O LORD, thou hast spoken concerning this place, to cut it off, that none shall dwell therein, neither man nor beast, but that it shall be desolate for ever. 63 And it shall be, when thou hast made an end of reading this book, that thou shalt bind a stone to it, and cast it into the midst of Euphrates: 64 and thou shalt say, Thus shall Babylon sink, and shall not rise again because of the evil that I will bring ³upon her: and they shall be weary.

Thus far are the words of Jeremiah.

¹ Or, one book   ² Or, and shalt see, and read...then shalt thou say &c.
³ Or, upon her.   And they shall be weary: thus far &c.

arrangements for quartering the king at the various halting-places¹. LXX. reads *ruler of the presents*, that is to say the official in charge of the tribute or of the gifts prepared by Zedekiah to mollify his offended suzerain.   The AV. somewhat quaintly renders *a quiet prince* (cf. Vulg. princeps prophetiae).

62.   This *v.* interrupts the connexion between *vv.* 61 and 63 and should be omitted.   It seems to depend on l. 3, 26.

64.   Cf. Rev. xviii. 21 *b* 'Thus with a mighty fall shall Babylon, the great city, be cast down, and shall be found no more at all.'

they shall be weary. These words—in Heb. one word only—are to be separated from those which go before, as is done by the rendering of mg.; they come originally from *v.* 58 and have been placed here by error.   It is generally held that the concluding phrase *Thus far* &c. once stood after *v.* 58 and when it was transferred to this place the last word of the *v.* (in Heb.) was either by accident or design transferred with it.

Thus far....Jeremiah. These words were inserted before lii. which is an appendix mainly borrowed from parts of 2 K. xxiv. and xxv. (see below).

CHAPTER LII.

The Fall of Jerusalem.

This ch. with the exception of *vv.* 28—30 is taken almost word for word from 2 K. xxiv. 18—xxv. 21, 27—30.   The present narrative also bears close resemblances to ch. xxxix., and indeed *vv.* 4—11, 13—16 are identical with

¹ The Heb. (שַׂר־מְנוּחָה) lit. means *prince* or *ruler of the resting-place. Enc. Bib.* 4373 compares several Palmyrene inscriptions set up by the senate and people 'in honour of the leader of the caravan' (רב משריתא).

vv. 1 f., 4—10 of that ch. No account, however, is given here of Nebuchadrezzar's
command that the prophet was to be preserved (xxxix. 11—14), but on the
other hand details concerning the temple vessels, not given in xxxix., are now
related (*vv.* 17—23). There is some reason for supposing that in the cases
where the text of this ch. differs from that in 2 K. the latter is less well preserved. LXX. omits *vv.* 2 f., 15, 22—30. The object of the ch. was perhaps to
shew that Jeremiah's prophecies against Jerusalem were fulfilled, and it is
interesting to notice that a similar historical appendix is placed at the end of
the first Isaiah, though the reasons for this addition were not the same (Is.
xxxvi.—xxxix.=2 K. xviii. 17—xx. 19)[1].

LII. 1 [1]Zedekiah was one and twenty years old when he began
to reign; and he reigned eleven years in Jerusalem: and his
mother's name was Hamutal the daughter of Jeremiah of Libnah.
2 And he did that which was evil in the sight of the LORD,
according to all that Jehoiakim had done. 3 For through the
anger of the LORD did it come to pass in Jerusalem and Judah,
until he had cast them out from his presence: and Zedekiah
rebelled against the king of Babylon. 4 And it came to pass in
the ninth year of his reign, in the tenth month, in the tenth day
of the month, that Nebuchadrezzar king of Babylon came, he
and all his army, against Jerusalem, and encamped against it;
and they built forts against it round about. 5 So the city was
besieged unto the eleventh year of king Zedekiah. 6 In the

[1] See 2 Kings xxiv. 18, &c.

LII. 1. *Zedekiah was one and twenty years old.* According to 1 Ch.
iii. 15 Zedekiah was older than Shallum (i.e. Jehoahaz), and since the
latter was twenty-three on ascending the throne (2 K. xxiii. 31) Zedekiah
must have been well over thirty by this time.

Hamutal. The mother of Jehoahaz (2 K. xxiii.), to whom Zedekiah
was therefore full brother; the mother of Jehoiakim was called Zebidah
(2 K. xxiii. 36).

Libnah. The scene of the destruction of Sennacherib's army (2 K.
xix. 8 and 35).

4. *the tenth month.* 'The numbering of the months was a late
usage introduced with the Babylonian calendar, in which the beginning
of the year was reckoned from the spring season. Hence the investment
of the city commenced in the month of January, 588 (or 587).' Dr Skinner
on 2 K. xxv. 1. Cf. Zech. viii. 19.

6. *In the fourth month.* The numeral is missing from the text of
2 K. xxv. 3.

---

[1] The natural and earlier idea that the compiler of Kings made use of these chh.
of Is. in collecting materials for his history is no longer held by scholars; see Driver,
LOT.[8] pp. 226 ff.

fourth month, in the ninth day of the month, the famine was sore in the city, so that there was no bread for the people of the land. 7 Then a breach was made in the city, and all the men of war fled, and went forth out of the city by night by the way of the gate between the two walls, which was by the king's garden; (now the Chaldeans were against the city round about:) and they went by the way of the Arabah. 8 But the army of the Chaldeans pursued after the king, and overtook Zedekiah in the plains of Jericho; and all his army was scattered from him. 9 Then they took the king, and carried him up unto the king of Babylon to Riblah in the land of Hamath; and he ¹gave judgement upon him. 10 And the king of Babylon slew the sons of Zedekiah before his eyes: he slew also all the princes of Judah in Riblah. 11 And he put out the eyes of Zedekiah; and the king of Babylon bound him in fetters, and carried him to Babylon, and put him in prison till the day of his death.

12 Now in the fifth month, in the tenth day of the month, which was the nineteenth year of king Nebuchadrezzar, king of Babylon, came Nebuzaradan the captain of the guard, which stood before the king of Babylon, into Jerusalem: 13 and he burned the house of the LORD, and the king's house; and all the houses of Jerusalem, even ²every great house, burned he with fire. 14 And all the army of the Chaldeans, that were with the captain of the guard, brake down all the walls of Jerusalem round about. 15 Then Nebuzaradan the captain of the guard carried

---

¹ Heb. *spake judgements with him.*   ² Or, *every great man's house*

7 ff. See on xxxix. 4 ff.

10. *he slew also...in Riblah.* Missing from 2 K. xxv. 7.

11. *and put...death.* Missing from 2 K. xxv. 7.

12. *tenth.* In 2 K. xxv. 8 the *seventh* day is mentioned. Jewish tradition says that Nebuzaradan entered the temple on the *seventh*, profaned it on the ninth, when it was set on fire, and that it burned till the *tenth.*

nineteenth. Cf. *v.* 29 *eighteenth*; the chronology of this period is very confused and different traditions seem to exist; in *v.* 28 the date of the first fall of Jerusalem is given as the seventh year of the reign of Nebuchadrezzar whilst in 2 K. xxiv. 12 it is the eighth. It seems probable that one tradition reckons from 604 the first complete year of Nebuchadrezzar, the other from 605 the year when he came to the throne.

15. Missing from LXX.

away captive of the poorest sort of the people, and the residue
of the people that were left in the city, and those that fell away,
that fell to the king of Babylon, and the residue of the ¹multi-
tude. 16 But Nebuzaradan the captain of the guard left of the
poorest of the land to be vinedressers and husbandmen. 17 And
the pillars of brass that were in the house of the LORD, and the
bases and the brasen sea that were in the house of the LORD, did
the Chaldeans break in pieces, and carried all the brass of them
to Babylon. 18 The pots also, and the shovels, and the snuffers,
and the basons, and the spoons, and all the vessels of brass
wherewith they ministered, took they away. 19 And the cups,
and the firepans, and the basons, and the pots, and the candlesticks, and the spoons, and the bowls; that which was of gold,
in gold, and that which was of silver, in silver, the captain of the
guard took away. 20 The two pillars, the one sea, and the twelve
brasen bulls that were under the bases, which king Solomon had
made for the house of the LORD: the brass of all these vessels
was without weight. 21 And as for the pillars, the height of the
one pillar was eighteen cubits; and a line of twelve cubits did
compass it; and the thickness thereof was four fingers: it was
hollow. 22 And a chapiter of brass was upon it; and the height
of the one chapiter was five cubits, with network and pome-

¹ Or, *artificers*

of the poorest sort of the people &c. These words should be omitted
as inconsistent with the next *v.*, they are not found in 2 K. xxv. 11.
    17. The larger vessels were too bulky to be carried away as they
were and so had to be broken up.
    the pillars...bases...brasen sea. See on xxvii. 19.
    18. *The pots...shovels.* Mentioned in Ex. xxvii. 3; 1 K. vii. 45.
    snuffers. Cf. Ex. xxv. 38; Num. iv. 9.
    basons. For tossing the blood of the victims against the side of the
altar.
    19. *the candlesticks.* Better *lampstands.* These stood before the
oracle (1 K. vii. 49).
    20. *one sea...twelve brasen bulls.* The *sea* may have represented the
'water above the firmament' from which the rain came; and *the twelve
bulls* were perhaps the signs of the zodiac. The making of the *bulls*
was a technical breach of the second commandment.
    21—23. See 1 K. vii. 15—18.
    21. *cubits.* A cubit was about a foot and a half in length.
    22. *a chapiter.* This is a capital, the head of a column or pillar.

granates upon the chapiter round about, all of brass: and the
second pillar also had like unto these, and pomegranates. 23 And
there were ninety and six pomegranates [1]on the sides; all the
pomegranates were an hundred upon the network round about.
24 And the captain of the guard took Seraiah the chief priest,
and Zephaniah the second priest, and the three keepers of the
[2]door: 25 and out of the city he took an [3]officer that was set
over the men of war; and seven men of them that saw the king's
face, which were found in the city; and the scribe of the captain
of the host, who mustered the people of the land; and threescore
men of the people of the land, that were found in the midst of

[1] Or, *on the outside*   Heb. *towards the four winds*.
[2] Heb. *threshold*.			[3] Or, *eunuch*

unto these.   The word for 'network' has evidently fallen out.   The
opposite omission, strangely enough, has been made in 2 K. xxv. 17 and
and pomegranates omitted.

pomegranates.   The shrub was common in Palestine and suggested
the ornamentation for the embroidery of the robe of the ephod[1].   The
pomegranate appears very frequently in Assyrian and Egyptian sculpture
(see Dr McNeile's notes on Ex. xxv. 31 ff., xxviii. 33).

23.   *on the sides*.   The Heb. is *towards the four winds* or *windwards* as
Driver renders it.   No certain meaning can be given to the words which
have been interpreted in various ways (*a*) *visible outwards*, that is the
ninety-six could be seen in contradistinction to the four hidden between
the pillar and the wall (Rashi); (*b*) *hanging loosely*, that is four of the
pomegranates were fixed and the others hung down from them.

24—27.   These *vv*. contain a list of officials and others who were
taken to Nebuchadrezzar at Riblah and there put to death by his orders.
These men may have been selected for punishment because they had
been more directly concerned with the rebellion than their fellows, or
they may have been selected more or less at random according to the
summary methods of justice employed by oriental monarchs.

24.   *Seraiah*.   The name is a common one and possibly there is
some confusion between the various people who bore it.   This chief
priest was according to 1 Ch. vi. 4 ff. a descendant of Aaron through
Eleazar and the father of Jehozadak (cf. Hag. i. 1); according to one
account he was the father of Ezra also (Ezra vii. 1).

Zephaniah.   See on xxi. 1.

keepers of the door (better as mg. *threshold*).   See on xxxv. 4.

25.   *seven…that saw the king's face*.   In 2 K. xxv. 19 the number
given is *five*.   These men were apparently in the king's confidence and
had much to do with shaping his policy; cf. Est. i. 14; Matt. xviii. 10.

[1] Flinders Petrie (*HDB*. I. 158, 269) suggests that the bell and pomegranate
ornament on this robe was an adaptation of 'the old Egyptian lotus and bud border.'

the city. 26 And Nebuzaradan the captain of the guard took them, and brought them to the king of Babylon to Riblah. 27 And the king of Babylon smote them, and put them to death at Riblah in the land of Hamath. So Judah was carried away captive out of his land. 28 This is the people whom Nebuchadrezzar carried away captive: in the seventh year three thousand Jews and three and twenty: 29 in the eighteenth year of Nebuchadrezzar he carried away captive from Jerusalem eight hundred and thirty two persons: 30 in the three and twentieth year of Nebuchadrezzar Nebuzaradan the captain of the guard carried away captive of the Jews seven hundred forty and five persons: all the persons were four thousand and six hundred.

31 ¹And it came to pass in the seven and thirtieth year of

¹ See 2 Kings xxv. 27—30.

28—30. These *vv.* are missing from LXX.; they do not occur in 2 K. but instead there is a very brief account, based on Jer. xxxix. 11—xliii. 7, of the governorship of Gedaliah (*vv.* 22—26).

28. *seventh year.* If the text stands this refers to the first capture of Jerusalem when according to 2 K. xxiv. 14 more than ten thousand were deported. The simplest solution is to read 'seventeenth' and to take the figure as being the number of those who were carried away at the beginning of the operations of the second siege, the captives from the towns outside Jerusalem.

30. *three and twentieth year.* No other early account of this deportation has been preserved though there is no reason for doubting the substantial accuracy of the statement. The deportation may have been in connexion with the disorders in Palestine organised by Ishmael and as a punishment for the murder of the Babylonian governor. Josephus records (*Ant.* x. ix. 7) that Nebuchadrezzar in the twenty-third year of his reign deported Jews from Egypt.

31—34. The parallel narrative with 2 K. is now resumed and these *vv.* with a few small differences are the same as the last *vv.* of that book (xxv. 27—30). The reasons for the action of Evil-merodach are obscure¹, but none the less would excite hopes in the people of the captivity. Herodotus records (III. 129—132) that Darius gave the privilege of sitting at the king's table to a Greek physician named Democēdēs as a reward for his having restored to him the use of his foot which had been injured whilst hunting.

31. *the seven and thirtieth year.* That is 560 B.C. and the second year of Evil-merodach, who succeeded Nebuchadrezzar in 561.

¹ According to St Jerome, *Comm. on Is.* xiv. 19, Evil-merodach met Jehoiachin in prison where he himself was confined owing to his having offended Nebuchadrezzar.

the captivity of Jehoiachin king of Judah, in the twelfth month, in the five and twentieth day of the month, that Evil-merodach king of Babylon, in the *first* year of his reign, lifted up the head of Jehoiachin king of Judah, and brought him forth out of prison; 32 and he spake kindly to him, and set his throne above the throne of the kings that were with him in Babylon. 33 And he changed his prison garments, and did eat bread before him continually all the days of his life. 34 And for his allowance, there was a continual allowance given him of the king of Babylon, every day a portion until the day of his death, all the days of his life.

five and twentieth day. Cf. 2 K. xxv. 27 which says *seven and twentieth.*

Evil-merodach (Bab. *Amēl-marduk*). The reign of this king was cut short after a little more than two years by assassination; according to Berosus he had alienated his people by his debauchery and extravagance (see Canon Johns, *Anct. Bab.* p. 129).

lifted up the head. The same phrase is used of the chief butler in Gen. xl. 13.

32. *the kings.* The court of a great monarch like the king of Babylon would include amongst its members a number of conquered sovereigns whose presence there, whilst it added to the glory of the conqueror, also prevented any attempts which the vanquished might have been disposed to make to recover their former powers. Such incidents as the friendship which developed between Evil-merodach and Jehoiachin were probably not uncommon. Cyrus formed a similar bond with his captive Croesus.

34. *until the day of his death.* The successors of Evil-merodach did not withdraw the privileges granted to Jehoiachin.

INDEX

CAMBRIDGE : PRINTED BY
J. B. PEACE, M.A.,
AT THE UNIVERSITY PRESS